IS·MR·RVSKIN· LIVING·TOO·LONG?

SELECTED·WRITINGS OF·E·W·GODWIN ON·VICTORIAN·ARCHITECTVRE· DESIGN·AND·CVLTVRE·

'I shall ask you to go to the theatre and the circus, to attend ecclesiastical functions, to go to all sorts of studios, to accompany me to sanitary exhibitions, to workshops and to picture galleries.'

'To Art students. Letter No.1', *The British Architect*, 2 May 1884, p.215

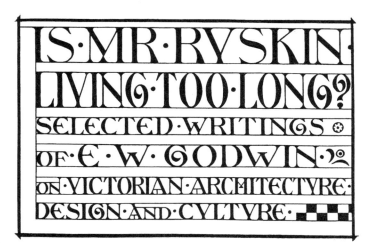

IS·MR·RVSKIN· LIVING·TOO·LONG? SELECTED·WRITINGS OF·E·W·GODWIN ON·VICTORIAN·ARCHITECTVRE· DESIGN·AND·CVLTVRE·

Juliet Kinchin and Paul Stirton

White Cockade

Published by

White Cockade Publishing
71 Lonsdale Road
Oxford OX2 7ES

Tel. 01865 510411
www.whitecockade.co.uk

British Library Cataloguing-in-Publication Data
A catalogue record for this book is available from the British Library.

ISBN 1 873487 12 6

Juliet Kinchin is Senior Lecturer and Honorary Reader in History of Art at the
University of Glasgow. Previously a curator at the Victoria & Albert Museum and
at Glasgow Museums, she has published extensively on international exhibitions
and on European architecture and design of the 19th and 20th centuries.

Paul Stirton is Senior Lecturer in History of Art and Fellow of the Centre for
Whistler Studies at the University of Glasgow. He has published extensively and
curated many exhibitions on European art and design of the 19th and 20th
centuries. He is also the author of the *Blue Guide to Provence*.

*White Cockade Publishing gratefully acknowledges support from the Paul Mellon
Centre for Studies in British Art for this publication.*

Opposite title page: Photograph of E. W. Godwin, probably late 1860s.

Cover art work E.W. Godwin and Nicholas Oddy
Design and editing Perilla Kinchin
Typeset in Monotype Photina
Printed and bound in Great Britain by Advance Book Printing, Northmoor

Contents

Editorial Preface

Godwin's published work is not to be found in a few substantial books. There is no easy access to his ideas on architecture and design, his principal profession, and even less to the numerous related interests he pursued at different stages throughout his career. We describe them as 'related interests' because Godwin saw dress, theatre and archaeology, as well as architectural style and practice, as part of a larger pursuit. This in itself was not unusual among Victorian architect-designers, but Godwin chose to explore these aspects of 'art-culture' through writing as much as through his own design work. For many he was a promising architect who became distracted by trivial pursuits like theatre and journalism. For others, he seemed a model of the aesthete who engaged with various media while upholding a higher, unattainable ideal of art. What was often overlooked, both at the time and subsequently, was the sheer range and extent of his output as a journalist and critic.

For this anthology we have pieced together Godwin's literary output from hundreds of articles, reviews and lectures published over a period of twenty or so years, most of them in journals long since defunct. These articles were not written, or read, as a sustained exposition of his design philosophy, but in the overall selection we have tried to communicate both his idiosyncratic writing style and a sense of his totalising vision. One of the most appealing aspects of Godwin's journalism is his ability to touch on so many facets of Victorian culture, and to relate his design thinking about the theatre, housing or dress to contemporary political concerns or academic debates, while also invoking such issues as history or national character. He had a formidable range, with an ability to move from discussion of sewage treatment to the structure of the architectural professions to an advertisement for writing ink within the space of one article. Our aim has been to select and edit this flood of newsprint in ways which draw out key themes, and give a sense of how his ideas developed over time, without losing the integrity either of individual articles or the cumulative thrust of those conceived as series.

We have also tried to give an overview of his writings, while avoiding excessive repetition. Like any journalist, Godwin recycled ideas and material, and related his discussion to topical events in other areas of the media. This anthology represents but a fraction of his overall output. Some of Godwin's more erudite writings in the areas of theatre and archaeology, for example, have not aged well and we are aware that the selection does not fully represent the range and depth of his interest in these fields. Conversely, some of his shorter 'Notes', 'Jottings' and 'Scraps', his more flippant asides, have been included to indicate variations in the tone of his journalism and the immediacy of his responses to topical issues. His expressive, witty, and often colourful use of language finds a parallel in his design philosophy. While rarely preaching in the mode of many Victorian sages, he is serious about the values he is communicating and aims to make these ideas fresh and accessible. The architectural environment and visual culture were to be enjoyed, not endured.

The organisation of this book

The 'Chronology' outlines the framework of Godwin's life and work, followed by an essay discussing developments in the Victorian press, and his particular literary and visual style. Thereafter the texts are arranged in fifteen thematic chapters, each with its own introduction and suggestions for further reading. For each extract, introductory notes on the specific context appear in italics, while the original title and source is indicated in the margin, together with reference to the relevant 'Biographical Notes'. These are included at the end of the book, before the cumulative index.

As far as possible the punctuation and layout of the original texts have been retained, bearing in mind that the various journals and magazines for which Godwin wrote adopted different conventions. In the longer articles he shared with many nineteenth-century writers a seamless flow of prose: to facilitate comprehension by the modern reader, additional paragraph breaks and sub-headings have been inserted in some of the longer extracts. The omission of phrases and sentences is indicated by three dots in square brackets. We have used engraved and lithographed illustrations from the period: those without captions are from drawings by Godwin that relate directly to particular articles.

The texts are followed by as complete a listing of Godwin's published output as could be made at the present time. In the process of compiling this book a number of previously unidentified articles has emerged, and there are doubtless others. It has not been possible, for example, to source all of the press-cuttings to be found in papers of the Bristol Society of Architects and at the National Archive of Art and Design in London. Moreover Godwin did not always sign articles. Where an extract has been included in this book, the citation is followed by a square-bracketed reference to the page on which the extract begins. The three journals for which Godwin wrote the majority of his articles are abbreviated as follows: *Arch.* – Architect; *BA* – *The British Architect and Northern Engineer*; *BN* – *Building News and Engineering Journal*. The standard monograph, edited by Susan Weber Soros, *E. W. Godwin, Aesthetic Movement Architect and Designer*, Yale University Press, 1999, is cited throughout as 'Soros 1999'.

Acknowledgements

We are grateful to Dr Susan Weber Soros for her generosity in sharing research material with us and facilitating our involvement in the retrospective exhibition, *E. W. Godwin, Aesthetic Movement Architect and Designer*, held at the Bard Graduate Center for Studies in the Decorative Arts, Design and Material Culture, New York in 1999. Prof. Gavin Stamp, Prof. Barry Bergdoll and Janie Munro have offered invaluable advice and feedback during the project. Our grateful thanks go to Jolyon Hudson for permission to use images; and to Perilla Kinchin without whose support this project would never have been completed.

We are also pleased to acknowledge support from the Paul Mellon Centre for Studies in British Art towards this publication.

Chronology

1833   Edward William Godwin born 26 May, Bristol; son of William Godwin, a leather merchant.

1846   Father dies, 12 September.

c.1848   Articled to William Armstrong, City Surveyor, Architect and Civil Engineer, Bristol.

1851   First publication, *The Architectural Antiquities of Bristol and its Neighbourhood*, written in collaboration with two fellow apprentice architects, W. C. Burder and J. Hine.

c.1852   Establishes his own architectural practice in Bristol, concentrating on church restorations and furnishings.

1856   Moves to Ireland for two years.

1857-60   St Baithen's Church, St Johnstown, Donegal, the first new building to be designed and completed by EWG, and the first of three churches designed and built in Ireland over the next three years.

1858   Meets William Burges with whom he establishes a close friendship until Burges's death in 1881.

1859   Marries Sarah Yonge, daughter of Rev. W. Yonge of Henley-on-Thames, Oxfordshire. EWG's architectural practice expanding, based on modest domestic and ecclesiastical commissions.

1861   Wins competition for design of new Town Hall at Northampton; completed 1864.

1862   Moves to 21 Portland Square, Bristol, which is decorated and furnished in new 'proto-Aesthetic' style, incorporating oriental carpets, bare boards, plain wall coverings and lightweight furniture. Elected Fellow of the Society of Antiquaries.

1862   Begins writing occasional reviews ('Jottings') of theatre performances in Bristol and London for the *Western Daily Press*.

1863   Studies Gothic architecture in France, visiting Amiens, Paris and Chartres. Meets Ellen Terry, for whom he designs costume of Titania in production of *A Midsummer Night's Dream*.

1864   Forms partnership with Henry Crisp. Wins competition for design of Congleton Town Hall; completed 1867. This is the last of EWG's competition designs to be realised despite numerous successes in open competitions over the next two decades.

Wife dies. EWG establishes London office in Baker Street, leaving Crisp in charge of Bristol office. Publishes *A Handbook of Floral Decoration for Churches*. September to March 1866 writes controversial 12-part series 'Art Cliques' in the *Building News*.	1865
Dromore Castle, County Limerick, Ireland, for Earl of Limerick; completed 1873. Travels round Ireland with his friend Burges.	1866
Designs first 'Anglo-Japanese' furnishings for his London chambers. Begins association with the firm of William Watt, furniture manufacturers and decorators. Designs Glenbeigh Towers, County Kerry; completed 1870.	1867
Elopes with actress Ellen Terry, at that time married to the eminent painter G. F. Watts. The couple set up home at the Red House, near Harpenden, Hertfordshire. Designs for short-lived Art Furniture Company.	1868
First child 'Edy' (later known as Edith Craig), born to EWG and Ellen Terry.	1869
Partnership with Crisp dissolved.	1871
Designs own house, Fallows Green, Harpenden (demolished).	1871-2
Beauvale House, Newthorpe, Nottinghamshire for Earl Cowper.	1871-3
Birth of second child, 'Teddy' (later known as Edward Gordon Craig). Collaborates with R.W. Edis and J. P. Seddon on unsuccessful competition designs, and enters agreement to design furniture for Collinson & Lock, Art Furnishers. Writes 6-part series 'Modern Architects and Their Works' in the *Building News*.	1872
Further travels in Normandy, reports of which appear in the *Building News* the following year. Exhibits furniture for Collinson & Lock at the Vienna Universal Exhibition. Interior refurbishment of John McLaren's Kensington house, and of Grey Towers, Nunthorpe, for mayor of Middlesbrough.	1873
EWG and Terry move to 20 Taviton Street, London; office relocated to Adelphi Chambers. Collaborates with James McNeill Whistler on installation of the artist's works at 48 Pall Mall. Designs a 'Co-operative Home' for Mrs King. Developing association with several manufacturers to produce wallpaper, fabrics and furniture to his designs. Begins period of prolific journalism, writing mostly for the *Architect* and *Building News*, including a series of 33 articles on Shakespeare's plays.	1874
Designs houses for new planned estate at Bedford Park, Chiswick. Advisor to the Bancrofts' production of *The Merchant of Venice* featuring Ellen Terry. EWG and Terry separate.	1875
In January marries Beatrice Philip, a pupil in his office and daughter of a leading Scottish sculptor. Son Edward born in October. EWG's 'Anglo-Japanese' furniture displayed by Collinson & Lock at the Philadelphia Centennial Exhibition. Writes a series on the furnishing of his London house and chambers for the *Architect*. Designs for Coleman's production of Shakespeare's *Henry V*. London interior for photographer Frederick Hollyer.	1876

1877   First edition of William Watt's catalogue, *Art Furniture from designs by E. W. Godwin F.S.A.*, published by Batsford. Designs houses in Chelsea for Gillow & Co., and begins design and decoration of The White House at 35 Tite Street, Chelsea, for James McNeill Whistler (demolished 1960).

1878   Becomes London editor of *The British Architect*. Designs 'Butterfly Suite', in collaboration with Whistler, for William Watt's stand at the Paris Exposition Universelle. Second edition of *Art Furniture* catalogue. Designs two other studio houses in Tite Street, for Frank Miles and for Carlo Pellegrini and Archibald Wortley (demolished). Studio for Princess Louise, Kensington Palace (demolished). November, Whistler–Ruskin trial concludes.

1879   Designs new masthead and establishes an Art Club (ends 1884) in *The British Architect*. New studio house for Wortley in Tite Street; completed 1883 (demolished). Whistler bankruptcy and sale of the White House to the critic Harry Quilter.

1880   Collaborates with J. P. Seddon on unrealised designs for a People's Palace and a hotel, and designs costumes for two Shakespeare productions: *Othello* at Sadler's Wells and *Romeo and Juliet* at the Olympic Theatre in London. Publication of *Artistic Conservatories ... by E. W. Godwin*.

1881   Designs the 'Shakespeare' dining-room suite for William Watt, and costumes for several theatrical productions in London, as well as wallpaper, textiles, furniture and ceramics for various manufacturers. Designs new facade for the Fine Art Society premises in New Bond Street, London, and the Tower House, a block of four studio houses at 46 Tite Street, Chelsea; completed 1885.

1882   Undertakes redesign of several interiors in London for aristocratic and theatrical clients. Founder member and honorary secretary of the Costume Society. Relocates office to 7 Great College Street, Westminster.

1883   Writes *Dress and its Relation to Health and Climate* for the 1884 International Health Exhibition in London. Designs sets and costumes for several theatre productions.

1884   Manager, designer and art director of open-air production of Shakespeare's *As You Like It* for Lady Archibald Campbell at Coombe House, Surrey. Appointed consultant to new Dress Studios at Liberty's of London. Remodels and decorates house at 16 Tite Street for Oscar and Constance Wilde.

1885   Work in the theatre expanding to take up most of EWG's time. Producer, designer and adaptor of the text for second open-air theatre production at Coombe House, as well as designing for five other theatrical productions in London, despite ill health.

1886   Designs for several plays including adaptation of Hengler's Circus as Greek theatre for *Helena in Troas*. Dies 6 October, aged 53, after operation to remove kidney stones. Buried in unmarked grave at Northleigh in Oxfordshire.

E. W. Godwin and the Victorian Press

IN THEIR first issue of 1878, the proprietors of the weekly magazine *The British Architect and Northern Engineer* introduced readers to their newly appointed London editor and sometime graphic designer, E. W. Godwin: 'whether it be a large and important building, a charming suite of furniture, a racy article or a diminutive piece of ornamentation, he seems equally at home and is equally effective' (see p.372).

Biographical notes:
Langtry
Swinburne
Terry
Whistler
Wilde

Journalism was the one area in which Godwin's creative versatility came into its own, uniting his diverse interests as both a critic and a practitioner. Throughout his career, on point of principle, Godwin resisted the tendency towards professional specialisation, and the fragmentation of knowledge and skills that seemed to characterise modern life. *The British Architect* and other magazines gave him considerable power to control the way in which his own work was discussed or illustrated; also a platform from which he could articulate his wide-ranging concerns, and extend the interest of architects to related areas like the theatre and dress, or to interior, furniture and garden design. The 'racy articles' poured forth, and within a year Godwin could reasonably claim that 'We have fought against the many evils which surround and clog the practice of modern architecture and have bent our bow against the bad client, the bad builder, the bad assistant, the sham architect, and the bumptious amateur' (see p.47).

By the time he joined *The British Architect*, many had already experienced the brunt of such criticism. He could claim specialist authority in a formidable range of fields – from theatre, literature and architecture, to archaeology, art, design and household taste – and as a society figure he gained visibility through association with the likes of the actresses Ellen Terry and Lillie Langtry, the poet Algernon Swinburne and the artist James McNeill Whistler. There were few commentators at the time with Godwin's breadth of experience as a writer and designer, combined with his flair for pithy insight, accurate observation and clear reasoning. 'Certainly Godwin was as gifted in his power of imparting knowledge to others as he was in his accumulation of it', commented *The British Architect*. 'He arrested attention, first, by showing his readers he had something to tell them which they would like to know, and then he retained their interest by imparting it to them in that pleasant, crisp style, so peculiarly his own' (p.377). Since co-authoring his first book as a teenager, his services had been in growing demand from a great variety of daily, weekly and monthly publications, to the extent that he became better known to many, particularly those outside the architectural profession, as a critic rather than a designer.

Yet Godwin's status as a critic and editor has become obscured over time. Understandably perhaps, given that the majority of his writing is so difficult to access, the scholarship on Godwin has prioritised the study of his more

[1] See J. Kinchin, 'Godwin and Modernism', in Soros 1999, pp.92-113.

[2] A view expounded in Wilde's now famous essay, 'The critic as an artist. Some remarks upon the importance of doing nothing', in *Intentions*, London, 1891.

[3] *The English House*, London, 1979 (first published Berlin, 1904) p.194.

tangible output, and has taken a compartmentalised approach to the many fields in which he operated. Today if people have heard of him at all, it is usually in connection with his ideas on the theatre or with a tiny number of works – his Anglo-Japanese furniture, and the famous White House designed for Whistler in Chelsea – works that have established his popular reputation as one of the earliest 'pioneers' of the Modern Movement.[1] Through excavating a selection of his writings, one of our aims has been to suggest that Godwin exerted a wider influence on Victorian architecture and design through magazines than the limited number of his realised projects would suggest. Also that his writings were both a significant and integral dimension of his creative output, rather than just a 'transparent' record of his design philosophy. Like his young protégé and friend Oscar Wilde, Godwin came to view his journalism as a form of artistic expression in its own right, rather than a mere adjunct to his main practice.[2] Writing honed his artistic sensibility and sharpened his powers of creative observation. Working through the Victorian periodical press he was able to reorganise his professional practice, reaching out to disparate audiences and new types of client, and creating a media persona with a distinctive voice and graphic identity.

No art or architectural critic of the High Victorian period could escape the shadow cast by John Ruskin. Godwin frankly acknowledged his debt to the 'great sage' but, as a critic and observer of modern life, he did not aspire to produce works of permanent literary value like those of his mentor. Ruskin had been the inspiration for Godwin's generation in their approach to art and life, but as Ruskin's range and published utterances moved into areas of economics, education, morality and religion with a firm and censorious tone, one might understand why the great man began to appear less as a guide and more as a stern schoolmaster. There was a sense in which, by 1878, Godwin could justifiably ask, 'Is Mr. Ruskin living too long?' (p.133). While Godwin had his serious and high-minded side, his criticism was certainly funnier than Ruskin's, and his lighter often scintillating idiom seems inherently modern. Also different are the signs of his proactive engagement with the developing character of the Victorian periodical press, with newly fashionable forms of commodity culture, and the changing configuration of the design professions. Reflecting in 1904 on the genesis of Britain's 'modern' style of architecture and design, the German critic Hermann Muthesius looked back to the 1860s and 1870s when the 'unheard-of modernity, the modernity that upset people, because it was in direct opposition to the familiar, had its day [...] Those were days of sensation and strife, when the patient shook their heads and the impatient condemned.'[3] Godwin lived through, and was part of, those stirrings of modernity and that period of 'sensation and strife'.

The Victorian press

Concomitant with a rapidly expanding market for art, design and theatrical entertainment was the proliferation, and increased specialisation, of the Victorian press. In 1866 'this wonderful engine of mind-culture' was described in the *Journal of the Society of Arts* as 'among our modern wonders.'[4] Technical improvements in printing and distribution, the expanding middle classes' appetite for self-improvement and entertainment, and the abolition between 1853 and 1861 of 'taxes on knowledge' (advertising, stamp and paper duties), all contributed to a massive expansion and diversification of periodicals from the 1860s.[5] A dedicated architectural and art press had already begun to emerge from the 1830s, with the start of titles like J. C. Loudon's *Architectural Magazine* in 1834, followed by other stalwarts like the *Art-Union* of 1839 (renamed *The Art Journal* a decade later) and the *Builder* in 1842 (whose editor from 1844 to 1883, George Godwin, was no relation). The three titles in this specialist field to which Godwin contributed most frequently were the *Building News* (which added *'and Engineering Journal'* to its title in 1863), the *Architect* edited by T. Roger Smith from 1869, and a newcomer in 1874, *The British Architect and Northern Engineer*, which was published out of Manchester.[6] Some of Godwin's articles were syndicated, reaching new audiences in the context of magazines like the *Furniture Gazette* or *American Architect and Building News*.

Theatre criticism evolved rather differently and, like the British theatre itself in the nineteenth century, was slow to be taken seriously. Many reviews, like Godwin's early theatre criticism, were placed in local and national newspapers or general interest magazines until the emergence of titles like the *Dramatic Review* and *Illustrated Sporting and Dramatic News*. It is obviously difficult to assess the relative impact of Godwin's criticism in periodicals with such varied circulation and audience profiles. It goes without saying that there was a marked contrast between the readership of a lengthy article in the *Ulster Review of Archaeology*, and one of his well-targeted letters in the *Times*, *Athenaeum* or *World*.

'Art, although losing in individual force, is every day widening in its influence, appealing to a larger audience, becoming more popular', wrote Godwin in January 1878 (p.46). 'From Cabinet ministers weighed down with serious affairs of State to young ladies who have just learnt how to arrange a little blue china on a mantelpiece, we receive lectures on art'. In the competitive environment of publishing, Godwin found himself besieged by a 'swarm of writers ... presuming amateurs and inexperienced artists ... self-appointed apostles of domestic art.' The art and architectural press had begun to spawn a new genre of books on household taste. The first and most important of these, Eastlake's *Hints on Household Taste* 1868, originated in an article in the *Cornhill* magazine followed by a series in *The Queen*.[7] Similarly, writers like Christopher Dresser, R. W. Edis, Mrs Haweis and Lewis Day all repackaged magazine articles on domestic art into book form. Godwin never got round to maximising earnings from his journalism in this way. Plans for pulling together articles on the Paris International Exhibition in 1878 as a spin-off publication, and an 'Art Students' Yearbook' in 1879 came to nothing, although *The British Architect* did reissue his articles on the Temple Bar as an illustrated pamphlet.[8] For magazines, advertising was another increasingly important means of generating revenue and defining a mar-

[4] *Journal of the Society of Arts*, 31 Aug. 1866, pp.656-7.

[5] J. Black, *The English Press 1621–1861*, Stroud, 2001, pp.178-9.

[6] See F. Jenkins, 'Nineteenth-century architectural periodicals', in J. Summerson ed., *Concerning Architecture. Essays Presented to Nikolaus Pevsner*, London, 1968.

[7] *Cornhill Magazine*, 9:51, 1864, pp.337-49; *The Queen*, 37:965, 1865, pp.411-12 (under pen-name Jack Easel).

[8] Victoria & Albert Museum, Archive of Art and Design (V&A, AAD)4/285-330 – 1988.

Biographical notes:
Du Maurier
Leighton
Pellegrini
Watt

[9] Letter from Raffles Davison to Godwin, April 1878. V&A, AAD 4/285-330 – 1988.

ket niche, and there was a growing convergence between journals and trade literature, both in terms of graphic identity and critical language. In his design for *The British Architect*'s new masthead in November 1877, for example, Godwin established a clear visual resonance with the Anglo-Japanese character of his *Art Furniture* trade catalogue published by William Watt earlier in the year (see p.47, compare p.295; pp.194-224 *passim*). Individual plates from the catalogue were also taken up in the British and American press, and went on reappearing in *The British Architect* and *Building News* until Godwin's death in 1886. Godwin's connections with commercial concerns like William Watt, and the success of this catalogue added to his marketability as a critic. He received a 20% commission on all new advertising and subscriptions he brought to *The British Architect*, and 'specially good advertisers' were described 'in a specially excellent way'.[9]

Apart from the periodicals to which he himself contributed as a critic, Godwin's architectural, design and theatre work was featured and discussed in a still further range of magazines in Britain and America, not least in *Punch* and the *Illustrated London News*. As a prominent figure on the London theatre and art scene, he was on intimate terms with editors and critics in many different sectors of the press: among his architectural clients was Carlo Pellegrini, cartoonist for the society paper *Vanity Fair*, a weekly finger on the pulse of upper-class society that started up in 1868. George Du Maurier, whose *Punch* cartoons regularly featured Godwin's unmistakable spindly furnishings, was another personal acquaintance. Moving in such circles, Godwin was conscious of the fashionable notoriety that came through his association with high-profile actors, writers, painters and dealers. Sensitivity to the reciprocal relationship between the professional, social and domestic lives of prominent artists was evident in his 1866 critique of Frederic Leighton's studio-house: 'To the readers of this journal it matters very little whether Mr. Leighton or Mr. Snooks builds an uninteresting mass, which he is pleased to call his house ... But outside the professional journal the thing assumes a totally different aspect ... To these people Mr. Snook's villa is a matter of indifference; but Mr. Leighton's is an example of everything that belongs to the Good, the Beautiful, and the True.' (p.251)

This was a trifle disingenuous on Godwin's part, in that professional journals did not exist outside the forces of capitalism and celebrity, and he clearly understood that readers were not encountering his articles in a vacuum. While professing indifference to the growing cult of artistic 'personalities', and expressing contempt for the vagaries of fashion and commercialism, he was self-consciously and deeply implicated in the system of which they were part. Magazines were an important mechanism within this larger system that governed the manufacture, marketing, retailing and consumption of art and artefacts.

From 'Groovy Goth' to 'Artistic Spirit'

At the start of his career, while still living in Bristol, writing had been secondary to Godwin's developing architectural practice, and virtually dried up altogether as he became embroiled in the design and building of Northampton and Congleton Town Halls (1864–7), then Dromore Castle (1866–73). These commissions had established his reputation as a rising star of the architectural establishment, but Godwin felt increasingly caught in a professional and provincial rut like the 'groovy' Goths for whom he expressed contempt.[10] From the mid-1860s, however, his personal and professional life took a distinctly unconventional turn. In the view of many, a promising architectural career was derailed by his move in 1865 to the big city with its fatal distractions, one of which was the young actress Ellen Terry, then married to the eminent painter G. F. Watts. Yet it was his engagement with the dynamic conditions of the great metropolis and his scandalous six-year affair with Terry, with whom he eloped in 1868, which clearly triggered the transformation of his career and lifestyle.

From the autobiographical content of his articles one gets a sense of how Godwin began to explore different ways of working and of living, all the time refining his ideas about modern design, its role and its audience. It was around this time, for example, that he wrote his first two major series of articles – 'Art Cliques' and 'Painted Decorations' – and began designing the furniture and wallpaper for his own use that were to provide prototypes for commercial production, and the subject of articles and illustrations over the next twenty or so years. Meanwhile his architectural practice began to falter. With no further major commissions forthcoming, his partnership with Henry Crisp ended in 1871 and he exhibited at the Royal Academy for the last time in 1872. In addition, several clients were becoming legalistic. Hounded by bailiffs, Godwin went to ground for a few weeks in 1873 leading to rumours that he had 'cut the country' for good. Financial worries forced Terry to return to the stage in the following year while also coping with two illegitimate children by Godwin, Edith (Edy) and Edward (Teddy). Despite such personal and professional uncertainties, these were intensely creative years. Shortly after their shared triumph in the Bancrofts' production of *Merchant of Venice* Godwin and Terry separated, and by January 1876 he had married his eighteen-year-old pupil Beatrice Philip, who produced a second 'Edward' nine months later.

Against the backdrop of this increasingly chaotic work and home life, Godwin's involvement with the Victorian press assumed significance on a number of counts: first, as a reliable and significant source of income, particularly in 1876 when he published a huge spate of articles in the *Architect* and the *Building News*;[11] secondly, as a means of maintaining visibility within the architectural profession; and thirdly, as a means of accessing a broad, dispersed and largely anonymous middle-class market with artistic aspirations. In other words, magazines helped him to mediate the shift between working on prestigious 'top-end' commissions like town halls and country houses,

[10] 'Groovy' in this sense was a favourite Godwin adjective, applied on several occasions to what he saw as dead-end Gothicism: see for example p.83.

[11] For Godwin's substantial earnings from the *Architect*, particularly in 1876, see Godwin ledger in V&A, AAD, 4/12-1980.

[12] In an 1877 letter to the *Building News*, (2 Feb., p.134), Carr described how he selected Godwin on the basis of designs for a parsonage which had been published in that magazine in 1874. When Godwin's preparatory designs for the Bedford Park development were published in December 1876 and January 1877 issues of *Building News* they were instantly criticised by William Woodward.

[13] '... one of the most artistic spirits of this century in England', O. Wilde, 'The truth of masks', *Intentions*, London, 1891, p. 232.

and addressing a middling market through the design of Art furnishings. A remote audience did not have to engage directly with his dubious morality, abrasive personality, and undeniably large ego. From Godwin's point of view this meant liberation from dealing face to face with committees, ignorant builders, or troublesome clients. At the same time, journalism enabled Godwin to advertise his services as an architect or designer indirectly, without having to tout for custom in an unseemly way. In the right magazine the successful launch of a design or publication targeted a huge potential audience. It was through skimming past copies of the *Building News* that Jonathan Carr hit on Godwin as architect for his famous Bedford Park development (although ironically it appears to be in the light of adverse criticism in the press that Carr also then dropped Godwin in favour of Norman Shaw).[12] In the absence of favourable coverage Godwin did not shrink from writing his own, while adverse criticism incurred instant retribution (see e.g. pp.77-9, 97, 253-5, 260-1).

In developing a multi-faceted persona through the periodical press, Godwin could reinvent himself as a free-floating 'artistic spirit' (a phrase used of him by Oscar Wilde)[13] whose role was incidentally that of interior designer, critic, theatre director, architect or teacher. His journalism provided a vehicle for this performative engagement with his public. By temperament a loner, and a hopeless financial manager, he was unlikely to have made a success in any case of running a large architectural office. On the other hand, in working with journals like the *Architect* and *The British Architect*, or with 'culturally prepared' Art manufacturers and retailers like William Watt and Liberty's, Godwin found a framework within which his flamboyant character and diverse interests could flourish.

Modernising architectural criticism

By the time Godwin turned to journalism in earnest he had developed a distinctive writing style, partly from the experience gained in archaeological scholarship and theatre criticism while living in Bristol. In his earliest writings one can hear him experimenting with two 'voices', the one academic and a touch pedantic, the other more combative and sensationalist. Articles for various archaeological journals honed his eye for significant detail and academic argument, and by 1851 he had co-authored his first book, the rather dull *Architectural Antiquities of Bristol and its Neighbourhood*. More influential in the long term were the off-the-cuff and opinionated 'Theatrical Jottings' in the local *Western Daily Press* in 1862–4. These punchy reviews blended analysis of set and costume design, performance and literary criticism in an engaging mix. (So successfully in fact that one enraged actor responded by coming round to Godwin's house with a horse-whip!)

Godwin felt that architects had to find new ways of communicating both within the profession and to cultivated members of lay society, by adapting the more entertaining language as well as the editorial and pictorial strategies of the popular press. For better or worse, architecture, like dress or furnishings, was becoming increasingly prone to the dictates of fashion and the consumers' appetite for novelty. This being the case, Godwin felt that people were more likely to look to the latest novel for inspiration than the turgid pronouncements of a staid organisation like the Royal Institute of British Architects (see p.270). What Godwin brought to criticism was a new sense of immediacy and intimacy, activating the readers' sensory imagination and physically inserting them into the text: 'I shall ask you to accompany me ...' (p.2); 'the master is known to exist through certain mysterious whistles and sounds which reach us' (p.112). With Godwin at their side readers become armchair *flâneurs*, relishing the sights, sounds, tastes and smells of modern life, all the while cloaked in anonymity, and eavesdropping on the artist's private musings and sparring matches. Vicariously they enter an unsanitary Paris studio, spend an afternoon shopping in Liberty's, or relive the experience of a Homeric house, learning to look and observe through an intensified sensory experience of the topic.

In the 1870s Godwin's barbed critiques of various organisations and figures of authority were invariably entertaining, although T. H. Wyatt disparaged the growing tendency to indulge in 'violent and personal language' as a cheap gimmick; all very 'exciting or amusing at the moment', but of no real value.[14] A colourful and opinionated style of writing was characteristic of the 'New Journalism' then developing in British periodicals and newspapers, just as quick witticism, parody and cultured repartee was becoming a hallmark of the Bohemian and Dandy.[15] Although Godwin was quick to dismiss pretentious 'twaddle about art' as he put it, one can see how he and his friends Whistler and Wilde were to feed off this combination of strong opinion, sophisticated ideas and facetious delivery. He could harangue, chat, complain, or philosophise, while introducing topical references to daily news-coverage. Titles like 'Chats', 'Afternoon Strolls', 'Rambles', 'Jottings', 'Notes' and 'Scraps' accentuated this informal and apparently spontaneous style. The lengthy format and often dry, not to say obsequious, tone of articles that had characterised the art press of the 1860s and early 1870s, increasingly gave way to bulletin-style paragraphs and catchy titles.

Controlling the visualisation of his designs was an additional strategy for defending authorship and positioning interior design as an architectural and artistic activity. Godwin was very fussy about the way his drawings were reproduced, and openly criticised illustrations that fell short of the mark. Referring to a *Building News* illustration of interior mouldings in St Lô, Normandy, he remarked to his readers that the beauty and workmanship of the original detail could not be appreciated, 'as the reduction of my drawing by photolithography has resulted in an uncertain outline.'[16] In a record of books bought as a teenager in the 1850s he noted the names of engravers and illustrators as well as the authors, and being an embryonic archaeologist, studied other people's illustrations for their accuracy.[17] Commercial photography was in its infancy during Godwin's lifetime, although he was quick to recognise the advantages of photomechanical forms of reproduction, and photography's potential as a recording tool. For his own drawings he favoured 'scientific clarity', developing a linear, diagrammatic style that lent itself to re-

[14] His 1872 series on 'Modern Architects and their Works', for example, generated a barrage of correspondence. T. H. Wyatt, 'General conference of architects: open meeting, Monday June 10', *Building News*, 14 June 1872, p. 475. See R. Hayes, 'An Aesthetic education: the architectural criticism of E. W. Godwin', in Soros 1999, pp. 115-25.

[15] The 'New Journalism', a term coined by Matthew Arnold, emerged in the early 1880s largely due to T. H. Stead's sensational articles for the *Pall Mall Gazette* (a magazine to which Godwin contributed).

[16] *Building News* 14 Aug. 1874, p.194.

[17] Godwin Notebook, V&A Prints and Drawings, E.225-1963, p. 10. More than twenty years after purchasing A. C. Pugin's *Examples of Gothic Architecture*, for example, he still admired 'the careful architectural drawings, with their dimensions clearly indicated, and their details elaborately and scientifically displayed': 'Gothic Revival', *Architect*, 2 Dec. 1871, p. 271.

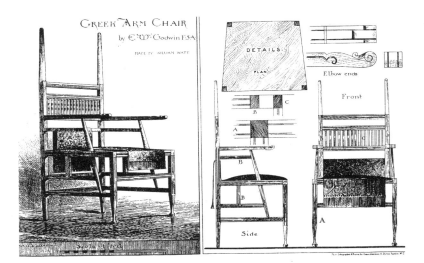

Godwin design for a Greek arm-chair, BN 29 May 1885.

production by both engraving and photo-lithography. Typically Godwin's furniture designs included one view showing the piece in relation to the interior, alongside elevations and constructional or decorative detail. On the printed page all architectural drawings, interior detailing and furniture designs were given comparable weighting and reduced to a similar format, emphasising the inter-relationship of these activities. His stress on constructional detail and controlled proportions also emphasised furniture and interior design as a conceptual, artistic activity, to the extent that the drawing style with which he became associated seemed to attract more general resentment against architects' high-handed incursions into trade territory. One seething furniture manufacturer spoke of architects as 'singular beings with hobbies ... who do not practice architecture, but devote themselves to furniture, pottery, sewerage etc., etc. Their marvellous doings in the former direction are occasionally witnessed in the productions of Gillow, Collinson & Lock, and other grand firms; but luckily, they are not often seen in use out of their — the architects'— own chambers.'[18] In case readers were in any doubt as to whom he referred, the correspondent went on to lambast designs by Godwin and his pupil Freeth Roper: 'the proudest boast of their producers seems to reside in the fact that they are *intensely geometrical* [...] of all the nightmare horrors in the way of architects' furniture I have yet seen, it is about the worst. If you have artistic talent, versatility, genius and picturesque imaginativeness enough for your composition to enable you to rule a piece of paper with numerous strictly parallel straight lines, and then cross them with as many or more parallel lines at right angles to the first, being very particular to secure a fair degree of squareness in all the spaces between the lines, you will have this identical and wonderful "DESIGN" [...] Its candid angular lines stare grimly out at you, shouting 'We are SIMPLE, We are STONEY, We are STRONG! ...We are *Architectural*! ... bow down and worship us.'

[18] 'Architects and furniture', *Furniture Gazette,* 7 Jan. 1874, pp. 72-3.

Remodelling *The British Architect and Northern Engineer*

Established in Manchester in 1874 by the brothers Oliver and Thomas Raffles Davison, this journal was prepared to give Godwin a freer rein than more established titles like the *Building News*. Even they, however, occasionally had to pull him into line, removing a vituperative reference to Eastlake, for example, that they felt would endanger their advertising income. Nevertheless his appointment was a departure from the opening pitch in 1874 that claimed the journal would 'give more prominence to facts, data and principle in connection with actual practice than to theories, opinion and criticisms upon general topics'. Godwin was nothing *but* 'opinion and criticisms upon general topics', and immediately set about putting his stamp on the image, range and format of the magazine.

On the pages of *The British Architect* he could construct a client map that drew together his demi-monde associates, the occasional aristocrat, and the nameless middle classes with artistic aspirations who might live in one of his Bedford Park houses or buy a Godwin wallpaper, thereby obliterating the social lines between these groups that would have pertained in day-to-day life. He used his influence in London clubs and theatrical and artistic circles to consolidate support discreetly for the magazine.[19] From the start he gave space and enhanced editorial coverage to repeat advertisers, to employers like Gillow's and Liberty's, and to friends whose outlook and preoccupations matched his own. By playing up his persona as 'artist' and scourge of the Philistines, Godwin was able to fashion an identity distinct from that of commercial concerns like Liberty's or Watt's, while simultaneously promoting their interests. William Watt for example was able to tie in advertising and product lines to the articles Godwin wrote about his home and other artists' houses. Consumers could buy into a celebrity lifestyle by acquiring copies of the furnishings that Godwin had described and illustrated.

'Notes on Current Events' became the backbone of the magazine ('this is pretty much the only kind of reading that professional men have time for now-a-days', wrote Davison in an advertising flyer for the magazine). Visually the layout was pepped up throughout with illustrations, using sepia ink and toned paper for the photo-lithographed pages, some of them designed as double-spreads. The generous font size and wide margins contributed to a modern and self-consciously 'artistic' layout that distinguished it from the denser look of more established titles like the *Art Journal* or *Building News*. From the outset Godwin pressurised the proprietors of *The British Architect* to improve the size, quality and range of illustrations, many of which he himself provided. He was fortunate in being able to work with T. Raffles Davison, himself a talented illustrator and expert printer. Davison wrote proudly about his perspective illustration of Godwin's Chelsea Houses in January 1878: 'a double page requires a great deal of extra care. The drawing it is reduced from is a large one in brown ink & has copied extremely well ... This is the largest print we have yet done. None of the other Building journals could produce so long a one'.[20] Raffles Davison also contributed perspective sketches of Godwin's houses and

[19] Godwin noted subscriptions he had sold in his diaries.

[20] Letter from Thomas Raffles Davison, V &A, AAD 4/12-1980: 47-8.

interiors, in a new, loose and self-consciously 'artistic' style, which encouraged readers to mentally inhabit these domestic spaces, and to see them as part of a modern lifestyle to be emulated. The aesthetic dress and posture of the illustrated figures emphasised the psychological identification of the individual with his or her surroundings. By contrast, the *Art Journal* and trade journals such as the *Cabinet Maker and Art Furnisher* tended to treat particular objects in isolation, omitting any indication of the user or interior context.

Godwin made sure that his name was visibly and prominently associated with his designs, frequently authenticating and personalising the images with the addition of his lithographed signature. This was accepted practice for architectural projects, but less so in the trade press, which tended to present designs under the manufacturers' or retailer's name. Significantly, Godwin's contemporary, Christopher Dresser, began to brand products emanating from his design studio with the stamp or print of his 'handwritten' signature from around the same time.

The British Architect was published simultaneously in London and Manchester every Friday morning and was targeted at a modern, professional and mobile readership. Copies were sent to railway waiting rooms and five hundred 'first-class hotels' in London and important towns in the north, 'where copies are placed in handsome morocco Reading Cases provided by the proprietors'.[21]

[21] Advertising flyer c.1878.

Conclusion

Godwin was a key player in the emergence of a critical discourse around design that looked to the paradigms of architecture and the theatre, and to architects as the ultimate arbiters of taste. For Godwin, as for his friends Whistler and Wilde, the published word was the vehicle for a dynamic engagement with the public, showcasing his wit and intellectual credentials in ways that in turn influenced perceptions of his design work.

Unlike Whistler, who lived on to become a grand old man of the artistic establishment, Godwin died in 1886, just as the backlash against Aestheticism was gaining momentum. Without being there to fight his corner or redefine himself through the press, Godwin sank from view until his rehabilitation in the 1950s as a pioneer of the Modern Movement. 'If a painter of easel pictures dies', he once observed, 'you can gather his life's work together in one place, and at loan exhibitions from time to time, even centuries after his death, they can command new, diverse and large audiences' (p.133). By contrast, he pointed to the difficulties in trying to summarise the varied achievements of a designer, in particular the scattered, apparently inconsequential, and often anonymous examples of their creative energy. We hope that the extracts that follow will help a modern audience recapture something of the vitality, complexity and modernity of Godwin's criticism, and to grasp the essential unity of his artistic philosophy and practice.

I Autobiography

IN A LECTURE to young architects from the Manchester Architectural Association on 26 November 1878, Godwin talked informally of his preparation for 'this battle of life, this battle of art', surveying the highs and lows in more than twenty years' experience. He had accepted the invitation to lecture because it was not to 'a full-blown body of architects, of whom he had a horror', but to assistants, pupils and young men embarking on their careers, whom he was always at pains to address. Even in this report of the event written in the third person one gets an impression of Godwin's charismatic delivery, his disarming self-criticism, and the authority with which he invariably spoke.

At this point his reputation had become enmeshed with that of James McNeill Whistler and with the Aesthetic tendencies now apparent in all the arts. He was at the height of his powers as both a critic and designer, publicly waging his 'battle of art' against the Philistines on several fronts. As London editor of *The British Architect* he was continuing to whip up the controversy surrounding his designs for two studio houses in Tite Street, one of them Whistler's (see Ch.X). The Metropolitan Board of Works had rejected the preliminary schemes for both as too radical. Godwin's status as an avant-garde, anti-establishment figure was also confirmed by the ongoing press scrutiny of his notorious collaboration with Whistler at the Paris Exposition Universelle that year, the famous Butterfly suite – *Harmony in Yellow and Gold*.

At half-past four on the very day of Godwin's lecture, the Whistler-Ruskin libel trial concluded with an award to Whistler of one-farthing damages. This was yet another *cause célèbre* that served to polarise the English-speaking art world and that seemed with hindsight to mark a watershed in Victorian attitudes to art, design and culture.[1] As he was at pains to admit in this lecture, Godwin was of a generation profoundly influenced by Ruskin, although by this time he was asking elsewhere 'Is Mr. Ruskin living too long?' (see p.133).

'Verdict for plaintiff. Damages one farthing', J. M. Whistler, The Gentle Art of Making Enemies, *1890.*

[1] See L. Merrill, *A Pot of Paint: Aesthetics on Trial in Whistler v. Ruskin*, Washington 1992.

LECTURE: 'THIS BATTLE OF LIFE, THIS BATTLE OF ART' (1878)

Childhood

Godwin began his lecture with a reference to his youthful enthusiasm for architectural antiquities, a passion borne out by his sketch- and notebooks of the 1850s. A modern building designed by Butterfield (an architect to whom William Morris was likewise drawn as a boy), had also triggered his imagination. Initially his parents, like those of Whistler, tried to propel him towards a career in engineering.

He intended his lecture to be discursive and rambling, and one could hardly begin to tell about one's own works in this battle of life, this battle of art, without saying something of the preparation received for the fight — what they

Source:
'On some buildings I have designed', *The British Architect*, 29 November 1878, pp.210-11

Biographical notes:
Butterfield

would call the education — because one's surroundings in childhood had much to do with art and with the ultimate art outcome.

He remembered two things particularly. First, his father's garden was surrounded with all sorts of curiosities — cusped fragments and quaint crumbling bits from old churches arrested his attention whenever he was allowed to enter this carefully secured paradise. His next education in art was derived from seeing Highbury Chapel, Butterfield's first work, built opposite the house where he finished his school days. He used to watch that chapel going up without the slightest idea that he would ever become an architect. He had, when young, what is called a taste for drawing, and it was designed that he should be a civil engineer — a more paying business it was considered, than that of an architect [...]

Architectural training

In around 1848 Godwin was articled to William Armstrong in Bristol, an experience that clarified his views on architectural training and the distinction to be drawn between engineers and architects. Reading the account of his architectural apprenticeship makes clear the extent to which he drew on direct personal experience in subsequent discussions about the profession.

Biographical notes:
Bowman and Crowther
Brunel
Nesfield

He was articled to an architect, who was also a civil engineer, and a great friend of Brunel. That "architect" knew nothing whatever about architecture — a thing by no means of rare occurrence; but he did know something of engineering. His walls were all right and his construction, generally, was good; and so it was not altogether a bad training for him (Mr. Godwin). In this office he became literally his own master, and before he had been three years at work he was, in fact, the architect of the place; that was to say, everything done in the office was designed by him; the details were drawn out and the specifications written by him — a most unwholesome thing viewed in one aspect, yet wholesome in another — unwholesome in the fact he had no master's teaching, yet wholesome on the other hand, because he was thrown upon his own resources, and became all the more earnest and anxious about his work. Whenever he had a holiday he went out to the villages and neighbouring towns, and was content to spend his days not merely in sketching old buildings, but in measuring and carefully analysing their details; because that was before the days of Bowman and Crowther, Nesfield and others, whose wonderful books now saved the student such a lot of trouble. Having passed through this sort of ordeal he obtained at last a commission, and made his final bow to his master. This first work was a school to cost only a few hundred pounds.* [...] There he was — a full-fledged architect now! He built the school, and there was something about it he was proud of to this day. The extras amounted to *nil*; there was, in fact, a deduction of £5 or £6 upon the contract. But, somehow or other they did not seem to believe at that time in an architect who had not a good bill of extras. There was something un-canny about it — something to be avoided; so he did not for a long time get another commission.

* The small, Gothic Trinity Branch School, 1852–3, in Easton, near Bristol for the Rev. D. Cooper (now demolished).

His brother was then practising as a civil engineer in the North of Ireland, and he (Mr. Godwin) was invited to go and see him. He went, intending to remain a month in order to assist in some competition drawings for a railway bridge. The competition, of course, failed. But he stayed in Ireland for two years, and during that time built a church or two and some small villas. None of them was of much account. As to the church he passed it about three years ago, and it looked, from the railway, perfectly new and somewhat like cast iron.* [...]

* Saint Baithen's Church, St Johnstone, County Donegal, the first of Godwin's designs to be published (*Builder*, 9 May 1857).

Ruskin and Northampton Town Hall

Having tired of Ireland, Godwin returned to England where his career took off with his winning entry for the Northampton Town Hall in 1861. Like William Morris, who was to describe Ruskin's chapter on 'The nature of Gothic' as 'one of the very few and inevitable utterances of the century', the young Godwin came under the spell of The Stones of Venice *(1853). Despite publicly debunking his aged mentor in 1878, on this occasion Godwin was at pains to point out his profound debt to Ruskin.*

Now it was he began to read Ruskin. From studying the "Seven Lamps" he got a fit about plate tracery — a kind of work very good for Verona, but very inappropriate and very wrong to apply to a country like ours, that had no sun, because the delicate shadows, the markings on the marble, and so forth, which the weather produced in Verona were a very different sort of thing from what was produced here. It got black — a black thing against a black thing — whereas in Verona, and under an Italian sun generally, there were stains of gold and red, flushed with light gleaming like new ivory against the black openings. However, he did not think of that at the time: he was strong, nay obstinate, on the subject of plate tracery, and did all he could to ruin himself therewith. After the "Seven Lamps" he read Ruskin's "Stones of Venice," and it was about the time when he read that work that there came out a competition advertisement for the Northampton Town Hall.

He went in for that competition, and determined to fight it upon Ruskin's "Stones of Venice."** [...] He did not know a soul in Northampton. Eighty designs, or thereabouts, were sent in, and his was selected, Mr. Tite (afterwards Sir William Tite) having been called in to adjudicate. He was very exhilarated with this success; it was delightful; and here he began his career, truly and practically. One gentleman on the council, an architect, criticising his drawings, said, "They are very fine, no doubt, but I should like to see all the details of that carving and of the figures drawn to a large scale." When, therefore, he was put to it to draw those figures of kings and other personages which stood along the front, it rather staggered him. However, by the aid of various books, he managed to draw one figure — Richard Coeur de Lion — and very bad it was [...], but it satisfied his critic; so he took courage, and when the specifications and working drawings were ready to be signed, another gentleman, who by the way, was in the iron trade — an alderman of the town — got up in the

Biographical notes: Ruskin

** Godwin's brief enthusiasm for Italian 13th-century Gothic was also indebted to the detailed drawings in Sreet's *Brick and Marble Architecture in the Middle Ages: Notes of a Tour in the North of Italy*, 1855.

Sculpture on Northampton Town Hall, BN *10 Nov. 1865.*

council and said, "I observe there are certain things reserved in this contract, the carvings, *e.g.,* ornamental ironwork and sculpture. I entirely object to that; it must be left open to competition". [Godwin] saw what a mistake he had made not to look after the local tradespeople. Still he could not give up his carving, the man who was his carver at the time having been really educated by him, having done a number of things for him in the West of England, and having, moreover, studied Ruskin which was an important matter [...] He told the meeting that, although it was perhaps premature for him to be so decided for his own man, as if there were none who could have done better, yet there was a time when it was well for an architect to be extremely firm about these things. Dilettante clients, who had pets of their own, were apt to interfere with them in a most woeful manner, whereas if you have been ten years in the profession, and have a carver who has been working all the time with you, he has got to understand what you want by a simple sketch. To throw that man over and get a new one was simply to double the architect's trouble, if the work is to be done as he intends [...].

Eventually the building started, and he had very little trouble about it from the beginning of the work to the end. It was finished as they saw it in the competition drawing, nothing was altered; it was decorated throughout from his designs, and he also designed the furniture. When it was completed the townspeople were proud of their building. Ruskin wrote him two or three very complimentary letters about it. But when it was up he (Mr. Godwin) began to see that there were two or three errors which he would specify. The first error that struck him was [...] the upper storey was top-heavy. The mass of stone in the pillars and in the statues really tended, optically, to give the impression that the whole thing was lightly tipping forward. Had the upper part been set back a trifle that imperfection would have been optically corrected. What hurt the thing still more was the appearance of the canopy. The canopy in flank appeared just the same as it did in front; so that the string course, first of all, projected more than the wall, the statues more than the string course, and the canopy more than the statues, an arrangement he considered to be defective.

But there was one point about that Town Hall to which he would like to draw special attention, because Mr. Ruskin was in a measure responsible for it and it was good. The façade was divided into seven bays. No doubt at first sight the seven arches appeared to be all about the same span; but he had read diligently what Mr. Ruskin had said about the charming building produced by having a series of arches of different widths. He (Mr. Ruskin) went into ecstasies over the arches of the west front of St. Mark's, at Venice, because they were of different widths, producing a beautiful wave-like harmony. In the Northampton Town Hall that idea was carried out. The effect was good; but it was not his — it was due to Ruskin. The narrow arches, being at the end, were the strength of the building, and it wanted precisely that appearance of strength which those arches gave. Another thing he was rather proud of in the building was the vestibule, of which he exhibited to the meeting one of the large working drawings. But practical men would say, What was the plan like? [...] Well, the plan was the best part of the whole business; it had been copied for another Town Hall,* by a gentleman in another competition, and it had won that competition [...]

At the time when he was building the Northampton Town Hall the mayor of the borough gave him a commission — and he was the only man in the town who ever did give him a commission — which was to build a couple of villas.* Those were the first villas of any importance he had built; they were, in fact, the "Stones of Venice" over again. They had a heavy character, but not so bad, he thought, as some other villas in the same neighbourhood. In some other villas not above twenty yards from them, which he built for the same gentleman later on, he avoided that heaviness.

* Saint Martin's Villas, 43-44 Billing Road, Northampton, 1863-4, for the mayor, Pickering Phipps; followed by Rheinfelden, also on Billing Road, and a cottage on the Collingtree Estate, both also for Pickering Phipps, 1868–9.

Travel in France and Congleton Town Hall

From the late 1850s many architects were beginning to explore France, particularly Goths of a 'muscular' persuasion like Godwin's friends Burges and Nesfield. (See Ch. VII, 'Travels with an Architect'.) By this time Viollet-le-Duc was replacing Ruskin as the leading pundit of the Gothic Revival, a tendency reflected in Godwin's second town hall of the early 1860s, Congleton.

After that he made his first visit to the Continent — not on a sketching tour, for he made no sketches worth seeing. He went to Paris, and stopped at Amiens on the road. He looked about Paris and Chartres, and on returning all that he had to show was a drawing of a bit of shadow — nothing else — not the ornament, but the shadow of the ornament cast on the string course. The result of that trip, of course, was that he had great respect for French Gothic. No one could go over exactly the line just pointed out without having a great respect for French Gothic; but he was not old enough then quite to see the glory and the beauty of the transepts of Chartres Cathedral.

Upon his return to England he entered into competition for the Town Hall at Congleton. That was a very small business. But they saw in that building, perhaps, a little of the influence of the French Gothic. The "Stones of Venice" already had been dropped. But the great fault of Congleton — its towering defect, if they would forgive him for saying so — was the top of the tower. It looked right in elevation, as things often did, but in perspective was so bad that if he were a rich man he would offer to rebuild the whole top at his own expense. But with regard to both the Northampton and Congleton Town Halls he would say this — that they were, whether by the subtle preparation of the architect, or whether by a fluke, he would not say, but they were wonderfully good for sound. He had been complemented on both halls — especially Northampton — by prima donnas who had sung there. The reason, he thought, in the case of Northampton, was because the entire wall on each side, above the head of the singer, was broken into a series of arcades recessed between the principals of the roof. The hammer beams [...] were open iron work, offering slight but not, of course, solid resistance to sound; and there was a boarded ceiling at a tolerable height. There was a recess at one end, broken by an organ, and projecting balconies, and it was, he believed, to these breaks — not

Biographical notes:
Burges
Nesfield
Viollet-le-Duc

Congleton Town Hall, 1864: R. Head, Congleton Past and Present, *1887.*

being very great, but being at regular intervals — and to the simple proportions of the hall, that its excellent acoustic properties were due.

Domestic architecture: Dromore Castle to the White House

'When offered a commission in Ireland, refuse it' was the lesson Godwin drew from Dromore Castle (1866–73). In this first major domestic commission following Congleton some of the blunders had been of his own making, but his most serious adversary was the weather. The roofs leaked and 'Somehow the walls always sent out a kind of fur' that defeated his attempts to implement a comprehensive scheme of painted decoration with his friend Stacy Marks. More successful in terms of embracing the 'Sister Arts' and expressing colour harmonies was his famous design for Whistler's White House, nearing completion at the time of this lecture.

Biographical notes:
Chaucer
Limerick, Lord
Marks
Whistler

Perspective of Dromore Castle by Axel Haig, BN *29 March 1867.*

His client in the case of Dromore was Lord Limerick; and he selected the site of the castle with his lordship one autumn morning — a site on the edge of a wood, overlooking a lake, which reflected the castle 100 feet below. It was a charming spot, commanding a distant view of the river Shannon, with old ruined castles and towers in the vicinity. He had not *carte blanche*, he was, in fact, limited as to expenditure. He could not convey the slightest notion of what that castle looked like. He had seen it by moonlight, seen it from the lake, from the road, and at a distance, at every angle, and the silhouette was about as charming a thing as he ever saw in his life, notwithstanding that it was his own work. Nevertheless there was in the construction certain blunders which the young architect should carefully guard against. One thing was that when he made an archway it should be a practical archway, capable of taking in what we in these days use, and not what we used in the days of Edward I. The archway exhibited in the drawing might have been perfectly right for that period, but was decidedly too low for the time of Queen Victoria. A four-in-hand, for instance, with a lot of passengers on the top, could not go in there; and gentlemen would drive four-in-hand sometimes. Of course his noble client was extremely delighted with the place. He was fond of Chaucer and of the mediaeval authors, and it realised his taste exactly. He regretted that the internal decoration of the castle was not carried through. Somehow the walls always sent out a sort of fur, which he got a distinguished chemist to analyse. The chemist said "Oh, it will go away in time," but the time had not come yet. He would strike a note of warning to all young architects on that point. Of course he could not be expected to live at Dromore whilst the work was in progress; so he had a clerk of the works, and an English builder took the contract. The walls were from 3 feet to 6 feet thick, and they were to be built with an inside lining of brickwork, covered with pitch, and the cavity was to be perfectly ventilated, and so forth. Well, the work was done, but then it was found, whenever it was going to rain, that the walls showed it like a weather glass. This bothered him exceedingly; he could not make it out; and he asked a London architect, who was in the neighbourhood at the time, as to the cause, and was told that it was due wholly to the climate. Ireland was sea-girt and always damp, and they could not help it. There was, therefore, an end to decorations. His experience at Dromore and elsewhere led him to give this general advice to young architects — When offered a commission in Ireland, refuse it. He had known no end of architects come to grief by touching Ireland. Once when staying at a noble mansion there, he observed that every room, without exception, was festooned at the ceiling with paper hanging from the walls. They could not keep damp out in Ireland. Go into a house having a stone staircase, and they could tell if it was going to rain the afternoon because the stones suddenly got darker in colour. Altogether, therefore, Ireland was a place to be avoided by the architect, he thought.

Mr. Godwin then called attention to his designs for the Castle Ashby lodges* — in connection with which he remarked upon the necessity of an architect being also an archaeologist and an artist — and also described other examples of domestic architecture in which he had been concerned. One of the principle works referred to was Mr. Whistler's house on the Thames Embankment at Chelsea, which, he observed, everybody knew, and of which they would know more next week. It was built entirely of hard white brick, slated with green Eureka slate (which he believed was a good slate and would last), and the doorway was of Portland stone, the doors, window-frames, sashes and other woodwork being painted a pale grey blue colour. The entire effect of the house everybody he had met said was simply what they would expect — original and pleasing. He did not know how the white would last, but when the house was first built it has a lovely effect with the green Eureka slate.

* Designed 1867–70 for the 3rd marquess of Northampton.

The White House, BA 6 Dec. 1878.

Self criticism – Architectural art – Historical style

Godwin concluded his lecture with some remarks upon the need for constant self-criticism, and careful study of the past 'in all its different phases and countries'. At the same time he urged his audience to be wary of fads and fashions, expounding a view of architectural style that would express the sensibility of the individual, modern designer, a sentiment echoed in 1902 by his admirer, Charles Rennie Mackintosh, who urged his fellow art-workers to 'Stumble, stagger ... go alone'.

Remarking upon a cemetery chapel in Nottingham, he said he had a fashion — which he thought would be a good one for young architects to exercise — when his building was in progress, or completed, of noting in his pocket-book what struck him as being better or worse than he thought it would come out. He had made notes on that cemetery chapel. They were very brief. The practice encouraged a critical faculty of mind very useful to the architect of the present day who did not criticise his own work as he went on sufficiently. It would be well if they all looked at their work as if it were that of an outsider upon which they were to publish some criticism.

Mr. Godwin in the course of some observations upon architectural art, said there was no building in the country that they could refer to and say, Look at this painting, or this sculpture; it is all one — one glorious work of art. Their sculpture was a disgrace, wherever they turned — whether they went to Northampton or the Manchester Town Hall, or wherever they went, it was uniformly dull. Hardly a man in England yet knew how to sculpt architect-

Biographical notes:
Burges
Jones
Street

Egyptian Court at the Crystal Palace, Sydenham: M. Digby Wyatt, Views of the Crystal Palace, Sydenham, *1854.*

* Following the Great Exhibition an expanded version of the Crystal Palace had been erected at Sydenham in June 1854. The spectacular Egyptian Court arranged by Owen Jones was hugely popular.

urally. It was impossible to find three sculptors who could properly fill a pediment. Yet the Parthenon room at the British Museum existed for them. Sculptors count on sculpting busts, but we had no architectural sculpture. We were not at the top of the ladder, and do not let anyone suppose that we were, or were even half way up. Let us encourage more simplicity, and the time would come, perhaps, when, having an architecture developed out of the wants of the age, we should have artists ready to come in, also simply, in the same quiet and modest way to decorate that architecture, whether in painting or sculpture, in a manner also appropriate to the age. It was in that matter of appropriateness to the time that he thought architecture was so utterly at fault. For instance, take Northampton Town Hall, or Dromore Castle. Was there anything in either that was appropriate to the time? He ventured to say there was not. Northampton Town Hall, logically carried out, should have been vaulted all throughout the ground floor. Very well, then, it was not a piece of logical building to begin with; and if not logical it was not satisfactory at all, because architecture must be logical, or it was nothing. Happily the decorations for Dromore Castle were not Gothic decorations, and they were not Mr. Burges's decorations. Mr. Burges would reproduce the decorations of the Middle Ages, and apply them to a Gothic building, which in its lines and arches was also completely mediaeval. Well, that would be simply to archaeologically treat a reproduction, which was very interesting — very charming. He was very fond of seeing reproductions. He would like to see the Parthenon itself reproduced, stone by stone, line by line. He would like to see an Egyptian temple reproduced. He liked to go to the Crystal Palace and see the courts there, to wander through the Egyptian pillars, the Pompeian Court, and so forth, but that was not architecture, that was not what they were to try for.* Be archaeologists — that was to say, to know all about the past; study Greek, Gothic, Renaissance, the Roman and later developments, study it in all its different phases and countries, but don't take up any one and say, "That is my line of departure; I will work on this line", because, after they had worked for a time the fashion would change. Depend upon it, Gothic architecture had had its knell sounded. As long as Mr. Street lived we should have a little of it, now and then. So of Queen Anne architecture; we should see much of that. It would develop much more rapidly than the Gothic developed, because it was much more easy. They had their specimens all cut and dried — all ready to their hand; then, having played all the scales and variations, Queen Anne architecture would die before they had time to turn round. Already they saw gas being superseded by electricity. So Queen Anne architecture, depend upon it, would be superseded by something else. He asked his audience to be independent of fashions, by simply being architects and artists, taking up work and doing it as their own. Study all; take what good they could from every country and every age; but work in no particular style. If asked what style their work was, to say — "It is my own."

II Aesthetic Theory and Criticism

GODWIN was not much given to abstract theorising and, as a practising journalist with deadlines to meet and columns to fill, he rarely went into print
with lengthy accounts of his views unrelated to the concerns of a specific article. Nevertheless, he clearly had original ideas about the role of art in society, about the need for higher thinking on contemporary culture and the possible long-term solutions to problems of which he was all too aware, as both a
designer and a commentator. If his journalism tended to address immediate
issues and practical problems, he always communicated a deeper set of values
lying behind his opinions. His list of useful destinations for the true student of
architecture, embracing as it does the theatre, the circus, ecclesiastical functions, art galleries and sanitary exhibitions, might seem like a provocation to
the casual reader but it was a genuine indication of his own interests. Time
and again one finds the metaphor of physical health and sanitation being used
to describe the intellectual or aesthetic state of the nation. What is more,
Godwin believed this to be the case literally, since both were essential to a balanced 'healthy' life. In this he belonged to a tradition of Victorian commentators whose views on any single point were at the same time an expression of a
greater, interconnected set of values. Architecture lay at the centre of a net-
work of disciplines extending from ideals of beauty to sewage systems, and
from matters of style to the role of an individual in society. This was why design and architecture carried such a burden of moral justification to the Victorians and appeared to professionals and amateurs alike as an arena of vital
debate on a par with politics or the church. An architect's practice impinged
on so many aspects of mental, physical and social life that, for Godwin as much
as for Ruskin or Viollet-le-Duc, to talk of style or building technique alone would
have been to deny the great and inspiring part of architecture – the part which
touched and shaped modern society.

Although he retained the emphasis on practicality and usefulness that was
a legacy of the Gothic Revival, Godwin increasingly turned away from the
moral earnestness and preaching tone of the movement. Instead, his evolving
Aesthetic interests drew him to different issues that he nevertheless pursued
with the same zeal. The role of the independent critic was one of these, a key
factor in maintaining the health of the profession. Like other Aesthetes, Godwin
regarded criticism as a creative act but only in so far as it influenced practice
and was effective in correcting the failings of his fellow architects and designers. In fact, professionalism in architecture was one of Godwin's recurring
themes, despite (or perhaps because of) the reputation he had gained as an
outsider to polite society. It was not the professionalism of learned societies
which engaged him, however, but the proper ways for an architect to conduct
himself and his business in full knowledge of the responsibilities which were
attendant upon this essential task. Above all, Godwin sought to promote the
emerging role of 'Art' as a 'permeating culture power' and a civilising force at

all levels in society. Whether this was expressed in questions of style, in the relationship between architecture and the fine arts, or by extension to such areas as dress, theatre or domestic decoration, Godwin was keen to uphold a higher ambition in his criticism: that of infusing everything with a quality of 'Art'. This was never restricted to one field alone. Godwin regularly emphasised the 'unity of the arts' and the ways in which the essence of artistic sensibility ranges across different media. Properties of 'rhythm and harmony' are common to all art forms, he writes in 'Frozen Music', going on to remark that the architect is merely 'building with stones instead of sound'. One can sense the emergence of this new outlook in 'The Sister Arts', a lecture Godwin delivered as early as 1863. At that time he was a 30-year-old provincial architect with only one significant building to his name, and that still incomplete. Although hardly developed at this early stage in his career, the ideas expressed would come to dominate Aesthetic views of the next two decades. It fell to others like Whistler and Wilde, themselves benefiting from the model of Pater, to write the polished performances that would elaborate Godwin's original ideas about 'Art' as a force in society.

Further Reading

R. Hayes, 'An Aesthetic education: the architectural criticism of E. W. Godwin' in Soros 1999, pp.115-25

A. Reid, 'Dromore Castle, County Limerick: Archaeology and the Sister Arts of E. W. Godwin', *Architectural History* 30 (1987), pp.113-42

Victorian architectural and art criticism:

M. Belcher, 'Pugin writing', in P. Atterbury and C. Wainwright, eds., *Pugin: a Gothic Passion*, London, 1994, pp.104-16

S. Casteras et al., *John Ruskin and the Victorian Eye*, New York, 1993

J. Codell, *The Victorian Artist: Artists' Lifewritings in Britain, 1870–1910*, Cambridge, 2003

P. De Montfort, '"A Sagacious Policy": The artist and the press in the Victorian Art World', *Inferno: St Andrews Journal of Art History*, 1994, pp.46-61

R. Ellman, ed., *The Artist as Critic: Critical writings of Oscar Wilde*, Chicago, 1982

P. Faulkner, 'The writer', in L. Parry, ed., *William Morris*, London, 1996, pp.44-8

F. Jenkins, 'Nineteenth-century architectural periodicals', and P. Thompson, 'The writings of William White', in J. Summerson, ed., *Concerning Architecture*, London, 1968, pp.153-60, 226-37

N. Pevsner, *Some Architectural Writers of the Nineteenth Century*, Oxford, 1972

Aesthetic theory:

C. Harrison and P. Wood, *Art in Theory, 1900–1990*, Oxford, 1992

K. Psomiades, *Beauty's Body: Femininity and Representation in British Aestheticism*, Stanford, 1997

I. Small, *The Aesthetes: A Sourcebook*, London, 1979

PROFESSIONAL TENDERNESS: THE ROLE OF ARCHITECTURAL CRITICISM (1872)

This lacerating attack on the leaders of the profession focuses attention on the independent critic as the true idealist and guardian of standards in architecture. After listing the failures, hypocrisy and incompetence of the officials, Godwin's remedy for the situation is 'criticism, plenty of it, deep, broad, and technical, general, and specific'. Ironically, while this clearly served to justify his own position as a critic, his primary aim was to defend Ruskin, an upholder of principles in architecture whose writings were often dismissed because he was not a practising architect.

It may be taken almost as an axiom that the architects of the present day are eminently thin-skinned. If an amateur with artistic and scholarly qualifications like Mr. Ruskin expresses an opinion at all condemnatory of this or that modern work, or of a past phase of art, the elder members of the profession rush together to find some Philistine to oppose him. So, too, if a professional man gives utterance to opinions which may be considered unfavourable, the favourable things he may have said are forgotten, and some Goliath is invited to shake his weaver's beam to make every endeavour to frighten him from the field. It is well known how Mr. Garbett and Professor Kerr, amongst others, resented Mr. Ruskin's criticisms. What could an amateur know about architecture? What dogmatism! what ignorance! what presumption! Even men like Mr. Burges were sometimes found to be wrath: professional teaching had been interfered with, a new prophet had arisen, and we were solemnly assured that such writing, and such criticism would do inconceivable harm to the young men, the fledgelings who were to be our future architects. Mr. Ruskin ceased to apply his mind to architectural matters, and after the short lull which ensued, architects themselves took up the pen, and both in anonymous and signed articles, in general and specific charges, many weaknesses, shortcomings, and backslidings in art have been exposed. For ourselves, we are free to confess that we have reaped no little profit and pleasure from these charges. The discomfiture of pretension is always a delightful thing to contemplate, and we have over and over again expressed our determination to prevent as far as in us lies the safety of incompetency under the shield of "respectability." Professional critics are now disliked — we might almost say hated — with an energy equal to that once bestowed on amateur critics. Sir M. D. Wyatt whitewashes Mr. Ruskin in one room, while his elder brother sneers in another at those who, having formed opinions on art questions, are bold enough to utter what they think, and who, we know from their works, have as much right to be listened to as the President of the Institute or the Slade Professor. Meanwhile, where is architecture? We turn to the public Exhibitions, to the Royal Academy, and the International. We examine with anxiety the new buildings which are springing up by thousands around us; and we ask in all seriousness are there ten that give promise of a better architecture in the future? Are there twenty which show any worthy advance on what was done ten years ago? If the dignitaries of the profession had only shown the same anxiety for the development of art as they have for developing their business; if they had had as

Source:
'Professional tenderness',
Building News, 28 June 1872,
p.515

Biographical notes:
Architectural Association
Bowman & Crowther
Brandon
Burges
Garbett
Kerr
Pugin
Royal Academy
RIBA
Ruskin
Slade School of Art
Verdier and Cattois
Viollet-le-Duc
Wyatt, M.D.
Wyatt, T. H.

much care for quality as quantity of work, such criticisms as we have lately read would have been groundless, and would have met with the ruin which sooner or later attends on weak foundations. But, unfortunately, there is no escape from the sad conclusion that architecture, generally speaking, is degenerating, and has degenerated even within the memory of the youngest practitioner.

Is there, we would ask, a single building of to-day founded on Classic, Italian, or Renaissance principles of design, which can compare with the works of the last generation? [...] Have the architects of the Gothic party done any better for the encouragement they have met with? Do their later designs show a greater power of composition and a greater grasp of beauty than heretofore? Is not the book of patterns as much resorted to as ever it was, with this difference, that, instead of English examples from Pugin, Bowman and Crowther, and Brandon, we have French from Johnson, Verdier and Cattois, and Viollet-le-Duc? These are questions which would, no doubt, be very convenient to leave unasked; but we have a duty higher than any personal considerations — a duty which is all the more incumbent on us to fulfil, watching as we do day by day the growth of indifference, the spread of superficiality, the want of anything like energetic life, and the increasing desire for taking things easy in matters artistic, characteristic not merely of the leaders of the profession, but of the whole body down to the poorest assistant and the youngest pupil. As is natural to such a state of things, good drawing is becoming every day rarer. Art is turned into business, and young and old endeavour to escape from it as much as ambition to get money permits. Spare time now is devoted to anything rather than to the mistress we have elected to serve, and even the Association finds it hard to whip up its usual classes. Seeing this, is it possible to suppose that the elders in the profession have nothing to answer for? We are imitative beings from the cradle, and yet look at what we have to follow! Men who are afraid of criticism, men who are prepared to give up their opinions and the lessons they have taught for a quarter of a century, rather than sacrifice the chance of a commission; men who we know never make a drawing, and who spoil their clerks' designs only for the sake of satisfying their elastic consciences. These are prominent members of the profession — these are our examples. No wonder a professional critic is regarded as cantankerous or spoken of as disagreeable. The sting of his criticism [...] lies in its truth, and the thin-skinned professors no doubt feel the sting, but do not exactly perceive the truth.

The cure for this unwholesome sensitiveness, we believe, lies in criticism, plenty of it, deep, broad, and technical, general, and specific. It is because architects have been so long exempt from hearing opinions of their works freely expressed that they have become so tender about them. And yet what art is so public — what so justly open to praise or censure? Pictures and busts one may avoid and yet live; but one cannot shut out building, — it forces itself on us in the country, and hems us in the town. The newspapers and periodicals may be deluged with critiques of the first that no one need see; but that which we are all bound to see is far too sacred for animadversion. Architecture must be in a deplorably bad condition when its professors must needs shrink from the caustic to the extent lately exhibited. [...] It is quite possible we may tread on a few tender places, but we admit at once that we shall care nothing about that, for architects have no business to be afflicted with any such encumbrances. They hurt us with their works right and left. They take little heed of the annoyance their designs cause us, and we, in our turn, shall not stand measuring terms or seek for words to soften our opinions when they do not happen to coincide with the dulcet notes of plaintive professors.

FEARLESS CRITICISM (1873)

Again Godwin makes the case for the harsh, impartial criticism needed to break through the stultifying complacency within the closed ranks of the architectural profession.

In these times of carping, cavilling, and motive-mongery, it is as well, if we wish our opinion to be taken for what it is really worth, and not at considerably less, to state clearly the personal relations of the critic and the criticised. If there be any relation, no critic is altogether above suspicion, because no one with memory can put himself beyond the reach of association. [...] Not consciously by any means, but *unconsciously* by all means, is everyone biased, and true judgment is altogether a myth. [...]

Source:
'The Works of Mr. R. Norman Shaw', *Building News*, 24 October 1873, p.449

Biographical notes:
Smith

We are constantly being reminded of *esprit de corps*, as Mr. Roger Smith calls it, although I question the existence of any corps whatsoever. We are told that our profession is a brotherly union, and everything that is pleasant, if the discontented ones would but leave off their unseemly wrangling. The Medical Faculty and the Law are held up to us as examples of behaviour: that is to say, we are invited to see how Dr. Brown cherishes Dr. Jones, conceals his little error when Jones kills a patient by sheer ignorance, and places the aegis of his reputation between the fool and the world for the sake of *esprit de corps*. The amiable men may talk as much as they please about esprit, and all the other nice things they pick up as they sup together in their private societies, or hobnob over a cup of weak tea in their public reunions, but all the amiableness in the world, and all the talk, will not alter the fact that ninety-nine in a hundred colour their criticisms of architectural works with pigments extracted from their prejudices for or against the author of such works. Architects are perhaps more hungry for praise than any other class of men outside the green room, and if once you begin to feed them, woe betide you if you stop the supply.

THE SISTER ARTS (1863)

In this lecture, first delivered to the Bristol Society of Architects, Godwin pleads for a more balanced and unified approach to the 'sister arts' of painting, sculpture and architecture; the musical resonance between them had been undermined since the Renaissance. Along the way he works in a few customary side-swipes at the Art establishment: first at the outmoded coverage of the Art Journal, *and secondly at the bias of the Royal Academy towards painting, which he felt limited the institution's potential role as a 'national school of art'. In this extract, he argues for enlightened patronage within the modern home in order to make the symbolic representation of the sister arts a living reality once more. Although not fully developed at this early stage in his career, these views would come to dominate aesthetic ideas of the next two decades.*

Cover of the *Art Journal*

Source:
'The sister arts and their relation to architecture,' 1863 news-cutting in Archive of Art and Design AAD 4/561.

Cover of the Art Journal *1866.*

I have here the paper covers of a well known monthly periodical. Inside, it announces to us that it has attained its "full age," and that it is "the only publication in Europe by which the arts are adequately represented." Large as these statements may sound, and inaccurate as the last of them may be, I must for the present pass them by in order to draw your attention to the picture on the outside of the cover. [...] First of all then, there is a huge circle, with a highly-enriched Greek border, possibly intended to represent the mirror which art is supposed to hold up to Nature; or it may be intended for one of the plates belonging to the dinner service of the Cyclops, for it stands upon a kind of sideboard which is also enriched after the Greek manner and flanked by gryffins and harpies. Ranged on each side of this sideboard are some half-a-dozen vases and a couple of candleabra [sic], and in the centre appears the singular and mysterious part of the whole design, to whit, three ladies, apparently on the very best of terms, leaning on one another in the most affectionate and sisterly manner, and evidently intent on one common object. We are told that this object is art, and that the three ladies are sisters, and represent Painting, Sculpture, and Architecture, thus called the "sister arts."

Now I ask you seriously, does that united and affectionate-looking group *really* present to us the true state and relationship of the three arts just mentioned? [...] For some five centuries, gradually, but too surely, the position of these figures has been changing so that, instead of that equality and unity which constituted the majesty and the strength of past times, we have now nothing but miserable jealousies and low time-servings; instead of one great consonant common chord reaching, like the music of Apollo's lyre, to the heart of beggar as of prince, we hear each note *singly* at the *best*, and this oft-times out of tune; and mark you this evil which has accrued, and is still progressing, in consequence of this disruption of the arts, is somewhat deeper than the mere surface. [...]

After a discussion of the role of the Royal Academy, and then of the mutual dependence of the three arts in the ancient world and the Christian middle ages, Godwin turns to the contemporary need to move beyond superficial applications of architectural style and the mindless following of fashion. In the language of mid-century Design Reform he advocates the cultivation of a truly artistic sensibility.

We are not such heathens as to require pictures of Dives and Lazarus, or St. Martin and the beggar, to keep alive our sympathies as we sip our claret in the soft light of crimson-curtained dining rooms. Wild unmannered scrolls of red and yellow torture themselves into madness on our walls, impossible flowers in the most impossible of positions climb frantically over the most impossible of trellises but we care not. In our self-satisfaction and luxury, and pride, we never *see* such things in any other light than the last French fashion, for which we have paid the very best price. You will say, perhaps, that we are advancing from this sluggish condition, and that I have taken an extreme view of the case. I wish in my heart it were so. I am rather inclined to fear that we are but changing from one fashion to another — going through the same diluting and stereotyping process with the Gothic and Italian as we have gone with the Greek and the Roman, without taking so much as one step towards the reconciling of the sisters, or the unity of art. I am well aware that there are exceptions, but, as a rule, I feel assured the public take no living interest whatever in ART, taken in its fullest sense, and freed from all the shackles of style.

When the authors of those suburban villas which are scattered in discordant ugliness amidst our dearest bits of scenery, shall have learnt to express, by the harmony of their works, the love they bear, or ought to bear, for one another; when Round arch, and Gothic arch, and straight lintel shall meet together in amity; when perfect and grotesque humanity, and natural and conventional beauties shall be chiseled in their proper place; when our mantel-pieces shall incite us to thankfulness by its sculptures, picturing winter so that it may be deservedly likened to winter itself; when our walls are diapered by paint or paper, and powdered with medallions, or hung with pictures guiltless of heavy frames; when each room and each article of furniture shall be found to be but resolutions of the same key-note; when Royal Academicians and painters and sculptors of equal merit shall stand upon our scaffoldings, side by side with our architects, to hold affectionate counsel together, moved by the same principles, and actuated by the same motives — then may we hope to have an art of our own — then, and not till then, may we hope to see realised the picture on the *Art Journal* cover. There is nothing, believe me, visionary in this. Every man who desires to build himself a dwelling-place which shall be to him as a home (for I refer not now to speculative building) may have all that I have said at no much greater cost than the ordinary outlay. And yet it is wonderful to note what little interest men take in their houses [...]

The need for artistic patronage

I am sure there are artists — professors of each art — who, if they but found you valued their studies and their services, would soon rival, if not eclipse, the works of the former times, noble as they are. It is upon the public mind that the fate of art depends, and therefore the public must be indoctrinated with art. If, however, people will continue to prefer ancient Greece to modern England, if they have more love for heathen Rome than for their own fatherland, if they will listen to ignorant upholsterers' opinions rather than to artists' suggestions, if they are determined to be advised by the jobbing mason instead of the educated architect, if they will still purchase their enrichments and decorations at so much a yard, if they are bent upon machine-made buildings and manufactured ornament, then artists may strive and starve, for in spite of all the zeal, and labour, and patience, and longing of the painter, sculptor, architect, the age will be virtually unrepresented in the history of art. I say "*artists may strive and starve*," for the title is far too noble a one to be applied to those self-styled artists who are nothing more than panderers to and flatterers of that gross darkness and ignorance (all the more dark because of the glitter of its gold), which have taken root in so many hundreds of houses in this land, where because it is fashionable the so-called arts are, as a matter of course, patronised, and which, under the cloak of art, conceal the assassin's knife, ever ready to destroy, if it could, that reality and truth which constitutes, as it were, the life-blood of the sisters.

I know not why it should be so, but there seems to be a feeling that art is a luxury with which we may indulge ourselves according to our pleasure and our means, and that artists are our slaves, to minister to that pleasure. The feeling is by no means new. It arose with the spirit of renaissance, and until that debased spirit of wild voluptuousness and unrestrained freedom be subdued and cast out from among us as an unclean thing, the position of art, in all its nobility and in all the power of its moral and religious teaching, will never be fairly and fully realised. If, on the other hand, the arts were but united again, how great would be their influence upon one another. Painting would teach architecture to avoid those *sudden* transitions of colour which she has lately been indulging in, and no longer to riot in ill-arranged bands of red and white, having no earthly meaning unless it be to keep up a lively interest in the bacon trade.* In our interiors she would teach us to subdue the colour of the walls and curtains, to note well those constant allusions to green and gold in the liberate rolls,** and if there be any pattern to keep that pattern flat, conventional, and unobtrusive. She would tell us that flowers were not made to be trampled on, that green harmonizes with dark woods, and that purple is friendly inclined towards maple and the lighter woods. She might, perhaps, warn us to be jealous of ormolu, to guard against gold, white, and the three primary colors, and to use them like nature with such wise economy that their great glory may be seen and known. [...]

* A reference to the structural polychromy of architects like William Butterfield.

** Manuscript records of medieval society.

Reuniting sculpture, architecture, and the fine and decorative arts

How absurdly puerile must that practice appear which indulges itself in copying those very architectural features which were created by the exigencies of sculpture, and yet ignores the latter art altogether. Most of you can, no doubt, call to mind many a modern structure treated in this meaningless way — niches that were never intended to be filled; blank, idiotic-looking pediments, and crocketted canopies covering nothing; and the worst of it is that all this is received by the public as the art of architecture, while its patrons, in pitiable foolishness, congratulate themselves on having obtained an "ornamental building." They hang their walls with no end of picture frames, but they utterly ignore the pictures. Depend upon it, true and good architecture cannot long exist divorced from sculpture. [...]

I know there are many persons who, in reply to what I have urged, would say that I have confounded the true artist with the "mere carver" and house decorator — in plainer language, the educated gentleman with the ignorant mechanic; to such, however, the unity of art and the liberty of labour are incomprehensible; their pride of art blinds their eyes to the grand law of gradation in all things, and they see not how "one star differeth from another star in glory." It is quite true that carving and house decoration have been forced to the lowest depths of degradation, and there they will remain, utter outcasts from the pale of art — if you continue to grind out their lives in everlasting twirls of volutes, or spin out their souls into one endless row of eggs and anchors. [...]

And now, what is the practical outcome of all this? In the first place, we should learn to look upon the fine arts (the knowledge of which an older writer has described as "the ultimate polish of a man") with reverence, and in a broad catholic spirit; and, in the second place, we should endeavour ourselves to know more of art, in order that we may see that artists have a higher mission in this world than the bare business of lodging us or ministering to our individual whims and fancies; and, lastly, we should all use the influence which we possess, be it great or little, in doing one act of love and kindness to a family which deserves to be treated well at our hands, but which, unfortunately, is at discord within itself, by labouring to unite its scattered members, to bring once more together the hands of the art sisters, that they may again rest in tender leanings upon one another's shoulders. History will tell you that it is *good* to do this. Your common sense and your own conscience will tell you *how* to do it.

ART: 'PERMEATING CULTURE-POWER' OR 'FASHIONABLE COMMODITY'? (1876)

Godwin viewed the archaeological concerns of the Gothic revival as having deeply – and on the whole positively – influenced artistic culture of the mid-1870s, whether one looked to architecture, painting, dress or theatrical productions. In this extract, however, he goes on to express his distaste for the inappropriate and superficial use of vernacular forms in the context of modern, urban life. If Art was to thrive as a 'permeating culture-power' rather than a merely 'fashionable commodity', it would need to draw in a more profound sense on developments in scientific and progressive thought.

The articles written on the "Hope of English Architecture;" the revival of the red-brick sash-window style of Queen ANNE; the Robertsonian comedy* and the school of painters represented by the followers and admirers of MASON, WALKER, PINWELL, and MILLET, illustrate although in different degrees of excellency, one and only one artistic pulsation, one social movement — the artistification of existing commonplace. This is but the natural reaction from the archaeological movement, which, beginning nearly half a century ago, has given us Houses of Parliament after the manner of Henry VI., which has restored nearly all our cathedrals, and made possible a MACLISE. That this archaeological movement, this recurring to the past for study and for exam-

Source:
'Some stray notes on the modern field of art', *Architect*, 1 January 1876, pp.2-3

* A form of naturalistic domestic comedy developed by T. W. Robertson in the 1860s, also known as 'teacup and saucer' comedy.

ple, has had a profound influence on the latest phase of art culture — however much some young artists may affect to despise it — is, I think, abundantly manifested in the best work of the new school. Mr. BODLEY and Mr. NORMAN SHAW, as architects for example, show a power even in the plainest, most commonplace structure which less accomplished men strive for in vain. They have sounded all the depths and shoals of building. They have learnt the story of their art and have found out much of the vanity of employing forms and detail which have no longer any *raison d'être*. In all their works we can trace this knowledge; in other words, the science of archaeology.

[... W]hatever the art form — architecture or acting, painting or poetry — it is idle to shut our eyes to the fact that the Farm-house School — the cup and saucer style, as a certain kind of art has been called — does not wholly satisfy. The idyllic is all very well in its place. The field, the river, and the mountain are some of Heaven's gifts, and will remain with us forever. But the moated grange, the thresher's flail, and much of what we have been accustomed to look on as the picturesque of country life, must inevitably follow in the path of many another bit of picturesque in the world's history that we still take pains to revive or to preserve, and some pleasure to contemplate. Village schoolchildren, tramps and paupers are no doubt far more interesting and easier to paint than the ladies and gentlemen who wear WORTH'S dresses or POOLE'S coats. But the village school and the workhouse are not quite all England [...]

Some may say, however, that our English life is so monotonous, so black and white as to be unworthy the painter's palette and is fit only to be shown through the medium of printer's ink in the *Graphic* and such like illustrations; this is no doubt the feeling of those who seek in Greek myth or mediaeval story a channel for their art. But it surely must be a bad time for painter and poet when their art hinges on a question of tailoring. So, too, if the art of architecture is to depend on the size of the panes of glass or that of the drama on blue china and tapestry, the harvest of our modern field of art will prove but miserable at its best. I venture, however, to assert that our life, colourless as it may be in comparison with Classic, Mediaeval, or Renaissance times, has yet much in it for art to record and translate that has hitherto passed unnoticed or worse than unnoticed. Science must not and will not be ignored, and if Art is to thrive again, not as a fashionable commodity, like the fictiles of Bristol or Chelsea, but as a permeating culture-power, it must be through the lively companionship of the thoughts and knowledge and development of the sundry thinkers and leaders among the men and women of our own generation.

TWADDLE ABOUT ART (1875)

Source:
'The "Daily News" versus Art',
Architect, 20 November 1875,
pp.281-2

Musing on a speech of Mr Gladstone, the then Leader of the Liberal Party, Godwin urges his audience to abandon a partisan attitude to style, to cultivate all their senses, and to consider beauty in whatever form it might take, from a tea cup to a cathedral.

The year's twaddle about Art has risen to its highest flood within the last fortnight, and culminated in a daily contemporary that is usually very clear-headed about everything it takes into its columns.

Now these are some of the things we are told by the critic of the *Daily News*:-

"We cannot be Classic Greeks, and we could not feel to Art as they did without becoming like them."

"We cannot give ourselves up as a people to the worship and culture of mere beauty."

"It is quite possible, sometimes, to combine in a wonderful degree the purposes of utility with the purposes of beauty."

"Any great cathedral will make this evident; as will a really artistic tea-cup." […]

To tell us that we cannot be "Classic Greeks" is just as futile and as unnecessary as it would be to say that we cannot be Hebrew apostles. To cease the practice of Christian virtue or the good because we cannot be Galilean fishermen and be crucified, would be just as reasonable as to cease the practice of natural virtue or the beautiful because we cannot be PHIDIAS, ICTINUS, or APELLES.* No one wants to be a Galilean fisherman, and no one wants to be a "Classic Greek," and yet we may well long for the virtues of both.

Nor am I aware that any, the most visually-sensitive, among us want the English people to give themselves up "to the worship and culture of mere beauty." The word *mere* in the expression "*mere* beauty" means, I suppose, much about the same as the word *really* in the expression "a really artistic tea-cup." What the difference may be between an artistic tea-cup and a *really* artistic one may not be so self-evident as the critic of the *Daily News* seems to think. And so, also, the distinction between the culture of beauty and of *mere* beauty. […]

It is quite enough for those who *can* see, to suffer, as they are compelled to suffer in almost every place, every waking hour, from the disquieting, ill-proportioned, inharmonious, discordant outcome of the insensible or careless modern worker without its being insinuated that their desire for beautiful form and colour proceeds from the later exercises of the Greek gymnasia. You may, if you choose, read the life of every nation in its *cloacae maximae*.** You may also, if you choose, read it on the brows of its noblest matrons, and on its temple fronts. You may, if you like, suppose that beauty has been fully reached, that the limits of human power are marked on the Athenian Akropolis and in the Greek rooms of museums. You may assume the Parthenon to have been perfect, and reap the rewards of your assumption for your pains. But, on the other hand, you may, if you like, hold that a limit to human power has *not* yet been and can not be defined; that beauty has *not* been fully grasped and never will be; that a perfect work was and is impossible in the very nature of things, because it implies a perfect workman; that beauty and perfection are ideal, and that it is only in the *endeavour* to reach this ideal — in the act of moving ever and ever onwards — that a living Art is possible. For the moment we assume the ideal to be reached — the moment we pause for self-gratulation, that moment we die to Art, fit only to consort with him whose satisfied self-sufficiency so swells him that he sees nothing to sorrow at in ugliness, does not think it worthwhile to seek to be artistic, struts in a vain show of "intellec-

Biographical notes:
Carlyle
Gladstone
South Kensington

* Pheidias, the most famous sculptor of antiquity, active c.450–30 BC in mainland Greece; direct contemporary of Ictinus, architect of the Parthenon; Apelles, Greek painter, active c.340–300 BC.

** *Cloaca maxima*, the 'great sewer' of Rome.

tual departments," and flatters himself with the false doctrine that Art can not "act directly on the mind" or help "to make men's lives easier and happier."

[... T]here is spreading among us, in spite of *Daily News* criticisms, a broader view of art and utility. There is, it is true, much dense unconsciousness in, much lazy indifference with regard to, the finer and more sensitive parts of our organisms. We townsfolk have most of us been surrounded from our infancy by, if not the absolutely ugly, at any rate the non-beautiful, and in the exercise of the senses as avenues to the mind habit counts for much. "If," as Mr. GLADSTONE very appositely remarks, "the nurse who carried you when you were three or six months old had continued to carry you until you were forty, you would not be able to walk." And what is true of the leg is equally true of the eye in a higher degree. If we have had nothing worth looking at, nothing for the subtle nerves of vision to divide and exercise themselves withal, then the faculties of seeing will not keep pace with the rest of our organism, and will end in a dull non-excitable death-like condition akin to the legs of the forty year old nursling, for seeing we shall not perceive. To furnish us with things that are worth looking at, to give the eye pleasant food that this sense may know what it is to live, that it may grow up at least as vigorous as the ear, able to discover discords in form and colour as readily as its companion sense distinguishes discord in sound — this surely must be a useful thing to do. If there is any respect left among us for the human body, it must surely be among the very highest utilities to minister to its keenest sensibilities, and through them to contribute to the enjoyment of the hidden faculties — intelligence, mind, soul, or whatever we please to call them. If by means of the Department of Science and Art, the City Companies, our Schools, Museums, Exhibitions, Manufactures, Criticisms, Architecture, Poetry, Sculpture, or our Stage, we can at least excite into action the eye of the nation, well for us. But if we fancy that we yet possess qualities in any one of the means I have enumerated sufficiently strong to produce the desired excitement, we are grossly deceived. The most advanced are still — to use Mr. GLADSTONE'S leg simile — often tottering and occasionally toppling over. Our principle painters build for themselves houses that are wanting in every quality which we look for in Art; our architects trade on their past success, and repeat, *ad nauseam*, the things they drew — I cannot say designed — years ago; our sculpture stagnates; our stage decays. This is not an exaggerated view, nor intended to be a despondent one. [...] But the self-laudation, the passing applause awarded to the favourite of the hour, the high value we put on our most paltry work are stifling us and the little Art there is develops but slowly under the terrific shadow of pretence. But it does develop, and it is because of this hope that is left us — that the little leaven shall in the end leaven the whole lump — that I plead here for Art — Greek, Hebrew, Christian, of whatsoever nation and whatsoever time; "not," as CARLYLE says, "because of its effect, but because of itself; not because it is useful for spiritual pleasure or even for moral culture, but because it is Art and the highest in man."

FROZEN MUSIC (1876)

In 1877 Walter Pater described all art as constantly aspiring towards the condition of music, a concept to which Godwin, like Whistler, made frequent reference. This article discusses the need to sharpen critical faculties and to examine rigorously sensory responses to existing phenomena: only then is it possible to move beyond 'accidental' details and focus on the development of broader compositional harmonies, whatever the style. Godwin clearly wished to distance himself from the popular view of fashionable Aesthetes whose rhapsodic and pretentious utterances were ridiculed so effectively in Punch, *a magazine to which Godwin himself subscribed.*

It is a well worn hackneyed expression that saying wrongly attributed to Madame de STAEL which describes architecture as frozen music. Reading lately the lecture delivered at the Architectural Association, and looking carefully at the illustrations which have appeared of new buildings, I certainly have not discovered any sign of the usual characteristics of music frozen or otherwise. No one seems to be in tune, there is a decided lack of harmony, and the time is more than "peculiar." It is somewhat noteworthy, this discord which rages so furiously round about arts whose excellences are generally supposed to destroy discord and disarm rage. It seems to me that all the smart talk we are perpetually hearing about the virtues of this style and the vices of that — of the abominations of Sir CHRISTOPHER WREN and the desolation of Queen ANNE is getting a trifle monotonous, for smartness itself may become troublesome and a bore if unsupported by more solid and enduring qualities [...]

It is all very well to be told that a certain building lifts up your soul or makes you stand fairly aghast with admiration. It is very fine to throw up the reins within ear-shot of fine music or eye-shot of cathedral vault, and let ourselves free to revel in the mere sensuousness of eye and ear, not caring to divide nor troubling to separate the evil from the good; for there is evil side by side with the good in the best of things, and the worst is not altogether without some sign of hope. We may sigh or speak in whispers, and our eyes like the poets' may roll in a fine frenzy; but we shall not move a step onwards by such pleasurable indulgences as these. Let us, while reaping the pleasure, deny ourselves indulgence therein, that we may find time to discover the *reason* of the satisfaction which any special form of art gives to any special sense.

To give a *reason* for your faith or judgment is what we now want. Those results of certain sounds in certain succession which, by way of the ear, enwrap the brain in heavenly dreams or rouse it to fiery action, are not accidental. They have come in obedience to the men who are not masters of copyism, but diligent students of the laws of time, tune, and harmony, by which they build up their sounds into noble structures of music. So, too, that lifting up of the soul and that standing aghast with admiration which certain architects tell us is their experience within certain old churches — so far as such experience results from a real nervous action of the eye on the brain, and not from some sentimental association — are not accidental, but have arisen in obedience to, and sympathy with, the men who, building with stones instead of sounds, wrought out their architectural symphony in well apportioned rhythm

Source:
'Frozen music', *Architect*, 5
February 1876, pp.76-7

Biographical notes:
de Stael
Pater
Punch
Royal Academy
Scott
Street
Waterhouse
Wren

Aesthetes aghast with admiration, Punch 9 Oct. 1880.

and delightful harmony.[... T]here is this advantage which this view of our art possesses, and whatever may be the work and whatever the material — however costly or however much the reverse, however elaborate or however simple — these properties of rhythm and harmony are common to all and cost nothing but thought. But thought, or in other words the power of composing, is not so common as one would like to see it, and so it happens that the architect of to-day, anxious to make a mark, and by much sound to cover up all other deficiencies, indulges to excess in shakes, *fortissimo* passages and the like. These are the "ornaments" which give what is now called *style*. I think it would be well for Art to set our faces wholly against such ornamentation, and if needs be against all enrichment. To know the function of the building we are called on to design, and to give expression to its purpose in life, well apportioning its divisions and balancing its masses with judgment, are lessons which all of us, pupils and masters, the most accomplished of practitioners as well as beginners, may go on learning with advantage to the end of their days. That the so-called Queen ANNE architects have managed to make some modern dwelling-houses look more like houses to dwell in than any modern Gothic houses I wot of, is in itself no doubt a bitter draught to those Gothic architects who are still wedded to the accidents of building development which are called the *details* of architecture. The architect whose life seems pinned to a large round moulding with a hollow each side of it — he whose time is mostly taken up with cusps — the man who has always on hand a banded shaft with cap and base complete to pop in at every available and unavailable opportunity — the R. A. whose glossary has different illustrations for different sorts of clients, and whose details are as elastic as his indiarubber — these men are all dealing with and depending on accidentals; their composition is thus a heap of details, a stringing together of mere prettiness at the best, without due relation of even prettiness to prettiness, and if deprived of the mouldings, caps, and cusps would not possess a line or mass to tell of delicate or strong proportion, of lively or solemn rhythm. In the name of all that is artistic I ask my student friends to give up these vicious details, these meaningless fritterings of arch and string-course and jamb. The sharp edge of your material for protection's sake must be taken off; well then, take it off at once, and have done with it — don't worry yourself to death over it, for no one cares or will care two straws about it. If your building is be all-glorious without and within, turn you to figure sculpture and painting to make it so, for depend upon it no one in the world cares or ever will care for the tons of carved capitals and polished shafts, the acres of inlaid trefoils, or the miles of round and fillet and hollow you think so desirable... Not that I wish to taboo capital and column and string-course, far from it. In the hands of men who know how to use them these may be as securely trusted as a shake may be to BACH; all I wish to insist on is, that the details of these features should not be taken as the measure of the goodness or badness of the work. I know well how a good mass or pile of building may suffer from an ill-conditioned detail, and how very good detail often atones for ill-considered or awkward mass, but if a building is spoilt or suffers overmuch from the badness of its detail, you may depend upon it the architect relied too much on his detail.

Queen Anne's Gardens, Bedford Park: M. Conway, Travels in South Kensington, *1882, p. 224.*

There are three buildings in London, one of which does contain, and the other two as far as one can at present judge will contain, greater mass and a larger amount of detail than any old building in the country. Sir G. G. SCOTT at St. Pancras, Mr. G. E. STREET at the Law Courts, and Mr. WATERHOUSE at South Kensington, are scoring hard at their symphonies, and trying to show the world what their respective notions may be of "frozen music."[...] For whatever there may be of music in these mighty structures, by all means let us try and find it out. If there are divisions and subdivisions ordered in well marked time and balanced rhythm; if there are harmonies of solid and void; if there are contrasts of curve and straight; if there are subtle resolutions of what might have been discordant angles; and if there is one motif through all, by all means let us enjoy them. But if the whole mass of each is mere discordant sound, or if without being discordant it fails like tons of musical composition from insipidity or dull monotony, from frivolous trickiness or manifest copyism, these also let us know, that our rising generation of architects may have a reason not only for the faith, but for the want of faith that is or may be in them.

Street, Law Courts, Art Journal *June 1887.*

Meanwhile, in the ordinary everyday pursuit of architectural study, where monster hotels, museums, and courts of justice are unknown — might not the student try his utmost — little enough perhaps at the best — some simple harmonies, some unaffected and wholly un-"ornamented" compositions of "frozen music." He need not, as many students do — notably the competing young gentlemen of the Academy and Institute — venture as yet into the sonatas or symphonies or fugues. There is no great anxiety to see what music he can make out of town mansions, guildhalls, or cathedrals, but much interest on the other hand to see what simple ballad or joyful carol he can freeze into fixity on middle-class house or suburban church. And this middle-class house need be but of the lowest denomination. A detached house of some ten or eleven rooms, to cost from seven to ten hundred pounds, with all sanitary advantages in the provision of bath, position of closets, drains, &c., which can be devised is the sort of thing we want to see done, and done artistically. With such a problem the student will soon find out (as I have, because I have after some sort of fashion done it) that the sash window and other common inheritance of the last century are more friendly to his cause than the leaded casement, transoms, mullions, &c., of earlier times. It is true that if you build with very low ceilings to your rooms, the long, low, mullioned window with lead and iron casement, such as we see in every old cottage and farm-house, is better for light and ventilation, but then it is very rare indeed that modern rooms, even in cottages, are so low as to make this sort of window practically preferable. If, after solving this problem, the young architect can find an opportunity for expending something more than the minimum cost per cubic foot, the question may then arise whether a few hundred pounds judiciously spent in encouraging our young promising and encouragement-lacking sculptors and painters would not be a wiser and more musical thing to do than to go on adding to mere mechanical production.

Waterhouse, Natural History Museum, Magazine of Art *1881, p. 359.*

A MANIFESTO FOR ART (1878)

In January 1878 Godwin became the London editor of The British Architect. *He immediately set about putting his stamp on its appearance, journalistic style and content. In this extract he sets out his agenda for the magazine, which restates his inclusive approach to the arts and many of the themes that had preoccupied him since the 1860s. In the fluid conditions of the late nineteenth century, groups were jockeying for position within an increasingly codified hierarchy of skills and professions, threatening to limit the artist to ever more one-sided accomplishment. Godwin actively resisted such compartmentalisation, canvassing to extend the interest of architects to related areas.*

Source:
'To our readers', *The British Architect*, 4 January 1878, p.1

Art, although losing in individual force, is every day widening in its influence, appealing to a larger audience, becoming more popular. Decoration and furnishing and other arts more or less influenced by architecture have been made the subjects of popular handbooks, and a swarm of writers has sprung up, including many amateurs, whose zeal occasionally requires some tempering. From Cabinet ministers weighed down with serious affairs of State to young ladies who have just learnt how to arrange a little blue china on a mantel-piece, we receive lectures on art. It is a subject no one seems to hesitate about, and, therefore, one of our new resolves is to criticize freely and fearlessly the presuming amateur and inexperienced artist, who in these latter days have developed the knack of posing as apostles of domestic art, endeavouring by noise and crowd to fill the place of those whose works and experience are warranty of their judgment. [...]

Hitherto we have rarely allowed ourselves to step beyond the professional limits of one art, but for the future we hope to take a wider range, and without slackening our watchfulness in the field of architecture, we shall embrace in our survey the border ground of painting and sculpture, taking note the while of that art which involves all others, namely the art of the Stage.

That branch of archaeology devoted to the Fine Arts will always find a welcome in our pages, and we shall be thankful to our country readers for any local notes relating to this department of art culture.

[...] Every day bears witness to the presence of a discordant element in modern art. The unity that once was its strength is ruptured, and art, especially household art, has become too much a question to be played with — a question of odds and ends. To reconcile the decorative and constructive to work for greater harmony and unity of thought in the surroundings of modern life will be therefore one of our aims.

For the architect's work should not be confined to the mere bricks and mortar of a house. The decorator, the upholsterer, and the cabinet maker should be as much subject to the architect as the joiner, the plumber, or the glazier. It is only here and there at rare intervals that this thoroughness is to be found, as in the case of an architect's house described in another part of the paper, where the interior and exterior, the building and its furniture, the enclosed as well as the enclosure, are in full accord.

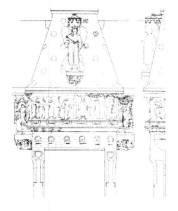

Drawing-room fireplace, in William Burges's Tower House in Melbury Road, London (see p.142).

Godwin's new masthead for the manifesto issue, BN 1878.

[... W]e have in the lines and colouring of our new heading the clearness and decision, the *black and white* of Truth — in the foliage over the initial, the expression of elegance and grace — and in the laughing kingfisher perched below may be symbolised our flight over the world and our pleasantry.

LOOKING BACK (1879)

A year later Godwin could note an increase in the journal's circulation and some progress in the direction of his manifesto.

We have fought against the many evils which surround and clog the practice of modern architecture and have bent our bow against the bad client, the bad builder, the bad assistant, the sham architect, and the bumptious amateur.

Last of all, believing that a healthy mind demands a healthy body, we have been diligent to record and assist, as best we could, the progress of sanitary science, and to this end have exposed the vicious systems under which so many of our towns still suffer.

Source:
Looking back', *The British Architect*, 3 January 1879, p.1

UNITY OF THE ARTS (1884)

Godwin used The British Architect *as a vehicle to reach the younger members of an increasingly fragmented profession. Here he takes up one of his favourite metaphors, linking architecture with the human form and its clothing. Another recurrent theme emerges in the concluding paragraph, that of the artist as* flâneur, *an anonymous, dispassionate observer roving the city.*

You may note that I address my letter to *art students*, not students of architecture. I do so because I wish it to be clearly understood between us that Art is one body, not half-a-dozen bodies, and that it is a bad look-out when we find one part, whether it be Architecture, Painting, Sculpture, Music, or dress, or any other member proclaiming in its pride that it has no need of the others.

To be a good architect — to be at all fit to take your place beside the men who set out the lines of the building on the Athenian Acropolis, or directed the masons at Evreux or Florence — you must know something more than the mere osteology of art. The whole anatomy of the body, even to the preparation, so to speak, of the nerves must be gone into. It is one of the

Source:
'To Art Students. Letter no. 1', *The British Architect*, 2 May 1884, p.215

greater defects of the modern study of architecture that it is nearly wholly limited to a contemplation of the skeleton. The architects of the present day who can fitly clothe the framework of a building with muscle and flesh, and infuse into it the life and final beauty of colour, are so few and so little understood owing to this ignorant method of separating one art from another, that I doubt whether the most diligent seeker would discover half-a-dozen in any country in Europe.

To lead you where you may observe and profit by the more or less disjointed members of the body of which you form a part will be, therefore, one of my chief duties. I shall ask you to go to the theatre and the circus, to attend ecclesiastical functions, to go to all sorts of studios, to accompany me to sanitary exhibitions, to workshops and to picture galleries.

REVIVING THE NATION'S SENSIBILITY (1878)

Godwin subscribed to the Liberal political emphasis on enlightenment through education, and what he saw as the necessary conjunction of science, health and art in improving the quality of life, at a national as well as an individual level. It was up to England's artistic elite to give a positive lead in this process. Like other Aesthetes Godwin believed in the importance of cultivating an artistic sensibility through the nurture of all the senses – hearing, touch, scent and taste, as well as sight.

Source:
'National art', *The British Architect*, 8 November 1878, p.177

Art-perception is a power that England as a nation lacks. Indeed England is not the only country where the people have lost all pride in the eye. But it is not only the eye that fails. How few among us have any genuine taste; a taste capable of separating flavours and of enjoying delicate distinctions. Does not the nation as a nation, prefer the jingle of the music hall to the harmony of a madrigal? Do we as a people take any real delight in encouraging the growth of sweet-smelling herbs and flowers? And do not the rough surfaces of dress fabrics especially for men's wear testify to the bluntness of our sense of touch? If as we suppose the answers to these questions must be in the affirmative, we find a verdict against ourselves of deficient sensibility. It is a very simple issue this we have to try, and everywhere, throughout the moral as well as the physical world, the answer is the same *deficient sensibility*.

Time was when our muscles were in the same plight of deficiency, and so we took to muscular novels, muscular Christianity, and all sorts of other muscular exercises, and it was just as well for us that we did take to them so kindly. An improved state of general health is certainly possible and assuredly desirable. Hygienic development means more life, and this must eventuate in art. We have grown degenerate and flabby, but as surely as our muscular activity revives so surely will the higher or more subtle functions of our organisation recover. It may and will take time, there may, and will be, much stumbling, many falls. But happily science is working to improve our general health — general health always meaning the lower health. And in proportion as drainage is perfected, water purified, food unadulterated, the commoner functions of life will be more pleasurably fulfilled, and there will be time and opportunity for the development of that highest gift of creation — the true and healthy gratification of the senses.

But the sense of sight cannot be fully gratified without art, and art will be ready to minister to our chiefest pleasures when our eyes can see. To this end the eyes, like the muscles, must be trained, and as this training is rapidly becoming an integral part of national education, so we hold it possible that the nation may become artistic. [...] But the nation will never be trained to see, or hear, or taste, or feel, or smell — (public parks and gardens are doing something) — if those who can teach are either always on stilts or ever desponding. People of fine sensibility no doubt suffer more than words can tell. One sense or another is outraged the moment they go out into the world. They grow discontented with that condition of life in which it has pleased GOD to place them; and so, instead of endeavouring to bring themselves to the level of the weaker, many with the object of raising them by simple modes and easy stepping stones grow sad and dispirited. Everything they do and say is toned with a dark grey tint of melancholy. Nature loses her colour; life is deprived of its spring; and love saddens without virility. It has pleased certain people to indulge themselves in this washed-out fashion, and it has grown to be the thing for others who know nothing about it to applaud them and all their dull sad ways and gloomy awkwardnesses. We want something healthier than this; we believe in its possibility; it will be always our fervent business to make it possible.

EXPRESSION AND FITNESS (1878)

This editorial expands on the two 'common-sense necessities' of expression and fitness in architecture, qualities advocated by Ruskin since the 1850s. Godwin laments the lack of progress on these issues, and ponders 'does writing do any good?'

Fitness should be the end and aim of all architecture. If a building is to serve ornamental purposes it must be an ornament. If it is to be a hold for goods and merchandise, it must take the form which will best serve that purpose. If a monument be wanted, it must be monumental. Now, what can be said but a repetition of such truisms as these, when we see erections intended to serve as public ornaments violating the delicate and subtle laws of real ornament and decoration, from their outline to begin with, down to the minutest detail and moulding of every portion [...] Market halls like municipal palaces — town halls like private and sedate unofficial structures — the homes of wealthy squires like jumblements of many mean and ugly dwellings rolled in one — Congregational chapels taking apish forms of the erections of the mediaeval worship, which was full of mystery, dimness, and sensational impression of place and form — rows of dwellings to house, cheer, and comfort working men, with no more expression or fitness for such purpose than mere stables or warehouse rooms. [...]

Some town halls, some churches, and some homes, in a certain very limited proportion, do express their character and are fitted to their purposes.

Source:
'Expression and fitness', *The British Architect*, 11 January 1878, p.15

Biographical notes:
Ruskin

Nearly every public-house and gin palace in the country (most of them innocent of an architect) do express their character and are fitted to their purposes. There is an invitation in their painted signs, their decorations, and their sumptuousness, in the brilliant furnishing and lighting, in the ample counter-room, and ready, easy entrance, in the well-placed bars and parlours. And this, whilst the real art value of any portion of them is *nil*.

There is a great deal of practical fitness in the railway erections all over the country; and yet Mr. RUSKIN may well sigh over the proportions and decoration of their metal columns.

So expression and fitness are not the sum of architecture, and fitness is a practical thing after all. We know well that a number of practising architects have no art feeling at all. But have not the bulk of them, at any rate, sense of fitness and expression of purpose? If they have employed a clever draughtsman for a set of competition drawings, — can they not tell him that the reservoir-looking space in that tower is not wanted in that house; — that the grand and imposing front he has enthusiastically produced is not exactly fitted to the client's purse, who only wants a well-built, plain, and well-proportioned warehouse for the storage of his goods, and that a good telling brick cornice will do instead of a balustrated parapet and row of flower vases; — that this building will be in a narrow street, and that, though there may be money enough, it is absolutely unnecessary to spend it in an ornamental top story, but that, displayed on the entrance, which can be seen and should be impressive, it may be very wise to spend money; — that he knows a simple and dignified building will be wanted because there is a limited expenditure, and the building is to memorialise a deed of the utmost dignity and grandeur.

It is not so much a question of high art, as of common sense and ordinary business perception, and a man cannot lay claim to the name of architect who is not able to give to all his work these two important common-sense necessities of EXPRESSION and FITNESS.

Godwin, design for baths and wash-houses in Manchester, BA *4 Jan. 1878.*

III Style

GODWIN was recognised by his contemporaries as a formidable critic of architecture. The combination of first hand experience of the profession at a high level and a willingness to express strong opinions in print, regardless of whom it alienated, was a worrying and potentially disruptive force within an architectural establishment still anxious to bolster its prestige and respectability. In a stream of articles Godwin held up the design tendencies of the day and the shortcomings of many leading architects to close scrutiny — much of it not very flattering. The *Building News* and the *Architect* were hardly the yellow press of their day, but as professional journals they were widely read by architects as well as potential clients and those in the trade. Godwin could be reckless in so far as he made very pointed comments and occasionally rude remarks about buildings which, even when not specified, every reader could recognise. Behind this deep and often personal criticism, however, he was anxious to maintain standards in the profession. He frequently castigated his colleagues for opportunism and succumbing to the 'lure of mammon', yet he would quickly leap to the defence of architects who were being attacked by ill-informed commentators outside the architectural world. His defence of G. E. Street over the Law Courts is significant here, especially since Godwin had been a supporter and assistant to Burges's losing entry in the competition.

A large part of Godwin's criticism of contemporary architectural style appeared in two series of articles in the *Building News* during the 1860s and 70s. The first of these consisted of twelve articles published between September 1865 and March 1866 under the general heading of 'Art Cliques'. Godwin was then a promising newcomer to the metropolitan scene, having recently moved from Bristol to London. The young architect who had made his name in the competition for Northampton Town Hall was swimming with the tide of Gothicism and keen to offer opinions on his own and rival schools which would help make his mark. The 'Battle of the Styles' was still current at this time but the issues of the debate were shifting. 'Muscular' Gothic was no longer accepted uncritically and a new strand of thought was emerging which questioned the validity of revivalist styles in general. Godwin was familiar with the sources that informed these debates and, although still writing from within the Gothic camp, he was increasingly critical of the factionalism which dominated architectural thinking. Rather than being a descriptive survey of the various groups, therefore, 'Art Cliques' was intended as an attack on the 'cliquishness' which hindered architects from achieving their full potential.

By the time he came to write the six articles which comprise 'Modern Architects and their Works' (1872), Godwin had adopted a different tone. To begin with, he was a more experienced journalist. But one is also tempted to see in this series something of the frustration, even bitterness, which grew in Godwin's mind as his career faltered. His affair with Ellen Terry had put him outside the polite society where most architectural business was conducted and, as a result, he had gained no major public commissions since Congleton Town Hall in 1864. Anxious as he was to participate in the ferment of debate within the profession, journalism was one activity that gave him a high profile and a role as an engaged participant in the issues of the day. This was not merely expediency, however. Like his friend Oscar Wilde, Godwin saw the critic as a key figure in a healthy art culture; what was needed was 'criticism, plenty of it, deep, broad, and technical, general and specific'.

It is doubtful if Godwin could ever have prospered in the way that figures like Waterhouse and Norman Shaw did. His personality was unsuited to the professional habits and business skills at the centre of High Victorian architecture. Unable to work in the systematic way that could have spawned a larger practice, and unwilling to compromise his views or kow-tow to uninformed clients, he became increasingly disgusted with the activities of those of his more successful contemporaries who he felt had betrayed their art. Some of this appears in the merciless assaults in the second series which are couched in language that many found difficult to take. Thomas Henry Wyatt, President of the RIBA, and Professor Robert Kerr, first president of the Architectural Association, were just two of the leading figures whom Godwin attacked, drawing strongly-worded complaints from both. Here, as in other contexts, however, Godwin felt he was waging a campaign against the stultifying effects of officialdom and the consequent loss of the 'art-sense' that was the soul of architecture.

Beset on all sides by complacency, cynicism, amateurism and downright stupidity, Godwin traced many of these vices to corruption of style. In some cases he felt the issues were misunderstood, but his own pronouncements can seem contradictory. On one occasion he seems to advocate flexibility in style while on another he presses for stricter adherence on the part of architects to their camp. The point is not so problematic, however, when one remembers that, as a lapsed Goth, Godwin respected the moral principles that accompanied each style. At the same time he sensed a deeper quality in architecture, the aesthetic or 'art-content', which transcended style and which he felt had been misused by bad architects in all camps. From that position, good quality buildings were possible in all styles but could only be developed from a thorough awareness of the function of the building, and the individual attributes of the style adopted.

Nevertheless Godwin reserved his most severe criticism for architects of the classic school, in all its forms, and remained to the end more sympathetic to the Gothic. He was also aware of the ways architects hid behind style as an excuse for thoughtless design, and freely attacked those who merely adapted their designs from a formulaic repertoire. One of his greatest complaints of classicism was that it lent itself to rules, sources and models freely available from any book of patterns and measured buildings. This was not to say that the Gothic was above that sort of thing but, as a style, it left more room for creative use of the forms and, importantly, required serious attention to the 'sister arts' to be brought off successfully.

If Godwin retained the kernel of his early inspiration from the Gothic, he was also actively involved in the quest for a new style that would express the spirit of the age. 'The Ex-Classic style called Queen Anne' (1875) appeared at the height of this debate when Godwin was himself veering towards this new taste. Around the same time, however, Godwin could also suggest there were lessons to be learned from Japan, and that the future of modern architecture would lie not in any revivalist styles but in matters of 'practical utility'.

Further Reading

J. Archer, ed., *Art and Architecture in Victorian Manchester*, Manchester, 1985

P. Atterbury and C. Wainwright, eds, *Pugin. A Gothic Passion*, New Haven and London, 1994

J. Bassin, *Architectural Competitions in 19th-Century England*, London, 1984

C. Brooks and A. Saint, eds, *The Victorian Church, Architecture and Society*, Manchester, 1995

W. Brooks, *John Ruskin and Victorian Architecture*, London, 1989

D. Brownlee, *The Law Courts: The Architecture of George Edmund Street*, Cambridge Mass., 1984

J. Mordaunt Crook, *William Burges and the High Victorian Dream*, London, 1981

C. Cunningham, *Victorian and Edwardian Town Halls*, London, 1981

R. Dixon and S. Muthesius, *Victorian Architecture*, London, 1978

C. L. Eastlake, *A History of the Gothic Revival: An attempt to show how the taste for Mediaeval architecture, which lingered in England during the last two centuries, has since been encouraged and developed*, London, 1872

J. Fawcett, ed., *Seven Victorian Architects*, London, 1976

J. Franklin, *The Gentleman's Country House and its Plan, 1835–1914*, London, 1981

M. Girouard, *The Victorian Country House*, revised edn, New Haven and London, 1979

M. Girouard, *Sweetness and Light. The 'Queen Anne' Movement 1860–1900*, Oxford, 1977

R. H. Harper, *Victorian Architectural Competitions: An Index to British and Irish Architectural Competitions in 'The Builder', 1843–1900*, London, 1983

P. Howell and I. Sutton, *Faber Guide to Victorian Churches*, London, 1989

R. Kerr, *The English Gentleman's House*, London, 1864

H. Muthesius, *The English House*, with introduction by D. Sharp, London, 1979; originally published in Berlin, 1904-5

S. Muthesius, *The High Victorian Movement in Architecture, 1850–1870*, London, 1972

S. Muthesius, *The English Terraced House*, New Haven and London, 1982

N. Pevsner, *Victorian and After.* Vol. 2 of *Studies in Art, Architecture and Design*, London, 1968

A. Saint, *Richard Norman Shaw*, New Haven, 1976

Style: Art Cliques (1865–6)

Flush with the success of Northampton Town Hall, and having moved his practice to London following the death of his first wife, Godwin confirmed his 'young Turk' status in a series of twelve articles on architectural 'cliques' for the *Building News and Engineering Journal*. This was his first major series in the architectural press, and it established him as a critic to be reckoned with. Godwin saw himself as an independent and therefore above the various factions which he described as 'detrimental to the progress of art'.

THE MUSCULAR CLIQUE

As if to emphasise his impartiality, Godwin opens the series with a few jabs at his friend Burges. A recurrent criticism throughout the series is of the way architects adopt 'peculiarities' to assert or maintain their visibility. This is individuality attained in a 'second-hand kind of way'.

Source:
'Art Cliques', *Building News,*
15 September 1865, pp.642-3

Biographical notes:
Burges
Pearson
Taylor, G. Warington

J. Pearson, elevation of St Peter's, Vauxhall, BN 24 Dec. 1875.

To be the head or leader of a party — no matter how small and unimportant that party may always prove to be — appears to be one of the chief aims of some of the most promising artists of our day. Should the chief of the clan happen to be a man whose power is recognised by other clans and other chieftains, he is sure to have followers or disciples always ready to accept his dogmas as the only possible truth, who borrow his light and never repay him, who lead him to destruction by that delicate art flattery, imitation, which is of all kinds of flattery the most insinuating and deadly. There are no doubt artists (architects and others) whose works have a strong family likeness, but who are not to be ranked in any cliques. Similarities of temperament and similar studies often produce similar results. No one for example would [...] place Mr. Burges and Mr. Pearson in any set, and yet no two men perhaps run more closely together. It is quite possible that when the last two-named architects have had their proper share of public works, one or the other of them may have the misfortune to be elected leader of what may be called the muscular clique, for there are still plenty of young students fond of change, who are always on the lookout for new leaders. Let it not for a moment be imagined that we wish to depreciate mutual admiration or the reverence of the student for the master [...] But when we speak of mutual admiration we must not forget that, in order to be honest, this involves criticism, or the admiration ceases to be of any value. As a rule we have always spoken favourably of Mr. Burges's work, but Mr. Burges would, we feel sure, be the first to complain if our remarks were all equally sweet. Our admiration of the general simplicity, proportion, solidity and power of Cork Cathedral does not prevent us from condemning the composition of the west front; and the merited success of his design for Lille Cathedral, admired by us in common with everyone else, by no means pledges us to unqualified praise of his design for Bradford Exchange. As, however, Mr. Burges's opponents regard him as the leader of what is called the Early French Gothic style, and as it is quite possible he may have many followers, it may be well perhaps to take the Early French Gothic clique first [...] But before doing this we ought perhaps to state what we consider to be an art clique.

There are certain countries, and even certain districts of countries, which at certain times were distinguished by marked characteristics illustrative of the temper and habits of the people and the period; these characteristics or peculiarities some lynx-eyed architect picks up on his travels, and on his return writes a book or reads a paper, and forthwith becomes himself a marked man in a second-hand kind of way by adopting and exaggerating the aforesaid peculiarities. One gentleman takes the brick districts of Italy; another the brick districts of Germany. One goes in for the stones of Venice, and another tries the timber of Cheshire. [...]

Now it is in the bigoted adherence to any one of these forms that we discover the origin of our rival schools or narrow cliques. [...] We quite agree with Mr. Warington Taylor that an extreme development of some Early French Gothic might result in coarseness. It is just as possible to have too much muscularity as it is to have too little. [...] We may dwell too much upon one phase of the art until our works become unnatural and strained. We may believe that architecture has only to be muscular in order to be good, or delicate in order to be graceful [...] Of the two errors, we must confess we prefer the first, for in these days of cheap expedients, and thin walls, and shams of every descriptions, even an excess of strength is rather refreshing than otherwise. [...] With Mr. Burges, we are dealing not merely with an architect as the world goes, but with a consummate artist, who can draw figures, and what is more group them to tell any story he has to tell. As with the architect of Wells, so with Mr. Burges, his sculpture has the peculiar characteristic ascribed by St. Paul to the virtue of charity — it covereth a multitude of sins. What Mr. Burges needs is just what he most probably will never take, a course of Ducal Palace study. There is something in a capital more to be desired than "horns," and strength is only truly noble when it is united to gentle graceful beauty, alike supportive of it and protective. But whilst we say this, we are far from endorsing the opinions, or rather dogmas, set forth in these pages by correspondents who need strength much more than Mr. Burges needs gentleness.

Ruskin, capital from lower arcade of the Ducal Palace, Venice: from The Seven Lamps of Architecture, *1849.*

THE EARLY FRENCH GOTHIC CLIQUE

'Steam and electricity have brought men and nations closer together,' writes Godwin. While welcoming the breakdown in British insularity that such modernisation entails, he deplores the degeneration of architecture into 'an advertising medium' for the dominant spirit of competitive and vulgar display. That said, Godwin pins his hopes to the Early French Gothic clique around Norman Shaw and Nesfield as the most likely to generate modern architectural expression of a positive kind.

Source:
'Art Cliques', *Building News*, 22 September 1865, p.657

The difference between the old Gothic architecture of England and that of France or any other place is possibly owing, as Mr. Warington Taylor says it is, to the difference that exists between the tempers and habits of thought which are characteristic of one nation and those which are characteristic of another. This being so, it follows that the architecture of a country is an index among others of the national character. There are three questions arising out of this — First, what are the national characteristics? second, how can architecture reflect them? and third, why should the peculiarities of a nation, any more than the peculiarities of a man, be regarded with unquestioning and indiscriminate admiration. [...]

Whatever the characteristics of England might have been, it is very certain they are not the same as they were when Tangmere Church or Salisbury Cathedral were built. If the architecture of to-day reflects anything, it is [...] a vulgar desire to appear rich. We live in an age of severest competition. Company vies with company, and man with man, in endeavouring to persuade the vulgar that they are not only well to do, but better to do than their neighbours. And to effect this desirable object it is necessary that the language used should be such as the audience can understand. Wealth of thought is exactly that kind of riches they cannot appreciate, but costly stone and glass and manual labour, such as they can see for themselves, are things of which they can form some sort of estimate. Nor is it only architecture which is made an advertising medium; the self-same vulgarity broods like a spirit of evil over the sacredness of our homes, and its evil offspring is visible in the upholstery of every room, and the millinery of every woman and child in town and country. People of all grades have larger notions nowadays than their forefathers ever had; the manager of a bank lives in greater luxury and greater state than the manager of a kingdom did a thousand years ago; and recognising this fact [...] would it not be the wiser course to endeavour to direct the tendencies of the age into purer channels, to acknowledge the nation's love for big houses and plate glass, to turn the big houses into stately architectural monuments with the assistance of good painting and good sculpture, to bring plate glass into reasonable limits by combining with it the use of stained glass in the upper parts of the windows — in fine, to set the cross upon the idol stone rather than break it, to work and sympathise with one another in a liberal catholic spirit rather than cry "no compromise?" It is precisely this cry of "no compromise", this bigotry of opinion, this obstinacy and determination not to look through any other spectacles but our own peculiar green ones, that encourages the growth of those art cliques which we hold to be so detrimental to the true progress of art. [...]

To return to the Early French Gothic clique. Although Mr. Burges may be the most powerful advocate of the style, he has at present the advantage of being alone in his glory, the true representatives of this school being Messrs. Shaw, Nesfield, Johnson, and Blomfield. For it must be borne in mind that there are two kinds of Early French art — one stately, grand and sculpturesque; the other piquant, quaint and picturesque. In the first we have large masses, an equal balance of parts, the horizontal element as strong as the vertical, and the sculpture and ornament kept pretty much within the surface boundary of wall or moulding. In the last we have more change and irregularity, the verti-

Shaw, Bradford Exchange
1864, BN 24 March 1871.

cal stronger than the horizontal, the sculpture projecting and less frequent, and the ornament masoned rather than carved. It is in its dependence on this last-mentioned characteristic that one of the main faults of this clique is to be found. Another fault of equal importance is to be traced in the eccentric surprises which are occasionally met with in the works of this school. A deeper knowledge of the sister arts would tend much to dissipate these errors. Architectural art does not consist in the production of quaintness, however sparkling, and good decoration means something more than severe conventionalising of foliage. [...] Nevertheless, as it is, we are more likely to get good buildings from men of this sort than from any of the other cliques.

ANGLICAN PECULIARITIES

With some grudging respect for Butterfield's 'architectural character', Godwin nevertheless shows little sympathy for the followers who lack artistic direction.

Few architects are more popular with High Church clergymen than Mr. Butterfield. Although regarded by many as the head of the Anglican school, he yet possesses so many individual peculiarities, and those of such an extraordinary character, that it might be perhaps more just to set him by himself. It is true that Messrs. Bodley, W. White, and Webb have much in common with the architect of All Saints' and St. Alban's. The ascetic temperament may be traced more or less in all of them; but for extremity of oddity, Mr. Wm. Butterfield stands unrivalled — nay, unapproached — amongst the English architects of this century. And this oddness is to be remarked, not only in one peculiar treatment of one particular feature, but in constructional features where no one would suspect it. How many people, for instance, are there in Oxford who imagine for one moment that the red shafts of Baliol [sic] College Chapel are hollow, were made by Mr. Minton, and are nothing more or less than field drain pipes? So accurate, however, had they to be made, that the cost was considerably more than the expense of marble would have been. We regret this all the more, because Mr. Butterfield began his professional life with a "feeling" for the tender simplicity of English Gothic, and a sympathy with all its quiet grace, which few, if any, ever equaled. It was only when he began to studiously copy those accidents of our old country churches and manor-houses, which are chiefly entertaining because they are so refreshingly rustic, that art languished under his hand.

For example, the irregularity of parti-coloured voussoirs seen in old buildings was never purposely designed, and, whether the irregularity was pleasing or not, was quite a matter of accident. But Mr. Butterfield and his imitators seize upon this innocent and accidental arrangement as something to be made much of, and to be trotted out on all occasions. The free work of the mediaeval mason is twisted and tortured into an irregularity so violent that there remains no longer any chance of the irregularity being pleasing, but every parti-coloured arch becomes a discord and an offence. As with the arch, so is it with much of their wall decoration. Plain surfaces of red brick wall are

Source:
'Art Cliques. No. III.', *Building News*, 29 September 1865, p.673

Biographical notes:
Butterfield
Bodley
Minton
Webb
White

Butterfield, interior of All Saints' Margaret Street, London, 1850–9.

Butterfield, St Alban Church, Holborn, London, Builder 1862.

no doubt much improved by an occasional band of black brick; but if the banding is only to be used in such excess that it is almost a question which is the band and which is the ground colour, then we had much better eschew bands altogether. Such work, at the best, when done by such a thoughtful man as Mr. Butterfield, is not satisfactory, but when done by the scores of thoughtless men who indulge in coloured brickwork it becomes a mere higgledy-piggledy of incompetence manifested *usque ad nauseam*. [...]

Then, too, in whatever Mr. Butterfield does he gives us something more than wall and roof, for, however much of a recluse he may be, he does not forget that the province of the architect comprehends something more than mere building. This is not the case with some of the younger members of the clique, for, looking at some of their works which have recently come under our notice, no one would think of asking for the architect, for the simple reason that there is no evidence of artistic direction. It may be all very fine to be different from all the rest of the world, to discard as vanities shaft and capital and arch and moulding, to deny oneself all sculpture and carving, and to practise nothing but what may be called the very rudiments of building. All this may give a certain kind of pleasure to lazy or weak minds [...] but to call such simple effortlessness art, or to suppose that the absence of all those forms which are the common property of every style, from Egypt downwards, indicates only that repose and that restraint which are characteristic of strong minds, would be an insult to the common sense of every one of our readers. And yet it is precisely this sort of thing we are invited to contemplate as the only legitimate style of architecture for nineteenth century England.

COMMERCIAL ENGLISH GOTHIC

This early discussion of George Gilbert Scott's architecture treads a fine line between respect for the master and contempt for the school which he spawned. Commercialism, repetitiveness and respectability were vices to Godwin and he took every opportunity to attack them in later articles.

Source:
'Art Cliques. No. IV.', *Building News*, 13 October 1865, p.707

Mr. George Gilbert Scott, R.A., is unquestionably the leader of the popular English school of Gothic. For, although we have taken Mr. Butterfield as the representative of the Anglican clique, it may be remembered that just as we have two phases of French Gothic so we have two phases of English Gothic — the one eminently monastic, the other as eminently commercial. The great distinction between these two schools is, that whereas the first-mentioned is characterised by peculiarities so markedly severe as at times to be positively ugly, the latter is characterised [...] by the presence of a careful correctness and an anxious desire not to rise too far above the level of the public mind. The architects of this school are generally men of middle age, who have learnt the balance of money and the wisdom of that dictum of St. Paul about being all things to all men — scraps of knowledge, which are both very desirable possessions, and which, combined with a knowledge of "Parker's Glossary", go a very long way in producing what the world calls a successful architect. The great copyists belong to this clique. We knew a very successful church architect who kept the plates of "Brandon's Analysis" loose, had the details numbered, and sent them as occasion required to his clerk of works. He had an unbounded reverence for Mr. Scott, and always looked upon himself as one of Mr. Scott's party. No doubt there are many such men [...] who flatter themselves that they are really great art-workers in the same groove as their popular leader. A careful examination of Mr. Scott's principles cannot fail to convince every one who knows anything about art that, however much sameness there may be about them, however much they may lack what we call the power of speech, they possess unquestionable evidence of their author's power. It is true there is never any humour, any real fun, in anything Mr. Scott does, and grotesque is very unhappy in his hands; but then, he never descends to frivolity or trickiness, and very rightly discountenances the quaint dodges of smaller minds. On the other hand, [...] Low Church and High Church may trust him with equal safety, and rest confident that nothing will be done beyond their instructions. And, however much we may regret the lack of humour, we cannot but be thankful that there is at any rate no bigotry. Could Mr. Scott imbibe a little of the fun of Mr. Burges, and a little of the religious zeal of Mr. Butterfield, he would probably produce works quite as powerful, and certainly more interesting. [...]

With Mr. Scott architecture is undoubtedly a fine art, and he tries — as far as is compatible with his multitude of engagement — to be an artist. With the majority of his followers, however, architecture never rises above the level of an ordinary commercial pursuit. To tout for customers is much more congenial to their minds than to learn wisdom or acquire knowledge of their art. These are men who, with their respectable (well-to-do) brethren on the Classic side, are always talking about the dignity of the profession; possessing nothing in themselves, they naturally cling to every accident which, in the eyes of the world, is likely to make them appear something. These mystic letters conferred by chartered societies — those knights of the T-square, Sir John Soane, Sir Sydney Smirke, Sir Charles Barry, and that Knight of the Garter, Earl de Grey — these royal patrons who seem so necessary to all the arts, because they neither know nor care about them — these things are worth dwelling on; under the shadow of these high and mighty sounds we may "rest and be thankful." Thankful or not, the men of whom we are writing undoubtedly take their rest. Now and then Mr. Scott, [...] appears at the Institute's rooms, armed to the teeth with a rousing speech and a bold resolution about some wrong in the art-world, which cries aloud to the Institute to be set right. But Mr. Scott, with all his prestige, is found to be powerless. Those two grand schemes, which had for their respective objects the conservation of historic monuments and the education of architectural students, are just where they were when Mr. Scott first brought them forward [...]

Hitherto in these articles we have only given our attention to architects, but the title we have adopted involves something more. The names of art-manufacturers, decorators &c., with which an architect is most familiar, are sure indices of the clique to which he belongs. The spirit which animates Mr. Warington Taylor when he says there is no architect but Webb, no poet but

Biographical notes:
Barry
Brandon
Burges
Butterfield
Clayton & Bell
Crace
Heaton
Hardman
Moore
Morris
Nesfield
Pugin
RIBA
Rossetti
Scott
Shaw
Smirke
Soane
Taylor, G. Warington
Webb

G. G. Scott, additions to New College Oxford, Builder *19 Oct. 1872.*

Morris, no painter but Rossetti, and no art-works but such as come from the firm of Morris, Marshall, and Company is just the same as that which animates in a lesser degree most of the architects of the present day. The names of Hardman and Crace are inseparable from the name of Pugin. Where Mr.

Burges works we may expect to find Mr. Nichol carving, Mr. Holiday painting, and Messrs. Harland and Fisher decorating with mosaic, or paint, or furniture. With the Shaw and the Nesfield school, Mr. A. Moore is associated, and also Messrs. Heaton, Butler, and Bayne, who have added to their stained-glass works the business of general decorators in mosaic wall-painting, painted furniture, &c.; and so far as they have practised, they have worked with considerable success. But, perhaps, the most decided connection between architecture and the subsidiary arts is that which exists between the studios of Mr. G. G.

Mural decoration by Heaton, Butler & Co., from Eastlake, Hints on Household Taste, 4th edn 1878.

Scott and Messrs. Clayton and Bell. To this firm the name and influence of one who is popularly styled the leading Gothic architect of the day must have proved very valuable; and in their turn, no doubt, Messrs. Clayton and Bell have proved faithful allies. All this is, no doubt, very convenient and comforting, but it is a question whether art prospers, or is likely to grow under such treatment. Far better, it seems to us, would it be could Messrs. Clayton and Bell be made to feel practically the value of decision by working sometimes under the iron rule of an over muscular architect like Mr. Burges, whilst, on the other hand, the mild sway and softening refinement of Mr. Scott, might be found still more serviceable in the studio of Messrs. Harland and Fisher.

GIMCRACK GOTHIC

Extravagance in architecture was something that Godwin felt uneasy about, even in the realm of the music hall. This attack is directed at Bassett Keeling although the deeper criticism is against the 'maddest architectural follies' that Godwin detected in many sections of the Gothic camp. He concludes with a test of power in architecture based on a chair and a town hall – the fact that these were both areas in which he himself had excelled would not have been lost on many of his readers.

Source:
'Art Cliques. No. V.', *Building News*, 20 October 1865, pp.725-6

Biographical notes:
Keeling

Perhaps no architect living has been so severely criticised as Mr. J. Bassett Keeling. We by no means intend to run a tilt on his behalf, because we think that the author of the "Strand Musick Hall" deserved many of the hard things that were said of him. It is possibly true that we live in an age of extravaganza. [...] But until Mr. Bassett Keeling appeared, no one probably so much as dreamt that the sober profession of architecture would be infected by the spirit which has called forth such a being as "the Great Vance", or made popular such a performance as "Ixion". We do not, however, deny that even in an architectural extravaganza there may be much artistic excellence. The architects of the fifteenth and sixteenth centuries, both abroad and at home, were rather fond of this sort of thing, especially in stone work, and produced pieces which even yet are regarded as attractions. But buildings like the music-hall above mentioned — happily, not many — are, in brief, vain pretences. Their authors, like the authors of some written extravaganzas, pretend to a cleverness which they certainly do not possess, and endeavour to conceal their incapability under a heap of word-splitting or stone-splitting. Quick retorts and sharp angles are the things to be desired, the absence of real wit or of beauty being alike matter of indifference.

Now, sooner or later, this question must inevitably arise in the mind of everyone who thinks at all about the subject, — is Mr. Bassett Keeling an exceptional man, alone responsible for the gimcrack stuff which goes by the name of Gothic, or is he only one of a clique, and representing to a superlative degree the extravagances of the set? We think the question admits of but one answer, and that, [...] whatever tricks and vagaries young architects may practise, it is not on the last, youngest, and most daring disciple of the notch and chamfer school that we must lay the blame, but on the more prominent members of the profession who are looked up to as leaders of the clique. [...]

We have heard it said, and quite concur with the opinion, that the two best tests of an architect's power would be, first, to plan a simple, comfortable, inexpensive chair, and then to design a town hall or Government offices or cathedral, or, in fact, any public building which demands *largeness of scale*, whatever its comparative dimensions might be. The last problem has been solved by the free architects who belong to no clique, and by one or two in the French Gothic school, and the Scott clique; but the chair, if it has been done, remains to be made public. From the other cliques, however, either from lack of opportunity or lack of power, no public work of any magnitude of scale has as yet issued. Nor are we likely to have any from students of farmhouses or architects whose practice is so essentially rural that even their city churches cannot escape its influence. We have repeatedly called attention to this crying defect in our modern town churches, viz., that they have nothing in common with their position, but look like buildings transplanted from villages [...] When we find some of our most popular Gothic architects persisting in this sort of thing, we are tempted to ask whether it is possible for any architect to be equally successful in town and country.

J. Bassett Keeling, Strand Music Hall, BN 1863.

'RASCALS'

Godwin was a harsh critic of the provincial hack and the suburban opportunist, perhaps because he had experience of this type of work in Bristol. Throughout his career he attacked those architects who, instead of upholding aesthetic principles, responded slavishly to the demands of a speculative builder.

There is yet another class numerically very powerful, which comprehends what Spenser would call "the rascal many," "architects" — so-called — and recognised as such by courtesy, but whose sole claim to the title is long usage. Many of these "architects" have never had any professional education of any sort. They mostly frequent county towns, and the suburbs of cities. In the former they have a certain local authority founded either upon white neckcloths or a long and intimate acquaintance with the bar of the chief hotel. In some cases

Source:
'Art Cliques. No. VI', *Building News*, 3 November 1865, p.767

we have even known them to be appointed to the dignities of a Dogberry, and they go down to their graves with the delicious consolation that wherever and whenever they had the chance they failed not to improve their native town by sweeping away every projecting gable or spar, porch, or lean-to, every half-timbered structure or tottering mediaeval wall, all such luxuries as high roofs and arched doorways, and all such Jesuitries as thick walls and mullioned windows, to make room for the light and elegant brick front, with its compo quoins, its plate glass and girder below, its low roof and parapet above, and between the two 18ft. super of sash window at intervals. The city-suburb architect, although of about the same mental calibre as his county-town brother, is, however, in an altogether different position. He is more or less a creature of the builder's. He makes the speculator drawings under the superintendence of the speculator — who, by-the-way, may be a lawyer or a lawyer's clerk as well as a builder. In this little, low, and avaricious world, he manages to eke out a wretched existence, under the thumb of some heartless money-breeder, and goes down to the grave with the happy reflection that he has been a humble instrument in the erection of a host of shaky shams upon the ruins of bright fields and shady walks and woodlands. Land and building societies have much to answer for by continuing and developing through the powers of association many of the evils involved in this suburban system. Their architectural advisors are too often selected from the very lowest class in the profession. The leading men in these societies are not uncommonly themselves speculators, and buy their art and science as they buy everything else, in the cheapest, if not the nastiest, market.

CLASSIC VERSUS GOTHIC REVIEWED

While suggesting that quality in either Classic or Gothic architecture is on a par, Godwin makes his sympathies clear when stating that the main weakness of the modern Classicists is their inability to incorporate decoration into their buildings. For Godwin, decoration was the area where architecture could combine with the sister arts of painting and sculpture.

Source:
'Art Cliques. No. VII', *Building News*, 8 December 1865, p.843

In reviewing the different cliques of that school which for the sake of distinction is called Classic, there are three things which at the very outset demand attention.

Infusing Gothic with Greek

1. Many have imagined, and possibly still imagine, that the two parties or schools known as Gothic and Classic are genuine rivals, after the fashion of the houses of York and Lancaster, that all architects belong to one side or the other, and would damage one another's cause most heartily in the firm belief that their gods were the only true gods. Many again, believe these two schools can be separated after a much more solemn fashion, and stretch somewhere between the two an impassable barrier or great gulf, so that they who would pass from Classic to Gothic cannot and vice versa. There is, in fact, no such

barrier or gulf, but wherever we look for it, whether on this side or that, we find a merging of one school into the other, a reconciliation of Pagan and Christian, a transition, or an eclecticism, call it what you please, which is full of promise for the architecture of the future. We doubt whether any style possesses sufficient vitality to last for ever. [...] Those Gothic architects who are not slaves to picturesqueness and those Classic artists who are not finally pledged to pediments — if they are both artists — stand very nearly on the same high level. [...]

Parallelism

2. And not only is there close relationship between the two schools of Classic and Gothic in their highest and noblest form, but in the various cliques of these so-called rival schools there is a wonderful parallelism. [...] The picturesque Early French Gothic clique finds its parallel in what we may be allowed to call perhaps the Venetian clique. The notch and chamfer mania is not confined to Gothic practitioners, we see its counterpart in the pillar and truss mania of the French Renaissance, for the Louvre — than which no building has ever been so shamefully overrated — may not unfairly be regarded as the Strand Music Hall phase of modern "Classic".

Neglect of the Sister Arts

3. The third point in connection with this school [...] is the neglect — we might almost say the uniform neglect — of the sister and subsidiary arts. Plaster "enrichments", and stone and wood carving of the same set of enrichments, may often be met with; but, unfortunately, there is no possibility of extracting an atom of *art* from an acre of such stuff. The dry bones of their art are the only things the architects of the Classic school possess, and even these are rapidly being pulverised under the wheels of the Juggernaut of Sensationalism. It is only just that it should be so. When all that is left of life is the bleached and sapless skeleton — when sculptor and painter are put on one side, and all that is left of art is cold and barren proportion, it is high time to bury it up altogether. A thousand times better would be to content ourselves with farmhouse architecture, or no architecture at all, provided only that, whether it be farmhouse-like or nothing but mere *building*, it should, at least, be consistent from cellar to garret, and have a unity and honesty of purpose about it.

VENETIAN GOTHIC

Ruskin's ambivalent role in the formation of modern British architecture emerges in this extract although at this stage Godwin does not feel the sage can be held responsible for the weakness and stupidity of his followers.

Another young clique which promises to be of larger growth than it deserves is the Venetian Gothic set. The architects who practise this style flatter them-

Source:
'Art cliques. No. VI', *Building News*, 3 November 1865, p.767

Biographical notes:
Ruskin

Details of Venetian Gothic from
Ruskin's Stones of Venice,
vol. 1, 1851.

selves that they at least are *en rapport* with the great art-critic of the age. It would be manifestly unjust to call Mr. Ruskin their leader, and yet it is doubtless to Mr. Ruskin that we are indebted for their very existence. We can scarcely select one architect from this clique as a representative man, but whoever will take the trouble to glance at the illustrations in the volumes of the BUILDING NEWS and other architectural journals will soon discover that all Anglo-Venetian Gothic is pretty much alike, that one example is as tame as another, that they are utterly opposed to Mr. Ruskin's real teaching, and that they are as far removed from the Gothic of Venice as a bleached mutilated skeleton is from the glowing living body. We do not for a moment mean to say that this infliction is Mr. Ruskin's fault. It is his misfortune, but not his fault, that his work should be skimmed instead of read. Books like "The Stones of Venice" are to shallow minds as strong meat to babes, with this unfortunate difference, that whilst the babe has to be helped and few are such fools as to give it strong meat, the shallow mind invariably helps itself and almost as invariably comes to grief.

INDEPENDENTS

Godwin did not include himself in this category, yet within a few years this would come close to his own preferred position. In 1878 he was encouraging students to take 'what good they could from every country and every age'.

Source:
'Art Cliques. No. VI', *Building News,* 3 November 1865, p.767

Biographical notes:
Deane
Stuart & Revett
Woodward

The independent Gothicists are just those who come in for the heaviest share of some people's displeasure. They are as a rule men of great antiquarian knowledge, and know more about Classic art than even the so-called Classicists. They have large sympathies and can appreciate a joke from Aristophanes as much as a jest from Shakespeare. Their hearts and brains are too big to be satisfied with a county for a world. Farmhouse life at the farmhouse is keenly enjoyed by them, and palatial life at the castle or chateau is just as keenly enjoyed; whilst quite alive to the beauty of the Sussex village church, they are equally alive to the grandeur of scale and greatness of thought visible in the remains of the chief commercial towns of the middle ages. The great Greek works — temple, theatre, and monument — find in these men their truest admirers. To them the shattered portico and broken wall is something more than mere proportion, and Stuart and Revett are not quite the end of the gospel according to Phidias. Good Renaissance work has, too, the best chance of being treated kindly by such as these, who seek in all phases of art those enduring principles, sometimes very patent and resulting in the noblest architecture, at other times covered and concealed by a mass of peculiarities or the over-development of a feature which was unworthy of such emphasis. Mr. Woodward, had he lived, would probably have been one of the few independent architects, and the loss of the Crown Insurance Offices in Bridge-street is one for which no amount of Messrs. Deane and Son's polychrome and pretension can ever compensate.

Deane, design for the Law Courts
competition, BN 28 June 1867.

IN NEED OF GREEK REFINEMENT

The Anglo-Classic clique, 'remnant of a school which not half a century ago was superbly supreme', is not spared criticism because it once included such figures as Soane, Smirke, Wilkins and Cockerell. Instead, Godwin attacks the central principles of the Classicists – unquestioning acceptance of certain models and a dry adherence to rules.

The life of the Anglo-Classic school — if it can be said to have had any — was very brief, and necessarily so. There was no stamina in it, no energy, no backbone, no love of life for its own sake, no fullness, because no spirit; but with an assumption of classical lore and an incessant fund of copy! copy!! copy !!! Architects humbugged the world for a time into the belief that they were men of fine "refined taste", grand masters of the mysteries of classic beauty, and initiated into all the mathematical subtleties which governed the marvellous loveliness of Greek proportion.

There was a grand, solemn pompous march about the old gentlemen of this school which when viewed from the present appears amusing enough, but which at the time was very crushing in its influence on the younger members of the profession. Orthodoxy and respectability bowed their heads in reverence to the wonders which patience and the measuring tape brought forth. The skeletons of the Erechtheium, the Choragic monument of Lysicrates, and the Temple of the Winds were suddenly found to be applicable to all sorts and conditions of buildings; the original scale and situation were matters of no import whatever. To magnify the order of the monument to three or four times its real size was a common occurrence. *Per se*, it was good, and it was impossible to have too much of a good thing. To say that climate, site and relation to surrounding buildings were ignored — that in our manners and customs there was nothing in common with those of the people who reared them, would be condemnation enough; but when we add to this neglect of scale, purpose, and position [...] there are no words in the English language, or for that matter in any other, strong enough to express our contempt of such puerile performances [...] We do not for a moment mean to say that we are faultless — nay, it is quite probable that a future generation may think (the present one might if it were accustomed to the operation) that the church architects of the Gothic revival were no better, but on the contrary rather worse, than the architect of St. Pancras, Euston-road.* [...]

The British Museum, the Leeds Town Hall, the Egyptian Hall, the Alhambra, the Brighton Pavilion are possible even nowadays. We have given up our allegiance to the Classic, cleared the house of one evil spirit, and swept and garnished it — for what? — the return of seven spirits worse than the first. In the pompous, grandiose work that passed for art knowledge in the beginning of this century there was a reticence which went far to make men believe that there was something in an architect after all, but in the trumpery trivialities of the present time there is no room left for reticence; whatever building we select its architect is sure to be "all there" as the modern phrase goes. About

Source:
'Art Cliques. No. VIII.',
Building News, 15 December 1865, p.876

Tower of the Winds from J. Stuart & N. Revett, Antiquities of Athens, *vol. 1, 1762.*

* St Pancras Church by H. W. and W. Inwood, 1819–22.

the very best buildings there is a lack of real stateliness which a multitude of columns cannot disguise, and no amount of Flora and Fauna can conceal. [...] what we want in this [Renaissance] school is just that which we require, and which we have pointed out as a desideratum in the Gothic school — refinement.

THE BARRY OR RENAISSANCE CLIQUE

*Godwin reserves some of his fiercest criticism for the Renaissance revival which he sees as both morally bankrupt and culturally inappropriate to the national traditions of England. Later he would caricature it as 'a style based at its best on a series of inconsistencies and shams where one kind of architecture is piled up on another, where portico rests on portico, and where a building is no longer individual but aggregate, not a man, complete in one, but as a pyramid of acrobats capable of infinite extension'.**

* 'The Rival Schools', *Globe and Traveller,* 27 June 1872, pp.1-2.

Source:
'Art Cliques. No. IX.', *Building News,* 19 January 1866, p.33

Biographical notes:
Barry
Sansovino
Scott
Smirke

** G. Bradshaw 1801–53, author of the first railway timetable in 1839 which became a Victorian institution.

Barry, Reform Club, Pall Mall, 1837–41, from The Surveyor, Engineer and Architect, *1840.*

The Farnese Palace, Rome, may be taken as the *point de depart* of the Roman Renaissance or Barry clique. But (as in the case of Geometrical Decorated of the Gothic school) this style remains in nearly the same position now as when the late Sir Charles Barry broke in upon the dull uniformity of our street architecture by the erection of the Travellers' Clubhouse. There is very little sign of growth or development in one or the other. Some of Mr. Scott's earlier works, like Sir Charles's works in Pall Mall, are wondrously true to their *point de depart.* [...] Unfortunately, however, there is a strong likeness between these two cliques and certain railway trains in *Punch's* edition of Bradshaw** — they start but never arrive. Up to the present time, it has been all *point de depart* with the clique to which we have just referred. Had Sir Charles Barry lived, it is possible — we may say probable — that he would have worked out an Anglican style from the particular phase of Italian art which he selected [...] Whatever Sir Charles did or might have done, it is certain that his death was an irreparable loss to the clique of which he was such a powerful leader, for his mantle has fallen on no one of his followers. His sons and old pupils may have parted his garments amongst them, but we should find it difficult to say which had made the most of their allotment. [...] Of course everyone knows that the leader of the Astylar revival, like the pioneers of the Gothic revival, was as close a copyist as the circumstances of the case permitted. Nor must it be supposed that it is any detraction to the first revivalists to say this; for, strange as it may sound, it is only the best architects who are really capable of copying, in the full sense of the word. [...]

[W]e doubt whether, if all the decoration employed in the Italian buildings which the English architects have erected during the last ten years could be gathered together, there would be found one truthful statement about one natural fact. Italian buildings, as we build them, are voiceless. They may be covered with figures and foliage, but both are dummies, for the foliage has nothing to do with the English flora or fauna, and the figure or scene is altogether foreign to the history and traditions of the country. Or they may possess neither one nor the other, and be not only voiceless, but expressionless. [...]

Next to the Barry or Farnese clique, is what we may call the Sansovino clique. In considering the numerous modifications and idiotic changes that have been made on the original designs of the Venetian architect, we cannot help coming to the conclusion that the Sansovino influence has been more detrimental to the true interests of art than any influence to which modern architecture has been subject. We need hardly say that the extent of this influence has been enormous. And it was very natural that it should be so, for the Sansovinian architecture is big and pretentious, its windows do credit to the manufacturers of plate glass, its many columns suggest the use of polished granite, serpentine and other inappropriate materials, and as it possesses little accommodation for the exercise of the true sculptor's genius, it not only looks more costly than it is, but exactly suits that large portion of the community who are indifferent to art, and therefore heedless of sculpture. Like many other revived styles, the first examples remain to this day the best. In Mr. Sydney Smirke's Carlton Clubhouse [...] we discover none of those violent exaggerations which some later works in this style exhibit. The Carlton Clubhouse is chiefly blameable for its poverty of detail and partial richness of material. Red Mansfield stone — or, indeed, any stone — would have been preferable to polished granite. The colour, the host of reflected lights, and the texture of polished granite are enough to destroy the best design, when used to any extent. In the case before us we have also an exaggerated entasis to swell the discord. [...] One cannot help thinking, too, that the Classicists — and especially the great clique we have been considering — are not so established in their faith as the great Gothicists are in theirs. One cannot always be certain of the most steady-going. There is a sort of cosmopolitishness about everything they do. They start with us at Venice or Rome, and we scarcely know where they will land us [...] whilst those of the Gothic party have strongly-marked boundaries, those of the Classic party appear to have none at all, for the severe Roman Renaissance fades into the luxurious Venetian, the Venetian mingles with the stately Florentine, and the Florentine passes into the picturesque French; and it is impossible to draw a line between them. The last-mentioned style is, however, rapidly becoming more and more popular, and the Louvre clique will probably soon be the most extensive and influential in the Italian school.

Smirke, Carlton Clubhouse, Builder 8 May 1847.

Barry, Wykehurst House, Sussex, Builder 20 July 1872.

THE HIGGLEDY-PIGGLEDY CLIQUE

The 'French Renaissance or Louvre clique' attracted Godwin's contempt, perhaps more than any other. It was a style which he disliked in general, partly due to its 'inferior' sources, but also because he felt it demonstrated a deliberate and tasteless display of wealth.

Source:
'Art Cliques. No. X.', *Building News*, 2 February 1866, p.62-3

W. Frame, design for a nobleman's town residence (awarded RA gold medal 1875), BN 11 Feb. 1876.

To manage the skyline so that we may not only avoid the dull, wearisome monotony of a Harley-street, but secure an ordered variety, is one thing. To twist the roofs into a maze of opposing lines and angles is quite another thing. [...] Roof-planning is, therefore, a part of the architect's business as important as the distribution of wall or window space, and must not be confounded with the practice of [...] what we can only call roof-dodging.

The French Renaissance or Louvre clique is especially characterised by this weakness. And even in works where something like propriety and discipline are manifest in the walls, the architect very often forgets himself in the roof. Nothing, for instance, could be much more temperate than the treatment of the walls of Montague House, Whitehall, but temperance ceases at the parapet, and we are introduced to an overcrowded congregation of dormers and chimneys, and mansard roofs, in which all that dignity of roof covering which such a mansion on such a site demanded, is sought for in vain. To prove our position we need only illustrate our meaning by a sketch of the skyline as seen from Hungerford Bridge, where the angle roofs and chimneys group themselves into a mass which can only be likened to a stunted heap of glasshouse chimneys. [...]

We have in former articles endeavoured to point out the great weaknesses of many of the Gothic school in this particular. The ultra quaintness of Mr. Nesfield and Mr. Shaw, the trickiness of Mr. Bentley, the notching of Mr. Bassett Keeling, the rural simplicity and emptiness of Messrs. Butterfield and Bodley, and the uncompromising obstinate adherence to over massiveness visible in everything which comes from the hand of Mr. Burges, were cited as instances of want of discipline and refinement. But the architects of the clique under consideration are unquestionably superior to all in the (bull) dogged grip with which they have clutched the French Renaissance roof [...] French roofs everywhere and anywhere towering over the angles, popping up in the centre, and sometimes appearing to cover the whole building. The monster hotel, the medium mansion, and the narrow street front are all made subject to its yoke. [...]

In the Chateau de Lyons, the Chateau de Criqueville, and even in the Chateau de Maisons near Paris, we may perhaps pardon the extravagance of roof, for the sake of picturesque results. But when the merit of picturesqueness is exchanged for a fussy pretentiousness, the most leniently disposed critic can scarcely be expected to discover an excuse. Unfortunately, too, it is not every one who, like the architect of Montague House, has the sense to limit what Petruchio would have called the apple-tart style to the boundaries of the roof. In Holborn, in the city, and in Westminster, we have numerous examples,

Roofline of design for War Office competition by H. Garling, Builder *1 Aug. 1857.*

to say nothing of those in our country towns, of the rapidity with which the fever to slish and slash spreads from roof to parapet, and from parapet to basement, covering the walls with an eruption of column and cornice, and capital and console, which the scholar in Rabelais would call cacophonous and contemptible. The crying defects of this clique are then, to put it mildly, over anxiety about the skyline and a weakness for heaping together architectural members disconnectedly and unconstructively, a method which simple folk describe by the two words higgledy-piggledy.

THE OPPORTUNISTS

Commercialism is the main theme of this article, architects who place business before principle being dismissed as 'pattern drawers for builders'. However, Godwin also touches on corruption in architectural competitions and the notion of stylistic loyalty being an expression of faith.

In a former article I had occasion to remark, in considering the Gothic cliques, that there were, unfortunately, men who viewed Gothic architecture chiefly from a commercial standpoint — men who possessed no claim to the title of artist, whose main object in life was to hunt up commissions, not because they imagined themselves to be better architects than their fellows, and could thus, by increase of work, do more for the advancement of art; but simply because money-making and riches were their delight. Happily, for the comfort of the Gothic men, there is a parallel clique in the Classic ranks which counts among its members men far superior in commercial activity to those who take the fourteenth century as their *point de depart*. [...]

Source:
'Art Cliques XI.', *Building News*,
9 March 1866, pp.146-7

It is astonishing with what gleeful alacrity these men will scent a job, to use their own sort of language. If work does not find out you, say they, you must find out the work, and stick at nothing in the process. [...] There are architects whose sense of etiquette is so delicate that they can so far rise superior to the ordinary mind of man as to sit in judgment as members of religious communities on plans submitted in anonymous competitions when they themselves were competitors. The furious haste to acquire that base sort of grandeur which is dependent on money is the real cause of all this unseemly strife. The genuine grandeur which crowns all work earnestly thought out and zealously done, is a commodity which stands very much below par now-a-days, and conscience is one of those things which we have gradually learnt to do without for six days of the week [...]

I am amongst those who believe that there is no such thing as genuine art to be expected from men without faith in what they do; and for this reason, I am by no means sure that a Gothic architect is justified in undertaking even the painted decoration of a Classic building, for he must feel, if he be honest, that all the ornament he uses is a mistake, and that it is opposed in principle and form to all that he has taught or has been taught. I can quite understand, however, that some architects may lay the flattering unction to their souls that by following all styles they are but exemplifying the true spirit of

Catholicity, and I can even understand that, like certain churchmen, they may glory in what they call their breadth of view. This principle in art is, to say the least of it, without precedent in the history of the world, and violent experiments in things whose very existence depends on their being allowed to develop gradually, may be looked on with gravest suspicion.

THE PECKSNIFF PARTY

This somewhat bitter attack is directed not so much at a style as the professional behaviour of successful architects. The smug self-satisfaction of some elder members of the profession alongside the rising practice in large offices of delegating work to younger assistants were, to Godwin, blights on the architectural profession as a whole (see also 'The architect's assistant', pp.109f.). Another vice was the exploitation of pupils for their fees – a recurring topic in Godwin's criticism – which offered poor practical training and thwarted any true artistic development.

Source:
'Art Cliques XII.', *Building News*, 23 March 1866, pp.177-8

Biographical notes:
Pecksniff
Tredgold

Mr Pecksniff, illustration by 'Phiz' to Charles Dickens's Martin Chuzzlewit, *1844.*

There is yet another clique which, if it can be said to belong to any party at all, belongs to the Classic. Mr. Pecksniff is its great representative in fiction [...] The writer of these articles is confident from personal knowledge that the race of Pecksniffs is by no means extinct. There are, however, degrees even in the Pecksniff clique, degrees owing more to varied circumstances of position than to any variety of principle. The natural history of these old birds (young Pecksniffs are never found) is somewhat curious. In appearance they are generally stout and comfortably-looking [...] They have an amiable weakness for old port and young pupils, and rather than pay qualified clerks, will take in youths for merely nominal premiums. Their chief occupation consists in writing letters and specifications, their designs and drawings always being prepared by the "young men in the office". That portion of the business hours which is not devoted to writing is usually spent in looking up clients, or in friendly chat with those builders of the town who pay them little delicate attentions in the way of fees or commission. They have a great horror of Medieval art, which they regard as one of the outward and visible signs of what they call Puseyism. In white neckcloths they stand unrivalled; they patronise with an unctious [sic] self-satisfaction the infants of the Sunday-school, and go in heavily for tea-meetings and missionaries. Nicholson's Five Orders is their *vade mecum*, and Tredgold's Carpentry is their ideal science. Like the majority of the Classic school they view all high class decoration in colour or sculpture as the trifling frivolities of youth, quite unworthy the consideration of serious minds and dignified professors. They look with an amusingly comic air, half parental, half supercilious, on the rising young architects of the day, for whom they keep a good stock of snubs and reproofs to be used whenever and wherever they can shelter themselves from reply. Criticism of their works they view as gratuitous impertinence, and art criticism in general, except when levelled against Mediaevalism, is to them an abomination.

One of the most wonderful features, however, in connection with the men of the Pecksniff clique, is the facility with which they obtain pupils, very often too with heavy premiums. There is either some marvellous mystery in it, which it is hopeless to try and fathom, or the British public is very gullible. [...] Modern papas and mammas have not yet got rid of the old-fashioned notions about art, which they still believe to be indissolubly united to poverty. The little ones — and be it remembered that every goose is a swan in the eyes of his own fond parents — have a "taste for drawing", their genius is early manifested in the portrayal of chickabiddys and moo-cows; and at a later stage the transparent slate shows what wonderful art proclivities they have. Mamma says that the child's genius must not be thwarted, so after sundry extras being paid for drawing masters, and the usual routine school-studies being completed, the all-important question is asked, "What is he to be?" an artist is out of the question, for no one ever dreams of an artist being other than a painter, and a painter in the eyes of most people is only another name for pauper. Then, too, paintings are not necessaries of life — houses are. Architects make drawings for houses, have offices in the city, and are always vainly supposed to have plenty to do. In architecture, then, the genius, which delighted fond relations with its efforts on the transparent slate, and in French chalks, finds a worthy field for the exercise of its power.

Having disposed of the genius, the next thing is to look after the bread and cheese; and here the question arises — not who is the greatest artist, or who knows the most of architecture, but who has the reputation of having a large business? [...] the only matter of interest is to find out a steady, respectable practitioner with lots of work in hand, the quality of the work being no consideration whatever, and the art principles being of very much less account than the regularity of his attendance at church or chapel. Now it is well known that in this last-mentioned accomplishment the Pecksniffian architect is very great; generally too, he has the reputation of having a large practice, for if work does not come to him through the ordinary channels, he has worldly wit enough to put on a show of business by creating work for himself, and goes in for imaginary restorations and visionary competitions. Then, too, he is either too much preoccupied with his professional avocations, as he calls them, or with religious meetings, to find time for any light amusements as attending the meetings of the Institute, the Architectural Museum, or any other mere art society. And in this imposing attitude, all sham and hollow as the plaster pedestal upon which he has placed himself, he awes the unsuspecting parents and catches the hopeful offspring.

Sometimes it so happens that the young victim discovers the true character of his master before his time expires and has wit enough to see that his wisest course is to escape as soon as possible from the shackles of Pecksniff to find refuge with some one who, without having used his religion or his profession as an advertisement, has happily learned more about architecture as a constructive science than could be gleaned from a whole race of Pecksniffs; and, what is almost of equal importance, is able and willing to impart what he has learnt. To such a man a youth presents his 50 or 100 guinea fee, and has a year's "improvement" — in other words, six months to unlearn what he has spent from £1 to £500, and from one to five years to learn, and six months' real study of architecture.

Style: Modern Architects and Their Works (1872)

Appearing in the *Building News and Engineering Journal* between July and October 1872, the six articles which make up 'Modern Architects and their Works' did not offer a comforting picture of contemporary architecture. The early 1870s witnessed an eruption of bad feeling in the profession, much of it focussed on the competition for the new Law Courts but actually touching on disputes which had been simmering for some time. Godwin's contribution to this stoked the fire of controversy because he took this opportunity to revive some of the issues from Art Cliques, while adding a few of his more recent complaints. The series appeared at an uncertain time for Godwin himself. Poised as he was between his faltering career as an architect and the mixed opportunities in art manufactures, one might have expected him to take a more conciliatory stance if only to increase his professional options. This was not to be the case. By this time he had mastered the techniques of the polemical journalist and was ready to address the issues of the day in a public forum. This was just the moment that a committed critic should speak out. As he wrote in 'Professional Tenderness', a preface to the series, what the architectural establishment needed at this time was 'criticism – plenty of it, deep, broad, and technical, general and specific.' (p.33)

THE PALLADIAN PARTY

The first group to come under attack is the Palladian party represented by T. H. Wyatt and Robert Kerr, both powerful establishment figures who had already protested at Godwin's 'violent and personal' style of criticism. The Palladians are presented as unprincipled 'style-mongers' ever ready to submit to the dictates of ignorant clients, and more like surveyors 'dealing in the manufacture of curiosities' than true architects.

Source:
'Modern Architects and their works.—I', *Building News*, 5 July 1872, p.13

Biographical notes:
Kerr
Wyatt, T. H.

Of this Palladian party [...] the first thing we have to notice is the strange admission by very many of them that their art is unequal to the wants of the age, and that for ecclesiastical purposes they must adopt the style of their opponents. Now in the whole history of the world there has never been a weaker admission. Imagine an architect living in the first days of Pointed architecture, always designing his secular arches pointed and his domestic gables high, suddenly making the one round and the other low, when called on to build a church. [...] Of course such a thing was no more possible to such a man than it is possible to be dead and alive, or sane and insane, at the same moment. You may borrow the Gothic features as a thirteenth-century man has borrowed Roman ones, but if you believe in yourself and your work, you are bound to Palladianise the one just as he Gothicised the other, and in so far that you do not, your principles are worthless, and your art is a sham and a pretension. To the young man who has nothing but his profession to support him, these words may sound extremely harsh. His employers, overflowing with twaddle about styles, and utterly ignorant of the art which creates style, dictate to him. [...] There may be some sort of an excuse for such as these, although it would be far better in the end for themselves, for their art, and for the world, if they could summon courage enough to protest against dictation, and if needs be decline commissions that tend to degrade the architect from the position of the artist to that of the style-monger. But for those whose worldly position is secured there can be no excuse in their accepting any form of dictation whatsoever. [...]

If, on the other hand, the architect denies the dictation, and says "Of my own free will and choice, I do these things; I, a Palladian, build Gothic Churches, and like it", or, "I, a Goth of the Goths, live in Palladianism and enjoy it", we warn our readers to mistrust him. He is no architect — he is but a surveyor dealing in the manufacture of curiosities, or, at the very best, a constructive antiquarian. That [Robert Kerr] the author of "The English Gentleman's House" could deliberately and seriously publish ten designs of a mansion in as many different "styles", are illustrations of what we mean, although it would have been more to the purpose if the attempts at reproducing Gothic forms had not been so sublimely ridiculous. Still more ridiculous is it to call such childish archaeological exercises eclecticism. When you have learnt to feel the refinement of the Greek, the strength of the Roman, and the common sense of the Goth — when you can see how to harmonise principles without becoming a slave to precedents, then you may lay claim to the title of eclectic. Mr. Wyatt, Mr. Kerr, and others of their party, would be more respected if, instead of complaining of the critics, they made an effort to see that for which the critics are contending. Let these gentlemen be but consistent — let them rest their case on its merits — let them adopt whatever principles they like, provided they adhere to them. [...]

[Mr. Kerr's] most important building has windows with mullions and transoms, "remains evidently [at least so he says] of the Ecclesiastical character, and this is decidedly inconvenient in the case of the present generation". Is not this enough to show the obliging sloppiness of modern architects, and how ready they are to wash their hands with invisible soap in imperceptible water? If our professors would talk somewhat less and learn more of art — if they would give to the studio even half the time they give to the counting-house, they might do more than a thousand Institutes and ten thousand congratulatory addresses to raise the position of architects and improve the condition of architecture. [...] Whatever may be said in excuse or palliation, the dignity of art is perfectly incompatible with any-thing like dictation. If employers are to dictate to architects the sooner the latter give up all pretensions to the name of artists and call themselves surveyors the better it will be for the honesty of the profession. It is to us the greatest sign of a master when we are able to recognise his hand in all his works, but unfortunately for architecture most of its nominal masters have no hands to recognise. Such individuality as there may be is derived, sometimes from the employer, sometimes from the assistant, and sometimes even from the pupil.

'Palladian', from R. Kerr, The English Gentleman's House, *1864.*

THE ELIZABETHANS

The 'Elizabethans' are damned with faint praise as an inoffensive compromise party attracting the 'mild Palladian' and the 'uncertain Goth'. They specialise in a picturesque 'cardboard style' of country-houses and parsonages.

Source:
'Modern Architects and their works.—II', *Building News*, 12 July 1872, p.35

Biographical notes:
Brandon
Burges
Smith

'Elizabethan Revived' from R. Kerr, The English Gentleman's House, 1864.

Next to the Palladian group of architects we find what Mr. Kerr calls the "Elizabethan-style-revived". It is par excellence a country house set, and, being so, its edges are not so sharply defined as are those of other groups, for on one side they are overlapped by the mild Palladian, and on the other by the uncertain Goth. Elizabethan-revived country houses are mostly gentle looking things, without much character either bad or good — a cossetty kind of architecture, with little or no back-bone in it, and quite too inoffensive to rouse much adverse criticism. There is about it a simple restful spirit of repetition. Not merely do we recognise the same handwriting and the same thoughts, but we have over and over again the same phrases and sentences, occasionally, even, whole verses. In plain architectural words, the detail drawings of (say) an Essex house, built in 1860, appear to have been found convenient for a dozen others in as many different counties. The plan is usually a long one, that is to say, all front and back and no ends or sides. The materials are generally red brick, with white wrought-stone dressings; the latter so much admired that they are even applied to the angles of the walls. There are square and semi-octagonal bay windows in all the enjoyment of plenitude, and now and then an angular or circular oriel peeping out in a timid shrinking fearful sort of way, as if there was something not quite right in the liberty it was taking with the delicate wall it overhangs, and making up for its timidity by a more than usual boldness in its corbel mouldings. The gables have nearly always considerable difficulty in keeping quite straight, for the Elizabethan-revived architects have a notion that the notched and curved lines of some old examples, if not characteristics of the style generally, are, at any rate, features of such beauty and excellence as to be well worth perpetuating. And they perpetuate them accordingly in their usual mild manner, a manner which culminates at last — if it can be said to culminate at all — in the shrunk shanks of the east terra-cotta chimneys.

The name of Mr. David Brandon is identified with this modern product in a marked degree; others have adopted it to some extent, but they have adopted it more in a playful spirit, and with less apparent conviction as to its real merits. Among the playful and amusing examples, we may note those buildings where the manufactured Elizabethan-revived detail has been mixed with trefoils, quatrefoils, and other bits gathered from earlier styles. These, I suppose, are attempts at eclectic art, but, like all the experiments hitherto made in the Elizabethan-style-revived, they are wanting in vigour, and cannot even make up for this deficiency by any claim to refinement. So many modern country houses and parsonages have been erected in this style that it would be difficult to single out any special example, but we may be quite sure of this, that an architect whose chief works are graced by meek details, whose notions of decoration can be traced in little bits of pierced parapets, jagged or stepped gables, lean, ready-made chimney shafts, unnecessary dormers, and useless but-tresses, is not a man likely to advance our art or induce either the critics or the public to look with favour on our profession. A crying defect in nearly all modern works is this same ready-made look of many details. Mantelpieces and internal joinery generally furnish us with innumerable examples of this kind of stuff, but what a man does to the internal fittings of his house is entirely a private matter. Not so, however, when he challenges the observation of every traveller by rail or road. Our gables and dormers, our turrets and chimneys, are often the only features of our residences which are visible to the public.

T. Searancke Archer, Harewood, Kingston Hill, Arch. *13 May 1876.*

Is it well, then, to invite comparisons which can only possibly tend in one direction? Apart from all question of offence to art or disappointment to artists, is it well to proclaim upon the housetops mean pretentiousness or architectural laziness? For I cannot help thinking that such architects, for example, as Mr. T. R. Smith, must either be the victims of their employers or unaccountably indolent in working out their designs when they present us with the toy-like details which we sometimes see above the tree-tops of our modern manors. Mr. Burges's engineering massiveness is the last thing one desires to see imitated; but there is a vast difference between expensive elephantine hugeness and mean microscopic littleness. [...] It is just possible that Nash's picturesque plates* and Richardson's scratchy sketches are the authorities for most of this Elizabethan revived work. If there are no carefully measured drawings to be got, it is quite time that one of the supporters of this style should proceed to make them.

* J. Nash, *The Mansions of England in the Olden Time*, 4 vols, London, 1839–49.

ACADEMY GOTHIC

Characterised as copyism and a 'flavourless réchauffé' of formulaic Gothic detail, this branch of modern architecture inspired some of Godwin's most vociferous and wide-ranging criticism. It was not so much bad design that incensed him but lack of thought and commitment in a field where he felt these were basic requirements.

Modern Palladianism and the Elizabethan-style-revived occupy in point of date the first and second places in our list of modern styles. The third place must be assigned to what for the sake of distinction may be called *Academy-Gothic*, and by this phrase I do not mean to implicate in any way our own Academy at Burlington House. What I wish to convey by the use of the word is that kind of Gothic which comes from a cold formal obedience to a circumscribed and set rule of precedent; an obedience that at its best is just as unlikely to produce a living style of Gothic as it is for the most careful regard of the minutest fraction of a module to result in perfect Greek; a style having no more of real Gothic art in it than the church in Euston-square has of Greek art. Careful measurement of old examples is all the study required for such work. An engineer or surveyor, or, indeed, a builder's clerk, can belong to this class of architects at a moment's notice. Possessing Bowman and Crowther's "Churches", and a few other kindred works, he may even dispense with personal measurements altogether. For just as Stuart and Revett's plates formed the only stock-in-trade

Source:
'Modern architects and their works.—III', *Building News*, 26 July 1872, p.67

Biographical notes:
Bowman & Crowther
Brandon
Kerr

of most "Classic" architects, so in the case of many a Goth, the early-measured drawings of our old churches, colleges, &c., have served precisely the same useful end. [...]

The only argument I have ever heard seriously advanced in support of this kind of modern architecture is that it is better to copy good things than to design bad ones. I am not altogether sure that it is not better to attempt to walk alone, even though stumbles be inevitable, than to rely for ever on leading-strings.* But for the present let us admit the argument in favour of copying to be sound; does it not in plain terms imply a high degree of critical knowledge? What are the good things, and how do you know them to be good? Is it merely after all a question of individual "taste"? or is there really such a thing as a right proportioning of solid to void, lateral and vertical, beyond the limits of which the best of us must come to grief? And by the right proportion of solid to void, I mean much more than is involved in mere consideration of wall space. The bars of a sash, the tracery of a window, the projecting and receding mouldings of arch or architrave, base or abacus, are all questions of solids and voids, and even the distance between intrados and extrados of a perfectly plain arch in a perfectly plain wall may come within the meaning of the phrase. If, then, there be such a thing as fitting proportion, surely the sensual and mental condition of an architect able to receive it, measure it, and judge it must be acute, critical, and strong [...]

The truth is we are not critical. We are overgrown with antiquarian rust. We admit, according to our party prejudices, all Mediaeval or all Classic Renaissance work as above the reach of question, and beyond the touch of analysis. We are the slaves of those who will employ us and not their leaders. In the witness-box there are of our most prominent men those who find it easy to forget the dignity of their profession, nay more, all that their art teaches them, for the low profit of partizanship. We have grown too rich and too mighty for the service which art so rigidly demands from all who profess to follow her. We are advocates, not artists, and the bend of our minds is to do anything rather than devote ourselves to architectural study. Thus it comes that we shirk all critical inquiry, and adopt the easiest method of producing what we have the impertinence to call "designs", by following a system of wholesale copyism, and then inventing fallacious arguments to show that it is the very best course to pursue.

Now, who are those who have thus taken the name of architect in vain? Who are those who, if we had the simplest elementary examination in design to-morrow, would incontinently fail? Their name is legion. Of all men they do the greatest harm to modern Gothic art, because the shallow multitude take their poor copies for original designs, and are utterly incapable of seeing the difference. To name them would be wasting time. To single out leaders is impossible, because they have none. How far the apostles of the Revival are to blame is not the question. It may be that the character of the criticisms in the *Ecclesiologist*, and the long reign of precedent, when an unfortunate architect was nearly always scarified by one or more of a coterie of sharp writers unless he could show Mediaeval chapter and verse for everything in his design, have been the cause of much of the evil we now deplore. But there are, I need scarcely

* Compare Charles Rennie Mackintosh who urged his fellow art-workers in 1902 to 'Stumble, stagger ... go alone.'

say, degrees of copyism. There is the "copy" which is nothing but a ridiculous travestie of the original, and there is the copy which may even deceive one of the critical few. This last is amusing and clever, and show that its author is at least learned as an antiquary, and may be capable of better things. The first is altogether contemptible, and not unfrequently leads to the final disgrace of travestying the designs of contemporaries which, in their turn, may have been more or less copied from old work. Such is the class of design which Mr. Kerr has taken the trouble to put before his readers at p. 367 "The English Gentleman's House" (third edition). To say that it is a parody or burlesque of Gothic would be untrue; it has not the cleverness of the one nor the fun of the other. It is, without the faintest exaggeration, nothing but a coarse *réchauffé* of scraps of Gothic, picked up, as it seems, by accident; and yet Mr. Kerr has the consummate assurance to say (A.D. 1871) that it shows modern Gothic "at its best." I venture to say, without any qualification whatever, that it shows it at its worst [...], for the grossest error of the feeblest Palladianism is better than such Gothic as this, and the wildest ugliness of the rococo works of the age of Louis Quatorze deserves less censure. Mr. Kerr professes to be serious, so here we can estimate with tolerable accuracy his artistic qualifications. How admirably fitted he is for an examiner of candidates for the Institute certificate, and how well entitled he is to be listened to, will be manifest to any architect of fair abilities who will take the trouble to refer to that part of his work which treats of modern Gothic. Criticism that in its ignorance *can* not, or in its injustice *will* not, distinguish between the works of the most accomplished architects and those of the miserable ruck of copying clerks who set up as architects, is worthless, and the only course to be adopted when we find architects systematically speaking, writing, and acting in ignorance or in contumaciousness of the fine art of architecture, who can take scornful delight in boasting that they are no artists, and do all in their power to depreciate the art position of those who are more favoured, is to oppose them at every turn, and to carry on a war *à l'outrance*.

'Mediaeval' from R. Kerr, The English Gentleman's House, *1864.*

THE ARCHITECT AS HIS OWN CRITIC

Keen to insert himself into the survey of modern architects, and knowing that no-one was going to do it for him, Godwin published an apparently 'objective' review of his own work, comparing it with that of his friend William Burges. 'Such are the opinions I have heard retailed in more or less roundabout language', he comments at the end of the article, playfully revealing his strategy to the reader. 'I suppose that I ought not to give an opinion of mine own one way or another. That I should have taken the trouble to write them down may be considered bad taste. Let it be so. There is so much good taste visible everywhere, so much modesty, so much consistency, that I shall not mind the impeachment for the sake of the change.'

Source:
'Modern architects and their works.— IV', *Building News*, 30 August 1872, p.167

Biographical notes:
Burges

The *Times* has lately pronounced an opinion that all the designs of Mr. Burges and Mr. Edward W. Godwin seem "conceived in the most exclusively and enthusiastically Mediaeval spirit". But the reviewer adds that it is a "grave question if the professors of this school have hit on a way of exemplifying their favourite truth which can be tolerated, except by a public of special bent and education." The gravamen of this judgment lies in the word "exclusively". It would not be too much to say that no modern architects are more ready to appreciate the good things of *all* past styles than those just named. But always the precious things they collect from Classic or Renaissance, from East or West, from old tradition or new fact, they pass through their own Gothic crucibles. [...]

But the great faults to be observed in nearly all the works of these architects are faults quite independent of Mediaeval enthusiasm, faults which it may be feared are becoming stubborn for want of pruning. There can be no two opinions that all Mr. Burges's works, no matter in what material they are designed, suffer from a certain coarseness, the result, no doubt, of a wholesome desire to avoid the weaknesses of modern Gothic. But in the constant desire to secure the expression of strength, an over-development takes place, and a character of stunted growth is stamped on every feature. To such an extent, indeed, is this carried that he has almost created a kind of Pollard Gothic where all grace of branch and leaf has been sacrificed to mere trunkiness. Not but what there is much to admire in a pollard, but yet no amount of beauty of spur-form and twisted knot, no quantity of golden lichen, nor mass of variegated moss, will ever compensate for the loss of true healthy growth, or of those proportions which belong to complete natural form. There may be much quaintness in the short bow-legs and long body of the dwarf: we may see a piquancy of effect in a tailless bird, and school ourselves into admiration for the hippopotamus. But there is a higher aim than quaintness, and proportion is not altogether the same as piquancy. This fault of stuntiness is the more remarkable because in sculpture and painting, as applied to architecture, no living architect is a greater purist, or has a greater appreciation of the Greek ideal, and yet, the skeleton of the dodo clothed in the feathers of the love-bird appears to be his particular weakness. Whether this aim is deliberate, or whether his best thoughts are observed by the feathers, and the skeleton is left to others, are questions which it is impossible for me to answer. It is true enough that strength real, and expressed, is an essential if we wish to establish a good school of architecture for the future, but the graceful strength of an Apollo is a very different sort of thing from the bicep force of a blacksmith. The Cardiff tower is as good an example as one could wish of what I have endeavoured to point out as the radical defect in Mr. Burges's work. From ground to finial it is an exhibition of every architectural muscle strained to the utmost, and would be far more appropriately situated on the west coast of Lundy than in a quiet street of a peaceful seaport town. There is no question that its author has knowledge, daring, and even originality, but he lacks refinement and grace, qualities by no means absent from the best works of the early part of the thirteenth century, from which he confessedly takes his *point de depart*.

Mr. Godwin's error is of a different kind: he starts from the same strong faith in Early thirteenth century work, but his vision is as too far-sighted as

Burges, Chancel of St Mary the Virgin,Studley Royal, Ripon, from R. Pullan, The Architectural Drawings of William Burges, *1883.*

that of Mr. Burges is too near-sighted; he dwells so long and so hyper-critically on proportion and mass that he has no time left for detail, and thus with one exception all his works suffer from blank spaces. They look, indeed, as if they had been designed with the scissors instead of the pencil, for distant observation rather than for close examination. One would imagine that, feeling disgusted (and not without reason) at the manner in which his first highly decorative work was executed, he had "sworn off", as Rip Van Winkle* would say, and was growing cynical towards the sculptor or carver. Be this as it may, I for one cannot help thinking that some of his later works would have been all the better for a little of those ornamental accessories which Mr. Godwin seems to scorn. With these added, and something taken off the solids and given to the voids, considerable gain would be effected. But, while saying this I am quite conscious that this over attention to mass has been brought about by the excesses committed by other architects in the contrary direction. The excess of weakness in so many modern works has driven Mr. Burges to the opposite extreme of unmeaning strength; the excess of fenestration has driven Mr. Godwin to a Spartan-like severity, which is certainly not in harmony with the spirit of the age. The architecture of the first reminds us of a Doric column reduced to half its lowest height, that of the last to a Corinthian column without its acanthus. We ask the one to be more graceful; we ask the other to be less severe.

* Character in a short story by Washington Irving who fell asleep for twenty years.

COUNTRY GOTHIC

Dullness, complacency and compromise are the faults of the 'general practitioner' held up here for condemnation, just as they were in the series on Art Cliques. It is not merely the lack of art that Godwin finds depressing, however, but the damage done to the provincial towns now populated by 'crude, pretentious and lifeless buildings'.

A successful class of modern architects is that Country Gothic class who look on Sir George G. Scott as their prophet. This sort of architect indulges in no kind of speciality. He makes no experiments: churches and houses, town halls and shops, theatres and markets, are all one to him. [...] A steady-going Gilpinish sort of citizen life makes him blossom forth at tea meetings. He is great on missionaries and the efficacy of prayer; modern science he hates, and he inwardly curses the artist architect. Possessing these, amongst other virtues, he can command the suffrages of hopeful mothers, and his office is thus always well stocked with pupils. These save him clerks, and to maintain a constant supply he is not particular as to the amount of the premium. He would always like to get his top price, a hundred pounds, but rather than lose a chance, he has been known to accept less than a fourth of that sum. His works are extremely various. Parsonages and Schools are favourite subjects, and for these he has always his prescription ready. Shops and street fronts, too, are profitable patients, and the very name of warehouse has a soothing sound in his ears. His library contains Scott's "Secular Architecture", Sharpe's "Parallels", the "Glossary", and above all, "Designs for Church and Villa Ar-

Source:
'Modern architects and their works.—V', *Building News*, 6 September 1872, p.187

Biographical notes:
Ecclesiological Society
Scott

chitecture", by Brooks and other distinguished artists. His works, wherever they are, may be identified by the coarseness of bead and fillet in all his mouldings, for the nosings of buttress, and stringcourse, and gable, are always from five to ten times as thick as they ought to be, and every other fillet and bead follow suit. In other words, detail is eschewed — that is to say, the poor young pupils make the drawings, and detail, unfortunately, is the very last thing a pupil picks up, even, indeed, if he ever finds it. The general practitioner, however, depends very much on external aid, and his incapacity either to design or draw has resulted in the establishment of numerous manufactories where all this is done for him, and thus the land is flooded with rawnesses and crudities springing from the great English commercial maxim — Buy in the cheapest, and sell in the dearest market. Sometimes the pupils fail, and then our family architect has recourse to partnership. An old pupil of his who has, since his pupil days, distinguished himself at the Architectural Association, or who has laid up a great store of foreign sketches, is generally preferred, and in a few years the pupil is absorbed, loses all his old energy, gives up the fight, and sinks into the merest echo of his quondam "master".

It is curious to note how very little the general practitioner cares for art or anything belonging to it. To be well in with the old family solicitor, to know the leading doctors to be the familiar friend of the most influential of the clergy, and to be on good terms with possible mayors, are his chief ambitions in life; for he knows well that it is by cultivating the friendship of general practitioners in other walks, and by a careful adjustment of the give-and-take principle, and not by any study or knowledge of architecture, that the country architect succeeds. Now and then he comes across some one who dabbles in ecclesiology, and on these occasions he covers his own deficiencies by the most fulsome adulation of the fashionable architect of the day, and utters all sorts of vapid platitudes about the purity of his style, his genuine sense of English Gothic, and his freedom from all the vagaries of his *confrères*. Among the architectural forms which our country friend is found most to favour, we cannot fail to notice the flat stone-coped gable, the two-stage buttress, the square chimney set diagonally, the cheekless dormer, and a *very* pointed arch. His materials are selected with the same love for art as that he exhibits in his choice of form. If the work is of wrought stone, the depth of the courses are from 15in. to 24in. If the building is of brick, there are sure to be dressings of stone to every quoin and opening on the important sides. I say the important sides, because happily the kitchen or back part of the house is left to shift for itself without stone dressings, and sometimes (rare luck) without even drawings to guide the builders. Of woods, pitch-pine, with a large bold grain, is very highly favoured, and is an almost certain sign of the class. Oak is rarely used, but deal stained and varnished a deep resinous brown is an everyday mixture. To leave the wood alone, or to paint it, are courses to be deprecated; for if the family architect is ever eloquent, it is sure to be about bringing out the grain of the wood. Indeed, his notion of Domestic Gothic has always had some mystic connection with stain and varnish. His roofs, as a rule, are covered with slate, which he sometimes manipulates in a stripy pattern of two colours. Now and then, to be very cottagefied, as he calls it, he will use a dull brown or blue black tile with delicate roll ridges and hips, but he can never be induced to adopt red tiles, and as to vertical tiling, he holds it in utter abomination, whilst he luxuriates in ornamental crests of the fleur-de-lys type. But the thing which appears to cost his pupils the most trouble is the pitch of his roofs. He is never sure of it. Here it is low, producing even in the youngest pupil's eyes a squat square-shouldered look. There it is so sharp and spire-like that all the walls seem squeezed up, and the building has a pinched contracted spiny look. But when the general practitioner is called into a more than ordinarily costly work it is almost amusing to see how laboriously he flounders in his endeavour to copy the stately proportions and grand tone of his hero, Sir G. G. Scott. He aims too at securing in the execution the same kind of remarkable "finish" which is so characteristic of all Sir G. G. Scott's work, and the result is that he invariably produces a cast-iron expression. The ashlar, the brickwork, the dressings, are all done to a gauge; joints are reduced to the minimum, and no end of money is thrown away on a mathematical nicety which is totally out of place. The carving is chiselled and polished to that peculiar smoothness of surface and accuracy of line we nearly always recognise in cast-work. Not a fault is to be found in it; every boss and every curve are as true as if they were engine-turned. Such life as there is they file out of it,

G. G. Scott, St Ann's Alderney, Illustrated London News *5 Oct. 1850.*

and the character of the natural material they sand-paper away. There is, however, a depth lower even than this, where architecture sinks to a condition of hollow pretension under the professional guidance of the general practitioner and the fostering care of the friends of the local Athenaeum, Ecclesiological Society, or Philosophical Institute. Little coteries and cliques of local savans whose chief business in life seems to be to pet one another with fond congratulations, to give gratuitous lectures before admiring aunts and cousins, and to remain gloriously unconscious of everything in the way of progress or energy beyond the radius of their short tether. The architect-member of these coteries is quite a superior sort of person; he dabbles in archaeology, so far as to give him courage enough to attempt a lecture on the ancient architecture and antiquities of his town and neighbourhood. He is eminently "respectable", for he is also eminently thin-skinned. He dislikes, it is hardly necessary to say, all modern criticism which is not in the old-fashioned descriptive style, and he encourages the fine arts by employing carvers to produce life-size statues for his buildings at £10 per head. It would take up half a column merely to name the towns where one or other of these general practitioners flourish. For some, there is just the faintest excuse that they have not had the benefit of any local school, nor do they possess any modern examples whereby to profit. There are, sad to relate, many scores of towns which are barren alike of old or modern architecture that is at all worthy of the name. But no such plea can be advanced on behalf of the crude, pretentious, and lifeless buildings which have sprung up of late in such towns as Bristol, Leicester and Plymouth. The old works in all, and the modern works in one of them, might have been expected to have exercised a more salutary influence than they appear to have done.

THE CHURCH ARCHITECT

The huge expansion of church building in Victorian England offered many opportunities for architects but Godwin felt this had created its own problems – architects who could only produce designs fit for ecclesiastical buildings, and a taste for Gothic that was validated solely by its devotion to religious ideals.

Source:
'Modern architects and their work.—VI', *Building News*, 11 October 1872, pp.291-2

Biographical notes:
Gwilt
Scott
Street

To be a faithful son of the church and at the same time a good architect, is a condition of things which, so long as the world revolves at its present pace, can only be possible to the strongest men.

It is just a quarter of a century ago that I made the acquaintance of a young architect of more than ordinary promise, full of energy, fond of his art, rather too much given to work, and not without that sense which is so sustaining to a hard worker — the sense of the comic. Tractarianism, as the Anglican revival was then called, had begun its operations in the parish in which he lived, and before long the diligence he had hitherto applied to his art was transferred in a very wholesale manner to the new *ism*. He became a devout attendant at every service; he familiarised himself with fasting, scourging, and hair-shirting, and even his spare time was so given up to the church that he at last entirely neglected his art studies, and, with miserable enthusiasm pitiable to behold, worked away in Berlin wool at crosses, pelicans, monograms, and lambs, to decorate the borders of pulpit hangings, altar cloths, kneeling mats, and alms bags; Gregorian tones, ceremonial observances, and church millinery, absorbed him until the inevitable "tide in the affairs", &c., came, landing his Anglican priest in Rome, and stranding him in Australia. Change the details, and the story will apply to many a young architect once full of promise, but who, wanting ballast, has been led astray by the mere sentiment of a revival, the real value of which he has never apprehended. The enthusiastic spirit was not, however, all wasted on black letter or Berlin wool. Here and there, at rare intervals perhaps, but present nevertheless, were to be found students of an architecture a trifle in advance of Gwilt's "Encyclopaedia", men who were not content until they had unlocked the treasure-house of the middle ages, and learnt how architecture was only, after all, but one of the numerous actors in the great artistic drama of Mediaeval life. To the delight an artist would naturally experience as each new treasure of embroidery, furniture, armour, jewellery &c., dawned upon him, maybe traced many of the anachronisms in the best of our modern Gothic works. Thus we have one architect who has always seemed to design as if the yule log was something more than a subject for the Christmas number of the *Graphic* — another, as if noblemen (in their own houses) still wore long dresses heavy with embroidery, bound in by belts joyous with jewels; and another as if it was still a question whether some Albert-Edward might not some day withdraw the privileges of Magna Charta. There is a certain boyish romance about all this, no doubt, but in some cases it has degenerated, to what may be called trading in antiquities, and the architect, losing what little poetry he may once have possessed, and too wide awake to hold by the sham romance of the nineteenth century, becomes little more than the professional counterpart of the curiosity-monger, satisfied with driving a very good trade among the descendants of those who made Wardour-street a possibility. [...]

It is from such designs as Mr. Street's Law Courts and Sir Gilbert Scott's German Parliament House, imperfect as they may be, that development will flow, rather than from stereotyped models of big churches and tiny cathedrals, be they ever such perfect exercises in the thirteenth century schools of Cologne or Chalons, Westminster or Wells. Modern secular wants oblige the architect, from lack of precedents, to rely on himself for general composition and for many of those details which arise from the necessity for abundance of lighting, heating, ventilation, &c., and the church architect finds, when he has to deal with these things, that he has rusted in his groove, and is unequal to the demand that is made on him. No one who will take the trouble to examine the secular buildings of men much accustomed to ecclesiastical work, and who have produced very fair churches, can fail to recognise the truth of what I have just said, for there are few grooves in this groovy world so deeply worn and so dangerously rusty as those into which the fashion of a day has dragged the ministering artist. Let any one ask what influence these church architects have exercised on the life of the people. The answer comes to us from every new suburb, and an architecture that is only for churches is too like a religion that is only for Sundays.

W. White, a country church, BA 16 Sept 1881.

Godwin, design for a suburban church, BA 3 Jan. 1879.

Style: Modern Architecture on the Move

The period of Godwin's journalism coincided with some of the most intense disputes about architectural style and its relevance to modern Victorian society. He also witnessed the disillusionment with the stylistic certainties that had characterised the profession when he first embarked on his career. As a result, many of his individual articles reflect the challenges that were being mounted on the Gothic and Classic schools, the new sources coming into vogue and the disputes, bad faith and misunderstandings that Godwin felt had to be aired in the columns of contemporary journals if contemporary architecture was to move forward.

CHAMFER FEVER (c.1864)

The 'notch and chamfer school' became a general term of abuse for the crude, over-decorated Gothic of the 1860s. In this article Godwin reveals his hostility towards amateurs who presume to sit in judgement upon the professional architect and makes an appeal to architects themselves to avoid sensationalism and stand up for their art.

Source:
'Mr. E. W. Godwin on architecture and Somerset churches'. V&A AAD 4/560-1988

R. Johnson, details from house in Sevenoaks, BN 28 June 1868.

No one will deny that the notch and the chamfer may be rendered very useful as subordinate forms of decoration in their proper places, but lately there has sprung up among us a troop of men possessed with an inordinate desire for notching everything. [...] There is no limit to the capabilities of these gentlemen; they have got hold of a part which is nothing but roaring, and, like the Athenian cobbler, they are determined to make something striking and sensational; they think their ranting to be "fine and lofty", and finally sink into the hopeless conceit that their notches are artistic touches, and their chamfers strokes of genius. Besides these two forms of the artistic, the stripey and the notchey, there is what is called *the picturesque*, that is to say, anything which may be likened to a "pig with one ear" an ancient similitude much admired by the scientific, and much used by them with great force and brilliancy. It is unfortunate, but not the less true, that a very large majority of those who follow after Gothic art, both as students and admirers, have somehow or other been led into the belief that the first principle — the essence — the soul of Gothic — is *irregularity*. These are the men who stick chimneys in odd corners where they are sure to smoke, put dormers on roofs where they are not wanted, throw out large oriels to small bath rooms, and corbel out balconies to housemaids' closets. They fail to see that in the best ages of the past there is no evidence of any *desire* to be picturesque or quaint either in the cottage or the palace, the village church or the cathedral. Lastly there is the archaeological groove. In this line travel all those who swear by precedent, who would try to persuade you that amateurs know more about art than the professors; who believe in the "Glossary of Architecture" and "The Gentleman's Magazine" as authorities on all matters architectural; who take pleasure in having little or no opinion of their own, and in giving up what little they have at the mere nod of any clerical or lay amateur. I confess that the education of architects has been so miserably neglected that clergymen and other educated men might well be excused for trespassing on professional ground, and taking matters over which they had any control pretty much into their own hands. Nevertheless, it is most dejecting and miserable to think that architects should so far have forgotten their art and themselves as to be reduced to voluntarily submitting every design to a standing committee of half a dozen amateurs, and to be content to be publicly criticised by men who are ever running in an archaeological groove, and who, in any other period of artistic development would have been learners rather than critics, disciples rather than professors. This archaeological groove is, however, the deepest and widest, and therefore the most dangerous of all, nor do I think its influence on art will be materially lessened unless architects attain a very much stronger position than they have hitherto attained. The story of Lot's wife is a lesson for us. From the time of the Tudors we have been looking back regretfully, and seeking in Italy, then in Greece, then in Italy again, and now in mediaeval England and France, for an architecture ready made to our hands, rather than go on labouring and working for ourselves. Constantly looking back, with no faith in ourselves, no trust in the present, and no hope in the future, we cannot wonder if our power has declined, we cannot be astonished if our works possess no attractions for others whilst we, of all men, have the least right to complain of architecture if architecture has lost all influence over men's minds.

MEDIEVALISM IN ARCHITECTURE (c.1871)

The association of the Gothic with ecclesiastical architecture alone was a recurring complaint in Godwin's writings. Here he deplores the limiting effect this has had with regard to patronage and on the perception of architects by the public at large. But he goes on to lament the crushing effect of Medievalism in general on a culture of building which seems to turn its back on the modern age.

Many things besides the discussion which has just been started about St. Paul's Cathedral have lately arisen to justify the belief that Gothic architecture is about to become the creature of a creed. [...] One of the greatest living authorities on mediaeval art, M. Viollet-le-Duc, has shown that the base of Gothic or pointed architecture rests not on the learning or religion of the early monasteries, nor on the splendour of the later ministers, but on that foundation of civil freedom and commercial life which was laid towards the close of the 12th century. The churches have been preserved, but the palaces, the halls, the houses, the shops have disappeared, and thus arises the common but very erroneous notion that mediaeval art is essentially ecclesiastical. The Churchmen saw and profited by the freshness and vigour that the free towns — the cradles of modern civilization — imparted to the art of building. New forms and new developments grew apace as soon as a man could feel that he had a house of his own and liberty to maintain it, and on every new scaffold were to

Source:
'Mediaevalism', AAD unidentified news-cutting, possibly the *Globe and Traveller*, c.1871

Biographical notes:
Burges
Bute
Viollet-le-Duc

be seen in elementary shape the principles of those details which blossomed at Amiens and Beauvais, and in the earliest-completed shop might have been traced the child-life that grew and strengthened into the glorious manhood of the palaces and halls of Venice and Ypres. Could the people of the day at all realise what the great towns of the 13th century were, the notion of Gothic architecture as an architecture peculiar to the Church would be exploded in a moment. Art, we maintain, is of no creed, and it is the endeavour to identify a certain phase of it with some form of religious belief that much harm is done to both.

The revival of Gothic during the second quarter of this century will be remembered not so much for its works as for its influence in loosening the bands and fetters of the formula and the academy. The most rampagious opponent of Gothic to-day is absolutely licentious compared to the stiff formalist of free-revival times. There is hardly a single modern work that will endure the criticism of the future. Very many of them can hardly bear the criticism even of the present, not because of the style (for any style would have met with the same fate if similarly followed), but because what is sometimes called the "faithfulness" with which modern architects have wrought. This it is which has suffered anachronism to overgrow art, and allowed the accidents of time to crowd the everlasting. Had the architects of the revival been fortunate enough to have had for their clients civilians instead of ecclesiastics, not only do we think greater way would have been made in the development of a noble art, but the profession itself would have been more respected and honoured by the public at large.

Our school of architecture is not broadly national, however much it may follow the styles of the Plantagenets. It is divided against itself; and although some may be quite shocked at the notion, there is no use in concealing the fact that the divided art is allied to the divided Church, and that Gothic and classic are but other words for Ritualist and ultra Protestant. The cure for all this is, in a great degree, in the hands of the public. If they would compete with the clergy in the encouragement of architecture, and leave to the two parties in the Church those architects who have identified themselves with one or the other platform, they might bring to the front artists who are not partisans, and architects who follow their own craft with too much zeal to spare time for other pursuits. We have no quarrel with Gothic. We think it has always shown itself to be a reasonable, a practical, and an every-day mode when treated as a free and living style. But we object altogether to people confounding the substance of such a style with the thin shadows of mediaevalisms so often of late indulged in. Nor will the waxen effigy, the mere reproduction of a past age, satisfy us. There are a few antiquarian architects living amongst us who could make us, indeed, happy if such replicas were desired. What we want is this same Gothic living in our midst as it lived in old time, *a part of the time*. And it can only be this by becoming identified, not with a sect or a school, but with the general public mind. The mind may be a low one, but we had far better had a low form of life than a grand image of death. We may grumble at the utilitarian spirit of our age, but it is *the spirit* all the same. We may despair of ever rivaling such works as those we have referred to, but then there should be no such comparisons, for the difference should be one of kind, and not of degree. We may long for a time when there shall be no more railways, no steam engines, no gas, but that time is not for us. And, seeing all this, would it not be just as well for our architects and their employers to make the best they can of all these inventions? Would it not have been wiser for Lord Bute to have recognised the living modern Cardiff than to have endeavoured, through an antiquarian architect, to call back a bit of the Cardiff of Henry III.'s reign? Would it not have been a greater encouragement to art to have identified himself through his new works with everything that has made Cardiff what it is than to separate himself in an exclusive anachronism which few can understand, and fewer still admire? And as with Lord Bute, so is it with others. We mention him not for the purpose of personal attack, but as the representative of a class of men (mostly young and wealthy) who may fancy that they are encouraging the artist when they are but fostering antiquarian research. We have a dozen architects who could do the archaeology; there are but one, or perhaps, two who could direct the art.

Burges, Clock Tower, Cardiff Castle, BN 9 Dec. 1870.

THE *TIMES* AND THE NEW LAW COURTS (1871)

The competition for the design of the new Royal Courts of Justice in the Strand, the largest and most prestigious building project in the country, caused the principal architectural dispute of the 1870s. Won by G. E. Street in 1867, it was taken by many as proof that the Gothic style could be used for civic buildings on a grand scale. Almost immediately, however, opponents led by James Fergusson mounted a campaign in the architectural and mainstream press that undermined Street's position and required numerous revisions to the original design. The issues of the debate confirmed Godwin's distrust of the anti-Gothic camp but it was the lay critics who infuriated him and prompted this response to a series of items in the Times.

The articles and correspondence in the *Times* on the subject of Mr. Street's design for the new Law Courts brings into prominence a characteristic of the present age that has already attained threatening proportions, and one that unchecked must inevitably tend to the discomfiture of a cultured class of the community. The characteristic I refer to is the readiness with which all sorts of people will prescribe for themselves when the subject-matter is one of what they call "taste;" and not less noteworthy is the reluctance with which such people can be got to admit the possible existence of any physical imperfection calculated to incapacitate their judgment. Colour blindness we have all heard of. Are there not defects of the nerves of sight other than those relating to colour? Is *form* always rightly apprehended, is *proportion* an instinct, or is *scale* measurement a natural gift common to us all? I venture to think that these are all matters requiring, in the first place, a high degree of nervous sensibility, and, in the second place, not a little culture. [...] With some critics the opposition to Mr. Street's design is but a renewal of the Old "Battle of the Styles" — for, however much they may deny it, there are men who shut their eyes just as firmly against the merits of Gothic architecture now as they did 20 or 30

Source:
'The "Times" and the new Law Courts', *Architect*, 30 September 1871, pp.164-6

Biographical notes:
Street

years ago. No one who was present at the meeting of the Section of Art and Archaeology, held at the rooms of the Institute, during the Congress of last summer can for a moment doubt that the old spirit for war still burns, however much men may attempt to press it down out of sight. It is the policy of the losing party, and has been for some time, to work in the dark against the Gothic school. What they could not effect by a hand-to-hand fight they now seek to accomplish by sapping and mining. [...]

With these preliminary considerations in view, let us look at the sort of criticism which Mr. Street's design has evoked; and, first of all, let us consider the leader in the *Times* of September 11. The *Times* assumes (upon the authority, I suppose, of a criticism which it inserted three weeks previously) that the design before us exhibits weakness, want of dignity, poverty of idea, and is unworthy of its purpose and position; that Ecclesiastical Gothic and Secular Gothic are two distinct styles; that Mr. Street is well up in the first, but has not yet mastered the practice of the second; that Gothic architecture in England has been almost exclusively ecclesiastic; that the right buildings to study as models for our Law Courts are the Town Halls at Brussels, Louvain, Piacenza, Bruges, Ghent, and the Cloth Hall at Ypres; and finally the Times, like the rest of the amateurs, gives its prescription – "the main requirements designed for such a purpose as the Courts of Law are very obvious and readily comprehensible. We require the majesty that can alone be supplied by unity of plan, severe simplicity of form, and imposing grandeur of mass."

Consider for a moment the prescription and the condemnation. The design exhibits weakness, want of dignity, poverty of idea, and is unworthy of its purpose and position.

By "design" the critics mean the front towards the Strand. The amateur critic has not, and never had, any notion of architecture more solid than the front wall or the façade, as the fine writers are so fond of calling it. Now this front is about 507 feet in extent, and, as most scientific people know, 507 feet of building against the Strand on the side of the Law Courts could never be seen as whole, for the simple optical reason that it would be beyond the angle of vision. No perspective of the entire front is therefore possible. Mr. Street, like some other architects in the competition, has divided this front into two compositions, separated by the gateway to the great quadrangle, yet bound together by a belt of carved work just above the open arches of the gateway. Of course in this we see nothing but poverty of idea. Well, then, the next step seems to have been dictated by the purpose of the building. Every one who knows anything about the requirements knows that a vast mass of the building has to be devoted to offices such as Lunacy Commissioners and so on, and that the real Courts of Chancery and Common Law, with their waiting and retiring-rooms are not so numerous as to require to be scattered all over the ground. The western parts, therefore, of the site has been devoted to the Courts, and the eastern part to the Offices. Each composition is uniform in itself. [... There is] not a feature from ground to topmost finial for the treatment of which a precedent could not be found in the secular buildings of the Middle Ages. The perfect balance of parts shows unity of plan. The absence of all small features and the fewness of large ones show simplicity of form or composi-

Street, The Great Quadrangle, New Law Courts.

tion, whilst the dimensions alone of the great gable will show whether it is mean or imposing in its mass. The eastern part of the Strand front looks just what it is — five storeys of offices *attached* to the Law Courts. No doubt the *Times* would like to see the windows in a frontage of 507 feet all of uniform shape and size. This possibly is the only idea of architectural unity which art amateurs possess — closet and council chamber, court and corridor, all lit by a regulation pattern window.

But then the *Times* has made the discovery, that there is such a thing as a Secular style of architecture, that the Ecclesiastical style is wholly unfitted for secular uses, and that this Secular style has a theory of its own, which, however, Mr. Street may have studied, he has not yet mastered. To many of us who remember the early congresses of the Archaeological Institute, these words of the Times sound refreshingly simple. To the *Times* now, as then to the youngest student of archaeology, every vaulted cellar of a merchant's house becomes a chapel, and every pointed arch savours strongly of a dark and superstitious faith. To this day the tradesmen of such cities as Bristol, backed up by the imposing grandeur of the *Times*, still cling to the notion that their shop-cellars were once the gloomy haunts of cruel priests, and that their vaults re-echoed the Abracadabra of ghostly monks. Surely it is high time for every one to know that a groined vault, whether built for storing merchandise or supporting the floor of a banqueting hall or church, was built to fulfil its purpose *as a groined vault*. We may be sure that its architect or builder never paused to ask ridiculous questions about ecclesiastical shapes or secular forms. [...] Another discovery made by the Times is that "Gothic architecture in England has been almost exclusively ecclesiastic." Does the writer seriously mean that he believes this? If so, then he is ignorant of the thousands of schools built in the Gothic style, of the multitude of parsonages, of the modern college buildings in our universities, of the Bishops' Colleges, and the Proprietary colleges, of the many houses of charity, and the scores of town halls and private houses and, being ignorant of this, is not aware that he has made an unconscious but unpardonable misstatement of fact. In truth Gothic architecture in England has been almost exclusively Secular.

But it is not enough for the *Times* to judge the present, to make out of the *use* of the building a *style* of architecture, and to misstate a fact. As it warms to its work it rises to the dignity of a professor and lectures us on what to admire, and tells us what is pure and good in art. The town halls of Brussels and Louvain "are pure Gothic!" Fancy being told that even by a school-girl! Buildings that stand on the very confines of the decadence of Gothic Art, from which but one step leads to the miserable travestie of the transitional period that immediately followed them; buildings which have, it is true, the advantage, such as it is, of being the most lavishly ornamented of any in the world, but ornament of which not an inch has any meaning and very little merit; buildings that have not a square foot of repose about them, where everything is repetition, and where mass is sacrificed to lines; buildings such as these, that could be manufactured to any extent at so much the square yard. These are

Street, Law Courts west side, BN *28 June 1868.*

the pure specimens of the Gothic Secular style in which the *Times* sees "majesty and simplicity." Of course, all this bombast about utility of plan, grandeur of mass, subordination of ornament to outline, would mean nothing if found in any other paper. It means nothing, even where it is [...]

Godwin then takes a series of published correspondents to task before returning to the central issues of the debate.

Let us, in conclusion, try to see to what it all amounts. The accepted design for the Law Courts must show majesty begotten of unity of plan: Simplicity, Purpose, Grandeur, Purity. Three courses have been suggested for the attainment of these virtues: 1. A new competition; 2. A revision of the present design by competent authorities; and 3. A return to the forms of the Renaissance. It is this last suggestion which lies at the root of the whole agitation. It is not really to Mr. Street's design that all this discontent is directed, for the criticisms, where they assume any shape at all beyond mere shrieks, resolve themselves into a question of detail. Thus "Anti-Gothic" and Mr. Denison condemn the design, by way of hearsay, for its "laboured and useless detail;" the Times calls it excessive and cumbrous; Mr. E. W. Pugin hints that its fault consists in trappings and gewgaws, "piled on to make a gorgeous show;" and "X.Z." describes it as an aggregate of highly ornamented almshouses. This, briefly, simply comes to this — that the details are too extravagant. Now let us examine the detail, and see how far fact bears out the criticism. To begin with the windows. With the exception of those in the great hall and upper part of tower, there is not one which has more than two simple orders of mouldings, and many of them have only one order. Will any of the critics who talk about "excessive" detail be good enough to point out to us any important Gothic building, old or new, where the details of the windows are less excessive? [...] The quantity of tracery in this 500 feet frontage is less than many a single church window, is less than that in the comparatively small frontage of the Manchester Assize Courts, and considerably less than that in the great halls at Ypres and Louvain, &c. Clearly, then, the useless ornament is not to be found in the windows. Turn now to the wall-space between the windows. Here, from the criticisms, we should expect to find shaft and statue and canopy, traceried panel and carved diaper running riot, and covering every inch of wall surface. What is the fact? Why, the wall-spaces between the two openings throughout the entire length and height of the building are of perfectly plain, unbroken masonry. [...] Again I ask, Where is the excess of laboured detail? where is the excess of ornament? [...]

I have written thus much, not for the purpose of examining the merits and demerits of the design in question, nor for the purpose of defending Mr. Street, who is more than able to defend himself when the battle requires it, but because of the readiness I noted at the beginning of this article with which all sorts of people will prescribe for themselves when the subject-matter is art. There is nothing of which the laity are so supremely ignorant as they are of the art of architecture, and this is most emphatically so when the art is only before them in the shape of technical drawings.

THE CLAIMS OF THE 'QUEEN ANNE' STYLE (1875)

This response to a lecture by J. J. Stevenson on the attributes of 'Queen Anne' indicates both Godwin's early support and his reservations about the style, some of which he would elaborate in a longer article the following month.

I quite agree with Mr. Stevenson in thinking neither pure Greek nor pure Gothic is suitable for domestic buildings, but that something more homely should be applied in our ordinary buildings. There are some features in the "Queen Anne" (as the woodwork) that may be well adopted; indeed, the style seems to have been largely suggested from wooden archetypes. Gothic joinery is heavy and thoroughly out of character for modern adaptation, and I know of no instance where it has been applied. On the other hand, the "Queen Anne" style is wanting in architectural solidity and mass. A correct masonry ideal is absent. Pilasters springing from keystones, solids over voids, corbelled pilasters, and other decorations, are certainly incorrect and unjustifiable methods of obtaining effect. With certain reservations, there are certain features well worth study in some of the early forms of Renaissance; there is a freshness and vigour about them, and the details are more in consonance with our modern uses than the Gothic.

Source:
'The claims of the "Queen Anne" style', *Building News*, 12 March 1875, pp. 304-5

Biographical notes:
Stevenson

THE EX-CLASSIC STYLE CALLED 'QUEEN ANNE' (1875)

The increasing popularity of 'Queen Anne' forced Godwin to take a stand and define his reading of the style. Using the extended metaphor of a marriage between buildings of different periods, he suggests how some hybrids may be successful while others are 'the prostitution of art'.

Now that there appears to be a lull in the storm which has been lately surging round us, anent what some very loosely call the *Queen Anne Style*, and others prefer to name the *Free Classic*, I venture to offer a few words on a revival which seems to me would be worthy of grave consideration were there nothing else to characterise it but the genuine feeling — I may even say zeal — that animates its more prominent disciples or professors [...]

Classic architecture is an expression which may mean anything or nothing. To some the word "Classic" has a very wide meaning, and embraces everything that is refined; to others its meaning is narrowed by the limits of the Doric civilisation, including its three periods of Archaism, Perfection, and Decline, marked architecturally by the temple at Corinth, the Parthenon, and the monument of Lysicrates. Both uses of the word are reasonable. [...] Now, as the word itself means nothing more than what City people would call in these days A1. or O.K., such an application of the terms as that just mentioned is not mere looseness of language, but comes at last to be absolute nonsense. [...] Mr. STEVENSON, will, I hope, pardon me for venturing to suggest the amendment contained in the title of this article. *Ex out of; from; in a downward direction* — [...] is the exact prefix which it appears to me is wanted to explain the relation of the Classic of all buildings in which the influence of Greek forms

Source:
'The ex-Classic style called "Queen Anne"', *Building News*, 16 April 1875, pp. 441-2

Biographical notes:
Champneys
Stevenson
Viollet-le-Duc

and details can be traced. Roman art is itself *ex-Classic*; nor can I see that there need be any limit to the *off*spring of the supremely Beautiful One [the Parthenon]. That her children should show degeneration, and that, too, heaped up; that one should be stiff-necked like the German; one not free merely, but lawless, like the French of Louis Quatorze, is but what might naturally be expected when we examine the characters of her several husbands. That our century should be signalised by a new marriage with her is the hope of many of us; but who is there for the bridegroom?

Four and a half centuries ago Gothic was wedded to her, and the new birth, the Renaissance — was a veritable thing, a living child; for Gothic old and decrepit as he may have been, was a properly-developed living entity, and not an electrified corpse as the every-day Gothic of our time unquestionably is. Nor will the revived "Renaissance" of Pall Mall or the city serve any other purpose than "a mockery king of snow." What, then, is left? Nothing but the vernacular, the builder's work, naked of ornament, void of style, and answering only to one name — *Utility*. Still, even this is a natural, living thing, though it be but a poor, unkempt-looking consort for the widow of Gothic. One of the Warwickshire Slys* wedded to Helen of Troy is the sort of union [...] I confess I can find no pleasure in [...]. Nevertheless, it is for those who sympathise with the Greek — who feel her delicacy, her refinement, her sweet sensitiveness, the everlasting strength of her beauty — to help her to bear this last infliction, which they cannot do in any better way than by befriending Sly, and endeavouring to keep him sober. By so doing it is just possible that the offspring of simple, unaffected Brutality and perfected Beauty may be as great and as strong, though not as elegant, as that of Gothic and Classic.

The latter family, which is described broadly under the word *Renaissance* is one where we may find almost every shade of character. [...] For example, the buildings erected in France during the reign of Francis I. are for the most part as thoroughly healthy and strong in idea and in mass as they are refined and tender in detail. And not only is this the case with the great, well-known examples, such as Chambord or Madrid (destroyed), but we see it to be so with nearly every *chateau*, or *manoir*, or *maison* of this period. The little loggia of the Manoir d'Ango near Dieppe, is an illustration of the power of design then prevailing. It is not easy to draw such compositions accurately, and to follow them in modern design is far more difficult than to follow the distinctly Gothic or Classic. Whether we wander through Calvados, ramble along the banks of the Loire, or walk through the streets of Rouen, Caen, Orleans or Toulouse, we shall recognise in all the works of the reign of Francis I. features which are no mean counterpart of either parent, but are the outcome and the resultant of the duality which produced them. In Italy, and in the later Renaissance of other countries, the Gothic parentage was in a very great degree ignored, and the ex-Classic of Rome, with all its faulty ostentation, protruded itself into what might have been a happy family. The union of Gothic with Classic was at an end, and the Mediaeval element sank lower and lower, until it was thrust from its last home by the influence of a new fancy. The prostitution of Art, which now arose — the wild license, the contemptible deceptions — are seen chiefly in France, Italy, and Spain, in the works of the time of Henry IV and

* Drunken tinker in Shakespeare's *The Taming of the Shrew*.

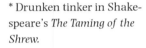

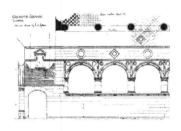

Godwin, drawing of Manoir d'Ango loggia, near Dieppe, BN *10 April 1874.*

Louis XIV, especially in the interior "decorations," and in such churches as SS. Paul and Louis, Paris (1627), and S. Maria Lobenico, Venice (1680). Lower than that it is impossible to go [...]

Now the ex-Classic or Renaissance of our own country, while it gives us nothing so outrageous as this, cannot present anything to be compared to the excellence of the French architecture of the first half of the sixteenth century. Longleat (1567–1579) — supposed to have been designed by John of Padua — is, like the town-halls of Arras and Beaugency, a combination of ex-Classic pilasters and entablatures with large mullioned and transomed windows. There is, however, a certain cold severity in the ex-Classic parts of the English example not to be found in the French buildings, and which, happily for us, did not prevail in England until the sixteenth century had fully passed away. Later on, even as late as the reign of Queen Anne, traces of the Gothic and Classic union are visible in many a country town, in some of our less important mansions, and in numerous farms and small houses scattered through the country. As a rule, however, they do not aspire to the rank of Architecture, but bear, at the best, a meek, modest appearance of quiet servitude, and, at the worst, possess only a wild desire for rusticated quoins and a fancy for balls. That many of these unpretending houses are picturesque is undeniable. Bricks of good colour, high roofs of tile, tall, stout chimneys, and full-grown dormers, are the elements to which they owe their chief attraction. I should have thought it quite unnecessary to insist that these elements are derived from the Gothic parentage, and not from the Classic, were it not that [...] Mr. Stevenson is reported to have said "*that the 'Queen Anne' styles were essentially Classic in character*,"* which is no doubt true of the large buildings designed by the leading architects of that day; but, then, these are far removed from the works of the new ex-Classics, as exhibited in the houses near the Albert Hall, Kensington, and at Bayswater-hill, or in the Schools in Seven Dials and at Greenwich. Whatever artistic value these buildings may possess — and far be it from me to say they have none — is due, as it seems to me, entirely to the material, the pitch of the roof, the presence of dormers, and the absence of large sheets of plate-glass. In some, as in No. 3, Bayswater-hill, we have an arrangement of solids and voids, and a disposition of horizontal divisions, which could hardly fail to produce a good effect, no matter what detail was applied. This "order in variety" is neither essentially Classic nor Gothic, but belongs to both, and may be studied on the Athenian Acropolis as certainly as in any Mediaeval town.

It is when we come to examine the *special* characteristics of these new buildings we perceive that the ugly features of the paternal family have somehow mingled themselves with forms familiar to us in the refined features of Classic art. The exquisite perfection of contour seen in Greek mouldings is marred; a bulbous Bardolphian moulding takes the place of the echinus; roofs are marked by gables compounded of broken-backed scrolls; and pediments are introduced in a nervous, fitful sort of way astride the narrow top of the gable, or, mural-tablet-like, placed against the wall. Some of the buildings have not even thus much development, and the creed of the school may be broadly, but not inaccurately stated to be, faith in *brick and red tile, high-proportioned sash windows painted white, and outside Venetian shutters painted green*. With careful adjust-

* *Building News,* 12 March 1875.

93

Champneys, Newnham College, Cambridge, BN 4 Sept. 1874.

ment of solid and void, much may be done, even with such a limited faith as this. Artistic excellence we need not expect. We need not hope to see works rivalling Chambord, or the brick-built Hotel d'Assezat, at Toulouse; but I think, on the other hand, we should be spared ugliness introduced for nothing but oddity's sake, [...] such intolerable crudities as those exhibited all over the south front of Newnham Hall, Cambridge [...]

Again, it has been argued that the new ex-Classic, although admirably adapted to the social and domestic requirements of the present age, is not so well suited for churches or houses of public worship as Gothic is. This, it seems to me, is the greatest confession of weakness in regard to a style of architecture that could possibly be made. From such a confession it would appear that this new form of ex-Classic seeks our suffrages not on any ground of abstract right either in construction or detail, not by reason of its superiority scientifically or artistically — for if it did so it certainly should be applicable to all classes of buildings — but rather on some foundation of mere sentiment, the stability of which is, to say the least, open to doubt. In the new birth derived from the last genuine union of Classic and Gothic there was no such limitation, and no such want of confidence as is now exhibited. The *Renaissance* of the churches in Dieppe, of the church of the little town of S. Florentin (1611–1632), of the organ of the cathedral of Rodez, and of scores of churches and parts of churches scattered over France and England, shows clearly enough how thorough was the movement, and how it permeated the whole body of sixteenth and seventeenth-century life.

It is the absence of this thoroughness which is the essential weakness of all modern work. Had Mr. Stevenson and his party been strong enough in their faith to have effected a new union — not a revival, for revivals are only fashions of the hour — a union should be something more than a barren love-in-a-cottage sort of sentimentality, they, as its promoters, would not have shrunk from incurring the responsibility such a union involves. If the ex-Classic of today is not big enough to embrace town-halls and law-courts, chapels and cathedrals, as well as suburban villas; if it is not strong enough to influence the whole character of modern manufacture and make itself felt in the works of the potter, the glass-maker, and the smith, in the looms of Yorkshire and Lancashire — in a word, if it has not vitality enough to permeate the whole body of Society, then this last attempt will end, like so many others, in the merest sham, and this new endeavour to beget a living style must perforce prove futile.

CURIOSITIES OF ARCHITECTURE (1875)

Source:
'Curiosities of architecture',
Architect, 17 July 1875,
pp. 30-1

Fitness for purpose and context is the theme here, with Godwin attacking the 'mock-modesty' and 'snobbish hauteur' of buildings which ape inappropriate models.

Every nation and every age that may be said to possess an architecture of its own has also its chapter of architectural curiosities. By an architectural curiosity I mean that which results from an architect or designer being too eager, over-busy, careful or laborious in his work. The anxiety to do some new thing; the eagerness to devise novelties; the effort made to be singular — to force individuality into one's work, are no doubt manifestations of a most unhealthy state of mind — a state of mind, moreover, that may be traced in great periods of art-culture. [...] Extremes in proportion are to be found filling up a great space in our museums of curiosities; in old Greek days represented by the Doric of Corinth and Agrigentum, and the Doric of Delos; in Mediaeval England, by the first Pointed of Wells and that of Salisbury. [...]

Coming down to the present time, we find, without going any further than our own country, all sorts of curious things, "Gothic" as well as "Classic". We have heavy pillars thrust out in front of a building to support — nothing; we have stone lintels and jambs stop chamfered, as if the stones were morticed and tenoned together, and the shoulder was wanted for the sake of strengthening the tenon; we have enormous street fronts built so slightly that they are unable to balance the cornices which crown them, and we also have look-out towers built so extravagantly strong that that they might well rival the great keeps on donjons of our mediaeval fortresses. But of all constructive curiosities perhaps the greatest is to be found in the great salon of the Star and Garter Hotel, at Richmond,* where the massive stone pillars of a heavy stone arcade have no resting place, but are absolutely *suspended*, so that a piece of thin metal can be passed under every base! [...]

Turning to the region of ornament [...] the central refreshment-room at South Kensington Museum has on shaft and wall and window abundance of rich well-larded ornament in form and colour, and if one desires to see how blindly and mechanically the designs of the later Renaissance period can be applied to modern structures, the same building will furnish us with touching examples. [...] Mr. COCKERELL'S new entrance to the Old Water Colour Societies' rooms at the other end of Pall Mall is also a little curious, it poses to us a little bit, not altogether stagey but in an amateur theatrical sort of way, and for fear we should not take enough notice of its attitude, which is by no means ungraceful, it gives us a glance that says as plain as can be — "*Do* look at me, for I have put on these window shafts and other knick-knackeries, got at great trouble, all on purpose to attract your attention and show you how much finer I am, and how much greater taste I have than any of my neighbours." [...]

In modern domestic Gothic architecture one of the most curious things is the constant recurrence of the pointed arch [...] under flat ceilings. How long will it be before architects understand that the purely domestic or civil Gothic of the Middle Ages was as much a trabeated system of construction as the Roman or Renaissance? Even in military and palatial structures, in the castles of Conway and Carnarvon, and in the palaces of Venice, the windows — however much filled with tracery — are nearly all constructed with *square heads*, whilst in all ordinary house building the lintel predominates over the arch, and in the vast field of timber construction supersedes it altogether.

It is not, however, in his construction, still less in his detail, that the modern Gothic architect is most distinguished. Bad or even erroneous construction, bad or even doubtful detail, are rarely, I may say never, seen in the works of the leading men of the school, or even of their immediate followers. The curi-

Biographical notes:
Phipps
South Kensington Museum

* Designed by C. J. Phipps in 1874.

95

ous thing about their designs is that they are so often out of scale with modern life and its surroundings. [...] For not merely in suburbs like Kensington or Haverstock Hill, but in the very heart of the city, we find, as it were, dropped on the ground or squeezed in between its neighbours, a house that is not merely countryfied — for there are many market-towns and village streets whose houses would put to shame these modern paltry affectations — but a house where every crudity, every spokeshave, every rough expedient of the hamlet and the farm are carefully, laboriously, curiously, expensively wrought out by the skilled artisans of the greatest metropolis in the world. This sort of thing may be taken as a protest or reaction against the pretentious palatial superficialities of the vulgar imitations and parodies of Italian Renaissance. This is the most we can say for it; but it should be remembered that the vulgarity of pretension can be shown in mock-modesty as well as in snobbish hauteur; that *any effort* to be singular, whether that effort takes the form of childish simplicity or philosophical profundity, is unhealthy even in the least degree, and in the highest becomes insufferable.

THE END OF ARCHITECTURAL REVIVALS (1875)

This preamble to a discussion of Saxon building allows Godwin to outline his ideas on the demise of revivalist styles, a theme which had engaged many progressive architects and critics since the 1850s. Invoking 'practical utility' as the true test, he seems to anticipate the principles of early Modernism.

Source:
'Old English or Saxon building', *Architect*, 7 August 1875, pp.70-1

Shaw, Alliance Insurance Offices, Pall Mall, Art Journal *June 1887.*

It must be admitted that there is a tendency just now among refined, art-cultured folk, to encourage simplicity in building — encouragement arising chiefly from a wish to discourage pretension to palatialism. This pretension is all the more offensive because it is due partially to the possession of an overwhelming money-wealth, and partly to a lack of soul-wealth, or what some would rather call mental culture. The day of architectural revivals may be near its setting — I for one sincerely hope it is — Classic and Renaissance, early Gothic and late Gothic, Tudor and Stuart, it matters little which we select to imitate, we have shown enough of each to prove how thoroughly competent we are to deal with all. The latest phase insofar as it avoids style is perhaps the most hopeful sign for the health of the future of English architecture. How long those who have introduced and work at this particular phase or revival will have Spartan courage enough to resist on the one side the witcheries and enticing prettiness of Gothicism, or on the other hand the passionless grace of measured Classicism, it is impossible to say, but that those who have already begun to trust in detail will ere long leave that detail whatever it may be, and that they will do this in the cruelest and most faithless manner we may be quite certain. For no part of the building styles of the past which depends on detail can ever really live again until the condition of society be the same as that when such detail was produced. The only style of detail that can possibly be a living reality with us, the only one to which we could attach ourselves to our life's end, must be therefore one founded, as all other style and detail have been — on building questions of practical utility — founded first on these, developed day by day by our own culture, or feeling, or both, and culminating in fitness and beauty in exact ratio to the kindliness of the feeling or the sensitiveness of the culture.

BLENDING STYLES (1881)

Always sensitive to any misunderstanding of his own buildings, Godwin takes a school-masterish tone with a critic over the new entrance to the Fine Art Society.

Who is the architectural critic or expert on the staff of the *Art Journal?* This is what he says in the current number (page 377) — "We have to note the new entrance to this (the Fine Arts Society) gallery, designed by Mr. E. W. Godwin, F.S.A. Without confining himself to one style, but by the judicious blending of several, the architect has," &c. &c. Now, really, this is too funny. What is every architectural style the world has yet known, but a judicious (or injudicious) blending? We do not go so far as to say, with the *Art Journal*, that this little front in New Bond-street is a blending of "several" styles, but any — even the unfledged student — can perceive it is a blending of two, just as the first outcome of the Renaissance was a blending of Gothic and Classic, and just as was the Roman order, commonly called the "composite", a blending of the Ionic and Corinthian styles. When will people understand that the art of architecture *is* an art, and, therefore, a living growing thing, and not a fixed scientific formula?

JAPANESE BUILDING (1878)

Godwin's fascination with the principles of Japanese design had been apparent in his interiors of the 1860s. It took longer to manifest itself in his architecture but by 1872 the Building News *could report that 'Mr. Godwin has gone beyond most people's notions of the boundaries of civilisation, and has added Japan to the list of authorities worth copying'.* Apart from studying the stock of importers like Liberty's, Godwin also consulted a range of printed sources that informed his design and writing. He owned a copy of Aimé Humbert's* Le Japon illustré *(2 vols, 1870), for example – the book referred to in this extract – and illustrated two earlier articles on 'Japanese wood construction' in the* Building News *(1875) with details taken from Humbert and volume 5 of Hokusai's* Manga.

It is surprising how little is known of Japanese Art outside that which is simply and purely decorative in the modern sense of the word. Dining the other night with some artists whose knowledge of Eastern Art is superior to that possessed by most of their brethren, we ventured to remark that the architectural lesson Japan could teach us was as yet unlearnt. Some years ago we hinted in a company of artists that the Japanese artists knew perspective and that their ideal of female beauty might possibly be as good as ours. This hint drew on us a torrent of the severest condemnation for which we were in a measure

Source:
'Notes on current events', *The British Architect*, 9 December 1881, p.612

Godwin, Fine Art Society, BA 16 Dec. 1881.

* 'Wall-papers', 11 October, p.291

Source:
'Japanese building', *The British Architect*, 30 August 1878, p.85

Godwin, details of Japanese wood construction, BN *19 Feb. 1875.*

prepared, knowing how readily English people accept the lowest, cheapest, and most archaic productions of the Japanese market as illustrations of art in Japan. We know better now, and therefore we were not quite prepared for the attack which our artist friends launched against Japanese architecture. "A flimsy wood and paper construction", said one; "A congregation of pagodas", said another. Indeed, the estimate formed by most people of Japanese architecture rests on no better or surer foundation than that exhibited years since in regard to their perspective or their ideas of female beauty — an estimate based on most deficient premises.

As we write we have before us, *not* a collection of cheap and modern fans or hand screens, too often the only illustration of Japanese art with which Europeans are familiar, nor have we specimens of cheap lacquer, roughly painted crapes, or still rougher printed books; the authority lying open on our desk is a work on Japanese building, an elementary book, it is true, but still a work devoted to the speciality of architecture. [...] it is no more than an introduction to the art, the merest sketch, the barest outline of a very limited area of the Japanese mode of building either of form or construction. In this limited field, however, we have post and lintel construction, both plain and rich, cylindrical and square; balustrades right-angled and curvilinear; elaborate eaves cornices; many panelled doors; screens and windows; gable ends, ornamental ridges, and finials, together with illustrations of a combination of iron and wood construction; all utterly different from the modes of western Europe, but yet quite as appropriate to our climate as the forms with which we are most familiar, and yet only last week a writer in the Saturday Review — curiously like our artist friends above-mentioned — thinks the Japanese do not understand perspective, while all he can tell us of their architecture is that they make everything of wood and "raise their houses on stages or platforms under which the air can blow," — information of the cheap book and twopenny hand-screen type. That it was by no means a universal practice to build of wood, even the cheap books will show to eyes that can see, for the platforms as well as the houses built on them were sometimes of solid construction and of stone. Indeed the object of raising the ground floor was not for the air to blow under it but to escape the flood, the overflow, and the heavy rainfall. One word more, — Japanese architecture is not to be judged downwards from the Tea houses and the inferior Temples any more than we should judge the domestic architecture of the Greeks upwards from the Parthenon or even the Propyleion. To do one or the other would be to estimate falsely, for we should be taking Japan at its worst and Greece at its best. But even assuming that Japan possesses only timber constructed buildings, is there, think you, no style — no architectural art — in that wood construction worthy of our admiration or even of our emulation? We are bold to say that there is, that in their wood building there is an art full of refinement and capable of wide adaptation: that we may learn much from their arrangement of masses, their shaping of outlines, the combination and the opposition of delicacy and of strength, that they exhibit in all their detail: and that nowhere shall we see a simple building purpose fulfilled with greater propriety, more modesty, or a keener sense of beauty.

IV The Architectural Profession

GODWIN was writing at a time when the status, responsibilities and education of architects were in a state of flux. The Institute of British Architects, which had been established in 1834 to secure 'uniformity and respectability' in the profession, was run by a small group who conducted their business 'behind closed doors' (p.24). This organisation was unable to address the growing external pressures on the profession, or to unify the spectrum of opinion and activity among architects. It should be remembered that architecture was still an unregulated activity in the early 19th-century and was largely the preserve of gentlemen-amateurs or 'tradesmen' who freely raised their ambitions into the sphere of architecture as opportunities arose. In the competitive world of the building industries, different groups – surveyors, engineers, building speculators, house agents, measurers, cabinetmakers-turned-decorators – were all jostling for power and contesting the authority of the architect. Many factors had a bearing on this, not least the steady diffusion of wealth among the middle classes which fed the building trades. Alongside this rapid population growth and industrial expansion caused unprecedented urban development which created both opportunities and pitfalls for architects, as manifested in the increasing diversity of building types, the proliferation of regulations, and introduction of new technologies and materials.

Since the late eighteenth century most architects had come into the profession through the pupillage system, and Godwin was no exception. As a young pupil then assistant in Bristol he experienced little formal education and found himself tied to many of the dull and uncongenial aspects of architectural practice (see p.24). Along the way he encountered plenty of 'Pecksniffs' (from the smug and deceitful architect in Dickens' *Martin Chuzzlewit*,1843–4), who for Godwin came to stand for the hypocrisy and narrow-mindedness that seemed endemic within the profession. On moving to London Godwin pitched in to the debates about professional reform, regularly exposing cases of malpractice and incompetence while at the same time attempting to set a tone of idealistic debate that upheld issues of beauty and quality. Like many young architects, he had a vested interest in campaigning on questions of authorship, copyright, and competitions. The last of these was a source of particular exasperation. Competitions had become the most common way of allocating major public commissions but they were plagued by local and national pressures and, if not actually corrupt, often adjudicated on mysterious criteria. Even when professional assessors were employed there was nothing to ensure that their recommendations would be followed.

Godwin was among those who felt themselves pressed into 'one-sided accomplishment' by the increased specialisation and commercial pressures within the profession. In 1857 G. E. Street had warned: 'We architects are in great danger of endorsing the popular view that we are "professional men" and not artists!' It was a view echoed by Godwin on several occasions and expressed most succinctly in 1876 when he wrote, 'The world will not let an architect become an artist' (p.111). Indeed, his central concern in this sphere was to define the education, practice and image of the architect in relation to a broad concept of Art. As institutions he felt not only the RIBA but the Architectural Association (established 1847) and the Royal Academy were failing the profession, and expressed his contempt for establishment figures like Robert Kerr to whom he refers, sarcastically, as 'Professor'. The RA was a particular source of disappointment. As early as 1810 there had been attempts to establish a separate academy dedicated to architecture which might raise its status to that of the fine arts. By the 1860s, however, little had changed, and architecture was still being under-represented in both the elected membership and annual exhibitions of the RA.

By using the architectural press as a medium to engage directly with an increasingly fragmented and geographically dispersed profession, Godwin was able to side-step the hierarchical authority of such organisations. Arguably his prowess as a journalist gave him more power in setting the agenda for architecture than he could have exerted from within the committees and institutions of the architectural establishment. An anti-establishment stance was part of Godwin's media persona, not kow-towing to agencies of one form or another that tried to constrain his practice or his opinions. In 1878, after becoming editor, Godwin set out to make *The British Architect* 'more and more a medium of inter-communication' providing a forum within the profession for debate, instruction and dissemination of information. It was not only a mouthpiece for Godwin's ideas about 'art-architecture'. An equal amount of space is devoted to practical matters and to keeping architects up to date with the latest technical, legal and commercial developments. As he reported a year later, 'We have fought against the many evils which surround and clog the practice of modern architecture and have bent our bow against the bad client, the bad builder, the bad assistant, the sham architect, and the bumptious amateur' (p.247).

While lambasting his direct contemporaries in the two early series, 'Cliques' and 'Modern Architects', Godwin used a lighter touch on the younger members of the profession in whom he found a more receptive audience. He was particularly concerned to address those whom he felt were open to reform and could shape the future. The series 'Scraps for Students' (1876), and 'Letters to Art Students' (1884) were specifically targeted at this audience, an audience that also included women. Despite his vehement criticism of authors like Mrs Orrinsmith and Mrs Haweis, Godwin was one of very few architects to take on a female pupil and to encourage women's entry into the profession.

In the absence of an effective educational system or broad-based 'academies', Godwin took it upon himself to foster some form of higher education among the young architects and pupils across the country. The 'Art Club', which ran in *The British Architect* between 1878 and 1885, set briefs like the 'design of a cheap chair' or 'an artist's studio', and published Godwin's critiques of the designs submitted – very much like the student-centred competitions that *The Studio* magazine was to organise from the 1890s. The feedback he offered to letters and designs submitted by young architects was more like a modern correspondence course but it supplemented the training and experience of pupils in the office. Godwin had a fairly traditional view of the education a young architect needed, based on his own memories of pupillage. He set great store by student-centred learning and self-improvement through extensive reading, measured drawing, model-making and visits to museums, old buildings and demolition sites. Practical advice was leavened by his informal tone and by his frequently humorous accounts of social life inside and out of the architectural office. Godwin was an acute observer of professional behaviour and the shifting values and identities that people adopted, especially among clients and builders. Likewise, his revelatory discussions of the 'secret manufacture of architecture' had the ring of truth. The characters and situations he describes are still recognisable, as are many of the issues surrounding education and professional organisations that he flagged up. On the one hand he could suggest an idealised vision of a united profession marching forward with the 'unstoppable power' of a Prussian army (see p.128), on the other he depicts life in the architectural profession as it was, 'warts and all', giving tips about how to get on in life. When speaking to students he was neither an aloof artist nor a prosaic journeyman but recognised that the successful architect had to inhabit both worlds. While deploring the development of architecture into an 'advertising medium', for example, Godwin recognised the importance of exhibiting a flashy drawing at the Academy or writing a popular handbook as a strategy for attracting clients.

This contact with young architects must have given Godwin some sense of community and influence at a time when his own practice was shrinking. He took on very few assistants even at the height of his success. Through his journalism and the Art Club, however, he was able to promote his integrated approach to architecture, interiors and furnishings, and to suggest to the generation including Voysey, Mackintosh and Ashbee, an image of the modern architect who was able to move freely between different areas of design without the restrictions of the High Victorian architectural office.

Further Reading

R. Hayes, 'An Aesthetic education: the architecture criticism of E. W. Godwin', and A. Reid, 'The architectural career of E. W. Godwin', in Soros 1999, pp.115-84

A. Saint, *The Image of the Architect*, New Haven and London, 1983

R. Norman Shaw and T. G. Jackson, eds, *Architecture: A Profession or an Art?* London, 1892

ARCHITECTURE AND THE ROYAL ACADEMY (1869)

Written as part of a longer review of the Royal Academy's centenary, Godwin returns here to his theme of the sister arts and their unequal representation both in the annual exhibitions and elected membership. Exhibiting at the Academy was an important means of attracting clients that architects like Norman Shaw were beginning to exploit with a new flashy style of drawing.

Source:
'The Royal Academy',
Architect, 1 May 1869,
pp.229-30

Biographical notes:
Royal Academy
Roberts
Turner

The painters tell us that it is their *pictures*, and these alone, which draw the visitors — the architectural drawings and sculpture are as nothing; that the shillings are drawn by the moveable art (easel pictures), so the honours must go to the men who provide these easel works. This is in effect to say that the Royal Academy is nothing more than an exhibition. Architecture never did and never can be represented on the walls of an exhibition. It can be symbolically set forth by means of certain drawings. But these drawings have no more right to be considered architecture than have those bits of pasteboard called 'keys' (which painters sometimes use to explain their works) to be considered paintings. The country's annual progress in easel painting may be seen in the summer months on the walls of the Academy, and similar exhibitions. But to see the progress of architecture we must look on rather wider walls than those at Burlington Gardens. If the value of art to a nation depend upon the number of shilling sight-seers it can attract, architecture is valueless. [...]

The injustice consists in this — that whilst the works of the painter and sculptor are seen and examined, the *works*, not the drawings, of the architect are, comparatively speaking, ignored, because, unfortunately, they cannot be put in gilt frames, nor placed on pedestals. An architect's drawings are to the public little more than cabalistic signs. What non-professional man ever yet understood a 'section,' or that mysterious compound 'half plan looking up, half plan looking down?' It is no doubt possible to produce a picture of an architectural work by giving a commission to some young painter; but, after all, it is the young painter, not the architect, whose work we see upon the Exhibition wall.

What we really want is a real practical union and sympathy between the sister arts. Every one is in agreement thus far. The question is, can this be done by the present machinery, or must some new plan be adopted? If it were true, as some affect to believe, that one man has been, and could be, at once architect, painter, sculptor, there would be no difficulty about the matter. An architect would depict his works with the pencil of a Roberts or a Turner, and get praised for his painting, even if his building were never seen, or not worth seeing. Life is much too short for this sort of thing. [...] But, though the union in one man of the practice of the three arts may be regarded as generally impracticable, it is much to be desired that there should be more sympathy between the several practitioners — less marked division and more dovetailing. Painters are unquestionably woefully ignorant of architecture. Sculptors know nothing about it, and very few architects can draw their own perspectives, fewer still their own decoration, even in little. These shortcomings ought not to be. We must all be set to work if the Academy would be a living working institution in our midst; the question, how? is not for THE ARCHITECT to decide. That is essentially an Academy's business. This much, however, may be said: no advance will be made by glorifying exhibitions at the expense of schools, nor will the brotherhood or sisterhood of art be strengthened by electing only three architects in forty-four elections.

BROTHERLY ASSOCIATION (1872)

From the 1830s, moves to establish national guidelines for the professional training and practice of architecture had been fraught with factional disputes. Godwin was not alone in his hostility towards the RIBA, the principal professional body for architects in Britain, established by Royal Charter in 1866. While socially ostracised on account of his notorious liaison with the actress Ellen Terry, however, and not part of the 'inner circle' that seemed to run affairs behind closed doors, Godwin was beginning to exert considerable influence as a critic.

It is almost proverbial that architects not only do not support or back up one another as the members of other professions do, but they seem to delight in frustrating each other whenever they have the chance. The history of architectural competitions and law cases affords abundant proofs of this. Nor is it very surprising, considering the absence of anything like an effective system of organisation. In fact, we have no body representing the profession. There is, it is true, the Institute of British Architects, which is entitled to speak with such authority as may be established on a royal charter. But against this authority there is arrayed a very formidable majority — for it is as well to remember that there are over 1,700 practising architects who are not members of the Institute, and that amongst them are many of the most accomplished architects of our time — Butterfield, Bodley, Shaw, Webb, Nesfield, &c. Some have always held aloof — some have tried it and found it wanting, but the majority see plainly enough that there is as much jealousy, and opposition, and unbrotherliness within the family circle of this society as there is without. [...] the great practical service which was supposed by many would have arisen from the establishment of a professional practice committee has proved to be a delusion. To a question of doubtful practice, a definite answer was indeed rare [...]. The President and his supporters flatter themselves, no doubt, that this is an unwarrantable sketch of a very valuable and worthy society: we only wish it was. [...] It is too surely a sign of decay and feebleness when the chief of a chartered society finds it necessary to deprecate public criticism. If the art and the profession flourish better by virtue of such association, and if the practice of architecture aesthetically and economically suffers by non-association, we should like to have the example pointed out to us. If, too, modern design is the genuine work of the man who fathers it, what has he to fear from adverse critics? Either his design is bad, in which case he may reap benefit from the condemnation, and should be thankful, or it is good, and he can punish the critic by publishing it. [...]

There is another point. We have not the exact statistics by us; but we ven-

Source:
'The "British Architects"',
Building News, 21 June 1872,
p.505

Biographical notes:
Butterfield
Bodley
Nesfield
RIBA
Shaw
Webb

ture to say that the Fellows of the Institute of British Architects do not number one seventh of the profession. And in the face of this numerical weakness they yet think it to the interests of the profession to discuss, and, for all who know, settle schemes of general practice with closed doors. What guarantee have the outsiders that arrangements and understandings have not been made in the discussion of this last document which will never appear on the face of it? Is it not well known that its predecessor was looked on as nothing more than a foolscap sheet of suggestions even by those who drew it up? Is it not too well known that many members never paid the slightest attention to it; and that those who, in their *esprit de corps*, as it is called, were fools enough to sail according to its instructions, were only laughed at for their pains? It is verily surprising that even in the simple matter of a schedule of charges unanimity of action is impossible! Let us hear no more of comparisons between the architectural and other professions, for until some ground of unanimity is discovered by the "British Architects" such talk is but presumption.

ARCHITECTURAL EDUCATION (1874)

In Godwin's view, architects were in danger of being railroaded into one-sided accomplishment by the fragmentation of the arts and increasingly narrow specialisation of the professions. To adjust this tendency there was a need to supplement the hands-on training offered through the pupillage system, with exposure to more expansive teaching within the context of a broad-based Academy of the Arts.

Source:
'Architectural education', *The British Architect*, 22 May 1874, p.1

Biographical notes:
Architectural Association
Royal Academy
Spiers

The question of Architectural Education has been before us for some time, but only in a vague sort of way. It is trotted out sometimes by young men like Mr. SPIERS, and sometimes by somewhat older practitioners; but, wherever it appears, there's a shambling gait with it, — a shilly-shally sort of movement; in brief, a want of backbone, which must be supplied before anything important can be developed.

This want can only be supplied by constant iteration and by uninterrupted and systematic agitation. When, therefore, I am told that an Architect's office is of such a nature that we must accept it as it is and give up the idea of reforming it, I reply that if this be so we must look elsewhere for Architectural training, and oppose the system of pupils altogether. But is an Architect's office necessarily no school? This is the question we have to answer. To say that the majority of Architects' offices have degenerated into mere business premises may be true; but for technical education — the education, that is, which results from intelligent observation of the practice of our Art — the office is, and must be, the only true school. Let us recognise thus much, and the path before us becomes smoother. [...]

But the office of the present day is, and still more the office of the future will be, far too busy a place for the full realisation of what we understand by Architectural Education. This is felt on all sides to be true, and everywhere efforts more or less successful are gradually being made to supplement the office, so that side by side we see growing up in our larger towns associations of practising Architects and separate associations of non-practising Architects and Pupils. This division, I confess, seems to me a dangerous one, one calculated to weaken rather than strengthen the common cause, which is no less than the advance of Art and the higher education of the Artist. More Utility and less separatism is what we want. In great towns and great centres of industry and wealth the Artists, under whatever speciality they may be described, should be brought more together. The education of the Painter would be all the higher for communion with the Architect, and the Architect would gain no little from intercourse with the Painter and other Artists. This has been tried to some small extent, and with much mutual advantage; but all such associations soon degenerate, unless there is real work to be done and zealous hands to do it. No better work can be found than the education of those who are to be our successors; and taking this as the very foundation and prime reason of our associating, no name can be better suited to such an association than that of the central school so well known as the Royal Academy of Fine Arts. Setting aside for the present the chartered prefix, an Academy of Arts embracing professors, assistants, and pupils in each and every Art, perhaps even embracing a class of honorary members — gentlemen or ladies who take a real interest in Art — is the sort of thing one would like to see established in such towns as Manchester, Liverpool, Glasgow, Birmingham, &c. [...] To secure on the one side the genial help and encouragement of practitioners, and on the other the zeal and hearty co-operation of the students and assistants should be our aim. Establish an Academy on a broad, sound basis. Gather round it support of the strongest character. Make it such that everyone may deem it an honour to belong to it. Let its membership be a passport to other things. Accumulate funds by annual exhibitions of every kind of local Art. Encourage by proper fees sound lectures and careful teaching. Above all, let there permeate through the body a spirit of Unity and of brotherhood, and the result is certain. [...]

The course of study is a matter of vital importance. Whatever it be or be not, it must before all things be practical. Work must be done within the walls; the art of design must be followed not at home, with books and papers to refer to, but before the eyes of the director or professor, if we would judge rightly and desire to encourage the power of composition.

LADY ARCHITECTS (1874 and 1879)

While Godwin was critical of most female amateurs and writers on household taste, he openly supported increased educational and professional opportunities for women in the arts. Indeed with the exception of Whistler, his most productive collaborations were with women. He was unusual in admitting a female pupil to his office, Beatrice Philip. Under his supervision she carried out the kind of work described in this article, including decorative panels for architecture, furniture, stained glass and painted tiles. They married in January 1876. This article was reprinted from the first issue of a new paper Women and Work: a Weekly Industrial, Educational, and Household Register for Women, *edited by one of Godwin's friends, Miss Emily Faithfull.*

Source:
'Lady architects', *Architect*, 13 June 1874, p.335

Biographical notes:
Garretts
Philip

A young man, or youth is 'made' an architect by being allowed to study under an architect in his office for three, four, or five years, for which his friends pay a premium or fee to the architect, varying from 100*l*. to 1,000*l*. His sister may be better qualified for an architectural student than he; may have the power of design in her; may have a special eye for colours, or at any rate greater powers of adaptability. I see nothing to stay the exercise of these powers. I know of nothing that could impede her progress as an architect. Its suitability is the first question — its chances as a means of livelihood is the next. In discussing the question you must keep clear of the notion that an architect is anything else than an artist in that full sense that implies science or knowledge. There are many 'architects' who are only such in name. I am not thinking of these when I say my profession is suited to women. We want refinement, delicacy, great sense of fitness, the sense of the beautiful, imagination, or at any rate sufficient mental activity to be able to picture in the mind's eye the result of given proportions and combinations of the three elementary figures — the circle, square, and triangle. Accuracy is essential, and repose is desirable. An impulsive, gay, free-as-air, lightsome sort of girl is not the stuff for an architect. The right sort of being found, there is before her a wide field of usefulness.

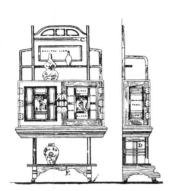

Godwin, 'Beatrice cabinet' with panels decorated by Beatrice Philip.

Architecture including Furniture and Decoration.

Public Buildings.	Carpets and Hangings.
Private Houses.	Painting on Cabinets.
Monuments.	Painting on Walls and Ceilings.
Illustration of Old Works.	Wall Paper Designs.
Cabinet Work.	Tiles.
Metal Work.	

Such are the chief features of my own practice, and as last year I realised a clear profit from one firm in the City of 600*l*. for furniture and decoration designs alone, made without trouble or leaving my room, I conceive that in this branch alone the architectural student of the future will find more and more opportunity of employment. Cabinetmakers always prefer architects to design for them when they can get them, and it is the architectural, or mother art, which is so necessary first of all to master before we are ready to deal with the numerous arts subject to it.

Beatrice Philip, design for carved brick panels for Gillow & Co. houses in Chelsea, BA 9 May 1879.

Source:
'Notes on current events', *The British Architect*, 21 March 1879, p.121

We shall have lady architects yet, and the sooner an Architectural School is established for the purpose of educating girls in the technics of the art, the better for the art. Even as it is, lady architects are not so rare but they may be found practising in the quiet of their country homes, both in England and her colonies. We know of three who have so practised for years, making plans, sections, elevations, details, and superintending the workmen. One a titled lady, one the wife of a bishop, and the third belongs to the family of a country rector. Although their designs for schools, cottages, farm buildings, and church decorations are lacking in many things, especially in construction and proportion, they may yet fairly hold their own in comparison with the majority of works of this class erected from the designs of male architects.

THE SECRET MANUFACTURE OF ARCHITECTURE (1873)

In many respects the architectural office was becoming like a factory production-line for drawings, which reduced the assistants to anonymity. Godwin could speak from his own experience at the hands of William Armstrong, the Bristol architect to whom he had been apprenticed. For the creative artist to maintain visibility it was vital that he received due credit for his work, and that the public was made aware of the way in which architecture was being 'manufactured'. As a test case, adopting the legalistic tone of the law courts, Godwin takes the part of one of his assistants, G. F. Roper, in a dispute over credit for drawings in the Edinburgh Cathedral competition. (Ironically Roper went on to irritate Godwin by copying his furniture too closely.)

The processes involved in the production of modern architectural design have been familiar to me ever since I was eighteen years old, for at that ripe age, before the time of my apprenticeship (or pupillage if you prefer it) had expired, I occupied the proud position of making my own designs for the works my master's customers — or clients — intrusted to him. Nor did my advantages stop here; for the whole of the details, and on some rare, privileged occasions, the specification, superintendence, and management of the work were freely placed in my hands. [...] When my venerable master signed my first design, not seen by him before the minute he fathered it, I was possessed by conflicting emotions hardly possible to describe. Pride in my work was uppermost in me. And I felt, too, a decided satisfaction at his endorsement — a feeling which, as time advanced, I regret to say, faded away — but there was a sense, or a glimmer of a sense, that I was being deprived of something, and I would have given him gladly an extra year's service to have placed only my initials in the corner of my drawings, or to have been allowed to sign them as letters are signed — So-and-so, per So-and-so. These little weaknesses of youth soon passed, for in other offices I saw the same sort of thing at work and taken by the assistants as a mere matter of course. The production of modern architectural design I found, therefore, to be mostly a manufacture in which the head of the business might or might not take part, and when he did act, that it was chiefly in matters of accounts and correspondence.

If I am rightly informed, this system still prevails in town and country; no one grumbles, no one objects, because it is taken for granted that architectural work is a business to be conducted by business men in a business manner, and the best architect is naturally enough he who employs the best hands. Sometimes the *hands* are unruly and strike. Sometimes they set up a manufactory on their own account, but it is only very lately that the *hand* has signed his own death-warrant by laying claim directly or indirectly to the credit of the work he has produced, as something he is entitled to over and above his wage. In what is known as the manufacturing districts this claim is beginning to be recognised, and in exhibitions we have seen the names of the workman joined with his work, without in any way discrediting the manufacturer or reducing his business. Now the cases are exactly parallel; for it was the veriest bunkum that was ever uttered to talk about architects being individual artists and jealous of their art-honour; that assistants are too apt to lay claim to credit

Source:
'The secret manufacture of architecture', *Building News*, 7 February 1873, pp.145-6

they are not entitled to, &c. The profession, from John o'Groats to the Land's End, know this right well, and the correspondence which has enlivened the pages of THE BUILDING NEWS has told *us* no new tale.

The general public, however, seem not to know, or if knowing, not to care a pin's-point about the process of manufacturing architectural designs. There are certain so-called art-patrons, who, backing up a few manufacturers that happen to be their personal friends, occasionally utter sonorous phrases about the fine art of architecture, making plentiful use of powerful adjectives. But these phrases, rooted neither in knowledge nor in faith, are not quite so much trusted now than they were in the early days of this journal.

It would save a world of trouble and vexation if architects would only admit, recognise, and adopt the principle of professional advisers, or consulting referees. It is, however, just possible that some architects [...] might shrink from exposing their emptiness even to the most liberal of advisers, for it should be clearly understood that the consulted is not to do the work of the consulter, but to advise with him as to the improvement and development of a well defined subject. If otherwise, that is, if the consulter comes empty-handed, he should either go away empty-handed, or subside into a superintendent of the works, leaving all the art honour and emoluments to him to whom they fairly belong; the credit of the work to be to the workman whatever the nature of the work may be — the design to the inventor; the representation of the designs to the artist who draws it out.

Edinburgh Cathedral competition: Ross v. Roper

A. Ross, competition design for Edinburgh Cathedral, Builder *7 Dec. 1872.*

For example, if Mr. Ross, of Inverness, made the sketch-design, however roughly, which was developed by the drawings in the Edinburgh Cathedral competition that bore his motto or name, Mr. Ross deserves the credit of the design in inverse ratio to the degree of roughness of the first sketches; for when we talk of sketch designs or preliminary sketches, or rough ideas, we use very elastic words. My own notion of a sketch design is such a drawing as a man might jot down with pen or pencil on a sheet of note-paper or in his memorandum-book, with no more accuracy, detail, or finish than the oscillations of an express-train would permit. But most careful eighth-scale elevations in pencil I have heard described by their authors as sketch designs, whilst the merest scrawl of a plan, little better than a child's first scribble, I have heard honoured by the same much-abused title. In all disputes, therefore, of authorship of design, it is essential, in order to arrive at sound judgement, that the first sketches made by the several claimants, and the dates thereof, be brought into court.

In the disputed case of Roper *v.* Ross, Mr. Roper's "sketch" was a careful pencil elevation of the west front, and was almost line for line the same as that exhibited. This I know, for I saw this "sketch", directly after it was prepared. Now, if this was not altogether Mr. Roper's design, where is the prior sketch he copied, imitated, or developed? That such a sketch exists, we are assured both by Mr. Ross and his bishop. The bishop even saw Mr. Ross making it. What is it like? Where is it? When did the bishop see the performance? And why has it not been produced? These are the questions that one would think ought to be easily answered. They must be answered if Mr. Ross wishes to maintain his right to be considered the author of the Edinborough [sic] Cathedral design under his name.

It is neither Mr. Ross's fault nor Mr. Roper's that this disturbance in the architectural atmosphere should have taken place; but it is the fault of a system which has grown too rotten to hold together any longer. [...] we can feel nothing but satisfaction at the exposure, and only hope that we may have yet more of them, so they that the secret manufacture of architecture may ultimately become a dangerous trade.

THE ARCHITECT'S ASSISTANT (1878)

Godwin's autobiographical references to his own training evidently struck a chord with student readers, many of whom wrote him private letters on the subject.

He belongs to a class which is somewhat various. Last week we had a note or two touching that kind of assistant who "assists" the lazy or the ignorant, who fulfils nearly all the professional duties and quite the whole of the artistic requirements of the architect in whose office he works, and who for the sake of a poor salary is content to remain unknown, watching from day to day the fame and profit of his labours fall to the share of his paymaster. No doubt the assistant in such a case has ground for complaint, and yet if his position is so hard to bear, [...] why does he suffer it to continue? Is he not free to set up for himself? Questions very easily asked by the tribe of PECKSNIFFS but not so easily answered by the assistant who has perchance a mother or a sister or a young wife dependant on his earnings. An architect's business is not made in a week or a month or even a year by merely fixing a brass plate on his street door. If he has neither influential friends nor capital to back him up he must perforce become an assistant whose only hope in life is a partnership with his master or some brainless youth who fortunately possesses a family connection. To wait for this is often dreary work for the zealous assistant [...]

The unscrupulous assistant

There is another class of clever assistants, — men who have no one but themselves to care for, who work out of office hours in a very quiet way for architects other than their masters, who go in for competitions on the sly and occasionally do odd designs on their own account for some of the most trusting in the limited circle of their acquaintance. There are among them those who do not hesitate to put their master's time, office, and even materials and clients to their own private use.[...] They stick at nothing. They enter your office to make the most of you; they will even work up your own sketch designs for others before you have had the opportunity of using them for yourself, and are not over particular in appropriating other things besides designs. As a rule they avoid the PECKSNIFFS and endeavour to obtain a footing in the offices of easygoing men more or less accomplished, and are sometimes found at the desks of very eminent architects. [...]

Source:
'The architect's assistant',
The British Architect, 25 October 1878, p.157

Biographical notes:
Pecksniff
South Kensington

The business assistant

The shrewd business assistant whose art knowledge starts at zero and rarely gets beyond is a very valuable servant. He sometimes begins humbly enough; he has cost no one any premium or articles, he remains generally in one office and becomes at last something more than the *alter ego* of his master. Builders stand in dread of him for he is conversant with all their ways and is familiar with figures. His master has now and then to propitiate him; he understands the ledger which no one else does, and is as a rule a valuable man who grows old and respected in the same office. An occasional fault found in this type of assistant is the assumption of a mock dignity and superiority which his master would not dare to exhibit and which would be amusing if it were not sometimes impertinent.

The mediocre assitant

Another class of architectural assistants is one that is largely filled with young men of various shades of mediocrity. They can do nothing well, their drawing is bad, their measurements are inaccurate, their writing slovenly, and their notions of art or of the science of construction, though great and brilliant in their own estimation, are in reality most vague and uncultured. Among these may be found the gentleman assistant, who is condescending to the profession, looking on art with ill-concealed contempt, and the "Kensington" assistant whose fair friends paint still life at art schools and whose eidolon of architecture is found only in the keeping of the "Department" as a sort of oracle at Delphi.*

* The South Kensington School of Art administered through the Department of Art and Science.

The pupil in disguise

Then there is the assistant who is only a pupil in disguise. He has been articled at a small premium to some one who cannot teach him anything beyond the most miserable office routine, and when the days of his pupilage are over he seeks to enter the office of some one who can teach or whose designs are at any rate worth studying. Here his real architectural studies begin, and for this he is bold enough or silly enough to ask a salary perhaps as little as twenty shillings a-week when he ought in common justice to pay at least the premium that has been sacrificed to his ignorant master.

There are other varieties that possibly some of our readers may know or remember, but amid them all there goes on his way the quiet, unpretending, diligent, careful student, ever ready to assist but wholly free from any desire to assume a part that he is not cast for, a true disciple of his chosen master, most faithfully serving him, fitted to succeed him, and the best of all assistants.

THE OFFICE OF THE ARCHITECT (1876)

Source:
'Scraps for Students.—IV. "The Office"', *Architect*, 13 May 1876, pp. 303-4

The furnishing of the office speaks volumes about how architects view their practice. The dominant image of the architect is more akin to that of a surveyor or lawyer than an artist. Good manners, an orderly environment, and a degree of pragmatic cynicism are nevertheless essential for those who wish to get on.

There are usually three distinct epochs in the office-life of a young architect. Pupil, assistant architect; apprentice, journeyman, master; it matters little what we call them, each has its peculiar work, its own pleasures, its own troubles.

Biographical notes:
Pecksniff

The office environment

As to the office, it is still essentially the office; the long desk, the high stool, the bare floor, the walls innocent of all forms of art, or at the best hung with feeble perspectives of feeble designs or rubbings of well-known brasses. Here and there, so few as to be hardly worthy of being quoted as exceptions, are to be seen rooms more like artists' studios, where in the midst of elevations and specifications we may meet with a fragment or two of glorious colour, a cast of some Greek statue or bas-relief, some good examples of eastern pottery, and perchance an easel. These few exceptions you had perhaps better know nothing about, for whatever you may think, however much you may desire to cultivate yourself by cultivating your eye to the habitual reception of the beautiful, however strong may be your conviction that in joining our profession you became a student of that *one* art which includes within itself all the principles of beauty [...] you may be quite sure that the intelligent people of England will not regard you as an artist, and that in any question of artistic work which may perhaps arise in the conduct of your work, you are as likely as not to find to find that those who are kind enough to entrust you with the great and responsible work of welding stone, brick, timber, and metal into mighty compositions, will not ask your advice as to the finishing of the walls, the hangings, or the furniture, but will prefer to consult even the amateur painter in water colours. *The world will not allow an architect to be an artist*. You must learn to understand this at the very outset. To dabble in watercolours so as to make effective and rapid views of your designs, or to have a free use of pen and ink, are accomplishments which you will undoubtedly find very useful, but do not suppose that the most superb composition in way of absolute building will ever induce a human being to look upon you as an artist therefore. An architect in the world's eyes is a man of business on the same platform as a surveyor or land agent. Some of us seem to have an ambition for a diploma so as to make us nearer the level of the lawyer and the doctor. Indeed the private office of many an architect is very suggestive of that of a conveyancing attorney. The table in the centre of the room is crowded with letters, reports, specifications, quantities, accounts, &c., tied up with red tape. There are the ponderous volumes of the Messrs. KELLY;* there are tin boxes with large white letters painted on them, telling us that they are honoured by having been made the receptacles of papers relating to the estates of Lord This and Sir Somebody That. On the walls are two or three large coloured views of noblemen's country seats, and there is a general untidy crowded look about the place as much as to say, "it is impossible to keep things in order when one has so much to do". Your first experience of office life may possibly be gained in such quarters.

* Trade and post-office directories

One such office presents itself vividly to me as I write. There are three rooms *en suite*. There is the large room for the pupils and general assistants with the bare floor, the long desk against the windows, the high stools, and the general workhouse look supposed to be so eminently conducive to respectability of practice. In this room a high nest of drawers forms a sort of counter screen near the door to keep builders and casual callers at bay. Here, too, are dusty piles of the architectural periodicals, uncut, but with many of the photo-lithographs missing. On the mantelpiece is a plaster cast of a font, some small squared specimens of building stone, and three villainous-looking tiles. The colour boxes are always in the last stage of dried-up decay — the enamel gone, the colours hard and cracked. The windows are grimy with dirt, and there is a good deal of dust everywhere. In this general office plans are inked in and coloured, specifications and letters are copied, tracings are made, and caricatures abound. The master is known to exist through certain mysterious whistles and sounds which reach us, but his visiting the general office is an event of such rarity that the pupils have ventured to caricature him on the desk and drawing boards in various positions on horse and foot.

The head assistant

The head assistant, who has a little room to himself and who really makes all the designs, occasionally amuses himself by looking at the pupils' work. This splendid young gentleman has generally a profound contempt for pupils, and at our office he is no exception to the general rule. He is rather fond of jewellery, wears an eyeglass, and indulges in a back parting. His knowledge of design is limited, *very* limited. There is not much power of drawing either, but he manages very well between his assistantship and some outside work done on the quiet to secure £500 a year. It is curious to see how the process of designing goes on in his little room. After consultation with his chief as to cost and accommodation he retires to incubate his design. Unlocking a drawer he takes therefrom a pile of selected engravings of other men's work that have been published in this and other journals. He has them all arranged in bundles — churches, town houses, town halls, country houses, farm buildings, cottages, and so on. If it is a town hall, he has recourse to the bundle of town halls, and placing them before him, considers deeply which of them best meets the requirements of his case as to cost and accommodation. One, perhaps two, being selected, he proceeds to adapt their features to the special site and arrangement he has to deal with, and then, after the front elevation is made, the engravings are carefully locked up until a new job demands a new consultation. This practice is by no means confined to our office; indeed so common is it that I believe it is the reason why some of our most artistic and original architects decline to publish their designs. So, then, as far as drawing and design are concerned the pupil need expect but little help in this kind of office.

Self-help and conduct in the office

But there is such a thing as self-help, and to this he must look. He need not despise such help as he can get from the periodicals. The illustrations of modern works he would do well to pass by, and keep his attention fixed on those old examples which often enrich the pages of this and other journals. He will have to learn by observation, and not look to be directly taught.

Among other things he will mark well the servile manner, and practise it. The rich man expects a servant in his architect to obey his behests, and not a teacher to direct him. Remembering this, the pupil may derive great profit from observing the action, voice, manners of his master when in the presence of rich clients. You should be careful, too, how you reply to visitors.[...] Pupils, especially those in country towns, are extremely apt to be curt and brusque in answering inquiries from strange visitors. Hawkers of pens and publishers' touts are no doubt a great nuisance, and take advantage of the slightest laxity on your part, but you may be civil and yet firm to all, and not jump over embryo premises to unjust conclusions. The manners and convention of architects' pupils are often not merely ungentlemanly, but eminently prig-gish. Even very mild young gentlemen, in the first flush of their new case of instruments, with the consciousness of being brought up to something which is somehow not exactly like a retail shop, are prone to indulge in trumpery airs and paltry juvenile smartness. One trick pupils have is not to turn round when addressed by a caller, another vulgarity is, in replying, to repeat the whole or part of the question asked; for example, a gentleman called at an architect's office not long ago, and this was the scene:—

> A Clerks' Office. At the desk, with their backs to the door, three young gentlemen, looking at French prints:—
> *Enter* STRANGER, *after knocking twice*: Is Mr. So-and-So in?
> ELDEST YOUNG GENTLEMAN, *without turning to interlocutor*: Yes, Mr. So-and-So is in.
> STRANGER: Can I see him?
> ELDEST Y. G., *in same position, curtly*: No, you cannot see him.
> Exit STRANGER.

And Mr. So-and-So, who was talking to a builder, lost an introduction to an influential but modest man.

You may have a large quantity of writing to do in your first office. Do not let the quantity encourage carelessness on your part as to the quality. An illeg-ible or almost illegible hand is not a sure sign of genius, and may some day involve much trouble to you and others.

In all your office work, whether writing or drawing, mixing colours, or tying up your papers, learn to be cleanly or even precise. Nothing is got by slovenly habits. You may fancy that, because among a certain class of artists the studio is kept in the direst confusion, and litter, litter and mess are some-how signs of art; but they are nothing of the kind; they are only signs of the lazy, the idle, and the ill-bred. [...]

The first job

The second office experience of the assistant is oftimes what the first ought to be — the real probationary time of the student. [...] These raw assistants are often willing to serve for quite a nominal salary — even as low as ten shillings a week. Their object, openly avowed, is to improve themselves by seeing the work and getting the oversight of some one whose designs they admire. In a word, they desire to enter a real school, and serve under a master they can readily acknowledge. Of course, it is disheartening to them to be told, that instead of being paid they will have to pay; that we whose designs they admire are really not paid by the Department of Science and Art to rectify the errors and make good the shortcomings of young Pecksniffians. [...]

When an assistant, however, is capable and is successful in getting a salaried engagement, his one rule of the office should be to make his master's interests his own. There are some assistants who have in store a strong connection, and who from the first are introduced to us with silver spoons in their mouths. They are sure to succeed, and are almost as equally sure to know nothing of their art. There are some masters who possess the power of self-reliance to an enormous degree, and are almost independent of the regular qualified assistant. But the majority of architects are very dependent on clever young men. The active man of business who is hand in hand with successful company promoters, who is an authority on school boards, who talks profoundly at tea meetings, or takes the chair at missionary gatherings, is not as a rule partial to the drawing-board. His individual practice consists chiefly in valuations, arbitrations, dilapidations, rights of light, and other semi-legal functions. To such an one the young assistant who knows how to get up an effective set of drawings, who can design fairly well and has a faculty for etching perspectives [...] should prove extremely useful. So useful indeed that in some cases master and assistant have been known to share the credit as well as their fees for successes in public competition, and eventually to arrive at some sort of partnership. Only, in preparing for this happy consummation, the assistant should be particularly careful not to hurt the professional pride of his master. In cases where the latter is wholly innocent of design and drawing, having not so much to do with the work as the client — where the assistant has been in effect the sole architect — your master has not only a right to sign the drawings and speak and write of the design as his own, but will be grievously annoyed if you venture, even among friends, to claim it, or any part of it, as yours. Much of modern sculpture is managed on the same wise principle, and you will find it in various callings — dentistry, law, and others — whenever the business is of an extensive nature. For, remember that everything is purchaseable nowadays, and an architect has "a right" to the authorship of everything done by the assistants in his office. So if you are wise you will encourage other branches of art, and thus, in dull times, be enabled perhaps to add new lustre to your master's name by writing a book or painting a picture. The gentleman who is gratified in putting his name to your designs for churches and town halls would be even more pleased to scribble it in the corner of one of your pictures if you could but command a place for it on the line at Burlington House, and would reach perhaps a higher degree of satisfaction could he append it to your title of a treatise that would be sure of popularity.

STUDENTS AT HOME (1876)

* 'To Art Students. Letter No. 8', *The British Architect*, 4 July 1884, p.2.

Architectural education does not end in the office. Here and elsewhere Godwin advocates more 'plain living and high thinking', and offers tips on self-improvement at home – what to read and how to study.*

Balancing work and play

Architectural "students", whether pupils or assistants, may be broadly divided into two classes — those who work and those who play. It is far too common to find illustrations of the latter kind. Young gentlemen with well-to-do parents, and, indeed, many others who are not obliged to work for mere sustenance, are much too apt to look upon office hours as the beginning and the end of the time due to study or work. The best of them will sometimes venture on what they call "work" during their summer or autumn holidays. But the work consists in making pretty sketches of old buildings, interesting only to the young ladies of their acquaintance and — themselves. With such students, for the most part, architecture is put on and off with the office coat. The many hours at their disposal before 10 A.M. and after 5 P.M. are sacrificed either to the drudgery of laziness or the hard labour of "pleasure". In summer the river and the lawn possess irresistible attractions, and to talk of book or study in fine weather is suggestive to them of cruelty to animals. In winter, besides the all-absorbing rink, there are the attractions of theatres, music-halls, and sundry more or less exciting sports, to say nothing of evening parties and bachelor entertainments, where the discussion of art is thrust on one side by the competition of meerschaums or briar-woods and much exercise of the judicial function on bad claret and worse whisky. It is the young — the very young — gentlemen of this class who are fond of expending the exuberance of their animal spirits in places of public entertainment. They delight in applauding loudly, not to say uproariously, the wrong thing and at the wrong time, and there are among them those who appear to be especially proud of the acquaintance of some ancient ballet girl, or the equally distinguished serio-comic, who is forever reiterating some such excruciatingly funny phrase as "Tommy make room for your uncle".

Opposed to this class, running sometimes quite to the other extreme, is the working class of students. I am not certain that it is not almost as painful to watch the overstrained seriousness of the continual grinder of knowledge as it is to follow the wretched monotony of those vacuous evenings consumed by his opposite. Unsatisfactory as it may be to see the architects of the future engrossed in the idiotic follies which constitute the bulk of our public amusements, to know that they are undermining their health and their mental power by an excessive use of tobacco smoke, by late hours, and by inhalation of most villainous compounds of various kinds of vitiated air, it is almost if not to the full as unsatisfactory to see the freshness of youth pale day by day before what is called the consumption of the midnight oil. For there are students who neither smoke nor drink, to whom theatres and music-halls are unknown, who have never skated on ice nor on ashfalte, whose hands are innocent of oars, foils, guns, who dread evening parties and have an absolute horror of balls. When not in the office they are nearly always to be found at home with a book or drawing: their little recreations consist partly in occasional visits to South Kensington Museum, where after a bit they come to anchor in the reading-room, and partly in attending lectures. Now it seems to me that it would be very desirable if the excesses characteristic of these two classes of student could

Source:
'Scraps for Students.—VI. At home', *Architect*, 27 May 1876, pp. 338-9

Biographical notes:
Architectural Association
Bowman & Crowther
Brandon
Burges
Gwilt
Johnson
South Kensington
Viollet-le-Duc

be made advantageous to both by interchange. It is not altogether an affair of temperament, for there is no temperament that is not open — at any rate in early life — to the modifying action of education. [...]

Reading matter

If you can afford to buy books you can hardly do better than adopt the means afforded by them for self-culture. Moreover, the formation of a library, however small, is in itself a source of considerable pleasure. But an architectural library is a costly matter, and it may not only be costly but next to useless. If you live in London all the very expensive works may be consulted at the British Museum and some at the Kensington Museum. You should exercise therefore great caution as to your purchase, for there is a vast mass of rubbish included in the general heap of architectural publications. Especially useless to you are the popular treatises; the illustrations are as a rule woefully inaccurate, and the letter-press is produced for a class of readers in which it is hoped you are not included. BRANDON'S works, VIOLLET-LE-DUC'S Dictionaries of Architecture, Furniture and Costume, some good work on Greek Art one on Renaissance, with the best edition of GWILT for practical common-place — are the books best suited for your outfit. A careful study of the Greek rooms in the British Museum, and of one or two of the large German works on Greek art, may, however, do more for you than any English work on Greek Architecture with which I am acquainted. If you have the means to do it, you will no doubt like to increase this list considerably. Mr. JOHNSON and Mr. BURGES have published carefully measured drawings of medieval architecture, mostly French, which you will find valuable supplements to VIOLLET-LE-DUC. BOWMAN and CROWTHER about twenty years ago issued a series of measured drawings equally valuable from an English point of view. [...] The *Moniteur des Architecte*s, the *Gazette des Beaux Arts*, *L'Art*, and *L'Art pour tous* are nearly always worth examining for their architecture, which is not the case with our English magazines devoted to art. The *Art Journal*, the *Portfolio*, the *Art Monthly Review*, and others of the same group, are singularly backward in their recognition of architecture, and curiously deficient whenever its illustration is attempted. [...] The student, whatever maybe the extent of his library, should early engender a habit of cautious analysis. It is greatly to be feared that not only very many architects now in practice, but many pupils [...] take up architectural books solely for the sake of "the pictures". Of the large number of architects and students who possess copies of VIOLLET-LE-DUC'S "Dictionnaire l'Architecture" [*sic*], how many, or rather how few, have taken the trouble to read the admirable articles on *Construction* and *Maison* and *Pan de bois*? We have unfortunately nothing comparable to them in our own language, either in clearness of description, in logical argument, or admirableness of illustration. In all your reading, especially in reading of construction, you should have pen or pencil and a good-sized note-book at hand. For, however copiously illustrated an article on construction may be, it will not profit you to the extent it might if you neglect to work out, step by step, the reasons for this and for that, applying past processes to present problems. For this reason above all, I have more faith in home study than in attendance at lectures.

R. Brandon, illustration from An Analysis of Gothick Architecture, *1844.*

Lectures, visits, demonstrations and model-making

The only good of a lecture on architecture, as far as I am able to see, is when it limits itself to the condition of a direction-post, pointing out to you the readiest means of obtaining the best information. More than this must be simply the recapitulation of what you might read [...]. It is true that the Architectural Association have Saturday visits to various important buildings in progress. One week it may be the Midland Hotel*, the next week St. Thomas's Hospital; today it may be the Law Courts, next Saturday the Natural History Museum, and so on — a sort of feast where the dishes are removed so rapidly that you get nothing to eat. Of course it would be delicate work for a professor to lecture on a brother architect's construction within the very walls that he might feel called on by his conscience to condemn. But I do not ask for this sort of vivisection. There are hundreds of subjects that I think are much better fitted for students' study, and I venture to throw out the suggestion, which for all I know may be far from new, that where buildings are condemned and are about to be broken up the professor and his young friends may have free use of the subject beforehand, and for such a time as would be ample for thorough investigation, for complete measurements and drawings, and not merely for one lecture, but for half a dozen if needed. In such lectures the professor would have his assistants — a joiner, bricklayer, and so forth — to remove panelling, &c., and, in fine, to lay bare the skeleton piecemeal.

* Designed by G. G. Scott in 1867. Godwin supplied a scheme of painted decoration in 1877, reworking his earlier designs for Dromore Castle.

Among other home work the architectural student might very well employ some of his time in making models of buildings and parts of buildings. The architectural model is, I fear, too much neglected now-a-days. As a means of study it will be found full of help for you. There is no necessity to expend much time in the completion of minute detail, for the model is chiefly valuable to the young architect in enabling him to look all round the masses of his building, and is in this respect superior to a cartload of perspectives. When you translate your design into the solid, it is astonishing what surprises you will meet with; how wonderfully low the dormers will look, how attenuated the turrets and spires. You will not infrequently find that your beauties have a way of crowding into one corner, and that there is but one prospect of your building that can lay any, even the lightest, claim to be artistic. All this the model will correct for you, and you will learn from it more about your defects of design, and obtain more suggestions for their remedies than by attending any amount of lectures and classes as at present conducted.

COMPETITIONS AND CLIENTS (1876)

Godwin had extensive experience, both good and bad, of entering architectural competitions. Early success with the Northampton and Congleton town halls had made Godwin's reputation, but disappointments and controversial judgements followed.

Source:
'Scraps for Students. —V. Competitions and clients', *Architect*, 20 May 1876, p. 320

The transition between the office life of the assistant and that of the newly-fledged master is really but slight, although to all appearance it sometimes seems an enormous change. The change is, however, wholly, or almost wholly,

Biographical notes:
RIBA
South Kensington

*J. Salman, design for Congregational Church, Chertsey, Surrey,
BN 17 March 1876.*

one of externals. Instead of having the range of a suite of rooms the young master often finds that one or even half a room is quite sufficient for the needs of his professional practice. Instead of an unceasing flow of work, the days hang heavily from week to week with nothing to do. He looks out for architects who are more fortunate and who do not mind putting out their work. [...] Should he be obliged to have recourse to this sort of architectural pot-boiling, he will have the opportunity of learning a good deal about warehouses and workhouses. Dissenting places of worship and Board schools may also very probably come within his range. Meanwhile the youthful professor looks sharply out for "*likely*" competitions, and depends chiefly on this game of speculation as his main chance for the exhibition of his art prowess. Now competition in itself is not to my mind the entirely bad thing some among us would try to make it out. If the two chief points of the contract — cost and accommodation — are strictly adhered to, then much may be hoped for from the system; but if glaring departures from the stipulated cost are permitted, as I believe to have been the case in the late competition for the Derby Free Library and Museum, and not long ago in the selection of the Town Hall at Hastings, then the system is debased [...]

But we will suppose that the young architect has entered himself for a race which is to be conducted in a fair manner. If he would wish to succeed it is of first importance that he should visit the site. [...] Not only have you the advantage of understanding your problem better, but you may be able without acting in any, even the slightest, underhand way to gauge the prevailing sentiment of the locality, whether, for example, the committee is biased by an antiquarian consideration, by an overwhelming sense of utilitarianism, local associations, or what not. Moreover you can make yourself acquainted with the surroundings of the site, and, by showing them in your drawings, exhibit a touch of local knowledge which will weigh much in your favour with many committeemen. You can also learn by a visit easier than by any other process all about the material which may be best suited and its proper treatment. In fine, a visit will enable you to collect information far beyond what you can derive from correspondence or books. [...] The competitions in which you are most likely to succeed are those for public buildings where the cost ranges from 5,000*l.* to 20,000*l.* The drawings for such works you can prepare single-handed, and yet have time for pot-boilers. The cost out of pocket will be a trifling one [...]

Professional charges

When the young architect is fairly on the wing, and his first client, employer or patron has appeared, he should be particularly careful not to frighten him through the channel of his cheque-book. Not merely should he be careful to avoid exceeding the stipulated cost; not only should he guard attentively the avenue of extras, but he should be particularly cautious in his own professional charges. [...] It is quite true that the Royal Institute of British Architects published a long time since, and continue to sell, a printed paper called a *scale of charges*, from which it would appear that the Institute considers an architect to be fully justified in claiming for preliminary sketches and designs that have not been carried out, for travelling expenses, and, in long journeys for time occupied in travelling at the minimum rate of three guineas a day. [...] You would do wisely not to cumber yourself with any such scale, for if you imagine that the members of the Institute are governed by it, and that it would be a breach of professional etiquette, or a lack of *esprit de corps* on your part were you to depart from it, you must be profoundly ignorant of the ways of your profession. Make your mind up from the first never to charge more than the 5 per cent commission. [...] In private houses, especially, you should always leave a margin in which your patron, or your patron's wife, may disport; thus the wall papers, the final cost of the paint, grates, and even mantelpieces may well be left untouched by you. They are delicacies which the rude architect is not generally supposed to properly appreciate, and although in your youthful ambition and in the early days of a green hope you may plan and design rooms with a view to a certain colour and so on, it will nevertheless be well for your peace of mind, and especially satisfactory for your business, to give any such ambition or hope the least possible encouragement. For it is necessary to remember that the mantelpieces, wall papers and the general internal finishing of a modern house have latterly come to be considered as more or less belonging to the artistic, and you will find a host of competitors in this path to stop your way, especially among the painters who exhibit what are called decorative subjects. It will be time enough for you to attend to such things when architecture shall have become as fashionable as its sisters. Of course your work will thus often be reduced to dry bones, but however disheartening this may be to you, it will be found in the end much more lucrative to deal with the hard mechanism of skeletons and scantlings than with those graces of contour, those tones of colour, and those refined uglinesses more or less represented in the art fashions now nourished at Kensington, whether cornice, or costume, or needlework.

Godwin, prize-winning competition design for Leicester Municipal Buildings (not built according to Godwin's design), Arch. *13 Jan. 1872.*

ARCHITECTURAL POACHING (1877)

The unacknowledged appropriation of designs was not confined to the master-pupil relationship, but took place at every level of the profession. The proliferation of architectural magazines and publications at this time meant that published designs circulated rapidly around the country, as evidenced by the examples Godwin cites in this article. Having assisted Burges with his design for the Law Courts competition, Godwin was in a position to judge the extent of J.J. Burnet's appropriation.

An evil which is rapidly gaining ground in our profession is the barefaced appropriation by certain architects of the studies of their contemporaries. In the majority of cases it is only a certain feature or particular combination of features that some student architect has developed from one or more than one old example which we find "conveyed" by others. From Mr. R. Norman Shaw much of this sort of thing has been conveyed. We can hardly fail to recognise, for example, the New Zealand Chambers in Mr. Collcutt's design for

Source:
'Architectural poaching', *The British Architect*, 13 July 1877, pp.16-17

*Especially galling to EWG as he had been placed second in the Winchester competition.

Burnet, Glasgow Stock Exchange. BA *13 July 1877.*

Burges, competition design for Law Courts.

Wakefield Town Hall. Many of Mr. Stevenson's peculiarities have been present in Mr. Robson's designs since these two architects combine their talents in the production of the design for the board schools at Greenwich. In Mr. Brydon's work Mr. Shaw is repeated over and over again. Some very young gentlemen have gone so far as to copy plans in every particular of contrivance, as witness Mr. McLaren's appropriation some time ago of Mr. Shaw's house at Shortlands, near Beckenham on which a public correspondence arose. I do not care to make any comments on the manner in which some of my own designs have been conveyed before they have been published, but I may mention the Guild-hall at Winchester as a remarkable example of architectural conveyance, its ground plan being a strained reproduction in all the important points of that at Northampton Town Hall.*

The instances to which I have referred are, however, no more than delicate recognitions of the merits of certain works when compared with a case that has just come under my notice. On a corner site in Buchanan-street, Glasgow, there has lately been erected a building for the Stock Exchange. Nominally (and virtually, so far as the general public of Glasgow is concerned) its architect is, I believe, a Mr. J. Burnet, a fellow of the Royal Institute and president of the Glasgow Society of Architects. Really and truly, so far as artists are concerned, its architect is Mr. W. Burges, also F.R.I.B.A., of 15 Buckingham-street, Strand. What the plans of the several floors may be like I have no means of knowing. The arrangements of the rooms may or may not be highly creditable to the gentleman who devised it. What I wish to call attention to now is the exhibition in the external ordinance of a deliberate appropriation of Mr. Burges' work as shown in the illustration of his design for the Law Courts published ten years ago. When such a liberty as this may be taken, when an artist's thoughts may be traded on unrequited — nay, even unacknowledged, and that too, by one fellow of the Institute as against another — it can be no great matter for surprise that certain accomplished architects should so rarely exhibit their work through the medium of our professional journals. [...] There is just one important difference between the Glasgow building and Mr. Burges' drawing, for the first floor of the latter is erased, the upper part of the Law Courts design being dropped to the ground floor arcade in as cruel a way as if the cook were to take the oyster from the pâté.

Mr. Burges' design has been, in fact, cut down to suit the circumstances of the case; but its merits — and it certainly possesses not a few, are, so far as they go, quite as much to be credited to Mr. Burges as if his Law Courts design had been carried out line for line. I appeal to the profession whether it is not time to endeavour to put a check on this sort of thing. [...] Do the leaders of our profession regard these conveyances as merely jokes, amusing incidents, rather complimentary than otherwise to the real but unremunerated author? I trust not. On the contrary, I hope that by calling their attention and the attention of the whole profession to a case so patent, some steps, however small, may be taken towards remedying this growing evil of copying contemporary designs that have no existence except on paper, and which as a rule are only published by the courtesy of the designer.

WHO DESIGNED BEDFORD PARK? (1879)

Godwin, design for Bedford Park, BN 22 Dec. 1876.

The Bedford Park estate at Turnham Green in London was an immediate success with middle-class residents aspiring to 'artistic' taste, and much to Godwin's irritation, the architect Norman Shaw was generally perceived as being solely responsible for the design of 'this new and interesting colony … delightfully suggestive of Old England and country life'. Having set the record straight regarding his authorship of the White House in September (see p.255), Godwin now used the columns of The British Architect to seek acknowledgement for his design of the first houses at Bedford Park, and to protest at the repeated use of his plans by the developer Jonathan Carr without consultation.

The real fact is that this Bedford Park Estate was started, so far as design and the employment of red brick and tile are concerned, by Mr. E. W. Godwin in 1875. His design for a corner detached house has been repeated over and over again, and his design for a double or semi-detached house has also been repeated. Mr. Godwin sold his designs and the copyright of them to the freeholder; who intended to superintend the erection of the houses without the aid of an architect.

Source:
'Notes on current events', *The British Architect*, 24 October 1879, pp.160-1

Biographical notes:
Carr
Shaw

ARCHITECTS' RIGHTS (1878)

Interference in art from clients or committees was not to be tolerated, whether the artwork was a building or a painting. In this editorial Godwin interweaves his art and architectural criticism, thereby reinforcing his view of architecture as art. A year had passed since his article on Whistler's Peacock Room, a subject to which he returns here in support of a parallel. Readers would also have been aware of his ongoing dispute with the Metropolitan Board of Works regarding his designs for studio houses in Tite Street.

An architect designed a facade for a town hall at a considerable distance from his office. When the work was nearing completion he visited it and found that certain windows had been made considerably lower and wider than shown on his drawings. He found also that the change had been made deliberately by the town council, and that the artistic intention of his work was, in a word ruined. Do the gentlemen of the town council think they have done their architect an injustice when the latter points out to them that the work that goes under the architect's name has been to a certain extent remodelled by them? No: on the contrary, the town worthies think they have improved the facade, and that the architect should be grateful. The council think the building belongs to them because they paid for it, and that they have, therefore, the right to do what they like with it. To this view we entirely demur.

Is architecture a fine art? Does it rank with painting and sculpture? Is the architect responsible for his work? and is his name published in connection with it? To these questions no one, we presume, will dare to reply other than in the affirmative. The *building*, not the drawings which dictate its proportions, is

Source:
'Architects' rights', *The British Architect*, 8 February 1878, p.63

Biographical notes:
Leighton
Leyland
Whistler

Leighton, The Arts of Peace *mural in South Kensington Museum,* Art Journal *June 1887.*

the art work. It is so, just as the statue is the sculptor's art work, or the fresco the painter's. It is true that the materials and the mechanical appliances in the first case cost as a rule much more than they do in the second or third cases, but the disproportion on the score of material makes no difference whatever to the art question. The *building*, wherever placed, is as much the architect's as the fresco is the painter's. Suppose, then, that the authorities of the Science and Art Department thought Mr. LEIGHTON'S fresco could be improved, and forthwith had the boat in the foreground of his "Arts of Peace" enlarged in his absence;— does anyone imagine that the doers of the deed would escape with anything less than an everlasting stigma of shame upon them ? Or conceive it possible that Mr. LEYLAND could be blind enough to cause Mr. WHISTLER'S peacocks that have made his London dining-room so famous in the history of modern decoration to be altered or obliterated;— why, we know well that all the wealth of Liverpool and Manchester to boot would not suffice to shield such an act from the opprobrium and scorn it would justly merit. The same measure that is meted to painters we demand for architects. That which would be unanimously considered injustice if directed against a painter or sculptor, should be equally considered injustice if directed against an architect. Because architecture so named has here and there sunk to a condition little better than the occupation of contractor's clerks: because the *business* of building has in many places superseded the *art* of building, it by no means follows that men who are artists or architects in something more than card or brass plate can give, are to submit quietly while their works are subjected to treatment which any painter or sculptor would very properly resent. We have drawn no fancy picture; we have indulged in no exaggeration. The case we have cited at the commencement of this article — names and titles being different — has just occurred to one of the most accomplished architects in Europe. The case is one that no doubt comes home to others: we know, in fact, that it does. In some instances the confessed and patent ignorance of the employer dulls the sensibility of his architect; in others, unhappily not rare, the artistic pretence and social position of the "patron" adds to the rudeness of the interference.

ART-ARCHITECTS OR ENGINEERS? (1878)

Engineers are just as capable as architects of culling historical 'trimmings' from pattern-books. True architecture requires the power of adaptation distilled from 'long artistic study' as evident in Burges's work.

Source:
'Notes on current events', *The British Architect*, 23 August 1878, p.79

In matters purely of plan arrangement and construction the civil engineer can have little or no difficulty in becoming the successful rival of the architect. The latter has in our day accepted the role of the mere manipulator — more or less successful in imitation — of sundry past phases of architecture; in other words, of certain historical styles. Here and there it is true there are men with individuality who translate the style of a past age in their own language, but at the best it is only a translation, sometimes coarse, sometimes refined, sometimes vigorous, but more often weak and verbose. No one, for example, could ever mistake the vigorous — too often over-vigorous — work of the architect of Cork Cathedral [William Burges] for the architecture of the thirteenth century. His designs are founded mainly on a close and exhaustive study of a few buildings in Northern France of that period notable for the unusual heaviness — we might almost say lumpiness — of their proportions, but the modern works are not imitations. The prime idea or thought may be found in the past, but the composition is emphatically of the present. In some few — very few — instances an architect has ventured on unconventional combinations of elementary forms, with detail entirely derived from long artistic study, and from no books or archaeological storehouse; but the difficulties which beset any originality of this kind are innumerable, and no one is more ready to resent any artistic success achieved thereby than architects themselves. If architecture is to be a reality, if grace and beauty are to clothe our modern buildings, architects *must* become artists in a fuller sense of the word than that accepted in Conduit-street or South Kensington. Repetition, however careful, of Gothic or Renaissance forms, is no more Art than a repetition of an Egyptian temple or a Roman amphitheatre would be. The engineer of to-day can have books to refer to, full of measured drawings and details of nearly all the best buildings of every age and country. Ancient construction is no secret now. The architectural publications of France, Italy, Germany, and England have brought past styles to the office of the engineer as well as to the private room of the architect, and made bare to him the minutest fibre. So far then as patterns go (and they go very far at times) the engineer is as well off as the architect. When, however, we come to those enduring qualities that constitute the foundation of all Art [...] in other words, from the local or temporary conventionalities of Art to the beauty of elementary form and simple masses, we find the modern architect as a rule no better than the engineer. Indeed it is only when the engineer follows in the path of the modern Revivalist, giving to his iron bridges details and "decorations" culled from the architects' pattern books, that he becomes ridiculous. London and Waterloo bridges are nobler structures than Blackfriars or Westminster, not so much because of the difference in material, not at all because of the difference in style, but because in comparison with the latter they contain so much less of that which is mutable and which expresses the passing fashion — sometimes good and often bad — of the mere trimmings on the skirts of the great Goddess of Art.

To open the eyes of architects to the building lessons taught in rocks, and mountains, and trees; to make the brains of architects capable of receiving impressions of the beauty of elementary form in simple combinations; to induce them to forego the stuff called ornament, so that the money now frittered away in miles of wearisome reiteration of meretricious moulding and carving, may be devoted to some work, however small, from the hands of our best sculptors, would be work far more worthy of an Architectural Association than to grumble at engineers filling our chairs, or indulge in mutual admiration of one another's copies and adaptations under the no doubt pleasing but dangerous hallucination that they are.

Biographical notes:
Architectural Association
Burges
South Kensington

'WANTED – AN ARCHITECT' (1879)

Butchers are not surgeons, and nor should surveyors be confused with qualified architects.

Source:
'Wanted—an architect', *The British Architect*, 7 February 1879, p.53

The *Improved Industrial Dwellings Company, Limited*, of which Sir SYDNEY H. WATERLOW, Bart., M.P., is the chairman, require the exclusive services of a duly qualified architect for £600 per annum.[...]

When will Sir SYDNEY WATERLOW and others understand that architecture is an art and that an architect is an artist? What the Industrial Dwellings Company really want is not *"a duly qualified architect"* but a surveyor or chief clerk of works. As well might one ask an accomplished surgeon to superintend the slaughter-houses attached to some meat market as invite *duly qualified architects* to perform the duties set out by Sir S. WATERLOW and his board.

SURVEYORS – STUPID OR JEALOUS? (1879)

Godwin was keen to distance the practice of the art-architect from that of surveyors and what he termed the 'drains and dilapidations men'. This outburst appeared in the context of Godwin's ongoing difficulties over the design and construction of his studio-houses in Tite Street.

Source:
'Notes on current events', *The British Architect*, 7 November 1879, p.179

Why are district surveyors either so stupid, or so jealous, that they persistently worry architects of known reputation, and leave jerry-builders almost to themselves? Perhaps something that is neither stupidity nor jealousy is at the bottom of it. Whatever the cause, it is undeniable that some of the metropolitan district surveyors meddle in things that do not concern them, neglect their official work, and send young assistants, who have never passed any examination, to inspect and to interfere with the works of architects in the foremost rank of the profession. These assistants have really no *locus standi,* and can legally be kept out of any building. There are two West End surveyors who are far too fond of flourishing their young assistants about, and we would, in all gentleness, advise them to be more cautious for the future. We have a case before us of the *laches* of another West End surveyor, who, having neglected to inspect the work at the proper time, had the audacity to demand that the foundations should be opened up. The architect in this case luckily knew the Act of Parliament as well as, perhaps better, than the surveyor did, and entirely refused to gratify him, adding, that he might think himself fortunate his *laches* were not reported to headquarters.

The fact is a district surveyor ought not to be an architect, and ought not to be allowed to practise as an architect. It is from the class of building surveyors that the district surveyor should be elected; but from whatever class he may come we should endeavour to compel him to mind his own business.

As it is, he practises as an architect, and keeps an assistant to attend to his district duties. We were ourselves for some years in the office of a highly respected district surveyor, and we know the ways thereof. Thus instructed we do not wonder that little speculative builders are encouraged by the district surveyors, and that architects who are careful to consider nothing but their duty, should find every attempt made to render inspection unpleasant and vexatious.

IGNORANT BUILDERS (1878)

The worst of assistants is not such an infliction to an architect as an ignorant builder. As a rule, the builder of to-day has no interest in or knowledge of architecture as art. This is the first trouble. The second is that few of them know anything, strange to say, of the history or science of construction. Left to themselves, they put together stone, brick, wood, metal, or what not, in accordance with a miserable half-starved tradition. The king post and queen post are the Alpha and Omega of their roof construction, and their only mode of escape from a difficulty is a bungle. There are, it is true, some few exceptions to the general tone of the class, but they are so few, that many — nay, most — architects go through their professional career without meeting them. Nor is it in ignorance of the principles of building or construction that the modern builder is alone deficient. He is grossly ignorant, in a general sense. Even in the conduct of the £. s. d. part of his business, he is always blundering from inability or carelessness. If the slate or timber merchant's youngest clerk quotes an absurdly erroneous price, he adopts it for his estimate without a thought, and loses thereby the work he is seeking. He fails to make inquiries at head-quarters, and becomes the slave of middle men. An architect's drawings are difficult things to them; a carefully divided scale is a mystery, and specifications they cannot understand. Are we too sweeping in our charge? By no means. When a specification directs in the plainest words an architect or his surveyor can use, that mortar shall be compounded in a certain way, that timber shall be used of a certain kind, that felt shall be so many ounces to the sheet, &c., &c., and finds not only one builder, but every contractor he employs failing to comply with these directions, it is surely not unfair to say that the builder's education — at least, in reading— has been sadly neglected. People inclined to judge more harshly than we are disposed to do might take possibly another view of the matter, and put down the faults that we ascribe to ignorance, to something usually regarded as a more serious defect.

Two marked characteristics of the bad builder are to be found in the barefaced and systematic way in which he breaks through the clauses of the contract relating to extras and time. These, however, are as nothing compared to the tricks he sometimes employs to obtain money on account that is not due. For example: The other day an architect of our acquaintance was absent on the Continent for a fortnight. During this time a builder who was engaged under him applied at his office for a certificate; at last writing, and even telegraphing, to the architect direct. The certificate was not granted. Thereupon the builder called on the client, insisted on being paid without a certificate on the ground that the architect was abroad and that he (the builder) was unable to communicate with him! *That builder was paid* by the client to get rid of his importunity. Could any of our readers furnish us with a case more

Source:
'Ignorant builders', *The British Architect*, 1 November 1878, p.169

fully illustrating the ignorance of builders? Another phase of stupidity is seen in the grandeur assumed by a builder who is lucky enough to have a few hundred men in his employ. He is served by a staff of clerks — the estimating clerk, the financial clerk, the drawing clerk, who is a sort of half-baked architect, and others of less account. To one or other of these he refers all small matters under £10,000, and expects that the architect is to give personal interviews to any of his young men that he may choose to send. Architects who are what the name implies — artists; who desire for their works the personal attention of the builder, and who give their own time to builders' questions in expectation of being met by the principals, will learn in time that the builder who is what is called in a large way of business is not always the best man to carry out their intentions.

BAD CLIENTS (1878)

Godwin revenges himself on Mrs Client and Mr Arrogance – those unwilling to pay for the true costs of an architect's services, or who constantly change their minds, interfere, and exclude architects from the interior.

Source:
'Bad clients', *The British Architect*, 18 October 1878, pp.149-50

Biographical notes:
Loftie
South Kensington

Of late years much has been written, spoken, and published against the modern architect. [...] In even one of the architectural journals have now and then been published without comment reflections on some modern work, that were calculated to produce nothing but contempt for the architect, only that the criticism being probed was found to be based, to say the least, on misconception. It may perhaps be profitable to direct attention to the other side. We have had dinned into our ears stories about bad architects until we are just a trifle bored; suppose for a change we turn the tables and look up stories of bad clients. We invite our professional readers to contribute. Meanwhile we point out, as much for the sake of the employer as the architect, some of the varieties of bad clients.

One of the most common specimens in the practice of young architects is the client who thinks, or acts as if he thought, that the pursuit of architecture was an amusement. Many country clergymen are of this type, and we have heard of certain wealthy country people who appraised an architect solely from the superintendence point of view. Thus what are called sketch designs are asked for with no intention of paying the architect, as if designing was the very least part of an architect's labours. These clients often hesitate before asking for working drawings and specifications. Details of construction and technical phraseology which they cannot and do not pretend to comprehend assume an importance in their eyes by no means commensurate with the subject. There is a mystery to them about a paper that speaks knowingly of *dragon pieces, scarfings, joggles, and rebates.* But there is no mystery at all in a composition of roofs and chimneys, or an arrangement of cornices and string courses, or a grouping of windows and doors. It is a mere drawing-room accomplishment, for has not the bishop's wife made the drawing for the new school in her father's parish, and does not Lady Marion design all the new cottages and farm buildings on the earl's estate, with her monogram worked in fancy brick? With

a painter it is well understood that to ask him for a sketch would be tanta-
mount to asking him for money. Of course neither painter nor architect could
object to furnish any amount of sketches if clients were prepared to pay for
them, and pay for them well; for the sketch is the artistic creation — if the
sketcher be worthy a client — and all the rest, whether in picture or building,
is technical manipulation or mathematical skill.

Another most objectionable sort of client is the man who is never in the
same mind as to what it is that he requires from his architect. He begins by
saying that he cares nothing about external appearance, that he wants so many
rooms for so much money; but that he is determined not to expend a shilling
beyond the sum mentioned, and that anything may be done, even the number
of rooms decreased, rather than add to the limit of cost he has prescribed.
This sounds all very well, and would be an exceedingly comfortable instruction for the architect to carry through, only no sooner has the building been
started than the client demands something that has been carefully excluded
because of the cost, wonders his architect never thought of it, grumbles that
he should have to pay for it, extra, then veers round completely and says he is
determined to have so and so, no matter what it costs: the result is a heavy bill
of extras, final dissatisfaction, and another illustration of the saying "fools
build houses," &c. Akin to this style of bad client is he who starts very moderate ideas of a house on a small scale of management; who cuts down his first
instructions to a hall, three reception rooms, half a dozen bedrooms, a bath-
room, a butler's pantry, kitchen, scullery pantry, larder, cellar, and two water
closets. The plans are completed, the estimate is reasonable, the contract signed;
and if the client could manage to go to sleep some two years or more, the work
would be completed, in nine cases out of ten, with few if any extras and to the
satisfaction of everyone concerned. Your bad client, however, never goes to
sleep; he grows restless, sets aside the wishes of his architect, introduces trifling changes perpetually — occasionally large deviations are made. He wants
a servants' hall, a housekeeper's room, a billiard room, a manservant's room,
in every corner and available roof space, a group of private rooms that can be
used independently of the rest — a sort of house within a house — in brief, a
"villa" turned into a mansion, and then rails against the architect, and tells
his friends that they are little better than thieves leagued with the builders to
rob the public, and that the bill of extras he had to pay amount to nearly as
much as the original contract sum. Again, there is the bad client who never
permits his architect to have a voice in anything that relates to the artistic
finishing of the work. The architect in this case is allowed to work only as a
surveyor; if any sculpture or plastic art forms part of the external design, it is
reserved for the client to do. The mantelpieces and grates, the painting and
mural decoration, the stained glass, and even the knocker and bell handles
are reserved to be considered, ordered, and perhaps designed by Mrs. Client,
who has such excellent taste, whose sister has been a student at South
Kensington, and whose most intimate friend has written no end of charming
twaddle about art at home.

When a client belonging to either of the above descriptions is inclined to be
arrogant or bumptious, the architect would be but ill paid if he received dou-

ble the usual commission. Such a client acts as if his architect had nothing in the world to do or think of, but the one particular work with which Mr. Arrogance has entrusted him. At all hours of the day the architect is summoned to attend his client, to discuss alterations that ought to be made, or re-open questions long since decided. Sometimes when time is more than usually precious the architect is kept waiting in an ante-room, or on the works until another engagement perhaps compels him to leave sooner than Mr. Arrogance wishes, and then there is an explosion which taken any way is sure to count against the architect. On the other hand, woe to the unfortunate man who by accident keeps his client waiting. Not very long ago a rector literally foamed at the mouth with rage and screamed inarticulately from the churchyard gate to the churchyard porch because his architect was an hour late — through a delay of the train. We would fain hope this is indeed a rare example, but it happens to be one of the experiences of the writer of this article.

There are other varieties of bad clients, such as those who object to pay travelling expenses, and those who never pay anything except on compulsion; but we have recalled quite enough for one week.

Michelangelo, prophet from Sistine Chapel ceiling, BN 5 May 1876.

MICHELANGELO ON BAD CLIENTS (1880)

Godwin invokes Michelangelo as an example of how to deal with interfering clients.

Source:
'Notes on current events', *The British Architect*, 2 January 1880, p.2

Michelangelo had just been appointed architect to St. Peter's; a cabal was organised against him, and the Pope Julius III. assembled a council to enquire. "Michelangelo replied triumphantly to all the criticisms of his adversaries. Then, turning to the Cardinal Marcello, who irritated him by his observations, 'I am not, nor do I mean to be, compelled to tell your eminence, more than any one else, what I ought, and what I intend to do. Your office is to give the money, and to remove rogues. As regards the building, this is my business.'" We only wish modern architects would adopt the same tone. The impertinence of employers now-a-days far exceeds that of Cardinal Marcello.

STRENGTH IN UNITY (1884)

Source:
'To Art Students. Letter no. 8', *The British Architect*, 4 July 1884, pp.1-2

Union is strength, no matter under what banner you fight, and if on certain well defined points everyone is content to set aside individual prejudices and adhere to a common united action the profession will be materially strengthened, and the pursuit of art in this great branch — or, rather, trunk — will be rendered more honourable and less uncertain. The great weakness which has hitherto marked the march of modern architects proceeds from a grab-all covetousness which over-rides all society rules directly there is any prospect of losing a possible client by adherence to these rules. Could any architect be sure of the course his brother architect would take under certain conditions, then the march of the profession, like that of Prussian soldiers, would possess the cohesion and sympathy that make it move as one irresistible and mighty machine.

V Contemporaries

AS A JOURNALIST and obituarist, to say nothing of his position in the London art scene, Godwin was well aware of the mechanisms by which critical reputations were constructed. His pen was frequently the instrument that propelled others towards recognition or anonymity. The last articles he wrote were reflections upon his friend William Burges who had died in 1881, and given the preoccupation with his own delicate health, he must have mused over how he himself would be remembered. 'If a painter of easel pictures dies', he once observed, 'you can gather his life's work together into one place, and at loan exhibitions from time to time, even centuries after his death, they can command new, diverse and large audiences' (see p. 133). By contrast he pointed to the difficulties of trying to summarise and publicise the varied achievements of a designer or architect. Their grander urban projects might attract acclaim, but what of the scattered, apparently inconsequential, and often anonymous examples of their creative energy; a power 'that was satisfied in creating, and is nameless, or shamefully carries credit to another's name'? Such remarks questioned the very nature of artistic canons and biographical recognition.

The reviews in this section indicate the uncertain and often tetchy relationship Godwin had with his more successful contemporaries. In many respects that attitude might be expected of an architect and designer who himself felt that he had failed to achieve the success that his talent and opportunities might have suggested. He was never entirely bitter, however, partly because he found new interests and pursuits to distract him from the patient building of a successful career. This also explains why Godwin always placed ideas of quality and artistry uppermost in his articles about his contemporaries, even when they might have been regarded as rivals. He was not above scoring points, nor was he entirely altruistic. Nevertheless, he maintained his ideals to the end and would rarely temper his criticism because of some professional advantage or personal association. On some occasions it seems to be the reverse: adverse comments about Burges's designs were often emphasised despite, or because of, their close friendship (see p. 78). It is only in the obituary of Burges that Godwin's personal feelings come to the surface in a heartfelt tribute to a designer who was both unorthodox and, by the time of his death in 1881, moving in the opposite direction to Godwin's own artistic interests. Through observing each individual's temperament in relation to the intellectual life and professional concerns of the age, he moves beyond the simple description of a personal relationship, a personality or a career. In the final extract of this section, for example, it is an eccentric piece of desk furniture that is taken to stand not only for the character and imaginative power of Burges, but for wider issues of cosmopolitan design identities and the shaping of the present through history.

Further Reading: See under Ch.III Style, and Biographical Notes.

THE WORKS OF MR NORMAN SHAW (1873)

Source:
'The Works of Mr. R. Norman Shaw', *Building News*, 24 October 1873, pp.449-50

Biographical notes:
Shaw

Shaw, Leyswood, Sussex, BN *31 March 1871.*

Shaw, Cragside, BN *10 May 1872.*

You have asked me, Mr. Editor, for my opinion on Mr. Shaw as an architect, and I have no hesitation in giving it, biased though it may be by the sympathy arising from mutual reverence for, and admiration of, good work in every age. Personally, I know nothing of him. I do not know that I have ever seen him, or that I am acquainted with any one who knows him. We have had no professional intercourse of any kind. We have not robbed one another of clients, nor have we entered into competition against one another. Whether he likes any of my work or not I do not know: I hope he does. So far, then, your readers may see that the reasons for what I am about to write have as little bias as may be, and certainly none of a personal nature. [...]

First, then, that your readers may the more readily follow me, I shall speak only of those works which have been illustrated in these pages. These are four country houses, one town house, two churches, and one town hall, or, more correctly speaking, exchange.

Of the country houses, those at Preen and Leyes Wood [*sic*], Sussex, are the best examples of modern half-timbered work I know. I had written this sentence without the word "modern," but here, I suppose, an antiquary's bias dictated the addition; for, of course, there is a charm about many of the old farms and manor places in Cheshire and Warwickshire which no modern can seize, however strong his grasp. Moreton Hall, in our own county, and the fragments of the farm-house at Mesnil-Mauger, in Calvados, have, perhaps, too strong a hold in my memory for me to be as enthusiastic as I might wish in praise of Leyes Wood and Preen. But when Moreton has been destroyed by one of our "restoring" architects, and when Mesnil-Mauger has been completely sawn up for firewood (a process it is rapidly undergoing), we shall, perhaps, begin to learn from Mr. Shaw's country houses what it is we have so long neglected, and at last irreparably lost. I have no space to describe as they deserve either Preen or Leyes Wood. Let my readers look at the illustrations in this Journal of March 31st and August 11th, 1871. Let them note the calm country simplicity, the unaffected picturesqueness which pervades them. What poetry lurks in that corner window! — in that widespreading roof, that towering chimney, what far-reaching hospitality and quiet enjoyment of life! I do not like altogether the crenellated parapet, flat roof, and skylight in the left foreground of Leyes Wood; they seem out of tune with all the rest, but as I have seen an engraving of the design showing a very different termination to this end of the quadrangle, it is just possible that the architect is not wholly responsible for them. It is rather odd that we have so little published of these charming homes. Why have we not the plans, an interior of the hall, a dining-room, and so on? They deserve illustration of the most complete kind, if any modern work ever does.

The house at Harrow Weald (B.N., Sept. 6, 1872), and the castellated mansion at Cragside (B.N., May 10, 1872), are also picturesque, and contain many exquisite bits, but both these works seem to me disjointed, each looks as if two or three houses had been brought together and shuffled up somehow into one. So far the style of Mr. Shaw's work is based on that old English half-timber domestic construction which prevailed during the latter part of the fifteenth and for a great portion of the sixteenth centuries, or, in other words, the architecture of the House of Tudor. Directly, however, we leave the country house, and go to the country church, or town house, or civic building, we find Mr. Shaw's style founded both on much earlier and later styles. Thus the two churches (B.N., Jan. 10, and May 23, 1873) are distinctly thirteenth century in character, as is also the Exchange (B.N., March 24, 1871), whilst, on the other hand, the town house in Leadenhall-street (B.N., Sept. 5, 1873) is at the opposite extreme, and is as distinctly founded on the Anglican form of the Renaissance. The churches, especially that at Lyons, are very characteristic, although based on a style now used and abused by every one. The porch and bell gable at Bournemouth are somewhat gaunt, and the latter-looks as if the designer would have liked to have made it a chimney. This building is wonderfully plain, and the great credit of it is that such character and dignity could be got out of such simple elements. The design of the Lyons example is also marvellously simple, but the way it solves the problem of making a small town church look dignified amongst the tall street houses adjacent is well worth the student's careful attention. Whether the acutely pointed arches in the gable are in accord with the rest may be a question; and I doubt the use of the enormous gargoyle, for, if it be not a water-spout, it is vain, and, if it be, I pity the good people of Lyons.

Shaw, house at Harrow Weald for Goodall, BN 6 Sept 1872.

The design for the Exchange at Bradford is, again, remarkable for its severe simplicity. The wide segmental opening in the tower, the angle buttresses, and the great irregularity of the fenestration, strike me as defects. But in the treatment of the dormers, the balcony parapets, and the top story of the tower, we see the hand of the artist as vigorous as in anything he has designed.

I now come to New Zealand Chambers, Leadenhall-street. And here let me say one word to those who are for ever droning in our ears against clever sketching, and who would have us believe that pen-and-ink drawings cleverly done, in the manner of Mr. Shaw, for instance, are all very well as drawings, but that they are gross exaggerations on the side of flattery if taken as representative of the architecture they profess to illustrate. Now, knowing the works and the drawings of Mr. Street and Mr. Shaw, I have no hesitation in saying that in regard to these architects the statement is entirely visionary. Let any one take the illustration of the New Zealand Chambers, and look well at it in all its detail, composition, effect of light, &c., then go to Leadenhall-street with as little delay and as early on a sunny morning as possible, and he will see an overwhelming proof of my assertion. Looking, only at the drawing, one might not unreasonably advance criticisms that an inspection of the building would prove to be beside the mark. Thus the effect produced by the chief colours — white, red, brown — is totally absent from the pen and ink drawing. And this question of colour, mind, is not to be pooh-poohed as having nothing to do with the architecture. Colour you *must* have, whether you admit it lovingly or turn a cold shoulder to it. Your grey-stock-brick architects do the last with a

Shaw, New Zealand Chambers, Leadenhall Street, London, BN 5 Sept. 1873.

result which is no doubt highly cheering to themselves and of advantage to the art. Mr. Shaw prefers the other course, and gives us, in a dull City street, regulated by stringent Act of Parliament, such charming cheerfulness of colour, such play of light and shade, such diversity of form, that — although I am not inclined to endorse all the detail (of which hereafter) — it appears, in my eye at least, the most satisfactory modern street front I have yet seen. But the building itself must be seen. No pen-and-ink drawing in the world could show it; for the lights and the darks have not, and cannot have, the same relation in the one as in the other. When we come to examine the detail, we find some crudities, or, at any rate, singularities, which might have easily been spared. For example, the pattern on the cove of the main cornice seems to me huge almost to coarseness. The projection, too, of the main cornice itself in such a high front in such a narrow street completely shuts out the roof from a near view. The loss of the roof, and the substitution of a straight skyline in the cornice, is the practical result. The doorway has also the appearance of coarseness, intensified by the delicacy of the wood bars in the adjacent windows. The little pediments over the oriel windows strike hard, very hard, on my retina, although many people might think them quaint. Above the main cornice the design falls off considerably — but as few will ever see it, it is not of much consequence. One practical feature in the design must not be overlooked, and that is, the easy gradation by which the lighting spaces are made to meet the several degrees of light from the open sky of the roof level to the shadowed pavement of the narrow street. To my mind, the design would have been far better without the square dividing piers, too large to be called pilasters and too small to act as *wall* space; but then the Act forbids oriels; so to get the undeniable charm of an oriel, the external play of light and shade, and the view up and down the street from the interior, it is compulsory on us that we cut them out of the wall, so to speak, like the apsidal chapels of Coutances and Bayeux, which, although distinctly apsidal, do not interrupt the great comprehending curve of the main chevet.

Whatever grumblings we may indulge in, we see in Mr. Shaw a master of the first half of his art — *i.e.*, knowledge of what has been done. It matters not whether he bases his work on thirteenth, fifteenth, sixteenth, or seventeenth century, it is all equally pleasing, free altogether from the faintest tinge of vulgarity, yet exhibiting often features that were once upon a time most commonplace and homely. I do not know whether I have not unwittingly just written the word that best describes in brief Mr. Shaw's power. The English homestead and all that it means was never hardly noticed as worth anything except to a water-colour artist, until Mr. Shaw revived its style as no style has yet been revived — revived it, that is, with a vigour which has rendered it almost a style of his own. Whether the New Zealand Chambers indicates a movement towards the fashionable Queen Anne style (of which some day I may send you a few jottings) is perhaps hardly known even to Mr. Shaw himself; but of this we may feel sure, that whether he takes up with this phase or that phase, the artist's impress will be no uncertain one.

ALFRED STEVENS (1876)

Of Alfred Stevens and his work, it is surprising how little is known. It is, perhaps, the unavoidable fate of an artist whose mode of expression is by sculpture or architecture (or both, for one almost of necessity involves the other in all noblest work) that little should be known. If a painter of easel pictures dies, you can gather his life's work together into one place; and at loan exhibitions from time to time, even centuries after his death, they can command new, diverse, and large audiences. But save for very exceptional works in our greatest cities, this publication of art is impossible, or, at any rate, impracticable, either as regards architect or sculptor. We know that the little iron lions outside the railings of the British Museum are by Stevens. We know, too, that some of the furniture and fittings in Dorchester House, Park Lane, are by him, and that the still veiled Monument of WELLINGTON in St. Paul's was the especial work of his life. But, besides these there are scattered about many examples of his power – a power, like that of some other architects and sculptors, that was satisfied in creating, and is nameless or shamefully carries credit to another's name.

Source:
'A painter and a sculptor',
Architect, 15 January 1876,
p. 30

Stevens, iron lion outside British Museum, Art Journal June 1887.

IS MR RUSKIN LIVING TOO LONG? (1878)

This dismissive item on Ruskin seems out of character in view of the praise Godwin heaped on the sage in previous articles. The date is perhaps significant – just seven months after Ruskin's intemperate comments about Whistler at the Grosvenor Gallery (Fors Clavigera, No. 79, July 1877), and nine months before the libel trial that grew out of it. Godwin's allegiances were with Whistler and this short piece further suggests the shift in modern sensibility that would make Ruskin seem dated to younger artists in the 1880s and 90s.

Is Mr. Ruskin living too long? The newspapers contain an "I-told-you-so" letter from him with reference to the present depression in trade. [...] The causes of the depression, he adds, are fourfold; first, the separation between masters and men, which is wholly the masters' fault. Secondly, the loss of custom through our bad workmanship. Thirdly, the spending of money by the fools of Europe (!) in iron constructions instead of wood, and in machinery instead of hand labour; and Fourthly, competition on the part of other nations. It is pretty plain we think that the professor knows more about the "Ethics of the Dust" than the laws and actual conditions of trade. We have heard before now of the unreasonable demands on the part of workmen as well as of the best work in the world being done in England, and it is many years since we abandoned the idea that the introduction of machinery lessened our comforts and made it more difficult for us to live. For ourselves, we should hardly like to go back to the "flail" and the "packhorse", but we should rather like to see our aged mentor seated on the one and carrying the other.

Source:
'Notes on current events',
The British Architect, 15
February 1878, p. 75

Biographical notes:
Ruskin

SIR GEORGE GILBERT SCOTT (1878)

As leader of the profession and the most successful architect in Britain, Scott was often the target of Godwin's criticism. When it came to the obituary, however, he was remarkably generous. Describing Scott's work as 'representative' rather than genius sounds like faint praise, but Godwin speaks up for the architect's character and his constancy in support of the Gothic style.

Source:
'Sir George Gilbert Scott', *The British Architect,* 5 April 1878, pp.155-6

Biographical notes:
Scott

SIR GEORGE GILBERT, SCOTT, Knt., R.A., F.S.A., Past President R.I.B.A., Gold Medallist, &c., died at his residence, Courtfield House, South Kensington, on the 27th ult. These letters and titles may be taken as so many tokens of success — a success as yet unequalled in the lives of modern architects. The question for us is, *of what nature was this success?* The just completed life of him who is the subject of this notice, was filled with so many formidable undertakings of architectural magnitude that we who are nearly all of us more or less his pupils may well hesitate on the threshold of the inquiry I have just ventured to put down. There are special reasons, too, why I might have still further hesitated to write this notice, for to him whose place among us has been so suddenly made empty, I owe much. We had our little fights about archaeological questions, art criticisms, and even competitions. Sometimes we hit one another perhaps a trifle hard, but over all and through all he was ever courteous, kindly, and pleasant. Always ready to acknowledge earnestly and gracefully the artistic powers of other architects, he was thus happily very unlike those whose opinions of their contemporaries find expression in a shrug of the shoulders or a lift of the eyebrows. [...]

It was this "gentil" courtesy that secured SCOTT in the good opinion of those he served, and which was one of the main things on which his success depended. That he was the son of a clergyman, and grandson of the well known commentator of the Bible, were circumstances rather favourable than otherwise in the eyes of those comfortable Deans and orthodox Rectors, who made up his vast clientele of clergy. But I well remember how the courtesy was predominant, for, at a deanery where I was staying a night, the talk turning on two distinguished architects, it was SCOTT'S kindliness and "gentil" qualities rather than his lineage or art that were dwelt on. [...]

I should hesitate to nominate SCOTT'S works as those of a genius. If he had not the great gift he however possessed others which in these days are perhaps even more conducive to success. He was indefatigable in business and a fervent worker. No chance was ever missed, no opportunity neglected, and thus he obtained a somewhat unenviable notoriety among less energetic or less industrious architects, of being over anxious to obtain commissions and of using means to obtain work which some of his less successful and, perchance envious brethren considered "infra dig." SCOTT'S architecture was thoroughly representative. It represented, in a word, the modern science — Archaeology. [...]

He lived long enough to see his favourite style of architecture travestied everywhere by wholly incompetent "architects" — men not only without a fraction of artistic power but wholly ignorant of the history, the general prin-

Scott, interior of St Mary Abbott's, Kensington, Builder *23 Nov. 1872.*

ciples, and the details of that mediaeval art he knew so intimately and loved so well. He lived long enough to see a new "revival" spring into being, grow rapidly into popular favour and entice to its banner some of the best men of that Gothic school with which his whole life had been bound up. He lived long enough to see the two sons who follow his profession work in this new fashion, the elder a master and a leader in the "Queen Anne" revival, the other following close upon his footsteps if we may accept his design in the Kensington Vestry Hall competition as a fair example of his quality. And he lived long enough to see even this latest fashion in its turn burlesqued, and to see the hope of English architecture, that with such unceasing care he had watched for nearly half a century, fade as the leaf that withers in the chill October.

GEORGE EDMUND STREET (1881)

Street represented more to the profession than the sum of his buildings. As the target of an intense and personal campaign in the press over his designs for the Law Courts he attracted much admiration from architects like Godwin who respected his integrity and courage even when they may have had reservations about his work. The respect was mutual. As assessor for the Leicester Municipal Buildings competition in 1871, Street had selected Godwin's design, although it was turned down by the town council. In this obituary Godwin speaks openly about the uneven quality of Street's buildings but leaves no one in any doubt that Street was a major figure and an architect of great power and sensitivity.

G. E. Street, BA *12 Aug. 1881.*

Source:
'George Edmund Street', *The British Architect*, 23 December 1881, p.643-4

Biographical notes:
Burges
Street

The year 1881 closes sadly to very many of us. The cold winds of this last spring were blowing when William Burges was buried, and before the gale of last Sunday had spent itself his old friend and rival in many an art contest, George Edmund Street, was dead. "I don't envy him the work," said Burges to me one evening, just after Street had received the commission for the Law Courts; "he won't take it easily, he will be too earnest, he will worry himself, and it will kill him."

This earnestness was Street's characteristic. He followed art at high pressure, and the mildest criticism from those whose opinions he valued was regarded with seriousness, if not with pain. He, more than any man I know, fought for art, and seemed never so much himself as, when in armour, with his lance in rest, he rode down with his strong array of words those whom he held to be the enemies of art.

It was the view of his design for Cuddesdon College [...] that first attracted me, then a student, to this accomplished architect; and from that time to but a few weeks ago, when he delivered his last address in Conduit-street,* to follow him and his work has been one of my chiefest pleasures, as it must have been for thousands.

Though not quite as determined a Gothicist as Burges, no two men were more opposed in their treatment of the style — for while the last-named "revelled in the somewhat rude and ponderous version of First-Pointed," Street's sympathies were for the chief part with the more graceful and elegant devel-

* Reported in *The British Architect*, 11 November 1881.

*Street, Wymering Church, BA
12 Aug. 1881.*

*Street, St James-the-Less,
Westminster,* Ecclesiologist *20,
1859.*

*Street, Crimean Memorial
Church, Constantinople, BN
21 Aug. 1868.*

opments of that phase of Gothic known as Second-Pointed. In his steeples particularly was this desire for elegance manifested. Take as examples those he designed for St. Mary Magdalene, Paddington; St. Peter's Bournemouth; and the Cathedrals at Lille and Edinburgh.

Many of his happiest efforts are to be found in his smaller works. A country church (like that at Wymering, or his own lovely one at Holmbury, a village school, a little convent (like that at East Grinstead) he seemed most thoroughly to enjoy. Again, in his larger buildings and designs it is in "bits" rather than in the *tout-ensemble* he chiefly excelled, as in the north porch of Bristol Cathedral, the open arcades in the first floor of the Strand front of the Law Courts, and a similar feature in his competition design for the Foreign Office, all of charming proportions and most refined in detail. As I said years ago in my review of the designs for the Law Courts, a very large building seemed every now and then to escape his grasp, and though perhaps gaining in picturesqueness lost in unity.

The best design for a large building, in my opinion, Street ever made, was that for the Cathedral at Edinburgh (1872). [...] At the end of the report which accompanied the drawings he wrote:— "to me it has been a real pleasure to work out the scheme to a certain extent completely on paper; but if I am so fortunate as to be deemed worthy of carrying it out in reality, I venture to say that no one would do so with more enthusiasm or more zeal, and *that with my own hand every detail and every part should be designed and drawn* so as to make the whole work as harmonious, as uniform, and as artistic in its character as it is in my power to make it." The italics are mine, and I have so marked these words because they show another strong characteristic of this artist — an absorbing love for his art, and a determination to do his work himself. Even when engaged on the plans for the Palace of Justice he was careful over the smallest buildings entrusted to him, that no hand but his own should meddle with their designs; and I have seen him engaged in his own room on sections of a little country church with T square and bowpen, as if there was no such thing as a drawing clerk in existence.

With the amount of practice he deservedly enjoyed, and under such a rule as that I have just mentioned, it was not to be expected that he should be different from every other artist the world has seen, or that all his works would be of equal merit. It would be absurd flattery to say they were. Cuddesdon College is better than the college at Burton on Trent. The English churches at Rome and Constantinople are inferior to some of his churches in this country, whilst St. Mary's, at Speenhamland, and the Wilberforce Memorial Church, are scarcely worthy of the author of the beautiful church at Toddington Park, or the new works at Christ Church, Dublin.

Many and various, however, as have been his designs carried out, or not carried out, all are comparatively of small account when considered by the side of his last great building in the Strand — a building in itself of unequal merit, and which, from its situation, its purpose, and very gigantic extent, it is, perhaps, unfair to consider too deeply as a whole. [...]

Quick-spoken and somewhat ultra-English in manner, Street was at heart most tender and kind, and consequently sensitive. This sensitiveness, which so many of us regard as weakness and try to hide, found a resting place in many a detail. No one fit to judge can fail to observe how subtle and delicate is the composition of his mouldings, how tender their shade. So again in the arrangement of plain surfaces, as in the slopes of buttresses, hipped roofs and base moulds, how right they are, how pleasing in their varied lights, how piquant in their keen lines of shadow! We know how to do it now, but when Cuddesdon College was built, how many of us possessed one tithe of his artistic vigour, his fresh picturequeness, his strong reality! This reality was the lesson he was always teaching, and the best we can lay on his tomb is — to use his own words — a "determination never to build anything which is not solidly and well constructed with the best art we can bestow."

Street, reredos, All Saints' Clifton, BA *12 Aug. 1881.*

MY FRIEND WILLIAM BURGES (1881)

The friendship of Burges and Godwin, as the latter writes in this obituary, was a major feature in the lives of these two architect-designers. On the surface they seem an unlikely pair, yet there was clearly great mutual respect, and they shared a similar facetiousness and Bohemian lifestyle. The ability to trace their art and ideas to a common base and to share a logic about the ideals and processes in their work also ensured their continuing friendship despite the divergence in their styles.

William Burges died at a quarter to twelve on the night of Wednesday, the 20th of April.

It is now more than twenty years since I first saw him. He was at that time a young architect, chiefly known by his work on paper; the decorations on his chamber walls, at 15, Buckingham-street (consisting of a study, a bedroom, and a little den for a clerk) were fresh and new. There were but few of the many books and objects of art he has since gathered together. I introduced myself; he was hospitable, poured wine into a silver goblet of his own design, and placed bread on the table. With a few words on either side we ate and drank, and thus began a friendship which was more intimate and sincere than any friendship of my life. We had our little tiffs, "we trod on one another's toes," as he used to say; we even quarrelled more than once, but we fought side by side the common enemy of art, discussed far into the night many a point of archaeology or art, and differed on little except his weakness for excess of strength in colour and proportion.

The thing that led me to call first on Burges was an illustration in *The Builder* I greatly admired; it was a design by him of a fountain for the city of Gloucester, with a bit of the old city as a background. In this I noted a realisation of the Middle Ages, such as no modern pencil had in my then very limited experience produced. Even then, however, the influence of foreign art, and especially of early thirteenth century French art, was manifest, and from a sternly antiquarian point of view, the scene was less like what we know Gloucester must have been than like some town in southern France or Spain. This and the quite wonderful bird's-eye view of a Mediaeval seaport town in *St. Simeon*

Source:
'Friends in Council: No. 15 William Burges, A.R.A., 1827–1881', *The British Architect*, 29 April 1881, pp.213-14

Burges, fountain in Gloucester, Builder, *29 May 1858.*

Stylites, it should be remembered, were drawn sometime before the appearance of Viollet-le-Duc's works, before Rossetti's illustration to Tennyson's poem of "The Palace of Art," and before the admirable Mediaeval revivals in the pages of *Once a Week* and *Good Words*.

His early years as a practising architect were not a little embittered by the lack of work. Luckily he was not in any other want, but to find year after year passed by, and to see men far his inferiors, or even wholly incompetent, receive important commissions, was galling to him, and often would he talk of it to me in tones of bitter disappointment. During this slack time let no student suppose he was idle or desponding. His energy, his vitality, his hope, were never more buoyant than at this period. Though in the way of business there was nothing for him to design, yet he never ceased designing. In his little pocketbooks then and throughout his career the cunning fingers were ever busy noting down the art longings and thoughts of the yet busier brain; and of the many lovely works he has left behind him, I know of none to compete in interest with these tiny memorandum books, containing as they do his first ideas of nearly everything he subsequently carried out, and of many a dream beside.

One of the first important designs he was engaged on was that for the new Cathedral at Lille, in a competition open to all the world. In this his friend, Mr. Henry Clutton, was associated, and their design met with the approval of the very distinguished committee of artists, archaeologists, and others, that gave judgment. Although, however, Messrs. Clutton and Burges were placed first, and Mr. G. E. Street second, the building was not erected by either of them. Another great disappointment to him was the Crimean Memorial Church at Constantinople (designed in 1856). Placed first in this competition, and indeed so far entrusted with the work as to be commissioned to prepare working drawings and obtain estimates, he was somehow unfortunate with the builders, and after some delay, failing to get a tender satisfactory to the committee, the work was given to Mr. Street, from whose design the building was finally erected.

In again another competition for an important church, he was placed first, but this time little or no disappointment was to cloud his success, and the Cathedral of St. Finn Barre, Cork, stands now well nigh complete in its minutest detail a monument of the genius of its learned architect. I saw the cathedral with him some years ago, when the shell was complete, and at that time told him what I thought of it — that its detail seemed a little heavy for its scale. What it is now, with its exquisite fittings and carving finished, with all its splendour of mosaic pavement, and its glory of painted glass, I can but sketchily imagine, not having seen them in their place. How earnestly he worked out every line of this most complete specimen of his art, is known to all those who were engaged in the realisation of his design. [...]

[I]t was always a pleasure to me to watch him probing any assertion concerning the past to its root. No second-hand evidence would ever fully satisfy him, and the why and the wherefore were ever on his lips. With the same penetrative intelligence that made him such a master of Gothic, he dug into the

St Finn Barre Cathedral, Cork, 1863, from R. Pullan, The Architectural Designs of William Burges, *1883.*

quarries of Renaissance and Greek art, and no one could be more keenly alive to the merits of the one and the super-excellence of the other. His knowledge of Renaissance found an outcome in Worcester College Chapel, Oxford, quite as excellent in its way as any of his Gothic productions, while his knowledge and appreciation of Greek art led him to an untiring pursuit of refinement and beauty in the drawing of animal life. All those who knew him will remember how persistently he enforced on the architectural student the advantages derived from studying and drawing the figure, and his own efforts in this direction I always examined with immense pleasure, especially those drawn by him when his sight was at its best.

During the years Cork Cathedral has been slowly but gradually reaching completion its architect has been entrusted with commissions of especial interest. His church work in England has been chiefly marked by the two rich buildings erected at the cost of Lord Ripon and Lady Mary Vyner,* and by the new east wall and general restoration of Waltham Abbey Church. The sculptured and painted re-table for the latter will long be remembered as a prominent feature amidst his painted furniture in the '62 Exhibition; while his illustrated report concerning the restoration of the Lady Chapel at Waltham may be quoted as a model. Among other ecclesiastical designs, that for the altar screen, King's College Chapel, Cambridge, has always ranked, in my eyes, as one of the most beautiful combinations of architecture and sculpture of this or any other age. [...] With much that he did in the decoration scheme for St Paul's Cathedral I was at issue with him. [...] I afterwards learnt from him that he fully admitted my views to have been right. I mention this, partly I confess out of pride, and partly to show that strong as he was in his opinions he was always ready to re-examine them, to reason about them, and to leave the door open for conviction.

In domestic and civil architecture he has left his mark not less gloriously illuminated than in the page of ecclesiastical art. Lord Bute's castle may remind us more of Carcassone than of Cardiff, but putting aside the foreign influence and the somewhat excessive heaviness of certain features (a point on which we had many an encounter), no house of the Gothic revival that I know of, except his own at Melbury Road, could for a moment compare with it in the gorgeousness and completeness of its medieval splendour. The reconstruction of Castle Coch and the report on the fortress, written for the Marquis of Bute, are particularly interesting, as exhibiting the profoundest acquaintance with the military architecture of the Middle Ages [...]

But it was not only in architecture and its decoration that his artistic ability was made manifest; his own offices and house, Lord Bute's castle, and many other homes contain examples of his skill in furniture, in gold and silversmith's work, and indeed in every branch of art industry, from precious reliquaries to cheap paper-hangings. All were designed with vigour — sometimes, perhaps, too masculine — some exquisite in their refinement and delicacy, and most of them full of quaint conceits. Then there was the Mediaeval costume he had made for himself, with its hood and liripipe; his vellum sketch book made and filled after the manner of Wilars de Honecourt's celebrated book preserved in

Litany desk for St Andrew's, Wells St, London, 1867: from R. Pullan, The Architectural Designs of William Burges, 1883.

* Churches at Skelton and Studley Royal, see p.78.

Burges, escritoire for own chambers, Buckingham Street, London, 1868: Art Journal *Oct. 1886, p.301.*

the National Library at Paris; his many papers and drawings contributed to our archaeological and architectural periodicals; [...] and his own folio work of architectural drawings. These contributions to the history of art would have alone been sufficient to arouse the admiration and gratitude of us all, but behind, and unseen, remain a mass of unpublished letters, full of merry quips, quaint conceits, good advice to students, and kindly chaff — this also occasionally too strong perhaps, and leaving on some of the more sensitive among us unquestionable bruises. His advice to pupils and young assistants was always strong meat, and to the point; he would talk to them freely and expose the weakness of the style of drawing that went only for effect.[...]

His loss makes a gap in the world of Art no one can fill. As I write these last words, although I had seen him but rarely of late years, compared to our intimacy when we were bachelors together, I can hardly realise that his busy brain is at rest and that I shall hear his voice no more.

A MAN AND AN INKSTAND (1886)

Even by the standards of the Victorian architectural profession, which admits some fairly unusual characters, William Burges is one of the most curious and engaging of all the Goths. This pen-portrait reveals the patterns of his thought, the eclecticism of his sources and the mischievous sense of humour that made him such an excellent companion. Written in the year of Godwin's own death, this memoir is one of his most touching and personal tributes.

Source:
The Art Journal 1886,
pp.170-3

Biographical notes:
Burges
de Honecourt
Nesfield
Shaw
Street
Stuart & Revett
Willis

Take a Chinese bronze elephant incense-burner, with dumpy legs that are hardly more than feet, remove the pierced howdah-like cover, and in its place put a low circular tower of green porcelain, domed with a *cloisonée* cup reversed, and crowned with a Japanese *netzuki*. Combine these things with metal mouldings and machicolated parapets fashioned after the manner of the thirteenth century; arrange the ivory finial, the dome and tower so that each may turn on a pillar at the back, uncovering receptacles for matches, red ink, and black; mount the whole on a slab of marble and suspend chains, and rings, and seals from tusks and trappings, and you have the inkstand Burges had made for himself, which occupied the centre of his writing table all the years I knew him, and reminds me of him more than anything he ever achieved.

Observe the power of adaptation: the things he is dealing with are Chinese and Japanese, but the whole is thirteenth century-Burgesesque. A few pieces of metal in his favourite style to unite them, and lo! this strange group of Eastern things fall into their places as if they had been originally devised for the purpose they now fulfil. As one looks at it in admiration of its rich colour, its usefulness, its elephantine strength, one never thinks of its lovely dome as a cup reversed, or of the ivory figure group that crowns it as a Japanese button. But it is in the bronze elephant itself that we are chiefly interested. This short-legged, thick-set beast exhibits the power of conventionalising a natural object in a very remarkable degree. The thing is so like and yet so unlike; so false in detail, so true in essence. It was this power of the artist, whether exhibited in Chinese bronze or Egyptian granite, in Pentelic marble or Caen freestone, that Burges was so quick to recognise, to appreciate, to enjoy. And it was this mastery in conventional treatment, this power of governing natural form so that it should best serve the artificial purpose for which it was selected, that he possessed in a remarkable degree. Nesfield, Shaw, and Street, each in his own way, has produced architectural designs more beautiful and far more graceful than any building Burges ever designed or could design; but no one of the century in this country, or any other that I know of, ever possessed that artistic rule over the kingdom of nature in a measure at all comparable with that which he shared in common with the sculptor of the Sphinx and the designer of Chartres.

I often regretted that the Chinese bronze elephant, admirable as it was for an inkstand, should have so grown into his life that almost everything he touched partook of its thick-set, heavy proportions. Nor was mine a silent regret, for I spoke in no uncertain tones in those days when neither of us had much to do and when we saw a good deal of each other. That he was conscious of it I knew, for I well remember his delight one evening when he elicited unqualified praise on showing me a cup which had just come home, and chiefly remarkable because he had designed it with more graceful lines and on a lighter scale than usual. His head was slightly more inclined to one side than usual as he thrust the cup close to my eyes with the words: "There! is that light enough for you?" This heaviness might have been in a measure due to his short sight. How far the bronze elephant operated, or how much, if any, of this feeling of sturdiness may be regarded as having been inherited from his father, who was an engineer of eminence in his day, I am not prepared to say. The architecture of Cork Cathedral or Cardiff Castle, as well as of the smaller churches and houses he built, is in its quite unnecessary massiveness more than suggestive of engineering construction as we see it in breakwaters and bridges. This, no doubt, was a fault in the right direction, a conviction or expression of his architectural faith, but partly as a protest against the flimsy work of our time. The pity was that in making this protest he was led into exaggeration—a not unusual accompaniment in the language as in the work of all protestants.

Another influence which had a marked effect on Burges was the discovery, among the MSS. in the National Library in Paris, of the sketch-book of Willars de Honecort, a French architect of the thirteenth century, who with his friend, one Peter de Corbie, designed some important buildings. It was published in fac-simile in Paris under the editorship of Lassus, and in London with notes by Professor Willis. Of course Burges lost no time in seeing the original, and forthwith equipped himself with a book of similar material, dimensions, and make as that of Willars. This he eventually filled with original designs and sketches drawn in the manner of the thirteenth-century architect: and a fac-simile publication of this sketchbook, with notes by a competent hand, would form in my opinion the best monument we could raise to his memory. A keen sense of the comedy of life was another characteristic of my old friend. I remember how at a remote Irish hotel (August, 1867), after a long dispute on

Burges, elephant inkstand, Art Journal *June 1886, p.171.*

some architectural matters, I found he had sketched on the margin of a newspaper two thirteenth-century architects in a most comical pugilistic encounter, with the legend in Old English text, "Willars de Honecort et Petrus de Corbie inter se disputantes." Then, too, although he believed the French first-pointed to be the best school of architecture for us to work in — the type best adapted to our climate and requirements, his faith was by no means bigoted. His appreciation of the beauty, the picturesqueness of Greek architecture was intensely genuine. At the Conference of Architects held in London in June, 1876, he contributed a short paper on "The Importance of Greek Art and Literature to the Practice of Gothic Architecture," in which he said: "I would earnestly recommend a careful study of Greek Art and Greek Literature to my Gothic brethren. It is really the key to the position; but in studying Greek Art it will not be sufficient to consult Stuart's 'Athens,' and other like books. The actual buildings must themselves be visited. It was not until I was actually on the spot that I understood how beautiful Greek Architecture was, and how nearly it was allied in spirit to that of the thirteenth century. From that time I took a new view of the latter art, and things which had before appeared arbitrary and confused became clear and logical. I saw the same mind working at Athens as at Chartres, but in a different climate, under different conditions, and with different material."

When therefore the time came for the realisation of his long day-dream, and he began to work out on paper the designs of his house in Melbury Road, those who knew him were neither surprised to find that the building differed not from other modern houses in its general arrangement, nor that its Gothic character bore the impress of his Hellenic studies. [...] A red-hot mediaevalist would have ignored modern life and its advantages, such as they are, and would have perpetrated the anachronism of hall and solar, [...]; but Burges, as I have already endeavoured to show, was no such revivalist. He could distinguish between Archaeology and Art, and while the most conservative of antiquaries, was in all new works an evolutionist or developist rather than a revivalist [...].

Burges, The Tower House, Melbury Road, London, Art Journal 1886, p.170.

Describing the garden building, 'an open lesche', Godwin goes on:

Here on a summer's afternoon, Burges would delight to give tea to a few friends, who lounged on the marble seats or sat on Persian rugs and embroidered cushions round the pearl-inlaid table, brilliant with tea service composed of things precious, rare and quaint; one thing alone wanting to complete the picture — a fitting costume.

VI Archaeology and Conservation

For Godwin archaeology was a lifelong passion. As a mental discipline, an analytical method combining aspects of science and art, it informed the way he thought about material culture, and his approach to all forms of design. Moreover archaeological study underlined his views about the essential unity of all artistic expression, whether manifested in architecture, dress, theatre or poetry. 'As became a man who had made a speciality of Gothic, he was an archaeologist, but not in the usual sense of that word', wrote the *Architect* following Godwin's death (see p.374). 'To his mind the past was something more than a mouldering skeleton. It lived for him, and buildings were only a background for figures. It was an easy transition when EDWARD GODWIN passed from the architecture of the fourteenth century to the poems of CHAUCER, and when he passed from a study of SHAKESPEARE'S characters to the buildings in which they were supposed to live. He was learned without having a particle of the DRYASDUST about him.' In fact, some of the articles in which Godwin airs his scholarly credentials are rather turgidly written, but on other occasions he talks about the past with an immediacy and intimacy that reflected this sense of continuity with the present.

While recognising the nostalgic lure of the old – a charm 'we all more or less feel' (p.171) – Godwin was part of a generation reacting against the piecemeal appropriation and 'skimming' of historical detail by earlier Romantic artists and architects. Archaeology could be a progressive force, a source of imaginative inspiration and principles that could inform modern design. 'Be archaeologists', he urged young architects, 'know all about the past' (p.30). At the same time he was all too aware that a deepened knowledge of the past could dampen creativity, or generate 'archaeological fads', and was wary of the antiquarian bent that automatically prioritised the old and traditional over the new and modern, regardless of beauty or use. History offered examples and principles to avoid as well as those to cultivate.

Inspired by the researches of Pugin's generation, Godwin showed a precocious interest in archaeology as a teenager, with his first publication in the field in 1851. His early partnership with Crisp, like that of many young Goths, relied heavily on commissions for the refurbishment and surveying of small parish churches, and in this sense archaeology was a tool of the trade. The accurate recording of historical dress, artefacts and buildings through the process of drawing was, for Godwin, vital to the development of a cultured architectural sensibility. As his interests developed beyond the sway of Gothic, so his archaeological method was applied to an increasingly diverse range of periods and cultures. Complementing his documentation of surviving structures, he made extensive use of archival documentation, literary descriptions and illuminated manuscripts in his archaeological studies.

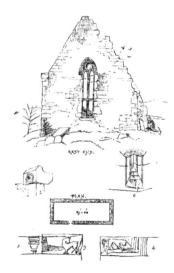

Godwin, sketches of Temple Douglas church, Ireland, Arch. 18 May 1872, p.249.

* Letter to W. C. Angus, 13 August 1884.

15 A XXI.   10ᵗʰ CENTURY

Godwin, drawing from a manuscript, BA 8 March 1878.

He was an inveterate list-maker, and in 1884 talked of producing a 'catalogue of all the illuminated MSS. in the Brit. Mus. annotated and illustrated by me'.* Similarly comprehensive publications were planned on Irish antiquities and Greek armour (looking at *every* Greek vase in the British Museum). The only one of these publications that actually came to fruition, however, was his handbook on *Dress in relation to health and climate*, an ambitious project on which he spread himself too thin, with disappointing results (see p. 321f.).

Godwin was writing at a time when the quirky antiquarian studies of individual amateurs and scholars were developing into a more widespread conservation consciousness among the middle classes, and a view of historical remains from the past as a source of communal identity, continuity and aspiration. By the 1870s issues of conservation versus restoration were being fiercely debated in the specialist and national press, leading to governmental intervention and the formation of local and national lobby groups like the Society for the Protection of Ancient Buildings, established by William Morris and a group of his friends in 1877. As a veteran campaigner on issues of archaeology and conservation from a practical as well as aesthetic and ideological point of view, Godwin was not overly impressed by what he saw as the amateurish nature of this 'ornamental society'. As in other areas of personal interest, he used his power as a critic and editor to flag up his own achievements and pet cases, and to mark out the territory as the province of the professional architect. The archaeologically informed architect was the only kind of 'doctor' fit to minister a programme of treatment to an ailing monument. His interest was never limited to the preservation of grandiose individual monuments, but extended to everyday artefacts and buildings, and to consideration of *context*. As an archaeologist he realised the importance of syntactical interrelationships in the study of material culture. Not all the past was worth saving, but its wholesale destruction in industrial cities and towns in the name of 'public improvement' was to be halted. A more planned and sensitive approach to selective retention, he argued, could achieve a viable balance between old and new, decay and growth.

Further Reading

C. Arbuthnott, 'E. W. Godwin as an antiquary', in Soros 1999, pp.45-70

C. Miele, 'The conservationist', in L. Parry, ed., *William Morris*, London,1996, pp.72-87

C. Miele, *Morris on Architecture*, Sheffield, 1996

G. G. Scott, *A Plea for the Faithful Restoration of our Ancient Churches*, London, 1850

C. Wainwright, 'The antiquary and collector', in P. Atterbury and C. Wainwright, eds, *Pugin: a Gothic Passion*, London, 1994

ARCHAEOLOGY AND THE LIVING PAST (1868)

Tinged with Romanticism, this extract captures Godwin's sense of the past as some-thing 'more than a mouldering skeleton', and archaeology as 'a science that clothes and reanimates the dead' (p. 334).

Archeology [*sic*] fills in the details of every picture of the past, it forges the links of the chain which binds together at all time; it brings into stronger light all those great events which have contributed to build up those blessings we now enjoy. It clothes with vivid reality all those noble ones whose figures would otherwise have but a shadowy indistinctness in the mighty procession of the world's issue. It tells us among many other things how the decoration of dress was once as much an art as the decoration of a temple. It tells us how both ladies' and gentlemen's dresses were once under the direction of artists [...] It helps us to a better appreciation of the wonderful picturings of such poets as Chaucer and Dante, and illustrates every page of our early literature.

Source:
'A lecture on dress by E. W. Godwin. F.S.A. 1868', *The Mask*, Vol. 6, No. 4, April 1914, p.350-1

Biographical notes:
Chaucer

NEGLECTED MEDIEVAL ARCHITECTURE (1861)

The somewhat stilted tone of this extract, from one of eight articles submitted to the Archaeological Journal *between 1853 and 1865, reflects the young Godwin's desire to engage in serious scholarly debate. Demonstrating that his interest was never simply in grandiose monuments and picturesque detail, here he focuses on the study and preservation of unassuming, domestic vernacular of the medieval period as a key to developing a national tradition of architecture. He shares the growing interest among architects like Street and Burges from the 1850s in less decorated, 'primitive' forms.*

Source:
'Notice of an example of domestic architecture at Colerne, Wiltshire', *Archaeo-logical Journal*, June 1861, p.125

Every one interested in the history of the past admits that this division of our study is well deserving attention, and that earnest exertion is required on our part, lest the few examples which remain should suffer more from the utili-tarianism of modern days, than from the wear and tear of centuries, or be sacrificed in so-called improvements by per-sons alike unconscious of their value and careless of their preservation.

It can scarcely be requisite to observe that it is not only in the residences of the higher order of the people, — the con-vent, the castle, or the manor-house, that we must look for specimens of our national architecture. [...] It seems, there-fore, desirable that greater attention should be directed to those long neglected examples of mediaeval art, — the dwell-ings of the comparatively inferior classes, which doubtless exist in greater abun-dance than may be generally supposed, and lift their pointed gables in pictur-esque irregularity in many a quiet village, and by many a lonely road.

Godwin, cottages in Ireland, sketched in 1870, BA 27 May 1881.

THE PERILS OF ARCHAEOLOGY (1864)

Godwin warns against 'surface skimming' of the past, and the mindless collecting or reproduction of historical 'odds and ends'.

Source:

'Mr. E. W. Godwin on architecture and Somerset churches', c.1864, lecture to the Bristol Society of Architects, V&A AAD 4/560-1988: cuttings book (probably *from The Western Daily Press*)

It may appear perhaps strange in me to warn you against archaeology. It is true I have always maintained that we must have a little of it, only to help us to recover certain principles of our art which have been lost, but, on the other hand, it is quite possible that we may have too much of it; that instead of its leading us to think for ourselves it may entice us into an almost boundless ocean of antiquarianism; instead of its bringing out our powers of design it may make us mere collectors and transcribers of the designs of those who have gone before us; our sketchbooks, instead of exhibiting our own fancies and thoughts, may become nothing more than mere pattern books, and this is especially to be guarded against in towns which, like Bristol, have been distinguished in the past for [...] noble work but which now enjoy an unenviable notoriety for their utter neglect of art, celebrated, perhaps, for their tallow, their loaf sugar, and equally celebrated for their disregard of everything other than a hard bargain and accumulation of gold.

[It is a town where] the field of archaeological research is rich and wide, but where the field for exercise of art-thought is narrow, hard and stony. Indeed so much has the spirit of antiquarianism been diffused — so far has the reverence for everything old and musty exceeded its useful limits — that it is positively dangerous to open one's mouth about anything older than the Georges. A building is found to be interesting to the antiquary or the ecclesiologist, and forthwith the architect must accept it *nolens volens*; nay, is vaunted heretical, if not impertinent, should he in his innocence attempt to dispute its value, to question the grace of its gargoyles, or to take exception to the weary repetition of parallel panels. Thus it is that so many of our new buildings exhibit nothing but the same windows, over and over again; the same mouldings, taken from the same page of the glossary; the same corbel heads, the same bosses — one dull, dead, sea of sameness, the best of them being little more than a piece of patchwork, made up of scraps from all kinds of buildings of a given date in all parts of the country, with a most amusing disregard of all conventionality, both of time and place.

I take this opportunity to warn our student members against sketching scraps — a thorough study of one good building, whether it be a small village church or a cathedral — a careful analysis of its entire scheme, of the general design, of the detail, of the construction, and of the workmanship, would be of more value to them, and more likely to reveal to them the principles upon which architects should work, than any collection, however large, of mere odds and ends picked up during a lifetime of surface skimming.

SPENSER'S KILCOLMAN (1872)

Godwin's interests in literary criticism and archaeology came together in his study of the poet Edmund Spenser's Irish castles.

Source:
'Spenser's castles, &c. Part I',
Architect, 27 January, 1872,
pp.41-2

Biographical notes:
Spenser

The last eight years of his life were passed at his "house of Kilcolman." Here Raleigh, when he went into county Cork to look after his estates, visited him. Here too his short dramatic life began and ended. Here his children were born; here his *Faerie Queene* was written. And yet not one of his editors seems to know anything about the place. I am not very much surprised at this, for it took me two days to find it out with the help of the six-inch Ordnance sheets. [...] Earl's castles are as few and far between in Ireland as anywhere else. Of tower-houses — and bear in mind that it is with Spenser "my house of Kilcolman" — there are plenty in all stages of ruin, and of all sorts of proportions. Many of them belong to as late a period as the reign of James I., and there are few of much earlier date than the middle of the sixteenth century. The general plan or arrangement is much the same in all, although no two are exactly alike. [... Spencer's] was one of the smallest of the tower houses scattered over the broad estates of the great Desmond, but it was no more one of the Earl's castles than a farm or manor on a royal estate can be said to be one of the Queen's palaces. The tower itself could scarcely have contained enough accommodation even for Spenser. Like a true artist he may have been content with little, and if his visitors were limited to a shake-down in the living room, it is just possible he may have managed. The rooms, however, must have been very dark and gloomy, and I am inclined to think that the refined, accomplished well-bred Englishman, accustomed to places like Penshurst, would not be long before he utilised some of the oaks upon his estate in the erection of a suite of rooms against his Bailey wall. Such wooden structures were very common appendages, and as these were almost invariably thatched, the record of destruction by fire is thus easily explained,* for the towers themselves being practically fireproof only acknowledged defeat before Cromwell and his iron shot. Kilcolman does not stand alone in the vale of Mulla. We can see from the top of its broken staircase the remains of neighbouring towers, one of which must have been large enough to have contained four or five such towers as Spenser's. All these have been used as quarries by the patriotic Celt, and the luck of Spenser's tower house resides in the fact of its basement being used as a storehouse for lime; but for this, the natives assured me it would long since have been pulled down. I spent two long summer days at Kilcolman, and dreading the uncertainty of lime, I plotted on the spot every fragment of the ruin. The woods have long since departed, the lake has dwindled to little more than a good-sized duck-pond, but Spenser's tower, even in its ruin, is fresh and green, with its ivy crown throwing back the golden sunshine, as if determined like its master, to be joyous to the end.

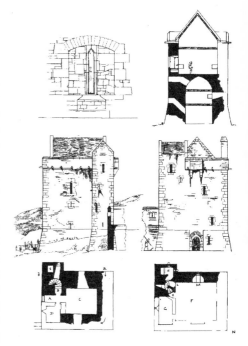

Godwin, drawing of Kilcolman, Arch. 17 Aug. 1872.

* The tower-house was burnt in October 1598 by the O'Neills during an insurrection.

147

CELTIC AND JAPANESE ORNAMENT (1879)

Like Owen Jones, Godwin attempted a comparative analysis of principles underpinning the ornamental design from different ages and parts of the world. On several occasions he wrote about the marked similarity in feeling as well as in form, between patterns in Ireland and Japan.

Japanese designs illustrated by Christopher Dresser, BA 21 March 1879.

  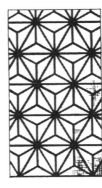 

Source:
'Notes on current events',
The British Architect, 18 April 1879, p.161

Biographical notes:
Dresser

There is very little invention in some of the patterns used by the Japanese or Ancient Celts. At least four of the twelve given by Dr. Dresser in our issue of March 21 are simply taken direct from matting, and belong to what may be called the rudimentary art of all nations. There are, however, some singular parallelisms between Celtic and Japanese work which are not traceable to such a primitive state of humanity; as, for example, the three incipient volutes within a circle — a form found among the illuminations of early Celtic MSS., and serving also as the arms, badge, or sign of an old Japanese family.

THE ARCHAEOLOGIST (1885)

While stressing the need for scientific rigour, Godwin also sees the exercise of the artistic imagination as essential to archaeology.

Source:
'Archaeology on the stage. Part 7', *Dramatic Review*, 24 October 1885, p.113

The Archaeologist or Antiquary [...] is something more than a frequenter of museums and a patron of pigeon-holes. His method or mental attitude is of special significance; and you can no more make him off hand than you can make an artist: indeed he must have some of the artist's qualities, or, at least, be able to truly imagine in his mind's eye the features of the past and interpret its records and memorials.

Godwin designs for production of Claudian, BA 7 Dec. 1883.

THE VALUE OF DRAWING (1884)

For Godwin, the archaeological recording of historic buildings through the process of drawing was vital to the development of an architectural sensibility, and there was more to be learnt from such drawings than from most modern plans or elevations.

From the North of Scotland a student writes to ask me to lend him any drawings of any of my work from which he may be able to make a perspective [...] If students, even in the far North wish to try their hands at perspectives, they have nearly always old examples near them which they can measure up and draw out carefully to scale, and then out in perspective — a course which would be of far greater value every way than to make drawings of the work of any modern architect whatsoever. It has too this great additional advantage, that by selecting an accessible point of sight the student can from time to time compare his perspective with the real one, and he will learn far more about the subject in one practical experiment like this than in half a lifetime spent over nothing but drawings.

If, however, there be no old buildings at hand, this paper has published within the last few years elevations and details of historical monuments, far more worthy of your attention than anything created by modern architects. For there is nothing which so entirely separates the buildings of the past and the present (admitting for a moment that there can be a separation in the chain of time or any historical sequence) as is to be found in the consciousness of the values of projection. As a rule, we, with our acres of feeble drawings, are unconscious of these values; while the old builders, with their simple diagrams, were so fully alive to them that I venture to assert no old building of worth can be appreciated from mere elevations of it. How different it is with us. Every artist knows and would be right glad if he could never see anything more of modern architecture than is revealed by the geometrical elevation.

Source:
'To art students. Letter no. 4',
The British Architect, 6 June
1884, p.273

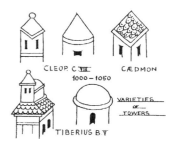

MANUSCRIPT ILLUSTRATIONS (1878)

Complementing his documentation of surviving structures, Godwin made extensive use of archival documentation, literary descriptions and illuminated manuscripts in his archaeological studies. The 13th-century manuscript of Wilars De Honecourt was a particular favourite that he and Burges studied in Paris.

We give this week illustrations of certain architectural features found in some of the illuminated MSS. of what is called the Anglo-Saxon period. Some people hold the opinion that the art of the illuminator is a fancy art of the painter's own, and not, as our old friend Wilars de Honecourt would say, "drawn from the life". We propose from time to time, to present our readers with careful copies of examples culled from the best MSS. in the British and other museums.

Godwin, drawings from manuscripts, BA 8 March 1878.

Source:
'Illustrations of Anglo-Saxon art', *The British Architect*, 8 March 1878, p.108

Biographical notes:
De Honecourt

A CHURCH IN THE WAY (1876)

Godwin's earliest publications related to archaeological studies in and around his native Bristol, and he had spearheaded the 'local opposition' to the demolition of St John's referred to in the opening paragraph. After moving to London he continued to campaign for a planned and sensitive approach to the city's overall development as an issue of national importance. It was time for householders to exercise more artistic discrimination in the public sphere, for town surveyors to take a more informed view of 'public improvements,' and for the House of Lords to query Bills facilitating the wholesale destruction of 'the history of our old towns and of old England'.

Source:
'A church in the way',
Architect, 25 March 1876,
pp.190-1

Biographical notes:
Lord Limerick

Every one who knows the city of Bristol knows that among the most prominent relics of the old town are the churches of St. John and St. Werburgh. St. John's church stands on the oldest of the town walls, and its steeple crowns the town gate at the north end of Broad Street. St. Werburgh's church stands at the angle formed by the junction of Small Street with Corn Street, on the north side of and parallel with the last-named thoroughfare. Some years ago it was whispered that the Corporation had cast an hungry eye on both these churches, and especially on the steeple of St. John and the archway beneath it. A local opposition was raised to this devouring design of the authorities, and the gate and churches were for the time happily saved. It now appears that St. Werburgh's church is to be the first victim to the Bristolian appetite for what is called "Public Improvement." [...]

The antiquarian case

Now this of course means, Lord LIMERICK to the fore notwithstanding, that before long the church of St. Werburgh will be added to the already long list of the destroyed churches of Bristol. From an antiquarian point of view this is a distinct loss to the city [...] There are very few people who, on being shown the limits of the old English (or Saxon) town extending from Bristol Bridge south to St. John's Arch north, and from early the end of Wine Street east to the bottom of Corn Street west, would suppose for a moment that as late as A.D.1500 this little area contained no less than ten churches. Of these ten there will, when that of St. Werburgh goes, be only five remaining; and of these five two have been entirely rebuilt (in 1762 and 1787), the old arrangements of the buildings being completely ignored. Such being the pace of the march of modern improvement, we may hope in a few more years to see Bristol a third-rate, prosperous commercial town with no silly marks of medieval life about her, and the shame of having once been the second city in the kingdom completely flushed away with other inconveniences from her streets.

The artistic case

Apart, however, from the historical and antiquarian aspect, the loss of St. Werburgh's church will be felt from an artistic point of view. [...] Now a church that was in great part rebuilt in 1760 has *prima facie* lost its interest so far as the purist is concerned, and there are many architects who would not hesitate to condemn it for what they would honestly enough consider to be purely artistic reasons. But the men who can only recognise the artistic when governed by a set of hard and fast architectural rules are happily few. The question is, does the church of St. Werburgh add an artistic element to the central street of the old town of Bristol? and if so is that artistic element worth preserving? To both questions I venture to give an unqualified affirmative. We are in this age far to ready to ignore altogether the artistic element in all public questions. Some of us are blind enough — I may even say foolish enough — to deny that there is any value, any good to be got out of any such consideration. We are all ready enough to encourage the artistic according to the limits of our understanding so long as it is confined to our own private houses. Much more money is expended now than in any former time on pictures, bric-a-brac, and what is called decorative furniture. Is this expenditure a mockery? Is this apparent revival of what is called taste a sham? Are we surrounding ourselves with these things for the sake of display, and not for the enjoyment, the happiness, the benefit we and our friends can derive from them? It would indeed seem so if we may form any judgment from the coarse treatment to which the old towns and villages of England are daily subjected.

Town surveyors and 'improvement'

I do not wish to be hard on anyone, but there are times when we must be harsh if we are in earnest, and I have no hesitation in saying that the town surveyors of England are a standing disgrace to all the efforts made towards their education by the government, by professional journals, and by central and local societies. With town corporations I will not attempt to argue; we can expect no more from them than what we get. If by any accident there is anything in the homes of its members that may be pleasing or refined, we may be assured that it is owing to the wife or the daughter. But with town surveyors and with town architects the case is very different. From them we expect — and in the case of our large towns where their salaries are 1,000*l.* per annum, more or less, we have a right to expect — the evidence of a culture something beyond the attainment of the three R's. And yet what are the facts? Putting aside the jobberies committed to get the appointment, the plans for "public improvements" made by or under the direction of the surveyor exhibit quite enough to convict the public improver of his utter incompetence to guide or direct with good taste and judgment those alterations necessitated by new wants and an increased population. It is in the experience of many of us that in cases where interesting and valuable illustrations of architectural history and beautiful artistic compositions have been destroyed because they were considered to be in the way of a public improvement, it was really because the surveyor who plotted the so-called improvement never heeded their existence. [...]

Take this case St. Werburgh as an example. [...] No plan could have been devised to make more money for the town surveyor in designing new frontages for the several owners and occupiers, than this brilliant one of effacing both sides of one of the chief streets in one of the most interesting and beautiful of England's historic towns. The work was begun, as was the fashion a quarter of a century ago, in a slow wedge-like movement, until now at last, the wedge has been driven home; the church of St. Werburgh must go, and the ground that has been hallowed for some eight or nine centuries must be given up to the traffic of buyers and sellers, tramps and thieves, and all because the town improvements were placed in the hands of men wholly incompetent to improve anything. The root of this barbaric action which is undermining the whole aspect of England, which is reducing the most lovely, picturesque, and happy-looking villages to a state of cold barren dullness beyond measure disheartening, and which will soon destroy every fragment of historical or artistic interest in our old towns and cities, must be sought, I believe, not in corporations or the inhabitants generally, but in the class of men from which agents, town surveyors and city architects are selected.

THE METROPOLITAN BOARD OF WORKS (1878)

Source:
'Notes on current events',
The British Architect, 11
January 1878, p.20

*T. Raffles Davison, Temple Bar,
illustrating Godwin's articles
reissued as a pamphlet in 1878
by* The British Architect.

*Right: Linley Sambourne
cartoon,* Punch, *18 Nov. 1876.*

The Temple Bar, an historic gateway designed by Christopher Wren, was dismantled amid much controversy to make way for the new Law Courts. Godwin had written about this on several occasions. Around this time he had a series of run-ins with the Metropolitan Board of Works which represented the kind of bureaucracy and officialdom he detested. Apart from issues of architectural conservation, he harangued them over environmental controls such as sewage treatment and, most famously, over the design of his studio-houses in Tite Street (also in 1878).

for the Metropolitan Board of Works than the destruction of Temple Bar; for now that the latter obstacle has received its *coup de grace* attention is more than ever concentrated on the Board. Every one interested in making modern London a city worthy to be ranked with the modern cities of Europe looks frowningly, and even the *Daily News* has opened fire on what it *calls a group of mere nominees* — nominees whose immense power has been neglected or misused.

In the smallest measure of reform contemplated it is proposed to make the new Board a representative body elected by, and therefore responsible to, the ratepayers, who are to elect by ballot-voting on the accumulative system. We should be content with this only on the principle that half a loaf is better than no bread, but whatever changes are made let us have nothing likely to reduce the courteous attention that distinguishes the official department in its business with architects and the public generally.

THE MANIA FOR CHURCH RESTORATION (1877)

Godwin responds to the debate sparked by J. J. Stevenson's polemical attack on 'Architectural restoration, its principles and practice'.* He was sceptical about the ability of the newly founded Society for the Protection of Ancient Buildings to arrest the mania for inappropriate church restoration that sustained many architectural practices in the 1860s and '70s.

In spite of the virtuous indignation of Messrs. Stevenson, Loftie, and Morris anent "restoration", we may be sure there may yet be plenty of cakes and ale to nourish the architects Mr. Stevenson has attacked. It will take more, far more, time and means than are at the disposal of any architectural party to place any serious check on work that is at the same time so profitable and pleasant to the modern architect as that of church restoration. We may be tolerably certain that the protest has come too late, and that the restorer's tools so mightily wielded by Sir Gilbert Scott and Mr. Street will not be stayed until the time come when no more subjects shall remain for dissection and preparation. The case of the preservation party is well-nigh hopeless, and being such, some of their long-delayed indignation might fairly and usefully be diverted into other channels.

* Royal Institute of British Architects. Papers 1876–77, pp.219-35; 242-68.

Source:
'Architectural poaching', *The British Architect*, 13 July 1877, p.16

Biographical notes:
Loftie
Morris
Scott
SPAB
Street
Stevenson

THE RESTORATION OF ST MARK'S, VENICE (1879)

The proposed restoration of this icon of Ruskinian Gothic in Venice seemed to capture the public imagination. Largely instigated by William Morris and the SPAB, meetings were held the length and breadth of Britain. The topic was aired in the nationalist and specialist press, with protests lodged at governmental level. Godwin was irritated by the prominence given to William Morris's views on the subject. As he noted in a subsequent article, 'The opinions of deans and poets, or Mr. MORRIS or Mr. BURNE JONES, on questions of stability in building, we altogether decline to accept' whether concerning St. Mark's or 'the most common-place piece of architecture in Oxford or London.'** The archaeologically informed architect was the only kind of 'doctor' fit to administer treatment to an ailing monument.

** 'A second note on St. Mark's', BA 21 Nov. 1879, p.199.

Mr. William Morris's letter on "The Restoration of St. Mark's at Venice" is too hurried for the object we suppose he, in common with all of us, has in view — the preservation of the west front of the building.*** "The proposal to rebuild", much as it may shock the author of *The Earthly Paradise*, seems to us the only proposal that could be reasonably made. Nor can we see that a rebuilding necessarily involves renewal or imitation of details, or even the obliteration of "the solemnity of the tone and the incident" that time has given to the marble. A "restoration" in the sense we too often have to deplore would be indeed an immense loss to the world, but it should be remembered that St. Mark's facade consists in great part of a fanciful grouping of detached marbles, held in its place thus long by a multitude of iron ties and cramps. These have not only added to the charm of the colour of the marbles, but they have

Source:
'The restoration of St. Mark's', *The British Architect*, 7 November 1879, p.179

Biographical notes:
Morris
SPAB

*** See Architect, 6 December 1879, p.333.

West front of St Mark's, Venice,
Magazine of Art 1880, p.116.

by the same process of rust that gives the delight of colour gone near to make of St. Mark's a heap of ruin. To arrest this ruin while there is yet time, to take away that disrupting iron net-work once and for all, can only properly be done by re-building. In this rebuilding it would be wise to make one, and only one, change, and that is to substitute for the original iron ties copper or gun-metal. There is no difficulty in taking down any wall or grouped pillar or arch, and putting every bit of it save its cement or mortar back again. This we have ourselves done, each stone in its own place, not a fraction of surface destroyed, and scarcely even a piece of grey lichen disturbed. It is one thing to be interested in your patient, to be always with it, and to restore it with patient, loving care, not merely for its architectural lines, but with reverence for all its silvery age; it is quite another thing to pay it flying visits, to mark it with your own notions of what it *ought* to be, that you may swell the cost and increase your percentages.

In the weeks that followed Godwin tried to turn public attention away from St. Mark's and back to conservation issues nearer home.

Source:
'Notes on current events', *The British Architect*, 14 November 1879, p.190

Biographical notes:
Morris
Pearson
Street

The Society for the Protection of Ancient Buildings has sent a memorial to the Italian Government, protesting against the proposed restoration of the west front of St. Mark's, Venice. If the Italian Minister of Works were inclined to make a telling reply, he might inform the memorialists that they would be more usefully employed in endeavouring to preserve our buildings at home, and that while in Venice the work to the west front would be carried out under the supervision of an architect directed by a commission appointed by the Government, we are about to hand over one of the most interesting buildings in this country to a rich parliamentary counsel, who considers he has a taste for architecture, and the right to do exactly as he pleases with a national monument, merely because he undertakes to defray the cost of what he calls a restoration. The west front of St. Albans is in no need of repair, and to alter its character to suit the fancy of Sir Edmund Beckett, is an outrage of which everybody concerned should be ashamed.

POOR PALACE! (1880)

Despite poring over Ruskin's Stones of Venice in great detail, Godwin never visited Italy. Nevertheless he had direct experience of G. E. Street's interventionist approach to conservation in the case of many English parish churches.

Source:
'Notes on current events', *The British Architect*, 21 May 1880, p.241

Not content with obliterating the art and history of St. Mark's the authorities have begun to clean and restore the Ducal Palace! "The weather stains (says Mr. Street) are being cleaned from the exquisite capitals and much new work is being done." Poor palace! We really are very sorry to hear of such sad work.

[...] There was once a little cross church in Somersetshire of great interest to us. We sketched it, and measured it, and photographed it till one fine day passing by we found it had been "restored." A curious passage cutting diagonally from the north transept to the chancel *had been wholly swept away*, moreover it was a mediaeval piece of work and had many weather stains on its picturesque three-cornered roof. Mr. Street was the architect. Between the simple village church in England and the few buildings of Venice there is really no more comparison than between a little ewe lamb and the beautiful daughter of Eliam.

Biographical notes:
Ruskin
Street

THE SOCIETY FOR THE PROTECTION OF ANCIENT BUILDINGS (1881)

As a veteran campaigner on conservation issues Godwin clearly felt that his own achievements and authority in this area were in danger of being obscured by this 'ornamental' society.

The annual meeting of the Society for the Protection of Ancient Buildings took place at the Westminster Palace Hotel, on Friday last, 24th June. His excellency the Hon. J. Russell Lowell presided, and as far as we could hear spoke with the ease of an accomplished orator, but hardly with the voice of one. The room, which was crowded by an audience chiefly composed of ladies, had its *open* windows looking into the street that flanks the aquarium where Miss Beckwith was disporting; and the constant rattle of cabs (for this much frequented street is not paved with wood) rendered the words of the speaker quite inaudible to us whenever the voice was lowered, which happened, unfortunately, whenever a point was made, judging from the applause these low tones called forth from Mr. Wm. Morris. Another time, if Mr. Morris or Mr. Newman Marks would get a quiet room adapted to the purpose of the meeting, we might so far assist them as to give some account of their proceedings.

Source:
'Notes on current events,' *The British Architect*, 1 July 1881, p.329

Biographical notes:
Morris
SPAB

The annual report contains (p.15) "a list of all the buildings concerning which the Committee have taken action since the last annual meeting." Sixty is the gross number of them, but in how many cases the Committee's action has been successful does not appear. This is just the one thing we should like to know. Sixty cases a year is not much for a Central Committee of a hundred, with more than twenty detectives scattered about the country. But is there not just a little too much of the ornamental in this Society? The object they profess to have in view is good, but it is one certain individuals have been exercised in for many years past; and the protection or preservation of ancient work, whether in buildings, furniture, in documents, or in any other form, is so much an element in art culture that we fear the dictatorial method adopted by the Society runs the danger of giving offence to those who were busy in protecting ancient work, when many members of the S.P.A.B. Committee were alike indifferent to Henry III. and Queen Anne.

LITTLE SOMERSET CHURCHES (1880-1)

Source:
'Notes on current events', *The British Architect*, 21 May 1880, p.241

Godwin used his editorial muscle by following up these notices with a reprint of his 1850s survey on the front page of The British Architect. *The restorer in question was G. E. Street.*

There was once a little cross church in Somersetshire of great interest to us. We sketched it, and measured it, and photographed it till one fine day passing by we found it had been "restored."

Source:
'Notes on current events', *The British Architect*, 7 October 1881, p.496

So one of the most interesting little churches in England — Clapton-in-Gordano, Somerset — has fallen prey to the restorer's clutches. Let us hope he will deal mercifully with it. We remember certain massive oak seats, old altar candlesticks of admirable design standing not on the altar, but on stone brackets, or rather capitals, attached to the east wall each side of the communion table. Then there was an old stone altar, and some curious thirteenth century features in various parts, notably a two-light window and a piscina. The church stands out of the way at the end of a by-road, and the manor house close by is of the same age.

LEGITIMATE VANDALISM (1881)

Source:
'Notes on current events', *The British Architect*, 29 July 1881, p.376

Strange that in our many visits to York we never noticed the church of St. Crux, and even now we do not know its exact whereabouts. Through the courtesy of a correspondent we have been favoured with a photograph and description of the church, which, as our readers are doubtless aware, is on the eve of demolition; the sooner the better say we, for the photograph shows about as poor an example of debased Italian Gothic, and other mixtures, as possible. [...] Strange we missed noting this singular (to York) piece of ecclesiastical ugliness. Its destruction is quite legitimate work to be undertaken by our modern Goths and Vandals.

ELASTIC CREDIBILITY (1878)

A response to a book on St Alban's Cathedral by H. Comyns Carr which cites Godwin, among others, as a source for the early history if the building.

Source:
'The Abbey Church of St. Alban', *The Athenaeum*, no. 2620, 12 January 1878, pp.62-3

Biographical notes:
Carr

I do not know whether Mr. Carr satisfied himself of the accuracy of the researches of those "others" whom he marshals against me. But one would have thought that a critic, even though he be no antiquary, might have taken the trifling trouble to have tested the one authority which precedes Bede in point of date, and given us at least chapter and verse for his assertion that the first church "is certainly mentioned by Gildas." I have twice gone through the work of Gildas and some of the original MSS. to which Mr. Carr refers. There is something in Gildas about the martyrdom of St. Alban and others, something of the changing of the cloaks, something of the Israelites, and something of the river Jordan; but not a syllable could be found about any structure that could by any possibility be called a church of St. Alban's. If Mr. Carr and his modern authorities are ready to go so far as to accept the general expression in a paragraph about the British church, "basilicas sanctorum martyrum," as implying that, a basilica or Church of St. Alban then existed, I would not desire for a moment to interfere with such an elastic credibility.

YE OLDE ENGLAND (1881)

The numerous commercial, philanthropic and international exhibitions of the late nineteenth-century presented many opportunities for historical fancy dress. Generally the results did not meet the standard of archaeological accuracy that Godwin was to set in his pageant of historical dress at the 1884 International Health Exhibition in London.

The "preliminary announcement" of the "Grand Fancy Fair", to be held at the Albert Hall, does not promise well for anything like an intelligent revival of an old English fair. The only point in the entire programme that savours of old English, being the constant substitution of ye for *thee*, an affectation so feebly puerile that it suggests nothing but dreary pretence and lack-a-day limpness. We are told that "Ye Elizabethan period is chosen for ye fête, and those who take part will be attired in appropriate costumes." Saleswomen in stalls or booths at a country fair [in the time of] Elizabeth were simple enough in their attire, but at the same time so like one another that we cannot suppose the rivalry of modern toilet will for a moment allow of any such *appropriateness* in this direction as that promised in the announcement.

Source:
'Notes on current events',
The British Architect, 27 May 1881, p.267

REPRODUCING 'OLD LONDON' (1884)

Since the 1870s there had been a vogue for recreating historic streets as part of international exhibitions. In 1884 it was the turn of 'Old London', where for three days actors in Shakespearian garb milled about and attempted to speak 'Olde English' to visitors.* There was some attempt at historical accuracy in the architecture – the architect George Birch won two gold medals for his reconstruction of landmarks like Dick Whittington's house and the Tabard Inn from prints and drawings of the medieval city — but Godwin was critical of the distortions of scale and inauthentic homogeneity in the streetscape.

One of the best modern attempts to realise the scenic accessories of a bygone time is no doubt the "Old London Street" at the Health Exhibition; but [...] it is to be regretted where money and thought have been spent so lavishly, that we have after all not a reproduction but a model to scale.* [...] one of the first things that strike the eye is a hanging tile on one of the old houses; the tile is

Source:
'To art students. Letter no. 6',
The British Architect, 20 June 1884, p.297

Biographical notes:
Bancroft

* It seems likely that a section of this 'Old London' street was transferred subsequently to New York. See C. Gray, *New York Times*, 3 Oct. 1999.

several times larger than usual, and dwarfs still further the house, already too small.

As long ago as 1862 I insisted on this matter of scale; and when Mr. and Mrs. Bancroft produced the "Merchant of Venice" at the Prince of Wales' Theatre two bays of the lower arcade of the Ducal Palace at Venice were portrayed with casts taken from those of the Ducal Palace itself preserved in the Architectural Museum at Westminster. But there is, archaeologically speaking, a graver error; the houses in the Old London Street are too much of one date and style. [...] Each style of building did not enter, nor did it depart, like the actor in a scene. But we should find a Norman house shouldered by a 14th century one and so on. And this variety would be necessary to a truthful representation of any city thoroughfare. Even now-a-days in some London streets we see 16th century, 17th, 18th, 19th century work side by side. [...]

The measure of the success of accessories is the faithfulness of the adherence to originals in architecture, in costume, in music. And the best authority for all these will of course be the man with the most varied and thorough knowledge where to find these originals. In architecture, at any rate, the accomplished architect will be the best seeker.

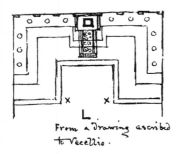

Godwin, plan of stage set for The Merchant of Venice, BA *13 Feb. 1880.*

VII Travels with an Architect

WITH GODWIN at their side, readers could relish the sights, sounds, tastes and smells of travel throughout Britain and on the Continent. His roving eye took them from Ireland to Liverpool, from Rye to Yarmouth, to Copenhagen, Lisieux, and Paris, pointing out overlooked charms and modern architectural horrors in passing. In Rouen he spends an afternoon gazing through his opera-glass at a small dormer which 'in its way and its degree, affected me more than did the grand piles for which the town is so celebrated' (p.168) and while several column inches are given to the discussion of table-ware in a modern Paris restaurant, the new Kursaal at Ostend is dismissed at a stroke as 'a compromise between a locomotive shed and a beehive' (p.186).

Increasing mobility was characteristic of the age, and like many middle-class architects Godwin was constantly on the move, travelling around Britain and Ireland to supervise architectural commissions, and within Europe for work and pleasure — to Normandy on holiday, installing an exhibition in Vienna, researching Hamlet in Denmark. Despite his evident enthusiasm for the cultures of Japan and Greece, however, Godwin did not have the independent means and leisure of his friend Burges to spend on extended periods abroad, nor did he develop the commercial side of his practice to the extent of his contemporary Christopher Dresser, whose business-related activities took him as far afield as Japan and the United States. Nevertheless, from his travels Godwin stocked his mental gallery with images and impressions that filtered steadily into both his design work and journalism. Obviously he was drawn to those formal values that he wished to express in his own creations. Sometimes details were transposed directly, as in the shaped gable added to the elevation of his studio house for Frank Miles, which self-consciously alluded to 'some reminiscences of a visit to Holland' (p.260). Less obvious, perhaps, was the role of travel in honing his analytical skills, advancing his views on conservation and urban development, and confirming his predilection for subtle coloration and austere, simple massing.

Godwin was not a particularly adventurous traveller. As these extracts show, he prized his creature comforts, and his architectural commentaries are interspersed with engaging detail about the experience of travel itself. On holiday in Normandy with Ellen Terry and two young children in tow, there is a litany of complaints about the unsanitary hotels and poor food. In Mantes, for example, the 'only hotel worth naming encouraged cats, and had a genuine old garden damp about it quite beyond the influence of wood fires. This dampness pervaded the whole house, even to the larder, and so gave a peculiar earthy-flavour to one's food' (p.168). With the exception of certain centres like St Lô that were extensively damaged during World War Two, the articles and sketches produced from this trip still provide the modern traveller with an entertaining

Godwin, sketch of Belleville church, Normandy, BN 23 Oct. 1874.

and informative guide to Northern France. Godwin rarely strayed far from the beaten track, yet still managed to avoid the tourist set-pieces. Where possible he travelled in the relative comfort of hansom cabs and trains from which he could concentrate on looking. With an opera glass in one hand and pencil in the other, he would home in on architectural details through the windows, rapidly sketching in his little pocketbook: 'Moral — don't bury yourself in your newspaper or novel when you visit new countries' (p.174).

For young architects he offered holiday tips on where to go, inns to avoid, and practical advice on how to set about making measured drawings. Travel for the young art-architect was about learning to look, and then to criticise, 'and by criticism I do not mean a volley of vituperation or an avalanche of ecstasy' (p.177). Nor was evaluating architecture like judging a pig or an ox. It involved a forensic dissection of construction and detail, and an intensified perception of context, atmosphere and patterns of use. The *slap-dash, flick-and-dot* and *vague* styles of drawing were all very well for producing pretty reminiscences to show off 'to mamma and the girls', but 'to be faithful and accurate and to really understand the *modus operandi* of the past', required plenty of time, and a more scientific approach. While exhorting his readers within the architectural professions to travel within Britain and abroad, he always emphasised in-depth study and relevance to the scope of their practice: better to focus 'on one or two buildings rather than the architecture of a whole province'. The student might well extend his studies to Persia, Hindustan, Japan, China and Mexico: 'Life is, however, perhaps too short for any such extended study, and very glad am I that it is so, for I have a horror of what is called English enterprise when art matters are in question' (p.178).

Further Reading:

W. Nesfield, *Specimens of Gothic Architecture*, London, 1862

E. Viollet-le-Duc, *Dictionnaire raisonée du mobilier français de l'époque carolinienne à la renaissance*, 6 vols, Paris, 1858–75

E. Viollet-le-Duc, *Entretiens sur l'architecture*, 2 vols, Paris, 1863–72

D. Mays, 'Sketching tours 1850–1914', *St Andrews Studies in the History of Scottish Architecture and Design*, 1991, pp.1-8

G. Stamp, 'High Victorian Gothic and the architecture of Normandy', *Journal of the Society of Architectural Historians*, 62:2, June 2003, pp.196-211

SKETCHING TOURS (1884)

For Godwin the archaeological recording of historic building through the process of drawing was vital to the development of an architectural sensibility, and there was more to be learnt from studying such survivals than from most modern plans or elevations.

The reason for sketching *old* buildings is twofold, first in great measure their picturesqueness, due to chance effects of weather or man's handling; this first reason is closely allied to that sense of association on which Alison founded the accepted theory of beauty;* the other reason should be the main determining factor in choosing the buildings we study — that is, their usually sound construction, the dignity of their composition, and a certain unspeakable feeling for beautiful outlines in the contours of their mouldings. We now refer more especially to the classics of architectonic art, the buildings of the ages of Pericles and the earlier Plantagenet kings.

And it is this construction, this dignity, this skilful outlining that is to be observed, and as it were probed, till we find out the hidden springs of so much loveliness; the beautiful construction and the constructed beauty, in these latter days so seldom found together.

Now, as to the buildings to be considered, in very many old erections, and good ones too for that matter, the beauty is rather in details than in mass. Here of course it would be unwise to more than study this detail; but when a building strikes you like a revelation, both of general effect and particular, then, I say, stop and study till you have dissected out the particles of proportion, mass, colour, outline which form the whole, and when the composition rests for its effect on repetition of features, measure similar bays one by one; you will, no doubt, find variations, which though unnoticed at first, are the chief agents perhaps in producing the life and play of a whole front. In all this bearing in mind that to put yourselves *en rapport* with the authors of a design is to be on the highway to similar art powers or otherwise; and the best way to attain this is by concentrating your attention on one or two buildings rather than the architecture of a whole province. Spend your whole holiday at Lisieux in itself a complete school of building art; or at Blois, or among the small Norman village churches, or at Flushing and Middleburgh, if you prefer the Low Countries; or if in our own country, one or two of the Yorkshire or Lowland Scottish abbeys will well fill a summer's holiday. Do not, because Jacobean work or Queen Anne is now the rage, pass by the far higher class work of the thirteenth and early fourteenth centuries; always remembering, however, that in all styles some fine work has been done. Few ages have been wholly dark and dreary.

Sketch your perspectives lightly, more as a test of perspectives made from your measured drawings; photographs are also very valuable for this. Before beginning on a building, try to grasp it in its entirety; walk round it, as you would a statue; note the points of view giving the best general effect, or those giving the worst, for a building is bad insofar as its defects of outline are the

Source:
'To art students. Letter no. 5', *The British Architect*, 13 June 1884, p.285

* Rev. Archibald Alison (1757–1839), author of *Essays on the Nature and Principles of Taste*, 1790.

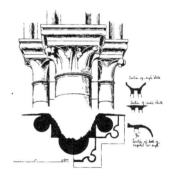

Godwin, drawing of a capital in Belleville church, Normandy, BN 23 Oct. 1874.

161

inevitable concomitants of the means used for giving characteristic beauties when seen from a changed standpoint; and in the avoidance of such defects lies the measure of the success of a building.

ULSTER ARCHITECTURE AND ANTIQUITIES (1872)

This series of articles and subsequent illustrations, many of which were recycled later in The British Architect, *are all that materialised of Godwin's plan to publish a book on the architecture and antiquities of Ireland. His interest was sparked during the time he worked with his brother, and on subsequent visits connected with projects like Dromore. He was concerned to tap into the most ancient traditions of settlement and architecture. Although some of his analyses have been subsequently disproved, his remarks are interesting in that he sensed in Ireland the reverberations of a common ancient culture linking east and west. His sensitivity to the political nature of heritage conservation is clearly articulated at the conclusion of the series, pointing the way forward to the full-blown National Romanticism that would flourish in Ireland as in many other small European and Scandinavian nations at the end of the century.*

Source:
'On the architecture and antiquities of the western part of the province of Ulster', *Architect,* 20 April 1872, pp.193-5

During a rather prolonged visit to the north of Ireland some few years ago, I was induced by the temptation of grand scenery to penetrate the wild mountains and shores of Donegal. Two or three professional engagements in the same county following upon this visit led me to enquire into the antiquities of the district, and the result of this enquiry I have put together in the following notes and accompanying sketches.

The wild grandeur of this part of Ireland, the majesty of its mountains, the solemn stillness of its lakes, and the deep, undercut, Atlantic carving of its coast-line, have attractions which tourists now and then seek out in spite of the almost barbaric condition of the inhabitants. Had they any peculiar charm for the tourists of Druidic Pagan times? That the country did attract them we have abundant proof in the traditions and customs of the people, and in the names of places. Unfortunately, however, the monumental record of this period is but slight and uncertain, a scarcity that may be attributed in some degree to time, but probably in far greater measure to the Christian labours of the first missionaries of the great Evangelist of Ulster, and his indefatigable disciples, who would naturally endeavour to root out the ancient superstition, or at least to change the character of the thorn and the oak by engrafting thereon the rose and the vine.

Godwin, round tower on Tory island, Arch. *4 May 1872, p.224.*

Cathairs

But although the monumental remains of these primitive days are few and far between, this fact only enhances the value of the little which is in existence, and gives us all the more time to examine one rude vestige of Pagan grandeur, which is in interest and association [...] I refer to the stone CATHAIR, or Fort of Grainan, a class of structure rarely met with except "in the more remote districts of Connaught and Munster." [...] The plan of the Cathair is circular, and its wall, like that at Staigue in the county of Kerry, is built of uncemented stones. At the time of my visit (March, 1858) the masonry was in very delapidated condition, owing in great part to the labours of some gentlemen who many years ago evinced more curiosity than care in searching after subterranean passages, &c.; since which this interesting work of antiquity has deplorably suffered by the summer invasions of visitors from the neighbouring city. Indeed, mere meddling and muddling have been permitted to such an extent that the drawings of the fort taken at the time of the Ordnance Survey have literally become matter of history [...]

Crosses

In hunting out early examples, Godwin describes how 'I cleared away the weeds and long grass which had well-nigh buried them, and traced out with my own fingers the long-worn channels and nearly obliterated incisions.'

I may mention that in Ireland, as in Cornwall, there is an unmistakeable eastern influence evident in the form of a great majority of crosses; nor in the cross alone, but also in the earlier masonry to which I shall refer hereafter. An influence so distinct in the early days of Irish art could not but have affected, more or less, the later times, and the wide difference discernable between the ancient monumental art of Ireland and that of England, whether in the lowly cross or towering abbey, arises chiefly, I believe, from the opposite influences brought to bear upon their early artistic efforts. [...] This influence is particularly marked in the county of Donegal, where there are crosses, the character of which, would almost lead us to suppose that they are either exotics or that the county itself had once been a colony of Greece. In Conwall churchyard there are two small examples of this Eastern character; both have distinguishing classic ornaments, the fret and the volute. But whilst one has only the fret and volute, the other presents us not only with a perfect Greek cross, but with four minor crosses in the exterior angles of quarters of the larger one. [...] The other example is but a fragment, the upper half having evidently been broken off. Both are incised in a shaly kind of slate — a material which seems to have been commonly used for the crosses throughout the country — more especially the older specimens.[...]

After Conwall the crosses next in chronological order are those at Dunlewey and Glen Columbkille. Here we perceive a decided change in the character of the ornamentation [...] from the simple Greek fret as we see it at Conwall to a system which, although resulting from the simple Greek type, has, nevertheless a character of its own essentially Irish or Celtic.

Round towers

The round tower on Tory island, probably owing to its position, is stunted in its proportions, and is of less altitude than any of the detached class now existing. Considering that it stands upon the shelving-shore of one of the most barren, wild, and rugged islands of this proverbially wild coast, it is somewhat remarkable that it should have retained so much of its original character — the north-eastern side, or that portion which is sheltered by the rising ground

Godwin, Irish crosses at Conwall and Glencolumbkille.

Source:
'On the architecture and antiquities of the western part of the province of Ulster', *Architect*, 4 May 1872, p.223

of the island is to this day in tolerably good preservation from the base to even within a few feet of the summit of the conical roof. The masonry is of granite, built for the most part in regular courses, but occasionally irregular [...]

Churches

Source:
'On the architecture and antiquities of the western part of the province of Ulster',
Architect, 18 May 1872, p.249

The peculiarites which are to be noted in these churches of Donegal are almost identical with those which charcterise many of the churches in the western part of Cornwall, and which exercised a peculiarly local influence on the ecclesiastical architecture of the whole diocese of Exeter. These are — first, the primitive simplicity of both Cornwall and Ireland; second, the absence of constructive chancels, attached towers, porches &c. (in West Cornwall all the older churches have had towers added to them at a late period, and are nearly all of one uniform style and design); and third, the paucity of fenestration, and the rare and exceptional use of buttresses.

An alphabet of indigenous architecture

Source:
'On the architecture and antiquities of the western part of the province of Ulster',
Architect, 1 June 1872,
pp.278-81

It may be said that Ireland possesses far more important examples of architecture in its midland and southern districts than those which form the subject of the above notes. This is perfectly true; but they are, for the most part, mere variations and enlargements of the type which Donegal presents us in the simplest form. It is because this county contains no large or elaborate work; because it exhibits elements of the national characteristics; because it exhibits the alphabet of indigenous architecture; because it presents us with the seedlings, so to speak, of those works which we find at Monasterboice and Clonmocnoise, at Cashel, Holy Cross and Quinn, in Galway and Limerick, Tipperary and Wicklow, that I have selected them to serve as a general introduction to the whole subject of Irish architecture. In this larger field there is room for many labourers; for in demanding the preservation of political nationalities, it might not be amiss to remember that there may be other national characteristics much better worth preserving than those dependent on the power of a Ministry or the wish of a British Parliament.

WHAT I NOTED IN PASSING THROUGH MANCHESTER AND LIVERPOOL (1874)

In 1874 Godwin travelled to Manchester to witness Ellen Terry's return to the stage. It was also the year in which The British Architect and Northern Engineer *started up, published out of Manchester.*

Source:
'What I noted in passing through Manchester and Liverpool', *Building News*, 10 July 1874, p.55

Biographical notes:
Marks
Waterhouse

I suppose there are people who judge architecture on much the same sort of principle a farmer judges a pig or an ox. To such, size and weight are easy of apprehension, and are elements about which they need take no trouble for neither education nor eye are needed to estimate the value of buildings when measured solely by the standard of feet and inches. It is much to be feared that this utterly base standard is beginning to influence the works of modern architects to an unwholesome degree. [...]

Now, the city of Manchester is throughout one vast illustration of this re-gard and reverence for mere size. Street follows street with uniform gloomy hugeness; flat dreary reaches of wall stretch on for miles without one square foot of beauty to gladden the eye, and the stone of which most of it is built — fair and beautiful at first—becomes in a few short years of a funereal tone, giving to the monotonous masses an aspect which in the quiet and silence of early morning is depressing and sad almost to the degree of horror.

If we look closer, we shall find that this sense of gloom permeates every-thing — not merely the general street architecture, but the special buildings with which the readers of this journal are familiar through the illustrations that have from time to time appeared. Whether we take the Free Trade Hall or the Assize Courts, the Exchange or Manchester Town Hall, we are conscious more or less of the presence of some such sort of (architectural) infliction as that under which Sinbad the Sailor suffered.* Primarily, I have little doubt that this is owing to an over-development of the first-floor at the expense of the ground-floor, the result of which is that the buildings look as if their huge weight had partially sunk them, and consequently dwarfed the ground-story. The full extravagance of this is seen at the Exchange and in the principal front of the new Town Hall, where the height of the first-floor windows preponder-ate in an undue degree, even for Manchester. [...] If we leave Manchester and charter a cab along any of its endless suburban roads, the eye, in search of the artistic, has to suffer to an amount unparalleled in any town in England. [...]

Fresh from Manchester oriels and plate glass Gothic, the "Classic" build-ings of Liverpool give quite a pleasing sensation even to a Goth like me. The style, with its many unmeaning features, may be objectionable on the score of climate and creed and common-sense; but still it seems to me that there is more thought — that the buildings have been more carefully worked out here than in Manchester. [...]

Of St. George's Hall there is nothing new to say.** It remains as it always was, and I suppose always will be, the best thoroughly Classic work in this country. Being such, it is strange that the authorities have not made up their minds before this to subdue the white glare from the end windows of the Great Hall by introducing glass of a golden tone. I saw a few panes, put up by way of experiment, I suppose; but if this is the only way to do it, I hope the authorities may ever remain undecided. By the way, a small piece of gutta-percha or indiarubber on the legs of the chairs placed on the tiles would prevent the disagreeable scraping noise visitors seem compelled to make, and which are so jarring to the ear, during the most delicate passages of Mr. Best's recitals. To keep them off the cold tiles, gentlemen *will* put their feet on the bars of the chairs in front of them; hence occurs the movement, and the inevitable offen-sive scrape. Of ordinary domestic architecture Liverpool seems to know noth-ing. When you have marked off its few public buildings and the Lime-street Station Hotel, you come to the end of architecture as far as the town is con-cerned. [...] The churches in and about Liverpool, in general composition, in proportion and detail, show a higher appreciation of Gothic art than that which apparently exists in the neighbouring city.

Waterhouse, Manchester Assize Courts, 1859, Builder 1865, p.136.

* Free Trade Hall (1853), designed by Walters; Royal Exchange (1869–74), by Mills & Murgatroyd; Assize Courts (1859) and Town Hall (1868–77), by Waterhouse.

** Designed 1841–56 by Elmes (completed by Cockerell).

If, however, the churches of Liverpool have the advantage over those of Manchester, the latter town has the superiority in places of amusement. The Prince's Theatre in Manchester is altogether in advance of any theatre I know in the United Kingdom. Such faults as it has are mainly superficial — *e.g.*, the colours and patterns on the pedestals of the proscenium piers, and a trifle too much warmth and solidity of colour in the general effect. The winged figures on the ceiling are not altogether satisfactory, and can scarcely be said to harmonise with the painting over the proscenium, one of Mr. Marks' happiest works, both in colour and composition. On the other hand, in Liverpool the art of the drama is just barely housed, and not one of its five so-called theatres is other than a disgrace to the town: some of them would even be a disgrace to a half-civilised village, whether we regard the construction or the "decoration," the fittings or the sanitary arrangements. In theatres, new or old, town or country, there is a strange blank on this sanitary question, and officers of health seem to be everywhere totally unconscious of the wretched condition in which these buildings are suffered to remain.

SOME NOTES OF A MONTH IN NORMANDY (1874)

'When you go abroad, begin with France', Gilbert Scott told students at the Royal Academy in 1857. 'It is the great centre of mediaeval art. Perhaps the best course is to take Normandy first, as most allied to our own country.' In 1874 Godwin, Terry and their two children spent a holiday in Normandy, already a well-established destination for British architects, particularly those whom Godwin most admired, like Burges and Nesfield. Godwin had studied Ruskin's inspirational discussion of the great Normandy cathedrals in Seven Lamps of Architecture *(1849), and had at his side the drawings of de Caumont, Viollet-le-Duc, Verdier and Cattois, and Nesfield.*

Source:
'Some notes on a month in Normandy. —I', *Building News*, 28 August 1874, pp.251-2

Biographical notes:
Scott
Shaw
Viollet-le-Duc

DIEPPE, Rouen, Mantes, Evreux, Lisieux, Caen, Bayeux, St. Lô, and Coutances, are towns I have lately visited, and it may be questioned whether there is any other equally extensive tract of country in the same latitude where the habits and homes of the people are more uniformly dirty, where the land is more consistently neglected, and where travellers are so incontinently surcharged. Sometimes you have the rare fortune to enter an hotel that has just undergone or is undergoing the process of refurbishing — in such cases, and in such cases only, can you rely with certainty on the absolute cleanliness of your apartments. But, as a rule, dirt and decay dominate over everything. The villages and small towns (as, for example, Conches) are quite on a par with the dilapidated wretchedness of the worst specimens in Ireland. Here and there, as in the country just named, you meet with pleasant surprises, pure exceptions to the rule. Such, for instance, is Beaumont-le-Roger, between Evreux and Lisieux, where you can get better coffee than at any of the so-called first-class hotels of Normandy at less than a quarter the price, and where, though appearances are simple and primitive, good rooms, country-fare, undiluted cyder, and cleanliness are provided at five francs a day. More developed in its cookery, but no whit cleaner, is the White Horse at St. Lô, a capital and reasonable hotel, where everything the host can do to oblige is done with alacrity. Commend me to his table-d'hôte, and his Curaçao is a pleasant remembrance. In Caen, too, one can get really good dinners. But at such towns as Lisieux and Bayeux, where I particularly wished to stay for the sake of the antiquities, the accommodation is either very dilapidated or very costly. If a man (unencumbered) can drink ditchwater for coffee, and take his meals in a place as gloomy as a charnel house, he may manage to exist in Lisieux for a day; after that he must resign himself to a system of slow poisoning, and is fortunate if, after a week, he has vitality enough left to reach the next halting-place in his journey.

Rouen

ROUEN, as a town, is still essentially medieval, in spite of its modern quays, new streets, and iron spire. Of its multitude of old narrow ways, there is scarcely one that has not a good morning's lesson for the young student. Of late work, especially note-worthy are the delicately-moulded beams, &c., of the Flamboyant houses, and the exquisitely-carved Renaissance work at St. Vincent's, as also that of the restored houses at the back of the tower of Jean D'Arc. [...]

The great church of St. Ouen and the Cathedral are too well known by photograph and otherwise for them to be fit subjects for my notes; and yet it is hardly possible for me to leave the latter without adding my contribution of praise to the unfinished north-western tower (Saint-Romain), perhaps the plainest piece of architecture in all Rouen, and yet to me the grandest in its mass, the most refined in its proportion, and the most lovely in its detail of moulded and carved work. The Cathedral, although so much shut in by narrow streets and tall houses, is far more interesting to the student than the show church of St. Ouen; and when added to this the visitor finds the custodians of the Cathedral more than civil, and those at St. Ouen more than obstructive, it is pleasant to reflect that the grand thirteenth-century church, with its twelfth-century heritage, is in every respect more worthy of regard than the more elaborated and bedecked abbey church of 1318–1518.

Of timber houses Rouen is still well supplied. In the Rue de la Viconte there are two or three good fronts — one especially good is divided into five bays, the main-posts covered with delicate tracery and pinnacles higher up the street, at the corner of the Rue aux Ours, is a very refined, though much battered, example. One of the best-preserved houses is that at the corner of the Rue de la Tuile. That at the angle formed by the Rue Nationale and Rue aux Ours is fine and well preserved; but perhaps the most complete of unrestored work is that at the corner of the Rue Malpalu and the Rue Tuvache, illustrated by M. Viollet-le-Duc in his "Dictionnaire" [...] Besides the restored Renaissance house already mentioned, there exists a rather tottering, but very beautifully-proportioned and delicately treated front of the same style at No. 146, Rue de la Grosse Horologe — a street, by the way, that has no very extensive or superior specimens to show us, but one that somehow overflows with an indefinable charm — a place where we rest as we walk, although it may be after many hours' exertion.

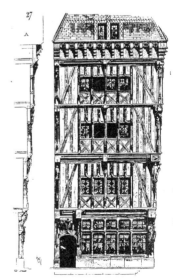

The Viollet-le-Duc illustration, referred to by Godwin, of a timber house in Rouen.

A little dormer

One feature in which Lisieux is particularly rich is here of scarcely any importance. The dormer or *lucarne*, I need hardly say, was a very great favourite with many architects in the fifteenth and sixteenth centuries. With Mr. Norman Shaw, and one or two others, it has influence enough to make its picturesqueness felt even in these days; but the great majority of modern dormers are miserable looking, weak, roof excrescences, as worthless for any practical value they are to the interior as for any architectural or picturesque character they give to the exterior. Of *small* dormers, one of the most piquant and most effective I have ever seen is to be found at No. 16, Place de la Basse. The roof overhangs considerably. The barge-board is moulded immediately under the tiles, and is then trefoliated under a semicircle, with the spandrils between them pierced. [...] Small as it is, this little window possesses nearly all the qualities of great and good work; its lights and shades are broad; intensified and concentrated round about its decorative features — the trefoliation of the bargeboard, and the three short lengths of simple mouldings. It may seem to some strange that I should pass by the famed structures of Rouen to note at such length a little dormer nearly at the top of a high roof in a low quarter of the town. I do so for the very simple reason that, in its way and its degree, it affected me more than did the grand piles for which the town is so celebrated. I studied it for more than an hour, partly by my unaided eyes and partly by the help of a powerful opera-glass, and I made a sketch of it as well as I could. There is still much for me to learn from it, for the power of this little thing lingers in my memory; and my chief regret on leaving the capital of Normandy was that I had not dissected and secured every measurement of the dormer of the Place de la Basse.

Mantes

MANTES was my next halting-place, and on a wet, cold, dark evening, when fires are welcome in every room, Mantes does not wear the most pleasant and inviting face to the unexpected visitor. The only hotel worth naming encouraged cats, and had a genuine old garden damp about it quite beyond the influence of wood fires. This dampness pervaded the whole house, even to the larder, and so gave a peculiar earthy-flavour to one's food. The church is the only attraction here, but then it is one of a kind not easily forgotten. Exteriorly, the want of good towers is a very great drawback, for from any point of view the western quasi-towers are weak and ill-proportioned to a surprising degree, considering their early date and the good qualities to be seen in the greater part of the building. The first and pre-eminent charm about this church is the almost classical purity of its interior. The curves of the vaulting sweep above our heads with wonderful grace; the section of the ribs and string-courses are proportioned with utmost skill — strong without being in any way coarse; refined, without a shadow of weakness. [...] With the exception of an admirable fourteenth century chapel, the church throughout is of one style, viz., the First Pointed, the design dating from the latter part of the twelfth century.

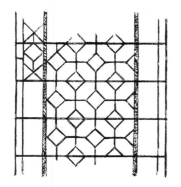

Godwin, drawing of glazing pattern in Mantes.

That the architect had his thoughts on painted decoration when he designed the interior of Notre Dame de Mantes, is an almost irresistible conclusion as we look at the broad, flat treatment of the vault and wall spaces. We should note well the grand simplicity of the composition, and what I may call the sensitiveness of the articulation — the life in shaft and arch and rib, whilst in so many old churches, and in all new ones, the arches and vaulting appear to press more or less heavily on the walls and piers, the groining at Mantes seems to grow and spring out of its supports. Words and drawings are equally incapable of expressing the peculiar grace and perfection of this work as a structural composition. I am ashamed to say I hardly noticed the carving and accessory arts, so absorbed was I with the general treatment.

It was not until I surveyed the outside where the general composition is questionable that details assumed any importance. Here one becomes conscious of a grandeur of proportion in the simple, almost unmoulded lancet-windows, in the great west rose without a solitary cusp in all its broad surface, in the west-central doorway and the arcade over, and descending even to the later work of the chapel in its broad buttresses, deeply -moulded arches, and exquisite tracery. This chapel, as illustrated by M. Viollet-le-Duc is very charming, but the brilliancy and the grace of the windows, and the strength and repose of the buttresses, are wanting, and even in the construction of the tracery, I am sorry to say the fourteenth-century architect does not receive the credit due to him. [...] I quote these cases, first because they are almost inexcusable, the original being so simple and well defined; and second, because it may be as well for those younger members of the profession who may follow me to learn to rely on their own eye-sight and measurements, and observations of even well-known examples, and whilst accepting as guides the authors of popular works, not to lean too heavily on their guides, or trust too implicitly to everything they may say.

Viollet-le-Duc, the illustration of Nôtre Dame de Mantes referred to by Godwin.

Patina on a tile roof

There is still another great charm about Mantes, which, to fully realise, we must retire to some distance, or mount one of the western towers (the south-western is the best). I can conceive of no coloured decoration in the external architecture of the Middle Ages to exceed in loveliness of tone the tile roof of this church. I allow for the additional effect of time, and odd tiles inserted haphazard, and I remember that it was a glorious day, and that the blue of the sky was of a deeper fuller tone than usual. But omitting these very important artistic aids, there remains a combination of three simple colours — green, yellow, and black arranged in a pattern common throughout Europe and the East, yet here so proportioned to the size of the roof, so piquantly placed at a slight angle with the horizon, and so harmonious in its colouring, that although acquainted with very careful drawings of it in Mr. Burges's work, I could not resist the temptation to draw it for myself, short as my time was. [...] Repairs covering a great number of years have resulted in scattering the colours a little, and throughout the whole roof we observe that black tiles had got amongst the green, green and black amongst the yellow, and red-brown or the modern tile everywhere. It is worth noting that the green glaze is far better preserved than the others, and very like in tone to some still used in the common water jars of the south of France.

En route to Lisieux

Source:
'Some notes on a month in Normandy. —II', *Building News*, 11 September 1874, pp. 307-9

Biographical notes:
de Caumont
Nesfield
Ruskin
Verdier & Cattois

We left Mantes reluctantly for EVREUX, but could not make up our minds to stay there, for with the exception of the house of No. 12, Rue Grande, and a fifteenth century domestic tower in the market-place, Evreux, in spite of its Cathedral, did not appear to me to be a place to take any delight in.

LISIEUX, on the contrary, is a mine of architectural wealth, and to the young man who can rough it, a fortnight or even a month devoted to the quondam Cathedral and the many interesting and beautiful examples of street architecture, would be time well spent. The hotels are of a very low order as regards sanitary arrangements, cleanliness of apartments, and quality of food. Servants are reduced to a minimum, for, besides the cook, one man and one girl were all the Hotel de France could muster in the month of April, although the price of a cup of café-au-lait with a morsel of sour bread and bad butter was 150 centimes, and a small not over-clean double-bedded room was quoted at five francs per night. But these are trifles, or, at any rate, only characteristic traits of a nation pre-eminent for its refinement. Hotels and all that they contain are happily forgotten directly we saunter out to look about us.

Timber houses in Lisieux

Down the principle street of the town, across the Cathedral square through the butter market and up that narrow lane where dormers most do congregate, is a short mile, but anyone who would walk it in less than two hours

need not stay at Lisieux. Setting the cathedral for the present aside, the timber houses of the town are more than enough to occupy the student for a week. The general composition of the roofs, the way they are arranged at the street corners, the variety of timber framing, the vertical slating and shingles, the carving, the glazed earthenware epis or hipknobs, the arrangement of the brick nogging and the moulded stone bases or plinths, are all the work of a people joying in their work, and imbued with a thoroughly artistic feeling. Foremost among these examples is the grand dormer-crowned house illustrated in "Architecture Civile et Domestique," by MM. Verdier and Cattois. "L'Auberge du Grand Turc" (its signboard still swings to and fro with a melancholy sound) is anything but an inviting place to mere sightseers or tourists, for from attic to ground everything is grimy with long neglect and accumulated dirt. I had not, unfortunately, time to examine anything more than the dormer itself. Of this I saw measured and plotted from the opposite window, by the help of a friend, enough to prove that the drawing by MM. Verdier and Cattois — exquisite as a drawing — has the failing common to a large number of

Godwin's drawing of a dormer in Lisieux.

so-called measured elevations — inaccuracy of observation. For instance, our neighbours and many of ourselves so often use straight lines and common or simple curves, where a little further time, a keener glance would have shown that such an off-hand treatment was unfaithful to the subject. In this dormer the front or barge rafters are not shaped by the line of a true semicircle, as shown by Verdier and Cattois, nor are the lintels and sills ever horizontally, straight, or level. All the horizontal timbers below the tiepiece are really cambered to the extent of one in sixteen — quite enough, one would think, to make it impossible for anyone but the most inexperienced eye to pass it over. [...]

These are not trifles, however much disposed some feverish scrambling minds may deem them such. These are the things which just make the difference between old work and new. There is a charm about the old we all more or less feel — a charm never, or very, very rarely, found in modern, and this charm, we may depend upon it, is not a mere question of age, but one owing altogether to the natural feeling and artistic spirit as opposed to the essentially unartistic mechanical modern spirit. It is the work of the artist-architect (or builder, if any one prefers the word) that the surveyor–architect can neither feel nor see, much less emulate. It is the eye and hand doing the work, borrowing now and then imperfect mechanical aids, instead of a box of perfect instruments, with eye and hand only as a sort of motive power.

But to return to our dormer. It is not by any means very easy to see it so as to make a drawing of it. The extreme narrowness of the street permits little more than a view of its soffits from immediately below, but if you are civil to the inhabitants of the opposite houses (and the young student should remember that civility and pleasant chit-chat go much further with the poor in Normandy than given silver coin in England) there will be no difficulty in getting direct views from two or three different levels, so close too, that you can make out much of the detail [...]

Lisieux cathedral

The cathedral is especially interesting to Englishmen, possessing many points of similarity with our own Canterbury. Built in the twelfth century, and yet designed in the early spirit of Pointed architecture, before multitudinous detail and elaboration of feature had dissociated most of those elements in architecture generally spoken of as simplicity — grandeur — strength — vigour — repose, it is the interior that exhibits these characteristics to the best advantage — single cylindrical shafts, or, as in the apse, double columns; deep square-planned abaci; broad soffits; large or bold mouldings to emphasise or strengthen arches and openings; delicate or small ones to tone and refine them; breadth of wall-space over arcade; still greater breadth of vault-space — these speak to us of its strength, its repose. [...] However brief our visit may be, we must linger for a moment before the doorway of the south-western tower. We shall see nothing like it for mastery of cusp-form in simple strong work for many a day. In the "Seven Lamps of Architecture," Mr. Ruskin has given a very powerful drawing of the arch and spandrel of wall-space between the arch, buttress, and string-course, and I cannot do better than refer my readers to his work.

Ruskin, detail of a spandrel in Lisieux Cathedral, as recommended by Godwin, from Seven Lamps of Architecture, *1849.*

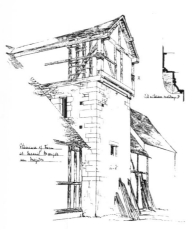

*Godwin, sketch of a farm at
Mesnil-Mauger.*

Source:
'Some notes of a month in
Normandy. —III', *Building
News*, 2 October 1874,
pp.395-6

Biographical notes:
Nesfield

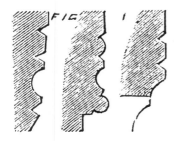

Fig. 1.

En route to Mesnil-Mauger

The country round Lisieux should not be missed. Pleasant walks up and down the river lead us to remains more or less interesting, among which the tiled and turreted gateway of the Chateau de Benvilliers stands out somewhat prominently. Pleasant drives can be taken to the Chateau Ouilly da Houley, where limited means compel the farmer proprietors to retain things nearly intact. The old wood casements and the glazing, the shutters, and the fittings generally, including even the kitchen andirons, still remain in use, happily unrestored. On the road to Mesnil-Manger [*sic*] we passed the manor-house of Houblonière, where we found some extremely charming bits of timber and shingle work, but unfortunately fast dropping to pieces. Through the pretty village of Creve-Coeur, and so to Mesnil-Manger, to meet with disappointment, for of its grand old farm, as M. de Caumont sketched it, three detached fragments are all now left standing, and even these will probably be cleared away before very long. One soon feels tired when disappointment meets one, and so somewhat dispirited I took my ticket and jumped into the next train for Caen.

Caen

CAEN is a town where, as I could not stop three weeks, I elected to stay only three days. The dates of the Abbey churches, Aux Hommes and Aux Dames, make them at once singularly interesting as archaeological studies, and these alone might well occupy more days than I had to spare for the whole town. Moreover the days were dull, with wind and rain, and so the interiors were dark, and sketching in the open was impossible. However, from the shelter of a friendly doorway I managed to secure some bits from the charming timber house, No. 94 Rue St. Jean, illustrated in plate 17 of Mr. W. E. Nesfield's Sketches. If a student has time and opportunity, it would be well worth his while to make careful drawings of the details of this front, for they are well preserved and remarkably simple and effective. Here (Fig. 1) are three rough sections indicating the style of the work. I cannot say I was much pleased with the Renaissance work in this town, for it all reminded me of the vulgar but expressive phrase, "butter upon bacon." No doubt the plentiful supply of an easily-cut stone tempted the workmen to go beyond the lines of legitimate ornament, and indulge in caprices to an excess that is in some cases fully bewildering. I confess I did not see much of the ins and out of Caen, nor can I tell whether I missed much by not doing so. The place had too much of a dull-modern-respectable look on the outside to make one very hopeful of finding much by penetrating deeper.

Bayeux and environs

Bayeux is altogether different. The cathedral, the museum, with its great possession of needlework, and the multitude of old houses, ranging from almost cottage proportions to the fully-equipped town-house; the old Norman character of the town, its hilly streets, narrow lanes, old courtyards, and that indescribable quiet so very far removed from dullness that is characteristic of small cathedral towns, all combine to make Bayeux a very pleasant resting place. It has, too, a great advantage over Lisieux in possessing a really good hotel, where, although the prices are maintained at a higher rate than usual, there is every comfort except spring mattresses, and not a few luxuries. The cathedral and the celebrated tapestry having already been well illustrated by photography and otherwise, I contented myself with merely looking at them.[...]

In the main streets most of the houses have had their fronts modernised, and, therefore, it is necessary to pass through into the courtyards in order to rightly estimate the wealth of old domestic work this little city of Bayeux possesses. The special feature in nearly all the examples I noted is the turret staircase. This is built as high as the eaves of the main roof, on a semi-octagonal plan; but at this point the canted sides are corbelled over, and there results a square, or nearly square, room, with gabled roof at the crown of the turret, access to which, in the large examples, is obtained by a small newel staircase, corbelled out from the wall of the main staircase turret.[...] The plans of the houses, the position of the staircase, and the treatment of the corbels, vary considerably, but through all there is a striking family likeness. There is one style for the one little community, but each man's house has its own individuality; and this individuality is nearly always expressed in the crowning glory of the staircase. [End of article]

At Bayeux we must still linger for a little while, in order to see the timber houses in the street leading from the west-end of the Cathedral to the Rue St. Malo. I give here a diagonal sketch elevation, to scale, of the angle house, the effect of which is exceedingly bold.

From Bayeux, as a centre, the student can work a highly-interesting district. The Priory of St. Gabriel, a small, but fine twelfth-century ruin, will be one of his first attractions [...]

St. Lô

St. Lô was our next halting place, and although still picturesque, its architecture, I am sorry to say, is at a very low ebb. [...] So that, speaking from experience, I would advise the student to give St. Lô a day, stay the night at the White Horse — a charming and wonderfully cheap hotel, where every one is on the alert to please the guest, and where a really good meal can be got at a really rational price. Go on the next morning early to St. Gilles, on the main road to Coutances after mastering the very simple yet novel beauties of an interesting village church.

Coutances

At Coutances we "stand all agaze," like the shepherds of our madrigals were said to do when they met Diana; for the Cathedral is, in one word, a *wonder*. It holds the same place with me, relatively to other cathedrals, that a comet does among stars. I need hardly say that this effect is solely attributable to the steeples, for the main structure is both in general design and detail almost commonplace. But in the steeples, the western ones especially, there is noth-

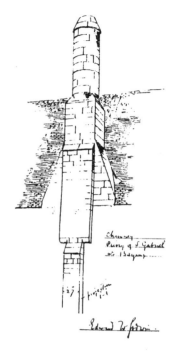

Godwin, sketch of the Priory of St Gabriel.

Source:
'Some notes of a month in Normandy. — No. IV', *Building News*, 13 November 1874, pp.572-3

Biographical notes:
Nesfield

173

ing at all commonplace. Indeed, they look rather as if they had dropped from above, stalactite-like, than as built from below. The three ideas of pinnacle, shaft, and crocket are here carried, one would hope, to their extremest limit, and yet so masterly are these extravagances treated, that it requires perhaps a course of such structures as St. Pierre Lisieux to fully appreciate the enormity of this at Coutances. Mr. Nesfield gives us an admirable drawing of it, as seen from the Bishop's garden, but the western view of the towers is by far the best. There are plenty of photographs to be obtained of these, and so I passed my time in searching out some of the delicate grisaille glass in the Geometrical windows of the chapels [...]

Unfortunately the horses at St. Lô are not inclined, by any course of treatment, to proceed at a greater rate than $3\frac{1}{2}$ miles an hour, so that as I had to return the same day, I had very little time to search the by-ways of the city.

Mancelier church

From St. Lô it is a pleasant row up the river to the quaint thirteenth-century village church of Mancelier. The tower is at the west-end, battered from ground to summit; it has a gabled roof looking east and west, and is very plain but very well proportioned. In the chancel is a barrel vault with king-post and tie-beam. [...] Here also are preserved the churchyard cross and boundary wall. As yet the hand of the restorer, hardly that of the repairer, has not touched this river-side church, and this is no small merit in a land where almost every old building bristles with scaffolding, and echoes the monotonous scrape of the masons' defacing tools. From St. Lô we started back again for home, but not without two rests — one *at Beaumont le Roger*, and last at *Dieppe*. [...]

View from the train

All along the road — for the country was new to me — I sought where I could put my sickle. The pretty spirelet past Affray; the little church at Bonneville; the steeples between Caen and Bayeux; the quaint large pyramidal spire near Bernay; the bell-turreted church of Poissy; the charming wooden spire of Serquiny; the strange steeple between Longueville and Dieppe; the effective large spire-roofed tower near Mezidon; the tall spire in the wood between Serquiny and Elboeuf, are all full of suggestion, and, — thanks to my opera-glass and the slow travelling — are down in my sketch-book. Moral. — don't bury yourself in your newspaper or novel when you visit new countries.

The Manoir d'Ango, near Dieppe

Easily got at, this little quarry of brick, wood, and stone construction is doubtless known to some of your readers. Measured drawings of it there may be, but I have not had the good fortune to meet with anything but the flimsiest general view, badly drawn, and in the wrong perspective. The effect of time upon the flint, granite, and brick, has, in a colour point of view, done wonders for what, perhaps, when new was a trifle harsh, or, at least, sudden in contrast. Thus in the wall of the pigeon-house we see now a very large amount of dark-grey lichen where once a clearly defined black, and almost a glittering

Godwin, chimney at Manoir d'Ango.

Source:
'The manor-house of Ango, near Dieppe', *Building News*, 3 April 1874, p. 364

white, must have produced a dazzling chessboard effect. Nothing can surpass the subdued contrasts and quiet graceful harmonies of the work as it now stands; all the more interesting and artistically valuable for the framed timber barn which forms its nearest background. But the architectural gem of the Manoir D'Ango is not to be found in variety of brick and timber pattern, charming as they are. It is in the exquisite detail of the early Renaissance loge or loggia, situated just within the entrance gateway, and set askew on plan — just as people take pains in the hanging of pictures — in order that the visitor should at the first see the work from one of the best points of sight. Lest it might escape the observation of your youngest readers, I would direct attention to the way the arch mouldings are managed, just above the capitals or impost line. The effect, viewed from any point of the compass, is altogether satisfactory, and these are just the sort of things which are nearly always missed in modern work.

SELECTION OF STUDIES (1876)

The selection of a sketching ground is not always an easy matter to the architectural student. Even when the purse is long enough to compass all financial questions, it is not impossible for the young architect to make very grievous errors of selection. One of these errors consists in taking too high a flight. Some mighty minster is fixed on for our holiday study this year; next year it is a huge towering castle, the year after an episcopal or baronial palace, and so it comes to pass that much of even our leading architects' ordinary work is stilted, not to say affected. How often must it be repeated that the English architect's everyday work in these times is not to build castles or cathedrals? Indeed how very few there are who have experience, even genuine modern experience of palaces; for the bishop and the baron are not as a rule lodged now in palaces.

Modern requirements and modern society demand other exhibitions of the palatial than an architectural one. And yet, in spite of this the most commonplace wants of a very commonplace world are constantly being translated into extravagant, stilted, architecturally-Johnsonian, phrases. When it happens that we have a palace of art or palace of justice to build — palaces really palatial in character and purpose — we can go no further than we have already gone, having exhausted our powers of the palatial on linendrapers and licensed victualers. If however your connection is an influential one in high quarters you would do well not to neglect altogether the study of such buildings as cathedrals and palaces. The Italian Renaissance palaces sometimes very much reduced in scale, have supplied the architects of our London clubs with designs and details; they have also supplied the architects of insurance companies. To these structures we owe our Royal palaces called Buckingham and Osborne; we also owe to them the Manchester warehouse, the railway station, the vestry hall, and the public-house. The same general ordinance, the same detail, almost the same dimensions of door and window, may be found in the buildings here named, although erected for such diverse purposes. Our own mediaeval palaces at Wells, Westminster and Hampton, and the great French châteaus, especially that at Blois, have been well worked, and have

Brickwork, Manoir d'Ango.

Source:
'Scraps for students.—III. Selection of studies', *Architect*, 6 May 1876, p.285

Biographical notes:
Pecksniff

been used up indifferently for town and country houses, for guildhalls, alms-houses, and law courts. Even the Venetian palaces, built in a fashion peculiar to the city of the sea, a fashion which stood alone from all other mediaeval fashions, as it never moved beyond the precincts of the city that gave it birth, even these have been, so to say, dragged from their tombs to be mocked in London streets as insurance offices or restaurants.

If you think that you certainly will be called on constantly to design cathedrals and palaces, and such places as clubs, banks, town halls, law courts, and Government offices, which are all of the nature of palaces, it would be well to see what you can of the greatest and most important structures of Renaissance and Gothic art in Europe, not merely in your early student days, but every year even when in the full flood of professional engagement. But if, as is much more commonly the case, your architectural practise is likely chiefly to lie among schools, suburban villas, country houses, churches and chapels, you will be all the better for not crowding your mental art gallery with gorgeous pictures which can never be of any real service to you, but on the contrary only tend to make you an architectural caricaturist. The large number of sad examples of this course of study which London, Manchester, and nearly all our large towns exhibit is painfully depressing. Nor is this stiltiness by any means limited to the nobodies of the profession. There are men who take high, I may say the highest, rank, whose suburban villas are the offspring of baronial castles by palaces of justice, whose English hotels are nourished on foreign cathedrals and whose country houses are clothed in the second-hand toggery of the mighty town halls of mediaeval guilds. But you must be careful not to fall into the dangers of Scylla in steering clear of Carybdis [*sic*]. The impatience some artists have felt towards the stilted grandiose architect with his unbending and unbendable blank-verse compositions — blank verse for everything, for his letters and daily converse as well as for his high tragedies and comedies — has led to the opposite extreme, and there is therefore the danger of a reaction whereby the common-place brick and tile and wood construction — so admirably suited for the common-place — may also be pushed beyond its proper limits, and our palaces, guildhalls, clubs, banks, and such like be starved into the likeness of the country town inn, the manor place, and the farm house. Nevertheless, for *early* study it is these places you would do well to select. When occasion arises for you to design a large town hall or other important public building, there is always time for a few days' trip and a special study, if you require it.

To find the class of building to which I would direct your attention, you cannot have far to travel. The country town inn, the manor, and the farm house though not so plentiful as they were at the beginning of the century, are yet not so rare but that pupils or assistants of the most economical turn-of-mind may manage to reach them. Nevertheless students who live in a stone country, like Somersetshire or Yorkshire, must not expect to find close at hand the timber and tile of Cheshire or Sussex. Sometimes he may find stone and timber used in a free manner in the same town, as in Rouen and Caen; but he will not be long in either place before he finds out that in spite of its stonework

Godwin, sketch of church tower at Sompting, Sussex, BA 15 March 1878.

the first is essentially a timber city; and in spite of its woodwork, Caen is emphatically a stone town. So, too, Bristol and York are both rich in timber work, and yet they are decidedly stone-built. Were I a pupil at Leeds or Bradford, it would take a long time to tire me of York. The architectural food to be found in its narrow streets and back courts (I am speaking of ten years ago) is altogether nourishing and wholesome and very unlike the over-spiced rich dish which towers over everything in the city. I can conceive nothing more depressing in the way of sketching than to carry out in York the Pecksniffian order as touching Salisbury — to sketch its cathedral from every point of the compass. The huge building has its merits — what large old building has not? But apart from size all other merits must be searched out, for they are by no means so very apparent as people would have us think. My "pupil" reader in Bradford cannot do better than exhaust York, carefully avoiding the cathedral. He need not go out of his way to master the triple-horned leviathan in order to horrify the authorities and the public by a sort of ecclesiastical vivisection. The cathedral lives in popular favour, and by popular favour its gawdiness has outlasted many a better example of its own type and many a nobler specimen of a higher type of mediaeval art; so with an eye to business hereafter, young students should think twice before they disregard a popular prejudice, and be especially careful not to do violence to the art opinions of local dignitaries *in esse* or *in posse*, for the young architect may some day require the influence of the Rev. Mr. So-and-So when he becomes dean or bishop, or of busy Mr. — at the corner shop when he is graced with the chain of my lord or his worship, and the student's policy should be to steer clear of criticising either directly or indirectly their art leanings as he would the short measures of the one or the nasal intonations of the other.

In all your selections it should be remembered that the mediaeval revival having reached its limit, the future order of the day, if there is to be any order at all, will not be to blindly follow any given or past condition of architecture — Greek, Roman, Renaissance, or Gothic — but to follow ART. For this you will require an artist's training and not a stylemonger's. You must above all, as I said in my first article, learn to look, then to criticise; and by criticism I do not mean a volley of vituperation or an avalanche of ecstasy — the only two views of criticism possible to many people and especially to professed critics. When I ask you to criticise, I mean that before selecting a building for study you should weigh well the nature of its merits, and probe the depths of its failures or demerits. Of the site and its surroundings — their nature when the building was erected, their nature now — you should know and note. A house that might look wholly admirable in the narrow street of five or six yards width, for which it was designed, might very possibly look absurd in an open square, and contrariwise. In selecting subjects for study you may, also have already said, find towns with good examples of each of the three kinds of ordinary construction — stone, brick, timber. Yet, whenever you have the opportunity to see a town where one kind of construction has been so dominant as to have practically excluded the others, you should be careful not to miss it. If you wish to study stone architecture (it matters not in what style) take the West of

Godwin, drawing of brickwork at Someries Castle, BN *22 Jan. 1875.*

England and the valley of the Nene, the West of Normandy and the valley of the Loire for your chief hunting ground. Scotland, the border country, Yorkshire, and Ireland will teach you many things as touching the right and artistic uses of stone in building: I say *uses*, because there are many more ways than one of using stone; there is the Caen use, for example, and the Galway use, and the Veronese use; and between the extremely soft and the extremely hard many intermediate uses. If brick architecture is the object of your pursuit, the eastern counties, particularly Essex, may do much for you. Holland is not far off, and may be taken as a supplement to Essex. Indeed, for the later styles of building, such as the Renaissance of the eighteenth century, there are few towns in England which will not afford you some material. For timber construction go to Cheshire and Warwickshire, and after that to Lisieux and Rouen. You will find admirable examples in Kent, Surrey, Sussex, Shropshire, Suffolk and many other counties; but as Bayeux and Bath are cities of stone, so Lisieux, Coventry, and Chester are towns of wood, and in these towns you may select the most representative buildings from scores of examples. The student who has made up his mind as to the scene of his future practice or who may possess family influence in any special locality, had however better thoroughly grasp the natural and architectural characteristics of that locality, and do his best for its artistic development, than go wandering after fresh fields and pastures new. Of course if he has the ambition to live in London, to secure a general practice all over the island, reaching even across the Channels to Ireland and the Continent, and sometimes to the other side of the Atlantic or to India or Australia, then he would do well to go even further a-field than Europe. He might well extend his studies to Persia, Hindostan, Japan, China and Mexico. Life is, however, perhaps too short for any such extended study, and very glad am I that it is so, for I have a horror of what is called English enterprise when art matters are in question. Let us send what *material* we like abroad and receive in exchange what we can, but let us spare the nations of the earth the infliction of our architectural fads and archaeological art.

HOLIDAY TIPS FOR STUDENTS (1876)

For Ellen Terry the times spent in Winchelsea and Rye with Godwin were happy ones, and she chose to settle there permanently in later life.

Source:
'Scraps for students. —1',
Architect, 15 April 1876,
p.237

This week I venture to show you a way in which you can utilise your next holiday.

There are two towns not so far from the south coast but that the sea breezes can easily reach them, where few people go, and in whose streets you can draw and measure through the livelong day without attracting the notice of, or being incommoded by, any human being save a child who will speak of you and your work as if you were a being of another clime, and utterly unfamiliar with this island and its language. These towns are Winchelsea and Rye; each possesses a comfortable old-fashioned inn, and you may choose whichever you like for your headquarters. In Rye there is more chance for varied study, but

Winchelsea is perhaps of the two a cleaner and pleasanter place. Suppose, however, we sacrifice our bodily comforts a little and fix on Rye. To begin with, you will do well to make arrangements with the landlord of the inn or hotel; his usual charge is seven shillings a day — board, lodging and attendance — but he seems open to reason, and his notion of board embraces four, or at least three, meals a day, you may be able, by arranging for only two meals a day, to effect a considerable reduction. One or two Abernethy biscuits or a good crust of bread and cheese at midday, breakfast at eight o'clock, and dinner at seven will be generally found sufficient to keep the engine going. But do not miss midday sustenance. Your foot is not on the wild heather, you are not drinking the mountain air, and there are few things more exhausting than standing about in the narrow streets and back slums of an old town, trying to pierce the mysteries of, or concentrating your attention on accurately rendering by drawing and measurement its architectural examples. Before breakfast and for an hour or so after are the best times for the absolute handwork of outside drawing and measuring. The hot part of the day you can either devote to interior work or to *looking* quietly at the building you have drawn or intend drawing. To *look* well, is, I maintain, as important as to draw well. Glancing at things if they are at all worth looking at is little better than idling. The way in which your clever student in these express days will "do" a foreign town in order to hurry on to the next is, to my mind, a painful exhibition. You will learn far better how to master your craft by staying quietly in one small town than by scampering through a county. If you are preparing a treatise on the rise, progress, and decay of the cushion capital, it is altogether a different matter; the more examples you can bring from different places the better for your treatise; only remember distinctly and always that, however interesting and useful archaeology may be, it is not and never can be art. Thus at Rye, archaeologically speaking, the church dominates over everything else; but you had far better not go near it, unrestored as it is, if it is to distract you from the domestic work.

Planning a drawing campaign

My own way of working in an old town (i.e., if of moderate dimensions) is to perambulate it carefully first of all without using my pencil, except to note the position of any specimen of ancient art I encounter. And in this perambulation I never avoid taking advantage of open gates or doors to penetrate to the back court or garden. This is very essential, for there are towns like Bayeux of a dual character, almost wholly modern in their externals or street fronts, and as wholly mediaeval in their hind parts. The perambulation completed, every alley and lane examined, the next step to take is to select the fittest specimen for detailed study. And it is in this selection that the art of knowing how to *look* at a thing becomes so important. The colours of age, the accidental composition of angle and line which results from decay, things which are invaluable to the drawing master are often found to be dangerous temptations to the young architectural student. It is always a useful question to put to yourself when looking for the first time at an old work of art — "How would this look if it

179

were new?" For many a building that seems now pleasing enough with its overhanging roofs, uneven ridges, and so on, would be found stiff, gaunt, and, perhaps, absolutely ugly, if reproduced minus only its ruin. Now, at Rye we need not ask this question of every example, for half-way up the hilly street that leads from the quay to the church is a large deserted house of the sixteenth century with three overhanging gables towards the street, the front of which has been worthily prepared and re-edified, and the whole fabric isolated by the removal of a comparatively modern house. The repairs have been limited to the street front; the garden front and the interior being just in that happy state of half-ruin wherein the construction is laid bare, while the finished design and detail are yet sufficiently preserved for all purposes of architectural study. This house is almost entirely of timber construction, is planned in the form of the letter L, is quite devoid of anything like extravagant or even elaborate forms, and is of one character throughout; in fact, just the sort of house for a young student to study, from the scantlings of its angle posts to the finest moulding of the drawing-room door panels.

Assistance and equipment

And now comes the question — How had he best study it? Some students think it convenient to hunt up old buildings in couples. Two will sketch and measure up a house much quicker than one. But then it is doubtful whether either of them will understand the case so well as if each had done the whole of the work. The help of a companion who is *not* given to archaeology or architecture may, on the other hand, be of real service, but for all practical purposes a poor man on the spot to get ladders, to hold the tape, and to make himself generally useful is the best assistant a student can have. As to measuring instruments, it will be sufficient to take with you a 66-foot tape, and a 2-foot rule with bevelled edges for plotting to scale; rods and balls of twine can be generally found in the neighbourhood. I once, however, enjoyed the luxury of a walking-stick having a metal top which unscrewed and discovered two 5-foot rods with spring joints and divided into inches. I found these delicate rods very useful in measuring ruined buildings in remote country places. In towns, however, you can always get from a builder a roofing lath, which can be divided out into feet and half feet with V cuts made by your pocket knife, and rendered plainly visible by charcoal rubbed into the cuts. A large block book with metal square, and set square, or a small drawing-board, with some hot-pressed paper and pins, are all the appliances you need further have.

How to look

And now if you would rightly draw this Rye house for example. Begin by — *looking* at it. Go all round it and into it, pluck out the very heart of it. Probe it here, there, and everywhere, in a word, *understand* it as best you may before you put pencil to paper; and then when you have plotted or scribed or cymagraphed its last moulding full size, the mystery of it, if there be any, will be open to you. But if you proceed to take it up, as a draper's assistant would take up a roll of silk to measure it offhand, without looking to understand, it may very possibly happen, indeed it probably will happen, that measure as you may your drawings will never come right. There is a story told of Stonehenge that you can never count the stones twice and arrive at the same result both times; how far this is true I cannot say, never having tried it; but when I was a pupil, and ere yet I had learnt the value of *looking* well over a building before drawing it, I used to visit at a village in Wiltshire where was a very small but interesting and curious mediaeval house, of which I made at least six different sets of measured drawings, to find, always, that no two of them were alike. Old buildings are not always to be read off in the slap-dash style encouraged by some members of the architectural association. So if you wish to be faithful and accurate and to really understand the *modus operandi* of the past, take your time.

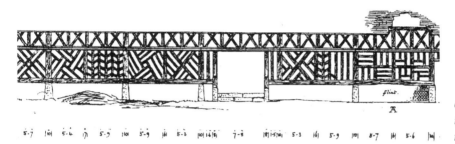

Godwin, measured drawings of timberwork at Manoir d'Ango near Dieppe, BN *27 Feb. 1874.*

Plotting measurements

It is not altogether hopeful when we see in perspectives of *new* buildings projections unaccounted for in the lines of the plan; as is the case in the published drawings of one of our popular church architects; but it is much more to be regretted when we see in the far more important drawings of *old* buildings similar discrepancies. The method of measuring I have usually adopted is — after a considerable time spent in examining my subject — to plot roughly to a small scale the general ground plan, dotting down on it all projections above the ground level, and to mark and measure doors and windows by their clear, and sometimes all by their extreme widths. Then to letter all the moulded angles or jambs and plot all the different ones to a large scale, or full size, if they are at all complex or peculiarly beautiful. This done a very few heights will generally enable you to make a rough elevation overnight, which next day you can fill up and explain by detail, always remembering that it is your *detail* which should hold imperial or paramount sway over general measurements. For if you are a few inches out in the length of the wing of a building, making say 20 feet 9 inches instead of 20 feet it is no very serious matter for you, but if you are careless in the section of your mouldings, making fillets coarser or hollows deeper or shallower than they really are, although only by a sixteenth of an inch, you had far better stay at home.

Measuring roof and arches

Among the chief difficulties you will have to encounter are those attending the measuring of roofs and arches. It is not always an easy matter to reach the ridge, but there is one plan you can always adopt if it is within a stone's throw, and that is to tie an ordinary penny ball securely to the end of a long light line, and after arranging the line in free open coils on the ground, throw the ball over the ridge. Now having got some one to observe when it reaches the eves on the opposite side you have only to strain the line to the base or ground level, and here mark it, for having the width and height of the walls already fixed, as well as the projection of the eves, there is only a little sum in subtraction from the line measurement to be done, and the position of the ridge is settled. The projection of the eves can be ascertained by letting out the line till the ball nearly reaches the ground, the line will thus act as a plumb-line, and you have only to find the distance the wall is from it to know the projection of the eves. The measurement of arches is not quite so easy.

OUT-DOOR SKETCHING (1876)

Source:
'Scraps for students.—II. Out-Door Sketching', *Architect*, 22 April 1876, pp.252-3

Biographical notes:
Prout
Pugin
Royal Academy

There are two vicious styles of sketching, both no doubt very attractive, over which mamma and the girls become so rapturous that the young architect may almost be excused for following them. One of these styles may be described as the *slap-dash*, the other as the *flick-and-dot*. PROUT and AUGUSTUS WELBY PUGIN were severally masters of these, and very happily for our art, there has not been a master in either since PROUT and PUGIN ceased. CONEY too, was strong in dots and doddering lines, carrying the viciousness of the style to its extremest limits. Most architects who have covered a great deal of ground in their "Continental tour" have brought home piles of *flick-and-dot* sketches. Mounted in frames or albums, with wide margins on delicately tinted paper, the little bits of vermilion or Antwerp blue on the foreground figures tell remarkably well in the sea of toned white paper which is called an architectural sketch. Very interesting are these sketches — as reminiscences. Do they not recall the free open-air jolly life we led there, or the dreamy quiet days among those half melancholy yet sweetly silent towns that lie far from the great highways of the world of commerce or of pleasure? Not less useful are they to put out on the library or drawing-room table when we endure the social penalty of "a few friends" for do they not serve as well as photos or chromos to engage the shy, the timid, and the awkward? But for all the architectural or art value they have been or ever will be to us, their authors, we might just as well have left the paper untouched, nay *better*, for has not the flick-and-dot way of looking at things infected to the core our own designs? We use forms and decoration that were the outcome of a certain system of construction, but this construction finds no favour with us, and of it we take no heed, for that worst of all possible reasons, because we have not really cared earnestly enough for our art to search into the rationale of it — the reason *why*.

Avoiding fudged drawing

Even in making measured sketches or drawings to scale the flick-and-dot should be guarded against. If there be a break in the stonework, if the timbers have started and the framing no longer meets, show it distinctly if it is desirable to show it at all A third kind of drawing to avoid is that ghostly, vague, undefined, and indefinable sketch, with memoranda and detail flying all around it, which we vainly suppose we can bring into its proper shape and consistency when we get home. I never knew an instance of this kind that was ever completed without fudging. And this process of fudging is one of the very worst snares that beset the path, or rather the drawing-board, of the young architect. He begins by fudging a sketch of some old building; then the perspective of his first competition, set up carefully, to begin with, from plans and elevations, does not somehow turn out as was expected; the tower looks broad and heavy, the spire weak and slim, the hipped roof low and squat, a turret he had hoped much from disappears altogether, the dormers have sunk into the roof, and so setting aside plan and elevation he fudges his perspective to his heart's content. This habit grows like every other one. When the young architect has got strong on the wing and commissions pour in on him, he indulges the appetite for fudging in the perspectives he makes or has made for his clients or the Royal Academy. If the perspective were made first or contemporary with the other drawings, and the latter made to accord with the former, then there would be no ground for the charge I bring here against the majority of Gothic architects, viz., that *they mislead the building world with cooked perspectives*. Thus arises the complaint so commonly heard from laymen — that the real buildings modern architects erect never look so well as the pictures of them. Let the student then be careful to avoid this fudging altogether at the outset, when he is, so to speak, his own employer. Whatever sketch or drawing he makes before an old building, let the work be done on the spot, be sacred to him, and let him never attempt to touch it away from the subject thereof.

Pencils and paper

Before we sit down to draw there is, however, a little preliminary which may as well be satisfactorily settled, and that is the choice of pencil and paper. First, as to paper, avoid extremes; the very rough and the very smooth are both objectionable. For the sake of an occasional bit of colour that you may find desirable to use in order to illustrate your subject properly it is as well to have a large block book of fairly rough paper, but the most useful for ordinary sketching is that which is moderately hot-pressed. Avoid cheap papers like *cartridge* or *continuous*; I have not found them conducive to sweetness of temper when a slight error has made it necessary to have recourse to that dangerous but sometimes necessary assistant the eraser or indiarubber. On the other hand there is not the slightest use in going in for such extravagance as to purchase the best and heaviest. Having secured your two books and two rolls of imperial (for you may require to plot larger drawings than the largest block book may admit) you have to select the pencil. The beautiful unpolished cedar pencils (I think they were BROADMAN'S that we used in my master's office) are not now to be had for love or money; they are unpolished cedar "pure Cumberland lead" and all the rest of it still in the market, but I have not yet discovered that they are worth the price charged for them. ROWNEY'S two-penny pencils are as good as any you can get, and if you mention to the shopman that you are an architect you get a liberal reduction on the cost of all your drawing materials. For the rough paper HH, and for the hot-pressed paper H, I have found in my experience to be the pencils best suited to my work. If you have a very heavy hand HHH and HH may suit you better, and if you have a very light hand H&F or HB may be more pleasant to work with. A small L-square is occasionally found useful in putting in long and parallel lines in the block-book sketch.

Scientific drawing of construction

And now your first care in making a measured sketch or drawing is to plot the chief constructional lines, and these oft-times you will utterly fail to do rightly until you have *mastered* the construction. Mediaeval groining, for example, will frequently demand much more *thought* than students are in the habit of giving before rib and impost can be accurately laid down on paper. Having mastered the main construction and drawn it, and you had far better content yourself with drawing a little thing that you *can master* than scramble through an apse or chevet over which even experienced and accomplished architects have come to grief, the next thing is to put in the detail. And here it must be remembered that the details of an old building, unlike the details of a modern structure, are mostly themselves constructional. So you will take great care with such things as the jointing of the stonework; only whilst you are careful to show all the joints in their proper thickness you need not mess your drawing by etching or scribbling over every other stone. Woodwork also need not be laboriously covered with wavy lines supposed to indicate

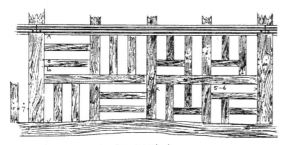

Godwin, drawing of timber construction at Manoir d'Ango, near Dieppe, Normandy, BN *27 Feb. 1874.*

the grain of the wood; a few light touches here and there, or at one end only of each separate piece of wood, are quite sufficient to indicate the material, and they have this advantage besides saving your time, that they leave the drawing clear and the jointing apparent. Lines on shafts to indicate their circular or polygonal section — and indeed all lines which are of the nature of shading — are by no means to be commended. For throughout your work it must always be borne in mind that your business is not — emphatically *not* — to make a pretty picture of an elevation or section. These, like the plan, are scientific diagrams, and should be treated scientifically. Not but that I have been guilty of the error I here condemn, for many a time I have been led away by the temptation to touch up the diagram, and have indulged in shaded elevations until I have almost thought them as good as perspectives, and nearly lost sight of the fact that an elevation is purely an architectural formula. It may, however, often be very desirable to indicate forms of solids shown only by mere boundary lines. In such cases as on round or clustered piers the plan or contour of the pier might be drawn on the elevation, and if these contour lines are put in very finely in red the value of the drawing is considerably enhanced. The fashion that obtains with a large proportion of young students of lining in or etching all openings, such as the unglazed arches of a cloister, is one that only adds to their labour, with the almost certain result of confusing the drawing. If you have a blank space in the elevation, you cannot do better than occupy it with some detail or explanatory perspective sketch. In drawing sections of mouldings and contour lies generally you would do well to avoid that vicious practice now so common of marking them with a thick black line. I have seen such drawings where the line or black shading has been so evenly drawn that it was hardly possible to tell to which side of the line the solid belonged. Cross hatching for sectional lines, if very finely done, is pretty but laborious work, and although colour in pale tint is best, the black should be adopted if you want to reproduce your drawings by any of the cheap processes, such as photolithography; only take care that the inner edge of the black is sufficiently broken or jagged to prevent confusion.

Rapid sketching in the pocketbook

There are many things one sees in the course of a long visit to a town, or indeed as one travels by road, boat, or even rail, that it is sometimes well to make a note of. For this purpose I always carry with me a good fair size metallic pocket-book (PERRY'S is the best). It has, I understand, disadvantages, from an artistic point of view, but there are two advantages attached to it. One is that your sketch will not rub or wash away, and the other is that as there is no opportunity for the operation of the indiarubber you are not likely to begin sketching without thoroughly knowing what you are about to do. It is in a book of this kind we can best store up the many suggestive compositions we see in travelling that are not sufficiently instructive to induce a special visit. Thus the few minutes' pause at way-side stations, so often the cause of restlessness and grumbling in others, may be turned to our benefit if we will only keep our eyes open. To be quick to seize the salient features of a building, or part of a building, and to jot them down with tolerable accuracy, is a faculty worth encouraging: at the same time you should know when and when not to put it into practice. For this faculty of rapid sketching too often induces carelessness, if not laziness, in regard to the more important study involved in detailed measurement and plotted drawing. In towns where the buildings are so notorious as to have attracted the attention of the public photographer it is a great waste of time to make general views of such celebrated structures. By measuring up one bay, and by expending a few shillings on photographs the young student will learn more of a cathedral than by making general views of it from every point of the compass. I know how it is said that the value of sketching is not so much in the drawing itself as in the act of looking involved by it, and that most young men never properly see a building until they have made half-a-dozen sketches of it. This may be; but if the student having eyes to see won't see till the necessities of his hand compel him the sooner he retires from architecture the better for our art.

Godwin, rapid sketches in Paris reproduced in BA *1 July 1881.*

185

BRUGES AND OSTEND (1878)

Source:
'Notes on current events', *The British Architect*, 5 July 1878, p.2

NOT content with a spick and span restoration of their Gothic Town Hall the good people of Bruges have seized the small Renaissance building to the left of it and are rapidly wiping out every old and valuable touch. Restorers are bad enough when they attack the village church, but when they fly at such noble game as the town halls of the middle ages of which so few remain, it almost makes us hold opinion with Pythagoras that souls of animals (at any rate the wolf and the ass) infuse themselves into the trunks of men.

A CURIOUSLY picturesque town is Bruges, but its chief merit, or what ought to be its chief merit in the eyes of architectural students, is the lesson it teaches on the value of masses of simple unadorned brickwork when well proportioned. The west end of St. Jacques is little more than a pile of brick, with square set buttresses finishing as octagonal turrets, all of the plainest description, but proportioned with such a sense of dignity that it satisfies the critical eye and makes one almost unconscious of the few square yards of weak tracery that does duty as a window.

House dated 1477, Place Jean van Eyck, Bruges, BN 21 Jan. 1876.

THE new Kursaal at Ostend, lately opened by the king of the Belgians, is a compromise between a locomotive shed and a beehive. The general idea of the plan is good and well adapted to the purpose, but the detail, like all the detail in Ostend, is meretricious, vulgar, debased.

A NEW corner house on the Digue with ambitious elevations and octagonal tower is even worse, with its trumpery dolls imitated from Michael Angelo's tombs of the De Medici. The architect of this work is A. Mennessier, and he is evidently proud of his achievement for he has affixed his name to it in a very prominent place.

OSTEND does not possess a single architectural merit, for even the old church has been altered until it has lost every beauty it may once have had.

AMSTERDAM: PICTORIAL EFFECTS AND HORRIBLE STENCHES (1878)

Source:
'Notes on current events', *The British Architect*, 19 July 1878, p.28

If anyone wants to study Dutch architecture he should avoid the large towns, and keep to such places as Haarlem and Alkmaar. Amsterdam is full of pictorial effects, horrible stenches, high prices, dirt, and inconveniences but no architecture worth a moment's notice in comparison with that at Haarlem, Alkmaar, or Deventer. In these country places, houses, streets, canals, and people are sweet and clean. The bells are not so discordant, and the huge wooden rattles not so frequent as in the narrow, ill-kept, ill-governed thoroughfares of the capital of Holland.

A NEW RESTAURANT IN PARIS (1881)

Presumably during the course of a leisurely meal, Godwin penned this analysis of his surroundings.

The *Lion d'Or* is the sign of a new restaurant in the Rue Helder, close by the Boulevard des Italiens. It is a novelty in Paris, being designed and fitted in the style Henri II. The plan is shown in sketch A, being an open court filled with plants and fountains, and B a side room not so rich in character as the main salon. In this latter the construction *appears* to be of wood, the windows and screens are wide and lofty and filled with greenish-toned roundels, the ceilings show joists of brown wood, edged with gold, crossing from back to front, and supported midway by a beam, which in its turn is supported by carved wood posts. The blank walls are covered with boldly designed tapestry, except only a low panelled dado. The tables, chairs, and furniture generally are in the same style, which is carried into the blue and greenish white dinner service, the greenish glass, the black-handled knives, the table cloths, with their open work and fringe, the napkins, the rich carpet, and even the hand-made Dutch paper on which your dinner bill is made out. The completeness of the idea is the chief merit, for the carrying out of the details is in many respects inartistic and clumsy, thus the carving in the façade is very badly designed and has a sham look about it; the stained glass — a plaque of blue with a gold lion on it, set in each window-light — is worse than a caricature, and indeed the drawing of the lion throughout, from the paltry-looking signboard to the powderings on the blue spaces between the joists in the ceilings, is stupid and weak, instead of being quaint and strong.

Source:
'Notes on current events', *The British Architect*, 1 July 1881, pp. 328-9

Godwin, sketches in the Lion d'Or, Paris.

PICTURESQUE ORDER IN COPENHAGEN (1884)

If ever you want a short sea trip, you might do well to pay Copenhagen a visit. Not so much for its architecture, which is of little account, ancient or modern, do I recommend this town, as for a certain characteristic which will soon be revealed to you, whether you walk through the town, streets, or the country roads, or skirt the coast in the steamer that plies to Elsinore. This characteristic is the systematic order that underlies the picturesque. In the larger cottages of ground floor and attic, in the farmsteads, in the castles or palaces this order or rhythm is preserved. [...] The central dormer of the cottage is developed in the farmhouse to a large gable, either springing from a higher level than the roof eaves or projecting slightly. But of all the projecting features, the most delightful are the towers and the tall bay windows that assume the form of low towers; and these the castles illustrate in no sparing manner.

Another feature worth your noting is that on roofs of any importance as to size, the main dormers are not the small, unimportant things known in modern architectural practice, but notes — semi-breves, or, indeed, breves — in the composition, which give immense dignity to the design, for their ridges rise to within a few feet of the main ridge, and they often include in their height two, and sometimes as many as three storeys. The facades of the Castle

Source:
'To art students. Letter no. 4', *The British Architect*, 30 May 1884, p. 262

of Kronborg, close to the town of Elsinore, exhibit the value of these noble dormers in a grandly simple way, the only drawback to one's enjoyment being in the continual regret that the architects of modern times cannot or will not avoid the disturbance and fussiness which are almost always present in their works, and found their designs more on those principles of order and bigness which we find at Kronborg, and, in a less degree, at Rosenberg and Fredensborg.

Since I have been here I have not had the annoyance of seeing one modern attempt to vulgarise these sixteenth and early seventeenth century castles by applying their features in a more or less degraded form to buildings of a very much smaller scale *e.g.*, the suburban villa. Had they been in England we should have had their angle towers degraded into pepper-box turrets, scarcely big enough for a flue, and their dormers dwarfed to the dimensions of a dog's-house. This reminds me of a certain rectory or vicarage house in Cornwall, where the occupant, being more or less poetical, and independent of all trammels and order (except such as he had a mind to) conceived the brilliant idea of rebuilding all his chimney stacks in the likeness of all the neighbouring church towers of which he could obtain drawings. The dining-room chimney was a tiny caricature of Probus Tower, the drawing-room was a ridiculous travesty of Launceston, and so on. Had this man been an architect he would have given us St. Michael's Mount, rocks and all, as the roof or covering of a tower 20 feet square, and, mark you, would have only been carrying out to its logical conclusion the principles on which much of your modern design is founded.

MR FAGAN'S CARAVAN (1881)

One way of avoiding poor hotels! Louis Fagan was a friend of Godwin and involved in the Costume Society.

Source:
'Notes on current events', *The British Architect*, 8 July 1881, p. 340; 9 September 1881, p. 448

To take a man with a horse and van, and to get leave from the owners of large parks to live among the ferns during July and August, is not a bad way of getting fresh air and quiet.

Mr. Fagan's van or land yacht is finished, and the private view drew together the few art-representative men who happened to be in town. Hospitably entertained by Mr. Bailey, the well-known wagon builder, they lingered over their cigars in pleasant chat till the afternoon was well advanced. The van is strongly, yet lightly built of oak and mahogany, is delightfully fitted up, and reflects great credit on the designer and builder.

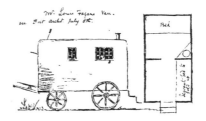

VIII My Houses in London

IN 1876 GODWIN published two remarkable series, the first on the decoration and furnishing of his London chambers from 1867, and the second on the house at 20 Taviton Street to which he moved with Ellen Terry and their two young children in 1874. The articles convey a vivid sense of the experimental and continually reflexive way in which he explored different ways of working and of living, and taken together, provide a unique record of these influential schemes and of his radical approach to interior design. This is Godwin at his most charming – erudite, witty and practical – offering comprehensible advice for those on a limited budget, while relating interior design to Aesthetic idealism and issues that reverberated outside the context of the home. During the emotionally turbulent but intensely creative years with Terry, his thinking on many themes – unity of the arts, synaesthesia, furniture and wallpaper design, the poetic use of colour, painted decoration, and the role of the artist as taste-maker – all coalesced into a coherent design philosophy (see Chs II, IX, X, XII).   The furnishings that he designed for his own use were to provide prototypes for commercial production, and the subject of further articles and illustrations up to the time of his death. His design sources reflect an eclectic sampling of different periods and cultures that, by the time of writing, had come to typify Aesthetic taste: modern 'art' furnishings blended with eighteenth-century furniture and second-hand carpets; oriental ceramics, textiles and printed ephemera; and the occasional vernacular item creeping into the mix. As pieces of writing, the innovative style and format of these series pioneered a new genre of 'through-the-keyhole' design journalism. Within a few years the formula was rapidly taken up throughout the fashionable and architectural press, with a flood of articles and interviews on the theme of the artist or celebrity 'at home'.

Like the majority of middle-class householders, Godwin rented his properties in London and therefore focussed his creative energies on the transformation of the interiors. A concentration on the domestic followed moves within design reform circles to break down the traditional hierarchy of arts, and demonstrated that this sphere could attract the highest level of aesthetic thought and sophisticated design. Moreover the reform of one's domestic surroundings went to the core of the issue about how to cultivate the senses. At home, Godwin clearly did not have to compromise his leaning towards pure joyous colour under pressure from 'apostles of the tertiary creed' (see p.193) and could control the way in which his art manufactures were collated. Given his awareness that such products took on a new life of their own when despatched to unknown destinations, the very act of writing about his interiors can be seen as an attempt to extend that control to the way the public encountered and responded to his work. By example Godwin educates the reader in art appreciation and spatial awareness, demonstrating how to analyse interiors using their common-sense, but also how to tune into atmosphere, emotion and sensation. The descriptions quiver with his heightened receptivity as he draws our attention to the smell of incense at one moment and boiled broccoli the next, to the sound of piano music or traffic on the street, and to the 'sticky-to-the-touch feel' of serge curtains in a polluted urban environment.

Godwin appears before the reader simultaneously as designer and consumer, presenting his interiors as the manifestation of an individual, cultured sensibility. He describes a disciplined process of selection, reordering and manipulation of the elements at his disposal — shunting furniture around in his own home between rooms, changing a wallpaper here, a colour there. In other words, interior design is presented as an exercise in artistic rather than formulaic composition, a process of constant adjustments towards achieving an overall balance and harmony in these three-dimensional, walk-through works of art. Yet while the interiors are highly individualistic, Godwin carefully avoids alluding to them as a form of autobiographical narrative; once items or finishes have outlived their usefulness, they are discarded without sentimentality. He confirms his attack on social norms through undermining the conventional coding of particular room-types. In particular he explicitly plays down the stark contrast between a dark, heavy, 'masculine' dining room, and a light, refined, 'feminine' drawing room as advocated by commentators such as Robert Kerr.[1] Godwin's schemes were designed to choreograph modern forms of lifestyle, manners, and gender relations.

[1] See Kerr, *The English Gentleman's House*, 1864, p.119.

In a world of unsettled habits, and movement from one place to another, there was a need for stability, and Godwin set out to shape the environment of the home into 'quiet, simple, unobtrusive' beauty (p.294). Godwin cuts through the suffocating accumulation of 'things' and signs of conspicuous excess to be found in more conventional middle-class interiors. The paring down of room contents and the lightweight design of the furniture create space in which the inhabitants, 'the actors', can freely move. He describes how the structural framework of his sideboard had been reduced to a minimum, for example, in order to facilitate cleaning and its movement in the event of a change being required. In fact the first version, constructed in cheap deal, was so light it fell to pieces. The delicacy of the colour schemes and scaffolding transparency of the furniture were dramatically different from the earlier art furniture of figures like Burges or Morris, let alone the more conventional furnishings of the middle-class home. The transformed domestic environment was not to become a retreat into medieval fantasy or claustrophobic, neurotic introspection. The harmonious, playful but often fragile balance of elements described in these articles highlights the inherent instability of interiors as three-dimensional entities. Indeed by the time of writing, only two years after moving in to Taviton Street, the rooms had been virtually cleared by bailiffs. (Godwin had also left Terry, moved house and married his eighteen-year-old pupil Beatrice Philip!)

In criticising the worst excesses of middle-class taste these articles followed the format of Eastlake's widely read *Hints on Household Taste* (1868), and an increasingly familiar 'before' and 'after' formula, while at the same time pioneering a novel kind of voyeuristic journalism. What distinguished Godwin's articles was the carefully constructed intimacy of their tone and the way they opened the recesses of his *own* home to the public gaze, challenging the self-contained privacy of the domestic ideal. These were not interiors discussed in the abstract, or at one remove. As an omnivorous reader, Godwin had recognised the power of the popular novel as a potential medium for instruction and psychological insight on matters of household taste (see pp. 270f.). In these articles he deliberately adopts the format of the serialised novel, developing a narrative structure, using 'chapter' titles, and building up anticipation towards the next instalment. It is quite possible that he intended to follow the practice of literary magazines in collating and publishing these series in book form.

From the start his tone establishes a 'dear reader' sense of intimacy and complicity with his audience. We climb the flights of narrow stairs from the front door of his chambers behind him, vicariously experiencing his first impressions. At Godwin's side we trudge the streets of Bloomsbury and Westminster in search of an affordable property with 'potential'. Over the series on 'My house "in" London' we tour the house room-by-room, from basement to attic, including spaces to which even the most intimate friend would not normally have gained access. The final article in the series effectively relates the experience of domestic interiors to the wider urban environment, and to issues of urban planning and environmental legislation. From the enclosed intimacy of the nursery and servants' attic-rooms, we emerge out onto the rooftop, to look through Godwin's binoculars over the surrounding cityscape. Such changes of scale and focal distance keep the reader's attention, just as on a single page in one of his sketchbooks, the detailed description of a doorhandle is juxtaposed with the section of an entire house. Godwin's view swivels round to a set of 'mansions in the sky' and he reflects on the empowering effect of the panoramic view that effectively miniaturises these colossal developments, containing them within the lens of his field-glass. For a moment he homes in on the disorder of 'sundry odds and ends' normally obscured from view – a flagstaff, a rotatory fan on a tripod, and fragments of large galvanised iron boilers. It is this ability to capture such fleeting impressions and incidental detail, rendering the familiar strange, that seems to encapsulate the modernity of his outlook.

Unless otherwise indicated the illustrations in this chapter are drawn from Godwin's designs for William Watt's *Art Furniture* catalogue published in 1877, the year after these articles were written (see p. 295). Many of these items were designed originally for his own use.

Further Reading

S. Soros, 'E. W. Godwin and interior design', in Soros 1999, pp. 185-223

C. Gere and L. Hoskins, *The House Beautiful. Oscar Wilde and the Aesthetic Interior*, Aldershot, 2000

L. Lambourne, *The Aesthetic Movement*, London, 2000

See also Further Reading under Ch. X Artists' Houses, Ch. XII Fashionable Aesthetic Taste, and Ch. XII Art Manufactures.

MY CHAMBERS, AND WHAT I DID TO THEM (1876)

Godwin had established a London office in 1865, leaving Henry Crisp to manage the Bristol end of the partnership. Two years later he moved from 23 Baker Street to 197 Albany Street in Regent's Park, the property described in the articles that follow. While retaining these chambers as his architectural office, the focus of his domestic life with Ellen Terry became the Red House near Harpenden in Hertfordshire. Despite their straitened circumstances, the improvident couple soon embarked on the building of a new house, Fallow's Green, also in Harpenden.

CHAPTER I. A.D. 1867

Source:
'My chambers and what I did to them. Chapter I: A.D. 1867', *Architect*, 1 July 1876, pp.4-5

They were not bad chambers by any means. It was a long way up, and over and above the physical exercise of mounting three flights of stairs three times repeated, there was the far greater fatigue of monotony; and yet, trying as all this often was, I am not at all sure but that it was fully balanced by the advantages of being a little more removed from the street noises than the floors below me, to say nothing of the view and air secured owing to my windows topping the roof levels on the other side of the way. The plan or arrangement of the rooms was somewhat after this fashion. I had two rooms (drawing and dining-rooms) in front, a bedroom on one side, at the back; servant's room, kitchen, &c., on the other side; and between these two was the lobby or hall opening onto the general staircase. Every room was well lighted, and my entrance lobby or hall, as well as the side or kitchen passage, were well lit by the light which came through a continuous sash above the door-head level from the staircase. The little side passage I found invaluable, as it completely shut off the kitchen and the servant's bedroom. Another great advantage I found was that by rigging-up a movable door and door-frame in my lobby, and a small sofa-bed in one of the front rooms, I could sub-let my bedroom and dining-room in the season for an amount almost equivalent to my whole annual rent. The absence of a bath-room was a decided drawback, and in the summer I often grumbled at the somewhat cabinned incomplete arrangements with regard to larder, pantry, and so on, which were too much of the nature of hanging cabinets, but, drawbacks fully considered, I repeat they were not bad chambers by any means.

What to do with the walls?

When I entered on their occupation, I found a crimson flock paper on the walls of the dining-room, where the windows looked south-west. In the drawing-room there was a satin paper of a yellowish ground whereon emerald green and orange red bouquets were drawn up in rank and file. The bedroom, which looked to the north-east, had of course (most bedrooms have) a cold paper, a blue lattice on a very light ground. Of course, none of this was endurable, and the first artistic question — what to do with the walls — arose *with all its importance* before me. [If the printer could only manage to print these italicised words in red they might be a little suggestive of the emphasis I wish to put on them.] I confess even now to some trepidation in choosing a colour for a room.

Personally, I might go so far as to acknowledge that I like certain yellows of a tone akin to old satin wood; that light red or Venetian red brightened by white and pure, or nearly pure, white itself are favourites with me. Professionally, I have of course to assume a gloomier style, for the apostles of the tertiary creed, the devotees of madder, brown, and terra verte are strong in numbers and loud in talk, and my little personal weakness for combining simplicity and delicacy and purity of colour is apt to be snubbed and even ignored by the very advanced young artists of the day who I am constantly meeting in studio or club. So at the outset of my work of decorating and furnishing I find myself in a quandary. My artistic friend — only one letter removed from LAUNCELOT GOBBO'S familiar* — at my elbow, tempted me to run after dirty light-absorbing greens, with the pattern printed in duller green. My conscience said "No; take heed!" But on turning to follow the counsels of my conscience, I found nothing but disappointment. I went to the painter stainer's works; I dropped in at every shop I passed where papers were exhibited; and I turned over patterns by the thousand. There was plenty of bright colouring, but I could not find it anywhere combined both with simplicity and delicacy or refinement. In a word, wherever a wall paper was bright, it was more than a thousand chances to one that it was crude. Under this stress of circumstances I had recourse to a house distinguished then, and which has since has become very distinguished indeed for its artistic "tone." Here I had a choice only of five papers, each of which was printed in two ways — *viz.* as dark and light. The more expensive papers were naturalistic in drawing, colour, and to a certain extent in shade, the others were conventional — a small square diaper, printed both in green and yellow, and a meandering pattern printed also in two ways — blue and yellow. I confess that even to this day these two small conventional patterns appear to me to rank as *patterns* among the most satisfactory wall papers England has produced. It is no detraction to say that the meandering pattern is a copy, or close adaptation from one, on an old Italian box or chest. The quick appreciation that prompted the copy or the adaptation, though not so deserving of credit as the artistic power of the original designer, has nevertheless claims on our admiration and gratitude; for, at the advanced age to which the world has reached, nearly all new designs must be sought more or less in adaptation and combination of existing natural form or of older designs. At the same time there is no absolute need to copy, for the power of conventionalising natural form is hardly capable of limitation. The fifteenth and sixteenth century patterns of Western Europe abundantly prove what wealth can be got out of one digging. Japanese work sufficiently proves that these riches are not confined to one groove, and that there is no need to work in the same mine.

But to return to my chambers —

I had now to arrange my walls and wall papers. And first of all I determined that as the rooms were ten feet high I would cut off the upper part of the walls by a band or string of wood, into which one could easily, and without help, screw brass hooks for hanging picture, tapestry, &c. This band I decided to carry through every room and passage at one and the same height. This for

* Gobbo was Shylock's clownish servant in *The Merchant of Venice.*

193

Godwin, wallpaper design.

Biographical notes:
Pugin

two reasons, firstly, because the height at which I placed it was within my reach, and, secondly, because when the doors were open there would be a sensation of greater space by maintaining an uniform level than by chopping up the level, now making it higher and then lower according to the nature and size of the room. The band itself was $3^{1}/_{2}$ inches broad and half an inch thick; the top of it had a moulding projecting altogether about 2 inches, with a groove on the top, so that it formed a ledge for brass dishes, plates &c. The top of this band, string, or ledge was 6 feet 9 inches from the floor, so that I could easily remove things on the ledge without getting on a chair or troubling to get steps. The skirting being 9 inches high, and the cornice 6 inches, the wall was thus divided into flat spaces of 5 feet $8^{1}/_{2}$ inches, and 2 feet 9 inches high respectively. Had the upper part been more, there would have been some risk of the walls *appearing* as if equally divided, which has always a bad effect. And here I may remark, that to divide a wall by a band placed *exactly* half way up has not by any means a bad effect, for the lower half being encumbered by furniture the upper part has invariably the *appearance* to the eye of being *more than half*, and the general effect is that of a high dado, rather pleasingly proportioned than otherwise.

In arranging my wall papers I selected a dull green diaper of small squares for the lower part of the walls in *both* sitting rooms and entrance lobby. Over the band in the lobby I left the wall unpapered, colouring it a sort of creamy white. Over the band in my principal sitting-room or drawing-room, as it is commonly called, I used a rich pattern of branches of fruit covering a toned white ground, and in my dining-room a trellis pattern of roses and birds, also on a light ground. For the bed-room I adopted the meandering conventional Italian paper in yellow below the band, and a somewhat formal flower pattern on a white ground above. Having settled these things, another important question arose — What should be the colour of the woodwork in the several rooms? Now I have always had a great horror of what is called "picking out;" I am not enamoured of the details of joinery, and I have never seen anything yet in a four or six-panel door, a shutter or a skirting, that I should wish to emphasise or see developed beyond the already pronounced development of their construction. I therefore selected plain colours, using cream white for the drawing-room and lobby, a dark green for the dining room, and a pale golden brown for the north-east bedroom.

Furnishing fabrics

When I came to the window and *door* curtains — for in this country where at least two-thirds of the year is winter *portieres* are almost a necessity — my troubles began afresh. Go where I would, neither in pattern, colour nor material, could I find anything altogether suitable. There were blue and yellow chintzes to be had where we got the papers, but to me they never seemed satisfactory either as to material or pattern. Then, too, there were serges in blue and green and red well-toned, but serge in London, no matter how admirable its colour, is such a dust-holding grimy-to-the-touch sort of fabric that, suitable as the colours were to the wall papers that had been selected, I could not reconcile myself to the feel of them. At last, after much search, I found in a house in Tottenham Court Road an old chintz of a flower pattern on a parchment-coloured ground. It had been put aside as a thing long out of date, and the shopman smiled quite pityingly when he understood how that was the sort of thing I wanted. This then I adopted for the drawing-room, the easy chair cushions and sofa being covered with the same. I could not find anything for the dining-room that was at all reasonable in price, except a damask designed or adapted from a fifteenth century conventional pattern many years ago by AUGUSTUS WELBY PUGIN. The colour was not good in itself, nor did it quite fit in with those already selected for the room, but by spreading out the stuff in the sun whenever one had the opportunity there ensued by the process of fading a change which, if it could have been arrested at a certain point would have given a tone as satisfactory as one could desire for the position and the circumstances. But unfortunately it could not be so arrested! (My curtains were hung by small rings to small brass rods of 1-inch iron tubing coated with brass, and pretty knob ends. I have seen many a room utterly ruined by the use of coarse wood curtain rods, and rings strong enough to suspend a bullock!)

Floors

Regarding fluff and dust in rooms as two of the great enemies of life, it was a matter of conscience to have the carpets sufficiently small and free to be easily removed for beating. In one room — the dining-room — the margin of the floor to the extent of three feet was stained and varnished. [Varnishing floors is altogether a mistake, when they could be beeswaxed; but I am speaking of 1867, when, although you ordered beeswaxing, it by no means followed that it would be done.] In this room there was a square, or nearly square Turkey carpet, the border of which was entirely free of the wall furniture, such as buffet, book-cases, cabinets, &c. Of course the carpet was *secondhand*. I say *of course*, because it would have been next to impossible to have found any Eastern fabric, especially a Turkey carpet, that would not have been far too rich and bright, when *new*, for the general tone, or scheme of colour adopted for the walls. On the drawing-room floor I had three Persian rugs, a large skin, and two pieces of Eastern matting, the *whole* of the flooring boards being stained and varnished. A large cheap rug nearly filled my lobby, and the bedroom floor was left bare except a rug at the side of the bed and two Eastern mats.

Furniture and ceramics

When I came to the furniture, I found that hardly anything could be bought ready made that was at all suitable to the requirements of the case. I therefore set to work and designed a lot of furniture, and, with a desire for economy, directed it to be made of deal, and to be ebonised. There were no mouldings, no ornamental metalwork, no carving. Such effect as I wanted I endeavoured to gain, as in economical building, by the mere grouping of solid and void and by a more or less broken outline. The scantling or substance of the

Godwin, wardrobe design.

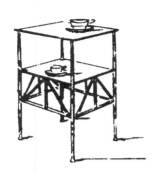

Godwin, design for coffee table.

Godwin, wicker chair design.

framing and other parts of the furniture was reduced to as low a denomination as was compatible with soundness of construction. This seemed desirable for two reasons — firstly, for economy's sake in making, and, secondly, for economy in cleaning. For by making all the furniture, the large pieces as well as the small, as light as they could well practically be, there was no particular effort required to move them either for the purposes of cleanliness or in the event of a change being desirable. Indeed, I found by experience that no man or extra servant was ever required, and that I could with ease, single handed, shift the whole of the furniture from one room into the next. All the furniture for the dining-room I designed specially, but I found deal to be a mistake, and had very soon to get rid of it, and have a new lot made of mahogany, also ebonised and decorated with a few gold lines in the panels. Since then my buffet, coffee table, and chair with cane back and seat, have been freely made, nor can I see wherein I can, to any very great extent, improve them as examples of cheap furniture. For the drawing-room I picked up two spindle-leg tables, got four Japanese cane armchairs from Baker Street, two porcelain seats, some tall vases on the floor, and, as I cannot live without music, I spoilt a really light and pretty effect by introducing that conventional lump of pretentious [...] ugliness, a modern piano. Some time after I found it not such a difficult matter to alter the ordinary piano case in such a manner as to render it so far from displeasing that it should at least not be out of harmony with its surroundings.

My bookcases I never much liked; bookcases never are satisfactory. The cabinets, on the other hand, were nearly as affective as the buffet; they, however, were rather expensive and as far as I know have never been repeated. I believe, nevertheless, its design was founded, as all designs for inexpensive furniture should be, on utility, and that it only required a little attention to have rendered it generally acceptable. It was a three-storeyed structure: the lower-most storey was devoted to a nest of drawers or trays for drawings, photographs, seals, &c., enclosed by folding doors; the upper floor had two shelves for books, enclosed also by doors; and the intermediate division was mostly of glass for the display of curios. Practically the end doors were often in the way, and although the four-square panels in each, filled with figures and other decoration in gold outline, were vastly superior to any combination of drawers, yet there is no doubt that from the utilitarian or modern point of view it was a nuisance to go through the process of unlocking one door, unbolting a second, and pulling out a tray every time one wanted to refer to a drawing. I can see now how capable of improvement it was, and how easily it might yet be done at a considerable reduction in cost.

Fenders and fire-irons were of brass. There were circular mirrors of various sizes on the walls, and a very large one flanked by sconces over the mantelshelf in each room. In and round the buffet a certain golden atmosphere was attained by the use of different yellows. Besides the gold lines on the panels there were a large round brass tray in the shadow, a large imperial yellow jar, two smaller yellow jars from Cannes, a bit of Chinese gold embroidery on yellow satin, and some yellow-green plates.

The bedroom furniture was exceedingly plain. The bedstead was of brass, very low, without any canopy, and the posts were alike devoid of taper or any other so-called ornament. My wardrobe was a compound design — half chest of drawers and half hanging wardrobe — and, like the trouser patterns of some years ago, required a pair to show the complete design. The wash-hand-stand was a poor sort of thing — a weak invention, like every wash-hand-stand that I have ever seen — and my dressing-table and glass which formed a part of it were not much better. The dressing-table and the wash-hand-stand of the period have to be designed, or at any rate if designed have yet to be made public. A light hanging bookcase, the best and cheapest thing I ever designed, and some Sussex chairs completed my bedroom furniture. Scarcely was everything settled and in order than I became conscious some huge mistake or mistakes had been made. No matter what the weather or what the time, the dining-room had always a touch of sadness in it. Even when the white cloth was on the table and vases were bright with flowers, after I had fixed up opalescent glass in the windows and saw all the colour of the place softened through clouds of Japanese incense, there still remained an effect which was unquestionably saddening in its influence. The cause of this effect, and the several changes I made in order to remedy it, will be considered in the next chapter.

Godwin, bookcase design.

CHAPTER II. A.D. 1872: CURING MELANCHOLY

Changing the wall paper

It was some years before I could find out what it was that made my dining-room look so melancholy. At first I thought it must be due to one thing and then to another, for it never occurred to me at that time that it might be owing to a variety of things. I began by fancying that the trellis pattern paper above and the square green diaper below did not work well together. So I sacrificed the trellis and substituted for it the light fruit pattern that I had already adopted in the adjoining room, where, although the effect was not absolutely exhila-rating, neither was it absolutely depressing. When, however, the freshness of the change had worn off I found the room drifting rapidly back to its old sad look. Again I had the upper part of the walls stripped, but instead of repapering it the plaster was merely coloured in distemper, the same tone as the ceiling — a creamy white. This was a great relief, so great indeed that I congratulated myself on having extirpated my enemy. I have since seen many rooms papered with an upper and a lower paper, and in no case have they appeared wholly satisfactory. It is now a general thing for decorators to indulge their customers not merely with two but with three papers — for dado, wall, and frieze — and the result is that we are so very much over-papered and over-patterned that it is a real pleasure to know some one in Bloomsbury or Westminster whose rooms have wood dados and plaster friezes, where the monotonous pattern of the paper, if there is any, is sure to be limited to one design and one division of

Source:
'My chambers and what I did to them. Chapter II. A.D. 1872', *Architect*, 8 July 1876, pp.18-19

the wall space. But the plain light wall also grew in time somewhat oppressive; the fact was there was too much of it, but this I entirely remedied with the help of a few Japanese-painted crape hangings placed at intervals. I may add that a similarly successful result might ensue from a fitting disposition of Japanese fans. From that day to this I have never had a better wall or frieze decoration than that of the Japanese hangings. Strange to say, however, the room largely improved as it was, continued true to its original melancholy expression.

Cheering up the colours

I was getting a little hopeless about the whole thing, when one fine sunny morning (sunshine, by the way, is often more melancholy than shade if your colours are not *en rapport* with *light*), a man I but slightly knew called on me. He was a blunt outspoken doctor of the pure air and fresh water school. Almost his first words were, "So you, too, have that light absorbing green paper that the artistic world swear by." I liked to be classed among the artistic folk, of course, but there was something in the tone of his voice which made me feel just a wee bit hurt. He was not long before he poured forth a whole vial of wrath on the Tertiary School in general, and this "dirt-mixed light absorbing green" in particular. "I have known," he said, "a considerable number of rooms papered with this green, and I have observed that every one subjected to its influence, as by using a room so papered more than another, invariably suffers for it physically in some way; next to the arsenic colour it is the very worst green I know. The bright green poisons you in an open, direct, active manner, but this dull one with the pleasing externals of quietness and repose robs you of that light which not enriches it, and makes you poor indeed."

I confess that I was troubled at this view of affairs. It is true that at the outset, five years ago, I had adopted these tertiary tones under mental protest, and that had there been any colours in the English market like the bright cheerful hues of Japanese manufacture I should have escaped contamination. But somehow, partly from habit, no doubt, and in some measure unquestionably from the virtues it certainly possessed, I had grown fond of my green diaper. There was no question that my rooms demanded a great expenditure in lamps or candles, for although the dining room was not more than 20 feet by 16, two dozen candles and two moderator lamps were barely sufficient to light it properly, and when reading alone with my solitary lamp, covered with a green paper shade, the outlines of the furniture were lost in an almost cavernous gloom. After five years' endurance of this I was at last induced to design some papers for myself. The diagonal H pattern, so well known both to the East and the West, I adopted instead of the green square diaper, and this I had printed in three ways — green, blue, red — showing on the drawing the colours I wished to see reproduced, carefully copied from Japanese work. As, however, I used transparent water-colour, the manufacturer was not much to blame for printing a green, blue, and red of his own, and which, I need hardly say, were very harsh translations of my Japanese tones. The green, instead of being merely quiet, was dull, if not dirty; the blue and red, instead of being

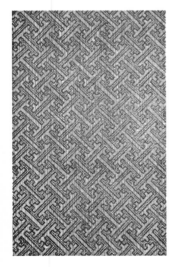

Godwin, wallpaper design.

pleasantly bright, were positively violent. However, I determined this time I would make two experiments. I therefore used the blue diagonal in one room, and the tertiary green in the other, keeping the wall over the green free of paper as before, and putting a blue Japanese bird pattern as a frieze over the blue diagonal.

Rearranging and changing the furniture

The blue room, after a lapse of five years, has turned out more or less, a success. The colour has been much softened, and the room being almost entirely furnished with Japanese things, even to the blinds, there is a oneness of design and colour, bright and cheerful without being garish, and quiet in tone without being dull. The dining-room, with its new green paper, was still a trouble. It did not look quite so melancholy as at first, but it still required a great expenditure in gas to illuminate it;

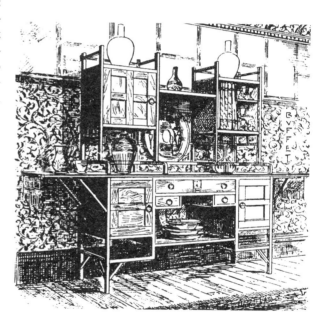

for four-and-twenty candles per night, to say nothing of lamps, had driven me reluctantly to adopt what an accomplished architect describes as the invention of the Devil. Now I have a weakness, no doubt a ridiculous one, for rearranging my furniture, sometimes going so far as to shift it from room to room. Moving the black buffet one day from end wall to side wall, it occurred to me that I might try the experiment of interchanging the rooms. To the horror of my servants and the amusement of my friends, who took no trouble to conceal from me the fact that they thought me "a little touched," I moved the black furniture into the blue room, and the Japanese into the green room. My blue room was spoilt, the ebonised furniture looked funereal; but the green room had both gained and lost, it had gained light, but it had lost colour; the room was less depressing, but the green looked dirtier than ever. I came at last to two conclusions: 1, that the tertiary green used by paperstainers was an unwholesome green and an artistic mistake; 2, that ebonised furniture, unless in small arti-

Godwin, sideboard design.

cles, or largely decorated with inlay of gold or ivory, or both, is not calculated, to say the least, to make a room look cheerful or even comfortable.

There now remained two things to do: to change my ebonised goods for some other kind, and to banish the tertiary green. Three courses were now suggested to me; I might have my own designs worked out in oak, and thus go to very nearly the opposite extreme of what I had already experienced. Light oak, brass mountings, brass trays and sconces, white cloths, blue and white china, Indian matting, &c., are suggestive of a certain brightness and freshness; but the London atmosphere is charged with dust and blacks, and London servants are, as a rule, careless and dirty. I might have American walnut, a very useful wood, half way in effect of colour between oak and ebony, with these special advantages over both — that it does not show dirty finger-marks so easily as the first, and does not reveal dust and bruises so readily as the second. The third course was to hunt up secondhand shops, for eighteenth century mahogany work inlaid with strips of satinwood. Whether it was that I had grown a trifle weary of modern designs in general, and my own in particular, or that I longed for more colour than was to be found in plain oak or American walnut, or that the cost of the eighteenth century work was so much below the least expensive of the specially made goods of the present day, or whether — as is most likely — it was from a concretion of these three thoughts, matters little; the eighteenth century won the competition, and my dining-room was refurnished with a bow-fronted sideboard, Chippendale chairs, flap tables, cabinets, bookcases, and a little escritoire, all of admirable colour, design, and workmanship.

Back to the wall papers

The difficulty now was to get a fitting paper or background for it. Tertiary green was out of the question. My Japanese patterns were too formal, and again I ransacked the decorators' shops for a really good naturalistic or semi-naturalistic paper. Good, that is, in pattern and good in colour. This time the show was very different from what it was when I first entered on my chambers. Since then architects and painters by the dozen had taken up the subject with more or less success. There were geometric designs and naturalistic designs, some even combined one within the other, on the principle of the trellis. The patterns were all effective, and some remarkably good; but there was no evidence that any advance had been made by the manufacturer in the important matter of colour. Where the tones were quiet they were also dull and unwholesome for the eye; where they were not quiet they were not simply loud, but uproarious. One set of patterns I accidentally stumbled across showed a slavish copying of Japanese books for details, and an application and combination of them wholly unartistic, and therefore thoroughly *un*-Japanese in character. The way in which Japanese "bits" are being worked up into modern English manufacture is not good in any sense for art. It is like the old way our forefathers had with the Greek honeysuckle and the key or fret pattern. The Japanese have taught us much, and de-

Godwin, peacock wallpaper design.

serve better at our hands than for us to trace one of their artists' designs for a swordhilt and sow it at 4-inch regular intervals all over our walls. All things considered, I found among the naturalistic papers nothing to surpass nor even compare with the old fruit paper that I mentioned in Chapter I. This, printed on a blue ground, I therefore selected for the walls of my dining-room, and had at last the satisfaction of sitting in a pleasant, cheerful room, where, although the tone was quiet and perhaps a trifle dark, it was yet neither dull nor dirty.

MY HOUSE 'IN' LONDON (1876)

Crippled by the costs of building and furnishing their house in Harpenden, and tee-
tering on the edge of bankruptcy, Godwin, Terry and their two children relocated to
central London in 1874, renting a property at 20 Taviton Street, Gordon Square
(now demolished). Here Godwin could accommodate his office, while Terry was
within easy reach of the theatre district. Despite Godwin's increased earnings through
his journalism and design of furnishings, Terry was compelled to return to the stage.
By the time he wrote this series Godwin had separated from Terry, and moved home
and office, marrying his pupil, Beatrice Philip, in January 1876.

Given the resources, Godwin would have liked to create 'one home for my art and
myself' from scratch, not in the suburbs, but overlooking a city park or gracious
square. One of the compelling features of this series, however, is the way Godwin
demonstrates how to make a virtue out of necessity, building on the lessons learned
in the furnishing of his chambers.

CHAPTER I: HOUSE-HUNTING

The exhilarating but often distressing process of finding a new home is an experience
with which modern city dwellers, then as now, can readily identify.

Avoiding the modern suburb

Decidedly, "in". That crowd of half-bred towns that belt about London and are
known usually by the name *suburbs* has always been to me the occasion for
distinct and unmitigated hatred. A modern suburb is a place that is neither
one thing nor the other; it has neither the advantage of the town nor the open
freedom of the country, but manages to combine in nice equality of proportion the disadvantages of both. Rookeries of detached and semi detached villas, a few terraces, a crescent, a batch of flaunting but ill-stocked shops, a new
evangelical church with a weak spire, half a ritual one without any spire, wide
shadeless roads, with flinty gravel paths to cut your boots on, an empty cab
stand, and a palatial public-house — these are some of the ingredients of a
well-to-do suburb. All this might well have been different, only unfortunately
the London suburb is the creation of the modern speculating builder, sometimes directed by a surveyor who thinks himself an architect, but more frequently alone in his ignoble work. In the course of a little time such suburbs
will be crowded up by further suburban reaches, until the house-hunter seeking after an open, airy situation, will find that the Embankment and
Bloomsbury have this attraction in excess of the overbuilt land that was once
bounded by fields and green lanes. Of course, where the great heaths and commons are preserved, as at Hampstead, there the suburb will retain much of
the virtue of the country, even though it be built over with streets and terraces
like some provincial town. But in districts where there is no common heath,
where the speculative builder is so mightily rampant that anything like an
open square is forbidden, and woodland trees are felled for the mere timber's
value; where the front "garden" is no more than a threshold to the front door,

Source:
'My house "in" London.
Chapter I', *Architect*, 15 July
1876, pp. 33-4

and the back garden not so large as many a West End drawing room: districts where the space left between house and boundary is barely enough for a wheelbarrow, and the "detached villas'" detachment is little more than a trumpery pretence, in such retreats as these to talk of enjoying the virtues of the country is to talk bosh.

Hunting in Bloomsbury and Westminster

When, therefore, I was looking out for a house I carefully avoided the suburbs. Besides, from a professional point of view, I rather like the mediaeval system of residing if possible where you have to work. For instance, were I a wealthy architect of deserved renown with an income of some 80,000*l* a-year, I should not be satisfied to have any studios or offices, or whatever I might happen to call them, at Charing Cross and my residence three or four miles west. I should not be happy until I had secured one home for my art and myself, with an outlook on one of the parks or one of the large squares. Art, it is true, has, like trade, dwindled of late into a mere affair of daybook and ledger. The tradesman no longer takes pride in his stock, nor the manufacturer in his goods. Indeed he knows nothing at all about them except what he derives from his books. The sculptor no longer uses mallet and chisel, and the architect no longer designs, draws or superintends his buildings; the designing and drawing is done by the gentlemen in "the Office," the superintending by the clerk of the works. It is not pretended that this practice has yet become invariable. There are happily some people remaining old fashioned enough to be proud of their art, work, shop, or trade, and who still think that to "talk shop" is not that wonderful offence against good manners that empty-headed women and very young gentlemen would have us believe. For "shop talk" is generally worth attention, being about the only talk most people have any title to use, although except among painters and stock-brokers it is now rarely or ever heard. No wonder then when a man has learnt to sink the charm of work in a sea of ink and figures that he should desire to separate his life from the means whereby he lives, and to put a two shilling cab fare between his house and the prop that doth sustain his house. Thus it comes about that street after street and square after square of houses, full of architectural beauty — beauty of inlaid mantelpiece, of carved staircase, of modelled ceiling and moulded panelling, are daily sinking lower and lower, many such having reached the depth of the low lodging-house, where every moulding is choked with dirt and every fragment of carved work is grimy with grease. The larger houses have a better class of tenants, some again are divided into bachelors' chambers, and not a few are let out in apartments; but the small houses are nearly always in the possession of Filth, often accompanied by Squalor and Wretchedness. This was, and is still to some extent, the case with the charming eighteenth century houses that fill the maze of little streets to the south of Westminster Abbey. These, however, it is satisfactory to know, the Dean and Chapter of Westminster are buying as opportunity offers, and letting on short leases to a good class of tenants. In Bloomsbury, the houses, where large, are of extravagant rentals; where small, they are almost wholly given up to a poor class of lodging-house keepers. On both sides of Tottenham Court Road, in the long parallel thoroughfares of Gower Street and Charlotte Street, as well as in the short cross streets, there are numerous houses with rich panelling, decorated plaster ceilings, wood dados, inlaid mantelpieces, ornamental staircases, &c., occupied by people who have not the remotest appreciation thereof, and under the control of surveyors who are doing their miserable utmost to destroy every vestige of old times. This can be seen wherever the leases of the brick houses of Fitzroy and Charlotte Streets have expired by the offensive stucco fronts and vulgar wavy sheet glass windows to which certain corner houses have already been subjected.

Very weary did I get as week after week I wandered round about Bloomsbury and Westminster; for house hunting after the first month is apt to become depressing. At last by the merest chance I found a delightful house in one of the large squares. It was an accidental sort of place, that seemed to have been the result of some mistake in setting out, for it was only half the width of its neighbours, the whole frontage of the ground-floor being taken up by the hall and cloak room. Now if there is one thing more than another which I dislike, and which is so common in small houses, it is the long narrow passage entry, devised in order to get two or three inferior rooms on the ground-floor with that doubtful advantage of being able to throw two rooms into one by means of folding doors. The plan of the Bloomsbury house was exceptional, or non-vernacular, and for that reason — a reason that was altogether to its advantage — the rent was wonderfully low. There were, it is true, some fixtures to be taken, and the price of them was wonderfully high *qua* fixtures, but looked at in its proper light, as a premium for the remainder of the lease, it was nothing out of the way. I need hardly add that I concluded my hunt with this prize, which we will now proceed to examine.

Elevation and layout

And, first of all, let us look at the outside. The entrance door is in *the centre of the frontage*. It is wide, and forms, as the entrances to Greek houses appear to have done, the one important feature of the facade. There is a narrow sash window on either side of the door, and above are three stories, with two very tall and narrow sash windows in each floor. The doorway is of wood, beautifully moulded and carved, but all the rest of the front is of red brick. By three steps we reach the threshold, which is sufficiently deep to serve very well as a quasi-porch, for under it one can be quite protected from rain, except when accompanied by a north wind. The door opens on a hall about 15 feet square; to the right is a fireplace; to the left a door leads into the cloak-room; and immediately opposite the entrance we pass through an archway into the second or staircase hall. This second hall traverses the whole width of the house, which is only 24 feet. The stairs are to the right, and to the left is the entrance to the dining-room, which measures 24 feet by 17 feet. Here are two sash windows grouped together and on either side doors — one leading down steps to a corridor communicating with the garden and my study, &c., at the back of the garden, the other to a small conservatory. My study and offices have also an entrance from a back street. On the first-floor are two rooms, each about 17 feet by 24 feet, communicating through an arched and domed vestibule, formed by cutting off the end of the staircase landing, an arrangement found eminently useful in various ways, especially for the free circulation of visitors on "at home" evenings. On the second-floor are two bedrooms, each 17 feet by 15 feet, a large linen closet, a dressing-room, a bath-room, and a w.c., which is in the front of the house and above the ground-floor closet, that I should have stated, adjoined the cloak-room. On the third-floor are four bedrooms, and in the roof two attics.

The interiors before

When I first looked over the house it was in the charge of an aged woman. Every window from attic to basement was carefully closed, and there was an uncomfortable sense of stuffiness on all the floors. The staircase lantern light had become obscured with dirt, and stairs and landing were consequently gloomy. There was a heavy crimson and oak paper in the dining-room, and over the windows were deep gilt cornices, covered with cast flowers and fly-specks. The fixtures throughout were in the large solid mahogany style, in adopting which it appears to have been found necessary to cut away the dado mouldings, and to cover the panelling with canvas. The old sashes, too, with their 1 3/4-inch sash bars, had been removed, and new ones with plate glass or thin 1/2-inch bars had been substituted. The sculptures of the mantelpieces had been taken away, and their places filled up with plain slabs of marble. Luckily, however, the plaster ribs and the beautifully delicate Greek-like scroll work on the ceilings remained intact, although somewhat choked with successive coats of white lime. It was in great part this Greek-like delicacy and tenderness in all the old detail that was visible which induced me to take the house, and which sounded the keynote for the decoration and furniture I have just carried out.

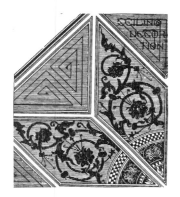

Godwin, ceiling design.

Introducing light, air and cleanliness

But first, as to the alterations.

These have been mainly designed for the purpose of securing abundance of light, air, and cleanliness. Thus:— 1, the partition between the outer and inner hall I have had removed and a panelled wood one put in its place, the upper panels being glazed casements; 2, every fragment of paper, paint, &c., has been cleaned off the walls and wood; 3, in the larders, pantries, dust-bins, water-closets, and bath-rooms, the walls have been covered with glazed tiles, the ceilings rendered in parian cement, and the wood finished with a surface like a coach panel; 4, the mahogany fixtures, the gilt cornices, and massive, handsome chandeliers, huge dust collectors as they were, no longer exist; 5, the gas-pipes have been emptied of gas, disconnected with the main, and a fresh arrangement made so as to limit the gas to the basement, hall, and stairs; 6, as regards the drains and soil-pipes, all the waste pipes that formerly led into them have been disconnected, and as the scullery sink-pipe passes through the wall and empties itself in the open air over an ordinary grease-trap, I am never annoyed when we have spring cabbage or broccoli; 7, an extra "dust-bin" has been constructed, so that one is now used for dust and ashes only and the other for the cook's refuse; 8, a special ventilating flue has been built for the kitchen; and, lastly, by a slight alteration to the staircase lantern, and keeping up a high temperature by means of gas constantly burning at the top I have secured a general ventilating-shaft for all the rooms above the ground level.

For the sake of preserving the architectural style so decidedly marked in the doorway, ceilings, and mantelpieces, I have restored the dados, but instead of restoring the old sashes, the bars of which, so thick in themselves ($1^3/_4$ inches) and so thickly set, would have always obstructed so much light, I have kept to plate glass, giving scale to the windows by a few bars placed horizontally, and two vertically, leaving large panes near the centre of each sash, a method of division which I confess to having borrowed from my friends of Japan. My painting and papering — the "decorations" as they are called — have been carried out with a leaning, perhaps in excess, towards lightness, and a simplicity almost amounting to severity. I have had a long experience in chambers, and hope I have profited by it. I have seen how easy it is to make one's home discomfortable, sad, and melancholy by following certain artistic principles dear to those artists who view nature from the owl's point of sight, and who are always painting the haunted house, the deserted mill, the solitary cottage, and this, too, not in sunshine, but under cold murky skies, or in ghostly uncertain lights. I have seen how next to impossible it is to properly light a room where the paper is of that fashionable tertiary green one sees in an old tapestry where the light of centuries has fed on the glory of its colour, and dust has been ingrained with the residue. I have learnt how hard a thing it is to find any wall paper that shall be wholly satisfactory in colour and pattern, and have experienced the worry, I may say the painfulness, of *exact* and formal repetition applied to large surfaces, all the more worrying when there is a pretence of *non*-repetition. These things, among others, have afflicted me, and I have avoided all risk of their repetition by painting the walls and avoiding paper altogether.

CHAPTER II: THE HALL

Expressing literary culture in the home

I said last week that my hall was something more than a passage. "Show me a man's books, and I will tell you what manner of man he is," is a saying which was current in the first half of this century, and is still occasionally used in spite of public libraries and reading rooms. It has frequently occurred to me that we might read *hall* for "books" and yet run no more risk of incurring an error of judgment with the change than without it? It will at once appear that whether the word be *hall* or *books* is a matter of very little consequence to the great mass of English people. The ordinary Englishman and woman are strangely indifferent both to one and the other — an indifference which is

Source:
'Chapter II.—the hall',
Architect , 22 July 1876,
pp.45-6

brought more or less prominently before us in almost every house we enter and every conversation we hear. Take the ordinary middle class society to which the *main* body of architects, painters, and sculptors belong — I am not at present quite persuaded that the society to which the *select* body of artists belong is very much in advance of the others — and what do we find? Why, an amount of ignorance and indifference on all matters not immediately related to their daily work and occasionally on some matters that are, compared to which the ignorance and indifference of English mechanics count for nothing. That ordinary men or women should know anything about history is not fair to ask, seeing what very second and even third-rate sort of knowledge of this kind some of the leading men of the time possess. But, as concerning English literature, what with public libraries and the wonderfully cheap editions to be had of most of our English classics, it is amazing that people should know so little. Grown up men and women as a rule may fairly be excused from reading the alliterative poems and other mediaeval lore published by the Early English Text Society. It is quite possible, too, that CHAUCER may be more plague than profit except to those who long to know and can find leisure to learn their mother tongue; but in the works of SPENSER and SHAKESPERE there are few or no difficulties to contend with. The language they speak is as familiar to us as household words, and the teaching and the art of them second to none. SHAKESPERE many have read and others pretend they have read. Some of his plays have been fairly well advertised, popularised and made knowable to man actors and actresses; but of the other Elizabethan dramatists and of that contemporary whom SHAKESPERE recognised as the king of English poets — EDMUND SPENSER — most of us know nothing or next to nothing, such *next* being only what we have learnt from "Elegant Extracts" or some magazine essay.

I do not wish at all to underrate the class of which I am writing. There are some architects and a few painters who have had a fair share of reading in their day. There are, I know, Spenserian stockbrokers, and the poetical "promoter" we may perhaps consider possible, and yet the mass of the men and women of the middle classes, I venture to affirm, remain illiterate. Where a household is given more than is usual to the cultivation of aesthetics we find the literary learning is generally in harmony with the dirty green colours used in modern wall papers, and with those toned — decidedly toned — green and blue serges cut after NOAH'S ark patterns, which enthusiastic young ladies affect. Similarly, as a rule, wherever the "idle singer of an empty day" has found a comfortable resting-place, you may be nearly sure to meet dull sad greens on walls or floors. Where the literary feast consists of ROSSETTI or SWINBURNE, taken without salt, of course, OUIDA and BROUGHTON, with BROWNING as an ornament in the midst, we may be sure that the house is pretty well in the hands of very young ladies, and that we must not expect anything outside the drawing-room beyond some white muslin blinds tied in at the waist — always dirty as white muslin blinds must be in London — put up as an outward sign of the inward spirit of the place. Where the master of the house is thoroughly saturated with the sad and the ugly the spirit of this

Linley Sambourne, cartoon of the novelist Ouida, Punch *20 Aug. 1881.*

sweet, bewitching, melancholic, glamourish kind of yellow-green art spreads all over the place, and finds expression in the passage-hall in the shape of a strip of coconut matting and one sickly green rush-bottom chair. But I need hardly say that this dreamy minor key in art is only thoroughly understood by a few, and that the halls and entrance passages of houses where the inmates have only just begun to acquire the twang still retain that conventional appearance which shows strongly enough that the Englishman's indifference to domestic art (he is really indifferent to all art as art — my Lord Mayor to the contrary notwithstanding — but no matter) is not less than his indifference to literature.

If men are careless to drink of the fountains of knowledge within easy reach — an entire fountain for three shillings and sixpence — it is not likely they will go out of their way to seek other refinements not so easy of attainment. If a man's literary cravings are satisfied by the morning paper, the "comic" journals, and an occasional novel — and some have boasted that they do not even reach so far — we can easily understand his indifference to refinement of all kinds. If he be married, the wife takes the drawing-room as a matter of course, under her special protection, leaving the dining-room, possibly, and the hall certainly, in the charge of her lord. And what a dining-room! What a hall!

The inartistic hall

Inside the front door is a mat that occupies the whole, or nearly the whole, width of the entry. Beyond this, in superiorly-arranged dwellings, is a second door or doors, forming what is sometimes called a *vestibule*. Both in cold and hot climates this is a very useful feature; so useful indeed as to be almost a necessary adjunct to every class of house. These second doors are often glazed with ground glass in large sheets, and have margins of stained glass, mostly of a strong orange tint, with squares of dark purple in the corners. Having passed this we are in the hall proper, rarely more than 6 feet wide, usually under 4. An oil-cloth, in imitation of fourteenth century encaustic tiles from some chapter-house or cathedral sanctuary, is occasionally varied by a kamptulicon that has caught the Greek fret and is determined to make the most of it. The woodwork is nearly always painted *and grained*: in quite new semi-detached "Gothic" villas it is stained and varnished. The walls are covered — hall, passage, and staircase to the top of the house — with a counterfeit presentment of large slabs of highly-polished Siena marble, or it may be smaller blocks of grey granite. These are among the cheapest wall papers in the trade, and if well varnished *can* be easily kept clean, only they never are so kept. Blocking up a full third, sometimes one-half the width of the hall, is a hat and umbrella-stand, a stool or form, or a table and two chairs. These are sure to be of oak. The hat and umbrella-stand has cheese-plate pegs all over it, has too an uncomfortable habit of tilting forward, offers no place for your overcoat except where your coat-tails may dangle against the umbrellas, while the place for the umbrellas is no better than a trap. The chairs have a hard heraldic look about them, the stool or form has twisted legs, and the table generally

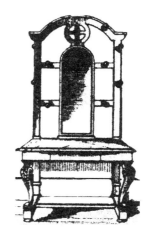

'Inartistic' hallstand, 1876, catalogue of Shoolbred & Co., Tottenham Court Road.

follows *en suite*. Passing all these not merely uninviting but repelling features we notice that at the foot of the stairs and at each of the two or three doors that lead from the hall to the rooms adjoining is a wool mat. No matter how many mats the entry and long passage-hall contain, no house is considered complete unless every door, from base to summit, has its mat. I suppose no one would dare to say that there is any use in these expensive appliances beyond their serving somewhat to exclude drafts. Aesthetically they serve no purpose whatsoever, and one soon gets over the sense of nakedness their absence at first engenders, a sense entirely depending on custom and habit. As it is, we not only suffer the first cost but the perpetual cost of servants' labour in daily shaking and beating of them, or the unknown cost of leaving them as dust-traps. In a word, the door-mat, except as a means of boot-cleaning near outer doors, has become an unmeaning relic, and the sooner we cease to use them the better for our pockets, our servants and our health.

The author's remedies

Godwin, hallstand design.

Now I hold that the furniture and decoration of the entrance hall is of the very essence of the house. And where we mark indifference there too we may be assured, as a rule, that the master of the place — he or she — is indifferent really to the maintenance of an art spirit among us, or in other words is careless about refinement. Where the flooring-boards are good, as in my house, narrow that is, and close jointed, there is perhaps no better way of treating the ground-floor (hall and the rest) than to oil and beeswax the boards. It is what I have done, and it has certain advantages on the score of cleanliness which I take to be the first consideration in all domestic design. I like, too, a contrast between one *floor* and another, and as I have Indian matting on the first floor I did not want it here, although in small houses, I am not over fond of changing the general colour of rooms on the same floor. One almost naturally prefers some kind of blue or green in rooms looking south, especially just at this time of the year, but then the weather we have in July reaches us only after June has begun and leaves us before the end of September. The large majority of our days out-of-doors are grey and cold, and it is of these we should think when we come to decorate and furnish, so as to get some relief indoors from their chilling depressing influence. For example, we should avoid grey or blue-white in marbles or paint. If ceilings are to be whitelimed, the white should be toned with yellow ochre, with perhaps a little light red, and possibly a pinch of black or blue according to the light. My hall ceiling, and indeed the whole of the ceilings, are coloured a creamy or vellum sort of white, and the plaster ribs defined with lines of amber. The flooring-boards in hall and throughout the ground-floor are oiled and beeswaxed, and the upper half of the walls above the dado is distempered in vellum colour somewhat darker than the ceiling; then comes a moulded wood rail; between this and the dado in the hall is a stencilled conventional pattern in umber and vellum of an alloverish design tending somewhat to a straight-diagonal effect, and the woodwork throughout the whole ground-floor is painted light red. The mantelpiece is old white marble and a little Siena mixed with it. Above the marble shelf I have simply placed a looking-glass with side brackets, and a deeply moulded shelf cornice. Five pieces of blue and white china (two on the marble shelf and three on the cornice) completely furnish it. A brass fender and fireirons, a high grate with brass mounts, a brass chandelier, and a couple of small circular brass trays supply the high lights.

Two mats, one coarse and one fine, are placed just within the front door, and in the centre of the hall is a thick carpet, about 9 or 10 feet square. There are two side tables, two stands for flowering plants, and two strong wicker arm-chairs. In the archway opposite the front door are heavy Tunis curtains, of which we have two pair. There is more traffic at this point than anywhere else in the house, and to have hung unwashable material, no matter of what kind, would have brought down on us the penalty of dirt — grimily greasy to the touch — in a very short time. In the inner hall the arrangement as regards the walls, floor, and ceiling is the same as that in the outer hall. One eastern rug fills up or nearly fills up the floor from the foot of the stairs to the dining-room door. The handrail of the stairs is of polished oak, the balusters are painted light red, and the stairs themselves are in the centre inlaid with lead, on treads and nosing, having a pattern tinned thereon. The advantage of lead is that it deadens the sound almost as much as carpet, and is infinitely cleaner and less troublesome. The cloak-room, which may be taken as part of the hall arrangement, is like the hall except that it has one small rug in front of the fireplace instead of a carpet, and that the furniture is limited to a chair and one long table against the end wall. The final result is that my hall, although looking due north, is warm and cheerful, and possesses the prime virtue of being cleansable without being too troublesome.

Godwin, flower-stand design.

CHAPTER III: THE DINING-ROOM

The weightiest of rooms

How is it that the conventional English dining-room is always heavy, not to say gloomy? Day after day only four people at a time occupy it; but there, day after day, a desert of white cloth is stretched over a table capable of accommodating at least fourteen people. The sideboard is what the trade truly describes as "massive," the table is massive, the dozen and a half chairs are massive, and the three-decked article which does more work than all the rest of the furniture put together is the lightest thing in the room. On the floor is the heaviest of Turkey carpets, with more than a tendency to red, and the margins of the boards beyond the carpet are stained and varnished as dark as they can be. On the walls is a paper of a "rich warm tone" — crimson and raw sienna, with a gold outline to the pattern. The curtains are to match. The upholsterer has revelled in sticky cut velvets. The chairs are obliged to have castors fixed to them, as they are much too massive and heavy to lift. As to the table, its weight is so great that the castors on its legs are quite formidable-looking contrivances of the mechanical engineer. The sideboard is im-

Source:
'Chapter III.—the dining-room', *Architect*, 29 July 1876, pp.58-9

Biographical notes:
Stevens

movable or next to immovable; its weight is simply beyond the power of any known castor to bear. Its usual office is apparently to support a group of black bronze horses under an oval glass shade, an office which could be effectually performed by a small bracket or the lightest of coffee tables. When we know more of the gloomy depths of its drawers and pedestals we discover that in its secret recesses it finds accommodation for one tablecloth, four serviettes, four decanters, a cruet stand, and a handful of silver. Nor are these massive furniture makers with a gross excess in *absolute* strength. The design of the drawer fronts is so contrived as to exhibit an apparent strength simply outrageous, that is, they would have us believe the thickness or depth of the top slab to be at least 6 inches! or as deep as the joists which support the floor in many an old house. To add to the weight of the scene, there is a black mantelpiece of very broad slabs of marble with enormous consoles or brackets; a black marble clock, and two more black bronzes enliven the mantelshelf with fits of gloomy flickering when the lights are lit; behind them, rising in awful state to the ceiling, is an oil picture with a very deep and very heavy gilded frame, round the room are half a dozen more oil pictures with more gold frames. Five have been family portraits, one is supposed to be sacred subject, and one a CANALETTI. Some dining rooms have a peculiar weakness for CANALETTI.*

Early English dining-rooms

If by chance you enter such a room in the intervals when the cloth is not laid, there are but two courses before you, either to finish the day with FOX's "Book of Martyrs,"** or fly to champagne. I have attended a few funerals, and I have had occasion to attend in a few conventional dining-rooms during their nonfestive intervals. Of the two I prefer the funeral. What there should be in the process of eating and drinking to demand all this heavy preparation does not appear. Indeed I venture to deny the existence of any satisfactory reasons for producing such weighty furniture or such heavy "decoration." In the thirteenth century, when what is commonly known as the *"Early English"* style prevailed, furniture was to a very great extent mere pieces of carpentry, often put together in the rooms for which they were designed, and rarely or ever taken thence until fire or decay reduced them to easily movable rubbish. The armoires at Bayeux and Noyon, the circular table and cope chest at Salisbury, and the kitchen table at Winchester are illustrations in point. These are no doubt very heavy, but then we must remember they are almost as much part and parcel of the carpentry of the buildings to which they belong as the heavy-planked iron-bound doors of the rooms, that are hung (not with rising brass butts to rebated linings or moulded wood frames, but) with broad strap hinges on huge iron hooks let into the massive stone jambs. Under such circumstances, taken with such surroundings, the furniture of the Early English period is no whit too heavy.

So again the enormous bulging legs, the many-moulded deep rails, &c., of the Elizabethan and Jacobean styles, now often described as *"Old English"* — an expression, by the way, rather wide for the limited reference it is intended

* Giovanni Antonio Canal (1697–1768), Venetian view painter.

**John Fox (1516–87), English Protestant, author of Acts and Monuments 1563, better known as the *Book of Martyrs*.

B. Talbert, *Early English sideboard from his* Gothic Forms, *London 1867.*

to bear — are no doubt massive and heavy to move, but then again we must bear in mind that the rooms for which they were made were also massive. The fireplaces were huge architectural edifices weighty with sculpture; the ceilings were of elaborate plaster work, or else they showed the thick joists resting on deep moulded beams; the windows were large, but heavily mullioned and transomed, so that the glazed openings themselves were rather small, and looked even smaller than they were owing to the glass being divided by numerous lead-lines and iron bars. In a word, the furniture and the architects were in accord. And what an accord it was! Big if you like, even to what we should now call coarseness, but big with joviality, not with pretence. The buffet and the table might well be of sturdy scantlings, for the feasts were in accord with them, and big like the rest. The very men too were big and blustering in their manner; they drank deep and quarrelled freely as deep drinkers needs must; chairs were consequently often overset, and then what may seem to us ultra solidity and strength of construction were not in any way too much, considering the strain often put on them, and the service to which they were habitually subject.

Old English sideboard for a house in Hampstead, BN *15 May 1885.*

Modern manners

We have changed things somewhat in these days. Our dining tables no longer groan under the weight of barons of beef. We dine altogether or in great part *à la Russe*, and the only weight the modern dining table is asked to bear is that of a few plates, some glasses, a vase or two of flowers, and half-a-dozen dishes of fruit. Men do not drink deep nor quarrel at table as of old; it is considered more polite to abuse a man behind his back, and should you publish your abuse, he no longer retaliates with a rapier, but with the law of libel, so that a modern Jacobean chair is quite a purposeless construction. Seeing that all this is so, that the feasts we now have are composed of dishes in succession small and light, that our dining tables are unencumbered except with fairy-like articles, that our manners are either so brightly effervescent or so steadily sober as to render us almost unconscious of support; the style of furniture suited for our dining rooms should also be light, and the architecture and decorations in accord with it should be cheerful and bright. Nothing can be more offensive than flock papers and woollen hangings, the usual surroundings of an Englishman's dining table. Who has not experienced in such rooms many a stuffy stale reminder of an exhausted feast? Where the men smoke after dinner — and where do they not? — there is the additional advantage of breakfasting in an atmosphere that derives a flavour of stale tobacco from the stores laid up overnight in wallpaper and curtains. The whitewashed, dimity or chintz curtained parlour of some poor wayside inn is the lowest form of the right kind of dining-room. The polished marble and glazed tile wall surface of some eastern palace, with hangings of finest linen or silk, is perhaps the highest form. There are, as my readers can imagine, many intermediate steps, and one of these formed the pattern of my dining room.

Godwin, dining-room furniture design.

My dining-room decoration

It may be remembered that there was an old wood dado to the whole of the ground-floor, and that my dining-room looked south. It looked on to a square and somewhat shut-in grass plot or lawn, bordered by one or two trees and some bushy evergreens. The view was bounded by my study wall, on which I fixed trellis work for such climbers as the situation would suit. The colour of the dado and the rest of the woodwork I determined should be painted a tolerably vivid blue. I had no little difficulty over this. Dull greenish blues, such as I had used before in common with many others, were fairly easy to get; turquoise blue and the blues of palatial residences generally were much *too* easy to get; but the blue which lights well at night, which *is* blue — by candlelight that is as well as daylight — perhaps rather more so, was what I wanted, and what after much trouble I eventually obtained. The ceiling and the wall below it to the depth of 18 inches, were already decorated by delicate plaster work when I took the house. The main lines of the ceiling design are drawn as a large circle within a square, and as the room measured 24 feet by 17 feet there is thus an oblong panel left at each end. The scroll work in the panels, and the radiating decoration in the circle, the outer diameter of which is 14 feet, are treated with a refinement and delicacy which we might well endeavour to emulate. One great charm it has for me is that its detail is not large enough to take up much dirt, for modern plaster enrichments, and what are called "centre flowers" are to be deprecated, apart from their intolerable ugliness, as reservoirs for dust.

Godwin, ceiling design.

The wall space between dado and plaster frieze is divided horizontally into two equal parts, the lower part is covered by irregular groups of broad parallel horizontal lines broken by small squares and oblongs at irregular intervals, boxed out just enough to allow for the reception under a glass door of small choice water-colour sketches. The colours used in this wall space are a cool yellow (which is the colour of the upper wall space), a pale brown red, and a deep or old ivory white. In the upper division are wall paintings in distemper on coarse canvas representing the modern labours of the months in relation to meat and drink. The drawing is treated naturally, and is taken from a point of sight lower than the ground on which the figures stand, as in many of MANTEGNA'S* decorative works. The conventional restrictions are confined to the background and the composition or distribution. My wall, therefore, instead of being dull, lifeless, depressing as even painted walls too often are when the figures are painted flat with strong outlines, are on the contrary always cheerful and sometimes even lively. The floor is covered with Indian matting (the plain yellow colour); an Indian carpet occupies the centre, and there are two rugs — one before the buffet and one before the fire as hearthrug.

* Andrea Mantegna (c.1431–1506), Italian renaissance artist.

The table is normally square, the leaf or leaves being added only in the event of a dinner party. As the table is always covered by a cloth which nearly reaches the floor the legs are not elaborated with ornament; the two important pieces of joinery or cabinet-maker's work in the room are the sideboard and the mantel at opposite ends of the apartment, the latter reaching sufficiently high to break into the upper wall space. In the recess each side the fireplace is a low bookcase. In the window are two large vases of irregular height, one containing a tree fern the other a palm. The chairs are all circular in plan, and made with arms, very light, very open, and fully equal to any work they may have to do, they have cane seats and movable leather cushions. The wood throughout is of Spanish mahogany, brightened by fine inlay of brass. The work over the mantelshelf is of common Honduras, painted blue like the constructive woodwork of the room, and here, and here only, has silvered glass been introduced, and that in one long central panel.

Godwin, dining-chair design.

Much of what we call artistic furniture is ruined, when otherwise excellent, by too free a use of silvered glass panels, which, instead of enlivening the monotony of, say, American walnut, too often tend to deepen its gloom. My sideboard has no silvered glass about it. Had it occupied a recess, I am inclined to think I should have followed Mr. ALFRED STEVENS'S example as exhibited in Dorchester House, and have had the entire background of the recess as glass, making the sideboard a fixture. As, however, there is no recess, and the buffet is a *movable*, I determined to have it such in fact as well as in name. The construction is as light as is consistent with the strength required and effect is obtained more by play of light and shade than by costliness of ornament. There is abundance of room, and yet some to spare, for all the different articles that usually belong to a sideboard; and I have this satisfaction, that as its lowest shelf is at least 9 inches from the floor, there can be no secret dust hole, and that even the dust on the skirting and dado behind it can be daily removed, if needs be, without calling in the aid of a second housemaid, in as much as the whole piece of furniture (and it measures 7 feet wide by 5 feet high) can be moved easily in any direction by one pair of hands. My chairs are light enough for a child to carry, and strong enough for a child to clamber on.

Godwin, buffet design.

A joyous modern room

Over the windows and each door are light brass rods ($^3/_4$-inch diameter), which are more than sufficient to support the voluminous linen curtains of pale brownish-yellow, banded and otherwise embroidered with blue and yellow. No words, however, can give an adequate notion of the joyous kind of light in this room, whether illuminated by sun or duplex lamp or candle. Joyous it is, without being in any sense disturbing, and this, I take it, should be the character of our dining-rooms if we wish to complete the light and improved *menu* of the present day with appropriate surroundings. To keep pace with the advanced style of cooking, and with the laudable efforts of the School of Cookery, its not enough to see that the manufacturers of our dinners have light hands; the palate is but one of many avenues to the counsel hall where things are approved or disapproved, and it behoves all those who desire to enjoy the high delights of art in every-day life to see that the *heavy hand* is transported without chance of ticket-of-leave not merely from the *entrées*, but from the furniture, the decoration, and the architecture.

CHAPTER IV: THE DRAWING-ROOM

Conventional middle-class formulae

Source:
'Chapter IV.—the drawing-room', *Architect*, 5 August 1876, pp.72-3

Cabinet and table, Cassell's Household Guide, *vol. 3, 1872.*

W. Blackie, high-backed chairs, Cabinet-Maker's Assistant, *Glasgow 1859.*

The drawing-room of the middle classes is quite as much a matter of course as the dining-room. Just as the latter is bound by some occult reason to be hot and heavy in its "decoration," so the former is bound to be cold and light. If the dining-room has a prescriptive right to a flock paper and a general tone of crimson and oak, it is as certain that the drawing-room has an equal right to a satin paper and a general tone of bluish white touched up with gold. While, however, we are consistent in our gloom of dining-room, and generally have dark furniture — Spanish mahogany or dark oak — there seems to be no such law to govern us in furnishing our drawing-room. No sooner have we selected our bluish-white satin paper powdered with a device in almost pure white edged with gold than we reveal at once the principle that guides us in the domestic art of the drawing room, the principle of contrast, by filling the room with the darkest woods we can select, walnut or ebony, the one intensified by being carved, the other by being partially gilt. The floor, instead of being the quietest, most unobtrusive part of the room, is made the reverse, by a carpet of large pattern and violent colour. The mantelpiece is of white statuary marble, with magnificent trusses, and from shelf to ceiling is a huge and costly plate of silvered glass, framed in a fearful and wonderful manner. The curtains are somewhat mixed — partly of imitation lace, winter and summer, and partly of damask with a good deal of a yellow floss expression. The chairs and other seats are covered with similar damask, with now and then a startling exception in favour of a prie-dieu, the back and seat of which serve as pegs on which, for the gratification of our friends and ourselves, is exhibited the handiwork in Berlin wool of the fair mistress or some other friends. It is noteworthy that the conventional drawing-rooms of people who are by no means given to Puritanical habits have a strong flavour of the rigid formality which the Puritan favoured. Thus the central table, even though the circle and swing legs modified to an oval and claws recalls the time in England when all kinds of past ritual arrangement, even down to that of a domestic chapel, were looked on as ungodly, and the family altar, (occasionally also the public altar) was only considered quite orthodox when it was capable of accommodating a broad party. To the same period may be referred also the straight-backed, high-seated, drawing-room chairs, with stuffed seats and rather substantial framing, suggesting family prayers and heavy teas.

Now, the drawing room is of all places the least suited to feasting, whether we use the word literally or metaphorically. It is a place to *withdraw* to in the intervals of the more serious business of life for the sake of wakeful rest. Here the light guitar may be as light as it likes, the flute may be as magical as you can make it, and the piano may vibrate to manifold beauties, provided only that you keep your heavy solemnities out of the way. WAGNER may do for the stage, the Requiem and the Mass for the church, but for the drawing-room we want no such profundities. It is the same with conversation. Few people are so wanting in the sense of the appropriate as to carry on serious discussions in a drawing-room. The room is, or should be, an exercise ground for the pleasantries of speech rather than a riding field for trained disputants. A touch of scandal, provided it be not ill-natured, is much better suited to such a room than the pulpit and water talk or the deadly silence that too often divide the empire of the middle-class drawing-room. On the other hand, we should guard against an excess of the appliances of physical luxury. A low, subdued light, capacious lounges, large soft pillows, velvety carpets, are apt to lead from the necessary wakeful rest to the unnecessary and unwholesome lazy sleep. Between the Puritanical or formal state of hard central table, attended by stiff upright chairs, and the ennervating luxury of a drawing-room all beds and bolsters, there are happy mediums, more or less reasonable.

The cluttered model

Again, a very objectionable habit with some people, especially among the higher middle classes is to fill up their drawing-rooms with furniture and knicknacks until a short-sighted person is placed in constant peril. The door, as it opens, almost skims a side table covered with odds and ends; then comes a folding screen; after safely doubling this, you find yourself in an archipelago of large dumpy easy chairs, all frill and upholstery; moving then to the right and left at the risk (if not acquainted with the locomotive powers of their castors) of knocking over a light table covered with china, you may find a channel to approach the coast lines of sofa and lounge. Here, however, one has to be especially careful, as there are serious *table* rocks ahead surrounding the whole line of coast; one of these tables is so long, so pushed up to the seat, and so crowded with books and lamps, that it is out of the question even to attempt a landing on the sofa behind it. Besides tables and seats there are half a dozen cabinets, but no one can get near enough to see their contents. There is a piano in one corner, and the difficulties of circumnavigating this in order to reach the music chair, placed almost in the angle of the walls, must be experienced to be appreciated. I have seen a lady not very nervous and certainly not awkward in her movements, break a small table, smash two vases, and tear her own dress in accomplishing this passage. The floor is *covered* with Axminster, the curtains are of silk velvet and of lace, and the walls have a French paper on them. Now this is no fancy picture; it is a drawing-room wherein I have dawdled away many an hour, but I venture to be ungracious enough to say it is not altogether a model of refinement or good taste.

Drawing-room chair, Cassell's Household Guide, *vol. 3, 1872.*

The 'sensitive' alternative

Take another room, equally a reality, for an illustration of the opposite extreme. It is of much the same dimensions as the last. There are two or three light chairs, one easy chair, one small sofa near the fireplace, a piano near one of the windows, a Chinese cabinet of light wood marvellously carved, and filled with Chelsea china, a large Eastern vase as big as a font, a low Japanese screen, a few fans against the skirting and on the ceiling, and two small

Japanese cabinets about a foot high. There is one low small table about twenty inches in diameter just to receive the tea-tray, and for no other purpose. The floor is covered with Indian matting, the curtains are of whitish linen, embroidered with yellow silk, and the walls above the low wood dado are panelled in long panels with broad stiles, each panel containing a Japanese embroidery on whitish silk. No description, however, except perhaps that which may be conveyed in form of music, can give any idea of the tenderness and, if I may say so, the ultra-refinement of the delicate tones of colour which form the background to the few but unquestionable gems in this exquisitely sensitive room. I say *sensitive*, for a room has a character that may influence for good or bad the many who enter it, especially the very young. The influence of things seen is greater on some people than the influence of things heard. With myself I know that the memory of the eye's experience is far and away beyond that of the ear, and I do not for a moment imagine that I stand alone in this particular. The loud, the pretentious, the odd, the awkward, and the sensual can be proclaimed in a drawing-room by other means than by vulgar speech or personal manner. These latter are mostly variable, for nature even in the most vulgar man or woman occasionally asserts herself, and the natural is never coarse; but a room full of offensive furniture has never any such variableness. If it is pretentious at first so it always remains. If its look is awkward at first we may be quite sure the look will grow into a vacant stare. That use may breed a habit in a man is a statement for which we have not only no mean authority, but abundant experience. Many people doubtless grow accustomed to vicious things from their youth up — to villainous smells, ugly forms, inharmonious colours. The education of the senses of indeed most people has been so neglected that harsh discordant street cries do not even affect them. But until we are prepared to say that barrenness and dullness of perception are conditions superior to culture and light, we have no right to rest satisfied with any habit that can offer no better *raison d'être* than mere use. With these thoughts and memories in my mind, I set to work at decorating and furnishing my drawing-rooms.

Godwin, drawing-room interior design.

My drawing-rooms

The floor throughout both rooms, connecting lobby, and landing is covered with the best plain Indian matting. The best has a sort of trade mark in the shape of a fine red line woven into the matting at six-feet intervals which is, if anything, an improvement. In the room to the north the matting is freely covered with rugs; in the southern rooms there are only two. There are brass fenders and fire-irons, which I have had made from special designs, and which, instead of being upright, like our great-grandfathers' fenders, slope in curved section upwards and inwards. The woodwork is painted a rather dark-toned yellow, of which yellow ochre is the base, but combined with white, and sprinkled with gamboge, Prussian blue, and vermilion. The walls above the dado are divided vertically at tolerably regular intervals of about 3 feet by plain pilasters, which slightly project, carry a plain frieze, and stand on a plain base or step. This framework is painted a pale grey green (that

Godwin, table design.

green sometimes seen in the stem end of a pine-apple leaf when the other end has faded — indeed, I may as well confess that most of the colours in the room have been gathered from the pine apple). Within the spaces thus formed — spaces which may be regarded as panels, but which are not panels so much as intercolumniations — are painted trees and large birds, such as the peacock, pheasant, eagle, &c., against a background of thick foliage below, and a yellow sky changing gradually to a line or so of pure blue at the upper edge. The dividing pilasters are much wider than is usual: in fact, more like masses of wall than pilasters, and on each of these are sconces, with branches for lights. The curtains are of straw-colour silk, embroidered with amber and pale green. There are two sofas, one each side of the fire, and three *really* easy chairs. This portion of the furniture is all made with movable seats, so that there is no difficulty whatever in keeping the crevices free from dust. The seats are low (not too low) and deep, and the backs are low, being little more in the sofa than a pillow, and in the chair just high enough to form a rest for the head when seated well back. There is a piano — not against the wall, which has caused me no end of trouble, as piano makers are so stubborn and stiff-necked in the matter of appearance that they never will produce anything out of their well-worn groove, a groove which has been worn so deep that it is entirely out of keeping with all the other furniture grooves of the day. Mine has been made, works and all, specially for me. This, three small coffee tables, one long low cabinet, and the mantel-shelves are the only cabinet work in one of the rooms. They are made of Honduras mahogany, inlaid with ivory and panelled with cedar wood, carved in low relief. The other room has lounges against all the walls, some basket chairs, and light, easily movable easels of different choice woods to hold choice drawings, and easel pictures occupy the centre of the floor; the walls, &c., are treated as in the opposite room, and flowers and plants in large vases stand near the windows. I have thus plenty of free walking space, am in no way crowded, and yet have abundance of comfortable sitting room.

Godwin, piano design.

Godwin, detail of drawing-room scheme.

CHAPTER V: THE BEDROOMS

Luxurious rooms for the lazy

There are two ways of looking at a bedroom. It may be viewed as a sleeping place simply, or it may be regarded as a private sitting-room with a bed in it. This last is the view generally taken by the fashionable world. In such sitting-room bedrooms upholstery assumes an almost tyrannical position. The sofa, not merely with spring seat but with spring back and arms, draped to the ground temptingly, spreads abroad its luxurious undulations; easy chairs, all springs, low and capacious, invite you to be lazy. There are little tables for your refreshments, reading stands for your novel. The writing table is so crowded with the knick-knackeries of stationery that it is impossible to think of putting it to any practical use. The floor is covered to the remotest corner with a thick carpet, and the doors and windows are hung with voluminous curtains. It is well if the arrangements of laziness, which we

Source:
'Chapter V.—the bedrooms',
Architect, 12 August 1876,
p.86

'Queen Anne' bedroom, Cassell's Household Guide, *vol. 1, 1872.*

misname "comfort," end here for this luxurious style of furnishing is perhaps productive of nothing worse than an enervating effect. But there are houses where the ministrations of luxury reach beyond the intended refinement to a condition of piggish laziness, and I could point to more than one house where the windows of certain guest-chambers have been fitted with costly seats, elaborately upholstered, that lift up unexpectedly and reveal the usual blue landscape and other appliances of a well-ordered water-closet apparatus — a sort of clever death-in-the-box arrangement, that seems to interest and amuse the noble owner of the house not a little. It may be said that this drawing-room w.c. bedroom is exceptional save among the houses of the upper ten.

'Artistic' shams

Perhaps the middle classes have not yet thoroughly accepted it, but that they are doing their best towards its attainment in their favourite way, viz., by feebly copying those in the class above them, the furniture shops of the East Central and West Central districts, as well as the advertisements in daily and weekly papers abundantly prove. I take up a newspaper of last Saturday, for example, and among other Tottenham Court Road advertisements I find "bedroom suites in black and gold," and in "real ebony inlaid with ivory," one of the latter priced at 200 guineas. Now if there were any real art about any of this one would be ready to excuse the "taste" that finds pleasure in ebony bedrooms. Two hundred guineas for anything really and genuinely artistic among the rapidly increasing crowd of "artistic" shams is by no means much to a money-making people like the English, but I venture to doubt the existence of any really modern artistic furniture made of ebony inlaid with ivory. Who are the artists that are commissioned to design it? Do we not know the portfolios of the ordinary cabinet-maker, how they are stocked with a mass of rubbish, not one drawing indicating even the ordinary power of a draughtsman — not one but speaks plainly of the utter absence of anything like artistic excellence in drawing or design? Nor is this the case merely with the old-fashioned early "Renaissance," preceding the modern revival. Early English as it is called, with its quatrefoils and chamfers and cusps and ribs crammed with the detail of stone construction, has been drawn perhaps a little better, but the exhibition, to say the least, is a pitiable sham. "Old English" too is in the hands of designers equally unartistic. There are, however, more old examples and more published illustrations of them than of Early English, and so the designer of *modern "Old English"* (a sweet phrase!) is not so completely lost as in his attempts to revive, or build on the lines of, the older and purer style. One great drawback in the encouragement of anything like genuine domestic art is the mad desire for novelty which careers through every avenue of modern life. Another drawback of equal force is the general ignorance of even the rudiments of art among the ladies, which induces the manufacturer to employ a low class of imitators at a cheap rate, following, however, more or less (generally less) the lead of certain artists of the day.

Wardrobe, Cassell's Household Guide, *vol. 3, 1872.*

Healthy bedrooms for sleeping in

Haply for the race there are those who take a very different view of what a bedroom should be. Imprimis its floor should be scrubbed once a week, and in hot weather twice; it should therefore be carpeted only in parts, so as to be easy of removal. Then the curtains, if any, should be of some washable material, chintz, cretonne, or better than either, linen. Moreover, they should not be voluminous, but only just full enough to hold slight folds when drawn out. The bedstead must be of brass or iron, without tester or curtain; the dressing table and wash stand of plain light wood, deal or birch or ash, neither oiled nor varnished, and designed with plain surfaces so as to be capable of being cleansed and scrubbed like the kitchen table. The wardrobe and drawers of the same wood, but oiled or even polished, as they are not subject to the same splashing as is the wash stand, or to the accidents that invariably attend a dressing table. With folks that are wise enough to sleep in rooms so furnished, the bedroom is just what its name implies, a place for bed, and not a parlour or place for talk. If we intend to live in two rooms, and receive our friends in the bedroom, as the kings and nobles of the thirteenth century often did, and as the French do to this day, then there may be provision made to meet the requirements of a parlour, but until this has become a habit with us the clearer we can keep our sleeping places of furniture and hangings, and stuff of all kinds, the better for our health in all ways.

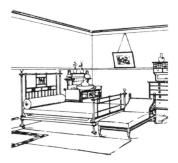

Godwin, bed design.

Rooted in this opinion, my bedrooms are what some would undoubtedly call bare and cheerless. They are large and airy, the floor has three rugs — one on each side of the bed, and one before the fire. There is a piece of matting before the washstand, and another piece before the dressing-table. The wardrobe is raised eight inches from the floor, as also the chest of drawers, so that all the dust can be removed from day to day. All the furniture has been fitted with powerful direct-bearing castors, so as to attain the minimum of labour in moving the articles from place to place for the purpose of the weekly scrubbing. The consequence of all this is that the room is never stuffy, and does not necessitate one sleeping in a thorough draught in order to avoid the disagreeable close atmosphere with which so very many bedrooms (especially those of hotels) are inoculated. I say *inoculated*, for I have been in bedrooms of the principal hotels of some of our country towns, where, in spite of door and window being open all day and all night for a week, there yet remained a peculiar and indefinable something which was not traceable to the drains, or, indeed, to anything except the unwholesome system of carpeting and general furnishing adopted. The walls of the bedrooms in my house are distempered, for if there be any sickness in a room I shall have the ceiling and walls newly done, and this would be financially impossible with any more costly and laborious process. The colour of the walls and woodwork is kept light, the woodwork yellow white, and the upper half of the walls a dark golden yellow. The blinds are brown, and the window curtains are cool brown yellow linen, something between gold colour and plain unbleached linen. Thus the room, though light, is full of repose; there are no patterns of any kind to distract the tired or sick brain. There is no positive colour to disturb the eye-nerves

Godwin, dressing-table design.

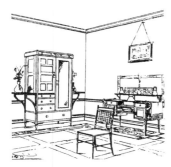

Godwin, economic bedroom design.

with unnecessary exercise early in the morning; at the same time there is no dull or dirty tone to induce melancholy or sadness; the matting, and the cane chairs, and cane couch, the brass bedstead, and even the ash wall furniture, partake of the fresh, clean, golden look that pervades the room. The toilet set is of light red earthenware, with a white glaze inside just lapping over the edge. There is one picture over the mantelpiece and some blue and white vases filled with dried rose-leaves, lavender, &c. *En suite* with the principal bedrooms are dressing-rooms and bath-rooms; these have small washable rugs, thick and warm, scattered over the floor, which is otherwise bare. The furniture is reduced to the minimum, and the water is laid on wherever water is required.

CHAPTER VI: TOPS AND BOTTOMS

Kitchen furniture

Source:
'Chapter VI.—tops and bottoms', *Architect*, 19 August 1876, pp.100-01

Biographical notes:
Crane
Harcourt

Kitchen furniture is nearly always sure to be of sound design, whether it be old or new. Take the simplest deal kitchen table, whether circular and three legged or oblong and four legged, it is manifest that both are made with the object of producing an article that shall combine the most serviceable of its kind with the least outlay, and the result is that the ordinary kitchen table is a satisfactory piece of furniture incapable of giving offence. It assumes nothing; it does the work it is put to do with a steady endurance beyond praise. If it gets dirty it does not hesitate to show its condition, and can be easily scrubbed clean without being any the worse for its ablutions. Indeed, to have by your side every morning a freshly scrubbed deal table, is a luxury in the appropriation of labour those only can fully appreciate who have enjoyed. My attention was first directed to this some years ago when on a visit to a certain nobleman, distinguished among his set for certain art proclivities. I remember well seeing his white deal drawing table brought to his room by a footman every morning, newly scrubbed, looking the very beau ideal of freshness and cleanliness. This table was every whit as plain as the plainest of kitchen tables, but somewhat lighter. There was always a plain easel of light wood (possibly deal) close by, and a cane chair; and, strange as it may sound, these pieces of furniture, so far from looking out of place on a Persian carpet, and surrounded by art treasures and valuable furniture, had from, I suppose, their very simplicity and the nature of their use — for art, say what we will, *is* the ultimate polish of man — a value not comparable with intrinsic worth. Nor does the charm of kitchen furniture end with the kitchen table. The Windsor chair and the dresser are designed and constructed on the same wise principle — a principle so little understood by modern architects — of the greatest utility at the least cost.

Windsor chair, Eastlake, Hints on Household Taste, 4th edn 1878.

Avoiding vulgar pretension

Few of us have watched with care the progress, as it is called, of modern design without noting that the failures are always or nearly always the result of pretension. In our domestic furniture and decorations Mrs. A. is determined, as it is vulgarly called, "to take the shine" out of Mrs. B., and only knows the one vulgar way of doing it, namely, by spending more money than her neighbour. In modern architecture, as may be seen in our insurance offices, shop fronts, hotels, &c., the same vulgar rivalry is at work, and thus architects too often become the slavish tools of a trade advertising mania. Now I am venturesome enough to affirm that the greatest-utility-at-the-least-cost principle is the only sure and certain road to beauty whether in furniture or architecture if, that is, we once thoroughly understand what is meant by the words *utility* and *cost*. To learn this we had better study in the bottoms and tops of houses — the basement and the attics — than in any of the rooms where guests are supposed to penetrate, and where the vulgar desire of exhibiting money's-worth seems to have grown into a necessity of existence. Moreover, it is worth remarking that the commonplace kitchen and scullery furniture of to-day is to all intents and purposes much the same as it has been for centuries past, the table, the dresser, the hanging shelves, the plate-rack, the three-legged stool are really of mediaeval design, and the Windsor chair is the only instance of the invention of modern times, having now in great part superceded the fifteenth century rush bottom chair still occasionally seen in cathedrals and churches. The Windsor chair was an invention supported by genuine merit. Its shaped wood seat is quite as comfortable as the rush seat and infinitely more cleanly; while in construction it is not only stronger than the older example, but sizes being equal it has the advantage of being lighter. The Windsor chair may be of *higher price* than the other, but considering its superiority in point of cleanliness and durability it may yet fairly be regarded as the *least costly* of the two.

The kitchen dresser

The dresser is the direct descendant of the lord's buffet, and its tiers of shelves recall a certain sumptuary law of the middle ages which prescribed the number of shelves for certain ranks, the largest number going with the highest title. At the present day, if measured mediaevally by dresser-shelves, the majority of ladies would be found to have assumed the rank, at least, of a countess. Dressers in the middle ages, or at any rate in the fourteenth and fifteenth centuries, were movables. We can still see in cottages and farmhouses the movable three-shelved dresser. In these examples, however, there are usually no cupboards, but in their place is a broad open shelf a few inches above the floor. This arrangement I like for its cleanliness sake, inasmuch as a movable dresser enables one not only thoroughly to purge the dresser — for joints of woodwork occasionally open and fill with dirt do what we will — but to wash and otherwise purify the wall behind it. To some extent this may be done with a fixed dresser, if the wall be not shut up by a wood backing. A dresser is like a plate rack, the more open it is the better. Again, if a fixture, the top self should not be much more than five feet from the ground. "What the eye don't see," — we all know the saying, and in a kitchen or scullery, shelves whose tops are out of sight are pretty sure to be thick with dust, dead flies, and other impurities. My dresser is carried the

Kitchen dresser, Beeton's Housewife's Treasury of Domestic Information, c.1862.

whole length of the kitchen, the top shelf is 5 feet 2 inches from the floor, and although its mediaeval rank is thus reduced, there being only two shelves, yet its cleanliness is established, made all the easier too by the shelves being arranged to slide in and out. Drop handles to dresser drawers are a mistake, indeed, drop handles to any drawers are objectionable. In the first place they are noisy; then the handle has a habit if suddenly pulled to leave the sockets. Box wood knob handles screwed in to box wood plates at the back of the drawer front, or hard white earthenware knobs with iron screws, such as are commonly used on cheap chests of drawers, are every way to be preferred to the drop handles as more durable and more convenient. The china or earthenware is, however, liable, under careless or impatient usage, to be chipped, cracked and broken, and therefore, although box wood would incur the greatest immediate outlay it may yet fairly be regarded as the *least costly*. In the offices of large houses, especially country houses, there are a vast number of articles or movables, more or less of the nature of furniture, that my readers will no doubt be able to call to mind, all of which are artistically satisfactory. As an example, among many I may mention the common beer barrel and barrel cradle or stand, which are much used "props" to the whole idyllic school of painters, and very rightly so, for taken together they have nearly as much drawing in them as a fishing boat.

Nurseries

If we leave the bottom of the house and go to the top we find that the law of economy reigns above as below, and prevents the pretence that turns furniture to folly. Nurseries are liable to invasions on the part of your friends and neighbours, and are therefore not under this law. The baby, especially if it be the first, is turned into a show, and the nursery must of necessity be a showroom. The sensible wicker cradle costs too little in its natural simplicity, and so it is unwholesomely trimmed with frills and furbelows, and thus made into a costly reservoir to catch as many impurities that may be floating in the air as by dint of fold and flounce, gusset and gather, it possibly can. The cot or berceau is canopied and curtained by the same foolish desire for show before health, and so on throughout everything in the miserable infants apartment; for to be satisfied with the purely necessary and right is almost as bad as to appear poor, which we all know is a crime; but to be unhealthy, unwholesome, or a fool are merely misfortunes. "To be a well-favoured man is the gift of fortune; but to write and read comes by nature." And the babbling and opinions of pretentious ignorance in these days are not a jot in advance of DOGBERRY.

The forms and colours of everything in the shape of nursery furniture and decoration should be as simple and as bright and graceful as possible. A few well-selected Japanese fans — but from an old stock, for the late importations are mostly bad — might be placed beyond reach upon the walls. A mantelpiece with a kindly story, fairy or otherwise, told in the lower tiles, easy to be understood, and with another more advanced fable painted in the panels above. A picture frame, capable of holding a series of pictures, so as to have a constant change, is another valuable feature in a nursery, for such rooms should be designed, not merely for the dawn, but for the sunrise of intellect, and the same old room, with its "ickle Bo Peep," its perpetual story of Red Riding Hood, and its everlasting Cock Robin, becomes at last a bore even to the dullest child. The nursery is the first school in this life, and the eyes of its little inmates are amongst the first leading channels of unconscious instruction or experience. Among others who have done good service to these little ones Mr. WALTER CRANE deserves our thanks for his charming toy books, the coloured plates of which, I find, are often used to decorate the panels of nursery furniture. The story of the dog Puffy, or Fluffy, or some such name, and "One, two, buckle my shoe," are perhaps the most successful from a child's point of view. His later books have been a trifle too elaborate, and in endeavouring to secure Greek form, he has wholly missed the spirit of that most refined of styles. Grown up, dowdy furniture, that may have belonged to you as a bachelor or spinster, ought on no account to be thrust into the nursery as if anything was good enough for children. Very much to the contrary, hardly anything is good enough for them that man makes. White deal furniture, not only well shaped, but refined, furniture that can easily be cleansed, every angle rounded off, no square legs, a free floor space under of at least nine inches, and a pleasing grace about everything, are the leading desiderata.

Crane, illustration from The Baby's Bouquet, *1878.*

Servants' rooms

But the attics are waiting for us, and through the open door of the first room we encounter we see at a glance that the mistress, untrue to her principles, has endeavoured to make her maid's room a sleeping place, but that the maid, unwilling that mistress should be false even in idea, has done her best to give it the air of sitting-room. Thus there are some tawdry imitation lace curtains at the window, a cheap American cloth "easy" chair, a little writing table with a writing case, and a coloured taper reposing thereon. Over the mantelpiece, photographs, chiefly tinted, of friends, markedly of one in the gay colours of a regiment on foreign service. There is little or nothing to find fault with; the danger lies not in what she has done, but in what she would do had she the chance. One can see clearly enough that this room, like the mistress's, would be a retiring room for the encouragement of laziness and luxury, and all that laziness and luxury lead to. The sleeping room, for it is that and nothing more, of the under housemaid is not far off. We look in and are at once reminded of Field-Marshall the DUKE of WELLINGTON. There is a small iron bedstead very narrow; if the under housemaid turns she, like her better, the DUKE, must turn out; there is a plain iron washstand occupying, skeleton like as it is, very little room; there is a chest of drawers which serves as a dressing-table; there are two chairs, a strip of carpet by the side of the bed, and all is told. There should have been a sponge or hip-bath, whether it were used or not, and the paper on the wall should not have been an emerald green sprig vilely drawn on a pink ground. One word as touching servants' bedroom furniture. Why should the deal be painted in vain imitation of a more costly wood, like maple, mahogany, &c.? The plain deal varnished, or if that necessitates better workmanship than the public will pay for, painted in plain colours would be immeasurably more genuine than the paltry imitations and frivolous pretences now in use. Again, why mould the legs of washstands in the unaccountably rich manner in which the vernacular deal washstands are now moulded? There is no beauty in it, and no use in it beyond being a harbour for the dust and a refuge for the insect. One of the most important reforms needed in the East End furniture factory is one that shall raise the chest of drawers sufficiently high to permit of the easy removal of dust, &c., from underneath. We go to sleep in bedroom after bedroom with the greatest nonchalance, while if we could only see the depth of fluff and filth collected within two yards of our mouths we should prefer a doorstep, and a shake down in a barn would be absolute luxury; so true it is that "what the eye don't see," &c.

Furnishing the architect's study

To revert for a moment to simple furniture for other use than that in kitchen or attic. If the ordinary stock four-legged deal kitchen table had the draw the whole length of the table, and the front portion of this draw — say 9 inches — were divided off from the rest; if a brass clamp were substituted for the awkward looking deal one over the draw ends; if the legs were rounded up to the squareframing, and fitted with castors, and if a brass rod handle were fixed to the draw, I know of no table in stock so well adapted for the use of architect or artist. The corners of the top slab should not, however, be rounded, as there might be times when the architect would like to use the table top itself as a drawing board. And the words drawing board remind me that I have not yet said a word about my study or office furniture and decorations.

First then, as to the furniture, I may at once say that book-cases, plan-cases, drawing-tables, and desks must be made to order. One would have thought that the simple necessities of the architect, artist, or engineer were so uniform and so apparent that it would have paid the cabinet makers to have supplied them with inexpensive useful articles. Only the cabinetmaker who attempts such a thing must guard, as he would his life, the introduction of anything like style. If he moulds legs in the manner of Elizabethan joiners and cabinetmakers, if he fashions them according to SHERATON or decorates them in the manner of a mediaeval MS. or extant example, it may be sure of failure. But if, in the spirit of the kitchen furniture maker, he sets to work to supply the demand for office furniture solely from a utilitarian point of view, with no adjuncts expressive in any degree of one style or another, he may be so equally sure of success.

The furniture in my present office is very plain, and has proved very costly from the fact of its having been made specially for me. Why it should be so I do not know, but it is a fact that if you ask a man accustomed to cut wood in 6 inch lengths to cut you *one* piece 4 inches or 8 inches long, for that one the charge (I will not say the cost) will be equal at least to that for four of the regulation 6 inch lengths. It is no argument to show that your new design has less material in it, less shaping, fewer joints than the ver-

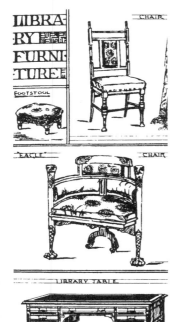

Godwin, library furniture designs.

nacular stock design. It is NEW, and that word is quite enough for the furniture maker. He knows, no one better — that his men are not so much men as machines. One man has passed the prime of life and will spend the fag end of it *in shaping chair legs of one pattern!* Another chains down his being to spindles and another to seats! And with this beautiful, inspiring, soul-raising system, countenanced by us and encouraged by the commercial, that is to say, the soul-snubbing, money-making, middle-men of society, standing between the buyer and the producer, we can find time to pat one another on the backs of swallow-tailed coats and congratulate one another in white kid gloves on the progress of our schools of art as we wander listlessly about at soirée and reception. There is much talk just now anent the Bulgarian atrocities; cannot some one — say Sir WM. HARCOURT — comprehend the atrocity of this machine-man system in English trade?* The wonder to me is not that there is brutality here and there among the people we are accustomed to class as British workmen, but that there should ever be anything else but brutality. The tenour [sic] of their working lives is based on a brutal notion, and until this has been broken up and a man, no matter in what position, is given a chance of joy and credit in his work, we must be quite content among other things to pay double and treble and quadruple the usual price for the execution of any new idea, even though the said idea may save double, treble, and quadruple of the usual material and labour.

* Harcourt, a Liberal MP, was an outspoken critic of Turkish maltreatment of its minorities, 1876-8.

CHAPTER VII: FROM THE HOUSE-TOP

It is not good weather now for observation. The heat in England is nearly always a foggy heat, but in spring and autumn, and on the few clear days winter vouchsafes us, the panorama from my nest among the chimney-pots embraces an extensive field of skyline and a perfect forest of building form. From the Crystal Palace at Sydenham to Haverstock Hill and from Chelsea to St. Paul's, is a fair sweep for my field-glass; and there are many curious things to be seen, of which the peripatetic philosopher has no notion. Prominent, however, among everything within this area, dwarfing church spires and making palaces appear squat, is Mr. HANKEY'S stack of yellow bricks at Queen Anne's Gate. The bricks look as if they were stacked in horizontal groups of II, III, III the number being prominently painted in different colours on each group. But on directing my field-glass to Mr. HANKEY'S stack, I find that what I took to be numerals are in fact window-blinds, each row being of one colour, red, blue, or yellow, with intermediate rows of white. There is no sloped roof. What appears, from its grey colour, to be a roof with two rows of dormers in it, turns out to be a vertical wall set a trifle back from the line of stack. At the top of this is a flat covering railed in. Just visible above this flat are sundry odds and ends, such as a flagstaff, a rotatory fan on a tripod, and fragments of large galvanised iron boilers. There is a slight irregularity in the block from my point of view, owing to the additional building Mr. HANKEY is now completing, and though there is not a

Source:
'From the house-top',
Architect, 26 August 1876,
pp.112-13

Biographical notes:
Smith
White

London skyline, BN 9 Feb. 1872.

scintilla of architectural character and not a trace of artistic merit, except what may result from a large mass of light and another large mass of shade disposed vertically, yet the building is by no manner of means offensive when compared with its neighbouring contemporaries. Its artistic failure is partly owing to the absence of horizontal shadows, partly to the treatment of the chimneys, but above all to the tame treatment of the summit. Failures which are nothing in comparison either with the stuccoed mass of sheer apparently deliberate ugliness in caricature of Gothic, just built between Mr. HANKEY and the Aquarium, or the pretentious balderdash of the last-mentioned public eyesore.

Mansions in the sky

Apart, however, from external appearance, there are errors, I venture to think, in Mr. HANKEY'S building at Queen Anne's Gate that may not unlikely be overlooked by Mr. HANKEY and his imitators amidst the first flush of landlord-success achieved. [...] Mr. HANKEY and the inhabitants of Babel are not the only folk who have encouraged tall building. This thing, like many other things, was once tried in ancient Rome but was suppressed by a stringent law regulating the height of houses to something like a reasonable dimension.* And if any attempt should be made to line our London streets with houses not only double their present height, but treble or quadruple, we too must seek for a stringent law. Manchester with its tall warehouses is gloomy enough, but the dullest of Manchester streets would be quite gay and lively in comparison with the gloom of a ten-storeyed Oxford Street. With plenty of vacant land round it, a high building with sufficient mass has no particular harm in it, but to shut in our streets by high buildings to the front and rear, to the right and the left, to wall in our narrow thoroughfares by stacks or piles of bricks 120 feet high and more, would be to overwhelm us with deleterious influences, the range of which would be almost impossible to over estimate. Even as it is the dwellers in large towns like London and Manchester are quite enough shut out from the sunlight and the free circulation of fresh air without architects and amateur builders devising plans for deepening the shadows and stagnating the air.

In the case of the Queen Anne mansions we find this huge stack of building erected on the very verge of the street, and I take it that there is nothing in the Building Act to prevent any number of Queen Anne mansions being erected side by side. If it be proved to be "good investment" for money we may rely upon it that the gaunt gloom of it will not be for a moment considered, and no one will stop to inquire as to whether it be a good investment for body or mind. Even were the Act amended so as to compel the modern Babel-builder to set back his building, say a quarter of its height from the line of street, although the public advantage would be immense, I doubt whether this piling up of residences would prove in the end to be the great social gain its advocates would have us believe it to be. I once lived for a short time in a "mansion" conducted on much the same plan as these near Queen Anne's Gate. I had a sitting-room, bed-room, bath-room, and w.c., with capacious lobby or hall. "The house" supplied all service, and food was

A. Bedborough, Royal Aquarium, Westminster, BN 21 Jan. 1876.

* See *Architect*, 1875, p.358

at a fixed tariff. The food was ill-cooked and expensive, the service was wholly inefficient, but I confess that many of my neighbours put up with it, some from unconsciousness, for the mass of English people are not yet fully roused to a sense of culinary art and cleanly attentive service; others, from that happy mental condition that is willing to do and suffer all things or anything for a quiet life. To people who are given to travel or to much visiting at country houses, a private suite of rooms in a private hotel at a good address in town is no doubt a great boon, but I fail to see the advantages possessed by these very private hotels, for such these "mansions" unquestionably are, over and above those to be secured at hotels like the Langham. In matters of cost they are not superior. In service and general efficiency they are decidedly inferior.

So long, however, as his neighbours refuse to follow his example, Mr. HANKEY may indisputably claim for his "mansion" an outlook which, in magnitude of extent, is unsurpassed by any inhabited building in the metropolis. This is no doubt a very great advantage from the Englishman's point of view, for it is astonishing how delighted the normal Britisher is with mere extent of prospect. "A panoramic view" as the guide book calls it, is always the goal of the British public in its excursions. The scenery of the wayside may be all very well for a poor artist, but other and more prosaic folk always like to see a lot of land at a glance. Their ambition seems never to lead them to the brook, the lilies of the hedgerow, or the cornfield, but always to exceedingly high mountains, or, failing those, to the pinnacle of the temple. Is it possible to entertain the idea on DARWINIAN principles that this general desire is indicative of a lost power, and that those who pay for a room on the tenth floor as much rent as for one on the second, third or fourth, are paying partly for the gratification of a dim indescribable sense that in the long, long past they possessed the power to cleave the buoyant air with soft grey pinions?

Kensington Gore Mansions, BN *9 March 1877.*

Waste in building

[...] But if any architects, say Mr. T. ROGER SMITH or Mr. W. H. WHITE, are plotting to overshadow us, I pray them, before it is too late, to pause, and reconsider what it is they propose to do. [...] That London is sadly wasted by an ignorant arrangement of narrow streets and low-class dwellings; that the best parts of it built for habitation are either wholly occupied by goods instead of human beings, or given up to rapacious hordes of lodging-house keepers; that acre on acre of buildings are under the tyrannical governments of ground landlords, are facts too well known to be disputed. The remedy for this state of things, is by hook or by crook to get hold of the ground landlord, and to educate him up to the architectural standard of the age and the wants of our metropolitan population. In doing this the milder our propositions are the more likely they are to meet with success. For example, the dwelling-rooms of houses let out as flats or chambers are almost invariably too high. One foot saved in the height of each floor would have amounted to the gross height of Mr. HANKEY'S mansions to a saving equal to the height of one storey! But here again the English middle class mind is so strangely prejudiced in favour of lofty rooms, that hardly anyone will be satisfied with less than ten feet as the minimum height. In most flats this is a deliberate waste of a foot; and some could well afford to be a foot and a half less. Moreover, high rooms (I am not of course writing of palatial buildings, where the height of rooms should be adjusted with regard to artistic proportions) give rise to a number of expenses — not only in building, but in furnishing and decorating — that produce no adequate return. [...] With the exercise of proper judgment in the use of ventilating appliances, and in the selection of wall papers, there is no reason whatever why such a height as 9 feet should ever *appear* insufficient, and no reason why it should be insufficient in *fact*. It is most absolute nonsense to suppose that a high room must necessarily have the advantage of a low room in point of wholesomeness and freshness. Stagnant water is not worse in a little pool than stagnant water in a large pond, the parallel is to the advantage of the small room; for the "natural" means of ventilation — door and window and fireplace — are *pari passu* manifestly more efficient in a low room than in a high one, and contrariwise. A 9-foot room too is artificially heated at considerably less cost than a 12-foot room — a consideration of no trifling moment to every one who has taken the trouble of late years to examine their coal-bills.

Fire-proofing

One thing of paramount importance in building high flats is to ensure perfect immunity from fire. Imagine the horrors of a large tower like Mr. HANKEY'S mansions in flames, with the staircase and lift cut off by smoke or fire! Our modern fire-escapes would be vain mockeries; our modern fire engines and appliances would be wholly insufficient as regards the upper storeys. For these reasons, if for no other, the Building Act should be amended as soon as possible in the next session of Parliament, and buildings of this character should not be suffered unless built not merely "practically fireproof," but *indubitably* fireproof, or at least in absolutely fireproof *compartments*, so that any fire arising in one set of chambers might be rigidly limited to the boundaries of that set. It is no answer to say that the precaution has been taken of storing water at the summit of the structure. When a fire once lays hold of such an enormous mass as Queen Anne's mansions, the cure by water is almost as bad as the flames.

London roofline, BN *9 Feb. 1872.*

IX Painted Decoration

PAINTED decoration was one of those subjects, like church ritual or historic costume, which engaged the Victorian architect-designer on both an aesthetic and an antiquarian level. For the generation of Pugin and Ruskin it was validated by reference to medieval prototypes and therefore part of the quest to recapture the values of the Middle Ages. Godwin came to this after the first flush of enthusiasm for mural painting in the 1840s, and his primary interest had less to do with a longing for the past and more to do with a commitment to 'art-architecture'. As such, painted decoration brought together two of his lifelong interests — the use of colour in interiors, and the promotion of the 'sister arts'. Architecture, in Godwin's view, was the presiding agent of beauty in society but it would be a sad, depleted medium if it did not employ painting and sculpture. By the same token he felt that the other visual arts were enhanced by their association with architecture. As he wrote in January 1868: 'Wall painting is, and must be, a relative art, and cannot stand alone'.

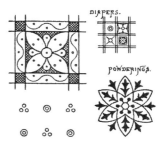

Godwin, designs for painted diapers and 'powderings', BN *19 July 1867, p.491.*

The campaign to revive English wall painting on a grand scale was given impetus in the 1840s with the plans for a series of large-scale murals at the Palace of Westminster based on the example of the Nazarene painters in Rome, although not even Pugin had control over these despite his comprehensive approach to all other aspects of the interior schemes. Although controversial in subject matter and technically flawed, this project at least put painted decoration on a national agenda. At the same time the concept of integrated, highly-coloured interior decoration was an issue among the Victorian Gothic Revivalists, much discussed in the pages of the *Ecclesiologist* and further advocated in the writings of Pugin, Viollet-le-Duc, Mandelgren and members of the Arundel Society. This debate took many forms, some technical, others theological, archaeological or aesthetic. In fact, many of the writers felt that they were engaged on nothing less than the re-invention of an art form in which everything had to be rediscovered and re-learned. The topic featured in discussions among the Cole group about provision for national design training, as well as the liturgy debate in the Church of England, and in the art criticism of John Ruskin. In the early stages most of the debate centred on church interiors but by the 1860s there were moves among the Pre-Raphaelite artists and especially the circle of William Morris to extend painted decoration to a wider range of buildings including the middle-class home.

Viollet-le-Duc, record of medieval painted decoration at Abbaye de Fonts Froids: Dictionnaire *vol. 7, 1864.*

Godwin grew up with this debate and he formed strong opinions that appeared in a series of twelve articles in the *Building News* between April 1866 and January 1868 under the general title of 'Painted Decorations'. This was his second major series of articles and the fact that it succeeded 'Art Cliques', his survey of current trends in architecture, gives some indication of the importance he attached to the subject. His aims were three-fold: to further revive general interest in an art form that had 'slumbered' for more than two centuries; to give an archaeologically informed account of the technical issues and aesthetic principles; and lastly to identify promising modern work while criticising examples to be avoided. Central to the modern revival of mural painting was the difficult process of redefining the respective roles and status of the architect and painter, especially since both groups now had institutions that conferred independent status on their activities. Neither side in this partnership would be prepared to abandon the hard-won gains that made them 'artists' rather than tradesmen, nor would they like to see their medium subservient to another. Godwin was optimistic that the new category of mural painting would attract serious artists, however, and before long there would be wall paintings and monumental art 'second only in drawing to the best Greek work, and second only in vigour of composition and dramatic interest to the noblest work of the Middle Ages'.[1]

[1] *Building News*, 19 July 1867, p.491.

In this series and subsequent articles Godwin pronounced on high-profile projects in his usual forthright manner. He dissects the murals in the Palace of Westminster and several other cases of modern wall painting, frequently as examples of bad practice. Easel painting, he claimed, was not the best prototype: 'The question should not be is it good painting? but, is it good decoration?' St Paul's Cathedral became another issue of national importance when proposals to complete its interior decoration were put forward in the early 1870s. Godwin's probing at the aims of this project laid bare the inherent problems but also emphasised the need for an artist-architect, like himself perhaps, to oversee the programme.

Godwin was constantly on the lookout for artists who would join with him in trying to practise what he preached, but had only mixed results. Today, the restored interior of Northampton Town Hall is one of very few surviving examples of this ephemeral side of his work that testifies to his integrated approach. Less successful was his collaboration with the artist Stacy Marks at Dromore Castle in Ireland, abandoned in 1869 on account of the severe damp: despite their best efforts, 'somehow the walls always sent out a sort of fur' (p.28). This experience did not diminish his enthusiasm. Godwin wrote repeatedly on the importance of wall painting in contemporary architecture and attacked the 'clerk-of-works mode of mural decoration' produced by the trade decorator and the builder. He balanced this with an appeal to artists to come forward when mural schemes were proposed, and felt protective of the limited opportunities for mural work. Godwin criticised much contemporary stained glass not only for its poor design but because it diverted patronage away from mural art, and in 1876 he campaigned on behalf of home-grown talent when two Belgian artists, Guffens and Sweerts, were engaged to paint the murals in Alfred Waterhouse's new town hall in Manchester.

Of contemporary painters who did undertake murals, Godwin was an admirer of Albert Moore and Thomas Armstrong, whose work chimed with his own preference for light colour harmonies and orderly forms. It was in Whistler, however, that he found an artist capable of producing the kind of modern painted decoration he had campaigned for since the 1860s. Both of them shared an interest in controlling the design of the environment in which their work was exhibited, and had collaborated over the installation of an exhibi-

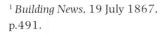

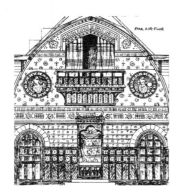

Godwin, proposed decorative schemes for Leicester Municipal Buildings, not executed: Arch. *13 Jan. 1872.*

tion at 48 Pall Mall in 1874, followed by the *Harmony in Yellow and Gold* suite at the Paris Exposition Universelle four years later. It comes as no surprise, therefore, to find Godwin weighing in on Whistler's behalf in the public debate over the Peacock Room for F. R. Leyland in 1877. Although clear about the scheme as a work of art, Godwin still had some reservations about the apparently narrative aspect of the fighting peacocks, but was unstinting in his praise of the distilled beauty of Whistler's 1884 exhibition at Dowdeswells' gallery (p.248). In his view the sensitively designed gallery space constituted a greater work of art than the individual framed images placed within it.

Further Reading

S. Soros, 'E. W. Godwin and interior design', in Soros 1999, pp.185-224

R. Asleson, *Albert Moore*, London, 2000

D. Bendix, *Diabolical Designs: Paintings, Interiors, and Exhibitions of James McNeill Whistler*, Washington and London, 1995

D. Curry, 'Total control: Whistler at an exhibition', in R. Fine, ed., *James McNeill Whistler: A Re-examination. Studies in the History of Art*, 19, Washington, 1987

L. Merrill, *The Peacock Room: A Cultural Biography*, New Haven and London, 2000

M. Harrison, 'Church Decoration and Stained Glass', in L. Parry, ed., *William Morris*. London, 1996, pp.106-35

J. Treuherz, 'Ford Madox Brown and the Manchester murals', in J. Archer, ed., *Art and Architecture in Victorian Manchester*, Manchester, 1985, pp. 162-207

C. Willsdon, *Mural Painting in Britain 1840–1940*, Oxford, 2001

Godwin, design for Dromore Castle dining room, Arch. 20 Aug. 1870.

FLORAL DECORATION OF CHURCHES (1865)

The building, refurbishment and archaeological analysis of small churches sustained the architectural practices of many young Goths like Godwin in the 1850s and 60s. In this extract from his little 1865 handbook on floral decoration one can already see the convergence of his preoccupations with archaeology, interior decoration, the use of colour, and the theatrical, ephemeral transformation of interior space. A scholarly analysis of medieval schemes is balanced by practical guidelines demonstrating how the colourful spectacle of the past could be adapted to relatively modest churches through the artistic manipulation of cheap and readily accessible materials.

Source:
A Handbook of Floral Decoration for Churches, London, 1865, pp. 5-7

There are few things in connection with the revival of Ecclesiastical art which have been more neglected than interior coloured decoration. In anti-puritan times, before men had found out the mystic significance of *vermilion*, the defiling influence of *scarlet*, the sin engendering qualities of purple, &c.— in a word, before Satan had been discovered in the rainbow, the use of colour as a decorative medium was universal. It was not as we see now, a Church here and there with a portion marked out for paintings, but every house of God, from the Cathedral to the smallest wayside Chapel, was not considered finished till all its walls, and floor, and roof, were united in the living throb of harmonious colour. But besides the decoration which was thus applied to, which was as much a permanency as the stones, and clay, and timber, and plaster beneath it, there was a vast variety of moveable decorations to suit special occasions. Amongst these were carpet stuffs, and other texible fabric, embroidered hanging, curtains, painted cloths, and stiff moveable panels, made of thin boards covered with canvass, upon which was laid a coat of gesso stamped with diapers of gold and silver, and painted with effigies or figure subjects. [...]

The records of many of our old Churches contain the items of expenditure for putting up and taking down the moveable decorations used on the great festivals of the Church. It is perhaps too much to hope that the dull cold walls of our Churches may occasionally be warmed into life and loveliness again by pictured cloths of tapestry or appliqué work, panels painted with the effigies of patron saints and angels, and banners and pennons all ablaze with the heraldry of the Christian life, bearing those glorious charges which the King grants to all who fight the good fight in his name. Of all internal decorations, however, the most lovely, and as a consequence, perhaps the most fleeting, is that which forms the subject of these pages. How flowers, fruit, and foliage, were treated in old times when used as decorations we have no direct testimony to show, but reasoning by analogy, I think we have sufficient evidence to convince us that the art feeling of the day entered even into floral decoration, and that in the very placing of flowers and leaves there was that which was characteristic of the style of art which then prevailed. [...]

Whatever the Church decorators of old did or left undone, of this we may be quite sure, that with them the Architecture was as a rule always supreme, and that whatever amount of moveable decoration they may have indulged in, it was all used to enhance the Architecture, and not to conceal or oppose it. To develop half revealed beauties, to hide with sisterly love false proportion, and emphasise with more than a sister's love the tender curve and quiet strength, are the duties of those who would rightly decorate our Churches.

It is to help, however slightly, in the accomplishment of this purpose that I have been induced to put together a few sketches and rules for general guidance. [...]

Here there are three patterns, which may be used in the chancel only, or all over the building according to the labour and material at our command. [...] The diaper itself, or the diagonal lines, may be formed either with wires, or coloured cord, or stout string. Rosettes, or patterns for rich work, should be pinned at the crossing points as in fig. 3, fixed to pasteboard, and fastened at AA, or the diaper squares may be fitted up by smaller squares of different colours, as fig.4. In the zig-zag work the strings or wires cross as in the diaper, and as shewn by the dotted lines in fig. 5. [...]

The principles of heraldic colouring are probably the best to adopt in floral decoration; that is to say, never let two colours touch, but always separate them more or less by silver or gold, otherwise white or yellow; black may sometimes be used for the same purpose, but black in all decorations requires very careful handling. [...]

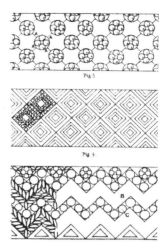

Figs 3–5.

In figs.10 & 11, I have given sections of an early English Church, with nave chancel, and transept in which the decorations assume a lighter character. Bands of calico covered with texts, scrolls, symbols, &c., may be placed under the wall-plates, and at the springing of the window arches, and immediately below the cells. These bands ought never to be much less than 8, or more than 20, inches wide. Red serge or white calico, strained on a thin board, with lines of white or red tape, and filled in with gold letters or bosses of flowers [...] always looks well.

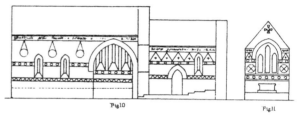

Figs 10 and 11.

WHERE ARE THE MODERN WALL PAINTERS? (1866)

From 1866 to 1868 Godwin published a 12-part series of articles entitled 'Notes on Painted Decorations' in the Building News. *For him, the revival of mural painting was a campaign which he waged for the rest of his life highlighting the unique merits of wall painting, as opposed to easel painting, the need for decoration in both ecclesiastical and secular interiors and the relative roles of architect and painter in collaborative projects.*

Few people who have mixed much in the society of architects can have escaped observing with what a grandiose contempt the English architect regards painted decoration. A large size railway station, a huge collection of pillars, or a multitude of pointed arches, present to the eye of the modern architect an idea of his art far more worthy commemorating than any union of the sister arts, however much it may approach completeness. It is the civil engineer versus the artist — the Roman against the Greek — quantity as opposed to quality — in a word, the material instead of the spiritual or poetical which

Source:
'Painted Decorations.—No. IV', *Building News,* 22 June 1866, p.405

Biographical notes:
Rossetti
Madox Brown

meets us wherever we turn. [... I]t is not in what is supposed to be the highest ranks of the profession that an architect must look for an artist to paint his walls and ceilings. Such men as Rossetti or Mr. F. Madox Brown for the highest work, and some of the younger men of the watercolour societies, are the only men we have that are capable of becoming painters in the strong broad architectonic sense. [...] An architect's work is something more artistic than to provide mere wall space or mere picture frames, and I desire to make this warning as emphatic as possible, for [...] there are indications already of how really talented architects by neglecting their own art for the sake of other arts, may be debased to the level of mere builders.

Widely separated in social position from the young artists who belong to West-end clubs and wear velvet and fine linen, are a large number of men who are chiefly employed by the trade, known as painters and decorators, and in a lesser degree by the manufacturers of stained glass windows and art furniture. Some of these, especially those engaged in the last mentioned trades, occupy a social and intellectual position not inferior to the gentlemen artists who have nothing to do with trades; but, the vast majority are in positions very little if at all different from the better class of masons and carpenters, having much technical knowledge but no artistic power, and are consequently of little or no use to the architect whose ambition may lead him to aim at something more than fleur-de-lis or quatrefoils.[...]

WALL PAINTING – HOW NOT TO DO IT (1867)

In the last two articles in the 'Painted Decorations' series, Godwin discusses the mostly disastrous murals for the Palace of Westminster and several other examples of modern wall painting, 'mainly as illustrations of what is not the duty of the painter.' Ironically, perhaps, Godwin's own subsequent attempt to show how it should be done, in collaboration with the artist Stacy Marks at Dromore Castle in Ireland, had to be abandoned in 1869 on account of their inability to deal with the severe damp.

Murals in the Houses of Parliament

Source:
'Painted decorations.—No. XI.', *Building News*, 18 October 1867, pp.715-16

Biographical notes:
Butterfield
Minton
Moore
Salviati
South Kensington

Of the Houses of Parliament it is almost enough to say that as the artists employed were men who had passed their days working primarily for a living, or, to use other words, in painting easel pictures, no sane person could expect that their wall decorations would be other than easel painting magnified. [...] They had always painted pictures which were, so to speak, independent objects, isolated by their frames from everything on the earth — separate existences having nothing whatever to do with the building in which they might chance to hang — having no local habitation, and not even a name, except to the very limited world of the sale room. When men's lives are spent upon such narrow work, it is not surprising that their grasp of art should fail to be large and monumental; nor can we wonder they should be blind to the interdependence of the arts, and thus fail to see that the primary object of all wall painting is not the exhibition of paintings — for that we go to the Royal Academy and Pall Mall — but the decoration of a wall and the addition of the glory of colour to the glory of architectural form. But apart from all this, the spaces devoted to the paintings are totally unfitted for such expensive decoration; gloomy recesses in gloomy corridors, with a gloomy climate, and gloomy costume bustling to and fro are scarcely the conditions required for the development of wall painting. The fact is the "Palace of Westminster," whoever designed it — Barry or Pugin, or both — is eminently unsuited, as is all panelled perpendicular architecture for high class painted decoration. Noble painting can only be suited to noble architecture. The architecture of the Westminster Palace, like the architecture from which it is copied, is anything but noble. The seeds of art estrangement were sown when architects began to interfere with what had been the province of the painter, and to substitute for broad wall masses of earlier days, narrow weak reiterations of mullioned and transomed panel. We see in the glass paintings how certain of the artists were not to be controlled, for though deprived of wall space they spread their pictures regardless of interruption by mullion or architectural framework all across the window. [...]

Butterfield's All Saints' Church

The east end of All Saints' Church, Margaret-street, is another instance of a union of the arts without affinity. Mr. Butterfield stands pretty much in the same relation with fourteenth century Gothic as the late Mr. Pugin did with fifteenth century. But the hardworking student, the good archaeologist, the devout churchman, is not necessarily the artist. The architectural composition of the east wall above-mentioned was purposely designed to receive paintings. [...] Were the subjects of the paintings settled before these arcades were executed? If so, was it by mutual consent of architect and painter? If not, to whom do we owe the awkward posing of the chief figure? [...] Even had the scale of colour been much lighter than it is, and had all the cavernous effect been avoided, the rounded and somewhat squat figures swathed in innumerable yards of Academic drapery, would still have been out of all harmony with the building. [...]

Butterfield, All Saints' Church, Builder 4 June 1859. This landmark church was funded by A. J. Beresford-Hope.

South Kensington Museum

At South Kensington Museum the artist's work is executed in mosaic by Salviati, Rust, Minton and others. [...] Indeed, it is a question whether we have any right to regard them as wall decoration in any sense, for the first impression produced upon my mind was that the mosaics were part of the museum, and not decorations of the museum *building*. [...] A gold background, beyond which conventionalism can no further go, is not enough to restrain the painter from aiming at a realism which is utterly destructive of his works as architectural decoration. Some too are not content with making the figure as realistic as possible, but must needs add accessories. Thus in the Hogarth panel we have the inevitable dog and a piece of furniture; with Phidias a distant view of the Parthenon; with M. Angelo a dome and some steps [...] but the best of these, wherever it might be placed, would fail to unite itself with the architecture. Why? Because it is, so to speak, *cut out from the wall* by the over dexterous use of what is called chiaroscuro, and has all the appearance of a painted statue *in suspensura*. [...]

Moore at the Queen's Theatre

It is clear something has gone wrong at the Queen's Theatre. When I first heard that Mr. Albert Moore had been commissioned to execute the chief decoration — a subject over the proscenium, containing fifteen figures rather larger than life size — I, in common with many others, rejoiced that such an opportunity had at last occurred to one who seemed so eminently qualified for the task, and I looked forward to the opening of this theatre full of hopeful expectancy that here, at last, we should see a fair result of the union of architecture and painting; but unfortunately we see nothing of the kind. [...] Had the painter's scheme been adhered to by the architect, in default of the architect not having a scheme of his own, the Queen's Theatre would have been a success. No one would have felt the want of colour or strength of line in the chief decoration, simply because all the rest of the house would have been in right subordination to the principal feature. Tender tones of grey and white and red would have occupied the place of violent blues and scarlets, and delicate pencillings and pleasing patterns would have made the house look light and spacious, and classic, where now coarse imitation Renaissance scrolls, and offensive overpronounced patterns swamp, with their barbarism, the exquisite Greek refinement of the only work of art our theatres possess.[...] In delicacy of colour (which can now only properly be seen with the glass) in loveliness of composition, in power of drawing, and in its thorough grasp of the spirit of wall decoration, this painting stands alone amongst all modern wall paintings. It is archaic, yet neither formal nor stiff; graceful, *yet in subjection*; monumental, yet animated and natural. It shows a most masterly knowledge of naked forms and drapery, and witness to its author's spirit of invention and his sense of the beautiful and fit. [...] The question whether Mr. Moore is right in adhering so rigidly to the Greek method is one which is far too important to be discussed in the final paragraph of an article; but this much we may be sure of — that until the nineteenth century can produce some distinctive art of its own, the single artist, be he architect, painter, or sculptor, who seeks a foundation for his work, either in Greek purity or thirteenth century common sense, is doing more for us than a whole army of artists who seek to immortalise the swallow-tail coat and all the other elegancies of drawing-room life, be their technical skill what it may.

THE DECORATION OF ST PAUL'S (1870)

Like the Houses of Parliament, St Paul's Cathedral was an icon of metropolitan and national culture, and plans to complete its interior decoration generated heated debate. Godwin pitched himself into this with his customary vigour, emphasising his scholarly credentials, and advocating more informed and developed proposals before the authorities proceeded to throw a quarter of a million pounds at the refurbishment. Without directly offering his services, his pointed questioning about the aesthetic and archaeological issues at stake frames the role of an artist-architect like himself to take on the co-ordination of the programme. In subsequent letters and articles on the subject Godwin supported the appointment of Burges in 1872 as

*architect for the completion of St Paul's (p.139). The responsibilities and contro-
versy caused Burges much trouble, to the point of despair.*

Shakspeare somewhere tells us, that in his time, when they meant to build they first surveyed the plot, then drew the plans or made the model, then counted the cost, and if this last was beyond their means, what did they do but draw anew the model? I appreciate that had Shakspeare been speaking of deco-rations, he would have in no wise changed the course of procedure. I call an authority for which Englishmen have generally some reverence because it seems to some of us that the nation is drifting into unknown seas of doubt and possible disappointment touching, in plain English, the *Decoration* — or what some choose to call "the complete restoration and finish" — of St. Paul's Cathedral. [...]

There are a few architects, and a still smaller number of painters, who have done somewhat towards the solution of the problem — how to decorate a given building. Where are their names? [...] Is it wise to form an estimate and ask for money before the contributors have any idea of the scheme pro-posed? [...]

Can it be that what has already been done is an example of what is in-tended to be done? I should hardly like to think so. Bad colour and caricatures of architecture in glass, mosaics badly composed and which, when on a bright day like Friday last, looked miserably dull and gloomy in colour, white and gold, with chromatrope patterns, and namby-pambyism over the altar, are not the sort of things for which we expect Bishops and Prime Ministers to turn beggars; but if a better scheme is contemplated — and we devoutly hope it is — we should like to know something about it. [...] Are the walls and piers to be painted? or covered with mosaic? — if painted, in what method? and by whom? Are colossal figures to be used? or will the space be cut up into panels or bands of figures? Are the windows to be filled with richly-coloured glass, casting a dim light? or will the light be freely admitted through pale tones or white grisaille, with here and there a yellow stain, and here and there some black? Will the figures have figure subjects as well as the walls? or will one be subdued into pattern-work to set off the subject-work? and, if so, which? Will the vaults be covered with mosaics? and if so, how? [...] Will there be one art-ist to design all the work in its detail, or will there be many? if the latter, can harmony be secured? And will there be a chief artist over them with supreme authority? if so, is he to be an architect? or will the walls be let out in frag-ments like the advertising panels at South Kensington?

Source:
'The decoration of St. Paul's Cathedral', *Architect*, 23 July 1870, pp.43-4

Biographical notes:
Burges

The dome of St Paul's, showing the inner conical wall to be decorated, Magazine of Art 1882, p.326.

WALL PAINTING – THE WAY FORWARD (1872)

*Reflecting on the 'unmitigated failure' of the mosaics and frescoes in the Houses of
Parliament Godwin once again returns to the need for harmonious colouring in interiors, and for architect and painter to work in unison. At the end of the article he
suggests that the first step in stimulating a national revival of mural art should be
a government-funded survey of technical and archaeological knowledge on the sub-*

ject, summarised in a compact and authoritative publication. By implication, Godwin would, of course, be the man to compile such a work.

Source:
'Wall painting', *Architect*, 24
Feb. 1872, p.87

What we want more than anything else — the first requisite in architectural and mural decoration — is a good colourist. [...] If it is possible to find a painter who can compose in colour without finding himself compelled to use dirty shades and black shadows well and good; but if such a man is not at hand, why, in the name of common sense, can we not leave the unfortunate buildings alone until the time and the man arrive? [...]

It has been made quite evident to architects that their brethren the painters take little or no interest in architecture as an art. It is quite hopeless, therefore, to expect that they (the painters) will take any trouble to find out the conditions under which they have to work when engaged in mural painting. However much the Royal Commissioners may endeavour to revive that large and monumental style of painting only found in connexion with architecture; however anxious our best architects may be to reunite arts which have been gradually wasted through two centuries at least of separate and independent action; however well-disposed the wealthy and cultured may be to fly from builders' architecture and upholsterers' decoration, there can be no practical outcome to all these desires and demands unless painters will come out from themselves, will throw off the isolation in which they have wrapped themselves, will assume the character of the Seeker before they put on the robes of the Professor [...]

Here we have an art that has been practically asleep for more than two centuries. In the Middle Ages it not only enjoyed a very active life, but it was so interwoven with daily affairs as to be as much a matter of business then as iron-casting or coal-lifting are now. It had its great men and its shoals of little men [...] It had its practical men and its theoretical men, and it found at all periods of its life most laborious and faithful historians. The contents of these histories and the remains of the art to which they relate, should be studied together.

COMMISSIONING MURAL DECORATION (1875)

There had been an upsurge in the popularity of painted interior decoration in the early 1870s, but Godwin was critical of what he termed 'the present clerk-of-works mode of mural decoration' resulting from the dominance of the trade decorator and the builder. He also rejected the popular perception that professional architects and artists would not be interested in taking on small commissions.

Source:
'The present aspect of decorative painting', *Architect*, 11
September 1875, pp.140-1

I suppose no one will dispute the statement that figure painting on walls has at last become a recognised branch of the decorator's business. Indeed there has been a growing tendency for some years past to merge art, in whatever form it may be manifested, into trade of some kind. Your rich men are no longer "patrons," much less worshippers, of art. They do not appear to know how to approach it; so the middle man, "the man of business," the dealer is created. From architecture downwards art has thus become a marketable commodity to which the grand trade rule — buy in the cheapest market and sell in the dearest — applies quite as a matter of course. Your surveyor and contractor now *deal* in architecture just as they do in theodolites or bricks. The large builder has often not only his own brickfield and hired brick-maker, but he has also his hired architect, and manufactures architecture on the premises. So, too, there can be no manner of doubt that for one case where an artist (be he architect or painter) is consulted by the owner or occupier of a house, there are a thousand where the tradesman, and the tradesman only, is called in to advise. Indeed, so much is this the case that the largest upholsterers and decorators rival the builders, and either retain an architect or keep a young one on the premises. Of course these shop architects are made of poor stuff. That independence which is always present in the real artist, whether working or waiting for work, prevents him as a rule from hiring himself out at a fixed rate. And this is even more the case with painters. "Our artist," as we find him on the decorator's premises, is made of even worse stuff than the kept architect. From nine to five or from ten to four his "designs" for wall paintings, tiles, stained-glass, hangings, and perhaps furniture and carving are daily rolled out between the two heavy cylinders of his brain with just as much intelligence and delight as go to the production of sheet iron or milled lead. It is therefore usual when the customer and estimate will bear it to call in some young artist from Marylebone or the northern heights beyond, and to give him the commission for the figure part of the work at a price *per* figure; that with background generally measures up at the rate of between twenty and forty shillings *per* square foot. [...]

Stacy Marks, mural at Eaton Hall, Cheshire, BA *Rambling Sketch no.70, Aug. 1882.*

There can be little doubt that we have among us some few artists willing, and, what is more to the purpose, able to make our walls live once again by their painting. But they will never do it so long as they have to work for the trade under art conditions imposed by men who measure art by the fashion of the hour, and judge the painter by the standard of the Academy. Set free from all conditions no doubt the reaction would at first be too great to be pleasant. No doubt the young artists, finding himself at perfect liberty to do as he pleased, would indulge that liberty to the degree of the licentious, and we might have at first all sorts of wild thoughtlessness and painful disturbing waywardness. [...] And is it not better that it should be so? Better that we should have Pagan stories told us again if only the painter is happier for telling them than see him fade into a painting clerk of works? Better to have free drawing of naked women lolling on clouds, than constrained elevations of wooden dolls dressed up in fancy costumes? That both are evils I have no manner of doubt; but if the choice is to be between the two, I venture to think that of the two evils the first is the least. [...]

It is in [...] smaller houses that the expansive nature of a decorator's mind, and the distant relationship between his estimate and his account, becomes especially manifest — more than ever manifest when, instead of wood veneers, the employer is venturesome enough to ask for wall paintings or figure subjects. I know as a matter of fact that young and talented artists are glad to receive commissions for this sort of work: that they have an ambition to do large and monumental painting; and that they readily accept prices at a less rate than that charged for veneers of oak and walnut. What, therefore, is chiefly wanted, both for the sake of the employer and the artist is, to shift the position of the decorator by placing the artist *before* him, which is only to be done by employers putting themselves first of all in direct communication with the artist, supposing that they persist in their suicidal policy of avoiding architects. Were landlords simple enough and bold enough to call at the studio or workshop of an architect-artist, or a painter-artist as freely as they now push open the show-rooms of the builder or the decorator-tradesman they would soon learn how easy it is to secure really artistic looking rooms at a moderate cost. They must not expect to be received with obsequiousness and rubbing of hands, or find every one's studio in Oxford Street, Bond Street, or Regent Street, but they may expect to find men absorbed in art and not in the business of making profits on other people's work; men who are ever ready to do more than they promise without any regard to extras or one thought of reward. Not by any means for the employer's sake; not because SMITHERS is affable and his lady gracious; nor because SMITHERS' sister-in-law can manage to get invitations for Chiswick garden parties; but simply and eternally because of Art, by the side of which SMITHERS is nobody and madam his lady next to nobody.

It must not, however, be forgotten that there are a few people who out of innate modesty fight shy of the architect in matters of decoration, alterations, &c., in the belief that such things are out of his line; or (if conditioned by small expenditure) beneath his attention. They hesitate to trouble him about such trifles. When they are ready to build a mansion, when they have thousands to spend, then the architect shall direct the expenditure for them; but in those alterations and decorations that are estimated by hundreds to call on him for advice would be like getting a steam hammer to crack their walnuts. This appears to me to be a great mistake, founded on the erroneous supposition that the importance of a thing is in exact proportion to its cost, which — in spite of our desire to make it so — it is not, never has been, and never will be. There are on the other hand others who, founding their opinion of an architect on their knowledge of a surveyor, take it for granted that he, the architect, is unable to guide them after a certain point in his work is reached. That what artistic power he may chance to possess is limited to the composition of walls and roofs, and to the fixed solids generally; but, that with regard to decorating the interior of the walls, or furnishing the rooms, he is not for a moment to be compared with her ladyship, hardly, even, with her ladyship's maid. Some of the most artistically designed houses of the present day have been utterly ruined internally by the application of this theory touching the functions of an architect — a theory that cannot but prove painful to any architect who possesses the sensitiveness of an artist and must in the end react on the employer for to blunt or chill artistic sensitiveness in one particular is to cool it in all.

To those therefore who desire to improve the present aspect of decorative painting my advice is, never approach the trade decorator or builder except through the professional artist-painter or artist-architect.

VACANT BELGIAN MURALS (1877)

In 1876 Alfred Waterhouse secured the agreement of the experienced Belgian artists, Guffens and Sweerts to paint murals in the Manchester Town Hall. Godwin was among those to protest against this, campaigning on behalf of home-grown talent. Having criticised them for shortcomings in archaeological accuracy, Godwin evaluates the 'art powers' evident in their work in the Chamber of Commerce at Antwerp. In the event they were not employed at Manchester, and after prolonged delays Madox Brown completed the murals – after Godwin's death.

Source:
'Mural decorations.— Guffens and others', *The British Architect*, 3 August 1877, pp. 54-5

Biographical notes:
Guffens

Guffens and Sweerts, 'Europe', Arch. 30 Sept 1876.

The typical figures which here represent Europe, Asia, Africa and America are so entirely undecorative, so stoggey [*sic*] in pose, so lumpy and dull in the arrangement of their drapery, so vacant of meaning and so void of beauty, that one can hardly bring oneself to believe that the designer of these could ever have produced the dignified representatives of the town of Ypres. Messrs. GUFFENS & SWERTS are, I regret, not the only artists whose treatment of typical figures reminds one of the architectural draughtsman or clerk of works. There are others both at home and abroad whose notion of making the human figure ideal, typical, dignified, is to draw a front elevation of a female model squatting on a seat much too low and swathed in a formal arrangement of blanketing.

As to the adoption of naked and semi-naked children in this Antwerp decoration, I feel that nothing could be much worse. Had the central full grown typical figure been dignified — as was no doubt intended — these naked urchins in all sorts of natural movement, and up to all sorts of childish and natural games, such as throttling the ostrich, hunting the lion, lassoing the bull, must have seriously detracted from the grand repose and the high monumental character essential to the maintenance of the dignity of throned figures in mural or any other pictures. [...] If children are to be introduced at all they should be identified with art, pleasure, relaxation; with music and the dance, the joyfulness of spontaneous song and action. Here, however, we see nothing but frowns, anxious looks, hard labour, dangerous pursuits; the only relief to this painful combination of child life and hungry commerce being in the illustration of America, where two precocious infants smoke Havannahs as long as their faces.[...]

Guffens and Sweerts, children rolling cigars, Arch. 14 Oct. 1876.

Whether as a question of selection or as a question of grouping or drawing, we have among us not one or two but a score of young artists — as yet too much neglected — who would put to shame such work as this Antwerp decoration. The Munich glass was bad enough. It is devoutly to be hoped that England's indifference to her own decorative artists, and that fashionable weakness she displays for all sorts of imperfections, if only accompanied by a foreign accent, may be so far modified by the failure of her Munich protégés, that her buildings may be spared for a while at least the infliction of Messrs. GUFFENS & CO.

BAD ART IN STAINED GLASS (1878–9)

Apart from trade decorators and builders, 'artists in stained glass' also threatened to debase, and divert patronage away from the development of inspiring mural art.

Source:
'The artist and the art manufacturer', *The British Architect*, 21 March 1879, p.121

Biographical notes:
Burne-Jones

The stained glass we have as yet seen that has been executed by distinguished artists — Mr. E. BURNE JONES excepted — may be generally described as failures. The restrictions imposed by the nature of the materials, and the changes in the colours of the cartoon, effected by the mode of lighting the picture, are not to be learnt except by experience, and thus it is we have the "artist in stained glass" practising only in this branch of art. [... T]he weary waste of window work that has been turned out of various houses in the trade during the last quarter of a century would not have been possible if artists of proven power had had the control of it. No doubt it might have been that the earliest specimens of even the best artists would have been bad as stained glass, however good as cartoons; but, the difficulties being technical, the painter would in time soon have gained experience sufficient to master them, and instead of the length and breadth of the land being interpenetrated with offensive transparencies we should have had an outcome or expression of artistic thought so diffused throughout the country that no modern exertion in the cause of art by the Government-Department or otherwise, could have equalled its influence for good on the whole Community.

Source:
'Notes on current events', *The British Architect*, 4 October 1878, p.134

Godwin, stained glass head of St John the Evangelist, Arch. 29 June 1872.

When is bad figure painting in stained glass to give place to good figure painting on walls? "The artist in stained glass" is everywhere, and of all mediocrities his is the most mediocre. We wish no harm to the artists in glass, but we wish they would turn their attention to something they could understand. The evil of it is, that so long as "the artist in glass", who in ninety-nine cases out of a hundred is no artist in any sense of the word, is encouraged, so long will he keep the real artist out of our buildings. We have among us young men who we are confident would prove to be of great power as mural painters if once people could take courage and trust them. We have had enough of coloured transparencies. We ask now that the money expended on glass, or at least a good part of it, shall be devoted to mural painting and the encouragement of art, which is incomparably more worthy than painted glass, even at its best.

No doubt if what we wish were carried out the herd of transparency manufacturers would only take down their trade signs and rewrite them. "The artist in glass" would change in a moment to the "mural artist" and our walls would be daubed with forms and colours no better than those which disfigure our windows.

WALL PAINTINGS: ARMSTRONG AND PRINSEP (1875)

The paintings of Thomas Armstrong, like those of Albert Moore, reflected Godwin's preference for joyous, light colour harmonies. To engage effectively in mural painting, he argued, modern artists would have to resist the contemporary fashion for depressing subject matter and muddy tertiary colours. Armstrong's novel collaboration with the architect W. E. Nesfield over the installation of his paintings in the form of a domesticated room setting anticipated a new style of exhibition gallery in which the artworks were harmonised with their immediate environment, a tendency developed most famously by Godwin and Whistler.

Two painters in the Exhibition of this season, and two only, show works which are so far obedient to certain conditions as to entitle them to a permanent or monumental position, and lift them beyond the range of movables. The noblest work Mr. V. PRINSEP has yet done that I have had the good fortune to see is the quasi procession of gleaners, in the Royal Academy. Given a room about 18 or 20 feet square, and not too high, and above all with *plenty* of light; panel it with long panels in the upper part and small ones below; put this picture of Mr. PRINSEP's in one of the long panels, and get the artist to paint the rest of the upper panels in the same key, and although the key is low — although the scale of colour inclines to the russety — it would be easy, by a proper selection of hangings and furniture, and by the adoption of quiet refined designs in the architectural details, to secure a room as satisfactory from an English art point

Source:
'Wall paintings in 1875: Mr. Armstrong and Mr. V. Prinsep', *Architect,* 3 July 1875, pp.2-3

Biographical notes:
Armstrong
Caldecott
Nesfield
Prinsep
Royal Academy
Stott

V. Prinsep, Gleaners, Magazine of Art *1875.*

of view, as the Propylaea at Athens, when POLYGNOTUS* had finished his pictures, was from a Greek point of view. This picture of modern village girls is, I am free to confess, far more interesting to me than the specimens usually met with of so-called *classic* or *mediaeval* times. [...]

No doubt it is far easier to secure unity and harmony in a painting when all the colours used are in a low key, than when they are vivid and bright. Nor from what I have seen of the modern treatment of the vivid and the bright in wall pictures, or in what is very inappropriately called "Decorative painting," do I greatly care to see many more examples of the English artist's notion of bright or joyous colour. But to avoid becoming riotous in primaries, we need not go so wide of them as some artists are eager to lead us — notably the

* Greek painter active c.490–460 BC.

painter [William Stott] of *The Ferry* and *Winter.* By all means let our painters keep to what they feel or know they can do, but let them not suppose that what they may happen to feel or know is the limit of that for which they should strive, namely, the power to make us happier. A large wet ploughed field, a strip of cold gray sky, a wretched hovel, and an old woman sawing wood compose a scene that may have for us a very salutary lesson. [...] Still, fill up the story how we may, and let the painting be wholly admirable, I venture to say that a room, however small, surrounded with pictures of such a tone, must be utterly unwholesome in its influence on those who might happen to live in it. I do not for a moment suppose that the author of *The Ferry* or *Winter* ever contemplated these works of his as parts of a series that should encompass a room, for they are entirely unfitted for any such purpose. I only cite them as strong examples of what even our wall painters may come to if they indulge (and certain symptoms give reason to fear they are indulging) in an intemperate affection for tertiaries.

Whatever anyone may have to say against Mr. ARMSTRONG, he is certainly not to be blamed for any such indulgence as that just mentioned. In general tone of colour this artist is pleasantly, and therefore not obtrusively, bright. There is daylight but no sunshine, and the daylight is wholesome and fresh, for happily there is nothing of that dullness — severe critics might even say dirtiness — which was to be seen in some of his early works. The paintings by Mr. ARMSTRONG at the Exhibition of the Society of French Artists, 168 New Bond Street, have been made for a room about 18 feet square.* A bay window nearly fills one side of the room, a sideboard, with a door each side of it, occupies the opposite space. On the third side is the mantelpiece, which like the sideboard, reaches nearly to the ceiling, and on the fourth side is an unbroken wall.

* Armstrong was commissioned by Henry Renshaw on the recommendation of W. E. Nesfield, the architect responsible for the remodelling of Bank Hall in Derbyshire. Armstrong's collaborator was Randolph Caldecott, who painted all the birds in the scheme.

As to the architectural character of the room, and its fittings, which are of light oak, it is sufficient commendation to say that they have been designed by Mr. W. EDEN NESFIELD. The panels which receive the paintings occupy the same position as to height that they do in Bond Street, that is to say, about 5 feet from the floor. And they are arranged in this wise — one long panel flanked by narrow ones fill the side described above as the fourth side; these only have figures in them: on each side the window is a narrow panel with large standing birds; over each door in the wall opposite to these is a panel with birds; and in the spaces each side the mantelpiece the background of the figure panels is continued, but instead of figures there are flowering shrubs in vases.

WHISTLER'S PEACOCK ROOM (1877)

In Whistler, Godwin found an artist capable of producing the kind of modern painted decoration he had campaigned for since the 1860s. At this point the collaboration and friendship between the two was at its most intense. The artist was in the process of commissioning a studio-house from Godwin, and they were to plan a joint installation for the Paris international exhibition in 1878. Here Godwin weighs in to the public debate over Whistler's 'Peacock Room' for the Liverpool shipping magnate,

Frederick Leyland, ostensibly to correct some popular misconceptions but also to assert Whistler's achievement over that of Thomas Jeckyll, the original architect of the room. Although he goes out of his way to compliment Leyland on his 'possession of this wholly admirable and unique work of art', Godwin reiterates the principle of the rights of the artist over those of the client, thereby implicitly supporting Whistler in the dispute between patron and painter over the scale and price of the work.

Source:
'Notes on Mr. Whistler's Peacock Room', *Architect*, 24 February 1877, pp.118-19

Biographical notes:
Jekyll
Leyland
Taylor, T.
Whistler

No. 49 Prince's Gate, South Kensington, has lately been visited by sundry art critics and many artists and amateurs interested in the progress of modern decorative painting. The *Times* amongst others has given a somewhat detailed notice of the work Mr. WHISTLER has accomplished there, and has, I think, fallen into such lamentable error that I shall venture [...] to contribute a fragment, however, little, towards the right understanding of such work as Mr. WHISTLER in his markedly original manner now and again sets before us.*

** The *Times* critic was Tom Taylor who was to appear in Ruskin's defence against Whistler the following year.*

But first let us examine the conditions, and see what room it was the artist had to deal with. It was not the very common-place South Kensington sort of room; neither was it altogether of any fashionable modern style, Jacobean, Queen Anne, or Japanese. To speak most tenderly, it was at the best a trifle mixed. This new room is to be used as a dining-room, and measures about 35 feet long, 20 feet wide, and 14 feet high. There is a fireplace at one end. If we stand in front of this we have a door at each end of the side wall to the right, three windows in the side wall to the left, and constructively a flat ceiling. Not bad conditions by any means for any scheme of decoration, and had the room presented to the painter this arrangement in its simplest possible form, so that it should have been left to him to design all the architectural detail or to associate with himself some architect who could and would have worked with and *for* him, we might have had a complete exhibition of the artist's power as a composer of *opera* in colour decoration, a full realisation of his "Harmony in Blue and Gold". It may seem a little bit strange that I should suggest the submission of the architect to the painter in opposition to the many words I have written tending all the other way. But, apart from my belief that architects have not of late kept pace with painters, that they are not so worthy of the consideration for which I once pleaded, this room was emphatically a case where the painter should have been sole director from the first. That he was not is the one fact to be regretted. [...]

Godwin goes on to criticise the failings in overall proportion, style and detailing of Jeckyll's design before proceeding to Whistler's contribution.

With blue paint, Dutch metal, gold-leaf, and various varnishes, Mr. WHISTLER, without taking down or cutting away anything, without altering one jot of the construction, has happily managed to obliterate some and modify many objectionable features. First, the leather, the vertical joints of which alone give evidence of its existence, he has covered with blue paint (in oil); second, *all* the woodwork except the shelf surfaces, he has gilded; and, third, the ceiling has been broadened and flattened by his colour arrangement. Now, as over

Peacock Room shutters, Art Journal *May 1892.*

* *La Princesse du pays de la porcelaine*, 1864–5 (Freer Gallery of Art, Washington).

the fireplace is a full-length life-size portrait of a lady in a Japanese dress,* the only broad surfaces left for painting were those formed by the window shutter when closed, and the upper wall space opposite the fire. These spaces are occupied by decorative drawings of conventional peacocks in action and rather larger than the life. The rest of the room is covered by patterns derived from the feathers.

Next, a detailed critique of the article in the Times, *before concluding with qualified praise of Whistler's quarelling peacocks. Knowing of their close association, one might assume that Godwin understood the symbolism in the battle of the peacocks, which ridiculed Leyland's wealth but lack of artistic sensibility.*

On the shutters of the central window are two peacocks in the air, one a little above the other, with tails sweeping down to the bottom of the panel. In the other windows are single birds standing on the ground with tails lifted high into the air, the bird covering the entire height. The central feature of the whole scheme of decoration is as it ought to be in the large wall surface over the sideboard, and here it is less a fight between the gold peacocks, as described in some journals, than a defiance. The scene is wonderfully dramatic, so dramatic in fact as to make one fancy that a story might be wrapped up in it. There is a haughty tremulous rage in one bird, the very feathers seeming to shake, a seeming secured partly by a shower of gold dots, and partly by force of drawing in the raised and re-curved tail, and in the erectile feathers of the throat. In the other bird, the one of the emerald eye, whose back is towards us and whose tail, depressed, sweeps over the top of the sideboard, one sees an outward calm, but a suppressed strength in the partly raised wing, the firmly planted foot, and the nervous tension of every feather of him, which would make us tremble for the life of the raging cock if once roused to retaliate. There is, indeed, more of ARISTOPHANES, more of the Greek satirist, here than of Japanese drawings on fans, or trays, or crapes. The birds are, in fact, human peacocks after all, not those of the ornithologist nor the peacocks of the Zoo, and as such give an interest to the work outside the drawing, the composition and the colour. It

Whistler, sketch of peacocks, Hunterian Art Gallery, University of Glasgow; Birnie Philip bequest.

is, in fact, the answer to the objection I have heard raised that the bird was not a high form to take for such costly decoration and that the human figure, and that alone, should have been used when the value of the painted decorations for one small room is to be estimated by thousands. This would have been a sound objection had Mr. WHISTLER been more careful in his ornithological studies, but he has drawn us something less and also more than a peacock. The drawing, the composition, and the management of the different toned golds in these birds are as finished and as perfect as need be. To me the one defect is in the framed easel picture over the fireplace. Its colour looks somewhat sad, not to say dirty, by the side of all the gold and blue, and is an interruption to the scheme that I, for one, do not much care for. I look for more wall space and more peacocks, and I fear the tendency of this want will be that the quarrelling peacocks will gradually be regarded too much as a picture instead of as part of a scheme of mural decoration.

Mr. LEYLAND is to be congratulated on his possession of this wholly admirable and unique work of art — art that would have been impossible but for the long peace and prosperity that have blessed this country — and Mr. WHISTLER may justly be proud of having composed and executed such a wonderfully lovely harmony.

THE VENICE PASTELS AT THE FINE ART SOCIETY (1881)

Godwin and Whistler shared an interest in controlling the design of the environment in which their work was exhibited, and had collaborated over the installation of an exhibition at 48 Pall Mall in 1874 followed by the 'Harmony in Yellow and Gold' at the Paris Exposition Universelle in 1878. Whistler's exhibition at the Fine Art Society was one of his most successful, marking not only his skill and innovation in exhibition design but also a return to critical prominence after his bankruptcy following the Ruskin trial of 1879.

We ought to add that the arrangement of the drawings in the room, and the colours of the room, the mounts and frames, are all due to Mr. Whistler. First a low skirting of yellow gold, then a high dado of dull yellow green cloth, then a moulding of green gold, and then a frieze and ceiling of pale reddish brown. The frames are arranged "on the line", but here and there one is placed over another. Most of the frames and mounts are of rich yellow gold, but a dozen out of the fifty-three are in green gold, dotted about with a view to decoration, and eminently successful in attaining it.

Source:
'Review', *The British Architect*, 4 February 1881, p.63

Three weeks later, Godwin compared Whistler's installation with the adjacent one showing work by Millais.

The gallery itself, though well lighted, is most unfortunately decorated. In the adjoining room hang Whistler's pastels against walls that have been subjected to the artist's treatment. In the Millais room the shrine of the paintings has been left to Messrs. Trollope, and to them we hear we are indebted for this crude arrangement:— First, a high skirting of black, capped by a bright bead of gold, then the wall to some feet above the tallest picture is covered with a crimsonish flock paper, not bad in pattern but destructive of much of the colour in the pictures. This is surmounted by a black moulded string, above which is a deep frieze of yellow flock paper; the yellow is repeated as a flat wash in the ceiling, and between them a large moulded and dentilled cornice sticks fiery off in startling terra-cotta red! We trust neither Mr. Millais nor Messrs. Trollope

Source:
'Notes on current events', *The British Architect*, 25 February 1881, p.99

Biographical notes:
Jopling
Millais

is seriously to be credited with such an arrangement, or rather *dis*-arrange-
ment, of colour, and the sooner Mr. Jopling, who is now installed secretary
and art-director of these galleries, directs the frieze and cornice to be distempered a warm grey, the better alike for Millais and the visitors.

NOTES, HARMONIES, NOCTURNES AT THE DOWDESWELL (1884)

*Godwin again calls attention to Whistler's exhibition design, introducing a regretful
note over the ephemeral nature of this class of interior decoration. He presents the
view, shared by Whistler, that the sensitively designed gallery space for pictures may
constitute a greater work of art than the individual framed images placed within it.*

Source:
'To art students, Letter No. 9.',
British Architect, 11 July 1884,
p.13.

I hope those of my readers who have had the opportunity have not failed to
possess the enjoyment offered by Mr. J. McN. Whistler, at the galleries of Messrs.
Dowdeswell, Bond-street. The collection consists of sixty-six small paintings,
drawings, pastels — stars of different magnitudes grouped around a blue moon
— a life-size full-length portrait, called by the artist "Scherzo in blue — the
Blue Girl." When, however, Mr. Whistler's "notes, harmonies, nocturnes" —
his moon and his stars — have departed to their several purchasers, there will
remain to Messrs. Dowdeswell a gallery specially prepared for this collection
in grey, white, and flesh-colour, which might be in itself an exhibition if the
people could enjoy colour. On a July afternoon, when the blind is drawn across
the skylight, there is no place I know of more grateful, more satisfying to the
eye. The restlessness of modern fashion, forever changing, that cannot allow
the best of things to last beyond a season, will, perchance, sweep away this
decoration, and it will be counted with the other delightful harmonies Mr.
Whistler has produced in Piccadilly and Bond-street, and indeed, wherever
his works have been exhibited. That these exquisitely lovely arrangements of
colour should live as memories only, gives to the very nomenclature our painter
has adopted a touch of pathos. The room in Piccadilly and the rooms at the
Fine Art Society have gone, as the vibrations of the last quartette; and thus it
comes about that a special and very significant value attaches to the little catalogues, with their brown paper covers and to the messages the artist sends us
wrapped up in them. A few see the pictures and drawings; fewer have the pleasure — the consummate joy — of seeing the room with its pictures; but all can
see the catalogue, and keep it to read and reread the forewords or "*L'envoie*," as
Whistler calls it in this his last message.

X Artists' Houses

FROM THE late 1860s the British market for contemporary art was particularly strong, and the rising socio-economic status of fine artists was reflected in the rapid development of a new building-type – the custom-built studio-house. Such houses were becoming viewed as works of art in their own right, a reflection of their owners' taste and creativity. The paradigm was Frederic Leighton, who embarked on the building of his own glamorous studio house in Holland Park Road on the strength of being elected an Associate of the Royal Academy in 1864 (see p.253). This developing interest among top artists and architects, including Godwin of course, was a distinctive phenomenon that contributed to Britain's world-wide reputation for artistic homes in the 1870s and 80s. Without the pressure of the commercial imperative driving speculative builders, architects and the now affluent artists could work together to create houses combining modern convenience and comfort with beauty and 'exquisite' poetic feeling. High profile coverage was accorded to these homes in both fashionable magazines and the professional press, rendering them an important means of projecting a public persona and influencing popular taste.

Certainly for Godwin, the artist's house was a model for both the practice of art-architecture, and for a new type of designer-client relations. In his manifesto for *The British Architect* in January 1878 he argued that 'the architect's work should not be confined to the mere bricks and mortar of a house. The decorator, the upholsterer, and the cabinet maker should be as much subject to the architect as the joiner, the plumber, or the glazier.' As an example he cited Burges's Tower House, 'where the interior and exterior, the building and its furniture, the enclosed as well as the enclosure, are in full accord' (p.46). In successive issues Godwin published a stream of his own domestic designs for artists like Whistler, Frank Miles, Archibald Stuart Wortley and Rosa Corder. The visual representation of such houses, and evidence of his intimate relationship with such individuals, consolidated Godwin's reputation for artistry, and reinforced his verbal campaign to re-colonise interior design as part of the architect's remit. Like Whistler, Godwin often resorted to musical analogies, and deliberately used artistic language in describing his studio-houses as exercises in colour harmony and the abstract grouping of solid and void.

Houses for Gillow & Co. in Chelsea, designed by Godwin, BA 15 Feb. 1878.

In his more practical commentaries Godwin emphasised that what most artists needed was light and space. In fact Signor Pellegrini told him 'I wish to have nothing but light – walls and roof and everything' (p.258). In this sense Godwin's studio houses became a vehicle for opening up the dust-infested gloom of the domestic home, and for combining the production and consumption of art into a single environment, thereby challenging the conventional categorisation of inside-outside, public and private, home and work. As noted in the preface to his designs for *Artistic Conservatories* (1880), 'the window has had more to do than any other feature, in bringing about the downfall of

* *Artistic Conservatories and Other Horticultural Buildings,* 1880.

the Gothic style for domestic purposes.'* The planning of his studio-houses was rationalised, and the number of rooms pared down. These were not palatial edifices, with stylistic pretensions, like some of the more elaborate studio-houses being built, but rather served to show how modest middle-class housing could develop. Godwin's emphasis on the perpetual motion of light, air and people, and the increasing transparency and spatial penetration of his domestic architecture through large windows and conservatories, were to become symptomatic of Modernism. In the next generation A. H. Mackmurdo, Charles Ashbee and Charles Rennie Mackintosh all went on to design studio-houses in Chelsea that built on the example set by Godwin in this self-consciously Bohemian artistic enclave of London.

When the Metropolitan Board of Works pronounced the first White House elevation for Whistler as 'like a deadhouse', and that for Frank Miles's house across the road as 'even worse than Whistler's', refusing to grant a lease on either property until the designs were modified, Godwin's whole architectural philosophy was put into question. Naturally he did not submit without wordy protest, keeping the debate alive in the national and architectural press throughout 1878–9. The Metropolitan Board were in his view too unimaginative and uneducated to read the elevations correctly, and they did not recognise 'Art' when they saw it, having 'never drawn a line, and never seen a drawing until they were elected on this ill-constituted board.'

In many ways the controversy sparked by the White House was a replay of debates engendered by the famous Whistler versus Ruskin trial of the same year, and the two were linked in public perceptions as part of a wider battle between Aesthetes and Philistines. Both incidents now appear as a symbolic watershed in the break with High Victorian values, and the emergence of modern attitudes to art and design. Through deliberate echoes in the arguments and language used, readers were encouraged to relate these events, and it is interesting to observe how Godwin and Whistler manipulated the press in tandem. In the *cause célèbre* of the Peacock Room in 1877, Godwin had supported Whistler's art over the claims of Leyland, the patron, just as Whistler supported him over the visual 'vandalism' of the White House first by the Metropolitan Board of Works and then by the critic Harry Quilter who bought the property in September 1879.

T. Raffles Davison, illustration of entrance to the Miles House, designed by Godwin, in Tite Street, Chelsea: BA 11 June 1880.

Further Reading

M. Girouard, 'Chelsea's Bohemian studio houses: the Victorian artist at home', Part 2, *Country Life* 152 (23 November 1972), pp.1370-74

D. Park Curry, *Godwin and Whistler: A Note in Time,* Fine Art Society, London, 2002

A. Reid, 'The Architectural Career of E. W. Godwin', in Soros 1999, pp.127-84

G. Walkley, *Artists' Houses in London, 1764–1914,* London, 1994

M. B. Adams, *Artists' Homes,* London, 1883

C. Dakers, *The Holland Park Circle,* New Haven and London, 1999

Mrs E. Haweis, *Beautiful Houses,* London, 1882

LEIGHTON'S HOUSE (1866)

As the home of a fashionable artist, the studio-house begun in 1864 by Frederic Leighton was highly publicised. In terms of architecture, however, Godwin had more time for the adjacent house designed by Philip Webb (architect of Morris's Red House) for the less well-known artist, Val Prinsep.

Take Mr. Aitchison's house in Kensington [...], and allowing for its completion, what can be said of it, except that from one end to the other it is altogether unsatisfactory? That the architect may have been trammelled by all sorts of whims and caprices on the part of his client is quite possible, until it may even be rash to say which is Mr. Aitchison's work and which Mr. Leighton's. [...] It may be, however, that even if desired, Mr. Aitchison had not to sacrifice much when he designed the doors in *one* panel and incised their architraves with mystic conventionalities. All, too, that Mr. Beresford Hope has said about skylines has been lost to the author of the work under notice. Nor has he gained by what he might have seen, and probably has seen, in Italy and elsewhere. And this barrenness of outline and defect of mass are all the more prominent from the fact that Mr. Webb's work, in Mr. Val Prinsep's house next door, comes into close comparison with it, and is chiefly admirable for the very things in which its neighbour is so utterly deficient — *viz* in beauty of skyline and pleasing arrangement of gabled mass. To the readers of this journal it matters very little whether Mr. Leighton or Mr. Snooks builds an uninteresting mass, which he is pleased to call his house, for as I have said before, as touching criticism, we look only to the work, and not to the man. But outside the journal the thing assumes a totally different aspect. There we find very many people who never by any chance think for themselves, who are well content to be led by the nose, and who having made a kind of god of Mr. A. or B., are agreed to swear by everything Mr. A. or B. may choose to do. These little gods are nothing more than the heads or leaders of coteries, and Mr. Leighton is in a position which warrants one coming to the conclusion that there are not a few who would be quite ready to open their mouths and shut their eyes at everything he said or did. To these people Mr. Snooks's villa is a matter of indifference; but Mr. Leighton's is an example of everything that belongs to the Good, the Beautiful, and the True.

Source:
'Three modern architects', *Building News*, 30 November 1866, p.799

Biographical notes:
Aitchison
Beresford-Hope
Leighton
Prinsep
Webb

House & Studio of F. Leighton Esqr

Leighton's house, BN 9 Nov. 1866.

PARIS STUDIOS (1881)

Damp, cramped and unsanitary, the studios to be found in Montmartre represented precisely what Godwin wanted to avoid in his own designs.

The way they build studios in Paris is not always on the most sanitary principles. Here is the plan of one of a set in Montmartre. A is the studio, B is the bedroom, with a window like a donjon window at D; C a lumber room open to the studio, with a water-closet "ventilating" into it, the w.c. having the further advantage of being without any water supply, and the little pavement window

Source:
'Notes on current events', *The British Architect*, 1 July 1881, p.329

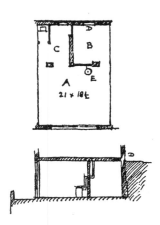

for C consisting of a piece of thick glass bedded into the stonework. The studio windows open to the ground and on to a terrace not many yards from a cemetery. The bedroom window is grated, and is hung to the lintel so as to open by a pulley and cord. The back wall is a retaining wall, and the damp earth makes itself felt inside the wall in the shape of dark irregular patches. There is no fireplace, but in the studio is a circular iron stove E, with a pipe that goes through a glazed partition and then on through the bedroom ceiling. Rather a sweet arrangement, considering everything. But the landlord gets 30 pounds a year for it. Fortunate landlord! Patient tenant!

MR WHISTLER'S HOUSES (1879)

These remarks on Whistler's colour sensibility and working habits come from a report of Godwin's lecture to the Architectural Association on 'Studios and mouldings'.

Source:
'The designing of studios',
Architect, 8 March 1879,
p.146

Biographical notes:
Whistler
Wren

Mr. Whistler used to paint in one of the ordinary first-floor rooms in a house opposite the British Museum. Mr. Whistler moved to Cheyne Walk, to a house built, Mr. Godwin believed, by Sir Christopher Wren. The studio woodwork was black, and the room had only one available window, and that window looked nearly west. They might imagine that the light in such a room was rather dull and foggy, and it was in such a room that Mr. Whistler painted what the Attorney-General in the late trial had such difficulty to understand. Mr. Godwin thought such a room was depressing to the painter, and did not allow his talent fair play. There was no one who had a more subtle sensibility for colour than Mr. Whistler, for he could see colour where others could see only black, and they, if they were not too lazy, would see colour too, and all the lovely gradations of it, in this artist's works. Mr. Godwin then described at length the studio arranged for Mr. Whistler in his new house, and went on to say that they should never design a studio without a little low window or lookout. The painter would work on hour after hour, but he must get tired at last, and he wanted a little relief from toil other than what the backs of his neglected canvasses staring him in the face afforded. It was, therefore, very important to have a little window, however, small, so that he could open his shutter, take his pipe, and look out; if it was only to look at the cats on the tiles or the dogs in the mews it was better than nothing. Mr. Godwin explained the design of the White House, Chelsea, as originally projected, without any panelling, ornamentation, &c. White bricks were to be used, and green slates, the woodwork was to be painted blue, so that in effect it was to be a simple colour harmony of white, green, and blue.

Godwin and Whistler at the door to the White House, BA 7 Nov. 1879.

WHITE HOUSE HERESIES (1878)

In the growing furore over the White House, Godwin was determined that his role in the design should not be obscured by Whistler's notoriety.

Who writes the "Various" in *The Examiner?* This is one of their "Variorum" in last Saturday's issue. "Mr Whistler's eccentric house at Chelsea, now in process of erection, is the despair of the Board of Works which is said to have exhausted every form of entreaty in trying to induce the artist to modify the fantastic nature of his designs. Mr. Whistler, however, holds to the belief that in a country where a man's house is his castle, the right to build that castle according to its owner's fancy should not be contested."

In a paragraph of only seven lines the *Examiner* has managed to get in about as many blunders as it well can. Mr. Whistler's house is *not* "eccentric", neither is it "fantastic", and it certainly is *not* Mr. Whistler's design. The building which is *not* "in process of erection", has been from first to last designed and superintended by Mr. E. W. Godwin, and until the Board of Works compelled the addition of sundry mouldings and carved panels, might fairly have been described as an artist's house having no vulgar pretension about it whatsoever. A farmhouse, or a bit of a monastery, or a wing of a Florentine Palace, it was not, and is not, sad to say. That it was not *Gothic*, nor *Queen Anne*, nor *Palladian*, was probably its crime before the Board of Works. It is unhappily of white brick and is covered with green slates — two heresies in the last modern faith that believes only in red brick and red tile. Then again, the architect has placed his windows and doors where they were wanted, and not with Baker-street regularity; and he has kept his walls comparatively low and his roof comparatively high, for reasons of economy both of space and money. Building thus with common sense, attending to the proportions of those features which were necessary, and content with one emphasis, a stone doorway of lofty dimensions and of delicate detail. Mr. Whistler as owner, and Mr. Godwin as author of the work must be prepared to be misunderstood in days devoid alike of simplicity and originality.

Source:
'Notes on current events', *The British Architect,* 19 April 1878, p.180

Biographical notes:
Whistler

Entrance to the White House, BA 24 Oct 1879.

AN AMERICAN CRITIC (1878)

Godwin was incensed by the following remarks about the White House that appeared in The American Architect and Building News *and were reprinted in the* Furniture Gazette *(a magazine noted for its hostility to architect-designers): 'The first design was so plain and ugly that the Metropolitan Board refused to grant a licence for it. It was then ameliorated enough to pass that most tolerant of critics. Its small front door opens directly on a landing of the staircase – an excellent way to break the necks of burglars, and of all who are not forewarned that their first step from the door will precipitate them headlong into the large atelier below.'*

Who is the English Correspondent of *The American Architect and Building News?* Is he a disappointed American architect or a juvenile just out of his time? Whoever he is no doubt he has been entertained by Mr. BURGES at Kensington, and unfortunately overlooked, possibly snubbed, by Mr. WHISTLER or Mr. E. W. GODWIN, perhaps by both. His misstatements concerning Mr. GODWIN'S work at Chelsea, especially Mr. WHISTLER'S house, and his extreme laudation of Mr. BURGES'S house at Kensington can, we fear, only be

Source:
'An American critic', *The British Architect,* 22 November 1878, p.197

explained by some personal motive, unless indeed the article was more or less inspired by Mr. BURGES. He speaks of that gentleman's library as a "symphony in gold" and of his bedroom so flooded with colour that the scarlet furniture is not too crude. Mr. WHISTLER'S front door is described as small, but as a matter of fact it is in every way larger than the front doors of the old Chelsea houses our American critic so much admires, as our readers will shortly see when we publish the design. He says the door opens directly on a landing of the staircase, when in reality it opens into a lobby or sunk porch; adding further, that steps lead down to "the large atelier below", when in truth the "atelier" is at the top of the house. He indulges in other equally wild, incorrect, not to say vicious statements which would be damaging if Mr. GODWIN'S reputation was not as much beyond the reach *of The American Architect and Building News* as Mr. WHISTLER'S painting is beyond the comprehension of this smart critic who "was not surprised to find on Mr. WHISTLER'S easel a 'symphony in blue'; . . . as vague as this vaguest of impressionists always is."

In this same muddle of misstatements figure Messrs. GILLOWS' large houses on the Embankment at Chelsea, which were also designed by Mr. GODWIN — "an octagonal front is recessed so that the side windows, instead of getting a wider oblique view, look upon the wall of the next house". This is a gross — we might almost add a deliberate — departure from that accuracy which, before all things, should be encouraged by gentlemen who set themselves up as critics. Again, "a brick architrave without suggestion of arch work", in which "there must be a hidden band of iron", offends. No doubt the appearance of the architrave is as described in the New York journal, but how is it the accomplished critic should have overlooked the fact that hidden bands of iron occur in horizontal heads to openings of brick construction from the sixteenth century down to the "*bona fide* Queen ANNE houses" he seems to admire, and about which he knows so much that he describes their roofs as "flat".

It is unnecessary to dwell further on the errors of a writer whose prejudices belong to the past, who adores the heaviest and stumpiest phase of the art of the middle ages, condemns Mr. GODWIN and Mr. SHAW, and is intolerant of originality — the characteristic, as he very truly admits, both of Mr. WHISTLER and that distinguished painter's architect.

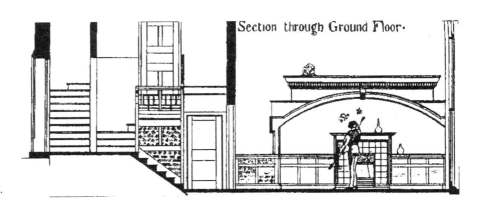

Godwin, lower studio in the White House, BA 6 Dec. 1878.

ARCHITECTS AND THEIR JUDGES (1879)

Although purporting to be written by someone else in support of Godwin, the latter's tetchy voice is unmistakeable in this front-page leader.

At the last meeting of the Architectural Association the Architect of the White House at Chelsea expressed indignation at the treatment to which his designs were subjected by the Metropolitan Board of Works and their Surveyor. We may well ask with him, Who and what are these judges of architects? Whether they congregate on the bank of the Liffey or the Thames, they are virtually the same, and the arrogance of them is never more amusing than when they run their heads against Art. A man's reputation as an artist and an architect does not wholly depend on the Board of Works any more than it does on the foolish utterances of people who cannot see that things which only partially intercept the view of the interior of a cathedral increase the apparent dimensions of the building. The error of these boards and protesters and objectors results from their inability to understand the difference between architecture and building between artists and builders. We know that there are so-called architects — gentlemen of experience, of travel, of even archaeological attainments — who are yet incapable of judging any art, least of all their own. Art is not in them, and an architectural design suggests to them nothing beyond the questions, whether it is in any past style, and, if so, whether it has faithfully followed the *precedents* of that style. Their archaeological studies have been of no artistic value to them, and of great hurt to others, for the jargon of the styles helps to blind those who trust in these architectural gentlemen to shape out opinions for them. These "architects" have rarely any works to show and generally fill lucrative posts as surveyors to some corporate body or some wealthy landowner. It is these men, we believe, who act as prompters to the ignorant judges of architects; and there is no greater enemy to the progress of architecture than the architect who is not an artist.

Source:
'Architects and their judges',
The British Architect, 14
March 1879, p.111

STUDIOS AND MOULDINGS (1879)

Following the controversy over his Tite Street studios Godwin delivered a series of lectures, this one to an appreciative audience at the London Architectural Association on 28 February 1879. Disingenuously perhaps, he claimed to have lost the paper he had prepared on 'Trimmings' between 10 o'clock the previous night and 10 o'clock that morning. Instead, he brought along five sets of drawings and proposed a chat about a few of his studios 'which he had lately built or which were in course of building.' Given the topicality of the subject, and the build-up towards Whistler's bankruptcy and loss of the White House in May 1879, Godwin's talk was reported at length in The British Architect, *the* Building News *and the* Architect.

Well, I am here simply to talk to you about a few studios — I see five sets of my drawings on the walls — that I have lately built. I shall divide my sermon into three heads (I am quite orthodox and regular, you see). Ist, Studios detached; 2nd, Studios in groups; and 3rd Studios in houses.

Source:
'Architectural Association.
Studios and mouldings',
Building News, 7 March 1879,
p.261

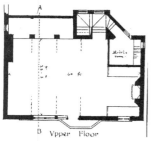

Studio and cottage for Rosa Corder, BA 3 Oct 1879.

Economical studios

The architect, like the tailor, should cut his coat according to his cloth; now there are hardworking young artists who have their pictures returned again and again, but who yet want studios built for them — places which shall not display any rare architectural talent. What is wanted is cleverness in designing something cheaper than the builder could manage by himself. At the back of most London gardens there is space for such studios. Thus in the neighbourhood of Gower-street there are stables, which let at from £20 to £30 a year. If the walls on the north side were raised, the south left low, and a lean-to roof or lid from the high to the low wall, with high lights, a working could be constructed which would cost very little and would easily let to painters at quite £40 or £50 a year. Nothing could be more simple, and nothing more effective. Competition with the builder on his own ground of cheapness is not a bad thing. I tried this some time since at Kensington Palace for Princess Louise, for whom a builder had volunteered to put up a studio for about £800. The Princess Louise thought this was rather too much for a simple building at the bottom of the garden, and a friend advised her to "go to Mr. Godwin". I built a studio 17ft. high and put over it a kind of Mansard roof, with windows looking into the garden. It is about 25ft. square, and has an ante-room attached for the Marquis of Lorne, a little hall, and three entrances. The walls are of red brick, there are green slates on the roof to match the old house, and few would notice anything had been added to the old building. It is quite as pretty as the builder's would have been. It is admirably suited for a studio, and we managed to put it up for between £600 and £700, including architect's fees. All the light is reflected so as to reduce the horizontal ceiling as much as possible. This studio seems perfectly satisfactory to the Princess, to Mr. Boehm, the sculptor (for it is a sculptor's studio), and also to myself.

Lighting the studio

Now as to lighting a studio, I use a so-called Mansard roof and keep it as steep as I possibly can. The artist is the most extraordinary client you can deal with — every individual painter has his individual idea as to what a studio should be. One tells me that he wants the light to come straight down from the roof, and another says that he must have a window light, while Pellegrini declares he will have nothing but light — walls and roof, all must give light. One would be driven mad if he had many painters as clients. Mr. Albert Moore has acted upon the principle of endeavouring to get rid of every right angle, and to reflect as much light as possible. He has designed his own building — I presume at a much greater cost than if an architect had been called in. The walls and ceilings of this studio are cut about in a most remarkable manner, so that when you go in you think you've got inside one of those many-sided figures used for mathematical demonstrations of angles and prisms. It has indeed, numerous sides, is very dodgy and well worthy of consideration by every artist. Detached studios may always be built for about £600 or £700 a-piece, and for much less if old walls can be utilised for part of the substructure. Studios thus arranged would be a vast benefit to young painters, most of whom live and work in little rooms of a very inferior character. Frith painted the "Derby Day" in a room which still exists over a French restaurant in Charlotte-street. Whether it would have been a better work had it been executed in a properly-constructed studio I am not prepared to say, but I hope so. Mr. Hamilton MacCallum says, "I should like to be in a conservatory when I paint, so as to get plenty of light all round". I fear that if it were anything like the palm-house at Kew he would spend half his time trying to shut out and adjust the light.

Whistler's house

On the wall are a series of plans and designs relating to a house I have carried out for my old friend Mr. Whistler (applause). He used to paint in one of those ordinary 1st floor rooms looking on the British Museum. Whistler moved to Chelsea, to a very different house in Cheyne Walk, built by Sir Christopher Wren; a small studio with black oak panelling, and looking nearly west with a light somewhat vague and foggy — just the terms in which the Attorney-General was pleased to describe his paintings the other day.* I thought he was working under studio disadvantages, and on my suggestion he took two plots of ground in Tite-street, which at the back looked north-east over Chelsea hospital grounds. My design showed two studios, one 48 feet by 30 feet, the other 30 feet by 20 feet, etching-room, dining-room, breakfast-room, and bedrooms, and was to be built in white bricks covered with green slates for £1,700.

> * At the Whistler versus Ruskin trial, 25-6 Nov. 1878.

The Metropolitan Board of Works, having let us proceed, at last objected to the design. Of what they said about it in council assembled, things were repeated to me which were positively shocking to one's morality. (Laughter.) They specially objected, I found, to my roof, which was at two different angles. I made a perspective with the utmost care, and I assure you I didn't fudge it one atom, showing that the upper part of the roof sloped at such an angle that the part they objected to would not be visible from the street. They replied that they did not judge by perspective but by elevation. Could you have believed that any body of men could display such crass ignorance as to think that a building would look, when carried out, like the elevation?

Frank Miles's house

There are on the walls two designs for Mr. Frank Miles's studio in Tite-street — a most unfortunate name, by the way. It is for a bachelor, is unpretentious, containing about nine rooms, besides studio. The latter is at the top of the house, and is in length the width of two plots — about 40 ft. The roof is very steep at base, and then falls off, light being got at the steep slope. The whole house was designed with balconies and other accessories to meet the tastes of a lover of flowers. When the first elevation was sent to the Board of Works, our respected friend Mr. Vulliamy, said, "Why, this is worse than Whistler's," that is would be useless to lay it before the Board, and that it would not do, and yet I consider it the best thing I ever did. I grant you there are no cornice, no parapet, and no string-course; but is architecture a matter of string-courses and parapets, and of following out to the letter every detail to which the provisions of the Building Act apply? Because I chose to do something different to

Staircase newel and rail from the Miles house, BA 11 June 1880.

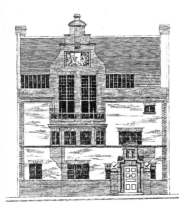

Godwin, design for the Miles House with the addition of a 'Dutch' gable, BA 6 Dec. 1879.

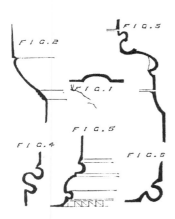

Figs 1-6.

the conventional, because I was not in the fashion, and because the Board and its offices knew nothing by experience of the nature of my work, the Board refused to let my design be carried out. Well, I made a second design, as you see, in which I introduced a number of reminiscences of a visit to Holland, and the thing was pronounced charming.

This is very sad. I am bold enough to say I am a better judge than the Board of Works as to what is right in architecture. There is no chance for art and originality when such things as that go on at Spring-gardens. It is a disgrace to the whole profession that Spring-gardens exists as it does. And who are they that dare to sit in judgement on my work? What "judgment" have retired farriers and cheesemongers, who never drew a line nor saw a drawing till yesterday? Well, here is another set of drawings of a double house designed for Signor Pellegrini and Mr. Stuart Wortley. In the elevation of the wall that I have submitted to the Board of Works, by talking in a language they have heard of, you will see the house is a double one, with balcony form one studio to the other, and various means of communication, all of which, should it be necessary, can be shut off.

Refinement in mouldings

Now let me diverge. It has been recently said in this room that there is a certain class of mouldings well suited for use in Greece, and another class that are eminently adapted for England; and the difference between the one and the other has been solemnly illustrated by a gentleman whose attainments are no doubt very great. Now, the class of mouldings which are said to be adapted for Athens, and not for this country, are those we see in the British Museum and in Stuart and Revett; they consist of very fine curves, hardly going beyond a straight line, with a slight turn at the end, as you see on the blackboard (Fig.1). In this (Fig.2) is another Greek moulding, like to the edge of the salvia leaf. These mouldings are of a subtle and delicate character, not to be copied by the use of instruments. Some of these delicate curves I have endeavoured to introduce into my designs, such as this (Fig.3), and I fail to see that they are not as suitable to England as to Greece. It has been said that our mouldings are bold or coarse because of our foggy climate; but on a wet day one doesn't care whether a moulding has been used or not. I never look at a moulding on a foggy day. When we talk about architecture as a fine art we mean refinement, finesse, gentleness; and these qualities we can always trace in Greek mouldings. At Whistler's house there is an entrance doorway in Portland stone, in which I have endeavoured to express these ideas; you will, it is true, find nothing forceful or bold about them. I do not speak without some knowledge about English mouldings. I have spent hours examining them, with Professor Willis; I have drawn them, measured them, felt round them — when we knew all the time just what we find in them. Here's a typical gothic moulding (Fig. 4). You may laugh, for there is next to nothing in it. Here (Fig. 5) is a moulding I have used. Had I been a few years younger I should have cut off the lowest member, and notched it. And here (Fig. 6) is a favourite moulding of Mr. Burges's. Most of us understand all about these, but we shall not know all the subtlety that makes the beauty of a Greek moulding till the end of our lives. They are not curves which can be struck with a pair of compasses. The best work of the thirteenth century no doubt approximates in feeling to Greek art. This I have seen in France, and especially at Lisieux some years since. I will conclude by expressing the opinion that earnest studies of the best Gothic work of the thirteenth century will lead us, step by step, back to Greek work.

IN DEFENCE OF THE CHELSEA HOUSES (1879)

Godwin responded to the somewhat lukewarm report of the Architectural Association's visit to his studio houses in Chelsea with characteristic sarcasm and attention to detail.

Source:
'Notes on current events', *The British Architect*, 18 April 1879, p.162

Biographical notes:
Gillow & Co.
Whistler
Wortley

* 'The Chelsea Embankment', *Building News* 11 April 1879, pp.373-4.

What a pity it is, too, that architectural critics should take the trouble to write leading articles about work they cannot, or will not, understand. Here are a few statements concerning some of Mr. E. W. Godwin's houses at Chelsea, selected from the *Building News* of last week.* The writer cannot think, *apropos* of Messrs. Gillow's houses there is "any peculiar charm in the arching over of the angular works, except the light and shadow obtained thereby", but that is just it: the light and shadow makes up much of the peculiar charm of most buildings worth looking at. The critic does not like *recessed* bays; Mr. Godwin and many others with him do not like projecting ones in rows of houses where, if you stand in your bay, you are exposed to the double-barrelled gaze of your neighbours. The corbels "have a rather feeble look", only they happen to be in every way stronger in fact and appearance than those our contemporary has hitherto admired. We know the houses well, and we affirm that there are no "Japanese" designs, and no "oriental zigzags" in the brass grates or anywhere else, and there are no "gabled niche-like projections" in the staircase partition, but there are bracketed shelves for vases. In Mr. A. Stuart Wortley's house the writer finds "slow combustion stoves, with a cast Japanese pattern", whereas there is nothing Japanese about either of the two patterns used. This flippant fashion of writing down "Japanese" to everything the writer cannot find a name for is pitiful. There is nothing of "the Queen Anne type" about the house and there is no such thing as an "oak chimneypiece". Of Mr. Whistler's house (the white house) the critic finds that architecturally he "cannot place it in any of the usual categories". No doubt, and this is its crown of offence. You cannot talk glibly of it, you cannot properly measure it by your only standard of art, an imperfect knowledge of past styles, and though you find "decided evidence" of "refined taste," and a "semi-Greek feeling" breathing in it, you "cannot speak in praise" of it, "for anything beyond this, either artistically or architecturally," whatever this subtle distinction may mean. *Rien n'est beau que le vrai.*

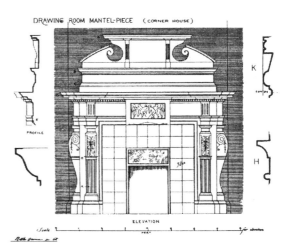

Godwin, design for drawing-room mantelpiece in Gillow & Co. corner house, BA 22 Feb. 1878.

FINISHING TOUCHES (1879)

Source:
'Notes on current events', *The British Architect*, 11 July 1879, p.14

Biographical notes:
Langtry
Miles

From ordering a plain white dinner service and brass hooks for the bathroom to mixing colours for the walls, Godwin was in charge of every detail of the Miles house interiors. Mentioning the involvement of Lillie Langtry, actress and mistress of the Prince of Wales, and other 'distinguished beauties', added to the glamour surrounding Tite Street

MR. FRANK MILES' house and studio at Chelsea is being decorated and furnished under the direction of the architect, Mr. E. W. Godwin, F.S.A. Mrs. Langtry is painting the glass for one of the windows; curtains are being embroidered by other distinguished beauties, and the house promises to be, externally and internally, one of the most attractive bits in New Chelsea.

Miles's studio, BA 11 June 1880.

NAME CHANGE? (1879)

Whistler made occasional puns about living in 'Tight' as opposed to 'Tite' Street.

Source:
'Notes on current events', *The British Architect*, 18 July 1879, p.25

We trust the Metropolitan Board of Works will not refuse to grant this simple request of the artists and others who own property in Tite-street, Chelsea, that the name of the street be altered to Holbein Walk or Turner's Walk or Prince of Wales Road. A memorial to this effect has been signed by Mr. James A.Whistler, Mr. Stuart Wortley, Mr. Frank Miles, and Messrs. Gillow, whose houses (all designed by Mr. E.W. Godwin, F.S.A.) face this street.

SOME FACTS ABOUT THE 'WHITE HOUSE'

While in some respects he relished the publicity that the White House generated, Godwin was anxious to put three things straight: first the fact that he, not Whistler, had designed the house; secondly, that his work as a designer enhanced the financial as well as aesthetic value of a property; and thirdly that he had fulfilled his part of the brief professionally, keeping within a modest budget.

Source:
'Some Facts About the "White House," Chelsea', *The British Architect*, 26 September 1879, p.119

Perhaps no house of its size and age has been the subject of so many notes as "the White House," Chelsea. "Society" journals, "comic" papers, and the press generally, even so far as America, have had their little amusement of it. Some have described it as an example of Mr. WHISTLER'S eccentricity — some have gone so far as to call it a fantastic arrangement, due to the painter's imagination. Simple, unpretending, almost cottage-like in design, it has excited the newspaper critic, until he has actually fallen foul of the outline of the party walls, visible *pro tem* only, owing to the tenants of the adjoining plots not having yet built. From the last notice of it we learn that the front is "a mere dead wall," "pierced promiscuously with square holes," which is possibly a comic way of describing sash windows 6¹/₂ feet by 3 feet. But then follows the serious and incorrect announcement that the house "cost the artist £3,500." Now, as the property was sold by public auction on Thursday, the 18th instant, at what would seem from the figure just noted to be an alarming sacrifice, or for £2,760; and as there has been scarcely one true statement in the press concerning either the design of the house or its cost, it may not be altogether uninteresting to put on record a few truths in reference to it.

As to the design (published in this journal for December 6th, 1878, and which it is proposed to illustrate in detail), whether it be good, bad, or indifferent, it is mine from first to last, and to its smallest detail. Whatever curious "fancy" or "eccentricity" there may be in it is mine, and not my client's; but to Mr. WHISTLER are due the colours and their arrangement on walls and ceilings, as well as on the wood inside and outside, and to him also are due the constructive colours, with bricks and Portland stone for walls and green slate for roof.

As to the cost: On September 9th, 1878, when the accounts were made up, the total cost, including architect's charges, *not only for the house but also for sundry drawings and designs for studios not carried into execution*, was not £3,500, but £2,726. 12s. 4d. The original list of tenders (October, 1877) was as follows:—

McMANUS & CO	£2,312
GILLOW & CO	2,153
STEPHENSON	1,950
SHEPPARD	1,870
NIGHTINGALE	1,783

The lowest tender was amended, and finally accepted at £1,910. The difference between this and the actual outlay was £816. 12s. 4d., apparently a most formidable addition, but resulting from — (1) the addition of fittings; (2) the erection of servants' rooms at the back of the garden, with a glazed corridor leading thereto; (3) experiments in painting; and, above all (4), rebuildings, delays, and additions forced by the Board of Works on an unwilling and combative client.

These are statements founded on testimony in black and white — statements, however, which I should not have ventured to make public but for the persistent misrepresentations, to use the mildest word, indulged in by so many of those who, in print or otherwise, have noticed this building.

The writer of the article I am specially referring to, after many inaccuracies arising from hearsay, and perhaps his own want of taste, did, however, do justice to one fact which took place before his eyes. He states that the lease was knocked down after a "keen competition" to a purchaser for £2,700. The house thus realised all that it had cost, including the extra expenditure above mentioned, which would not have been incurred under normal circumstances. The "keen competition" for its possession proves that its roof and walls and openings were extremely marketable, and that their alleged wryness existed probably only in the eye of the writer of the article.

A MASTERPIECE DESTROYED (1883)

Within three years of moving into the White House, the critic Harry Quilter embarked on a programme of major structural alterations. In dismay Whistler watched as the elevation 'that was the joy of the few and the bedazement of "the Board" crumbles beneath the pick as did the north side of St. Mark's and history is wiped from the face of Chelsea. Shall no one interfere?'* Godwin continues the protest.

* Letter to *The World*, 17 October 1883.

Source:
Letter to *The World*, 7 November 1883; written from the New Athenaeum Club

Sir — Is an architect an artist? Is architecture art? If not, why have they any place in the Royal Academy of Fine Arts? If they are, why does Mr. Harry Quilter outrage everything I did in the way of design for Mr. Whistler's studio, known as the 'White House' Tite Street, Chelsea? [...] The public is always crying out for a nineteenth century architecture and for originality. We endeavour, sometimes, to meet the demand, and lo, the encouragement which is prepared for us!

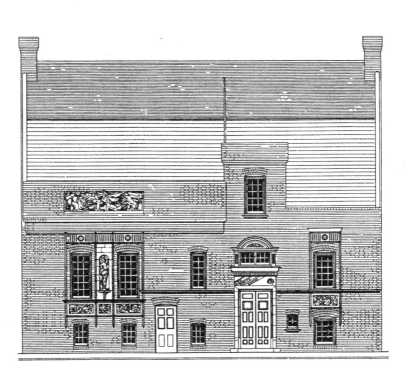

Godwin, design for the Tite Street elevation of the White House, BA 6 Dec. 1878.

XI Fashionable Aesthetic Taste

'ART, although losing in individual force, is every day widening in its influence, appealing to a larger audience, becoming more popular', wrote Godwin in January 1878. By this date the vision of a life infused with 'Art' was becoming a popular ideal, although one that was far from being realised. At every turn the Victorian town dweller was confronted with 'ugliness, filth and ignorance', to say nothing of the encroachments of industry and mammon which many regarded as the hallmarks of the age. Fear of cultural debasement was a major concern of sages like Carlyle and Ruskin and the crusade to restore moral and aesthetic values in modern society was picked up seriously after the 1850s when we might talk realistically about a 'movement'. The aim to make society better through 'art', however, and to make art available to all, presented a minefield of conflicting impulses, juxtaposing the ideal with the everyday, the elite with the popular, the aesthetic with the commercial, and high art against the emerging forms of modern culture. Nevertheless, this was a campaign that Godwin and other leading exponents of Aestheticism and Design Reform took up with enthusiasm.

The Aesthetic Movement was an urban, secular and middle-class phenomenon that drew together those with artistic leanings in rebellion against 'Philistinism' – all that was crass, ugly, joyless, smug and 'vulgar'. Art and aesthetic beauty would be the agents of enlightenment but even with this gospel there were, as ever, many differing interpretations. To some, art was a pure and transcendent ideal that could only be sullied by any attempt to make it practical or popular. To others it could be a 'permeating culture power' with the potential to reach all sections of society, bringing wisdom and taste as well as beauty to everyday lives. These contradictions run throughout the period and are apparent in the statements of many individuals, Godwin included. If there was one area in which the Movement seemed united, it was in the view that art and beauty of the highest order could be found in the practical and the decorative. As Godwin wrote in 1876, people were 'beginning to realise that art may exist in other forms beside pictures and statues' and that decorative art, above all, had 'a fresh start in life'. 'Art knowledge' and 'art power' could now be expressed in new forms of Artistic dress, in Art manufactures, in oriental artefacts, and in the collecting and arrangement of all these objects, as well as in a picture or statue. Unlike the revivalist styles that enshrined high culture for the traditionalists, Art for the new Aesthetes could as readily be found in a particular kind of verbal jousting and a cosmopolitan lifestyle. It could be smelled, and touched, as well as seen and read. It could even be a way of being, a form of sociability. Modern life could become art.

Godwin appreciated the new freedom that this concept offered and set out to explore its potential in his day-to-day life as well as his journalism. The extracts in this section expand on the dissemination of Aesthetic taste, including criticism of its superficial and pretentious aspects. Through Godwin's

Cartoon satirising Godwin's wallpaper design derived from a Japanese diagonal 'H' motif, Punch 2 Oct. 1875 (compare p.268).

eyes we catch glimpses of fashionable metropolitan life in action, at Liberty's oriental warehouse, the law courts, or a fancy dress ball. Godwin, alongside Whistler, Burges and Rossetti, was one of the first to collect Japanese goods, to develop a connoisseur's appreciation of their beauty and also to trace the decline in quality as the market caught up with this taste. As a habitué of the theatre, gallery and studio circuit Godwin was a regular visitor to London's many art clubs which provided a forum for lively intellectual exchange and gossip between artists, architects, actors and potential clients. An entry in the diary of the artist G. P. Boyce of 1867 gives some idea of this milieu: 'To Arts Club to dine with Edward Godwin. The others invited were Street, Madox Brown and W. Burges. Tremendous political discussion arose after dinner. Swinburne frantically joining in.'* Apart from providing Godwin with a source of journalistic copy, such venues also became a recruiting ground for subscriptions to *The British Architect* on which he received commission.

* Held by the Old Watercolour Society, entry for 24 April 1867.

As with many new movements, what began as an enthusiasm in a spirit of experimentation soon became hardened as its values were codified for conventional taste and ridiculed by its opponents. The Aesthetes were certainly newsworthy. Scandals like the Peacock Room and the courtroom drama of the Whistler–Ruskin trial gave the movement a sensational public image, compounded by satire in the form of popular novels, cartoons and stage performances. From 1874 the foibles and pretensions of Aesthetic taste were mercilessly parodied in Du Maurier's cartoons in *Punch*, and in 1881 two comic theatrical productions, Burnand's *The Colonel* and Gilbert and Sullivan's *Patience*, satirised Aesthetic taste in dress, manners and furnishing. By this time 'manuals of Aesthetic taste' were flooding the middle-class market and in 1882 Walter Hamilton published the first book on the movement identifying many of the new commercial, cultural and institutional formations that led its popularity. As one of the pioneers of Aestheticism, Godwin was caught between the popularisation of his ideas and the need to preserve his own individuality. On the one hand he was instrumental in promoting 'Artistic' tendencies as a designer-critic, willingly engaging with modernised forms of publicity, production and distribution. On the other, he was equally aware of the need to distance himself from rivals and from the more extreme and silly manifestations of Aesthetic taste. One can see him struggling to keep his name visible, holding his own against a growing 'swarm of writers ... inexperienced artists and presuming amateurs', constantly torn between trying both to develop and to regulate Aesthetic tendencies through his journalism.

Du Maurier, cartoon showing the Cimabue-Brown family of Aesthetes, Punch *20 Aug. 1881.*

Further reading

L. Lambourne, 'Edward William Godwin (1833–1836): Aesthetic polymath'; N. B. Wilkinson, 'E. W. Godwin and Japonisme in England'; S. Soros, 'E. W. Godwin and Interior Design', in Soros 1999, pp.19-43; 71-91; 185-223

E. Aslin, 'E. W. Godwin and the Japanese Taste', *Apollo*, December 1962, pp.779-84

M. Purslow, 'Grey Towers: an avant garde Japonaise interior in the north of England by E. W. Godwin', in P. Burnam, ed., *Architecture 1900*, London 1998, pp.218-29

Victorian advice literature:

Lady Barker, *The Bedroom and the Boudoir*, London, 1878

C. L. Eastlake, *Hints on Household Taste in Furniture, Upholstery, and Other Details*, London, 1868

R. W. Edis, *Decoration and Furniture of Town Houses*, London, 1881

R. W. Edis, *Healthy Furniture and Decoration*, London, 1884

R. and A. Garrett, *Suggestions for House Decoration in Painting, Woodwork and Furniture*, London, 1876

Mrs E. Haweis, *The Art of Beauty*, London 1878

Mrs E. Haweis, *The Art of Decoration*, London, 1881

Mrs E. Haweis, *Beautiful Houses*, London, 1882

Mrs L. Orrinsmith, *The Drawing Room*, London, 1877

Rev. Loftie, *A Plea for Art in the House*, London, 1876

Mrs Loftie, *The Dining Room*, London, 1878

General:

A. Adburgham, *Liberty's: A Biography of a Shop*, London, 1975

E. Aslin, *The Aesthetic Movement: Prelude to Art Nouveau*, London, 1969

D. Bolger et al., *In Pursuit of Beauty*, exh. cat., New York, 1986

E. Ferrey, 'Decorators may be compared to doctors', *Journal of Design History*, 16:1 2003, pp.15-31

P. Gay, *Pleasure Wars. The Bourgeois Experience: Victoria to Freud*, New York, 1998

M. Girouard, *Sweetness and Light: The Queen Anne Movement, 1860–1900*, Oxford, 1977

W. Hamilton, *The Aesthetic Movement in England*, London, 1882

A. Humbert, *Le Japon Illustré*, 2 vols, Paris, 1870

L. Lambourne, *The Aesthetic Movement*, London, 2000

D. Sachko Macleod, *Art and the Victorian Middle Class*, Cambridge, 1996

L. Merrill, *The Peacock Room, a Cultural Biography*, New Haven and London, 2000

J. Neiswander, *Liberalism, Nationalism and the Evolution of Middle-Class Values: The Literature on Interior Decoration in England, 1875–1914*, unpublished thesis, Westfield College, University of London, 1988

T. Sato & T. Watanabe, eds, *Japan and Britain: An Aesthetic Dialogue, 1850–1930*, London, 1991

T. Watanabe, *High Victorian Japonisme*, Bern, 1991

AFTERNOON STROLLS: A VISIT TO LIBERTY'S WARE-HOUSE (1876)

While living in Bristol, one of Britain's larger ports, Godwin had already been in the habit of frequenting the docks, observing the arrival of exotic imports. London continued to fuel his collecting instinct and curiosity about the material culture of different periods and places with exposure to a still greater range of commodities, old and new. In the 1860s he and a small group of aficionados including Whistler, Burges, Nesfield and Rossetti were regular visitors to Farmer & Rogers' Oriental Warehouse, the shop where Arthur Lasenby Liberty worked before setting up his own company. Here Godwin describes the spectacle of fashionable crowds gathering at Liberty's to watch the unpacking of the latest consignment from the orient, and reflects on the apparently inexorable deterioration in quality of the shop's stock.

Source:
'Afternoon strolls. —I. Visit to a Japanese warehouse', *Architect*, 23 December 1876, p. 363

Biographical notes:
Farmer & Rogers
Liberty's

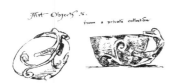

Godwin, sketches of Chinese objects from a private collection, BA *12 Aug. 1881.*

To be able to wander through a well arranged and well stocked warehouse is one of the delights of being in London. Being out for my usual stroll the other afternoon, I determined to seize another delight by a visit to the Winter Exhibition of Watercolours in Pall Mall East. But hearing of a new importation of Japanese fans, and that certain cases of them would be opened in a little shop near the top of Regent Street, I took the Anglo-Japanese warehouse first. There was quite a crowd when we arrived. A distinguished traveller had buttonholed the proprietor in one corner; a well-known baronet waiting to do the same, was trifling with some feather dusting brushes; two architects of well known names were posing an attendant in another corner with awkward questions; three distinguished painters with their wives blocked up the staircase; while a bevy of ladies filled up the rest of the floor space. It was some time before I could get sufficiently near to catch the eye of the master of this enchanting cave, and then only to learn to my disappointment, that the cases would not arrive till late that evening. Almost in a moment the swarm of folk vanished, and I was free to pick my way from ground-floor to attic, for No. 218 Regent Street is from front to back, and top to bottom, literally crammed with objects of oriental manufacture.

If it only had a little decent furniture to select from, an artist might almost decorate and furnish his home from this one shop. There are matting and mats, carpets and rugs for the floor; Japanese papers for the walls; curtain stuffs for windows and doors; folding screens small and large, chairs, stools and so-forth. There are necessarily some few things the banishment of which one could easily forgive. Most of the faience flower-pots, garden seats, vases &c, are positively crude, both in shape and colour. Now and then, too, one stumbles against a curtain or rug that is irritating in its sheer violence of colour. Such coarseness, however, is rarely or ever, to be found even in the *modern* products of Japan. I say "rarely", and I confess, with not a little sadness and misgiving, that the rareness is lessening every day. Either the European market is ruining Japanese art, or the Japanese have taken our artistic measure and found it wanting; perhaps there is a little of both.

Fans, screens and lacquer-ware

Take, for example, the common paper-fan of to-day and compare it with those found here ten, even eight, years ago. The market has been cheapened, and with this cheapening the inferior work has followed, as it always will. It is true we can buy for twopence to threepence the native fan that used to cost us from sixpence to a shilling, but from an artistic point of view the twopenny fan is as dear as the shilling fan was cheap. The fans of ten years ago are for the most part lovely in delicate colour and exquisite in drawing, but the great majority of fans of to-day that have come under my observation, and I have looked at a good many, are impregnated with the crudeness of the European's sense of colour, and are immeasurably below the earlier examples in both the qualities just mentioned. Let us hope that the new batch will furnish us with something better. Another article in which the decline of Japanese art is manifest is the folding screen. Here, however, no reduction has taken place in price; the six-leaf paper screen (hand-painted) of to-day that sells at five guineas, costs just as much as a similar sized screen did some years ago. The difference in the decorative work is perhaps not so immeasurable as that to be observed in the fans; but there is a difference, and that by no means slight, especially in the drawing and colouring of vegetable life, a difference which is wholly in favour of the earlier importations. Turning to the other side, there is one inexpensive article, the little lacquer ash tray-sold for sixpence — that bears the unmistakable impress of that artistic nation to which so many of us are directly or indirectly indebted. On one are a bit of old weather-beaten bamboo and a butterfly; on another one plant of the iris, with two blossoms and three buds; on a third a few naked branches; on a fourth, a baby bamboo shooting up like an arrow, each and all designed with a felicity and drawn with a freedom, that is unmatchable by any other nation under the sun. Here and there, maybe, a delicate stroke that just misses that certainty of execution, but with this exception the $4^1/_2$ inch cigar ash or pin tray is a marvel for its combination of beauty with cheapness.

Japanese fan and ceramic decoration illustrated by Dresser, BA 10 Jan. 1879.

'The Cheap Aesthetic Swell'. Punch 30 July 1881.

Japanese wallpapers

To an architect, one of the most interesting modern imports from Japan is the leather-like embossed paper made in pieces twelve yards long and one yard wide. The prices vary from two shillings to nearly seven shillings per yard, so that they are not likely to compete with our wall papers. That there are purposes connected on the one hand with elaborate and costly work, and on the other with inexpensive decoration to which these products may be most favourably applied, will be manifest to most architects who have thought twice on the subject. Among these papers there is one — a broad pattern of dark green meandering foliage on a gold ground — which is extremely beautiful, and, properly placed, might be well used in almost any style of building, and would of itself give style to a house that had none. There are others, again, that are more singular than beautiful, and seem far better adapted for filling up the small panels of cheap furniture than for any extensive area on walls. I

Godwin, wallpaper design derived from a Japanese diagonal 'H' motif, from the Art Furniture *catalogue, 1877.*

am told by an architect of much experience, who has tried this paper as ordinary wall paper, that in his case it was a complete failure from a practical point of view. There was not question as to its artistic merits, but after a very short time the paper became covered with a sort of efflorescence — some whitish stuff that appeared on the surface, and which, on being wiped off, revealed a mere ruin of the paper as first put on. There was no question of salt in the materials of the wall, for it was an old one, and the old paper that had been removed had shown no signs of anything like this; ergo, said my friend, it is the fault of the Japanese paper maker. On the other hand, it is but fair to those who import the material to say that they assert that the paper is free from any such fault as my architect friend would impute to it; that it has been used as a wall paper in new houses by a popular and deservedly-distinguished architect, who has found no fault at all; that it has been on one of the walls of the warehouse No. 218 Regent Street since it was first imported, where it can be seen by any one; that the importers are prepared to prove that the Japanese papers may be used as safely as our ordinary English wall papers; ergo, that the fault my friend complains of was not in the paper but in the wall or hanging. If these Japanese wall papers are to obtain favour with architects, it is of the utmost importance that we should be satisfied of their quality. It may be that they have as yet only been applied successfully to wood partitions or battened walls; it may be so, or it may not be so, but it would be as well if we could know all the details concerning the experiments and uses to which they have already been subjected, the fact that the Japanese live chiefly in houses of timber construction might go far to make an architect hesitate before using their papers on common plastered brickwork. Hence the desirability of our having a clear statement on the subject.

Japanese printed books

Godwin, drawing of Japanese wood construction copied from a Japanese book, BN *19 Feb. 1875.*

Talking of papers reminds me that as with the common fans, so with the common printed books, there has been a considerable falling off from the earlier importations. The books now on sale are neither so artistic nor so well printed as they used to be. Indeed I may venture to go so far as to say that the illustrations in some of them are so indifferent and the printing so abominably hurried as to render them only fit for the waste-paper basket. So long as the English buyers are without knowledge, judgment, taste, art — whatever we choose to call the distinguishing faculty that winnows bad from good, chaff from wheat — so long as they persist in cheapening art, looking for oddities rather than excellencies, alive to the coarse and violent but blind to the beautiful, so long will our Japanese importations go on deteriorating. Of course it is just possible that Japanese art, like Greek and Gothic before it, is dying out slowly but surely of itself; that its art-life has past its manhood and is all unconsciously but none the less certainly coming round again to its toddling time and final extinction. If so, then to this deplorable future every one of us has contributed who, thoughtlessly or ignorantly passing unheeded her good works, has purchased Japan's inferior products and helped to make a trade for them in the markets of civilised Western Europe.

JAPANESE ARTISTRY (1875)

Many consumers acquiring oriental odds and ends from shops like Liberty's have a skewed and superficial understanding of Japanese artistry.

In art circles in is by no means uncommon to meet with people who, while they admit the fact that the Japanese are endowed with a keen sense for colour, and with a great faculty for drawing natural objects, are yet rash enough to say that they have no knowledge of perspective, and are indifferent to beauty in the human form. Such people, and there are many of them, judge the Japanese from the standpoint of a shop in Regent-street, or Baker-street, and not unfrequently from a still lower level — to wit, a few pans and trays picked up at their family grocer's. Nothing can be more misleading than this, for no one who is at all acquainted even in the smallest degree with the best class of Japanese work — and by work I do not mean a fan, or a tray, or a cabinet — can for a moment have any doubt as to the high artistic excellence which permeates the entire country.

Source:
'Woodwork. —VI. Japanese wood construction', *Building News*, 19 February 1875, p.200

EXOTIC COSTUMES (1878)

BITS of the Japanese portion of the diversified entertainment entitled *Yolande*, lately produced at the Alhambra, were so unusually artistic that we venture to ask the enterprising manager to transport us to other countries besides Japan. Egypt, Assyria, and, above all, Greece in its best days might be presented to us in living pictures. The only real difficulty seems to be in securing figures suited to wear the artistic costumes, for it would never do for Greek maidens to clothe themselves in a bulging mass of garments as a groundwork for the outside chiton. It was bad enough to see the Japanese dresses thus puffed out into dull rotundities, but a panathenaic procession in petticoats would be too horrible!

Source:
'Notes on current events', *The British Architect*, 11 January 1878, p.20

Biographical notes:
Liberty's

TALKING of Japanese Art, we hear that Messrs. Liberty and Co., of Regent-street, are prepared to execute orders for the better class of Japanese furniture and joinery. In lightness of construction, finish of workmanship, quaintness and beauty of design, the Japanese wood-workers are supreme.

A FANCY DRESS BALL (1880)

In January 1878 Godwin created decorations for a masked ball using purchases from Liberty's, so it is quite possible that he provided the same service to the Hon. Mrs Brassey on this occasion. In other words one can view this notice as an indirect advert for himself and for Liberty's, a regular advertiser in The British Architect.

The Hon. Mrs. Brassey, of Heythrop, did the right and the artistic thing the other day for her fancy dress ball. The great hall was the ballroom, and Mr. Liberty, whose Japanese warehouse in Regent-street is so well known, sent

Source:
'Notes on current events', *The British Architect*, 13 February 1880, p.73

Biographical notes:
Liberty's

'Thoughts on a ball', Punch 31
July 1880.

down piles of valuable embroideries and other marvellous lovelinesses of the
East to clothe the hall and corridors. All the numerous lights in hall and conservatory were subdued by Japanese lanterns and shades. The whole effect
was simply glorious to the untutored eye, and to the artistic was exquisitely
satisfactory. But it does not require the riches of the East to produce lovely
effects. Great beauty may be attained by people of very moderate means if
they only knew how to use the simple and less expensive goods that are stored
in our Japanese warehouses. Lanterns, and matting, and cheap fans, with a
few six-fold paper screens, may be so arranged to give to any ballroom a look
of refined elegance and a tone of lovely harmony that no amount of European upholstery can equal.

THE POPULAR NOVELIST ON ART (1876)

'The art teaching conveyed in the form of a three-volume novel is sometimes vulgar',
wrote Godwin in 1879, 'sometimes silly, and rarely sound.'* Nevertheless he recog-
nised just how influential this kind of reading-matter was in shaping popular per-
ceptions of household taste, and elsewhere wrote about the parallels between liter-
ary and artistic leanings.

* 'Notes on Current Events',
The British Architect, 25 July
1879, p.34

Source:
'The popular novelist on art',
Architect, 8 April 1876,
pp.221-2

Biographical notes:
Disraeli
Hart
Horsley
Leighton
Royal Academy
RIBA
Scott, Walter
Thackeray
Whistler

The Art influence of the popular novelist in its lowest denomination is perhaps a greater power than that of the Royal Institute of Architects in its highest. Mr. Disraeli's young lady of twelve, whose remarks are deemed worthy a
Premier's quotation before the full House of Commons, is a typical young lady.
She learns about the nations of the earth from doubtful works on geography;
she swallows unquestioned the errors of a familiar almanac; and gathers her
Art knowledge from the latest novel [...] Neither the world in general nor that
part of it called society is any the wiser for the utterances of the Fellows of the
Royal Institute of British Architects. On the contrary, as far as I have yet gath-
ered, the world passes them by, society is unconscious of their existence, and
their own craft is indifferent towards them. But it is not so with the popular
novelist. It is to a novelist, and not to an architect or painter, that we really
owe the "Queen Anne" revival, and the style of the majority of London School
Board buildings is even more distinctly referable to the influence of WILLIAM
MAKEPEACE THACKERAY than the medieval revival was to Sir WALTER
SCOTT. I am not aware that any novelist has called upon the spirit of some
past time to furnish us with a new art-revival. A second Classic Renaissance
that would be Greek artistically and in spirit, instead of Greek architecturally
in modules and minutes, awaits its novelist. [...]

I am strongly induced to think the time has not yet arrived for this new
architectural revival or revolution, as I hope it may prove to be, from the way
in which architecture and other arts are written of in some of the latest productions of those writers of fiction who are most in demand. So long as an
English squire's daughter, of the ripe age of twenty-three, can think it "wonderful" to live in London in the midst of Academicians, "to live in the front
rank of intellectual progress" "to hear of famous pictures before they are

painted" [...] and to consider him incalculably blessed who has been among the first to see those marvellous illustrations of mediaeval life that Mr. HORSLEY delights in, so long as a novelist and her heroines can speak, think or write about this sort of thing there is little danger of the Queen Anne revival being supplanted.

An illustration of the novelist's art education

The book before me, which I have taken for an illustration of the popular novelist's art-education, has not been specially chosen by me for this purpose, and is by no means regarded as an extravagant instance one way or the other. The descriptions of architecture old and new, the approbation of certain styles of decorations and furniture, the mention of painters and paintings are rather above than below the intellectual level of remarks one has occasionally heard within the walls of privileged societies and institutes. [...]

As the Academy has been mentioned, it may be as well to begin with painting. A rich man of the world, speaking of an artistic lady's dress says, "pearly greys, changeful opals, amaranth, and primrose — gentle reposeful tints that remind one of LEIGHTON'S pictures". [...] Later on, the artistic lady, "a little off colour", "enters from the adjoining room, dressed in white cashmere — an opaque creamy white — with her hair loosely arranged, like a picture by WHISTLER." The satisfaction, power, and pleasure of being thus able to knock off, as it were, with two flicks of the pen the characteristics of LEIGHTON AND WHISTLER must be even more wonderful than the charm of hearing of Mr. SOLOMON HART'S "pictures before they are painted". Architects have not the honour of being mentioned by their real names, but architecture, with its attendant satellites of fittings and furniture, comes in for by far the largest share of our novelist's art utterances. Of the new buildings presented to us, a small fashionable theatre stands forth in such powerful relief as to be easily recognised. "All that there is of the most new; a house like a bonbonnière by SIRAUDIN,* all quilted canary satin and ground, with a background of Burgundy-coloured velvet."

* 19th-century Parisian patissier, famous for his elaborate confections.

Criminal, virtuous and elegantly extravagant interiors compared

Mr. Pipp, the architect, is ordered by the noble lord, his client, to make the manageress's dressing room "as perfect as art can make it", which is done accordingly. "POMPADOUR, in the plenitude of her power, with France at her feet, acknowledged protectress of the arts, may have had rooms as elegant, but not more costly. Walls upholstered in sky-blue satin, embroidered with butterflies and birds — birds and butterflies so artistic that they seem living creatures fluttering in a tropical sky; doors veneered with ivory, mantlepiece of Sevres, ceiling painted with more birds and butterflies, chairs and couches of white enamelled wood and quilted blue satin, toilet table, the crowning wonder of all, entirely of ivory and silver. There is not an inch of velvet or gilding in the room. All is cool, soft, reposeful. After the brightness and glitter of the theatre, the eye rests here as on a glimpse of dark blue water", and so on. [...] The manageress's house is furnished with the same art judgment that distinguishes the theatre. The drawing-room "has a cheerful glow winter or summer. The curtains and chair covers are of a rich amber, the carpet deep brown, shaded to palest yellow. These amber tones set off the ebony furniture, the majolica vases, and plateaus of turquoise blue, the water-coloured landscapes on the dove-coloured walls." The cheerfulness of black on palest yellow and the exquisitely refined harmony of majolica vases against dove-coloured walls are too manifest to require note or comment. But these reposeful dressing-rooms and cheerful drawing-rooms are not only theatrical property, but they belong to a lady who endeavours to compass the destruction of an unconscious rival. We may therefore suppose that the descriptions I have quoted are more or less symbolical, and that our minds are not intended to be directed towards the possession of this criminal kind of art, but rather to the attainment of the virtuous style described in the penultimate chapter of the novel made up chiefly of cretonne draperies, chromolithographs, pale green walls, point lace borders to chimneypieces, pitch-pine furniture, and a pair of Glastonbury chairs.

There is the middle course which may be described as the literary-artistic or extravagant style where the literary proprietor indulges his Pompeian or Elizabethan taste (it is oddly enough always one or the other) to the delight and benefit of — the upholsterer he employs. "There is an artistic grace about the river-side villa with its light airy rooms ... There is nothing costly, or that strikes the observer as costly; no gilding, except the slenderest line of unburnished gold here and there; no sheen of satin or splendour of brocade; no vast expanse of looking-glass, confusing the sense with imaginary space. The Pompeian vestibule and dining-room are deliciously simple; encaustic tiles, unpolished ebony, cretonne draperies of classic design and rich subdued colour. The walls are painted a delicate French gray, relieved by a four-foot dado of ebonised panelling, and the ceiling of palest primrose. A broad border of ebonised wood surrounds the Venetian glass over the chimneypiece, and on this broad framework there are brackets supporting small bronze figures which might have been dug out of the lava that buried Herculaneum." Then there are some more cretonne curtains, a lot of ebonised shelves, "a sofa of classic design," Etrurian beer jugs, an urn which might have belonged to ANTIGONE, and to sum up, "everything is artistic." Here, although we have not the viciousness of that perfection of art where embroidered birds "seem living creatures," and so beguiled and surprised is "as lively painted as the deed was done," so neither on the one hand have we any sign of the distinctly virtuous art — the humility of pitch-pine tables, the mortifying self-denial of Glastonbury chairs — unless, indeed, the cretonne draperies might be taken to symbolise the leaven of goodness which, even in his most thoughtless and extravagant days, was vouchsafed to the literary hero of the tale to prepare him for his future haven among chromos, point-lace, and pitch-pine. It is satisfactory to know that this last condition of things (chromos, &c.,) is due to the combined effort of two young ladies, the most active of whom the heroine has architectured not merely in a private way on her own greenhouses, but has amused herself with no less a public work than the village schools — "a pretty Gothic building." [...]

Such, then, are the three latest views of modern art to which this popular writer introduces us. First, we have a French costly luxuriousness of quilted satin and ivory and silver and Sevres — *perfect art*, but somehow identified with well-to-do crime; second, a Pompeian revival by an English upholsterer — *graceful art*, but distinctly extravagant; and third, a colourless, bodiless amateur arrangement of good, lasting materials or natural products which we are asked to regard as *pure art*. We are not allowed to suppose that our author is unconscious of the negation of art — of that which is sometimes illogically described as bad art, for early in the novel we are told how the hero and heroine as they roam about London on the look-out for that impossible article, a suitable home, are horrified by "the vapid square boxes," jocularly called houses, "which bear a remarkable family resemblance to one another, the very cornices sprouting out in the same architectural piccalili, a school of ornament which seems the result of a profound study of the cauliflower tribe. The mantelpieces look as if they had all been dug out of the same quarry, and chipped into shape by the same masons — mottled marble, like Castile soap, in the dining-rooms; statuary marble, with a little more of the cauliflower decoration in the drawing-rooms. Papers alike — graining alike — general newness and tendency to shrinking in the woodwork alike." This is intended to be severe; but why a profound study of the cauliflower should not result in just as pure an ornament as a profound study of the trefoil or clover is not altogether so apparent as the novelist seems to think; and I am much afraid that in the matter of modern art, the criticisms in this book, whether favourable or unfavourable, are founded on a profound study of those soul-stirring, convincing lines —

> I do not like thee, Doctor Fell,
> The reason why I cannot tell.
> I do not like thee, Doctor Fell.

Archaeology, antiquarian style, and a Queen Anne sitting-room

But it is not only on modern Art that the popular novelist ventures to express an opinion. Specimens of old work and archaeology generally furnish opportunities for some brilliant writing. Among other singular illustrations of past times we are told of a church yard in Wales that it "is a curiously one-sided Necropolis, the Welsh insisting upon being buried with their faces to the East, so that they may be ready at the great trumpet-call." It is certainly a strange perversity thus to follow a custom universal in Christian countries. Besides an old Norman church, called a "fane," which is dismissed for being as unpretentious as a barn, there is a picture of a country manor-house, drawn with much elaboration. Of course it is "of the Elizabethan era;" — every manor-house always was, always is, and, I suppose, always will be. It has steep gables, mullioned windows, and "an oriel here and there at a corner." It is built of brick, with stone dressings, is irregular in plan, having been enlarged a century or more ago. There is a fine old timber porch, and through the open door you "can see the hall, with its darkly-bright oak panelling." But oak panelling is nothing by itself, so there are flashes of armour and flickerings from painted windows playing on carved coats of arms. The dining-room is oak panelled like the hall, there are portraits by LELY and GAINSBROOUGH, and on the oak buffet are tankards, repousse dishes, and other specimens of old family plate. Last of all, true to the latest fad, comes a "Queen Anne" room — the prettiest sitting-room the literary hero, the friend of the RA, has seen for a long time. "Boudoirs blue and gold, chintz and satinwood, ebony and ormolu, he has seen without number," but this is new to him. "The walls are painted white, carved garlands of flowers and fruit adorn panelling and cornice, an old Venetian glass over the chimneypiece reflects a set of dark blue delf [sic] jars, quaint in shape, perfect in colour. In each corner of the room is a triangular glass cupboard, filled with rare old porcelain." Then there are Chippendale chairs and tables and curtains of embroidered muslin lined with rose silk. Near this interesting mansion we come across a Roman earthwork and a ruined priory, but the hero we are informed is too literary, too imaginative to be an archaeologist, and so these remains are disposed of by our novelist with a graceful brevity that might well have been exercised on those portions of the novel that relate to modern art and household taste. And yet this same literary hero tells us that Abbotsford jarred upon him because he "knew its mediaevalism was all carton pierre." Poor Sir WALTER SCOTT! whose mediaevalisms are so transparent that the literary minds of today, too imaginative to be archaeological, caring little and knowing less about Roman earthworks, old churches or ruined priories, can yet see through.

In defence of Walter Scott

Sir WALTER's archaeology was, no doubt, made up much after the style of the antique furniture of Wardour Street, but for all that it is to Sir WALTER and his powerful popular influence we chiefly owe the revival of the romantic spirit without which the revival of Gothic art would have been impossible. But then the author of "Waverley" was consistent. He, at any rate, did not go into ecstasies over Pompeian dining-rooms at luncheon, become eloquent over the bonbonnière style at dinner, and dwell with rapture over Glastonbury chairs before the cloth was removed. Carton pierre and sham, as nearly all the furniture, architecture, and armour of the old novelist undoubtedly were, still they illustrated a logical settled purpose. What Sir WALTER SCOTT tells us of Art is not in any way akin to the second-hand jargon of the clubs, nor to the paltry prattle of those art enthusiasts whose attainments are mostly limited by "Dyce's Outlines." His feeling, we know well enough, is heart and soul with the mediaeval times he loves to picture, and he himself is no sham, however unfaithful and imperfect his surroundings may be. Your modern novelist, however, is often just the reverse of this. His (and I may well include *her*) excitement about Art is just as transparent a sham as Sir WALTER's plate armour. All round us art *knowledge* and archaeological *science* are at high pressure, but the modern *litterateur* is too imaginative to care two straws about any earnest application of the knowledge of the science. To pick up a few technical phrases as they drop from artists on lawn or carpet; to remember, in spite of the Royal Academy, that there are such painters as ROSSETTI, WHISTLER, BURNE JONES; to be well posted in the studio slang of the day, or failing this, to make as much as possible of such words as "reposeful," seem to be the extent of the efforts made by the novelist to qualify in Art for the position he holds towards the ever-increasing thousands of the novel-reading public, a position in which he seems ambitious to figure as professor of *every thing* in Heaven or earth, or in the waters under the earth.

'ARTISTIC' FURNISHING (1876)

Godwin was an experienced collector who furnished his own house with eighteenth-century furniture and oriental ceramics, fabrics and rugs, but he always emphasised quality, usefulness and judicious selectivity. [Editors' note: this article cannot be attributed with certainty to Godwin, but the views are those he expressed elsewhere.]

Source:
'"Artistic" furnishing', *The Furniture Gazette*, 8 April 1876, p.222

Our rooms are becoming museums, and Wardour-street is a sort of Mecca to which the devout continually turn their faces. The man who sets forth innocently to pay a round of visits to half-a-dozen recently-married friends may calculate on a sweeping giro across two or three centuries, through mediaeval Germany and flowery Renaissance France, with a flight into the East, all in the course of an afternoon. In one house, old oak will frown on him from every side; in another delicate marquetry will thrust its curved legs in his way; in another he will have a Chippendale chair to sit down in, and a tiled fireplace to contemplate, and will not be able to move without brushing up against an array of old plates against the wall; while, last of all perhaps, he will reach a drawing-room decorated like an Eastern land, with Arab rugs on the floor, and cool mattings and sea-grass draperies to keep out the light of a November day — each of them being a sign and token of the absolute uncertainty of the general mind as to what is good or bad and at the same time of its timorous reluctance to leave the safe guidance of one dogmatism or another, and trust its own sense of what it requires. Among the motives for marriage nowadays, one of the strongest must be allowed to be (for those who can afford the luxury) the ambition of furnishing a house in some altogether aesthetical and exquisite way, with a perfection no one has attained before. Novelty, indeed, is very rarely attained, or if attained, lasts but a very short time, so eager are the next batch of neophytes to emulate and excel their predecessors. But oddity and inappropriateness are easily attained; and as houses unfortunately cannot be ordered in character, the contrast of the four-square London Victorian walls, looking down cynically and sturdily upon the outlandish garnishing to which they are subject, gives a point to the joke which nothing can surpass. And it is worth noting that these elaborate attempts to make the domestic circle "artistic", seem to be gradually pushing out altogether from the decoration of the English house the higher developments of art.

Old plates which one time in a hundred may be worth preserving in a collection, and perhaps one time in a dozen (which is liberal) might be an ornament to the dinner-table, are now strung up on walls where pictures once hung; or what is still worse than plates, gaudy Japanese fans made for the cheap use

'*The Ponsonbys at home*', Punch *25 Oct. 1879.*

'*Frustrated Social Ambition*', Punch *21 May 1881.*

of celestial peasants, but which English ladies and gentlemen arrange with simple pride upon their walls, and look upon with a delightful modest consciousness of superior taste. If, perhaps, these flimsy decorations take the place here and there of the staring portraits with which we were once familiar, there is a certain compensation in them, but surely a pretty water-colour drawing or a good print is a higher and more refined kind of decoration than paper-fans and dinner-plates? We have nothing to say against a dainty glimmer of old china in a corner, or the use of a Japanese fan where it may happen to serve a purpose, and give a quaint little touch of colour to a wall *en attendant* the moment when it may shield a lady's face from the fire, or even hide her yawn in a dull interview, or help a pleasant flirtation. Such legitimate and reasonable uses give a sanction to anything, but "the artistic feeling" which substitutes this foolish kind of ornament for pictures is surely anything but an improvement upon the old traditions of decoration.

THE 'ART AT HOME' SERIES (1876–8)

By the late 1870s there was a veritable flood of popular manuals on household taste that threatened to usurp the role and authority of the architect on issues of domestic decoration. Adopting a small-scale, relatively cheap format Macmillan's published twelve volumes in their Art at Home *series, 1876–83, many of them featuring the new 'lady experts'. Although supportive in general of women's professional involvement in interior decoration (see 'Lady Architects' pp.105f.), Godwin had no time for 'amateurs' like Barker, Orrinsmith or Loftie, and felt that the series was cashing in on both his ideas and his designs without acknowledgment. In his opening leader as the London editor of* The British Architect *he made pointed reference to popular handbooks on domestic decoration, resolving 'to criticize freely and fearlessly the presuming amateur and inexperienced artist, who in these latter days have developed the knack of posing as apostles of domestic art'.*

Rev. Loftie's 'Plea for Art in the house'

Whatever one may think of the present state of art and of the importance that should be attached to it, there is no doubt that now people take more interest in it than formerly. They are beginning to realise that art may exist in other forms beside pictures and statues, and consequently decorative art, which during the last century had been steadily sinking in the estimation of the world, seems as it were to have got a fresh start in life. The announcement of a series of books on art at home would therefore appear to be especially opportune. From the high reputation of the publishers we were led to anticipate a succession of volumes in the first place likely to be useful to those who are yet awaking to the fact that their education in art has been neglected, and who are anxious to free their houses from fashionable vulgarities and to make them beautiful; and, secondly, to those who are more or less engaged in the practice of decorative art. But such a series of manuals, to become of any real value, should bear the stamp of earnestness and thoroughness. They should be the work of men who are convinced of the value of art in the household as well as

Frontispiece illustration for books in the Art at Home *series.*

Source:
'The "Art at Home series"',
Architect, 9 December 1876,
pp.338-9

Biographical notes:
Loftie

elsewhere, and who are masters of the subjects about which they profess to enlighten us. If, however, the editor's volume is to be taken as a sample, the world is not likely to be much improved by the "Art at Home Series." Anyone who has sufficient culture to give literary expression to his thoughts may be excused for gossiping half playfully upon any but the most serious subjects. Indeed, there are few things more readable at certain times than one of those chatty papers, without beginning and without end, that discourse of all things under the sun, excepting that from which they take their name. But an essay published in the form of a book, and under the pretence of imparting information upon some particular branch of art, must be judged by a different standard. If the writer is not in earnest, or is incompetent to grasp his subject, or if he is compelled to hide his want of knowledge by relating anecdotes and drawing "morals", he is scarcely justified in the use of a title which, although it may be attractive, does not indicate the character of his book.

The first thing that struck us on turning over the pages of "A Plea for Art in the House" was a small woodcut representing one of the Seasons, which, unless we are mistaken, appeared some years ago in a penny weekly paper. Wondering what this illustration had to do with "art at home," we turned to the "list of woodcuts", and there we found that out of fourteen cuts that embellish the volume four belonged to this set of the Seasons, meaninglessly introduced as tailpieces, while five of them were initial letters from thirteenth century MSS. of no particular interest or merit, and bearing no relation to the text. There is also among the illustrations a reversed copy of Beham's* version of the Melancholia, which is given, according to the author, "partly because it is another rendering of Durer's famous subject, and partly because it seems to be less known than it should be." We fail, however, to see that either of these reasons account for its selection as an illustration of "Art at Home". There thus remain but four cuts which can be said to refer to the text, and we cannot say much of their quality. [...]

* Hans Sebald Beham, 1500–50, German printmaker.

There can be no doubt that suggestive books on household adornment would be an advantage just at present; but they must be the work of writers with taste that has been cultivated by practice, and possessed of that "sober certainty" of knowledge which cannot be secured by a sudden interest in a subject, or by the "bright ideas" which come to them by chance. Let the publishers obtain a series of books worthy to be placed on the same shelf with their primers of literature, science, and history, and they will be entitled to the gratitude of all who desire the promotion of art.

Mrs. Orrinsmith on 'The drawing-room'

Lucy Orrinsmith's little book sold over 6,000 copies in its first year.

In the *Art at Home series*, Mrs. Orrinsmith lectures us on *the Drawing Room*. In her last chapter she says (p.142), "The encouragement of original ideas has been throughout the motif of this book." She also trusts that certain of her readers are "convinced that personal perseverance in the search after pure decorative beauty will be rewarded by results apparently unobtainable except by those who have some gift of the nature of inspiration." This is all very fine,

Source:
'Notes on current events',
The British Architect, 8
February 1878, p.64

Biographical notes:
Orrinsmith

An illustration of 'inferior character' in Mrs Orrinsmith's The Drawing-room, *1878.*

Source:
'Notes on current events', *The British Architect*, 29 March 1878, p.144

Biographical notes:
Barker
Loftie
Royal School of Needlework

Source:
'Mrs. Loftie in excelsis', *The British Architect*, 22 February 1878, p.83

Biographical notes:
Burges
Garretts
Loftie
Mechi
Orrinsmith
Poynter

but if Mrs. Orrinsmith and her friends would have the grace to acknowledge the sources of their "original ideas," it would enlighten readers as to the method of searching "after pure decorative beauty." For example, at p.41 we read, "On the next page is a drawing of a fireplace ..." &c., but not one word of acknowledgement to Mr. E. W. Godwin, the architect who designed it, or to Lord Cowper, the owner of Beauvale, where he set it up, or even to the journal in which by courtesy of the architect, the working drawings were published, and from which it is manifest Mrs. Orrinsmith's illustration is directly taken. If Mr. Loftie and his friends want to play at "drawing rooms", can they not do it privately? and so spare us the infliction of these dissertations on *original ideas* until they can form some idea of artistic courtesy and justice, can learn to acknowledge the authors of original ideas, and can translate the idea themselves more seemingly. For there can be no question as to the inferior character of the illustrations generally and the utter worthlessness of some, markedly those on pp.33, 41, 69, and 76.

Lady Barker on 'The bedroom and the boudoir'

Here we have *The Art at Home Series* again! Its last effort is by Lady Barker. We have followed her into *the Bedroom and Boudoir*, and we're glad enough to get out again. Lady Barker is no doubt an excellent nurse, and lingers over a child's cot or a sick room with a pride and joy quite equal to that Mrs. Loftie takes in culinary cleanliness, but her views on art are mostly *réchauffés* of other people's fads. The writing is a literary mixture of a kind of Bohemianism and namby-pambyism. We have "dear, clean, old oaken walls", and other quite too charmingly delicious expressions on one page; and on another we find that Indian quilts "swear at everything else in the room", and that housemaids are actuated by "pure 'cussedness.'" Of course we are taken to New Zealand and "the snowy peaks of the Himalayas," and of course, as in the other books of this series, the designs of architects, who are totally unacknowledged, enrich the pages — *e.g.*, the frontispiece and figs. 11, 12, and 14; while the names of the Royal School of Art Needlework and certain "Art at Home" pets are dragged in for their accustomed butter.

Mrs Loftie in excelsis

Mrs. Loftie is the authority touching "the dining-room" in the *Art-at-Home Series*. The illustrations, though on the whole better executed than in Mrs. ORRINSMITH'S volume, are still very unequal, some being nearly as good as those of furniture published last year in *Scribner's Monthly*, and some as bad as the worst in *the Art-at-Home Series*. A bad, ill-proportioned copy of a well-known coffee table is again thrust forward in the woodcut at p.5, of course unacknowledged, and in chap. iii. is a description of a painted sideboard bought out of the 1862 Exhibition and now at South Kensington, the designer of which is also ignored. Indeed, it would seem to be one of the missions of the Art-at-Home people to turn their eyes away from the architects who have not merely paved the way for their Art-at-Home movement, but who for a full quarter of a century, have reiterated the precepts which the authors of these little books cackle over as if only just laid down by themselves. Mr. POYNTER, who, as a young man, painted, under Mr. Burges's directions, the sideboard in question is recognised by name. So also are Mr. Wm. BELLARS, for his writing; Mr. Wm. MORRIS, for his (melancholy) colour; Mr. MECHI, for his economical grate; and the Miss GARRETTS, for their "good" sayings and "charming" designs. There are true things here and there, and things worth remembering as in the other volumes of the series, but every chapter is crowded with platitudes and with error practical as well as theoretical. Here for example is an astounding statement: "Olive and sage greens, peacock and indigo blues, Venetian and Indian reds, are not modern inventions. [Interesting discovery; but now for the astounding part of it.] They were the colours chiefly used by all great paint-ers and illuminators of every country when art was at its best." "The back-ground of a TITIAN, the wall of a VAN EYCK, the drapery of a BOTICELLI [sic], the dress of an old Japanese figure", are then cited as illustrations of art at its best. Poor Mrs. LOFTIE! another victim of the crass ignorance that looks on an old master, and gives to the artist the credit of all the fading, dulling, dirtying touches that have fallen on it through the fingers of Time and his Assistants. Here is a bit of advice that runs counter to that fixed law of art, about material and design. Speaking of old chimneypieces, Mrs. LOFTIE says, "Many fine specimens in oolite are to be found in the Bathstone Country, which would look exceedingly well if imitated in wood." Again, there are suggestions that would shock the anti-restoration party. "If you can get four old balus-trades from the altar-rail of some restored church, they will do extremely well" for the legs of a made-up "old English" sideboard! Mrs. LOFTIE has discovered something about the history of Gothic Art, for she, says, "It must be clearly remembered that a Gothic table, that is, one actually designed and made be-fore the fifteenth century, scarcely exists." (p.65.) Gothic tables, therefore, were only made before the year 1400! This is really too delightful — this mixture of the most authoritative utterance with the most pitiable ignorance. We sup-pose some Gothic buildings were erected after 1400. In HENRY V.'S reign some folk sat on newly made Gothic benches and slept on newly made Gothic bed-steads, but it must be remembered that from the close of 1399 tables by a mysterious law were exempt from the art treatment of the day, and were made after an exceptional pattern familiar perhaps to Mrs. LOFTIE, but as yet unrevealed to the readers of Art-at-Home.

To be serious: do the publishers — Messrs. MACMILLAN and Co. — think that their reputation is too great to be affected by such foolishness and such weakness as these little books exhibit. In the one before us the only merit of it is in certain advice, which might well have been put into a tract of half the compass, and called The Housekeeper's Guide. To put forward a book like this as a contribution to art knowledge or culture is either the act of folly or pre-tence. Neither Mrs. LOFTIE nor Mrs. ORRINSMITH is fit for this sort of work. Looking through the dining-room volume we can easily see that the author-ess is a woman who would like, and possibly might be able, to get the greatest amount of creature comfort out of a given allowance. A good wife and kind mother with an eye for a healthy appetite with such sayings ever in her mind as — "the best decoration for a dining-room is a well cooked dinner" and "antique china will not atone for bad coffee" is after all a person of excellent parts and a pattern well deserving the imitation of young housewives. To write a good housekeeper's guide or servant's manual in such a compass as to be easily read, and in such a manner as to be well remembered, would be work within the capacity of many of the ladies who assume the role of public instructors on questions of art. We say assume because they occupy the position without sufficient and in some cases without any qualification.

ILL-ADVISED COLOUR HARMONIES (1879)

Mrs Haweis was another popular female pundit on aesthetic dress and household taste to attract Godwin's criticism. She had recently settled near her friends the Alma Tademas and Frank Dicksee at 34 St John's Wood Road (now demolished), known as the Amber House after she had the outside and her drawing room painted a warm yellow. Her book, The Art of Dress, *had appeared that spring.*

Source:
'Notes on current events',
The British Architect, 25 July
1879, p.34

Biographical notes:
Jackson & Graham
Haweis

MESSRS. JACKSON & GRAHAM are decorating the exterior of a house at the corner of Regent-street and Charles-street, and we trust the example, as far as it has gone, will not be followed. If people want to go in for colour on the outside of their residences, let them above all things use it gently — mixtures of ochre, light red, black and white, are quite enough to tax the decorative power of the present day. [...] But the house in Regent-street is quite elegant, lovely, appropriate — in fact, altogether praiseworthy when compared with a house in St. John's Wood, opposite Lord's Cricket Ground, inhabited, we believe, by Mrs. Haweis. This lady is supposed by some silly young people to be an authority on dress, and other things artistic, and the colouring of her house is, we understand, due to her notions about colour harmonies — poor Mrs. Haweis!

SHADES OF GREEN (1883)

In his 1863 lecture on the 'Sister Arts', Godwin had urged his audience to 'note well those constant allusions to green' in medieval sources when decorating their homes. Twenty years on Godwin returns to this green theme, and in analysing Chaucer's poetry for evidence of 14th-century arts and culture, reflects on the Aesthetic naming of colours.

Source:
'Colours and cloths of the
middle ages', *Building News,*
7 September 1883, p.357

What shades of colour were known by such names as *feu d'enfer, eau de Nil,* Magenta, Alexandra blue, and azuline? When we say "green," who is to distinguish between dark sage-green, pale grey-green, harsh arsenic-green, yellow mossy-green, sea-green, pea-green, unless such words as sage, pea, sea, arsenic help us out? The name of a princess or a town give us no idea of a shade of colour. Nothing could do it but a natural object which is likely to remain always with us — like the poor. But even when a sensible name occurs by chance, it never lasts long; peacock, terracotta, and cream colour have been spoilt, and are much ill-used.

PEOPLE WHO PRETEND TO HAVE TASTE (1879)

Here Godwin defends the rights of the architect and artist over unsympathetic inter-
ventions by the owner or patron, a topical issue given Whistler's bankruptcy at this
time and the auction-sale of the White House to the critic Harry Quilter. In fact, in
the passage preceding this extract, Godwin makes reference to an article that had
just appeared in the Cornhill Magazine *under the signature 'H.Q.', questioning*
whether architecture was an art.

Wherever we move, whether in the company of working artists or among amateurs, in studio, or in drawing-room, with critics, who talk a little sense, or with "Aesthetic" ladies, who talk only nonsense, of one thing we are soon made conscious, that not one person in a thousand who quote RUSKIN or ARNOLD and chatter and scribble about Art really knows what they are talking or writing about; for of the Art, that is the elder sister of Sculpture and Painting, without which the latter would never have been, they are [...] wholly unconscious. It is true that occasionally a well composed, charmingly proportioned house is admired for a time by the owner and his friends. What then? Do they ever even in their minds say of the architect what a consummate artist that man is, look how well he has balanced the solids and the voids, how pleasing are all the angles and the lines, from whatever point we view them? Do they observe with what admirable judgment he has found the right place for the sculpture or arranged the measures for the paintings? Do they ever note how he has given a path for the light, or that the shadows have been his creation? Not one such thought ever occurs to them; on the contrary, the owner and his family will enter just at the moment when the architect ought to be unfettered and permitted to complete his design. There are bare walls and ceilings inside upon which the owner seizes, as a child on some new plaything wherewith to amuse himself for a while. It matters nothing to him that the fashionable papers or the colours he applies are out of key with the architect's work. Nay, if he be so minded, he will throw out an oriel of his own devising, without leave or license from the architect, even without a word of consultation. Such an one cannot for a moment suppose that architecture is an art, and that a true architect is necessarily a true artist in the very highest sense of the word. And yet, those who are most blind in this particular have some sense of modesty when in the presence of the other arts. Before painter or sculptor they may now and then suggest, but certainly they never venture to add or alter. One of the finest series of apartments we have ever seen was lately made the victim of what is called the owner's taste, where the walls designed and lighted with a special regard to their future completion in a light key of decorative mural painting were finally covered with dark flock papers, as the result of sundry aesthetic consultations between the owner, his wife, and the local upholsterer. If people who pretend to have taste would have taste sufficient to leave unmolested by suggestions the architects, painters, or sculptors they are good enough to commission — if they would refrain from darkening counsel by words without knowledge, art would certainly not pine from any neglect of this kind they could possibly show her.

Source:
'Is architecture an art?', *The British Architect*, 14 November 1879, p.189

Biographical notes:
Arnold
Ruskin

Du Maurier, 'The Six-mark Tea-pot', Punch 30 Oct. 1880.

'INDIVIDUAL' BUT MEDIOCRE TASTE (1878)

Still smarting from the Metropolitan Board of Works' criticism of his designs for studio-houses in Tite Street, Godwin questions what is to be taken as the expression of 'individual taste'.

Source:
'Notes on current events', *The British Architect*, 27 September 1878, p.126

The writer in London says very justly — "A house furnished by a man of individual taste will bear the impress of his individuality; it will not be a mere blind collection of the good things made by this and that famous decorator, but a harmonious whole, assorted into consonance with the ideal of its owner. Whereas a house furnished under the sole direction of fashion will be nothing more than an undigested museum, often made up of shoddy in the worst of all disguises — the disguise which pretends to represent unvarnished truth." This is, no doubt, very true, but where and how is your furnishing husband or wife to prove it? Where is there a house furnished by a man of individual taste? The majority of the people who go in for individual taste are gentle minded folk of very limited power; amateur artists in some way or other; they paint or embroider, they work in silk or leather or wool; their friends look up to them as authorities, even on the subject of architecture; and it is not uncommon to find the drawings of the most accomplished architects subjected to that delightfully free criticism in which mediocrity delights to indulge.

COMPENSATION FOR AN 'ARTIST'S PARADISE' (1878)

'How pugnacious we all are nowadays', wrote Godwin. On 27 November, just a week after the Whistler–Ruskin trial he was back in court, this time as a witness for his friend Howell, the picture dealer. Howell was claiming compensation from the Metropolitan District Railway over the termination of his lease on Chaldon, a 'Queen Anne' manor house in Fulham from which he ran his business, claiming that his investment in the artistic decoration and furnishings had turned a 'wreck' into a work of art, 'a showpiece of domestic decoration'. Like the Whistler–Ruskin trial this event was a theatrical performance art in its own right, with a guest appearance by the Butterfly himself. (At around this time Whistler was painting a full-length portrait of Howell's mistress, Rosa Corder, and Godwin was about to design a studio and cottage for her, though the project never materialised.) The proceedings provide a fascinating insight into the creation of an Aesthetic ensemble, the blending of antique and modern art, and the domestication of gallery spaces as a commercial strategy. Although not signed by Godwin, this account would at the very least have been subject to his close editorial scrutiny as it reported his role in the trial.

Source:
'Compensation for an "artist's paradise"', *The British Architect*, 13 December 1878, p.231-3

Mr. Charles Augustus Howell, D. C. L., examined by Mr. Horace Browne, said: [...] I have dealt in works of art for the last twelve years, and have turned my attention to the artistic decoration of houses. I am the lessee of this house, Chaldon House, Fulham, It is a Queen Anne house of unique character. I took it about four and a half years ago. It was then the wreck of a fine house. It was not drained, and had neither water nor gas. It was an abandoned manor house.

[...] I have spent on repairs certainly £2,000 [...] In my £2,000 I do not count a single tile or decoration. I had to replace every fireplace in the house. Many of the rooms are panelled, and these had to be entirely repainted. I used Morris's papers, they cost from 14s. to 18s. a piece. I made every room a picture in itself, and managed it by using subdued colours. I could fill a room with drawings by Rossetti one day, and with a picture by Titian the next, and both would look equally well. [...] I put tiles in the fireplaces. Some of the tiles cost me £4 a tile. Those are Japanese. [...] The tiles in the fountain room are Portuguese. [...] One fireplace with Scriptural tiles I gave 10s. a tile for, they are unique. The price of these has advanced at least 50 per cent. since I bought them. In fact you cannot get them at all, and they are so sought after that manufacturers are imitating them. The whole of the tiles, independent of those in the fountain room, cost about £120. One window by Mr. Burne Jones is, of course, priceless. That is to be removed at my risk. Another window is after Rossetti. These windows alone were an attraction to the house. I used the house as a place of business, and there received privately the whole of my clients; they are gentlemen like myself who associate with me, and know that I make my living in this manner. People come to me to know how to fit up their rooms. This house is a showpiece of domestic decoration. Men of wealth and position see the house and wish to have rooms fitted up accordingly. I produce a photograph of a room I so fitted up, in which everything is a work of art.

Mr. Bidder [counsel for the Metropolitan Railway]: Is the lady represented in the photo a work of art? (Laughter.)

Witness [Howell] : The lady is the owner of the house and the gem of the room. (Applause and laughter.)

Mr. Bidder: She is not an old English lady, that is, I suppose the only old English thing you draw your line at. (Laughter.)

Witness: Certainly, on the most modest grounds, I prefer the young ones, merely for the sake of contrast. (Great laughter.) I have fitted up forty-three such rooms in the same way. My income during the last ten years from this business has never been less than £3,000 a year. I have had executed nineteen stained glass windows, reproductions of those in my house, at very high prices, and many of them, high as the price is, have been sold to the trade. If I succeed in getting another house of the same kind, with care and economy, and working myself, it will cost me at least £2,000 to redecorate it like this one [...] Mine is a genuine Queen Anne house. I know the collections of most connoisseurs. People come to the house because they like me, and because I make them comfortable. (Great laughter.) [...] A house for my purpose is always a mere carcass when I take it. A good deal of my business is done out of my house. I buy Whistler's picture at his house. I take it home and I hang it up and I never laugh, I never even smile. (Roars of laughter.) A man comes who appreciates a "nocturne", and he goes mad till he gets that particular one. [...] I was not aware there was a clause in the lease forbidding my carrying on any business there. I think that clause refers to butchering chops and such things. [...] The rooms are "arrangements" in blue and gold, or in green and gold, or other colours.

Mr. Bidder: I suppose the green is the customers, and the gold the money they bring. (Laughter.)

Witness: The gold is thrown in to show that there is no ill-feeling. It gave you pleasure to see it yesterday, and it would also please Mr. Ruskin, if he ever came that way. My bedrooms are beautiful "nocturnes". (Loud laughter.) [...]

At this stage in the proceedings Mr. Whistler entered the court.

Witness: We must be careful now. Here is "an arrangement in black and white", the keynote of all true symphonies is in court. (Roars of laughter.) [...]

Mr. E. W. Godwin, F. S. A. architect, Victoria-chambers, Westminster, examined by Mr. Grantham [counsel for Howell], said: I have considerable experience in houses of this character. Knowing the trade of Mr. Howell, I regard this house as one peculiarly adapted for this business. [...]

Do you think it is possible to get subscribers to a portrait of Thomas Carlyle in a common house? — It depends on the character of the house and on the social position of the owner, even when it becomes a question of getting subscribers for anything.

Can a "nocturne in black and gold" be only dealt with in a Queen Anne house? — I do not know how people deal with nocturnes.

Why is it necessary to pay £400 a year to carry on such a business? — The articles I saw in Mr. Howell's house were chiefly such things as furniture and pottery, which certainly look better when surrounded by architecture and placed in rooms appropriate to them, than when placed in an ordinary chamber or an everyday house.

Then, would he do better if he had a pagoda house to put old porcelain in? — I do not think pagodas are usually built for that purpose.

But that is the prevailing architecture of the Celestial Empire. I suppose that would be appropriate. — I have not been to the Celestial Empire. [...]

Re-examined: I could not produce a house like this for him under £400 a year.

CONVERSAZIONE AT THE HOGARTH (1877)

Godwin was a regular visitor to London's many art clubs, which provided a forum for lively intellectual exchange and gossip between artists, architects, actors and potential clients. Apart from providing Godwin with a source of journalistic copy, such venues were also a recruiting ground for subscriptions to The British Architect, *on which he received commission.*

Source:
'An art conversazione at the Hogarth', *Architect*, 6 January 1877, p. 5

Biographical notes:
Hogarth Club

Bohemianism with us in England is not what it was. Even the Hogarth Club is occasionally flavoured with the lardy-dardy. On last Saturday night I attended the closing conversazione for the year just passed away, and there, actually visible now and then through crowd and smoke, were the back partings and white ties of regulation-society. One does not wish to be ungracious, but it is quite possible even in a club to issue too many tickets.

[... H]aving chatted with a few and greeted many, we adjourn to the music room. There is a BROADWOOD's concert grand, and the room soon fills to suffocation; windows are opened, curtains drawn aside, but still the heat and tobacco smoke go on increasing. Seats are out of the question for the majority, and the lucky few are perched on chairs like birds on a rail. There are familiar faces in accustomed corners, but we miss not a few who used to contribute in no small measure to the enjoyment of the evening. The first song is over. Some members have wisely introduced friends who can sing or play, and as the evening grows these visitors ungrudgingly give us of their best. There are a few noisy members perhaps — good natured souls, but simple — who are easily forgiven, but who might nevertheless well moderate their ecstasy.

ACADEMY SOIRÉE (1878)

WHY IS it that the refreshments at Burlington House are not only so begrudgingly given, but what is worse are so disgracefully trashy — one glass of sherry was quite enough to upset the strongest.

Source:
'Notes on current events', *The British Architect*, 5 July 1878, p.2

THE DILETTANTE CLUB (1881)

So the Dilettante Club has collapsed; its start was quite too-too, and we noted at the time of its opening how unlikely it was to endure for long. Things of this kind to prosper must have artists or money, and this had neither to speak of.

Source:
'Notes on current events, *The British Architect*, 30 September 1881, p.485

A STAGE PARODY OF AESTHETICISM (1881)

In 1881 two comic theatrical productions, Burnand's The Colonel *and Gilbert and Sullivan's* Patience *satirised Aesthetic taste in dress, manners and furnishing. The set of the former, as described here, bore a marked resemblance to Godwin's own interiors, including an example of the ubiquitous little black coffee table. As an archaeologist Godwin realised the importance of syntactical interrelationships in the study of material culture, and was all too aware, therefore, of how the context in which his furniture and wallpapers were seen and used could affect their meaning. Myra Holme, parodied on stage for her Aesthetic costume, could pass unnoticed in the same Liberty dress out on the street.*

Is this not somewhat curious? Miss Myra Holme plays the part of an aesthetic lady (Olive) in Mr. Burnand's comedy of "The Colonel", and endeavours to burlesque the ways of the aesthetes. We met her just as she was leaving the Prince of Wales Theatre last Saturday afternoon, and her private costume, evidently quite new, was modelled line for line on that she had just worn as an aesthete in the comedy, and which the audience had been invited to ridicule. This is really worth noting, and the thought it suggests is that "The Colonel" will make more for aestheticism than against it. Indeed, if you set aside the clearly burlesque dress of Mr. Beerbohm Tree (*Lambert Stryke*), the sunflower carried to absurdity by Mrs. Leigh Murray (*Lady Tomkins*), the idiotic posturing of Mr. Buckstone (*Basil Giorgione*), and the occasional sing-song intona-

Source:
'Theatrical notes', *The British Architect*, 29 July 1881, p.379

Biographical notes:
Beerbohm Tree
Burnand
Holme
Morris
Padgett

Godwin, sketch of the actor
Beerbohm Tree playing Lambert
Stryke, an Aesthete critic, in
The Colonel.

Godwin, sketches of the actresses
Myra Holme and Miss Grahame
dressed by Liberty's for their
roles in The Colonel, BA 26
Aug. 1881.

tions that raised a certain amount of laughter but damaged Mr. Coghlan's part and had nothing whatever to do with the play, what remained of the so-called "sham art" we were invited to condemn was so largely superior to the stuff we were asked to accept as substitute, that we are afraid Mr. Burnand will have to acknowledge himself a complete failure as a satirist of fashion. The fact is, Mr. Burnand and his co-workers in the production of this piece have given us the really artistic for the sham artistic to such an extent that it is hard to see, save for the exceptions we have made, why the very thing he has attempted to destroy should not acquire by his mode of procedure a new lease of life. There are but two scenes in the comedy, both interiors, one supposed to be founded on aestheticism, the other on common sense. Looking round the last, we find it very much upholstered with yards on yards of curtain stuff of a staring, loud pattern; an entirely vulgar, uninteresting, unpleasant apartment. But it is *this* the moral of the piece indicates as right. Turning to the other room that is presented to us as wrong, we find it furnished with artistic and simple things: a charming cabinet in walnut designed by Mr. Padgett for the green room; some simple inexpensive black Sussex chairs, like those sold by Wm. Morris and Co.; a black coffee table, after the well-known example originally designed in 1867 by the writer of these notes; a quite simple writing table, matting on the floor, a green and yellow paper on the walls, a sunflower frieze, and a Japanese treatment of the ceiling (storks), and a red sun such as we see in Japanese books and on hand screens, make up a scene which, if found wanting in certain details and forced in sunflowers, is certainly an interesting room, with individuality about it, and, what is most important, harmonious and pleasing. Miss Myra Holme, with the one exception of the violent colour in her hat, is quite charmingly dressed, and the outrage to good taste is, as usual, committed by the "Philistine" *Mrs. Blyth* (Miss Amy Roselle), whose last dress is simply amazing in the ugliness of its arrangement.

XII Art Manufactures

'ART' or 'artistic' was a term liberally applied to furniture and decoration, indeed to the whole gamut of domestic products between the late 1860s and the 1880s. It implied an elevating concern for the design or appearance of products, the involvement of an artist or architect and, as such, became central to the whole concept of 'Aesthetic taste'. Reformers like Henry Cole had done much to reconcile art and industry through the Schools of Design in the 1840s and this had, at least, encouraged manufacturers to seek advice from professional designers to make their products more appealing to the middle-class market. Promising as this was, however, many designers including Godwin were wary of the new terminology, sensing a debasement of the aesthetic ideals which drew them to domestic design in the first place. In some cases the word 'Art' had become a casual prefix used cynically to confer status on some routine and often badly-designed item for the home. As he wrote in 1872, 'Under the name of art, traders flourish, manufacturers grow rich, and the man of the counting house secures to his own credit the brains of many a young and struggling artist' (p.289).

The term was made popular by Charles Eastlake who referred to 'Art Furniture' in his famous book, *Hints on Household Taste* of 1868. Thereafter it entered the common vocabulary of design and was soon used in connection with a range of decorative arts, including wallpapers, textiles, ceramics and metalwork. It is not difficult to understand why. The diffusion of wealth among the middle classes, allied to dramatic urban and industrial expansion, generated a huge demand for furnishings and decorating materials. Against this backdrop, the design of domestic goods increasingly figured in debates about the economy as well as social and aesthetic priorities. It was the latter, however, which engaged Godwin and the new breed of designers. Concern for hygiene as well as beauty, 'fitness' and economy are the ideas he chose to explore in his articles.

Simpson art tile advertisement,
Builder *27 Sept. 1873.*

'It is essential for true domestic comfort in these high-pressure, nervous times', he wrote in 1872, 'that the common objects of every-day life should be quiet, simple, and unobtrusive in their beauty.' For design reformers like Godwin, genuinely 'artistic' design was a means of countering the less palatable side of city living – the desensitisation, filth and chaos of the urban environment that had to be negotiated on a daily basis. When furnishing his London chambers in 1867 he had been driven by the lack of suitable furnishings on the market to design his own. In doing so, he built on his considerable experience of designing a range of decorative arts in connection with his major town hall projects and smaller-scale church work, including furniture and stained glass, tiles, fabrics and stencilling. Working with 'culturally prepared' manufacturers like William Watt and Collinson & Lock, Godwin was soon able to extend these innovations to a wider market. With modest expenditure smaller middle-class homes could now be furnished rationally and artistically – at least in theory.

This was the new territory of taste and fashion that journalists, designers and authors of advice manuals were beginning to colonise as part of the expanding field of domestic consumption. The magazines, novels and trade catalogues of the period were becoming the sources of informed taste and one finds Godwin railing against the false values and the simple wrong-headedness which he has either seen in some product or read in one or other publication. As in other fields of activity, Godwin was not above promoting products and ventures with which he was actively involved, although he took care never to appear as the mere puppet of his employers. As an experienced consumer and designer Godwin helped his readers to differentiate between the various alternatives on offer, advising on how to get value for money, and what to look for.

Godwin found the design of domestic furnishings a rewarding field in which to work. He was able to circumvent the tiresome committees and officialdom that dominated the architectural profession. Moreover he could avoid having to deal face-to-face with the snobbish and frequently politicised client networks that operated in the field of domestic architecture. Without stirring from his study he claims to have earned some £600 from supplying designs to a single manufacturer in the course of 1874. This is borne out by the record of increasing income derived from such sources in the mid-1870s. It was not without its pitfalls however. As a designer for industry, Godwin willingly engaged with modernised forms of production, publicity and distribution, but he fought a losing battle for control over the authorship of his reproducible designs, constantly struggling to keep his name visible, and to counter the distortions of plagiarism. To some extent he could see the countless imitations of his furniture as a form of flattery and positive publicity, but not when his design was travestied in the process. The coffee table manufactured by William Watt was a case in point. Godwin complained about meeting it 'almost everywhere I go, — in private houses, in show-rooms, in pictures, and in books.' (p.293) In Godwin's view the 'art' of such a design was not a question of the workmanship and materials so much as the synthesis of lines, proportions and colour in the composition. 'But I have seen the lines changed, the proportions altered, until that which I had regarded as a beauty became to me an offence and an eyesore', he wrote. Apart from aesthetic concerns, there was the equally important question of getting paid for ideas and drawings. It was one thing for an architect to position his designs as 'artworks', but quite another to recoup the kind of fantastic sums that fine artists were able to get for prints and engravings of their works.

In designing for Art manufacturers Godwin was never as well organised as his contemporary Christopher Dresser, who maintained a large studio to deal with his various enterprises and commissions. With the debasement of 'Art Manufactures' as a meaningful category in design, alongside the steady erosion of his most successful designs due to plagiarism one can appreciate why it must have seemed preferable to Godwin to immerse himself in theatre work in the 1880s.

Godwin, tile designs for Burmantofts, Leeds, BA 2 Sept. 1881.

Godwin, design for curtain fabric manufactured by Cowlishaw Nichol & Co., Manchester: BN 31 March 1876.

Further Reading

See essays on Godwin's furniture, textiles, wallpapers and ceramics in Soros 1999.

E. Aslin, *E. W. Godwin. Furniture and Interior Decoration*, London, 1986

S. Soros, *The Secular Furniture of E. W. Godwin*, New Haven and London, 1999

W. Watt, *Art Furniture, from Designs by E. W. Godwin, F.S.A., and Others, with Hints and Suggestions on Domestic Furniture and Decoration, by William Watt*, London, 1877

D. Bolger Burke et al., *In Pursuit of Beauty: Americans and the Aesthetic Movement*, New York, 1986

E. Aslin, *The Aesthetic Movement: Prelude to Art Nouveau*, London, 1969

E. Aslin, *Nineteenth Century English Furniture*, London, 1962

P. Atterbury and C. Wainwright, eds, *Pugin: A Gothic Passion*, New Haven and London, 1994

M. Donnelly, 'British furniture at the Philadelphia Centennial Exhibition', *Furniture History* 37 (2001), pp.91-120

C. L. Eastlake, *Hints on Household Taste*, London, 1868

C. Gere and M. Whiteway, *Nineteenth-Century Design*, London, 1993

J. Kinchin, 'Collinson & Lock', *Connoisseur* 201, May 1979, pp.47-53

L. Lambourne, *The Aesthetic Movement*, London, 2000

S. Muthesius, ' "We do not understand what is meant by a "Company" designing": design versus commerce in late nineteenth-century English furnishing', *Journal of Design History* 5, no. 2 (1992), pp.113-19

L. Parry, ed., *William Morris*, London, 1996

N. Pevsner, 'Art furniture of the eighteen-seventies', *Architectural Review* 112, January 1952, pp.43-50

M. Whiteway, *Christopher Dresser, a Design Revolution*, London, 2004

'Mutual Admirationists', draped around a Godwin coffee table, Punch *22 May 1880.*

MODERN MANUFACTURES FOR URBAN LIVING (1878)

Godwin returns to the themes of economy and hygiene in urban interiors. Modern artistic manufactures could contribute to a healthier and more pleasurable quality of life.

Source:
'Some modern manufactures',
The British Architect, 1 March
1878, p.95

Large towns, in other words places where the traffic is great, and therefore where dust is constantly on the wing, settling here, there, and everywhere, to be driven off only to make room for the next flight, are not so pleasant for the dwellers therein as they might be made. Not merely have townsfolk to suffer the ills that arise from constant disturbance of street dust, in itself bad enough, but in addition to this they have to reside in houses more or less vibratory, warmed by fires whose flues are more or less smoky, and open to an atmosphere more or less charged with smuts. Again, the loss of physical energy occasioned by having to ascend and descend the innumerable stairs which beset life in large modern towns, is a serious drawback to the enjoyment of social calls, or the profit of business visits. And the expense of furnishing and decorating a house or chambers so as to secure some degree of comfort, and at least a crumb of the beautiful is not uncommonly out of all proportion to the degree of comfort and pleasure of beauty attained.

Any modern manufactures that contribute towards remedying these evils of modern city life are to be welcomed, and deserve some more prominent recognition than that furnished by the paragraph formula — "We call attention", &c. Thus the evil of dust may be in no small measure counteracted by laying thin Parquet over the old floors, by using slow combustion stoves, by attention to the fitting of doors and windows, by selecting only such furniture as may be *easily* moved by one pair of hands, or so raised as to leave at least 9 inches clear space above the floor, and by the avoidance of woollen and indeed of all fluffy material whether in curtains, mats, carpets, or upholstery. Parquet floors, of which we have more than one advertisement, are made as thin as a Turkey carpet, and can be had at the comparatively trifling cost of thirteen guineas for a room measuring 15 feet by 18 feet. On such a floor one or two long and narrow rugs are sufficient, only these should be of the close hard texture of old Persian work, costing more to begin with than those of Turkey or Scinde, but cheaper in the end, not merely on account of their durability but because they take up much less dust than the softer fluffy kinds. Again, take the slow combustion stove, of which an illustration is given among our advertisements. Here the fire, besides being economical in the matter of fuel, requires little poking, and thus reduces considerably the supply of dust. This stove has advantages in other ways, and is one of the very few grates that does not contribute a more or less hideous patch to a room.

Advertisement for Doulton's stoves, BA, 10 Nov. 1882.

Large pieces of furniture placed against walls should always have clear spaces below. Thick dust, with all the unwholesomeness thereof, has no greater friend than the ordinary *cottage* piano, unless indeed it be the American organ. The *grand* and the *semi-grand* are the only pianos fit for the busy, dust-engendering life of to-day. They occupy, unfortunately, too much floor space to be generally adopted, but the inventive power of the age may succeed in reducing this. As a rule, we all have *too much furniture* in our rooms. If the constructive features — doors, windows, fireplace, floor, walls and ceiling — are only properly looked after, a rug, a small light table, half-a-dozen easy chairs, and a semi-grand piano, will often be found quite enough in the shape of furniture. To drag in side-tables and cabinets for no other purpose in the world but to carry the useless gimcrackery presented by foolish friends or fond husbands, is to lay traps for dust, to give servants unremunerate labour, and cause them ceaseless anxiety. If town folk would drop their old-fashioned prejudices, would insist on lifts instead of stairs, would consult architects about furnishing instead of upholsterers, and be content with simple but real comforts, with fewer ornaments, and with nobler art, we should have less dust and disease, less toil and trouble, and life in the busy towns of the nineteenth century might yet be made pleasurable and worth the living.

THE ART OF JEWELLERY (1872)

Here Godwin protests against the commercial pressures and modern system of manu-facture that inhibit the design and production of truly artistic jewellery. At best, noted artists are involved by manufacturers to add a note of authority and glamour.

As in architecture we are apt to lose sight of the design, in contemplation of the cost of the mere building, so in jewellery we too often forget that it is an art, in presence of the valuable material with which it deals. The public can appraise brick and timber, diamonds and rubies, with more or less accuracy, because they are tangible marketable commodities. When they attempt to value the mental force which turns the first into architecture and the last into jewellery, they nearly always fall into error. How is this? Simply because, as a people, we inwardly despise art. [...]

Source:
'Jewellery', *Globe and Traveller*, 22 June 1872, pp.1-2

Under the name of art, traders flourish, manufacturers grow rich, and the man of the counting house secures to his own credit the brains of many a young and struggling artist, only too glad to obtain his daily bread, even though it be at the price of remaining mute and inglorious. The experiments of the young and struggling soon cease, and the promising artist either rises out of his position altogether or sinks into a condition little better than a mechanical apparatus, from which is expected a certain amount of work in a stated time. Thus it comes that our so-called art-manufacturers are innocent of art. Here and there an impetus is given by one or two energetic firms, who occasionally rise beyond themselves to ask independent artists to design for them. But this rarely goes far enough to be of any practical value, for the hearts of our manu-facturers are not really set upon the encouragement of artistic work. The business is found to prosper directly the name of a popular artist becomes known as associated with it, the public taste is pandered to as before, but with this difference, that its viciousness is now endorsed by some noted authority. Igno-rance is made comfortable, and the world slides along unconscious alike of its great loss and of the extent to which it can be duped.

* Cellini 1500–71, Italian
Renaissance goldsmith and
sculptor known also for his
autobiography.

Ever since the time of Benvenuto Cellini* the jeweller's art has been degraded. For this Cellini himself is to some extent answerable; for whatever
executive excellence his works may have exhibited, it is tolerably evident that
his designs were too fanciful to be artistically great, and lost in refinement
what they gained in over elaboration. But whether we look at the goldsmith's
or jeweller's art through the puerile sentiment of the renaissance, or through
the sumptuous inventory of Charles V. (A.D. 1369); whether we see it
clothed in the over-muscular proportions of the 12th century or in the almost ethereal refinement of the best days of Grecian art; whether we turn to
the ancient Celt, to the modern Norwegian, to the museum of the Irish Academy, or the wedding presents of a Breton peasant; we find some degree of invention, some quality other than mere vulgar expression of wealth, which at
once classifies it as art, and separates it from the material costliness and
coarse display of most modem jewellery. So depressing is this mental blank
that we are almost wicked enough to long for a revival of the sad productions
which distinguished the reign of Louis Quatorze. Even backward movement
might be better than stagnation, and activity in evil is better than practising
sloth.

Look into any jeweller's windows, and the chances are a thousand to one
that there are not half a dozen articles exhibiting so much thought as that
required in setting up ninepins. There is the ever-recurring, ill-shaped oval
locket, with the ill-proportioned Latin cross. There is the iron gyve turned into
gold for a bracelet, with huge heaps of precious stones, sometimes semi-spheri-
cal in form, and thickly set like the very much magnified eye of a blowfly. Then
there are in special classes the fast jewellery of the turf and the billiard-room;
the ecclesiastical jewellery of the ring and morse; and the mystical symbols of
freemasonry — all of pitiable design and clumsy execution. In brief, the fashionable jewellery of modern society consists of batches of precious stones
lumped together for the bravado of the thing. A dozen diamonds on the wrist
of a fine lady, all of the first water, and each as big as the top of her little finger,
may possess the enviable merit of rousing even the envy of her grace, although
arranged by the unimaginative blockhead, while one stone choicely set in good
filigree, engraved, or beaten work, would pass unheeded, even though it were
made by a John of Pisa, a Ghiberti,** a goldsmith of Constantinople, or an
enameller of Limoges.

*Diamond necklace exhibited in
Paris 1878*, Art Journal *1878*,
p.18.

** Lorenzo Ghiberti 1378–
1455, Florentine sculptor and
goldsmith, responsible for the
bronze doors of the Baptistry.

The art of jewellery — that is, the setting of jewels, may possibly be lost, for
if the workman of to-day is only the workman, and can never again be the
craftsman or the cunning artificer, there is no hope. Here and there we may
find an architect, a painter, or some zealous amateur ready and able to design
a piece of jewellery in the true spirit — that is in the spirit proceeding from the
material and the purpose. Yet, such designs are vanity, for the executant has
nothing in common with the designer and the result is a dull and lifeless model,
wrought, not by force of active brain and nervous hand, but by such miserable means as compass and copy. The goldsmith's art, which includes the jeweller's, has always gone side by side with that of the sculptor.

RABBIT-HUTCH GOTHIC (1872)

By the early 1870s Godwin had considerable experience as a designer of ecclesiastical, institutional and domestic furniture. He was increasingly hostile to the self-conscious crudity and hackneyed reiteration of 'notch and chamfer' motifs that had come to be associated with Reformed Gothic furnishings.

Sir — You have recently published various illustrations of furniture in the "so-called" Medieval style. As your good taste in artistic matters is fully recognised by all who read your paper, and as you do not venture to eulogise these productions, I suppose I may safely infer that they are given as warnings of what should be avoided. At the same time, it is puzzling to understand why architects should take the trouble to produce designs for furniture which are evidently based on the harshest, crudest, baldest most angular and least interesting forms they can select; [...] also that they should so restrict themselves to a wearisome repetition of notches and stop-chamfers, almost always as angular and ungraceful as the general outlines.

Source:
Letter, 'Gothic Furniture',
Building News, 15 November
1872, pp. 393-4

When will designers understand that wood is a material susceptible of receiving the most delicate curves and mouldings, the most intricate and beautiful surface ornament, as well as the boldest relieved work, and that it requires only good and artistic taste to apply these agreeably; that there is no special merit in kitchen-dressers and plate racks, rabbit-hutches or washerwoman's clothes' horses, packing cases &c., which seem to be the inspiring "motifs" of our modern designers. Not only is this absence of elegance, grace, and beauty sought for, but we are presented with sections, plans, and details, to enable others to reproduce these abortions, though there is apparently no more need of such plans than there would be for a three-legged stool, or a butcher's block, with which these productions are about on a par in artistic treatment. [...]

GOTHIC FURNITURE.

George (on the arrival of the new cabinet). "Oh, Pa! do let me have it for a Rabbit-Hutch!"

Modern Medieval furniture as at present rendered, is both mean and ugly to the most intense and painful degree. There is no necessity to run to the other extreme of "rococo" extravagance, as we did fifty years ago, or less [...] A very little study of old examples will show how much enrichment can be used without in any way concealing, or even modifying, construction; designers may learn how long straight lines were usually relieved by curved or running patterns of great beauty, not by senseless notches. [...] In fact the lavish and senseless use of small shafts, and the exclusion or degradation of mouldings, is the bane of modern design. In old furniture the ruling principle of ornament appears to be that it is used to harmonise and soften the hardness of constructive lines. In modern furniture these are emphasised.

Gothic Furniture: 'Oh, Pa! Do let me have it for a rabbit-hutch!', Punch 18 Nov. 1865.

PROGRESS IN ART FURNITURE (1872)

While not averse to the use of ornament or vernacular forms, Godwin sought lighter, more elegant solutions to the integration of construction and decoration in his designs. Furniture should promote health and reflect modern manners.

Source:
'Furniture', *Globe and Traveller*, 15 June 1872, p.2

In ordinary houses the next important point to secure is to combine lightness with strength. Better have two cabinets your servants can easily move, than one which compels you to send out for help in order to manage it. Dispense with the bottom drawer in your bedrooms and your libraries. Better to have an extra set than all sorts of low organic dust poisoning the atmosphere. If, then, we are asked to select the style of the future from the new designs before us, we require, first, that the furniture be well lifted from the floor, and, second, that it be as light as is consistent with real strength. But this is not all. It is essential for true domestic comfort in these high-pressure, nervous times, that the common objects of every-day life should be quiet, simple, and unobtrusive in their beauty. Much of the furniture at the International Exhibitions from 1851 downwards, possessed a quality essentially vulgar, that quality which thrust every consideration on one side, and made paramount the question, "What did it cost?" We want no surprises of this sort. Indeed it is astonishing what a very little quantity of labour we really do want to secure the useful and the beautiful if only that labour be rightly directed. Let one of our best cabinet-makers furnish the world with a complete set of ordinary house furniture, where no moulding, not even a chamfer, no carving, no inlay, no painting nor gilding, shall have part; where genuine materials, genuine construction, shall combine with unobtrusive mass, pleasing outline, rythmical [*sic*] subdivision, and the practical desiderata we have already demanded as essentials; and more will have been done to make art, broadly speaking, popular than by a century of exhibitions. But it may be said, "You are depriving us of all the elements of beauty, of all arts, stock in trade, when you shut us out from the use of moulding, inlay &c." Some years ago we might have admitted this, but our own later experience has taught us otherwise, for we have seen that such furniture is not only possible, but is artistically preferable to the modern imitations of past fashions, and far more appropriate to the manners and customs of the age.

We must guard ourselves from misapprehension. We began by complimenting ourselves for the progress hitherto made; we must finish with a warning. Be careful of professedly Gothic or mediaeval furniture. Stop chamfers, Oxford frames, cabinets with shrine-like roofs, and all the other archaeological revivals of the last twenty years, with their host of miserable imitators. They have had their day, and the best of them have taught us something in presenting us with examples of solid wood construction, somewhat rough and carpenter-like it is true, but strong withal. Without losing the strength, let us cast aside the rudeness, and bear always in mind that the carpenters' fittings in a cathedral are hardly translatable into the furniture of a drawing-room or boudoir.

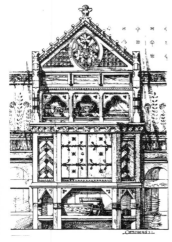

B. Talbert, cabinet from Gothic Forms, 1867.

THE *ART FURNITURE* CATALOGUE (1877)

The catalogue of Godwin's designs published by William Watt was an instant success, and acted as a manifesto for the new style of Art furniture.

I am in receipt of your letter announcing your intention to prepare and publish, a catalogue of your manufactures in furniture and decoration. I think it is quite time that something of the sort should be issued, so that the public may the better know what you have done, are doing, and propose to do.

Personally from an art point of view I am glad to hear of your proposal, as it may lead intending purchasers to come to you direct for things that I have designed for you, and which have fortunately secured such attention as to be copied by others in the trade; but have unfortunately been travestied, even caricatured, in the process. A marked example of this is the square coffee table you first made for me, nine or ten years ago. The lines and dimensions of the different parts of what seems to be a very simple bit of furniture constitute its beauty and its art — if it has any. But I have seen the lines changed, the proportions altered, until that which I had regarded as a beauty became to me an offence and an eyesore. I should not have alluded to this but for the large sale the table in question commands, and but for the fact of my meeting it almost wherever I go, — in private houses, in show-rooms, in pictures, and in books, very prominently in the frontispiece of Miss Garrett's "Suggestions for House Decoration" [...]

I do not know how it is with others, I speak only of myself when I say, that the commonest article of furniture — a chair or a table — cannot be an artistic work by any happy-go-lucky process whatsoever. Little things of this kind to be artistic imperatively demand no inconsiderable amount of thought, and much careful full-size drawing, sometimes done over and over again. But the labour of designing such things is so wholly disproportioned to the reward, that artists have but little external encouragement to devote their time to this class of work.

You are probably aware that in the middle of the fourteenth century a society of artists flourished at Florence, and that among the members were found "Decorative Artists," working in wood and metal. You will remember that the Institute of Painters at Venice included casket-makers, gilders, and varnishers. At the very dawn, too, of the Renaissance, we find that Dello, a Florentine painter of note, was not content to wait idly or dreamily for commissions to paint easel pictures. On the contrary, it is recorded of him, that he filled up the whole of his time for some years in painting and decorating furniture, seats, beds, caskets, &c. His work was not only well done, but the well-doing was much appreciated, and so, says Vasari, he amassed a considerable fortune. It is somewhat different now-a-days, the well-doing is evidently of small account, as anyone may see who will take the trouble to do so. Look at the worse than childish paintings on the panels of modern furniture. Why is it so? Because the appreciation that Dello enjoyed is not forthcoming. The majority of the few rich and cultured people who could appreciate, hardly ever look at new furniture, their way of encouraging contemporary artists who devise works

Source:
Letter to Watt dated 1 January 1877. Published in the preface to *Art Furniture from designs by E. W. Godwin, F.S.A., and others,* London 1877, p.iii.

Biographical notes:
Garrett
Watt

R. and A. Garrett, Suggestions for House Decoration, *1876.*

Godwin, detail of title page for Art Furniture, *1877.*

in wood and metal, being shown in patronizing the curiosity monger. This fashion of seeking in curiosity shops for mobilia, whether of carved work, of marquetry, or what not, is most pernicious to the development of what national art-power there may yet be latent among us. That artists should by example give currency to this fashion is to be deplored; but still more is it to be deprecated that the cabinet-maker should have given them cause, by neglecting or discouraging the artistic element in his work.

No doubt you will continue to do everything in your power to counteract this discouragement by producing furniture of refined design, of good workmanship, of reasonable cost; and that you will issue this Catalogue rather as an earnest of good things to come than as an exhibition of a work accomplished.

MANTELPIECES (1876)

Mantelpieces created an artistically dominant feature in the Aesthetic interior, providing an architectonic framework for the display of china and objets d'art. *Here Godwin talks of the mantelpiece as part of the permanent architecture of a room, to be distinguished from lighter, moveable furniture. In the spirit of Design Reform he urges his readers to dispense with ostentatious expanses of mirror glass and the 'vicious progeny of the modern marble mason'. Marble, pillars and cornices might be suitable for a palace, but not for the everyday rooms of a middle-class house.*

Source:
'Mantelpieces', *Architect*, 3 June 1876, p.353

Biographical notes:
Nesfield
Shaw
Stevens

Advert for marble fireplaces, Builder *28 June 1873.*

There are few features in modern houses so capable of improvement as the vernacular mantelpiece. Happily for the future, it is a feature which is arresting more attention every day, and where it once was thrust on one side into the limbo of "provide-and-fix" it now often forms an item for thought, if not for original design.

The hooded, flat and mean varieties

There are, broadly speaking, only two kinds of fireplaces — the hooded and the flat. To the first, or hooded class, belong by descent those wide, deeply embayed examples of the fifteenth and sixteenth centuries common in country cottages, and so much admired by the modern pastoral or farmhouse school of architects. To the last belong many of the grand town examples of the same period and the whole vicious progeny of the modern marble mason. The difference between the two classes is fundamentally the difference between an external and internal chimney breast. The earliest mantelpieces in this country were of the first or hooded kind, [...] mostly found in Norman castles and buildings, where the walls are of very great substance. Later on the wood becomes visible as an internal projection; in some instances very prominent, as in the early specimen illustrated by Mr. NESFIELD in his "Examples of French Architecture", where the fireplace is all wood and hearthstone. [...] As the hood receded in internal projection the opening for the fireplace became deeper, until it so thinned the wall at the back that it was deemed necessary to build a breast wall or flat buttress outside. This was the beginning of the great recessed fireplaces Mr. NORMAN SHAW appears to delight in. [...]

Shaw, dining room ingle, Cragside, BN 8 Nov. 1872.

If we have to choose between the varieties of hooded fireplaces, by all means let us have the capacious closed-in hood, the fire-room of the Tudor age, and not the corbelled-out hooded hearth of the twelfth and thirteenth centuries. The last is, I need hardly say, an archaeological fad. It has been a fad of my own; it is still a fad with one or two stubborn followers of a well-abused revival. [...] My object is rather to call attention to the flat mantelpiece with which we are all familiar, and to some improvements that have been made to existing examples.

Everyone knows the vernacular chimney-piece of the nineteenth century. How, by a succession of stages covering more than two centuries, the tall imposing mass of panelled work that was the chief feature of the room has dwindled foot by foot and inch by inch until the dwarf of our own time appeared, a dwarf that in spite of the richest materials was always so insufferably mean that it became a regular uniform practice to cover the chimney breast with a large picture or monstrous looking-glass. How far the law of leasehold is responsible for this deterioration in domestic interiors matters little to us. We take the facts as we find them, and the question for us is, how we can best treat them to render them agreeable.

Modern design solutions

If we accept as a rule that the mantelpiece should be the most important — the dominant feature in a room, the inquiry is narrowed to the question, How can this desirable consummation be best achieved? Some painters and a few architects have exercised their minds towards the solution of the problem with very diverse results. In some cases the difficulty of uniting an artistic superstructure of framed woodwork with the coarse ostentatious boxing of the modern marble mason's manufacture has been got over by altogether removing the latter and setting up a wood framework in its place. It is, I hope, manifest that to place a wood construction over a marble substructure is, to say the least, unsatisfactory. The edge of the incongruity may be taken off by overlapping the two materials in such a manner as to produce something like oneness or unity in the entire mass, as, for instance, by allowing the marble of the chimney-piece to appear in the panels of the upper part, which, for the sake of distinction, I shall call the mantelpiece, and by carrying, if practicable, the woodwork of the latter down to the floor.

Godwin, design for 'Jacobean mantelpiece' from the Art Furniture *catalogue 1877.*

One of the most common ways of treatment is to frame together a number of shelves of any height from about 2 feet to the entire height of the room,

Mantelshelves designed by Eastlake, Hints on Household Taste, *4th edn 1878.*

Godwin, design for mantelpiece, Art Furniture, *1877.*

without regard to anything beyond the sizes of certain pots and plates with which the shelves are intended to be covered. There are those whose *furore* for "collecting" has entirely outrun their artistic judgment, and whose mantelpieces are literally nothing more nor less than repetitions of the upper part of the vernacular kitchen dresser — a vulgar heap of costly china, where the close proximity of pot and plate interrupt the full appreciation of one and the other. A few well-selected and well-distributed specimens of *faience* show the cultured mind — the artistic feeling; but crowded shelves and piled-up heaps show little and often nothing more than wealth or clever buying. What I gave here, how lucky I was there, what I was offered for this, and what I refused for that, constitute the staple of the conversation one generally hears before a dresser mantelpiece.

Another objectionable kind is where, although the display of costly objects is by no means large, ostentatious, or vulgar, there is an amount of reflection and glitter which borders on vulgarity. If looking-glass or mirrors are used at all, it should be with considerable caution. It may be taken as a rule that wherever these are employed they should be boldly used, forming marked and important features in the general design, as pictures would be used, or wholly illusory for the purpose of doubling the composition, which would then be specially designed for this object. In this latter sense the late ALFRED STEVENS, who was a consummate artist in everything, has used silvered glass with very marked effect in the dining-room at Dorchester House. It is true it is in a recess which is fitted up as a buffet, and not in the mantelpiece which in such an important room is very rightly treated, not as furniture, but as a strong integral part of the architectural construction made artistically dominant by being composed with sculpture of a very high order. This is all very well for a palace, but in the small everyday rooms of the middle and lower-middle class house architectural masses of marble in pillar and cornice, however enriched, are inappropriate, more than ever inappropriate when, as is frequently the case, the rest of the room and, indeed, of the house is wholly unarchitectural and free from marble. The marble door-architraves and cornices of Italy we in this country have long since translated into wood for common use: the same can be done for the common mantelpiece without necessarily making it look like a cabinet with a stove stuck in the bottom of it. In a well-balanced properly-ordered room, the details of windows, floors, mantelpieces, and indeed, of all distinctly architectural fixtures, should be always bolder than the details of the furniture or movables. Where it is not so — and I have in my mind's eye a very charming house where furniture and fixtures were all carefully designed by one clever hand — one or two things must happen, either the furniture will appear coarse and heavy, or the mantelpieces, &c., weak, if not flimsy. [...]

Tiles and wood as a margin to the opening of a fireplace have lately become very common, but where a mantelpiece towers above the fireplace there are few more certain ways of destroying unity in the composition than by limiting the use of tiles to this margin. If tiles are used below, then they should be used in *some* degree above, not necessarily in a huge mass of equal-sized panels, [...] but with some feeling for the distribution and proportion of texture and colour.

FLOORCLOTHS (1876)

One of the articles following on from the series 'My house "in" London', in which Godwin surveys the range of available floorcloths, and primes the modern consumer about what to look for.

Of the various articles of domestic use from which the modern house furnisher has to select, there are some present few, if any, difficulties. The plainer fabrics of the East, for instance, whether in mattings, carpets, or curtain stuffs, are almost so invariably good that (apart from having to match with stuffs not so invariably good) it matters little which we take. Indeed, among such things the process of selection under ordinary circumstances might be performed in the dark, for although there is a vast amount of variety in these woven works, I never yet saw or heard of anything vulgar or offensive. How far European influence is operating to the deterioration of Eastern manufacture is a question that European civilisation is not likely to heed. Take two things — Indian matting and Japanese fans. As yet we have not reached in either the European level, but the manufacture of the present day as compared with the same manufacture of twenty or even ten years ago has unquestionably deteriorated. There may be still fan-painters and mat-weavers no ways inferior to their forefathers; all I insist on is that, owing to a general lack of artistic susceptibility among us, the best productions and the best artists of the East are unappreciated, and our markets being open to the sale of inferior, hurried produce, encourage from day to day the production of still yet inferior still more hurried work. The twopenny Japanese fan is even now, in spite of this, a marvel of beauty by the side of work of a like nature invented this side the world, and the decorations wherewith it is enriched, however much they may fall short in colours or drawing of those imported say ten years since, have nevertheless the merit of being as a rule fit.

Now it is this lack of *fitness* that is so much wanting in certain things of our own manufacture whereof the markets of the East are ignorant. If we want a floorcloth that shall wear well, and be washable, whether we call it by the familiar name oilcloth, or by some high-sounding title, we must have recourse to our own manufacturers, and the designs they choose to put before us. In wall papers, although the French compete with us, it is with less success than of old, so that practically for the floors of the halls and passages, as well as for the walls of the houses of the great mass of the people, English designs are, as a rule, selected.

To begin with floorcloth. I have open on the floor as I write books of patterns from most of the leading manufacturers. The earliest patterns, I note, are in the book of a very old-established firm. Two of these are even yet in demand; the one grey and white, in imitation of marble, the other in six colours, in imitation of the flowery Brussels carpet so commonly used during the first half of this century. Of course the demand for these patterns is nothing like what it was, and the retail sale is now mostly limited to lodging-house keepers and speculators in a poor class of furnished houses. What I mention these early productions for is to call attention to the fact that the designs for

Source:
'Floorcloths', *Architect*, 2 September 1876, p.128

299

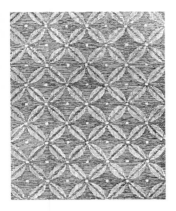

Floorcloth design from Eastlake,
Hints on Household Taste, *4th
edn 1878.*

these oilcloths were in almost every case taken from patterns of the marble mason, or from designs of the weaver of carpet stuffs. Before we examine the later and most approved patterns, we will pause for a second or two to look into the conditions of the case. These floorcloths are coarse prepared cloth, trowelled and printed all over in oil colours by means of wood blocks, cut to a design much in the same manner as wall papers are printed. The block pattern, as in paper, must be of certain dimensions a square of 9 inches being the most convenient, and that which forms the base of the large majority of patterns. The colours are, as a rule, limited to six; and as in paper printing, so here the greater the number of colours the greater the cost of production. But there is this important difference, that whilst papers vary in selling price according to the number of blocks or printings, a two colour or one print pattern selling, at say four shillings a piece, and a five print pattern at twelve shillings, the floorcloth always sells at a uniform price so far as regards pattern and number of colours. There is, it is true, a difference in the price of floorcloth, for at a retail house for the same pattern from the same maker you may give as little as two shillings and as much as four shillings and threepence a square yard — a difference owing to quality and age, and not at all to design or printing. This all sounds as if there were something wrong somewhere, for if it be logical for the paper printer to charge according to the rate of cost four shillings say for what has cost him one, and twelve for that has cost him three, it seems to me that it would be no less reasonable for the floorcloth printer to charge in like manner. If it pays the floorcloth manufacturer to sell all his products at a uniform rate, the six-colour as low as the two colour, then seeing that most of the work turned out contains three or more colours, it needs no strong powers of vision to see further — that we who are modestly inclined for grey and black, or who are happily artists enough to be rather shy of extensive palettes, must be paying for the lack of discrimination in those who are able to swallow any amount of vulgar inharmonious colour, and who keep up the demand therefore.

Modern sham products

If any floorcloth manufacturer would be bold enough to begin at patterns instead of colour, and pay for artistic and *fit* design rather than for the labour of repeated printings, there would be some chance for a production that will be otherwise soon superseded by a kindred trade. But as I have already said the designs must be FIT. Here is the last book out, plain tiles, encaustic tiles, marble in large slabs, marble in small cubes or tesserae [...] all with the joints accurately shown, recurring page after page. It was seemingly not enough that our churches, ancient and modern, should be given up to the designer of tile pavements. The architect, the manufacturer, the amateur, could use colour nowhere else, and so they had their fling on the floor; but we little thought that these apparently harmless amusements, open to everyone and "so artistic, don't you know", would have been an example to the sober manufacturer of a roll of painted cloth. For some of the patterns before me have not even the merit of being copied from old tiles. [... N]ot only are such patterns unfit for the manufacture, but they are wholly unfit for the ordinary middle class house, whether executed in tile or cloth or any other material. One reason why these tile patterns have commended themselves to the manufacturer is because they meet one practical necessity of the case, viz., that of separating or cutting up the colours as much as possible into comparatively small bits. There are, however, plenty of ways of doing this without having recourse to a system of slavish copyism, whether directed to marble or tile. One of the most enterprising houses in the trade evidently thinks so too and has given us something novel in the shape of a close imitation of India matting.

Wood floors have already been imitated in parquet patterns, so that we may now hope to have seen the end of this childish appropriation of the designs, construction, and texture of other materials to a fabric which, by the very nature of its manufacture, should have been marked from first to last by special designs fit and suitable to the materials used and the household purposes to which it is adapted.

[...] The powers of design exhibited may be estimated by the one word — *nil*. The resources of the adapter, whereby wall paper designs have been so much enriched, lately, have not been brought to bear on the patterns for floorcloths, or only in such a hesitating small way as to be practically worthless. If people can afford it, they can have their halls and passages floored with marble in one form or another, or covered with Persian, Brussels, or other carpet, or laid with mosaic of coloured or encaustic tiles, or made lovely with parquet of beautiful woods. And if their means are limited, lo! the manufacturer of floorcloth steps in and presents them with a fairly durable and cleanly substitute for all this in exact facsimile at 2s. 9d. per square yard laid. And thus certain avenues for artistic design are closed, and that vulgar pretentiousness which Charles DICKENS pictured for us in the villa of the VENEERINGS is perpetuated.*

* Characters in the novel *Our Mutual Friend*, 1864.

Where is the remedy?

And now where is the remedy? It is to be found, like everything else, in Nature. Say the pattern is limited to a square of 9 inches (which it is not, but this one will do as well as a larger or smaller one for my present object). The leading conditions practical are:— 1. That the colours shall not exceed six. 2. That the colours shall be cut up into small, or comparatively small, fragments. Now it is obvious that any pattern which is wholly of the nature of a powdering will be impracticable. Thus many of the patterns that are eminently suitable for linoleum are altogether unfit for floorcloth. But of those that are available there are three great varieties each of which — the diaper, the meander, and the stripe — contains an inexhaustible storehouse of lovely form. Beyond the practical conditions of the manufacture there are other conditions as to design. These [...] are yet so far implied by the materials used, and by the very name of the stuff, that we may well regard them as essential. For example, the design, however naturalistic, should always be perfectly flat. Again, there should be no tops nor bottoms nor sides, but the pattern should be readable, so to speak, in whatever direction we may be walking on it , like a daisy-covered mead. [...] But to apply these remedies an artist, not a draughtsman is needed.

Floorcloth designs for the Building News *Designing Club,* BN *16 March 1877.*

ARTISTIC STOVES (1878)

Source:
'Notes on current events', *The British Architect*, 1 March 1878, p.95

Biographical notes:
Jeckyll

While generally critical of Thomas Jeckyll's architectural scheme for Leyland's famous Peacock Room, Godwin was full of admiration for the artistic and affordable metalwork he designed for the Norwich firm of Barnard, Bishop & Barnard (faithful advertisers in The British Architect*). The firm's Anglo-Japanese stoves, fenders and other domestic products were exhibited to great acclaim in international exhibitions, exported in large quantities, and widely used by architects of an Aesthetic persuasion, including Godwin himself, Norman Shaw and Nesfield. By 1878, however, Jeckyll had been committed to a lunatic asylum where he died three years later in obscurity.*

Advertisement for Barnard Bishop & Barnard's artistic stoves, BA 3 Jan. 1879.

A paper called *The Looking Glass* has made the wonderful discovery that certain stove manufacturers make slow combustion stoves, and that these "ought to be as much a matter of necessity in a house as proper ventilation or drainage." The writer then launches his thunderbolt — "Architects are, however, notoriously ignorant on these matters and the public must look to themselves for a remedy". For more than a year the slow combustion stove of Messrs. Barnard, Bishop, and Barnard has been before the public. An architect — Mr. Jekyl [*sic*] if we mistake not — is the author of the charming Anglo-Japanese designs that render the manufacturer's work artistic. But architects may work until their very brains give way without one word of praise, nay, even of recognition, from those who are ever dinning into the ear of the public the merits of manufacturers whose articles the architect has rendered presentable and made therefore, saleable.

THE ARTIST AND THE ART MANUFACTURER (1879)

Godwin had long resented being channelled into 'one-sided accomplishment', and actively promoted the role of the independent professional designer able to work in different media, unshackled by manufacturers and middle-men.

Source:
'The artist and the art manufacturer', *The British Architect*, 21 March 1879, p.121

We are not of those who place implicit faith in the modern system that pertains to art-manufactures. In old times the artist had his workshop and his staff of assistants, and the place was generally known as that of the artist. In our time, as far as art-manufacture is concerned, he is generally sunk in the staff, — he has become "our Mr. So-and-So", and the place is known by the name of people whose money and capital and commercial capacity are exercised, not to produce the best art or to encourage the best artists, but to profit by the cheap productions of impecunious outsiders or the hurried thoughtless grind of the draughtsmen in their establishments. The art that results from such a system may not be altogether bad. The outsider however needy may have some sense of independence and honour, and may at times work *con amore*, looking only to art, and not at all to the few miserable coins the "art-manufacturer" will give him for his work. Nevertheless to know — and sooner or later the artist is sure to learn it — that the price he is paid is often less than half what the public pays, is sure to hurt and gall the sensitive man, and not infrequently tends to stay him from prosecuting or from further developing a course of artistic thought and labour that would have enriched the world. There are people among the art-purchasing public who are beginning to see this, and who are breaking through that icy reserve and false delicacy that have hitherto blocked their way of direct approach to the artist. This is a course we regard with unmixed satisfaction, as we believe it would be altogether favourable to Art if the manufacturers kept entirely to the chemical, mechanical, and other scientific questions arising from the nature of their manufacture, and carried out the designs of independent artists, under certain conditions, as builders carry out the designs of architects. The manufacturer who keeps his artists on or off the premises is like the builder who keeps his own architect. We can never in the nature of things expect that either one or the other will produce the best work, for Art before all things requires independence and freedom from all restraint, except such as she herself imposes. Of course in these rapid times the artist cannot bring his designs before the public except by way of commission; designs, therefore, which are capable of large repetition are practically shut out, unless there is some middleman to publish and sell them.

ART POTTERY (1878)

Like many Aesthetes Godwin was attracted to the tapered elegance and pure, balanced forms of Grecian pottery that lent themselves to mass production by Art manufacturers. As an example of good and affordable designs in this manner he picked out Woodward & Co. ceramics decorated by the artist Frank Miles (for whom he was in the process of designing a studio house in Tite Street.)

Source:
'Notes on current events', *The British Architect*, 27 September 1878, p.126

"LONDON" has made some sensible remarks on "spurious and shoddy imitations" of artistic handiwork. It is indeed much to be deplored that machine-made goods are often so exceedingly "decorative." Good form or shape such as that met with in the old red or black pottery of every local museum in the country may be reproduced by the thousand without the slightest injury to art in its higher flights. It is only where the artist's hand has delicately manipulated the surface of the clay into another kind of art which may be wholly independent of the general form that machine-made imitation fails. We want in fact less and less ornament, more and more beauty.

Godwin, design for toilet set, BA 14 Feb. 1879.

[Frank Miles's designs] are not to be surpassed in refinement of design by anything outside Greek collections...one small specimen we found [...] is, in its lines and colour, and sketchy decoration, quite fascinating, and is in our memory stored as among the best art work our age has yet produced.

Source:
'Notes on current events', *The British Architect*, 11 October 1878, p.142

CHINA PAINTING (1879)

Source:
'Notes on current events', *The British Architect*, 1 August 1879, p.41

Biographical notes:
Howell & James

Burmantofts art pottery sold at Howell & James, BA 7 Oct. 1881.

Source:
'Notes on current events', *The British Architect*, 30 July 1880, p.47-8

The 'chinamania' of the 1870s extended to a vogue for china painting among the middle classes, in particular women. In 1875 Howell & James instituted an annual exhibition of such work, which rapidly became an important artistic and social gatherings.

We looked at Messrs. Howell & James's, Regent-street, this week, to see the fourth annual exhibition of paintings on china, by lady amateurs and artists [... W]e venture to say that the workmanship far excels the decorative power [...] It is curious to observe how little design seems to be understood — how poorly it is appreciated. We miss it in architecture more and more, and have in its place a mere hodge-podge of forms gathered anywhere, and put together anyhow — we seek for this in vain in sculpture, and in painting its presence is rare. In this collection of china plates at Messrs. Howell and James's, a good design has to be searched for. [...] If young ladies and gentlemen wish to paint (in imitation) portraits, landscapes, sea pieces, and still life, canvas, panel and paper are at their disposal; a concave dish or plate of china is not the proper platform for their performances, not that we object to a head, a figure, or a landscape on a plate, if only they be treated with that convention and restraint that their purpose and position demand. And it is in this restraint, in this, so to speak, symbolic or shorthand drawing, that so much has still to be learnt from the Japanese artists.

WHAT TO DO WITH OUR WALLS? (1880)

Cheap, non-poisonous, hygienic and space-enhancing – Godwin endorses a new paint product.

What to do with our walls it still an unanswered query. Not the walls of palatial abodes, public buildings, and snug villa residences (though all these merit more thoughtful consideration than they usually get), so much as the millions of yards of wall surface in cheap buildings left without the tender mercies of an architect. Put an ordinary wall paper on your little parlour (about 12 or 13 feet square perhaps) and you reduce its size from what it appeared in the plain plastering by nearly a fourth. Good engravings are cheap now-a-days; walls may be covered with them by anyone, from the cottager upwards. What we want is a quiet tint of full, rich colour up to the chair rail, not to show the dirt of contact with dress, of a cheerful but subdued tint for the main bulk of the walls to show off the pictures and engravings, and of a lighter livelier shade if you wish for frieze and ceiling. [...] As to the choice of a decorative wall paint which shall have none of the poisonous properties of wall papers and their receptiveness of dust and dirt and shall be washable and of good colour, and moreover better than ordinary paint which is not always innocent, we have "Duresco". [...] Firstly it is cheap enough to be within the reach of everybody. Secondly, it is absolutely non-poisonous. Thirdly, it prevents the percolation of moisture. Fourthly, it is washable. Fifthly, it is applied in a simple manner, as ordinary whitewash, becoming excessively hard, and having the finished appearance of an oil flatted surface. What more do we want? We advise our readers to try it.

LIBERTY FABRICS (1879)

Godwin was a frequent shopper at Liberty's and became head of their costume department in 1884, employing the colour and drape of the firm's silks to the full. Whether considering textiles or furniture, a high gloss was to be avoided.

We have been shown some very beautiful samples of new hand-woven Indian silks, introduced by the firm of Lazenby Liberty & Co., of Regent-street. For artistic draperies and costumes these soft, pliant silks are invaluable, being full in colour without any approach to gaudiness, whilst the *matt* character of the surface of the fabrics gives sufficient of the sheen of silk, without any of that distracting glare so characteristic of the highly-gummed glossiness of French silks.

Source:
'Notes on current events',
The British Architect, 31
January 1879, p.43

A NOTE ON NEEDLEWORK (1879)

Art embroidery was another field in which upper and middle-class women, including Godwin's client Princess Louise, were beginning to achieve public and professional recognition. While approving the social aims of the Royal School of Needlework, however, Godwin still felt there was room to improve through designs for simple, inexpensive work.

We are well pleased to find that the present Winter Exhibition of the Royal School of Art Needlework, at South Kensington, shows in no wise any deterioration from the quality of design and workmanship hitherto shown there. There are still unquestionably many specimens of labour ill-bestowed — of multitudinous stitches squandered on designs which are not merely *ill-suited* to this kind of work, but that are quite unworthy of any art-labour whatsoever The greatest success is achieved in two very opposite schools of design, the Renaissance and the Japanese. [...] Among the naturalistic examples, the best both for harmony of colour and vigour of drawing, is the small lily piece designed by H.R.H. The Princess LOUISE, Marchioness of LORNE; but as a rule the naturalistic treatment is glaring and crude. Some of the larger panels in the Japanese fashion are ill-drawn, as if the designer had only seen the latest and most inferior screens prepared in Japan for the European markets. We think too much labour has been ill-spent in Mr. W. MORRIS'S specimen of wall decoration, for the design contains a vast quantity of needlework out of all proportion to the result obtained. On the other hand, we have to congratulate the Rev. S. IMAGE on his very excellent figure composition, in illustration of music. The subject is a wood, in which are four damsels and two or three small angels, all in outline; the wing of one of the angels is so nervously good in drawing, that it makes us regret more time was not spent over the angel's

Source:
'A note on needlework', *The British Architect*, 12 December 1879, p.229

Biographical notes:
Image
Morris
Princess Louise
Royal School of Art Needlework

'The Tidy Costume, a Hint to Art Needleworkers', Punch *12 Dec. 1879.*

face. After a careful examination, we come to the conclusion that the best designs as a rule are associated with the most elaborate, costly productions, and that in simple or inexpensive work the design, the drawing, and the colour arrangement leave much to be desired.

The institution itself is so good, and the work as a rule so well done, that there should be no doubt as to the ultimate success of this school being all that its founders and friends could desire. One of the objects in view is to give fitting work to those who, being by birth and education ladies, yet stand in need of the money they earn. Tenpence an hour — the highest rate the best needle-workers can reach — is little enough, and as there is no personal profit to the shareholders, work [...] comes out remarkably low in-price. What however is specially needed just now, is a higher class of *design* for the simpler kind of work.

Art needlework rightly understood demands like every other handicraft a special consideration of the materials in the preparation of the design. Ornamental tiles, wood block printing, wrought iron work, and even paintings have at present too much direct influence on those who are responsible for most of the designs of the needlework at South Kensington. The mania for *novelty* here, as everywhere, is undermining the true principles of art.

ELECTRIC DESK LIGHTS (1879)

As a frequent visitor to the British Library Godwin evaluated the interior from a designer's as well as a scholar's point of view, complaining among other things about the position of lamps that cast readers' shadows on their books.

Source:
'Notes on current events', *The British Architect*, 21 March 1879, p.122

We took our usual seat the other evening in the Reading-room of the British Museum to try the effect of the electric lamps. The two defects of noise and jerky interruption in the lights themselves will no doubt be remedied in the course of a short time, and therefore we do not intend to dwell on these conditions, unpleasant as they unquestionably are, to the reader.

INDELIBLE INK? (1880)

Another tool of the writer's trade receiving a less than enthusiastic endorsement.

Source:
'Notes on current events', *The British Architect*, 13 February 1880, p.73

We have before us a bottle, labelled Featherstone's black writing ink, which professes to be an indelible writing ink. We have made use of it, and find that the bottle we have used, at all events, completely belies its name. It is not only not indelible, but it moreover evaporates in the using and does not dry readily on the paper; in fact, it remained moist after being on the paper for twelve hours. There are so many nostrums in the market for this and that object, that we felt it our duty to inform each of our subscribers as have not yet used it that Featherstone's black writing ink is a good ink only in the quality of its colour — so far as our experience goes.

XIII Dress

'IF YOU really desire noble buildings', wrote Godwin in 1868, 'you must have an eye to your boots' (p.312). Dress was a subject too important to be left 'under the arbitrary power and sole despotic sway of the French milliners and the west-end tailors.'[1] It connected with Godwin's views about 'clothing' ideas and a cultured sensibility in tangible form, and presented a 'connective tissue' with the past. Such metaphors crop up repeatedly in Godwin's writing, drawing on a realm of experience that all his readers shared, and applied not only to fashion, but to discussion of topics as varied as drainage, or architectural construction and style. For men and women, dress could be an art-form, and Art was not something to be donned just every now and then. 'We must be drenched with it, through and through.' On a more theoretical level, fashion and clothing reflected the Aesthetic preoccupation with *surfaces* as expressive of content, a theme later taken up by Oscar Wilde in *The Truth of Masks; a Note on Illusion* (1891). As in matters of interior decoration, it was above all to Godwin that Wilde looked for sartorial guidance and ideas on dress. 'I hear you have been dressing our Oscar in plush!', wrote Whistler in a note to Godwin that found its way into the *World* (22 October 1884, p.18): 'why? That, I thought, ceased with the breeches — you know: "Knee plush ultra!"' Despite Godwin's attempts as both designer and critic to raise the visibility of dress as an art-form and academic subject, however, the institutionalised hierarchy of genres in the late nineteenth century meant that his contribution to this area was rarely noted. Significantly, not a single obituary mentioned that he was the director of Liberty's famous Costume Department at the time of his death.

Whether following the rules of sartorial etiquette, participating in amateur theatricals, tableaux vivants, or attending costume balls in full regalia, a passion for dress and dressing up permeated respectable Victorian society. As a child Godwin had been fascinated by illustrations in Planché's *History of British Costume* (1834) and had spent hours copying, colouring and cutting out figures from this publication. As it had been for Pugin, dressing up was a way of inhabiting the medieval past, and at home in Bristol Godwin and Burges entered into the world of Wilars de Honecourt by donning colourful hose, tunic and liripipe (see p.139). Such outfits offered a welcome release from the regulation black baggy trousers, frock coat and chimney-pot hat worn by middle-class men, all of which Godwin roundly condemned.

He was also a debonair figure in his everyday attire, immaculately turned out, and to be spied in the 1860s with felt hat, colourful floppy tie and velvet jacket or black cloak, frequently sporting a silk umbrella in one hand and cigar in the other. Later he advocated a Norfolk jacket, knee breeches and woollen 'combinations'. These dress codes were self-consciously 'artistic', 'healthy' and 'rational', and in fashioning a look that was distinct from the self-presentation of most architects as men of business, Godwin complemented his cam-

[1] 'A lecture on dress', *The Mask* 6:4, Apr. 1914, p.335

Fourteenth-century effigy of Blanche de la Tour, illustrated by Planché.

The worship of corsets satirised in Punch, *24 April 1869.*

paign to redefine the character of the profession. Likewise Ellen Terry 'dressed the part' with Godwin's assistance, both at home and on the stage. She recalled with affection the medievalising tabard dress he designed for her, inspired by Viollet-le-Duc, and also wore a kimono: both these forms of dress freed her from the restraints of corsetry.

In his Shakespearian studies Godwin emphasised how costume could be used for dramatic effect, both in affecting the audience and expressing certain character traits. For Ellen Terry's role as Titania in the 1863 production of *A Midsummer Night's Dream* at the Theatre Royal in Bath, Godwin designed and helped to make a chiton-style dress, first wetted and wrung out so that when dry, it unfolded in a crinkled and clinging manner. His designs for such clothing, both in and outside the theatre, incorporated movement as a dimension of the composition. His costume designs only 'worked' with a moving body and the dynamic this set up with the surroundings. This was clothing for modern life, not cladding for mouldering skeletons or corseted dummies (see p.324). To this end, like other dress reformers he looked above all to classical, medieval, and Japanese styles that he felt allowed dress to follow the natural form and movement of the human body. While the main dress exhibits at the International Health Exhibition in 1884, organised by Lewis Wingfield in association with Mme Tussaud, were arranged on life-size wax models, as the director of Liberty's newly established Costume Department, Godwin organised displays on living, moving figures.

Artistic dress for 'Young Geniuses', Punch *21 Sept. 1878.*

Further Reading

A. Holt, *Fancy Dresses Described, or What to Wear at Fancy Balls*, London, 1882

Mrs Haweis, *The Art of Dress*, London, 1879

Mrs Oliphant, *Dress*, London, 1878

J. Planché, *History of British Dress*, London, 1834 (3rd edn 1874)

J. Planché, *Cyclopaedia of Costume*, 2 vols London, 1876–9

H. Shaw, *Dresses and Decorations of the Middle Ages*, London, 1834

J. M. Smith, *Ancient Greek Female Costume*, London, 1883

T. Veblen, *The Theory of the Leisure Class*, New York 1899

S. Bennet and H. Stevenson, *Van Dyck in Check Trousers: Fancy Dress in Art and Life, 1700–1900*, Edinburgh, 1978

C. Breward, *The Hidden Consumer: Masculinities, Fashion and City Life 1860–1914*, Manchester 1999

C. Cruise, 'Artists' clothes', in P. Kirkham, ed., *The Gendered Object*, Manchester, 1996

J. Harvey, *Men in Black*, London, 1995

K. Psomiades, *Beauty's Body: Femininity and Representation in British Aestheticism*, Stanford, 1997

K. Montague, 'The aesthetics of hygiene: Aesthetic dress, modernity, and the body as sign', *Journal of Design History* 7, 1994, pp.91-112

S. Newton, *Health, Art and Reason*, London, 1974

M. Macdonald et al., *Whistler, Women and Fashion*, New Haven and London, 2003

DRESS, FASHION AND ART (1868)

In 1914 Edward Gordon Craig clearly felt that his father's lecture, delivered nearly fifty years earlier, was still relevant to a modern audience, and published the text in his magazine, The Mask.

Fickle fashion

The changeableness of 19th century fashion is perhaps not only the greatest evil, but the parent of all the other evils in modern costume with which we have to contend. There is no such thing now-a-days as contentment in dress, for if perchance a becoming hat, a graceful mantle or an artistic serviceable coat be approved by the world this season it must be given up next season, no amount of gracefulness or appropriateness being powerful enough to stay the restless hand of fickle fashion. The rule seems to be that directly a thing becomes vulgar in the old and true sense of the word it must needs be despised as vulgar in the modern and erroneous sense of the word. [...]

Source:
'A lecture on dress by E. W. Godwin. F.S.A. 1868', *The Mask*, Vol. 6, No. 4, April 1914, pp. 335-52

Fashion, like the true artist, may be unsatisfied by her best efforts and may be ever seeking to do better; or she may be desirous to keep up those social distinctions which many hold to be necessary to the well-being of the state; or she may be after all only a pander to the pride and vanity and deformity of the world.

> "When lordes and ladies ever do devise
> Themselves to setten forth to strangers sight
> Some frounce their curled hair in courtly guise
> Some prancke their ruffes and others trimly dight
> Their gay attire: Each others greater pride does spight."
>
> (Fairy Queen 1.4.14)

Male and female dress

Again the great difference which exists between male and female costume is another characteristic defect of the age in which we live. All natural relative proportion is ignored: the man is deprived of every vestige of drapery in the artistic sense of the word, and his limbs are disguised in bag-like coverings, whilst the woman copies the conventional short-skirted school-girl or clothes herself in a wasteful amplitude of skirt.

'What we must expect to see if the girl of the period keeps pace with the latest novelty', Punch 17 April 1869.

The difference between male and female costume is not, however, confined to form but extends even to material. We know how linen, wool, silk, satin, velvet, were used in old times for the clothing of men as well as for that of women; but, (as in the matter of drapery) the men have been forced by fashion to give up all claim to the richer materials and to encase themselves in gloomy monotony of broad-cloth.

Colour and costume

The general absence of colour is another important characteristic of our costume. An English crowd, (no matter how brightly coloured certain of its

A SUGGESTION IN BLACK AND WHITE.

Du Maurier's suggestion for flouting the black and white convention, Punch *4 March 1876.*

details may be), always resolves itself into a dull grey owing to the preponderance of black and white. In old times everyone had a wholesome horror of black and consequently we never find it employed except as the national colour of the Danes in religious habits and in heraldry. It was not till the reign of Edward III that black was used even for mourning, and then only as a cloak with a hood over the ordinary coloured garments. But now, as far as gentlemen are concerned, the evening dress at least of one half the world is black and a man who would dare to sit down to dinner in any other colour would be deemed guilty of a breech of etiquette, or, at the best, be smiled at as the victim of a weak and harmless eccentricity.

There are, however, two little bits of light flickering amidst this almost universal gloom. One of those is the coloured scarf now so frequently worn by gentlemen, and the other the scarlet tunic, to use a mediaeval name, worn by ladies, which is always visible when worn with the walking dress or short super-tunic and is occasionally revealed with admirable effect when worn under the long or trailing robe.

Shape and cut

The general shape of modern dress happily presents us with more hopeful signs than it did a few years back. Crinoline has vanished from the drawing room, and is gradually disappearing from the streets. Costume, more especially that adopted in country houses, is decidedly looking up. For instance, ladies' walking dress just now, consisting of tunic, super tunic with high neck, tight-fitting fur jacket and velvet hat with brilliant feather would be perfectly pleasing and picturesque if it were not for the short proportions obtained by the use of coarse trimming, extravagantly high boots and cut edges.

'The Crinoletta Disfigurans', Punch *6 Dec. 1881.*

A few years ago the male costume was equally hopeful; coloured stockings and knickerbockers with the short coat or Norfolk shirt and felt hat or cap were felt to be appropriate and artistic. What has become of this most artistic costume? A costume which only wanted a slight alteration in the sleeve to make it worthy to rank with the 14th and 15th century dresses. For the cut of the sleeve is the only point of difference between the cut of a modern Norfolk shirt and the very picturesque jacket or doublet introduced early in the reign of Edward IV.

It is some satisfaction to know that tight-fitting sleeves with loose or hanging sleeves over them are at last adopted by ladies. Will gentlemen see the advantage and follow suit?

Trimmings

But good form in shape or cut is of little avail unless we can get rid of the present system of trimming with all its higgledy-piggledy of furious exaggeration of band and button and bow. [...] One of the best modern braid borders I have seen was spoilt by an excessive use of little bits of jet. [...] If, however, we could get rid of braid altogether and adopt a closely-made silk or gold cord there would be much more chance for good plain designs. Indeed, very many of the best borders of the middle ages may be easily reproduced by sewing down cord in the manner shewn in the specimen of appliqué work before you, whilst the difficulty of treating braid in other than straight and continuous lines is manifested whenever anything else is attempted.

Nor is there any difficulty in securing artistic trimmings if ladies are so minded. I have seen some most exquisite little borders at Hellbronner's in Regent street. But the most glorious border the world ever saw would have no chance so long as there exists that passionate longing for mere novelty which is one of the great curses of modern society in each and all its phases.

Trimmings. Punch *13 May 1876.*

Evening dress

As regards our evening dress perhaps the least said the better. It is true the revival of the turn-down collar, by shewing the neck, was one step towards that right development of the human form which is characteristic of all good costume. The Prince of Wales, too, may be thanked for the revival of white waistcoats, for any relief to the dreary conventionalism of black cloth may be fairly regarded as a blessing; these are unfortunately the only exceptions to the corrupt taste which prescribes the usual evening dress of a gentleman of the present period.

Of a lady's dress I will not trust myself to speak, its indecency of cut being, as a rule, unequalled even by its ugliness of trimming. Time will not permit me to enter upon the subject of our official costume which, from the royal crown to the policeman's helmet, is utterly debased; nor can I now trespass any further on your patience to set forth the present promising aspect of children's dress or the uncompromising aspect of church vestments.

Modern dress as art

But before I conclude I feel tempted to express a hope that it is from lack of positive art instruction rather than from wilfulness of choice in this question of dress as in many other branches of art we moderns possess so little discrimination. If this be so, and if we in our better moments, deeming all things visible to have their varying degrees of power for good and evil, elect to labour for the good through the action of the Beautiful, our likenesses in the habit as we live may yet be handled by poet and painter, sculptor and architect, without fear of their being ridiculous. [...]

Artistic and 'Greek' dress, Magazine of Art *1882, p. 336.*

In spite of the many gross absurdities which mark the conventionalities of our present costume, in spite of the swallow-tails and chimney pots, of bastard embroidery and big buttons, I am satisfied we possess sufficient elements of beauty and appropriateness from which a costume might be developed equal to any of past times; and were such a development to take place our architects, sculptors, painters and poets would not have to seek, (as they now do), in ages long gone by for subjects fit for the artist, but would be content to be the chroniclers of their own age.

Of this much I am satisfied, that no art is possible to us unless we take a broad comprehensive view of the power and purpose of art. If you really desire noble buildings, strange as it may sound you must have an eye to your boots. It is idle to talk of art at the rate we do now-a-days unless we can feel it to be a reality to ourselves. We must be drenched through and through with it, not merely put it on now and then. We must have it in its proper degree in our servants' hall and our scullery maids' dormitory as in our drawing-rooms and best bedrooms; we must see it in the back offices as well as in the front elevation; in the table as well as in the front-door jamb, in the table cloth as in the table. And finally we must have it in lay vestments as well as in clerical vestments if we desire to have art present with us a growing, developing, living, joyous reality.

CRINKUM-CRANKUM FOOLERIES (1872)

While noting some improvements in artistic dress, Godwin returns to his rant against the dominance of trimmings in fashion.

Appropriating historical styles

Source:
'Dress', *Globe and Traveller*, 1 June 1872, pp.1-2

Biographical notes:
Leslie
Poynter
Viollet-le-Duc

* A coquettish character wearing 1780s fashions in Dickens's *Barnaby Rudge* (1841).

The only thing that is at all satisfactory about modern dress is that we are not so very bad in our present costume. We have learnt to appropriate and copy. The periods celebrated by two such beauties as Cleopatra and Dolly Varden* have been placed under contribution, so there is just hope that we may get our dress designers, whoever those mystic beings may be, to take a middle course. The 13th and 14th centuries have ceased to influence our architecture — we may possibly begin to feel their effect on our dress. But it matters little what past artistic influence is in season, whether Mr. G. Leslie's charming pictures of the love-sick damsels of our great grandmothers' time are operating on our fashions, or whether Mr. Poynter's Egyptian fancies take the lead; the great curse of modern dress is always dominant — the trimmings overpower everything by excess in quantity and vulgarity in design.

Modern trimmings

It is not that cords, cuffs, collars, buttons, borders, braids, loops, laces, fringes, or frills are in themselves offensive, we find them more or less in the sculptured capitals of the Doge's Palace, in the paintings of Fra Angelico and Giotto, and in the exquisitely artistic illustrations of the Arundel Psalter, and of that other known as Queen Mary's. But in all these there is delicacy of treatment and refinement of detail completely wanting in modern costume. [...] The exquisite cord or twine-patterns on the robes of Richard I. are impossible to us, because instead of cord we use rope. The enamel and other precious buttons used to fasten the front of the dress or tight fitting sleeves when lacing was discarded are magnified by us to such saucer-like proportions that we are forced to fashion them of common materials. Braiding is no longer fashioned in narrow widths laid lovingly round neck, and wrist, and skirt, but sprawls in riotous confusion here, there, and everywhere; and the gold and silver laces [...] have grown to the proportion of ship's tackle. As a matter of course, all natural form and fold are lost under such treatment. Dress is no longer decorated by a trimming, but is itself a bundle of trimmings.

Ancient Egyptian head gear drawn by J. Moyr Smith, BN 5 March 1875.

The frill is not limited to the edges — the emphasis is not on one or two words — but the whole dress is frill, and the whole speech emphasis. Your modern style then, my lady, can best be described by one syllable — you are loud. Moreover, your exaggerations have wrapped you in a tissue of falsities. Your buttons are not fastenings, your laces do not lace, your bows are a sham, your sashes are delusions, and your whole costume is a snare.

Ornamental dress, Punch *16 Oct. 1875.*

Artistic dress

Here and there we meet with most refreshing exceptions to the general condition of things. There are some ladies who exercise as much control over their milliners as they do over their gardeners; who can cut out the pattern, or direct the shaping and trimming of a dress, as artistically as they can plot a garden or arrange a bouquet; but happily for themselves, and unfortunately for the world, these costumes are generally for evening wear, and limited to the area bounded by the park palings. [...] The men who can and do wear velvet jackets are not altogether lost, and on these and the ladies who have united for the furtherance of simple attire — by which we suppose they mean natural folds and delicacy of trimming — our main expectancy for the future rests. In the more general use of real hoods we feel a slight elation [...] For the proper shape of this article, and for many other changing patterns, we have to thank M. Viollet-le-Duc, who has devoted a beautifully illustrated volume ("Dictionnaire Mobilier Francais") to the costumes of his country from the Carolingian epoch to the period of the Renaissance.

'Dorsal' from Viollet -le-Duc's Dictionnaire, *Vol. 1, p.95.*

The moral question

There remains what may be called the moral question. This is twofold. It affects the provider and the consumer in different ways. We are so gushing in our sympathies for the poor seamstresses that we have no time to look at the nature of their work. If we are in earnest — if we really desire to ameliorate their condition — we should give them work to do which may be to them a joy and a pride. Let a few plain lines replace the crinkum-crankum fooleries of our fashion books. Let us have leaves and flowers instead of a thousand loops; and more care in the division of nerve labour by taking from the fingers and giving to the brain — in other words more art and less mechanism. Then we shall be able to meet the other question. Our wives and daughters will not be mistaken by short-sighted persons. Modesty of attire will create a useful barrier in society, or what is as good, will discountenance the obtrusive altogether. The subject is not beneath the attention of the cultured.

THE COST OF FASHION (1872)

Here Godwin attacks the growing consumerism and social aspiration focussed on the fashion industry, making explicit the real costs involved.

This day week we discussed the question of dress from an aesthetic, to-day we look at it for a moment from the economic stand-point. No one will deny that

Source:
'Ladies' dress', *The Globe and Traveller*, 8 June 1872, pp.1-2

Biographical notes:
Worth

extravagance in dress is yearly increasing. Were it confined to the fashionable world comparatively little harm would be done. But unfortunately the infection descends through every class, down even to the maid-of-all-work. The whole population is influenced by the costly follies of the leaders of fashion and the great offenders are indirectly responsible for the errors of their imitators. The middle classes especially find it daily more and more difficult to dress "fit to be seen" on the sum legitimately available for that purpose, and which a few years ago would have been deemed ample. Passing to the class a step higher in the social scale, we find people ostensibly possessing a very fair income practically undergoing all the problems of poverty. [...] Some London ladies will never wear anything that is not made by the celebrated Worth, of Paris. This mighty potentate charges £79 for a court dress, without lace, and £20 for the commonest morning dress sent out from his establishment. A few ladies go so far as to obtain even their dressing-gowns from him, and however inexpensive the material, pay £15 for the sentiment. Again a garden party or Ascot costume which costs £35 is not deemed unusually costly. If on a visit to a country house, a fresh dress must be put on every morning and evening for at least a week, at the expiration of which time a little repetition is allowable. Now, as on a fair average each dress, with accessories, costs £20, the visit entails an expenditure in dress alone of £280. A velvet dress is a very common article of attire, and costs about 40 guineas. A lady, well known in London society, possesses a velvet dress of every conceivable shade. Half a dozen such dresses would soon make a hole in the handsomest allowance. A ball dress for a young lady would not be deemed extravagant if it cost twenty guineas. Fancy the unfortunate father of four grown up daughters, who during the season go out by alternate pairs every night except Sunday? It will surprise no one to learn that £150 is a moderate allowance for a young lady going out at all in London society. Those who have no talent for economy and set no bounds on their dissipation require a much larger sum. £1,000 a year is not an uncommon allowance of pin-money to the wives of noble personages.

To the uninitiated it might seem a difficult task to get rid of this sum without actual waste. A little consideration will show that this is not the case. A few years ago single-button gloves were the fashion. Now nobody wears them, but instead four-button gloves, costing 6s 9d a pair, or even eight-button gloves, of which the price is 10s 6d a pair. Bonnets cost from two to five guineas, and a lady, however economical, if she goes into society, cannot much do with less than eight a year. Then there is the fashion of having everything to match, which adds largely to expense. Formerly a bonnet or parasol was purchased which "would do" with dresses of several colours. Now, every appurtenance must belong to a set. Even in the matter of evening costumes, everything must match the dress. [... T]hough English ladies are not quite so extravagant as Parisian, they follow them on the path to ruinous extravagance at a distance which can by no means be termed humble. The excesses of fashion in Paris indeed almost surpass belief, considering that large fortunes are much more rare in France than in England, and that all classes suffered largely in pocket during the war. [...]

Engraving of a Worth dress, c.1880.

L. Sambourne, 'Mistress of Creation', Punch 18 Dec. 1873.

It is full time to awaken British husbands and wives to a sense of the folly and wickedness of emulating such profuse expenditure. Folly and wickedness it is indeed, for though a few millionaires can stand the outlay without running into debt, or having recourse to an unjustifiable pinching in other quarters, the large majority of their imitators cannot.

DRESSING-GOWNED MINSTRELS AND DOUBTFUL DAIRY-MAIDS (1875)

One of many articles in which Godwin draws attention to the 'grosser errors' of artists who have 'travestied and vulgarised' the representation of dress.

Whatever may be the value of the progress of the Art of Painting during the last quarter of a century, there can be no question that the painter's knowledge has increased, and that he has made some progress in that branch of science which we call Archaeology [...] we find a number of paintings exhibiting costumes mainly of two periods — the one founded on the Greek dress of three or four centuries before Christ, the other taken from the English of the last century [...]

There is something very suggestive in this, and taken in conjunction with the latest phase of architectural revival, and the extraordinary mania for delft and china of really worthless colour and design, it exhibits a condition of artistic feeling as narrow as anything yet manifested in the Gothic revival, and reveals a state of things which is as sad to contemplate, and as sure to be disastrous, as the Gothic chamfer mania of some years ago. [...] But let it not be supposed from what I have just said that the mediaeval costume — *of our painters* — would have been more welcome than Mr. G. D. LESLIE'S young ladies of A.D. 200 and 1780. Our great grandmothers' wardrobes we know, for the veritable robes may still be seen intact; and as to the others, they lived so very long ago that no great blame can be attached to Mr. LESLIE if his model's tunic is not exactly like an old one. Again, the later dress is so like many modern toilettes, and the earlier costume is so free and easy, and so little removed from an ordinary night-dress, that it is hardly possible for an artist's model to be other than thoroughly at home in them. On the other hand, the actual costume of the Middle Ages has only been seen at rare intervals, when the well-preserved long-buried body of some king has been exhumed, but —

> Which at a touch of light, an air of heaven,
> Slipt into ashes and was found no more.

So, we have to make anew the mediaeval dress according to the evidence supplied by picture and by description. These are so plentiful and so detailed that in the right hands and under certain conditions no insurmountable difficulties should ever be experienced. But somehow the tunic of the thirteenth century or the jupon of the fourteenth century never are made under the hands or conditions which would ensure success; for whether the subject of

Source:
'Notes on the costumes in the pictures at the Royal Academy', *Architect*, 29 May 1875, pp. 314-15

Biographical notes:
British Museum
Dicksee
Leslie
Long
Maclise
Moore
Royal Academy
Tadema

315

the painting be an afternoon's amusement in the reign of EDWARD III., or an episode in the life of his grandson, the costume is sure to be unnatural and stagey. Stagey altogether, not only in the Bow-street cut of it, but in the manner of wearing of it. Indeed, whether on the stage, at bal-masques, or in modern pictures, the human form seems to lose all life and sink into little more than a lay figure the moment it assumes a garb that at all approximates to those in vogue during the period of the Middle Ages. For quite apart from the defects in the pattern or shape or detail of the dress, neither actor nor masquer nor model can properly dress themselves; nor can they look wholly unconscious of what, owing to their ignorance, is to them a strange, not to say mysterious, novelty; nor can they cover up this sense of novelty, but, on the contrary, every motion and expression is a reflection of awkwardness and discomfort. If some reasonable amount of care were bestowed on the costume of the thirteenth century, and the people who have to assume the character of that time, or those who teach them, would only take a little trouble to familiarise themselves with its habits and with the general tone of its life, there would be opened to art a continent of beauty hitherto untouched. But let no one fancy that this sort of thing is to be done in a few weeks or even a few months. Gothic art, whether in architecture or dress, has been travestied and vulgarised until we sicken at the very name and turn for comfort to our great grandams. Nevertheless, the art remains, nor will all the scorn of a glorious art-period like ours, with all the brilliant wit, and all the sober wisdom, and the profound knowledge, and the acute sensibility that are so very manifest in the works and the conversation of modern artists be found sufficient to outweigh it; and so, in spite of that mighty advance we have made through which we may yet hope to see in London a collection of farm-houses and a population to harmonise with them, I would venture to suggest to our younger artists that in the works of the thirteenth century they may meet with the beauty of costume akin to that of the Greek, a naturalness not less than that of our great-grandmothers, a purity and freshness of colour which have never been surpassed, and accessories of architecture, furniture, &c., which have never been equalled in design either of mass or detail.[...]

Godwin (with exception of 'D' and 'G'), figures for dining-room murals in Dromore Castle, Arch. *8 June 1872.*

But perhaps the extremest height reached this season in the matter of costume, poetical or historical, is to be seen in [...] Mr. T. F. DICKSEE'S remarkable illustration of the second Scene in the fifth Act of "Othello". The stage costumes are bad enough. DESDEMONA'S ever recurring modern white satin dress and OTHELLO'S higgledy-piggledy of apostolic robes and guerilla jackets are ludicrous in themselves, and worse than ludicrous when they give occasion, as they not unfrequently do, to the exhibition of low-bred manners and unartistic action. Happily, however, the pictures of the modern stage are ephemeral, and therefore any violence or wrong done to Art in their production is not to be compared with the long-lived follies perpetrated on canvas. Mr. DICKSEE with his Georgian bedstead, his modern English little NELL which he calls DESDEMONA, his dressing-gowned minstrel that stands for OTHELLO, has outstaged the stage, and has produced a work of which the kindest thing I can say is that it is a feeble caricature. [...]

And now what is to be said of Mr. G. D. LESLIE and his host of followers? Have we had enough of the costume they affect, or do we want more of it? Are tippets, mob caps, and broad brimmed hats necessary accompaniments of the china mania and farm-house fancies? Or is there not something about this sort of thing that savours a little too much of the affectation of innocence and simplicity? Doubtful dairymaids and short-skirted sheperdesses may be all very well in Watteau-like ballet on the stage of the Alhambra or in Chelsea china, but modern life is artificial enough already without the addition of that worst of artificialities — the assumption of a rural simplicity and a sweet Arcadian *naïveté*, which are as foreign to the heart of modern society as are Greek refinement and Gothic strength. If Mr. LESLIE were the only artist who contributed illustrations of the costume of a hundred years ago, no complaint could justly arise, for there is no reason why our great-grandmamas should not have their representative, and certainly no one is better qualified to fill this post than Mr. LESLIE; but now when ten or a dozen artists follow in his wake it will require more power than we have yet seen in him to maintain his star in the ascendant. [...]

Leslie, Hens and Chickens, Magazine of Art *1881, p. 309.*

The Classic school in the Academy may be divided into the Dreamy and the Archaeological. Mr. ALBERT MOORE is pre-eminently the leader of the first as Mr. ALMA TADEMA is of the second. Mr. MOORE'S followers are few and far between [...] but no one will deny to the semi-Greek drapery this artist delights in a high degree of beauty — sensuous it may be — but still beauty, and that, too, far more refined, subtle, delicate, in a word far more Greek than any of the Classic costumes at the Burlington. On the other hand we have in Mr. ALMA TADEMA'S works the evidence of considerable archaeological research, evidence which is perhaps too prominently put before us by the exhibition of absolutely hideous but forgotten fashions. His women, too, are lazy, and massive like their costume; Mr. MOORE'S are also lazy, but the laziness of the first is as of the stagnant pool, that of the last as of the summer sea. Mr. ALMA TADEMA is one of the most correct painters of costume we have, but he is at times almost as oppressive with weight of facts as Mr. MACLISE used to be; Mr. MOORE gives us scarcely a single fact. We never see buttons or loops, girdles or sandals, or diplois, but yet in spite of all these omissions he recalls more than anyone else the essential qualities of Greek costume, and then he is happy in having models who can wear their thin many-folded chitons as if they had worn them all their lives. [...]

Moore, classical figures for title page of Nesfield, Specimens of Gothic Architecture, *1862.*

I have reserved for my last words Mr. E. LONG'S very admirable painting, *The Babylonian Marriage Market*. [...] Architecture, decoration, furniture, costume and personal ornament are here so carefully worked out that Mr. LONG may be said to challenge criticism in a measure which no one else has attempted. [...] There can be very little doubt that Mr. LONG has searched the Assyrian slabs in Great Russell Street, or illustrations of them, for most of his authorities. The bracelets, armlets, necklaces, mode of dressing the hair, girdles, &c., which are found in the picture, are also to be seen on the sculptures

Engraving after Long, The Babylonian Marriage Market, *1875 (Collection Royal Holloway College, University of London).*

of the north-west palace of Nimroud. Indeed, to such an extent has the Assyrian sculptor influenced the English painter, that the blocked-out, square-cut, conventional stone beard of the chisel has been painted, and not the hair beard of nature [...] but we may not unreasonably ask whether a Greek or any other warrior would walk about Babylon and attend sale-rooms in hot brass helmets and in full panoply of war? Again, the vest and chemise worn by the slave girls is made high in the neck and with a broad hem or band, for both of which I can find no sufficient warrant. The girl who is being sold has on a long thin semi-transparent fine linen skirt, held up by a deep embroidered waist-girdle, and a thin vest or veil is just being taken from her. This costume, both in form and material, strikes me as artistically and archaeologically wrong, and but for the girdle, would have an extremely modern look. [...] To take exception to details and to be critical about minutiae in this way only show what a strong hold the painting has on one. It is unquestionably the work of an artist who has manfully striven to be right, not to outrage a single point of history, and yet to keep his facts in due subordination to the human nature and human interest of his subject [...] Accessories of costume, &c., in pictures, whether on canvas or on the stage, should be either altogether wrong or wholly right, that is, if we wish to keep the humanity, as it ought to be, paramount. But when the worry of research, and the evidence of unfamiliar labour is proclaimed by the presence of little oversights and errors, the unquestioning satisfaction we might have enjoyed is no longer possible, and the pleasure gives way to criticism.

CONTEMPORARY DRESS IN ART (1876)

It is not the way to make our age artistic to be forever harking back to Greek chitons, Roman togas, mediaeval jupons, or even mob caps. WHISTLER has shown us that a dress suit can be translated into art; MASON has told us of the loveliness of cotton prints such as our country children wear, and here in Bond Street are grouped together 160 drawings from WALKER'S hand, telling us over and over again of the manifold beauties, in form and colour, which beset our everyday life if we have eyes to see and sensitiveness to perceive.

Source:
'A painter and a sculptor',
Architect, 15 January 1876,
p.30

Biographical notes:
Mason
Walker
Whistler

MODERN DRESS (1876)

Godwin praises the Bedford Park residents for having the courage to express their artistic convictions by dressing to match their 'Queen Anne' surroundings, but goes on to dissect the failings of modern dress.

There is in one of the suburbs of London a small settlement of "artistic" folk, including a few painters, some wood draughtsmen, one or two architects who, being more or less "artistic," have established a little world of fashion among themselves. Ladies and gentlemen, with a courage and a logic equally to be admired, have subscribed not merely to the architecture but to the costume of the eighteenth century. In the summer evenings the loafer about the quiet roads and lanes of this enchanting suburb may get an occasional glimpse of some strangely muffled figure, from beneath whose long cloak the glitter of silk stockings and buckle shoes reveals the harmlessness of the furtive look and hurried walk. That the Queen Anne fashion in building should have so strong an influence on any of its followers as to lead to the systematic use of knee breeches, silk coats and hair powder, for ordinary evening dress, no matter how limited the area of this circle of fashion may be, is remarkable. It is remarkable for standing alone in this respect among all architectural revivals, Classic or Gothic. It is not the less remarkable for exhibiting the length to which earnest thorough-paced disciples of a revival will go, and the dissatisfaction felt by some of the more zealous artists among us with the current *mode.*

Source:
'Modern dress', *Architect,* 10 June 1876, p.368

Biographical notes:
Keene
Tennyson

Fancy dress at Bedford Park fête, Lady's Pictorial *24 June 1882.*

Frock coats and baggy trousers

The sculptor, too, whether within or without the Queen Anne pale will not infrequently enlarge on this dissatisfaction. A statue of any modern worthy is always a trouble to him. Frock-coats and trousers are abominations over which he cannot even attempt to rise superior. There are accessories, it is true; there is the cloak hanging from the shoulders, the overcoat across the arm, the pedestal, and other architectural and furniture supports; but in spite of cloak and paletôt and furniture, the frock-coat, whether tightly buttoned and treated as a tunic, or loosely open and treated as drapery, is somehow as invariably a failure as the chiton of the Greek, and the tunic and jupon of the Middle Ages were as invariably successes. If the frock-coat is so much opposed to all that

Gorgeous Young Swells, Punch *21 Sept. 1878.*

constitutes the fine art of dress, if this highly respectable, dull and prosy-looking garment is in artistic eyes an abomination, what shall be said of the trousers? These, whether old, creasy, and baggy, such as CHARLES KEENE delights to caricature, or new and block shaped, as may be seen any fine afternoon in Piccadilly, or the Row, are equally offensive. In whatever aspect they are looked at, in front, at the side, behind, standing or sitting, they offend every nerve in the head that has ever pulsated to a form of beauty. In the general condemnation hurled at our modern statues we are too apt to forget that it is the tailor or rather the fashion of the day, and not the sculptor who is chiefly to blame. Not but that the sculptor is to be blamed, and that, too, in no small measure, for accepting commissions to execute that which he feels and knows must ever be opposed to the art convictions not merely of himself but of the whole world. How much longer the chimney-pot hat, the respectable frock coat, and the baggy trousers are to enslave one-half of the civilised world is a question not by any means without interest to art. They cannot go on like Mr. TENNYSON'S "Brook" for ever. A time must come when even the wearing of such long-lived ugliness will be quite as much of the nature of dissembling as the present adoption by a suburban coterie of the dress of our great-great-grandfathers. Now, as the best way of hastening that time is to hold the present fashion up to ridicule, we cannot do better than encourage the manufacture of statues to the utmost as so many pegs on which may be exhibited the ludicrousness of our attire.

Fringes, frills, bows and buttons

Yet while there is nothing artistic in the gentleman's morning dress, and very little in any of this other dresses, save in the free and easy knickerbocker suit which may yet be occasionally seen during the autumn or winter at remote country places, there is, however, much everyway admirable in the ladies' toilette of to-day. The revival of a certain form well known to the student of Assyrian art, together with its elaborate fringe, has been a markedly successful feature in indoor and outdoor dresses, and appears likely to continue the fashion for some time, although, of course, under certain new combinations and modifications. This is the basis, the ground-work, so to speak, of the dress of to-day. Love of variety, the desire to have a costume or toilet made expressly for herself, has led, and is leading, the lady of fashion into all sorts of inartistic devices, all kinds of violent and inharmonious combinations. The errors in modern dress are not so much in general form as in the exaggeration of this form (exaggeration peculiar to the English) and what I will venture broadly to call the trimmings. One very favourite trimming is the plaited flounce. As a rule, all plaited flounces, especially those that are bordered by frills, are destructive to the beauty of drapery. The long skirt of a lady's dress is full of the most lovely possibilities, but not if stiffened at the end and treated in imitation of an irate fish tail. The large *hanging* bow is another inartistic trimming to be seen everywhere; under no circumstance can such a bow look other than sloppy, washed out, distressed, and all the more so when placed, as is so often the case, in direct contrast with tench-fin plaitings. Although not strictly, per-

Women of Fashion, Punch 9
April 1881.

haps, a trimming, there is a useless but supposed ornamental addition, called a *pélerine* "Agnès", a sort of cape, which, leaving the arms free, is rounded on the back, and takes the form of a triangle in the front — a contrivance of which I find it impossible to say that one view of it is more inelegant than the other. Buttons are now almost as fashionable as they were in the days of the BLACK PRINCE or those of PIERS GAVESTON. With artistic regard to size, colour, material and position, buttons, besides being eminently useful, may become valuable as points of light or otherwise, but they can only become ludicrous when their office is forgotten, whether it be by edging them with lace or by allowing them to assume the proportions of rosettes. The latest fashion of placing half-a-dozen rows of extremely small buttons down the front is an extravagant fancy, with the one usual recommendation of novelty, and nothing more.

Tunics or jackets, cut with broad lapels or turn-down collars, are always an offence, they have a coarse, or at least a masculine, look, and the lines are altogether out of harmony with the rest of the dress. But the great danger attending modern dress is not so much error of detail, as detail, the overcrowding of one thing on top of another until every comely line of human form and every pleasing natural fold of drapery are dissipated. A well dressed lady is one thing, an animated heap of clothes is quite another, and the mistakes made in the application of lace and braid are often very prominent in these animated heaps. Among trimmings which are generally safe to be artistic are fringes, and these may extend to as great a depth as half a yard (see the Assyrian sculptures in the British Museum). Besides fringe, bands or borders may be noted as among the accepted decorations of the hour, and herein the Greek and the Mediaeval artist could teach the fashionable *modiste* many things she would be the better for knowing. One feature very observable in some of the dresses at the late drawing-room were certain flower trimmings used as waist garlands with trailing ends. And this we are assured was "a novelty which excited much admiration". A tablière, composed of one gigantic leaf, say a vine or fig, would be equally novel, and I venture to add, worthy of equal admiration. We can understand that simple toilet of old time when DAPHNE roaming through a thorny wood got her legs scratched by envious roses, we can picture the nymphs of Attic poetry all entwined with wild garlands and meandering branches, and we can recognise the appropriateness of the surroundings. But trailing garlands over silks and satins have too much the flavour of the stage sheperdess to commend themselves to the approval of the artist, and the only costume for which we have any art warranty to associate with trailing wreaths of flowers, is that very scanty allowance made familiar to us by Greek vase, Pompeian painting and their later imitators.

Colour

In colour we see here and there very considerable advance, and to the Japanese much of the advance is owing. A large check pattern lately to be seen in Paris was a direct copy in its form and in its colours — blue, grey, and black —

to one on a well-known Japanese fan. There is comfort, too, in the fact that ladies are becoming alive to the advantages of dressing in one *colour*, however much different parts of the dress are varied in *tone*. And it is pleasant to know that even for full evening when black is worn "long black gloves have made their appearance". One thing much affected by the PRINCESS OF WALES, and therefore worn by a great number of people to whom it is woefully unbecoming, is the velvet collarette. When its colour is pale it is eminently suggestive of a strip of flannel and sore throat, when dark it effectually separates the head from the trunk, and is destructive of one of the finest lines in the human frame.

SOIRÉE DRESSES (1878)

Henry Holiday painted a picture of an Academy soirée in 1881 featuring celebrities of all kinds (including Terry, Wilde, Trollope, Gladstone, Langtry and Huxley), and described how at this time 'certain ladies delighted to display themselves at public gatherings in what are called aesthetic dresses; in some cases the costumes were pretty enough, in others they seemed to rival each other in ugliness of form and oddity of colour.'*

* *My Autobiography and Reminiscences*. London, 1887, pp.256-7.

Source:
'Notes on current events', *The British Architect*, 5 July 1878, p.2

Biographical notes:
Royal Academy

There were three, even four, *really* artistic dresses at the Academy soirée. Many ladies, especially among the short statures of the throng, made evidently many struggles in their art-at-home efforts for effect, but with results that could by no stretch of gallantry be appropriated even to the outskirts of the domain of beauty. Apart from the truly artistic and the would be artistic there was one other remarkable dress that appeared at a little distance to consist of one shoulder-strap arranged diagonally.

DRAWING COSTUMES (1882)

Godwin was a founding member and Hon. Secretary of the Costume Society established in 1882. One of the main aims was to publish accurate illustrations annotated and 'approved' by authorities such as Godwin himself. As for architecture he advocated a drawing style of 'scientific clarity', and working from 'original sources' only. Godwin got estimates for printing 2,000 copies. In the end only one set of plates was issued.

Source:
Copy of letter dated 2 October 1882, to Louis Fagan

Godwin, drawing of costumes from the Column of Theodosius.

Concerning the drawings which may be made for the Costume Society I think we should be very careful to avoid the pretty picture style. Etched up effects are all very well for an illustrated magazine but our chief aim should be an accuracy that conveys itself and etching in shadows and tones often conceals the facts of the make. To enlarge the finely and minutely executed miniatures of the past so as to show clearly all the detail and to do this in as simple a way as possible seems to me more desirable than to elaborate the mere drawing.

Another thing — we have promised in our first circular to give drawings from original sources only. A picture of A.D. 1500 of a gentleman in the dress of 1500 is an original source but an engraving of 1700 or 1800 of that picture is no authority in our sense, at least not until some of us have compared the engraving with the picture & are prepared to certify its accuracy.

GAUCHE ARTISTIC DRESS (1881)

Appropriating dress styles regardless of the proper material and relationship to the living human form are doomed to failure.

Costume of any past time, or any really artistic modern dress, demands something more than figure; it demands knowledge and sympathy. An actor may put on the chain mail of King John's time, but it is one thing to put it on and quite another thing to wear it. Most actors and some actresses only put on their clothes. Any would-be-artistic people, your sham aesthetes, can go no further,— they in short are ignorant of the manners that accompanied a particular style of dress,— and become ridiculous by assuming a dress every line in which is a rebuke to "gaucherie" and every pleat a condemnation of "floppery." Material is an important factor, too. A quatro-cento or cinque-cento design with puffed sleeves, shaped neck and waist, cannot possibly look well cut out of the flimsy "eastern" silks, &c., so largely advertised. If architecture follows the suggestions of the materials of the country, it generally comes out right. For if an art founded on marble and monolith be applied to brick, the result is absurd; and if a form of attire that is the outcome of thin soft eastern stuffs be made in brocade or thickly embroidered velvet, it is just as absurd. The converse is equally true; and doubtless one of the most ignorant applications of art to be seen at the present day is the aesthetic lady's dress cut in a style adapted from the rich brocaded fashions of the fourteenth or fifteenth centuries, but made up of flimsy material that compels every energetic puff in the design to droop and hang in dull formless heaps.

Source:
'Notes on current events', *The British Architect*, 5 August 1881, p.390

DRESS, ARCHITECTURE AND HEALTH (1884)

At the 1884 International Health Exhibition, the chronological display of the History of Dress section gave 'an opportunity for the comparative study of civilian dress in its bearings on hygiene at different periods in the nation's growth'.* The exhibits were arranged in the Albert Hall on life-size wax models designed by Madame Tussaud. Godwin gave the main public lecture relating to this part of the exhibition which was published as one of the exhibition handbooks. In this ambitious survey he ranged from Samoan grass skirts to 19th-century crinolines, but it reads like a rushed job. This was not the definitive history of costume he had been asking for, but it does demonstrate his belief in the importance of dress and its inextricable relationship to architecture.

Source:
Dress and its Relation to Health and Climate, London, 1884

* *The Times*, 9 May 1884.

As Architecture is the art and science of building, so Dress is the art and science of clothing. [...]

*Du Maurier, 'Hygienic excess',
Punch 18 Oct 1879.*

*Artistic dress, illustrated in
Godwin's Dress and its Relation
to Health and Climate, 1884
(derived from a Du Maurier
cartoon).*

The scientifically-minded is too apt to look on art with a sort of pitying smile, as if it were something to play with; while the artistically-minded, though perhaps more sensitive and sympathetic, is still too often disposed to view *his* ideal as *the* ideal, and refuse to profit by the offices science might and, I venture to say, would gladly render him. Science and art must walk hand in hand if life is to be worth living. Beauty without health is incomplete. Health can never be perfect for you so long as your eye is troubled with ugliness. Of a surety there comes a time when custom breeds a habit; your eye ceases to be troubled with ugliness; you walk down Baker Street or Gower Street as happily as you would down the High Street at Oxford. [...]

The history of dress is curiously parallel with that of architecture; indeed we might almost say that to dress rightly, and build rightly, and speak rightly, are the three great primary arts. As speaking involves poetry and music, as architecture involves painting and sculpture, so dressing involves in principle all these. To dress well you must possess the gift of colour, and be a master of form. But this is not enough; with these accomplishments you might clothe a dummy or a corpse satisfactorily, but not a living human being; for there comes into the problem with this word *living* the element of motion. I do not mean the mere action of moving the limbs; but the action of breathing, of growth and of decay. And it is here that the laws of hygiene must be faced. [...]

To build architecturally we must have not merely proper materials, and sound construction, and pleasant handling of light and shade; but the ornament should be good in itself and well-adjusted, while the heating and ventilation, among other sanitary items, should be carefully considered. To build a dress or costume demands just the same kind of thought; and where the heating and ventilation are neglected we may be quite sure that we shall suffer. [...] whatever wisdom we may display in our selection of material and colour, healthy or hygienic dress will not be possible until it has at least as much beauty of form and cut to recommend it as that which may be seen on most lawn-tennis grounds. [...]

A well drained house, however awkward and ill-proportioned in appearance, is a distinct gain on the awkward house that is badly drained; and the converse is equally true, for a house of good proportions and interesting cut or shape, with inefficient drainage, is certainly health-giving to the eye, and to be preferred to an ill-conditioned looking shelter, with similarly defective sewers. So also is it with our dress.

XIV Theatre

GODWIN'S interest in the theatre dates to his earliest activities as an architect, but he first began writing about it in Bristol between 1862 and 1864, when he contributed a series of articles to the *Western Daily Press* under the heading 'Theatrical Jottings'. These were in the form of reviews of current productions but it is significant that, even here, he was formulating larger theories of staging, design, acting and direction which would eventually come to dominate his own involvement in the theatre over a decade later. What emerges from reading his early criticism is Godwin's high ideals and ambitions for the theatre as an art form equal, and in many cases superior, to the visual arts of painting, sculpture and architecture. This is surprising given the fact that he was a rising star in the architecture world and his career, if anything, must have seemed set within this profession.

Godwin's approach to theatre design and production has often been described as radical and innovative but he is perhaps better seen as extending an existing movement rather than introducing a new approach. The main tendency in Victorian theatre production was one of increasing realism in sets, costume and acting style, something which helped raise the status of drama and encouraged the middle classes to see play-going as a respectable pursuit. The most famous example of this was the 'Meiningens', a permanent company formed by the Duke of Saxe-Meiningen which visited London in the 1870s, but there was already a native tradition stretching back to Kean and Planché in the 1830s and 40s which sought to make stage performance more naturalistic and the sets and costumes more accurate and believable. By the 1870s the leading exponents of this were the Bancrofts, who in 1875 invited both Godwin and Ellen Terry to work on a production of *The Merchant of Venice* at the Prince of Wales Theatre in London. For Terry this was a simple, practical move: the stage was a more reliable way of life and source of income at a time when her relationship with Godwin was breaking up. From the Bancrofts' point of view it must have been equally obvious that Terry still had a considerable reputation, despite several years away from the London stage,[1] and any production which brought her back would attract popular attention. For Godwin, however, this was a new venture. At the very moment when he was writing his major series of essays, 'The architecture and costume of Shakespere's plays', he was given the opportunity to put his ideas into practice, albeit in a limited fashion. Godwin was engaged as 'historical adviser' but his influence extended only to the design of a few costumes. Even here, however, his work attracted considerable attention, Mrs Comyns Carr recalling that, on Terry's appearance in one costume, 'the whole house burst forth in rapturous applause'.[2] Many years later Beerbohm Tree described it as 'the first production in which the modern spirit of stage-management asserted itself'.[3] Despite the attention it attracted, the production was only a

[1] Terry had performed in a touring production of *Romeo and Juliet* for Charles Calvert in 1874.

[2] E. Adam, ed., *Mrs Comyns Carr's Reminiscences*, London, 1926, p. 31.

[3] H. Beerbohm Tree, *Thoughts and After-thoughts*, London, 1913, p. 44.

[4] *Morning Post* 19 April 1875 (quoted in J. Stokes, p.39).

Godwin, costume design after Amman for The Merchant of Venice, BA *13 Feb. 1880.*

Godwin, costume design for Claudian *from the column of Theodosius, 1883,* BA *21 Dec. 1883.*

limited success and Godwin's contribution, in particular, was singled out for some criticism. One writer commented that 'the play sinks beneath the load of its finery and is killed by the weight of its decorations'.[4] Nevertheless, this production marks the real launch of Godwin's career as a designer for the theatre, an activity that came to assume an increasing role in the final decade of his life.

One year after *The Merchant of Venice* Godwin advised Coleman and Phelps on a controversial although unsuccessful production of *Henry V*, and in 1881 he produced costume designs for Miss Bateman's *Othello*. The latter was notable for the sources which Godwin used, basing all his costumes, as he had already recommended, on those found in paintings by Titian and Veronese or prints by the 16th-century Swiss artist, Joost Amman. These were all somewhat frustrating experiences for Godwin because his designs were altered by the actors or producers and he was unable to carry through his ideas in a comprehensive or consistent manner. His aim thereafter was to achieve greater control, but this eluded him and his contributions to various productions, such as Irving's version of Tennyson's *The Cup* (1881), Wilson Barrett's *Juana* (1881), and the same producer's *Claudian* (1883), passed with only modest and mixed success.

Throughout this, Godwin sought to uphold the highest artistic standards and to emphasise the superior role that drama might play in an aesthetic approach to life. When he writes that the theatre offers a mode of beauty and enlightenment higher even than that of architecture this was not merely straining for effect. If his work in the theatre is anything to judge by, Godwin fully believed this and saw drama as the highest of all the arts, corrupted only by the short-sightedness, meanness and common stupidity that was endemic in the commercial theatre. In his writings he frequently returns to the failures and shortcomings which hold theatre back from achieving its full potential. Whether it was bad acting, poor design, inappropriate costumes, thoughtless stock props or inadequate stage machinery, they all served to diminish something that, in Godwin's eyes, should be perfect if the full artistic import was to be realised. Predictably, perhaps, he often commented on the design of theatre buildings, finding fault with the poor facilities for the audience, but more importantly he directed his fiercest criticism at the environment in which the actors and back-stage staff had to work. This touched many of his ideas on health and good design as a whole, but the main thrust of his attack is that these squalid closets and corridors where actors have to prepare and scene painters and costumiers have to work are detrimental to the art that the drama aims to produce in performance.

The dominant theme which emerges over more than twenty years of critical writings, however, is Godwin's belief in archaeological accuracy as something which will liberate theatre performance and enhance the illusion which is essential for the audience to be convinced of the drama. To some this has seemed an indication of Godwin's pedantry, as if he had merely extended his antiquarian interests to the theatre with no thought for the conflicting elements of drama in performance. Wilde and others found fault in Godwin's approach but it seems likely that they belonged to the 'idealist' camp which found the illusion of historical place and time an irrelevance to the experience of drama. Godwin's writings testify to the fact that his quest for archaeological accuracy was always driven by a belief in the potential for drama that this opened up. This was his ultimate aim in the last few years of his life when he was able to implement his ideas for a total work of art through the formation of a theatre company with Lady Archibald Campbell. For the first time he could control all aspects of the production, no matter what the cost. *As You Like It* (1884) and *The Faithfull Shepherdesse* (1885), performed by the Pastoral Players in the open air at Coombe Wood in Surrey, may have been seen by only a few wealthy socialites and, at £2,675 for only nine performances of the *Shepherdesse* alone, something of an extravagance, but many regarded them as a landmark. It was *Helena in Troas*, however, a production mounted in Hengler's Circus by Godwin himself, which points to a new mode of theatre in which the costumes, setting and acting styles were intended to revive a view of classical drama and the classical world that transcended mere accuracy of details. On this occasion Wilde was in full support, describing it as 'simply the presentation in Greek form of a poem conceived in the Greek spirit; and the secret of its beauty was the perfect correspondence of form and matter, the delicate equilibrium of spirit and sense'.[5]

The decade after Godwin's death was to see a revolution on the English stage, largely due to new influences such as Ibsen and Shaw and their drive to create drama based on the intense psychological interaction of ordinary people in contemporary domestic settings. It is perhaps no accident that Godwin's son and follower, Edward Gordon Craig should see *Helena in Troas* as a touchstone for his anti-realist approach to the theatre. When invited to Stanislavsky's Moscow Art Theatre to produce a *Hamlet* in 1912, he attempted a pared-down elemental setting inspired by the same austerity that Godwin brought to ancient Troy.

As You Like It *at Coombe House*, Illustrated Dramatic and Sporting News *2 Aug. 1884.*

[5] 'Helena in Troas', *Dramatic Review* 22 May 1886, pp.161-2.

Figures from Helena in Troas, The Queen, *5 June 1886.*

Further Reading

F. Baldwin, 'E. W. Godwin and design for the theatre', in Soros 1999, pp.313-52

L. Lambourne. 'Pyrrhic Success: E. W. Godwin and the Theatre', *Country Life* 80: 2 October 1986, pp.1024-5

J. Stokes, 'An Aesthetic theatre: the career of E. W. Godwin', *Resistible Theatres*, London, 1972

S. Bancroft, *The Bancrofts: Recollections of Sixty Years*, London, 1911

M. R. Booth, *Victorian Spectacular Theatre 1850-1910*, London, 1981

D. Howard, *London Theatres and Music Halls*, London, 1970

H. Maguire, 'The Victorian theatre as a home from home', *Journal of Design History* 13:2 2000, pp.107-21

E. Terry, *The Story of My Life*, London, 1908

A. Wade, ed., *Henry James: The Scenic Art*, London, 1949

COMPLETE DRAMA (1880)

Source:
'To correspondents', *The British Architect*, 13 February 1880, p.74

Certainly nothing would tend more to a refined and artistic enjoyment of life than completeness in dramatic representations. It is not enough to have good writing, or one or two first-rate actors, or merely picturesque scenery and dresses. It may be Utopian to expect it, but Art demands on the stage nothing less than an all-round completeness. The language must be good; all the actors, to the remotest "super," must be intelligent; their costume must have in it nothing to dispel illusion even to the most accomplished archaeologist; the scenery must never be less excellent and true than Mr. Bancroft's scenery in his production of "The Merchant of Venice;"* the properties should look genuine to the front row of stalls; and the stage management should always be in the hands of a quick-witted, cultured man.

*1875; Godwin was the historical adviser.

MISREPRESENTING SHAKESPEARE (1864)

Consistency and accuracy of period detail were central to the working practice of the Gothic Revival architect, but for Godwin they were equally important in the theatre – not as a form of antiquarianism but as an essential element of stagecraft if the audience were to accept the illusion of drama.

Source:
'Theatrical jottings', *Western Daily Press*, 11 October 1864, p.2

Godwin, costume designs for As You Like It, BA *26 March 1880.*

When we go to see a play of Shakespere [*sic*] we do not care to be presented with scraps or a piece of patch work, and if there were anything like unity we might excuse a century or so in two styles of costume, but we refuse to allow any commendation to higgledy-piggledy. The whole question lies in a nutshell. Is the drama an art? If it be so the great laws which govern the exercise of all other arts must govern this also. Every misrepresentation of a scene is a falsity, and it is manifest that there would be misrepresentation if either action, posture, costume, or other accessory were incorrect. The falsity arises out of the fact that the original scene is professedly reproduced in the representation. This is obvious, for if reproduction were not the aim why depart from ordinary evening dress — in other words the use of scenery, dress, and other accessories directly implies an intention to reproduce the original scene, and consequently an error in either of these vitiates the whole result, nor will excellence on the part of any actor atone for an inaccuracy of his personal appearance or of the scenery by which he is surrounded. I do not need to deny that a person totally ignorant of the past may feel himself satisfied in spite of the grossest anachronisms, but his satisfaction will be that of a man who is merely anxious to be amused, entirely irrespective of any desire to be instructed, whereas I maintain that we do not go to a theatre simply to hear passionate recitations and funny speeches, but to witness such a performance as will place us as nearly as possible in the position of spectators of the original scene or of the thing represented, and so gain information of man, manners, customs, costumes, and countries — and this result is only attainable where accuracy in every particular is secured.

ACTOR MANAGERS (1864)

The tradition of actor-managers like Garrick and Kean was still remembered fondly in theatrical circles long after they had died. It was a fairly radical statement, therefore, when Godwin chose to attack their legacy of overblown acting styles, not merely for its artificiality but for its failure to reflect the modern age.

There always have been people who, either from love of ease, or from some constitutional weakness, as sluggishness of blood or some natural infirmity, as defective senses, have been quite unable to appreciate the advanced position of the age or time in which they have lived. In these days we have abundant proof that this species of the *genus homo* is not altogether extinct. Now and then it so happens that one of this kind gets into some position of authority. To him *authority* is a synonym for *autocracy*, and so, owing to this confusion of words, the man becomes "possessed" with the dogged belief that he has a right to be absolute, supreme, and despotic. The results of this "possession" are more amusing than dangerous, and are sometimes very funny [...] The theatrical manager of the present day is, however, perhaps the best specimen of this sort of weakness, although it may be questioned whether the weakness is not rather a fault of the class than of the individual. They seem bound by nothing but the manners and customs of the last century. Garrick, Kemble, and Edmund Kean are the great lights [...] The conventional stilted staginess which flourished in the last century — in a word, the unnatural — is still encouraged. Superfine writing and speaking harmonises well with what the Americans would call "tall" acting, and there never was a time when the English language was made the vehicle for such bombast as the time of the dictionary maker Johnson. Of course the influence of the 18th Century is still felt, and there are still people who think much as their grandfathers did, and who still seem to be tied by their grandmothers' apron strings; but, happily, the education of the age, the progress of science, the earnest searching after truth, in fine, the nervousness of the public mind, shuts them out from our view, and their numbers are, consequently, diminishing day by day.

Source:
'Theatrical jottings', *Western Daily Press*, 11 October 1864, p.2

Biographical notes:
Garrick
Kean
Kemble

'Atlas': Kean as Richard III, etching by G. Cruikshank, 1814.

THE MERCHANT OF VENICE (1864)

This early note of praise for Ellen Terry appeared three years before they eloped. In this instance her performance is used to point up the uneven cast in many productions and the general lowering of standards which alienated the middle-class audience. Godwin also criticises the tendency of actors to play to the 'Gods'.

Dining in Bath on Saturday week I was induced by my host to visit the Theatre Royal. That Miss Terry was to appear as *Portia* would have been in itself sufficient inducement for most people, but I must confess to a weakness for Shakespere and all he wrote, and, just as a picture with *one* well-painted figure in a group where all the others are not only badly coloured but ill drawn would be offensive, so I have always fancied must it be with a dramatic repre-

Source:
'Theatre Royal, Bath: *The Merchant of Venice*', *Western Daily Press*, 18 October 1864

Biographical notes:
Ruskin
Terry

PAGANO
after
TITIAN

Godwin costume designs for
The Merchant of Venice, *BA
13 Feb. 1880.*

sentation where one character is, as the spiritualists would say *en rapport* with the author, and all the others — nowhere. [...]

It is no use mincing matters — the educated classes, as a rule, do not go to the theatre, and will not go until the dramatic art becomes an educational power and a living reality. They are not so particular as to require the palaces of Venice painted after Canaletto or Ruskin, but they do object to an English village street, with its wooden gables and low church tower, doing duty as a street-scene for nearly one-half of the play of "The Merchant of Venice." It is hard enough to realise the scene with the best acting of the best of living actors, but they give up the attempt altogether when the greatest of commercial cities is represented as an English village; moreover, an English village with *modern* houses! [...]

Mr. Robertson might have remembered, in putting on the Ducal bonnet, that the horn rises at the back, not the front, and the advantage of being *right* in this instance would not have cost anything but a thought. But it is just this expenditure of *thought* which is at the same time so rare and so requisite. It is not want of money, but sheer thoughtlessness or ignorance, which directs *Claudius*, King of Denmark, to trail royal robes in the dust, and wear a crown *all through* the play of "Hamlet," or which provides but one seat for *Portia*'s house at Belmont. Nor can I see that it would require any outlay of anything but brains, and very little of that, to do away with those wretched turn-about and wheel-about performances between *Launcelot* and his father, which are as unlike Shakespere or the characters as an English village is unlike Venice. But it is not Mr. Fosbrooke's fault — the action, in all its witlessness and unnaturalness, is no doubt traditional. [...] The "Gods" in most houses have it all their own way; the boxes think it infra dig to applaud; and, as actors and actresses can only tell how they are appreciated by the clapping of hands, they necessarily play to the gallery, and this accounts for all that makes modern acting, as a rule, low and despicable. To this we trace the ranting and bellowing of our "tragedians," the gags and indecencies of our "low comedians". The educated public must therefore make itself heard, either in the house or in the press, or give up the theatre altogether.

SPEND A SHILLING ON SHAKESPEARE (1864)

It was customary for actors in the High Victorian period to maintain their own wardrobes which partly explained the use, and re-use, of standard costumes regardless of the part being performed.

Source:
'Theatrical jottings. Romeo and Juliet', *Western Daily Press*, 5 October 1864, p.2

Biographical notes:
Chute

Is it quite hopeless to expect anything in the way of decent scenery and dresses upon the Bristol stage? On *Juliet* and *Romeo* we had sleeves of the period of Edward III., and bodices of a century or two later, with a scalloped hat and feather of no period at all. The nurse was in a costume two centuries later even than the time of Shakespere himself! *Lawrence*, the Franciscan or Grey Friar, in a costume compounded of the Benedictine and the Geneva gown! The soldiers were — Mr. Chute's. The scenery as of old — not the slightest attempt to improve in this any more than in the costume. As to the "proper-ties", the modern candle-sticks, the 19th century toilet table, the bed, the chairs — well, I have seen better in a booth at Henley-upon-Thames. Surely, if *Romeo and Juliet* is worth acting at all, it is worth *some* expenditure on the part of the manager. A sensation piece or a pantomime would soon set painters, costum-iers, and property men to work, and the manager would be active in superin-tendence — but Shakespere! who is he that we should care for him? What has he done for us, the stage or the drama that we should spend a shilling to render his works attractive to, or popular with the common people?

COSTUMES IN *HENRY VIII* (1875)

The series of thirty articles on 'The architecture and costume of Shakespere's plays' allowed Godwin to apply his ideas on historical accuracy to specific scenes and char-acters, as if providing directions to a theatre manager. In passing, he takes this op-portunity to advertise some of the fabrics that he himself had designed.

Costume in this play reaches the utmost limit of costly magnificence. The action is the movement of a pageant, the costume is the dress of a spectacle. In the text itself we are told that at Ardres every Frenchman was "all clinquant, all in gold," that every Englishman "show'd like a mine," that the "pages were as cherubins, all gilt." [...]

The third Scene of the first Act is devoted to Paris fashions, and in it we find mentioned not only the "fit or two o' the face" and the mincing walk of the travelled gallants, but such articles as the tall stocking, short blistered breeches, and those remnants of fool and feather that they got in France. The particular point, then, to remember in clothing the characters in Henry VIII is that the play opens immediately after the great meeting at the Field of the Cloth of Gold, and that London copied, with her usual exaggeration, the Parisian mode. Authorities for the period we have now reached are so numerous, so easily attainable, and so near to SHAKESPERE's own time, that error in costume is less to be excused than a failure in scenery. [...]

In stage representation there may naturally arise an objection on the part of the manager, be he ever so liberally inclined, to clothe his *dramatis personae* in velvet cut on real cloth of gold, but why the genuine patterns of the six-teenth century should be thought equally difficult to attain is somewhat strange, seeing that many of them were carefully reproduced in Birmingham under the direction of the late AUGUSTUS WELBY PUGIN about five and twenty years ago, and that one or two have been reproduced within the last two years under my own direction for Messrs. COLLINSON & LOCK. I have also seen at Messrs. GILLOW'S some remarkably good reproductions of early Renaissance fabrics and I believe Messrs. COWLISHAW, NICOL & Co., of Man-chester are directing their attention to the revival of genuine old designs in brocades, damasks, &c. So that, apart from the very costly materials, there are no difficulties in the way if any one wishes to revive HENRY VIII. and the world of his day—so close to SHAKESPERE'S own time that he might easily have

Source:
'The architecture and costume of Shakespere's plays. *Henry VIII* continued', *Architect*, 6 March 1875, pp.133-4

Biographical notes:
Collinson & Lock
Gillow & Co.
Cowlishaw, Nichol & Co.
Pugin

had it described to him by an eye-witness. On all sides authorities are to be found without any trouble to unearth them. HOLBEIN is especially to be noted, and his life-size cartoon of the KING at Hardwick Hall, made A.D.1537, must on no account be overlooked.

RESISTANCE TO ARCHAEOLOGY (1875)

Godwin's frustrations at the limited control he was allowed in theatre design came to a head over Coleman's production of Henry V *at the Queen's Theatre. Engaged as 'superintendent' of archaeology, his designs and advice were never fully implemented, prompting Burges to write an article criticising the costumes and sets. Godwin wrote two articles in* The Architect *on his experiences over* Henry V. *A third author followed this up (21 October 1876, pp.239-40) with an endorsement of Godwin's position, suggesting that his name should be removed from the playbills.*

Source:
'Henry V: a theatrical experience', *Architect,* 30 September 1876, pp.192-4

Beard of the Period.

Godwin, costume designs for As You Like It, BA, *26 Mar 1880.*

I propose now to give some account of the manner in which my drawings and archaeological directions have been carried out by all engaged in the work of production. I had intended doing this from the first, partly as a guide to other archaeologists who may hereafter be employed as I have been, and partly as an encouragement to those who have taken pains to understand one's meaning and to carry it out to the best of their ability.

The process of preparing drawings for the scenery, costume, and properties required in the stage production of any historical work of SHAKESPERE'S must perforce be pleasurable, howsoever laborious. The process of endeavouring to find out how your drawings and directions are being carried out is not so pleasurable. Among English artists, tradesfolk, and mechanics there are probably none so profoundly intelligent as those who are chiefly concerned in theatrical matters. And as a sure consequence of this profundity of intelligence, the beings so blessed are naturally enough apt to resent interference from any outsider. This feeling permeates the stage from one end to the other. It is not merely the costumier and the wardrobe women who look on the antiquary whom the manager consults as an intruder to be resisted; even the scene painter, whose knowledge of medieval art is of course boundless, and the well known actor or actress, whose ideas of historical personages are no less boundless, will scarcely ever listen to any mere antiquary, or deign to explain to him the reasons for the adoption of forms and combinations unknown to those whose study of the subject has only been life-long, and whose drawings from the architecture, sculpture, painting, or other arts of the past have only been faithful transcripts, wholly unattractive by the side of those delightfully-coloured studies for the stage that are superior to details and regardless of centuries.

The manager of a theatre venturing on a Shakesperian revival is somewhat like unto a man that means to build a house. Where a client arranges everything with his professional adviser beforehand, and then leaves the architect untrammelled to carry out his plan, whilst he (the client) carefully avoids all communication with clerk of works, contractor, or workman, we know that if the architect is only fairly competent the building will prove a success and the bill of extras little or nothing. Where, on the other hand, the client is always reviewing the plans, making alterations here in obedience to the suggestion of a one friend, changes there in fulfilment of his promise to another, the building will finally please no one, and the bill of extras will be almost endless.

CULTURED ACTING (1875)

Although Godwin directed most of his criticism at theatre designers and directors, he was well aware of the shortcomings of many actors. Vanity, ignorance and personal ambition are held up here as the most common faults, to the extent that the actors are frequently able to triumph at Shakespeare's expense.

It is quite time that I turned to the more personal, and, therefore, to the actor and actress, more interesting question of costume, and this sentence reminds me of a sense very much needed just now, even by the best of histrionic artists. They seem, no doubt, to be getting more conscious of their surroundings than they were when I first remember them some twenty years ago; but while their consciousness is perhaps immeasurable, their surroundings are unfortunately limited to their personal appearance in the pier glass. Of course it is the merest truism to say that the individual actor or actress, however popular, is after all only a part — often a very important one, I admit — of the picture the dramatist creates for us. The dresses, the positions, attitudes, and height of the other figures in the picture, as well as the background or scenery, are just as much surroundings as the embroidered robe or jewelled cap, the only difference is, they are not usually so near the distinguished star as to break its special rays. Of course there are plenty of situations, such as long embraces, &c., where costume and costume must mingle in one lump, and where we continually see the most harsh and violent discord; and these, good actors sometimes arrange beforehand among themselves when, as is too commonly the case, they have to find their own dresses. But beyond this I fail to see that sense of harmony or fitness one would naturally expect from the education, experience, and artistic resources of the chief actors and actresses. Their artistic faculty is so clouded by a narrow ambition to attract attention, and to obtain the excitement of applause, that they become wrapped up, not in their art, but in themselves. They are indifferent to the scenery, know nothing about the styles, dates, or colours of it, and after acting fifty nights can no more tell you the country where they have been supposed to live their brief life than they can map the back of the moon. If they would interest themselves in studies collateral and helpful to the one special study of acting, if, instead of spending their time in visits and in useless, and too often worse than useless, conversation, they would endeavour to attain to some degree of culture, to know something about the places, the times, the costume, and the manners of the play they undertake to act, to take some note of the stage picture, and hold due counsel with the scene painter, we might possibly some day really see a play of SHAKESPERE fairly represented on the stage.

Source:
'The architecture and costume of Shakespere's plays. Twelfth Night', *Architect*, 24 April 1875, pp.240-1

Godwin, costume design for Romeo and Juliet, *BA 21 May 1880.*

INHABITING STAGE COSTUME (1875)

Godwin stressed the importance of unity in all aspects of a theatre production. Accuracy in costume was not enough on its own; actors had to learn how to wear period dress and move in a manner that was natural to the period represented.

Source:
'The architecture and costume of Shakespere's plays. The Merry Wives of Windsor.', *The Architect*, 2 January 1875, p.3

Godwin, costume design for As You Like It, BA *26 March 1880.*

But rich gifts — soft kid, pearls, gold, and the rest — wax poor indeed when actors and actresses, absorbed in the finery of their situation, sink to the level of little more than lay figures for the exhibition of fashions. In ordinary every-day life the people who represent on the stage the fine dame, the noble duke, or the foreign potentate, are so little accustomed to art, or anything like good style in living, that it is with difficulty they can appear unconscious of their stage surroundings. Every movement of their bodies says plainly "this is a very telling sort of dress, and no doubt it must arrest attention; but I never wore anything like it before." Even in modern comedies we see the weak actress dominated by the sheer material force of millinery, and in the revival of old plays, when fairly genuine costume and scenery approaching reality are produced, the mass of actors and actresses simply look imbecile. We give them the benefit of the doubt, and assume that they are inside the clothes, but they certainly do not wear them. The human form becomes at last a mere peg with four movable peglets fixed in it and costume is thus too frequently brought into ridicule by the ignorant, and made the scapegoat for the incapable player. Scenery and costume we want to see progress until both shall be so natural as to be unobtrusive; but still more do we desire to see some signs of progress in those who stand between us and the past, as the living illustrators of the manners of that past, and the interpreters of its mighty dramatist.

AMATEUR ACTORS (1884)

It is somewhat ironic that Godwin should take such a harsh view of amateur actors in 1884, the year in which he and Lady Archibald Campbell formed the Pastoral Players. This company, and the one Godwin formed two years later for Helena in Troas, *were liberally supplemented by 'lady amateurs'.*

Source:
'To Art students. Letter No. 7.', *The British Architect*, 27 June 1884, p. 309

If lawyers generally were to adopt architecture as a profession in their old age, what an outcry there would be among the architects, who, having had premiums paid for their special education, fancy themselves to be trained professors of the craft! There is, I suppose, not less jealousy, envy, and vanity among actors who have paid their own premiums in the form of hard work than among architects; but the patience and the kindness the former exhibit towards amateurs is perhaps one of the pleasantest features in the increasingly busy life of the amateur actor.

I have been led to these reflections by witnessing lately certain attempts at dramatic representations by ladies and gentlemen who have had no training for the profession of the actor beyond a few lessons in elocution, and such very small practice as may be obtained by members of an A.D.C. Of some — especially of certain ladies whose bloom of youth has disappeared and left no mark — it may be said truly that they have no qualifications whatsoever for thus appearing before the public. Lumpish in form and movement, harsh in voice, spasmodic in every utterance, their presence on the stage, although only at long intervals, so annoys and vexes the onlooker that it makes it difficult to attend to or take pleasure in the performance in which they may happen to figure.

CRITICAL BLINDNESS (1880)

A critic in the December number of *Blackwood*, thus writes of the "Merchant of Venice" at the Lyceum:— "In scenery, appointments, and in stage arrangements, every reasonable wish is fulfilled ... the same may be said of the costumes, which *are well studied in contrasts of colour, true to the period, and handsome.*" The italics are ours. Does *Blackwood's* critic really believe this statement to be true? For the use of such words, if they be the honest expression of an opinion, shows that the critic manifestly understands nothing whatever about the fashions of past times or "periods;" so also the measure of his artistic culture is known to us when it allows him to give unqualified approval of such contrasts of colour, architecture, &c., as he refers to, and this, too, after he has passed a general condemnation on all critics for not tempering their enthusiasm with judgment, for wanting reserve and moderation in tone. It would be far better for the public and for art culture generally, if such critics were wholly to refrain from commenting upon things to which they are indubitably, because provably blind, lest their conclusions where sound should run the risk of being involved in the same mental cataract. [...] But the manners of a time and a people are like the costumes, and the architecture, and indeed the language, part of that genuine archaeology of the stage which authors, managers, and actors affect to slight. Indeed, action itself is more or less dependent on costume, weapons, &c.; for the style of action that would be general when loose easy dresses were in vogue would become absurd, if not impossible, in the tight-laced times of the second half of the fifteenth century. Let any fair reader remember, if she can, the days of crinoline, and think of the change wrought by dress in mere action and manner which this generation has witnessed.

Source:
'Notes on current events', *The British Architect*, 2 January 1880, p.2

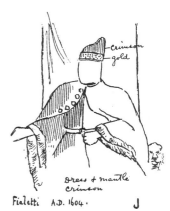

Godwin, design for The Merchant of Venice, BA *13 Feb. 1880.*

ARCHAEOLOGY ON THE STAGE (1885)

This extract comes from a seven-part series written a year before Godwin died, during the period of his most intense preoccupation with theatrical productions that brought together his lifelong passions for both archaeology and the stage.

Archaeology means, literally, the word about old things. This application of the sound principles of induction to the study of things of the past has re-

Source:
'Archaeology on the stage. Part 1', *Dramatic Review*, 8 February 1885, pp.19-20

sulted in our day in raising this study to the dignity of a science. A science that clothes and reanimates the dead, and gives colour to the pale shadowy forms of forgotten folk. The purpose of the archaeologist is to bring before us those old times, to make history of reality.

That is his purpose as touching the realities of life. The stage demands of the antiquary something more than this. Stage pictures of the past times should be treated *pari passu*, as life itself is treated by the dramatist. The archaeologist, in a word, must be *an artist*, endowed with the sense of form and colour, having constructiveness well developed, and in sympathy with the dramatic purpose. It follows that plays which run closely parallel to the life of the period of the action, as in society comedies, whether of the 18th or any other century, must be treated by the archaeologist with far greater accuracy of detail than romantic dramas in blank verse, or plays of high poetical value, for such comedies deal, as a rule, very largely with manners and customs, and these are much more intimately connected with the costume and externals than

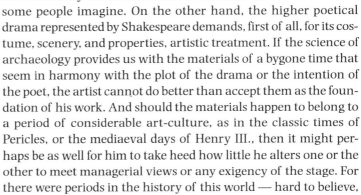
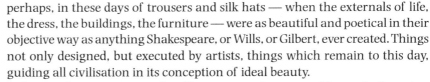
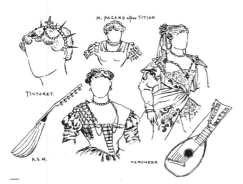

Godwin, costume designs for The Merchant of Venice, BA *13 Feb. 1880.*

some people imagine. On the other hand, the higher poetical drama represented by Shakespeare demands, first of all, for its costume, scenery, and properties, artistic treatment. If the science of archaeology provides us with the materials of a bygone time that seem in harmony with the plot of the drama or the intention of the poet, the artist cannot do better than accept them as the foundation of his work. And should the materials happen to belong to a period of considerable art-culture, as in the classic times of Pericles, or the mediaeval days of Henry III., then it might perhaps be as well for him to take heed how little he alters one or the other to meet managerial views or any exigency of the stage. For there were periods in the history of this world — hard to believe, perhaps, in these days of trousers and silk hats — when the externals of life, the dress, the buildings, the furniture — were as beautiful and poetical in their objective way as anything Shakespeare, or Wills, or Gilbert, ever created. Things not only designed, but executed by artists, things which remain to this day, guiding all civilisation in its conception of ideal beauty.

It is a paltry criticism on the effort to secure beauty and fitness in the externals of the stage to charge it with pandering to a vulgar taste, because actors cannot speak blank verse, or will not take the trouble to learn their art. You might quite as justly charge the architect or sculptor of a cathedral pulpit with pandering to vulgarity, because the dean has no idea of elocution. One would almost think, from the tone of some of our dramatic critics, that they resented the introduction of archaeology on the stage because the course of their studies had not, unfortunately, included this modern science, and they are, therefore, unable to write about it in any truly critical spirit. For if it be true that actors are also idiots, and endeavour to conceal their inability to act behind their dresses, then surely the critic might help to remedy this defect by simply ignoring the actor altogether for a time, and give undivided attention to the externals of architecture and costume, which have been gathered at an expenditure of thought worthy of recognition.

THE MISE-EN-SCÈNE (1875)

The trend towards greater realism in theatre productions raised many problems to which Godwin was particularly sensitive. More accurate props and costumes were all very well, but thought had also to be devoted to such matters as lighting, movement and the management of groups of actors if the illusion was to be maintained.

"MACBETH," as I have already shown, is an historical play, having reference to the time of EADWARD the CONFESSOR. The Management of the Lyceum has recognised this fact to the extent of adopting the ANGLO-SAXON Period, and this is no small gain to those of us who still stubbornly persist to look on the *mise-en-scène* of a dramatic representation as part of the intellectual enjoyment—or otherwise of the play. The dress of the actor, the shapes of the things he holds, leans against, or sits on, are at times so involved in the picture of himself that it is the merest wilfulness or blindness to regard them as unimportant. This is pre-eminently the case in "Macbeth" where the gloom of many of the scenes prevents the spectator, unless he happen to be in the front part of the house, from seeing any facial expression other than those which almost amount to contortions. Even when well-lighted scenes are before us, people in the back half of the audience in a theatre as large as the Lyceum are quite precluded from the study of facial expression save by the help of glasses.

Now as the most part of the audience is unprovided with lorgnettes, special study of a particular face is hardly possible, and so it comes to pass that we are learning to look at the stage more as a general picture, and to require in the surroundings of the figure, where possible, a reality as genuine as that of the figures themselves. This is, however, only absolutely possible in regard to costumes and "properties." But the more nearly the costumes and the properties approach reality the more difficult becomes the work of the scene painter and scene carpenter. Jarring effects sometimes amounting to the ludicrous are developed by the violence of contrast between a piece of realism and an old stage conventionality, effects which were not felt because they did not exist when everything was equally conventional. The noisy tramp of soldiers across a wild heath made of deal boards was unnoticed when the soldiers were so far removed from all likelihood that they recalled to us no living reality, and when the heath was as distinctly an apology as the sky was manifestly a cloth. So, too, anachronisms in architectural scenery or in furniture or costume are only acutely felt when we recognise features here and there which are sufficiently true to the past to furnish us with a fixed idea of date or style. When scene painters evolved castles from their own inner consciousness, and costume was invented for the occasion, and banqueting-halls were furnished with gilded monstrosities, the likeness of nothing that has been — *the mise-en-scène* — troubled us very little. [...] But it is very different when a manager attempts to be scholarly and archaeological; it is quite possible for him to seek proper advice and to be *wholly* accurate, yet he might fall short of this and still avoid such startling errors as are manifested in "Macbeth" at the Lyceum.

Source:
'The "mise-en-scène" at the Lyceum', *Architect*, 23 October 1875, p.222

C. S. James, set for the Bancrofts' production of 'Ours', Illustrated Sporting and Dramatic News, *1866.*

ADAPTABLE SCENERY (1875)

As with the crude and thoughtless use of stage costume, Godwin here attacks the similarly inappropriate use of stock backdrops.

Source:
'The architecture and costume of Shakespere's plays. *The Merry Wives of Windsor*', *Architect*, 2 January 1875, p.3

The usual street scene of the modern stage, if it has the slightest pretension to belong to the Middle Ages, is a wonderfully elastic and convenient device. For we find it in the hearts of populous cities, and we recognise the same old friend in quiet market towns and villages; to-day it serves, and perhaps, not altogether inappropriately, for Eastchepe in the time of HENRY IV.; to-morrow it does duty at Windsor. In the summer we find it at Venice, supporting with its picturesque gables the figures of SHYLOCK and the merchants, and in the winter the dear old scene turns up again doing duty in Canada, perhaps as the background of some modern trash or emasculated adaptation. Considering what small amounts are demanded by the most promising, painstaking scene painters, and what enormous amounts are paid for advertisements and monster placards, it does seem surprising that there should exist throughout the country such poverty of thought and such meanness of resource in almost every instance of an architectural scene being placed on the stage. The scene painter is not to blame, his order is to paint, not, mind, a scene altogether fitted to a certain play, but a scene that will serve the manager as a sort of general servant, attempting everything and doing nothing well. I venture to say that there is not a play put on the stage which might not have complete and special scenery of its own, without incurring any extra cost above its present gross outlay, and without reducing the receipts. A play properly represented on the stage makes every spectator a living poster and a

Scene shifters, Punch 20 Aug. 1881.

walking advertisement, for people are gradually learning to rely more on individual opinion of friends they know and to whose judgment they can trust, and every day less and less on the great unknown whose criticisms are written on printed forms of pleasant adjectives with blanks for proper names.

SCENIC ART (1879)

The Victorian age saw the emergence of 'Spectacular Theatre', involving huge sets, lighting and sound effects that attracted a mass audience. The alternative was the more realistic sets adopted by the Bancrofts at the Prince of Wales Theatre in the 1860s and 70s which appealed to a more middle-class audience. Godwin was himself associated with this latter tendency, but he could still be critical of its shortcomings. Recalling the great age of Romantic scene painting of a generation earlier, Godwin finds little to recommend the current state of the art.

Source:
'Scenic art', *The British Architect*, 28 November 1879, p.209

Biographical notes:
Roberts
Stanfield

Is scenic art improving, or is it on the wane? When one calls to mind the extravagant sets to be seen at the Prince of Wales's Theatre and elsewhere, the first exclamation of the ordinary playgoer will be "Most decidedly, progressing!" But is upholstery art? To a certain extent, no doubt, artistic tastes, and even what modern slang calls "aestheticism," are gratified by a show of carved chairs, damask stuffs, and embossed brasswork; but such additions to the completeness of stage decoration do not increase the talents of an artist, or call into play more than the taste to choose handsome materials and the will to purchase them. We speak of scenic art as the absolute painting employed on the canvas, which is to show forth, with more or less illusory force, landscapes, with all the perspective of air and outline, or interiors with their marble or wood illusions and carved ornamentation. The upholsterer is killing the artist. We once had men, like ROBERTS and STANFIELD, whose walks were as attractive in distemper as they still are beautiful in oils. Now and then one of their painted cloths, dull with age, makes its reappearance on the stage of Drury Lane, and stands out a monument of scenic talent and puissant effect, with its stereoscopic reliefs and subdued chiaroscuro. It is said that many of these scenes are stored religiously in the back docks of the old theatre; if so, an enterprising manager should revive them, and bring them to the light as a lesson to living scenic painters. [...]

All scenes are backgrounds to the figures in front, in whose action the interest centres. If scenery is so painted that while the action is going on, the eye is continually being called away to note details which rush into prominence, there is something wrong in the hand which has produced such a result. Even in spectacular tableaux the whole should be in harmony with the parts, and yet we see continually in the criticisms that appear in the daily press, lavish praise of the veriest daubs, where perspective is conspicuous by its absence, and where reds swallow up all tone, and vulgar chromes drive harmony out of the field. The worst fault of our School of Stage Painting is ignorance —ignorance of simple rules of drawing and colour, but more than all, ignorance of all science connected with art.

W. Telbin, 'The painting of scenery', Magazine of Art 12, 1889.

WOBBLY SCENERY (1882)

Of the scenery, quite the best set is "The Village Churchyard," by W. Perkins. Church and wooden porch are at last put on the stage to a right scale. The buttresses might have been advantageously omitted, and also the stupid looking pinnacle in the foreground of the churchyard. It might have been a second-hand drinking fountain got cheap for a tomb [...] only it is a pity the actors produce little earthquakes at every entrance and exit.

Source:
'Theatrical notes', *The British Architect*, 27 January 1882, p.40

THE GAIETY THEATRE (1869)

Described by Henry James as a 'striking example of the spirit of the age', the Gaiety was the leading comedy theatre in London. The decoration of the new theatre attracted much positive comment in the press but Godwin had reservations because it still fell short of true artistic ideals.*

* 'The London theatres', *The Nation*, 31 July 1879. Quoted in Wade, p.127.

Source:
'Mr. Marks's work at the
Gaiety Theatre', *Architect*,
2 January 1869, pp. 3-4

Biographical notes:
Marks

No seriously-minded person ever expects to see architecture at the opening of a new theatre. Building a modern theatre is essentially a *speculation* in the worst sense of the word. It is not merely a speculation with money — it is not merely a question of cheap materials and cheap manufactures, but always associated with these we find a style of construction never found in lasting, durable buildings — a style irreconcileable with any art principles and possessing no recommendations even to the theatrical speculator beyond the one and possibly the only recommendation it could possess for him — a narrow economy of money and of time. To build a theatre in three or four months may be a very noble ambition. The capital you expend does not long lie idle. You turn your money, as the phrase is, rapidly; your architect has no time to pause for thought; your painter and decorator have no time for the study of effects *in situ*; your engineer has no time for experiments; your masonry and brickwork, if you have any, have no time for settlement. In a dozen rooms in a dozen different parts of town men are working on the box-fronts, the ceiling, the proscenium, the act drop &c. Your artist-in-chief who paints your figures, has no time to talk about it. Thirty or forty life-size figures to be painted in two months is an order that makes any supervision of the ornament-painters, any consultation or experiment as to position and light, simply impossible. That all these *disjecta membra* should be rattled together at last and form a satisfactory and complete whole is one of those things no one could have expected, and about which therefore no one can be disappointed; but — it is a speculation. There can be nothing, then, left us but to sympathise with the unfortunate people who elect to take part towards the fulfilment of the theatrical speculator's ambition. [...]

Godwin's comments on the interior begin with the decorative painting by Henry Stacy Marks.

As to the scale of the figures in the main subject, it is manifestly out of all proportion to the building, and is, to say the least, dollish.

I cannot help thinking that under the conditions of site, the whole work would have been improved and more decorative had there been twenty-two instead of thirty figures. I am sure of this much — that it is not by a liberal use of figures in a given wall space that the artist is necessarily to produce good decoration. One figure with 'go' in it plus a few accessories with *meaning* in them would decorate a far larger wall space than is generally imagined. It is surprising how much space one really good figure will satisfy when well drawn in bright and lively colours. Had Mr. Marks fully realised this, we should possibly have had one figure to admire in the place of four which can scarcely claim that degree of consideration. Thus the dancing-girls — very difficult to compose, still more difficult to draw — are ill-composed and ill-drawn [...]

One word as to details. Of what use is the little embroidered shield on the back of the gold stick in waiting? It is a patch and nothing more. Why such a modern property shield in the hand of the player knight? Shields in the middle ages were as common as umbrellas are now, and players wanting a shield would surely have a real one, and not a piece of 3-inch plank. [...]

One thing I hope: that whatever opinions or criticisms may be published, all will agree in giving Mr. Marks credit for having produced an admirable decorative painting under trying conditions, and every one must join in awarding no end of praise to the theatrical speculator who could entertain the question of an artist's commission being an item in his speculation. I should add that the painting is executed in oil colour with turpentine medium on canvas — a process which, to my mind, is not one to be encouraged.

UTTER DEGRADATION IN THE THEATRE (1875)

In this, the first of two articles on the design of London theatres, Godwin's description of the squalid conditions which prevailed behind the scenes recalls the campaigning exposés of the Victorian poor by Engels and Mayhew.

Theatre and civilisation

[Theatre is] at once the most evanescent and the most comprehensive of any possible union of arts. It is only in the theatre that we see (or, rather, *might* see) the noblest results of civilisation. Poetry, music, architecture, painting, sculpture, meet in undisturbed harmony. It is true that in old times men might have seen in our churches and palace-hall something of this art-combination, but as we become conscious that worshippers and courtiers nowadays make up a mass of heavy incongruous grey, having in themselves or on themselves nothing in common with that modern art-renaissance that surrounds them, we soon discover that somehow there is no life left in any part of the picture; that the real glories of Classic or Gothic are impossible; and that our attempted revival in the real world of one or the other must result, at the best, in nothing more than a gigantic, and very expensively constructed set-scene. [...]

Source:
'Theatrical Jottings.—I.',
Building News, 19 March
1875, pp.311-12

Whether we look at the buildings devoted to the histrionic art from an architectural point of view; whether we take their interiors as illustrations of the art of coloured decoration; whether we examine the scenery either as construction or painting; whether we criticise the music, the costume, or the acting — we find in one and all a condition of things which is not far removed from utter degradation in every sense of the word.

A decade of criticism

Some ten years ago or more, thinking that an unprejudiced opinion, having in view a higher standard of excellence than any then prevalent, might, if published, do some service in the cause of those arts which the modern theatre is supposed to encourage, I ventured from time to time to publish notes or jottings (some said they were unkind) on the acting, scenery, properties, costume, and (in a rash moment) the management of two of our chief provincial theatres. And now, after the lapse of a decade, I do not hesitate to say that, so far from any art progress having been made in theatrical matters, the chief London theatres of to-day are wholly below the standard attained in those two provincial theatres. [...] How far it is possible, in an illustrated journal devoted to science and art, to operate on the inert mass of it enclosed within the boundaries of London theatres, remains to be proved. It may be worth while just now to try; for one of two things is imminent — either the theatre must disappear altogether from that art-platform on which for some time it has been allowed a place by courtesy, and so get at last to be quite hopelessly beneath the attention required for anything like careful or critical notice; or its moribund state may be the immediate cause of new life, and in this hope I write.

Purifying the theatre

Before I enter on my special criticism, it may be as well to take a brief general view of the present condition of things in the working part of the theatre, and at the outset there is cause for congratulation that the Lord Chamberlain should have expressed his determination to purify the stage. The indecencies of bur-lesque, extravaganza, or opera-bouffé may, for all I know, be so patent as to demand official interference. But whether the impurity is paraded or kept quiet, it is there; and it would be a marvel were it otherwise. When public attention was some years ago directed to the low, almost unconsciously indecent life led by the English labourer, his wife, his grown-up son and daughter, some com-mon-sense people suggested that it might be just as well, before we cried out upon their indecencies, to look to their dwellings, and give them cottages which should afford them the chance of living a little better than the pig, perhaps, though not so good as the horse. With equal reason we may suggest an in-quiry into the arrangement and construction of that miserable-looking por-tion of the theatre which lies behind the footlights.

Backstage

W. Telbin, 'The painting of scenery', Magazine of Art *12, 1889.*

Here the scene-painter is at work often from early morning until the theatre doors are closed for the night. Here the carpenters are busy with machinery, and men are modelling, making, and preparing most of the movables that are used on the stage, known technically as "properties." Here a host of dress makers are busy from morning to night altering old costumes or making new, if not for the principal actors, at least for the crowd of subordinates. Here also are the actor and actress for four or five hours every night, and often for an even longer time of the day. And now how are these people accommodated? Take the dressing room as an illustration. With a few exceptions these are nearly always a partnership business, sometimes as many as six dressing in one room of no more capacity than we should give to one condemned crimi-nal. Even in the better cases, where one dressing-room is given to two, it some-times happens that a gentle girl is the forced companion of one in every way the opposite. In very many theatres the chief dressing-room is little more than a close unventilated closet, while in the very best theatres nothing at all com-mensurate with the needs of the case is to be found. The approaches to the dressing rooms are sometimes even worse than the worst of the rooms. Thus, in one theatre the only approach to some of the rooms is by means of a nar-row platform under the stage, the basement of which is always more or less under water. This platform has no barrier of any kind, and the doors of the rooms open immediately from it! In some places the ladies' and gentlemen's dressing-rooms are side by side, and the partitions made of half-inch boards, or one piece of canvas strained from floor to ceiling. Of the sanitary arrangements it is hardly possible to speak calmly. One water closet to each sex is generally considered liberal; sometimes there is no such convenience in the establishment, and when there is, it is not unfrequently so placed as to be quite a way from external ventilation, opening on a landing or into a dressing-room.

The green room

It is generally believed that every theatre has a handsome, or at least a comfortable, green-room, where those not engaged in the passing scene can wait free from discomfort and annoyance; but this is by no means universally the case. In some theatres no green room exists, in some it is a mere passage-way, and in some it is little more than a wretched looking lumber-room. Then, again, ceilings are kept from falling on the actors and their dresses by a piece of loose canvas, slung from corner to corner. To these rooms the approach is often by a narrow, broken staircase, little better than a step-ladder; and I can assert that as a rule, the rooms devoted to the use of *all* the artists engaged behind the scenes are dirty, dilapidated, and uncomfortable. It would not be going too far to say that in no factory in the land are the common wants and decencies of life so little regarded, and the health and comfort of the workers so ill provided for, as in that workshop familiarly known by the expression "behind the scenes." To what is this condition of things owing? Is it to a laxity in the action of our sanitary authorities, or a deficiency in our sanitary law? Or is it to those who are responsible for the erection of our theatres—the proprietors and their architects; I do not hesitate to say that the money expended on the vulgar ostentation displayed in the auditorium and public entrances would be more than enough to provide healthy, convenient, and even comfortable accommodation for those who minister to our amusement or instruction.

STAGNATION IN THEATRE DESIGN (1875)

The design of theatres had relatively low status in the Victorian architectural world and was thus largely the preserve of specialists who worked in a conventional manner. Godwin regarded this as a missed opportunity since the design of the buildings had the potential to influence all aspects of the theatre from audience experience to the very nature of drama in performance. Three years later he would publish his 'New scheme for a theatre' in The British Architect, *and prepare plans for the Comedy theatre in the Strand (1881). Like his other speculative theatre projects, however, this was never realised.*

Theatres, as compared with other buildings, have been left in a miserable stagnation, and, as one of the properties of stagnation is deterioration, we cannot be surprised to find that this class of building has gradually fallen away from the control of the architect and the artist, and become the prey of upholster-

Source:
'Theatrical Jottings.—II.',
Building News, 18 June 1875,
pp.684-5

ers and paper-hangers. Thus, for example, theatres and town-halls are, I suppose, numerically equal; but, while from fifty to one hundred architects can be found to compete for the hall, five to ten only can be found to trouble about the theatre, and the reason is tolerably obvious, for it is proverbial that those who have the control of our theatres are the most tyrannical of clients. An architect may design and complete a town-hall, with all its numerous offices and law-courts, and arrangements for civic displays and large gatherings of people, without any interference whatever to interrupt the course of his thoughts; but I defy anyone to build a theatre in England without somehow or other getting the handcuffs of a paltry tradition put upon him by an ignoble conservatism; for, in theatrical matters, instead of being like civilised Europeans we are much more like the old Hindoo who follows in the track of his forefathers, and kow-tows to precedent as to a god.

Interior decoration

Seeing this groovy condition of things it is no great matter for wonder that theatre interiors should present us with nothing but spurious make-believes, temporary expedients, inflammable material, and offensive carton-pierre, which the lessee or manager expects us to accept as "decoration" — a decoration of which it may be said that it is chiefly made up of an unhappy mixture

Interior of the Royal Court Theatre in the 1870s, Illustrated Sporting and Dramatic News, *1872.*

of scrolls, imitation flowers, ribbons, and cords, at times elaborated by the introduction of heads and figures, the heads all of one type, and the figures all from one mould. In the province of colour, theatres are always wonderfully artistic, especially as regards the ceiling, which is generally constructed on a slightly domical plan. A not uncommon way of decorating this feature is by arranging highly-coloured figures round a central chandelier, said figures being supposed to be symbolical of all sorts of dramatic personifications. Sometimes the ceiling designer reaches the delicate idea of a tent-covering, with cords complete; sometimes (to such perfection can theatrical decoration attain) the central vault becomes more than transcendental in the quantity and quality of artistic thought portrayed in the marvellous imitations of such manufactured articles as ropes, fishing nets, lace, &c., and the still more wonderful achievement of representing in vertical perspective, near the centre of the ceiling a ring of those sweet things which bear the euphonious name of balusters.

Folly is cheap enough, and so paste-board and tinsel is the order of the day. An iota of wisdom costs thought if it costs nothing else, but we must not expect thought and wisdom in modern theatres, either before or behind the curtain. Your popular actor now-a-days is not the low comedian who had a faculty for real wit and true humour, but the meaningless slang-appropriator, whose cleverness consists in allusions to "that's the sort of man I am," and the introduction of such songs as "My Washee-Washee," or "Mother says you musn't." To be in harmony with this sort of thing our theatrical architecture and decorations are generally obliged to be on the same low level.

Mechanics

In the mechanical department the same stagnation prevails. After an inspection of an English theatre, below and above the stage, it requires an effort when we come out to realise the scientific powers of the age. After confusing ourselves with forests of posts and ropes, beams and cylinders and counterweights, we can scarcely believe in such things as steam engines or hydraulic pressure; but then it would be quite as heretical on the part of any architect or engineer to doubt the science of the master carpenter, as it would be to take exception to the art-knowledge of the decorator, the accomplishments of the scene-painter, the genius of the property-man, the completeness of the management or the perfection of the acting. Of course the public has no business to inquire into these things; the *mysteries* abide with us even yet, and in their modern dress must be kept sacred. Nevertheless, it may be as well for architects to try and see how the fine arts and mechanical sciences may be applied to this class of building, for this is our business, all managers and actors to the contrary notwithstanding: because the time may possibly come when public amusement may not be altogether vapid, not wholly founded on the assumption that ignorance is bliss.

We have only to look abroad to see how differently these things are managed. At Berlin, for instance, with a stage nearly 90ft. square, the mechanical arrangements, although far from what they might be, are of such a character that ten men are sufficient to work the stage, while in an equally large theatre here fifty men would not be too many. [...] A striking contrast to this is the noise, confusion, and crowding, orders and counter-orders, which pervade the English stage. I may add that a steam engine of eight-horse power works the machinery at the Vienna Opera-house, while, for the auditorium, a theatre in Central America, constructed inside of native woods, mahogany, cedar, etc., simply polished, with the construction visible, might afford us a useful lesson.

Lighting and ventilation

Again, look at the mode of lighting the stage:— If a painter or sculptor wished to exhibit his works would he admit the light from the floor? And even if *he* were foolish enough to do so, would the spectator place himself between the light plane and the object plane as in proscenium boxes? Look also at the arrangement of the audience. The best place in any closed theatre is unquestionably the pit, and the back rows of stalls. The Romans well knew it, and devoted that portion to the Senators and distinguished people; but we, because inn-yards were once used as theatres, must needs retain this pleasing historical fact, by rendering permanent the temporary arrangement that inn-yards necessitated, and charge the lowest price but one for the best seats in the house.

The sun-light chandelier is one of those cheap contrivances that infest theatres. It affords an easy way for the architect to escape from the two difficulties of lighting and ventilating by one simple line in his specification, and we are consequently either steamed or frozen out. In the stalls at Charing Cross, a

The flies at Drury Lane Theatre, Illustrated Sporting and Dramatic News, *26 Jan. 1884.*

English stage trap, from G. Moynet, La Machinerie Théâtrale, *Paris, 1893.*

Russian costume would be a luxury, while in the upper boxes at the Lyceum, the earliest dress on record would be more than enough. Again, the heating of a theatre is never thought of as a science, for it is almost impossible to make people understand that pure warm air may be as good to breathe as cold air, and may be made most refreshing without any of the evil results arising from chilly draughts. And so I might go on rehearsing many more evils — as, for instance, the stupidity of an orchestra being arranged across the whole width of the pit, instead of being concentrated. Indeed, the whole question of theatre-planning may well be taken up by a journal like this, and free criticism offered on the three plans at present before the public — the horse-shoe plan, the circular plan, and the semi-circular plan. [...] As to the lighting, a glass roof, with lights above, or a circle of star-lights with reflectors at the edge of the ceiling, seems to me to be better for the auditory than any of the usual plans. The stage should be lighted from above near the proscenium and arch, upon the same principle as a large picture is lighted.

Front of house and backstage

The contrast between that portion of the modern theatre devoted to those who are paid, and the portion devoted to those who pay, or are supposed to pay, is, at first sight, startling. But even in that part where the apparent luxuries of cushioned seats, curtained boxes, and carpeted stalls prevail, close inspection shows that slightness of construction, and cheap and weak makeshifts, are to be found, the same as behind the scenes. Assuredly the modern theatre before the curtain is nothing to be proud of: it is no more than a direct descendant of the inn-yard — is, in fact, a playhouse, and not a theatre, or in any way related to the theatre, in the Classic sense of the word. Indeed, there is no building of modern times to which so little attention has been paid to anything like permanency or durability of construction as in the playhouse, while, on the other hand, no building of Classic times can vie with the ancient theatre for the solidity of its architecture and the grandeur of its decorations. In the one case we see the enduring monuments of a people who were saturated with art, and had a profound faith in all that related to the drama, the movement of music, and the music of movement; in the other we see the creaking signboards of a people who for a long time have sat in darkness, knowing nothing of art, and having no faith in anything, save the narrowest of Sunday-clothed formalities.

A nineteenth-century renaissance?

May we not hope that in the train of revivals included in our nineteenth century Renaissance the theatre may find a place? Or is this last Renaissance too weak, too much of a sham, to give support to any revival? One might almost be inclined to take this latter and dismal view, judging from the present condition of those religions and arts which have been more or less resuscitated during this century. [...] The theatre, perhaps, more than any other building, presents the best opportunity for the architectural manifestation of the modern spirit of Renaissance, be it Gothic or Classic, but it may be as well to see first what sort of thing it is three centuries of playhouse-building has resulted in, and whether it contains elements capable of improvement, or whether it should be reformed altogether.

THE SPIRIT OF MOCKERY (1875)

The popular theatre of burlesque, pantomime and music hall may have had their place as mass entertainment but Godwin had higher ambitions for the English stage. He was not alone in this view. In a review of London theatre in 1880 Henry James described popular comedy as 'that infantile conception of dramatic entertainment which is the only contribution of the English imagination of the day to the literature of the theatre'.* This was in marked contrast to the next generation of artists, notably Whistler's follower Walter Sickert, who relished the bawdy humour and conventions of the music hall.

* 'The London Theatres', *Scribner's Monthly*, January 1881, quoted in Wade, p.159.

The dignity and beauty of art are old-fashioned things, quite out of keeping with the modern spirit that delights in chaff and mockery, and fondly believes them to be the outcome of wit. To mock at love, religion, education; to jeer at the unfortunate; to chaff the suicide; and ridicule the justice and majesty of the law are things which succeed if done with a sufficient amount of absurdity, and I may add accompanied by a sufficient number of pretty girls and pretty songs. This *mockery* is unquestionably the central spirit of the age, and those who take it and mould it for the stage into an hour's amusement for us are the artists who, perhaps, best represent, and who will be most identified with, the age. Of Mr. GILBERT and Mr. SULLIVAN we ought only to speak in words of praise: their works within the limits assigned is wholly admirable and altogether to be preferred to the dull commonplaces or the smart impertinences of modern English "comedy." But of the people who, having become tired with the burlesque of classic myth, and, bored with stagey reflections of their own lives burlesqued rather than demand the poetical drama, and by the demand cause the supply of the poetical or artistic actor — of these people one might fairly hold opinion with PYTHAGORAS, that souls of animals infuse themselves into the trunks of men.

Source:
'The architecture and costume of Shakespere's [*sic*] plays. The Roman Plays – I. Coriolanus', *Architect*, 12 June 1875, pp.344-5

Biographical notes:
Gilbert and Sullivan

THE SAVOY THEATRE (1881)

'Without adopting either the styles known as "Queen Anne" and "Early English," or entering upon the so-called aesthetic manner, a result has now been produced which I feel sure will be appreciated by all persons of taste.' This was how Richard D'Oyly Carte described his new theatre in 1881, but it was the facilities, especially the lighting, which attracted the greatest interest. The Savoy was the first theatre to employ electric 'incandescent lamps' instead of the traditional gas burners, although there were some teething problems which spoiled the initial effect. It opened on 10 October with a transfer of Gilbert and Sullivan's Patience, or Bunthorne's Bride, *a satire on Aesthetic taste in which Godwin was implicated by association.*

Source:
'Theatrical notes', *The British Architect*, 14 October 1881, p.511

Biographical notes:
Collinson & Lock
D'Oyly Carte
Gilbert and Sullivan
Phipps

The New Savoy Theatre, Illustrated Sporting and Dramatic News, *October 1881.*

The event of the week has been the opening of the Savoy Theatre. The private view took place on Saturday evening last, attended by gentlemen, mostly critical and professional, and a few ladies well known in the theatrical world. We arrived at the embankment or carriage entrance a little after ten o'clock, when the electric light was in full play as far as the auditorium was concerned. [...]

Of the general effect of the interior, whether viewed from the stalls or dress circle, we encountered but one opinion — that it was the prettiest and brightest theatre Mr. Phipps has yet built. White and gold, like Covent Garden opera house, is used on box fronts and ceilings; dark red is the colour of the walls at the back of the boxes, and the seats are of dark blue plush. [...]

There follows a critical overview of the decoration, the sight-lines, access space and exits.

Among the advantages promised, the patrons of Mr. D'Oyly Carte's new lyric theatre, is that of a staff of servants and a group of refreshment saloons under the immediate and sole control of the management, and no fees of any kind for programmes or cloakrooms will be permitted. "The attendants will be paid fair wages, and any attendant detected in accepting money from visitors will be instantly dismissed." We wish Mr. D'Oyly Carte every success in his new venture, and a happy outcome of any electric difficulty, which we feel sure can only be but temporary.

THEATRE HOLOCAUST (1878)

Source:
'Notes on current events', *The British Architect*, 29 March 1878, p.144

Another theatre gone wrong! The Elephant and Castle Theatre, built as lately as 1872, was early on Tuesday morning reduced to ashes. If every theatre in the country was to follow suit it would be no loss to architecture or art. The English people in their slowness are waiting possibly for a holocaust before they admit that the existing system of theatre construction is altogether an erroneous one.

XV Fine Art Criticism

ART CRITICISM, as a professional activity, came of age in the Victorian period. This was partly due to the rise of mass circulation newspapers and journals but it was equally related to the expanding market for contemporary British art among a substantial section of the population. The Royal Academy annual exhibitions attracted huge audiences, the sale of reproductive engravings soared, and in the wake of this numerous independent galleries opened in London's West End selling works by leading modern and historic artists. Godwin was intimately involved with this world. In 1876, for example, he designed the façade of the Fine Art Society's gallery on New Bond Street. By positioning himself as an 'art-architect' he also chose to move in circles of painters and sculptors, as well as actors, writers and other figures across the spectrum of the arts. This offered its own professional opportunities and Godwin became best known for his studio houses, designed for artists as diverse as the *Vanity Fair* cartoonist 'Ape' (Carlo Pellegrini) and Princess Louise, the daughter of Queen Victoria. Given this context, it cannot have seemed much of a step to engage in some passing criticism of the visual arts when Godwin was, in any case, writing for and editing architectural journals.

By the 1870s there was scarcely a serious newspaper or magazine that did not carry some sort of review of recent exhibitions and the gossip that attended on picture prices and acquisitions. Much of this was fairly descriptive, but it kept the visual arts in the public eye. Many leading writers and journalists of the period tried their hands at art criticism although, as with the various contemporary newspaper columns, it often had more to do with the author's favourite issues than the work under consideration. This is true of Godwin as much as it was of Charles Dickens, George Eliot or Oscar Wilde. Godwin's main themes were, somewhat predictably, the relation of the fine arts to architecture, archaeological accuracy, and the decorative aspects of pictures or sculptures, in so far as these could be separated from any aesthetic qualities. Aware that paintings were generally viewed within the context of public or domestic interiors, Godwin laments the tendency towards dull colours in much contemporary art, even when applied to subjects of hardship and misery, largely because he disliked the use of tertiary colours in interior environments. Like many of his friends in Aesthetic circles, he also found much of the tendentious and morally uplifting themes of contemporary art depressing, and preferred to ignore or make light of the hand-wringing social subjects which attracted middle-class audiences.

Two aspects of contemporary art did engage him seriously, however, and he returned to them on several occasions. The first was the relatively low position which sculpture occupied in high-art circles and the shabby treatment of figures like Albert Stevens. The latter's Wellington Memorial in St Paul's

Cathedral had been delayed for decades amid much bureaucratic wrangling, which Godwin regarded as a national disgrace. His other main topic was the art and activities of his friend James McNeill Whistler. The two men became close in the 1870s, leading Godwin to mount a sustained defence of the notorious Peacock Room (p.246) and engage Whistler to collaborate on the *Harmony in Yellow and Gold* for the Paris exhibition in 1878. At the same time Whistler commissioned the studio house in Tite Street from Godwin that became a *cause-célèbre* among architects when the first designs were turned down by the Metropolitan Board of Works. Throughout this time they saw a great deal of one another and must have shared ideas on contemporary art and culture. An entry from Godwin's diary of 22 July 1877 provides some insight into their connected lives: *'Called on Whistler, Pellegrini, Jopling & others. Saw Whistler paint full length of Mrs J. in an hour & a half an almost aweful [sic] exhibition of nervous power and concentration. Whistler with me home to duck and green peas.'* Godwin's support for Whistler was not uncritical. He rebuked Whistler in print over the latter's comments on art critics. Despite this, Godwin was a loyal supporter throughout the Ruskin trial and Whistler's bankruptcy, frequently praising his friend's work or advertising new exhibitions and print publications. This friendship endured, and it is significant that Godwin should write one of his most combative defences of Whistler in 1886, just three months before his death and at a time when his wife Beatrice had become, in effect, Whistler's pupil. Beatrice (Trixie), herself the daughter of an eminent sculptor, would marry Whistler in 1888.

Further Reading

S. Casteras and C. Denney, *The Grosvenor Gallery, A Palace of Art in Victorian England*, New Haven and London, 1996

R. Dorment and M. MacDonald, *James MacNeill Whistler*, ex.cat., London, 1994

L. Lambourne, *The Aesthetic Movement*, London, 1996

D. S. Macleod, *Art and the Victorian Middle Class*, Cambridge, 1996

L. Merrill, *A Pot of Paint, Aesthetics on Trial in 'Whistler v. Ruskin'*, Washington and London, 1992

J. C. Olmsted, *Victorian Painting: Essays and Reviews*, 3 vols, New York, 1980–5

E. Prettejohn, ed., *After the Pre-Raphaelites, Art and Aestheticism in Victorian England*, Manchester, 1999

E. Prettejohn, 'Aesthetic value and the professionalization of Victorian art criticism 1837–78', *Journal of Victorian Culture*, 2:1 Spring 1997, pp.71-94

B. Read, *Victorian Sculpture*, New Haven and London, 1982

J. Treuherz, *Hard Times. Social Realism in Victorian Art*, London, 1987

A. M. Young et al., *The Paintings of James McNeill Whistler*, 2 vols, New Haven and London, 1980

THE CLASSIC SCHOOL AT THE ROYAL ACADEMY (1869)

Godwin's review of the Royal Academy exhibition of 1869 praises the 'Classic School' for its suitability as architectural decoration. Each of Leighton, Moore and Armstrong were to practise as mural painters in collaboration with leading contemporary architects, and it was this aspect of their work Godwin sought to encourage .

If we seek among these for evidence of decorative powers, or, in other words, if we look at these pictures with a view to find if their authors would be likely to assist architecture in the capacity of wall painters, we shall have little difficulty in discovering much that must be regarded as favourable from an architect's point of view. Capacity and inclination are, however, very different things, although we see, or fancy we see, in certain works strong evidence of their authors' *capacity* for wall-painting. The decoration of architecture by colour, which means little more than wall-painting, is impossible unless the painter has some knowledge of, and love for, architecture, and an *inclination* to decorate it stronger, or at least as strong, as his desire to paint easel pictures, or his anxiety to appear on the wall of a fashionable exhibition-gallery. Gallery No. VII. is more than usually strong in presenting us with evidence of this capacity, expressed in three widely different ways, by three eminently modern artists.

Mr. Leighton, dealing with Greek Mythology, gives us, in 'Daedalus and Icarus' (469), what might be called 'the grand and monumental;' and although there is a great deal of perspective, and the drawing certainly has none of those flat qualities that are so desirable in wall-paintings, there is nevertheless strong evidence of the artist's power to conventionalise. It may be that the conventionalism is somewhat stagey — '*academic*' is, I believe, the proper word for it — still for any conventionalism we are grateful in these days of namby-pamby realism. If Mr. Leighton would think more of what the Greeks did, or would have done, and less of what the French do, he would find a conventionalism essentially belonging to his own art infinitely more satisfactory than that which he now feels himself compelled to borrow from another. It is hardly necessary to say, that Mr. Leighton's idea of colour is at total variance with that of all good wall painters, from the flourishing days of Assyria downwards. By the way, I must not forget to note that the pedestal in this picture shows us how the Greek masons utilised their defective columns.

Mr. Albert Moore revives the Greek element in form and accessories; he tells us no story, he gives us no expression, but he relies on his composition and drawing, and the exquisite loveliness of Greek costume. 'A Quartett: a painter's tribute to the art of music, A.D. 1868' (No. 483), is certainly very lovely. It is eminently decorative in its composition and general treatment, and had the painting been a little more careful, it would have had the rare merit of being a true easel picture as well. There are two great qualities which should place this work high in the estimation of architects, viz., its flatness and its brilliancy — a brilliancy attained (and this is especially noteworthy) with the most temperate use of colour, and by virtue of the most consummate knowledge of the value of white. It may be questioned whether, in this climate, where

Source:
'The Royal Academy Exhibition', *Architect*, 5 June 1869, pp.289-90

Biographical notes:
Leighton
Moore
Armstrong

'After a visit to the Academy', Punch *22 May 1869.*

two days out of three are dark and gloomy, such excessive temperance be desirable in painted decoration. The easel picture can be placed in the light best suited for it, and in such cases the tenderest tones may be adopted with success; but in wall decoration, or architectural painting, whilst we do not want such deep tones and rich Venetian colouring as would produce the effect of a dark hole in the wall, we at the same time as little desire to see such faint and undecided tints as would produce the effect of stained whitewash. Better figure-drawing it is impossible to get. The picture is really composed of valuable studies of seated and standing figures, and of Greek drapery; but the way in which these studies are united with musical instruments, and finally named, is as violent an anachronism as if an architect were to erect a series of Greek columns connected by an unmoulded entablature, and crowned by the spire of Salisbury Cathedral.

Mr. Armstrong's 'Hay-time' (No. 375) has a good figure in it: viz., the woman with the baby. The dress is exquisite — a delicate purple pattern on white. This is not the first drawing of short-waisted women we have had from this artist, and therefore it may be hoped it will be the last. The same feeling for colour and flat treatment which is evident here may produce much greater results, if combined with a costume less ungainly than that which Mr. Armstrong seems so anxious to immortalise.

The Water-colours are, generally speaking, so inferior, that it is matter for wonder why a room should have been set aside for them, whilst Architecture was thrust on one side. [...] When however, we turn to the sculpture, there are scarcely half-a-dozen works worth the marble out of which they are cut, and only one of this half-dozen worth exhibition. [...] There is probably no other art — not even the dramatic art — which in such a hopeless condition.

SADNESS AT THE DUDLEY (1875)

Taking advantage of his position as a regular columnist in the Architect, Godwin sought leave to air 'a few growls' about contemporary painting. He attacks the tendency for dull colour and sad subjects, as well as the artists' incompetence in depictions of buildings.

Source:
'First impressions on a private view of the Dudley Gallery', *Building News*, 5 February, 1875, pp.146-7

Biographical notes:
Dudley Gallery
Poynter
Severn

* Also known as *A Visit to Aesculapius*; exhibited at the RA in 1880 (Chantrey Bequest, Tate Britain).

First of all, it is worth noting that three of the most important pictures in the room — occupying places of honour — are unquestionably sad. To use the phraseology of the day, they are pitched in a minor key in subject and colour. "A Morass" (93), by Joseph Knight; "Camp Followers" (190), by Heywood Hardy; and "Venus before Aesculapius" (311),* by E. J. Poynter, A.R.A., are more or less the sort of pictures we might expect to find decorating the walls of the house of Spenser's "Griefe". [...] Now let us turn to Mr. Poynter's work (No. 311), described in the catalogue by the following verse:—

> "In time long past, when in Dianae's chase,
> A bramble-bush prickt Venus in the foote,
> Olde Aesculapius healpt her heavie case
> Before the hurt had taken any roote"

It is clear enough that the prospect, however momentary, of a *limping* Venus cannot choose but be sorrowful; and in spite of Aesculapius Mr. Poynter has determined to clothe it in colours so sad in tone that all life, health, and beauty are eliminated, and in their place we have an old-world look about it, interesting chiefly to those who only enjoy an old master when all its best colour has been dissipated. [...]

And now we come to a group of pictures in which the readers of this journal take especial interest, — I mean the architectural group. I regret very much that, although the number of the pictures is comparatively large, Mr. Arthur Severn is the only artist who attracts me. His work is faithful, and his buildings happen to stand upright — a very slight matter no doubt, but still one for which architects, at any rate, have a not unpardonable weakness. His "San Giorgio, Venice" (319) is a thing that has been *built*, which is more than can be said for the majority of artists' buildings, as witness the architectural horrors in 407 and 409, "The Side Door of Orvieto Cathedral", and the fig-tree angle of pillar of the Ducal Palace, Venice. While I am grumbling, I would ask why the Mersey (330), of all rivers, should have the rare property of flowing up-hill? and why the young gentlemen of the fourteenth century should handle a bow and arrow as one never did before or since that memorable afternoon which Mr. John Scott has recorded for us in No. 295?

Poynter, detail from an engraving after A Visit to Aesculapius, *1880.*

SOCIAL REALISM IN ART (1876)

In this extract Godwin addresses the issues of social realism in art and literature, concluding that it is a style in which the emotions are easily stirred. While the critic is moved by certain scenes of hardship and misery, and seems quite happy with the narrative and anecdotal content of such pictures, Godwin's principal complaint seems to be that there is simply too much of this sort of thing and the emphasis on dull, low-keyed colour has a depressing effect overall (see also p.198).

Mr. FILDES, Mr. W. SMALL, and Mr. R. MACBETH have gone for their subjects to the class which has so long furnished GEORGE ELIOT'S novels with rough and vigorous sitters [...] As a matter of personal "taste" I do not myself care much for cottage interiors, farm yards, agricultural labourers and the like; nor do I think that the tendency in modern times to paint sad subjects (sometimes in very sad colour too) is a wholesome tendency. The joy of life, the glory of work, may not perhaps be felt so keenly now as in old times, and few painters may have the heart, even if they had the power, to work in a high key or scale of colour, but from men like Mr. FILDES it may be hoped and expected that they will not forget the joy and the glory in the success that may await the trouble and the toil.

Mr. ROBERT MACBETH has devoted himself to the accomplishment of a larger picture than usual. Larger in absolute measurement, larger in *motif*, and larger than all because it is of the nature of the historical. Most of us know something of those troublous hard times English agricultural labourers experienced before Parliament interfered in their behalf. Mr. MACBETH takes

Source:
'In the studios of some "Outsiders"', *Architect*, 11 March 1876, pp.156-7

Biographical notes:
Fildes
MacBeth
Whistler

us back to an early morning of that time. The scene is laid in Lincolnshire; the background is mainly occupied by a farm-house; to the left of it we get a glimpse of the country and sky; and to the right a thatched stable or outhouse stretches from the back to the front. The ground is covered with straw, and across this a gang of labourers — men, women, and children — are moving, or, if one may apply such a word to English people, are being *driven*. We see against the chill sky at the back of the group of labourers the mounted figure of the "gang-master", as he was called. The farmer himself takes part in the scene, holding back a couple of greyhounds. He turns with more of curiosity than of any other feeling to the incident of the right hand foreground, where a sick, mayhap a dying, child is engaging the attention of a woman surrounded by the same quantity and quality of creature comforts usually allotted to swine. Here again we have a picture eminently painful in its subject, and no doubt full of attraction for that morbidly sentimental section of the public whose literary taste has been built on such foundations as "Uncle Tom's Cabin" and "The Ticket of Leave". Mr. MACBETH has, however, treated his subject in a much more wholesome manner than either novelist or dramatist and he has obtained, as the resultant of his pains, an artistic production which is more than can be said for the story or the play. Nevertheless, it becomes a serious question whether we are not having too much of this, however artistically managed. Early morning and late evening effects are easy to paint compared either with the full flush of daylight or the mystery of night. The latter Mr. J. M. WHISTLER is translating as no one among us ever yet has done, with a truth and subtlety altogether incomparable but of daylight how few there are who venture to give us the faintest glimpse. The sentiment, the story, or the human interest of the picture is an afterthought, however much we may endeavour to persuade ourselves to the contrary. We get a grey sea or landscape at the break or close of day — it matters little which, for we have only to make one cooler than the other — we find we can really paint it without much trouble, and having fixed on our scenic effect, we bring on our figures to give "interest" to the subject, and these, whether of geese or men, matter very little. I do not mean to say that this was Mr. MACBETH's process. What I insist on is, that it is a common process, and one likely to be encouraged by such subjects as he, among other good painters, have lately favoured.

Macbeth, detail of A Lincoln-shire Gang, Graphic, *15 July 1876.*

DEPRESSING LANDSCAPES (1877)

Source:
'An art conversazione at the Hogarth', *Architect*, 6 January 1877, p.5

Biographical notes:
Walker

Stagnant pools and badly cultivated farms find sympathising friends in Mr. WATERLOW, Mr. BROCKMAN, Mr. F. W. WALKER, and Mr. WILMOT PILSBURY. Mr WATERLOW is still among "the sad ones;" the yellow sky of evening reflected in the still pool, the shadow-bathed hill, the line of low roofs on its crest, the banshee's cry, the whisper of "Lenore." Nevertheless, little as I care for these sad effects, and ill as I think their tendency to be, one must admit that few young artists paint them with greater power than Mr. WATERLOW. Another stagnant pool under a more wholesome aspect, a summer day, two or three sheep, a corner of a field, overshadowing trees, all put skilfully together by Mr. W. PILSBURY, who has given us a third stagnant pool, not so good, and a wintry day on a rough common, rough sky, rough cottages, rough trees, rough geese — not altogether one of those aspects of nature that fits well with a gold frame.

FRED WALKER'S *BATHERS* (1876)

Walker was a very promising painter, much admired by Ruskin among others, whose death in 1875 was reported as a great loss to modern British art. This tribute identifies qualities that Godwin could appreciate in the realist school.

To see what we have lost in WALKER, let the student of art look at the figures of the old lady in black and the labourer in the picture called *The Old Gate*, and then pass on to the enjoyment of what I take to be the central work of the man's life, *The Bathers*.* By the time this will be in type doubtless many critics will have discovered, with the critic of the Times, that the figures in The Old Gate "suggest recollections of PHIDIAS" and that *The Bathers* is like a Greek idyll, or "Theocritus" done into English. I have already noted in an article, which appeared in this journal on January 1, the Greek— nay more, the high Greek — key in which much of WALKER's work is pitched. [...] In *The Bathers*, however, the composition from one end to the other is complete and altogether excellent, even if measured by the highest standard of excellence we know— the sculpture of PHIDIAS. [...] But let us go on yet further and note the curvy movement of the extreme figures outside this pyramidal group and the almost horizontal lines of the river banks, and I think we may confess that quite apart from the excellence of the painting from the usual painter's point of view, we have here an altogether noble work of decoration, which, like all good decoration, sets forth its nobleness even in its skeleton lines. I hardly know how to put into any form of words the praise I feel towards this picture. It is better perhaps that no one should attempt to give utterance to the sort of joy a work like this produces.

Source:
'A painter and a sculptor',
Architect, 15 January 1876,
p.30

Biographical notes:
Walker

* Lady Lever Art Gallery

Detail from an engraving after Walker's The Bathers, *1868 (Hunterian Art Gallery).*

THE 'TERTIARY' VOGUE (1876)

As in interior decoration, Godwin deplored the vogue for muddy tertiaries.

The labouring poor are, as usual, strongly represented. [...] I will say nothing of the ugliness of the line of the form or of the face of each individual thus handed down to posterity, because ugliness seems just now to be an accepted thing with a certain class of youthful artists in which Mr. MARSH is by no means singular. But if any artist can find any sea-shore so entirely devoid of colour as that here represented, it would be worth while to have a scientific expedition thereto, to discover the curious kind of life that must exist there. This doctrine of the "Tertiary" school is really being carried too far when it commands the sympathies of a man with so much promise of colour in him as Mr. MARSH. In the opposite extreme we have Mr. C. M. HEMY's *Mending the*

Source:
'Mr. Deschamps' Gallery',
Architect, 11 November
1876, p.276

Nets. Well! of the two evils, I think this perhaps is the least. Realism can hardly go beyond Mr. HEMY, but "Tertiaries" can come to, shall I say, mud and green slush as represented by J. A. HAGUE in *A Homestead*.

PAINTING AS THEATRE (1876)

Godwin's 'reading' of this picture reveals something of the Victorian attitude to anecdotal painting, relating it to contemporary staging in the theatre.

Source:
'Mr. Deschamps' Gallery',
Architect, 11 November 1876,
p.276

Taking the union of composition with colour, drawing, and handling, or as some painters call it, *painting*, the one picture that is good in all this and is pre-eminently above all the others is *Dawn* [by E. J. Gregory]. The background is the interior of an ordinary bay window of a vernacular drawing-room parallel with the plane of the picture, the Venetian blinds are down, and there are lace curtains; within the window is an azalia, and in front of the bay stretches a grand piano of the ugly every day common type. There is a brass chandelier of the kind now much affected by the disciples of Queen Anne. So far for the scene. The actors are — 1, an old and tired musician (of small account in the play), yawning, seated at the finger-board; 2, a young lady in a pale yellow tarlatan dress, leaning slightly against the curved front of the piano; 3, a blasé man of the world talking to her, and leaning well back with his right arm resting on the piano. The general light is yellow from the chandelier, but the blue-gray dawn is striking through the chinks of the Venetian blinds, and is reflected from the polished wood. There are two doubtful things about this work. First, it may be questioned whether the sort of finish or rather the absence of finish, especially about the lady's dress, here exhibited is right for an easel picture; second, whether a lady of such personal attractions as Mr. GREGORY has here meted out would ever engross the attention of the sort of man he has painted. But it is possible that the scene has another reading, and is a true record of modern life. If so, the fewer such records we have the better, for the love of beauty will never be encouraged if we make heroes of the cold, the sneering, and the calculating, and heroines of the scraggy, the dirty, not to say the ugly. The mise-en-scène is perfect, the stage management faultless, but the actress is not worthy; and there is an uncomfortable sort of feeling that the author of the drama has intended to represent a phase of life which a mediaevalist may have delighted in, but which greater artists, whether in Greece or anywhere else, would never have heeded. Viewed as painting, and not as story telling, there can be, I should think, no doubt at all that this is one of the most remarkable pictures of the year.

CHILDREN'S BOOK ILLUSTRATION (1878–9)

The new coloured illustrations which appeared in children's books of the 1870s attracted serious interest from art critics as much as from young readers and their parents. Led by Walter Crane, Kate Greenaway and Randolph Caldecott, these pic-

ture books introduced Aesthetic imagery to the nursery and played a significant role in the formation of taste. Godwin had strong views on suitable books for his own children.

THE *House that Jack Built* and *John Gilpin*, illustrated by Mr. Caldecott in outline and in colour, have just been published by Routledge & Co. They are two picture books of the children series which all should possess, no matter what age between four and fourscore. In tender beauty, in grasp of character, in power of expression, they are unrivalled. The "dog that worried the cat" is simply marvelous in expression, whether in his first sight of the cat or in his beaming satisfaction at the accomplishment of his purpose or in the awful and sudden catastrophe which came upon him from the crumpled horn. So also the cat in her fearful stealthy crawl and nervous pause, before the spring is hardly less admirable.

BUT why does Mr. Caldecott neglect brick walls and buildings generally? In no illustration of this artistic little production is this part of the scene fairly

treated. Everything else is as real as the nature of the drawing would permit, but the foreground wall in the coloured portrait of the dog and the views of "the house that Jack built" are really — well we are so pleased with the rest that we would rather not say what they are.

Kate Greenaway's 'ugly little girls'

Kate Greenaway sends two of her quaint, ugly little girls, cast in the usual mould, of which we are getting just a trifle weary, careful in drawing and rich in colour though they may be.

Walter Crane's *Baby's Bouquet*

The Baby's Bouquet, by Walter Crane (Routledge & Sons), true to the spirit of the day, savours more of the time of our great grandmothers than did the *Baby's opera*, the illustration of the *four presents* being the only one treated in the classic style Mr. Crane used to affect [...]

Another unsatisfactory feature of the book is the attempt to combine dark brown with bright red outline, as in Polly, put the kettle on, where the pretty red outlines of Polly are marred by the dark lumps of the kettle and grate, a contrast rendered even with worse effect on the opposite page where the little children are in red outline and their chairs in solid dark brown. Indeed the marginal figures and decoration generally are very much inferior to those of the earlier *opera*. By the way, we would ask Messrs Routledge to keep the children's sticky stuff in its proper place and not allow it to be put in the composition used on the covers of their books.

Source:
'Notes on current events', *The British Architect*, 22 November 1878, p.197

Biographical notes:
Caldecott
Crane
Greenaway

Greenaway, detail from Under the Window, *1878.*

Source:
'The Dudley', *The British Architect*, 7 March 1879, p.101

Source:
'Notes on current events', *The British Architect*, 17 January 1879, p.24

'CHOCOLATE BOX' ART (1881)

We do not care for the present smooth pretty manner of Marcus Stone, R.A. "Married for Love" has in it much of merit in the way the story is told, and in the drawing, but the colour is not quite happy, and the painting is polished up, and rubbed down, and smoothed over until it reminds one of a chocolate box.

Source:
'Notes on current events', *The British Architect*, 27 May 1881, p.267

Biographical notes:
Stone

WHAT IS THE MATTER WITH MR CAVE THOMAS? (1881)

A certificate is criticised for its bad draughtsmanship but Godwin was particularly irritated by the clumsy symbolism employed for 'Hygiene', a topic he was passionate about.

What is the matter with Mr. W. Cave Thomas? His name we find affixed to an amazing production, purporting to be a "Copy of Certificate Awards" [...] It is a placard about 30 inches by 22, printed in shades of brown, and represents the saving power of Hygiene, in the shape of a life-belt, about to be cast be a very stout woman, standing in a boat, emerging from a lofty *cloaca*. Agrippa, we are told, when he cleansed the sewers, passed through them in a boat, so that no objection can be taken on the ground of precedent for this part of the design. Our surprise arises from the character of the drawing — the brawny vulgarity of Madame Science and the wretched detail of the architectural portions, defects distinctly noticeable in this large scale plate. Mr. Cave Thomas did not commit such depravities as these years ago, when he decorated the dome of the little Greek Church in Welbeck-street.

Source:
'Notes on current events', *The British Architect*, 9 December 1881, p.613

Biographical notes:
Cave Thomas

SENSITIVE PRINTING (1878)

Godwin and Whistler had a shared interest in printmaking; both employed the master lithographer Thomas Way.

We have been favoured with an sight of an early proof of the mezzotint of Mr. Whistler's masterly portrait of Thomas Carlyle.* The painting has been translated with genuine and hearty sympathy by Mr. Josey. Indeed so truly has the engraver worked that at a little distance the proof looks like the brush-work arrangement in black and grey by the painter's own hand.

Source:
'Notes on current events', *The British Architect*, 27 September 1878, p.126

* Purchased by public subscription for the Glasgow Art Gallery, 1881.

'A SCREAMER' — WHISTLER'S ETCHING ALTERED (1878)

It is likely that Godwin is repeating Whistler's own views on this affair but we can be sure that Godwin shared the artist's attitudes to integrity of the art-work.

We have just read, in an American paper, an exhibition notice, in which are some remarks on a *"frame of signed etchings by the famous and eccentric Whistler, loaned by Mr. S. P. Avery."* One of the etchings is, *"A sketch of little Annie Haden,*

Source:
'Notes on current events', *The British Architect*, 22 March 1878, p.132

Whistler's niece. The legs, it appears, were etched in afterwards, by Seymour Haden, her father, between whom and Whistler there exists a strong enmity. The lines by Whistler on signing the proof will then be understood, and are very characteristic. 'Legs not by me — the impertinent work of another — J. Whistler.'"

Biographical notes:
Haden
Whistler

With Mr. Whistler's or Mr. Haden's quarrels, we are of course not concerned; but surely there is some mistake here. A brother-in-law's privileges are great, and a father's authority may be strained till it reach even the portrait of his child, but to alter an artist's sketch, and that artist such a master of etching as Whistler, is simply incredible? We hope for the sake of English amateur etchers that the story is of the nature of those Mark Twain describes as *screamers*. Anyhow, it is a veritable *eye-opener*!

WHISTLER VERSUS RUSKIN (1878)

The action of Whistler v. Ruskin, so long deferred in consideration of Mr. Ruskin's health, is now ripe for trial, and is expected to come before the court in the following month. We have no sympathy with a critic who speaks of any artist as an "imposter", but we pity the critic who is unable to recognise the power and originality of Mr. Whistler's genius — his handling and mastery of colour. We are glad the case has not been withdrawn, as some people hoped, for it is quite as well that the authority of the High Court of Justice should be invoked to declare once for all the boundary where art-criticism passes into libel.

Source:
'Notes on current events', *The British Architect*, 15 November, 1878, p.188

Biographical notes:
Whistler
Ruskin

WHISTLER ON 'ART AND ART CRITICS' (1879)

In December 1878 following the libel trial, Whistler published the first of his occasional pamphlets entitled Whistler v. Ruskin, Art and Art Critics. *In this response Godwin rejects Whistler's indiscriminate dismissal of all art criticism.*

Mr. WHISTLER having had "coxcomb" flung at him by Mr. RUSKIN, replies to his critic in the pamphlet just published entitled, "WHISTLER v. RUSKIN: Art and Art Critics." "We are told ," says the militant artist, "that Mr. RUSKIN has devoted his long life to art, and as a result — is Slade Professor at Oxford. In the same sentence we have thus his position and its worth. It suffices not, Messieurs! a life passed among pictures makes not a painter — else the policeman in the National Gallery might assert himself. As well allege that he who lives in a library must needs die a poet. Let not Mr. RUSKIN flatter himself that more education makes the difference between himself and the policeman when both stand gaizng in the gallery!" [...] All this is very smart, and is no doubt a very commendable and subtle way of not only calling Mr. RUSKIN an ass, but every one else who takes the trouble to separate the wheat from the chaff in the art of painting. [...]

Source:
'Mr. Whistler on 'art and art critics', *The British Architect*, 10 January 1879, p.13

Biographical notes:
Rossetti, W.
Ruskin
Taylor, T.
Whistler

Tom Taylor, The Magazine of Art, 1881, p.68.

Mr. WHISTLER boldly announces, and a host of painters will secretly agree with him, that he is against all art critics — "the art critic alone would I extinguish." This one can readily understand, although it is but a poor return to Mr. W. M. ROSSETTI for the evidence he gave at the trial. [...]

But Mr. WHISTLER is not satisfied in having only the scalps of Mr. RUSKIN and the critics. He hits out at all Englishmen. The poor Briton "is but rough-hewn and blundering," and "badly begun by nature," as compared with the Parisian. [...] No, Mr. WHISTLER, it will not do — this sweeping attack of yours, it overshoots the mark. There are critics — and British ones too — who have studied the fine arts as long and diligently as the engineer has studied his mechanics, and your vial of wrath should not have been poured out indiscriminately.

With some of the remarks of Mr. WHISTLER's sparkling and amusing brochure we entirely agree [...] when Mr. TOM TAYLOR comes under the lash, the painter seems positively to revel in the whips and scorns he scores on that poor critic's back, and surely the writer (Times, July 6, 1864) who "found VELASQUEZ 'slovenly in execution, poor in colour — being little but a combination of neutral greys and ugly in its forms,'" deserves all he gets. [...]

Whatever Mr. WHISTLER may say to the contrary, the ranks of every art are crowded with incapables and charlatans, whose works are ever thrust before us by the vanity or ambition of the producer, the pride of the purchaser, or the greed of the trader. So long, then, as this goes on, so long we trust critics will be found ready to expose the charlatans and point out to "blundering" Britons the work that is either weak or frivolous.

WHERE IS MR RUSKIN? (1879)

Source:
'The Dudley', *The British Architect*, 7 March 1879, p.101

Biographical notes:
Severn

A cheeky jibe at Ruskin in the aftermath of Whistler's libel action.

There is a true silver and grey effect in ARTHUR SEVERN'S "Ice on the Thames", so much in Mr. WHISTLER'S style that we involuntarily exclaim, where is Mr. Ruskin? has he quarrelled even with Mr. SEVERN? [...]

ALBERT MOORE'S *TIRED DANCER* (1879)

Source:
'Notes on current events', *The British Architect*, 28 March, 1879, p.142

Biographical notes:
Moore

In this aside Godwin brings out the central features of Moore's art: harmonised colours, 'diaphanous draperies' and a musical quality common to painting, dress and architecture.

[...] the most pleasant colour in the room is Albert Moore's Tired Dancer. Yellow greens of sundry tones mingle with flesh colour softened by white diaphanous draperies into exquisitely tender flesh-like colour. Note the deeper tones (still in the key of flesh colour) in head dress and floor, and the value they are to the picture — like the bass to a madrigal, or the keystone to an arch.

DIVINE BEAUTY OR SCROFULA? (1879)

Burne-Jones' androgynous figure types attracted a lot of criticism, and the heavy facial features of his women were often ridiculed in the press, particularly since they were intended to evoke an other-worldly beauty.

It is simply an insult to our knowledge of human nature to ask us to accept as "divinely beautiful", faces that, however intelligent, reflect — and that with no uncertain tone — a derangement we will not venture to describe. Nor is that particular construction of nose which Mr. Burne Jones affects, to be approved except by those who in themselves exhibit the painful marks of well-defined scrofula.

WITH WHISTLER'S CRITICS (1881)

The works which Whistler produced during his sojourn in Venice (1879–80) went far to re-establishing his reputation in the aftermath of the libel trial and bankruptcy. First to appear were the etchings, but it was the pastels that achieved greater success when 51 of them were shown at the Fine Art Society in January 1881. Many critics were still bewildered by Whistler's spare, economical style, so Godwin devoted most of this review to a survey of the mixed responses that had appeared in the press.

It is surprising, and at times amusing to read the criticism of any art work outside, or rather beyond, the general level of the crowd. The criticisms evoked by J. F. Millet in his lifetime, were mostly very curious as persistent examples of refusing to regard an artist *from his own standpoint*. They said Millet was revolutionary because he loved to paint the quiet, patient, enduring toilers of the earth! Corot was one of the objectors, who told us in plain words, that Millet's pictures were a new world to him; and he adds, "I don't know where I am; I am too fond of the old. I see there is great knowledge, style, depth — but it frightens me. I like my own little music better." Just so it is with even the favourable critics of J. A. McN. Whistler; they like their own little music better. He has piped unto them and they have not danced, mourned unto them and they have not lamented. "The Mother" was a sadly beautiful picture; it was the painter's art in the depth of its mournful cadence; a simple, earnest, soul-felt portrait picture of a widowed lady. Have the critics yet recognised the deep sympathy and the profound mastery in this work? They have not at any rate expressed any such recognition so far as I know. So again in the two exhibitions of Venice etchings and pastels. What have our confrères discovered? In two of the etchings, says the *Daily News*, he "has attempted to convey impressions by lines far too few for his purpose" — amazing insight. "He has cast aside his painstaking method" that in the earlier etchings afforded us an opportunity "of enjoyment in the technique of the artist of which we are now deprived;" — evidently looking not for artistic but mechanical skill. "The architectural ornaments and the interlacing bars of the gratings" are suggested

Source:
'Notes on current events', *The British Architect*, 6 June 1879, p.231

'Ars Longa', satirising Burne-Jones, Punch 19 Feb. 1881.

Source:
'With Whistler's critics', *The British Architect*, 25 February 1881, pp.98-9

Biographical notes:
Millais
Spenser
Whistler

'London paved with gold', Whistler's London success, Punch 19 March 1881.

Whistler, The Beggars, *etching,*
1880 (Hunterian Art Gallery).

rather than drawn, says the *St. James's Gazette.* An architect's clerk would have
done the trick better for you, no doubt. The spectator feels painfully the absence in these etchings "of any feeling for the past glory of Venice." His drawing, always masterly, is "sometimes that of a very slovenly master," architect's
clerk again needed; wants restored views. The *Portfolio* tells us that the twelve
etchings "have so little in them"; yet much more than the *Portfolio* can remember, as it complains of " absence of tone," light and shade, or chiaroscuro,
in the face of such fine examples of these very qualities as *the doorway* and *the
beggars,* and the artist who sent the notes on these etchings (see the *B.A.* for
Dec. 10th) too often lost sight of the beauty and the mastery in contemplation
of the mere method.

The fact is, Mr. Whistler's present mode of dealing with his subject is simply
the result and development of his past and vast experience. Just as in the case
of Mr. Millais, who now paints in half a minute what once took him half a day
to accomplish in, of course, a different manner. Let any one compare, for instance, "Isabella," painted in 1849 with "Cherry Ripe," painted in 1879. The
nutshells in the first took Millais longer to elaborate than the whole painting
of the last-named picture and yet the cabbage leaf in "Cherry Ripe" is quite as
much a cabbage leaf — has all its thick, cool, moist, succulent characteristics
— as the broken nut shell is an almond's serrated sharp sheath, rough outside
and smooth inside. So is it with Whistler's etchings of Venice, the method of
which is not new, but had distinctly been foretold in the dry point of Price's
candle factory. His later work on the Thames and Adriatic, as compared with
his earlier etchings, is as a Millais of 1879 to a Millais of 1849, and is as artistically superior. As to the few bits of architecture he has drawn, he has given
us — with what remains of the marble forms and details, which a knowledge
of architecture would have tempted the eye to complete and restore and spoil
— that most difficult of effects to render, its *gradual* decay. Of Venice as it is, in
the dethroned, neglected, sad, passing away of it, Whistler tells us with the
hand of a master who has sympathised with the noble city's suffering and
loss. This is not what our critics wanted. The Ducal Palace, St. Mark's, the
bridge of the Rialto, the Fondaco di Turchi, San Giorgio or Sta Maria Della
Salute — no matter whether vilely restored or not — are the familiar airs they
wanted played over again. They have sketches or photographs of them. They
or their friends have played them so often that they fancy they know them;
and this new music of Whistler's startles them and in some cases offends them
even to the point of direct misrepresentation.

The pastels of Venice, by the same artist, have been, on the whole, received
by the critics more favourably than have the etchings. But here and there have
been comments of exceptional absurdity. For example, the *Pictorial World* says,
"These works have been done with a swiftness and dash which precludes anything like care and finish." Well, you cannot trace the individual hairs in the
moustache of Philip IV.'s portrait (No. 745, National Gallery); "but," the *Pictorial World* adds, "every line has its full value;" and "there is nothing slovenly,
or badly rendered." Then why talk of care and finish? Is the staring evidence
of grinding labour a measure of art? The *Athenaeum* finds some "too sensational," a very odd term to apply to any one of them, except in its high sense.

Pan knows all about the aims and intentions of the artist and is really more absurd than all the rest: "His pictures do not claim to be accurate;" "form and line are of little account to him." What the pictures "claim to be," we will not pretend to say; what they are, is the exact opposite of what *Pan* declares. The perspective is singularly *accurate*, and an individual line is often of *superlative account*. *Pan* wants the brown paper in No. 4 (the *Zattere*) to be covered up, and calls it ugly. Poor *Pan*! Will he ever see that the picture wholly depends on this mass of brown! (for reason, see *British Architect*, p.61.) *Pan* talks much of the colour in these pastels, yet fails to see how the preciousness of it is reached. Here we have not a case of liking your "own little music better," but of absolute deafness. Of course such a critic is rudely familiar, even to the flippancy of saying that the artist he is incapable of understanding "has a sort of transatlantic impudence" in his "cleverness."

And now a word or two as to Whistler's selections. Critics grumble because the artist has gone into byeways and crooked little canals for his pictures, rather than place his easel and umbrella in the grand square of St. Mark. Let us not, however, suppose because of this that the painter has failed to appreciate the great architectural remains of Venice. No one who has listened as the writer of these brief notes has to Whistler's graphic descriptions of that fairy-like, open-arcaded, winding staircase that lifts its tall stem far into the blue sky, or of those remarkable facades yet unrestored that speak of the art power of the Venetian architects, can doubt that he who can so remember and describe has failed to admire. It is by reason of the strength of this admiration and high appreciation that he holds back in reverence and exercises this reticence of the pencil, the needle, and the brush. To etch the Venus of Milo, to paint the masterpieces of Pheidias, or make pictures of the splendours of architectural genius, would be, to use his own words, "an impertinence." Things that are in themselves mighty and complete works of art should not do service to other arts. Many years ago we suggested to one of the most accomplished artists of our day certain subjects from Spenser's "Fairy Queen." The painter took home our copy of the poem and after some time brought it back with the remark that the art of the poet was so complete and so great that no room was left for any other artist. Spenser has never probably received higher praise or more profound appreciation. Precisely of the same nature is Whistler's attitude before the master works of architecture, and it would be well for art if all other artists had the same reverence.

A REGULAR BUTTERFLY IN THE WORLD OF ART (1881)

In the late summer of 1881 Whistler took up watercolour painting seriously for the first time. The results were exhibited three years later at Dowdeswells' gallery in the exhibition 'Notes – Harmonies – Nocturnes'.

Source:
'Notes on current events,' *The British Architect*, 23 September 1881, p.471

Biographical notes:
Whistler

Mr. J. A. McN. WHISTLER — like his mark — is a regular butterfly in the world of art. As an etcher the world delighted in him, but when they cried for more he was off to other sweets. Dark canvasses with full-length portraits came for

Whistler, butterfly symbol 1883.

a time uppermost, then the most exquisite harmonies in colours and nocturnes of the brush were revived. Dull Britons, mostly of amateurish excellence, rail against him through the winter, and when the spring is fairly landed he bursts upon them with the fresh plumage of his pastels. And now, whilst all are wondering at the artistic mastery, the amazingly deft handling of these bits of coloured chalk, he is off again to another field, and is wooing water-colour for the first time. His first water-colour drawing is Swan Pier and London Bridge from a low point of view, just above the pier — dull sky, Thames reflecting it, dark smoke from the boat beside the pier, mist through the arches, and vapour of multitudinous chimneys; can you not see how precious he has made it all?

THE GOLD SCAB (1882)

* Museum of Fine Arts, San Francisco

Source:
'Notes on current events', *The British Architect*, 6 January 1882, p.2

Biographical notes:
Leyland
Whistler

At the time of his bankruptcy in 1879 Whistler painted a vicious satire on F. R. Leyland entitled 'The Gold Scab'.* When it came back on the market in 1882 Godwin described the picture in some detail which must have further embarrassed Leyland.

ON Thursday, the 6th, was sold at Robinson's in Bond-street, the famous life-size full-length portrait composition by J. A. McN. Whistler, known by the curious and historical title of 'The Gold Scab.' The Devil, in the form of a peacock-man, is seated at a piano playing a piece, the title of which is 'The Gold Scab: an eruption in frillthy lucre.' The music stool is an extremely uncomfortable one for men, whatever it may be for devils, for it is formed after the model of 'The White House,' Chelsea (illustrated in the *British Architect*, vol. xii) and the performer sits on the ridge of the roof. In one of the upper corners of the picture is the well-known butterfly with a very long tail ending in a sting that touches up the pianist in the back of the neck, producing wriggling contortions. As a satire in painting, the work stands, we should think, quite alone for the free and dexterous handling of it, and is especially curious as illustrating the characteristics of our Pictor-pugnax.

AN EXERCISE IN AESTHETICISM (1884)

Source:
'To art students. Letter no.1', *The British Architect*, 2 May 1884, p.215

Biographical notes:
Burne-Jones
Grosvenor Gallery
Lindsay

** Now Tate Britain

The Grosvenor Gallery, founded by Sir Coutts and Blanche Lindsay as a showcase of Aesthetic taste, achieved a high public profile after Ruskin's comments on Whistler's pictures there in 1877 which prompted the famous libel trial. In this review of the 1884 exhibition, Godwin highlights Burne-Jones' celebrated painting 'King Cophetua and the Beggar Maid' emphasising the pure aesthetic value of colour over content, morals or pictorial accuracy; views which Whistler had outlined in a letter in 1878 and would elaborate the following year in his 'Ten O'Clock' lecture.

From end to end of the Grosvenor galleries there is, with one rare exception no important piece of colour worthy of the name. The exception is to be seen in the picture of "King Cophetua and the Beggar Maid",** by E. Burne Jones. You need not look at the armour of the king which is utterly absurd and impossible; you need not enquire too closely concerning the architectural fittings of this visionary interior, nor waste your time in criticising the ungainly length and unwholesome look of the beggar maid. What we have to do is to absorb the undoubted splendour of colour which is here set before us. And this you could do quite as well were the picture upside down. If you patiently enlarged an illumination in one of the elaborately executed manuscripts of the fifteenth century to the scale of this picture, carrying on the finish of detail in the same laborious way, I am not at all sure you would not run our modern mediaevalist very close.

You will not accept this picture for anything more than its colour, and I would particularly ask you not to expect, or, indeed look for anything else. The drawing might have been better and the story told with truer effect, but if this had been done you would probably have lost the colour, which, after all, is the chief contribution Art expects from the painter. Walk in any direction from the King Cophetua, and observe — if you care to observe sad things — how deficient the paintings are in this all-important gift. Think it over, and tell me if you fancy there is any connection between this lack of colour in the painter and the lack of colour in modern life — in dress, in architecture, in the weary plodding of unenjoyable work, the dull monotony of the habits and manners of the age.

Burne-Jones, engraving after King Cophetua and the Beggar Maid, 1884.

A WHISTLER PORTRAIT (1884)

As Godwin had praised Burne-Jones in an earlier review for his colour, here he praises Whistler for his composition and handling in a portrait at the same Grosvenor Gallery exhibition. In this case, Godwin returns to another popular theme, the unity of the arts, to suggest that architecture students should emulate Whistler's technical excellence in their own drawings. The sitter for the portrait, Lady Archibald Campbell, was a wealthy socialite and aristocrat, part of a larger circle of patrons and friends whom Godwin and Whistler had cultivated since the 1870s. That year, 1884, she sponsored the first of Godwin's open-air theatre productions at Coombe Park with her company, the 'Pastoral Players'. The Campbell family found the pose of Lady Archibald too provocative and refused to accept the portrait.* Five years later it won a gold medal at the Paris Exposition Universelle under the anonymous title La Dame au brodequin jaune, *(Woman in a Yellow Buskin).*

* Philadelphia Museum of Art.

If the full length life-size portrait of Lady Archibald Campbell, by J. M. Whistler, had been placed with the bottom of the frame touching the skirting, I would have asked you to have taken a seat opposite it and within a few yards of it; as it is, you had better look at it from the further corner of the room, and inspect the mastery of painting here displayed through a powerful opera-glass, rather than by a near approach. If Mr. Burne-Jones gives us a wealth of colour, Mr. Whistler gives us execution; and the fact that this particular portrait is in a very low key of colour makes it all the more representative of the age in which we live. But beyond the mastery of the brush here shown there is a power and originality of design rarely seen. The pose of the figure has about it

Source:
'To art students. Letter no. 2.',
The British Architect, 9 May 1884, p.225

that mingled grandeur and grace that might have even been envied by the painters of the courts of Charles V and Philip II, artists who never failed to give us grandeur but often forgot the grace; possibly because they were not so fortunate in their models as the English painter of to-day.

Now, the technical excellence of Mr. Whistler's work is what I particularly wish to impress upon you this week. If you are architects, let your drawings be technically excellent, even though you may fail at first in design, and in everything else. The very habit engendered by the quality will be reflected on other qualities. I do not mean by technical excellence of drawing, the hard sharp line of engineers' work; but drawing which whether like that of W. Burges or Viollet-le-Duc, exhibits in the clearest way your knowledge of the subject. A few rough scratches from the hand of a very great master indeed may be very charming, and eminently suggestive, for they nearly always proceed from a profound knowledge, but scratches and dots from a young gentleman who is not even a little master are in no way entertaining in as much as they must proceed from an equally profound ignorance.

WHAT IS A 'MASTER'? (1886)

Godwin's last defence of his friend Whistler in their ongoing battle against the Philistines.

Sir,

That there should be now raging in the columns of a Society journal a word battle over the painter Whistler *à propos* of his election as President of the Institute of British Artists, is in itself evidence that the influence of this craftsman or master is acknowledged as a reality even by those who would like to persuade themselves — for they are without argument to persuade others — that the man who painted the Sarasate and created the peacock-room is not a master chief or Anax* in the realm of art.

In reading the correspondence I have been impressed with the, I will not say deficient logic, for of that there is none, but rather with the singular misunderstanding of one word which it has exhibited. The word <u>Master</u> to some folk as to children carries with it rather the sense of personal control than the sense of subject knowledge. The 'master' is the man who knows, and in every craft it is this knowledge or wisdom that compels the personal following — disciple, pupil, apprentice. These may or may not come within the master's direct personal control, but their belief and veneration are there.

The correspondence shows a certain set of people who, because Whistler has asserted his individuality, and declines to 'leave it with the porter at the gate', have already, with infantine instinct, begun to dread the ferule, and are fearing to hear the phrase, *palmam qui meruit ferat.*** Mr Whistler's physical prowess, remembered in many fields may have contributed to this. The long bamboo he bears may seem a symbol of something more than elegance, and this folk unable to distinguish art, and therefore unable to recognise mastership in art, dread merely the President as a tutor, perchance anticipating that his

Biographical notes:
Burges
Burne-Jones
Campbell
Viollet-le-Duc
Whistler

Whistler's butterfly symbol.

Source:
'Whistler and the Philistines. What is a "Master?" ', unpublished letter to the editor of the *Court and Society Review*, 22 July 1886. Library of Congress PWC 14/1336-7

Biographical notes:
Whistler

* Greek for lord or master.

** 'Let he who has won the palm carry it' – a play on Whistler's long cane.

anger may be roused. This is a pity, because all this diverts attention from the real issue that J. McN. Whistler is a consummate craftsman, able to do at once the noblest portraiture and the highest decoration the modern world has seen — e.g. the peacock room, which is a poem and a series of pictures, though never, for an inch of space, failing in its unity or entangling a link of the chain of beauty the great artist forged for the house in Prince's Gate. Had the 'Mother', the 'Carlyle', the 'Sarasate'* never been painted; had the gems of water-colour drawings and the treasures of etchings been all destroyed; had we forgotten the varied delicacy of those exhibition rooms in Piccadilly and Bond Street this man has created for our joy, we should still know him to be a master so long as wall or ceiling or shutter remained of the marvellous peacock decoration.

* Paintings now in the Louvre, Glasgow Art Gallery and the Carnegie Institute Pittsburgh.

THE WELLINGTON MONUMENT (1872)

Following the death of the Duke of Wellington in 1852 a competition was set for a monument to the great man in St Paul's Cathedral. Alfred Stevens was awarded the commission in 1858. For the rest of his life he laboured on this project, but it was beset with financial problems exacerbated by the sculptor's own procrastination. A reduced version of the monument was installed in 1912.

What are the Slade professors doing? We ask the question with some anxiety, for every year reveals more clearly the incapacity of too many members of our Legislature to understand or even apprehend any question of Art. Architecture, sculpture and painting will probably linger on for years before the ordinary M.P. becomes sufficiently illuminated to perceive them. But in the meantime cannot something be done to open his eyes to the position of the architect and sculptor, as they are already open that of the painter? The most uninspired genius would surely never dream of asking Mr. Millais to paint him 100 paintings by contract, or put a frame-maker over him as a quasi-taskmaster to be responsible for the fulfilment of his contract. Yet this is exactly what has been done with Mr. Stevens. To the average public intellect architects and sculptors are nothing more than tradesmen trading in stuffs too large, unfortunately, to be included in the ordinary shop. A commission is given, and the "patron" expects his order to be attended to with just the same sort of despatch that his grocer gives him. Only a few days ago we heard of a country gentleman who, after giving an architect instructions for some extensive work, asked (in all seriousness) whether he could not have the drawings on the following evening! After this it would be mere affectation to profess surprise at any honourable member confounding architects with cabinet-makers, or sculptors with contractors.

   The pursuit of architecture or sculpture as arts is quite beyond modern comprehension. To say that designs in one or the other should be and often are the result of much thought, much brain labour, much wrestling, much critical correction, and even, in some cases, an excessive desire to be perfect, is to talk as an unbusiness-like man — and to be unbusiness-like is to make one

Source:
'The Wellington monument', *The Globe and Traveller,* 17 May 1872

Biographical notes:
Stevens
Millais

Stevens, The Wellington Monument, *Magazine of Art, 1881.*

of the mistakes that are worse than crimes in the eyes of the great powers in modern society. We would venture to say to those gentlemen who are so fond of referring to contracts, that it is of the very essence of Art that its disciples should be unbusiness-like; nay more, that it is your business-like qualities, your man-machinery (well in its place) that is undermining the whole province of Art, and that, unchecked, will bring about a degradation in architecture and sculpture by the side of which even the Georgian era will be a shining light. We see already in the works of our most prominent architects that their thoughts cannot keep pace with their business; their early works which made them famous (always supposing them to be really their own) remain their best by very many degrees, for they have secured a thriving business and become business-like.

The country ought perhaps to be congratulated on the fact that Mr. Stevens cares nothing about contracts or any other purely temporal and artificial contrivances for the regulation of society, for he is thus the more free to devote himself to what the country wants from him — the fit expression of his thought. That Mr. Stevens should require money to proceed is the accident of his surroundings. In other times he might have had, besides a fee, a palace for a studio, have lodged in royal chambers, and fed from a king's table as an honoured guest. We compound for all this payment in kind by payment in cash and force our artists to become, to some extent, business-like, or to fall victims to the butcher and baker. The worry of keeping a house was mostly unknown to the artists of old times. Living in palaces and fraternities civil or ecclesiastical, their specialities could be nourished without taking thought for the morrow, or running any risk as to the future; and out of this peaceful, thoughtful life came the works we now so wonder at and fail to emulate.

We do not expect this state of affairs to return. But changed circumstances require changed treatment of the artist. As in literature, so in architecture and the sister arts, we have discarded the single patron. The great public has taken his place, only that the great public is not the patron but the pupil or *protégé*, to be cultured and instructed. Instead of having to consult the taste of one man as to the accuracy and purity of his work, the architect has now to work for and appeal to his generation. Public appreciation means to him, as well as to the author and actor, pecuniary profit. His practice, therefore, is likely to be influenced by his mode. What the age wishes he must supply, or fail in his profession — that is, regarding it as a craft. The favourable circumstances of the ages when Art was reverenced as well as admired do not exist for him. The consequence is that he too soon discovers the bent of his new master, and, instead of following his own genius, he becomes the body-slave of the public. This is a mistake, but the necessities of the case require some compromise. Under these circumstances perhaps it is not unreasonable to expect punctuality as to time, accuracy as to estimate, and relative fitness as to design. There are men who decline to become body-slaves of the public, and who, were they to try, would fail in their attempt. They listen to the conscience of their own genius and strive to obey it. Such a man is Mr. Stevens. He has undertaken a work for the nation which shall be national in character, and fulfil the conditions of true Art.

Stevens, original design for the Wellington Monument, Arch. *29 Jan. 1876.*

THE UNION OF SCULPTURE AND BUILDING (1878)

Lamenting the poor state of design for sculpture pedestals, Godwin calls for greater sympathy and collaboration between architect and sculptor to realise the larger ambitions of these two related arts.

Statues and busts, private and public, are the every day products of our sculptors. Modern architects have not sufficient of the artist in them to feel any lively sympathy for architectonic sculpture, and we fear that even the more educated section of the English public have not yet risen to the power of appreciating the union of high class sculpture with the fine art of building. As a consequence, even that small modicum of architecture which dwells, or may dwell, in a pedestal is oft-times cruelly neglected, sometimes grossly travestied, but never fairly treated. The architect as a rule knows too little of sculpture, the sculptor is too ill acquainted with architecture for us to hope that general success in pedestals can be achieved even though their efforts be combined. A walk through London or Manchester is quite enough to show anyone how much sculpture has lost by its divorce from architecture. If the sculptor were content even to submit to the architect in this department of his work, there is not one architect in a thousand who is artistically worthy of the submission. This no doubt some sculptors feel: for the general incapacity of architects when brought face to face with any little matter involving artistic sensitiveness is still extremely lamentable. And thus it comes that the sculptor roughs out his own pedestal, or takes counsel with the marble mason over ill drawn sections of Roman mouldings and inaccurate engravings of classic models. There are only two kinds of pedestals — the pedestal proper and the bastard form got by truncation out of pillar or obelisk. [...] To remedy this state of things the sculptor must either put himself through a course of architectural training under some artistic architect, or give up pedestal designing altogether and get the work done for him by competent hands.

Source:
'A note on pedestals', *The British Architect*, 2 August 1878, p.49

C. Morgan relief sculpture for Godwin's Gillow & Co. houses in Chelsea, BA 18 Jan. 1879.

ARCHITECTURE AND SCULPTURE (1878)

This bad-tempered reproach to sculptors was no doubt prompted by Godwin's *forced inclusion of sculptural decoration on the facade of the White House, for which he selected his friend Joseph Boehm.*

[...] one good piece of properly placed sculpture of the human form is more worthy than whole cornices and cartloads of capitals of carvers' work. But then, where are your sculptors? Mr. Boehm, A.R.A., is modest enough and artist enough to incorporate his work with that of the architect. Mr. McLean and Mr. Woolner, R.A., may be anxious enough to follow the same path, but a profound ignorance of monumental art — that is, of sculptural and painted architecture — is the special shortcoming of modern sculptors and painters. Like the easel picture, which is the beginning and the end of a modern painter's work, so the bust and the isolated statue are the beginning and end of the sculptor's ambition.

Source:
'Notes on current events', *The British Architect*, 15 November 1878, p.188

Biographical notes:
Boehm
McLean
Woolner

And it is not merely that they are ignorant; they are wilfully indifferent. They fail to see that there are architects whose artistic power in architecture is no less — sometimes vastly more — than theirs in painting or sculpture. And they are occasionally found — worse than all — interfering with bumptious self-assertion in architects' work, or bungling with amusing conceit over designs for mantelpieces and other internal fittings.

A LIFE-LIKE STATUE OF J. S. MILL (1878)

While praising the contemporary dress in this statue of Mill, a figure widely admired in liberal circles, Godwin finds the seating too commode-like for comfort.

MR. WOOLNER'S bronze statue of the late John Stuart Mill, erected on the Thames embankment, a little to the west of the Temple, was uncovered on Saturday. The figure is in a sitting posture; the right arm and left leg are drawn back and the body thrown forward, a situation that may be characteristic, but is open to objection on the ground that it suggests the straining of certain muscles, and lacks both dignity and repose. Mr. Woolner has worked in the ultra naturalistic spirit and admirers of Mr. Mill will be thankful to the sculptor for this life-like portrait, not only of face and hands, but of coat, trousers, and necktie. When, however, a sculptor goes so far as this, he should, we venture to think, go further as Monti, McLean, and other naturalistic sculptors have done, and provide the figure with an appropriate seat, such an one, that is, as the living man commonly used. In this case the figure of Mr. Mill is seated on a solid block of bronze, without back or arms, and is suggestive, in part of a sarcophagus wine cooler, and in part of another piece of domestic furniture, not much used in our day.

LADY SCULPTORS (1878)

Another instance of Godwin's support for women's professional involvement in the arts.

The committee for the Burns monument, Dumfries, have selected a design by Mrs. D. O. Hill, of Edinburgh.[...] The ranks of painters and sculptors are so rapidly filling up with ladies that architecture may fairly expect an early summons to open her gates. Indeed it is not a little surprising that no lady architect has yet appeared. Mrs. Hill and her pedestals will no doubt develop something. Meanwhile there is no reason why ladies should not be encouraged to enter the profession, which is certainly not less feminine than the occupations of the sculptor or the wall decorator, and not a whit more masculine than the faculty of medicine.

Woolner's statue of J. S. Mill, Punch 26 Nov. 1881, p.252.

Source:
'Notes on current events', *The British Architect*, 1 February 1878, p.53

Biographical notes:
Mill
Woolner

Source:
'Notes on current events', *The British Architect*, 1 February 1878, p.53

Biographical notes:
Hill

XVI *Tributes, Insults, Obituaries*

In both his professional and private life Godwin was fairly free with his opinions, so it is not surprising that he should have generated strong views in others. Like that of Whistler and Wilde, his artistry was widely recognised but the self-conscious pose of disdainful superiority that this group adopted towards those who did not share their values nade the Aesthetes anathema to mainstream taste. It was only at his death in 1886 that Godwin's career as a whole was reviewed and the fragmentary nature of his various interests considered as part of a larger pursuit.

EXTENDING THE BOUNDARIES OF CIVILISATION (1872)

Mr. Godwin has gone beyond most people's notions of the boundaries of civilisation, and has added Japan to the list of authorities worth copying. [...] He appears to be perplexed by a divided duty between Ireland and Japan, with an occasional leaning to the Mediaeval glories of Europe. The *divided duty*, as we have called it, may possibly turn out to be but one, for we believe Mr. Godwin has somewhere written on the marked similarity in feeling as well as in form, between Ireland and Japan in the construction of much of their ornamental design [...] One of these diagonal interlacing patterns in the Lambeth Aldhelm only wants the omission of the smallest fraction of a line to become the common diagonal T pattern of Japan, and China, and this it is which Mr. Godwin has enlarged to a useful scale for ordinary wallpaper.

Source:
'Wall-papers', *Building News*, 11 October 1872, p.291

A 'HARMONY' IN YELLOW AND GOLD? (1878)

Mr. E. W. GODWIN, F.S.A., has contributed a design, executed by Mr. WILLIAM WATT, of a drawing-room suite in mahogany, very light in colour, and absolutely without figure or grain [...] a brown carpet covers the floor, and the decorative work has been designed and painted in a very *yellow* yellow and gold by Mr. J. A. McN. Whistler. Like the celebrated "Blue Boy" picture, this room seems to have been designed chiefly with the view of overcoming self-imposed difficulties, and beyond the fact that the difficulties have been treated in a most masterly way and overcome so far as it is possible, this exhibit calls for no comment. To the "jaundiced eye" of a critic it is certainly not worth anything except as an example not to be followed; and as the wood becomes darker in tone, the yellow satin fades, the brown carpet turns grey, the gold tarnishes, and the wall paint gets darker, the effect, which entirely depends on the exact balance of yellows, browns and gold, will in the course of time become very peculiar. As an experiment in colour the whole is clever, and exhibits great knowledge; but as a room to live in day after day, it would never be bearable. The key is too high, and exerts a stimulating strain utterly destructive of any feeling of calm repose. Such a drawing-room after dinner might

Source:
The Furniture Gazette, 7 September 1878, p.l60

harmonise with the colour of the coffee and heighten the complexions of the ladies, but what about the digestion?

The Furniture Gazette, 15 February 1879, p.108

To justify so strong an opinion we publish sketches nos. 1 & 2 [...]. No. 1 represents the upper portion of "the Butterfly Cabinet," a design from the pencil of Mr. E. W. Godwin, F.S.A., made by Mr. Watt and decorated by Mr. Whistler. Knowing these gentlemen to be exponents of "furniture art," we were induced to compare their published opinions with their productions, and we give our readers the curious result. Mr. Watt remarks:— "We cannot fail to be conscious of an awakening of the spirit of the beautiful among us in our everyday life." As to the drawing-room:— "Here things that can lay claim to grace, elegance, and lightness should find themselves at home." (see figures 1 and 2.) He asks for "economy, utility, fitness, suitability, beauty," for instance, the Butterfly Cabinet, &c., price some two hundred guineas! "Look," says Mr. Godwin, "at the worse than childish paintings on the panels of modern furniture." And we look at the mysterious splashes of gold on the cabinet (merely indicated in our sketch) as we try to grasp the form of the butterflies and the subtle idea of Mr. Whistler. No doubt the number of mythical insects on the article may account for the "economy" of the production. [...] We may be told that the motif is Japanese; it may be Chinese; but there is no comfort to the perplexed and weary sitter in the thought and we object to such productions being credited to a people distinguished for suitability as well as pure art.

A RENAISSANCE MAN (1878)

Source:
'Notes on current events', *The British Architect*, 4 January 1878, p.8

... whether it be a large and important building, a charming suite of furniture, a racy article or a diminutive piece of ornamentation, [Godwin] seems equally at home and is equally effective.

THE GREAT MAN MILLINER (1886)

Source:
J. Coleman, 'The Fool's Revenge', *Dramatic Review*, 7 August 1886, pp.11-12

... let us now take our hats off to Godwin, the renowned; Godwin, the architect and archaeologist, Godwin the manager and stage manager; Godwin the scene painter and inventor of the Pastoral Player; Godwin the Great Man Milliner!

OSCAR WILDE ON *HELENA IN TROAS* (1886)

Source:
O. Wilde, 'Helena in Troas', *Dramatic Review*, 22 May 1886, pp.161-2

The historical accuracy that underlies the visible shapes of beauty that he presents to us, is not by any means the distinguishing quality of the completed work of art. This quality is the absolute unity and harmony of the entire presentation, and presence of one mind controlling the most minute details, and revealing itself only in that true perfection that hides personality.

A SOCIAL SNAKE

I have an intense objection to your being engaged in any scheme *whatsoever* in which you work hand and glove with Mr. Godwin [...]

Today for the first time Emmie asked me who this Mr. Godwin was — and when I told her 'the architect' she was *quite* horrified — utterly disgusted at the idea of my ever having known such a man. She knows something about him, I suppose — at all events says he is such a man as she would no more shake hands with than with a snake.

Source:
Letter from Maud Holt to her fiancé, Herbert Beerbohm Tree, August 1882

THE WICKED EARL

The architect E. W. Godwin—or "the wicked Earl," as some of his friends called him—was one of the most fascinating of men. He worshipped Greek art. He was the only man I knew who has a life-sized figure of the Venus of Milo in his chambers. [...] In looks he was like a portrait of Henry IV of France, but his soul must have been a reincarnation of a Greek sculptor.

Source:
Louise Jopling, *Twenty Years of My Life*, London 1925, pp.289-90

KING AMONG ARTISTS

> Man of men, born to be general king,
> By frank election of the artist kind,
> Attempting all things, and on anything
> Setting the signet of a master mind.
> What others dreamed amiss, he did aright,
> His dreams were visions of art's golden age,
> Yet self betrayed he fell in Fortune's spite
> His royal birthright sold for scanty wage.

Source:
Unpublished sonnet, perhaps by Ellen Terry, found among her papers

POET OF ARCHITECTS

Poet of architects and architect of all the arts, he possessed that rare gift, a feeling for the very essence of Beauty wherever and whenever it was found. The arts seemed to yield their secrets to him, and for him Nature opened her scroll, while with exquisite spirit of choice, and delicate tact of omission, he would, from both of these worlds of wonder, select all congruous elements of beauty and of strength and combine them into works of perfect symmetry and right proportion.

Source:
Lady Jane Campbell, *Rainbow-music; or, the Philosophy of Harmony in Colour-grouping*, London, 1886

OBITUARY: *THE BUILDING NEWS AND ENGINEERING JOURNAL*

A BRILLIANT, if somewhat eccentric, character, who might, under happier conditions of life, have become the first architect of his age [...] Mr. Godwin was in many respects a remarkable man, a facile sketcher, a good draughts-

Source:
'The late E. W. Godwin, F.S.A.', *Building News*, 15 October 1886, p.589

man, with a quick eye for harmonious grouping and proportions; a clear writer, an antiquarian, well versed in the architecture, furniture and costumes of all periods, a well-informed Shakespearian scholar, an excellent lecturer; as a setter of plays unsurpassed;— yet his life, though reaching nearly threescore years, has been, for the most part, one of unfulfilled promise.

OBITUARY: *THE ARCHITECT*

Source:
'The Week', *Architect*, 15
October 1886, p.217

EDWARD GODWIN was so distinct a personality in the little world of art that a void is left by his death which is not easily filled. Although he was neither painter nor sculptor, yet so well had he mastered their relationship with architecture that he might be said to belong to all three branches of art, and in that sense he resembled the Renaissance artists. As became a man who had made a speciality of Gothic, he was an archaeologist, but not in the usual sense of that word. To his mind the past was something more than a mouldering skeleton. It lived for him, and buildings were only a background for figures. It was an easy transition when EDWARD GODWIN passed from the architecture of the fourteenth century to the poems of CHAUCER, and when he passed from a study of SHAKESPEARE'S characters to the buildings in which they were supposed to live. He was learned without having a particle of the DRYASDUST about him. As an architect he was less fortunate than his friend BURGES in obtaining opportunities to prove his powers, and his best designs are to be found only on paper. There is enough of them to show that he could impart grace to small as well as large works. Like all men, he was not without his weaknesses. EDWARD GODWIN assumed an air of superiority at times, but he found many who willingly recognised his right to it. We have often thought that his removal to London did not help him as an artist. He found here too many distractions. If he had remained in Bristol he must have been more successful as an architect, and that means an enrichment of English architecture. Many of his friends believed that he might have been the first architect in England.

OBITUARY: *THE BRITISH ARCHITECT*

Source:
'Edward W. Godwin', *The
British Architect*, 15 October
1886, pp.347-8

Edward W. Godwin died on the 6th inst., at his chambers in Great College Street, Westminster, at a quarter to twelve, the day of the week and the hour singularly coinciding precisely with the time of the decease of his old friend William Burges, on the 20th of April, 1881. As yet, we can hardly realise the loss which has befallen the profession, so short a time does it seem since we met him apparently in his usual health. All the old enthusiasm lighted up his face as he conversed with us on the topics so dear to his heart, and the quips and anecdotes with which he generally enlivened his talk were told as vivaciously as ever. Outwardly, there was nothing indicative of the ravages which the harass and bustle of theatrical business were making upon his constitution. But we have no doubt in our own mind that it was this work which hastened his end. To sit down and design costumes and scenery for a play is one thing, and to superintend their production is another, especially where, as in Godwin's case, absolute correctness of detail is taken to be the essential and all-important element of success. Take for example, his work in the production of "Claudian" at the Princess's. The vivid reality of the scene in the prologue was surely never surpassed; no person, however insignificant in the plot, no portion in the scenery, and no article brought on to the stage seemed to have escaped his attention. In the same way, his Greek play, "Helena in Troas," showed an artistic ensemble the peculiar characteristic of which was its thoroughness. It was indeed this patient earnestness of spirit and painstaking attention to detail which gave to all Godwin's work that subtle charm of finish and completeness which characterised it.

But, besides his skill as an artist and his thoroughness as a workman, a prominent feature in Godwin's work in connection with the stage was his wonderful knowledge and grasp of archaeological details. This is evidenced in those carefully designed costumes for "Othello," "As you Like it," "Merchant of Venice," "Romeo and Juliet," and "Hamlet", which have been published in the *British Architect* (and in which, we believe, Mrs. Godwin, herself an accomplished artist, greatly assisted him), and in his criticisms of stage mounting which have appeared from time to time in these columns. Theatrical work seems ever to have had a fascination for him... he held strong views on the subject of theatre construction, and constantly insisted in this journal on the absolute necessity for a reform the usually accepted notions of theatre design. His own ideas as to how a theatre should be built were fully expressed in an article published in *the British Architect* of January the 18th, 1878, and there can be little doubt that, had he been called upon to put his theories into practice, the result would have been a unique example of this class of building construction.

Edward Gordon Craig, idealised portrait of his father, Godwin, from The Mask, *Oct.1910.*

Godwin's success as an architect is not to be measured by the standard of that attained by his more popular rivals. He was no more an architect than an archaeologist, and no more these than a decorator. It was this very versatility of his genius which at times led him into work which more or less interfered with a close abidance within the strict limits of architectural practice. Yet we know of no architect of recent times whose work has maintained such an even plane of the highest merit as that of Godwin's. His wonderful originality and power in design and his consummate skill were ever balanced by a keen critical judgment, which admitted of no slackening of individual effort to produce the best art of which he was capable. No one more fully realised or more adequately expressed in their work, the meaning of the "art of architecture" than did Godwin. His sense of proportion, colour and form in relation to style, and apart from and above all question of mere style at all, was a unique attribute of the man's artistic genuis. There was, too, a marvellous power of restraint in the decorative treatment of his architectural work. No useless bits of ornament found a resting-place on the exterior of his buildings, and he gave us instead beauty of outline and exquisite proportion, which were all the more thrown into relief by the absence of all fussy or meaningless ornamentation. His knowledge of Greek art was almost, if not quite, as extensive and thorough as that of Gothic, and we might perhaps say his appreciation of it as well. A list of his executed works would not indicate the extent of his powers, for his opportunities (and he had many) were not equal to his great capacity. Such a small and simple work, however, as the Congleton Town Hall would well suffice to show his skill in matters of proportion. [...]

Of all the cognate arts which go with and make up architecture Godwin possessed a masterly knowledge. The introduction of the specialist system, whereby one man designs the carcase of a building, another is responsible for the decoration, and a third takes in hand the furniture, he specially abhorred. If he for ever pleaded for a greater reconciliation between the decorative and constructive arts, and contended that the decorator and cabinet-maker should be as much subject to the architect as any other contractor about the building. He, however, went so far as to admit the possible good of one artist-architect consulting another artist-architect on artistic questions, such as proportion, distribution of sculpture, and the like. He designed a large amount of furniture, erring sometimes, we think, in what we might term over-elegance, the proportions being often too slight for strength. His Anglo-Japanese designs were, perhaps, more suited to a proper use of wood in design than any other modern furniture we have seen.

The present heading for the *British Architect* was designed by him in 1877. It was, perhaps, chiefly as an architectural art critic and a consulting architect that Godwin was best known to outsiders in the profession. As a critic of architecture we never knew his equal in some respects, and we imagine there were few men whose favourable judgment in architectural matters was more esteemed. He was a thorough artist, with all an artist's keen sensitiveness to the faults of others in work of which he was himself a master-hand. It worried and pained him dreadfully to look upon a badly-drawn picture, or an ill conceived design, and this sensitiveness often led him to give his opinion in somewhat strong and forcible language. But though he was vigorous and outspoken in his criticisms, sometimes even to bitterness, we never knew him to be unjust to others or untrue to his own convictions, and his conclusions were always logical. Criticism with him meant "the truth, the whole truth, and nothing but the truth" and if he could by his criticism lead anyone to do better things, or induce someone to abandon a hopeless pursuit, he counted it as a gain to art. But in all his writing there was the ring of true metal. Of masterly mind and intellect, and endowed with the instinctive perception of right and wrong which is the natural birthright of the genuine artist, he attached to his profession a dignity which, we fear, is not so generally understood and appreciated amongst architects as it ought to be. His views as to the position of an artist were widely divergent from those held by some, who would put architects and artists on a dead level with mere craftsmen, to count in rank and file with working carpenters and masons. This exaggeration of humbleness had no charm or meaning for him, who ranked a thinking, accomplished artist with princes and nobles, and who insisted upon the necessity for a modern architect having literary and studious accomplishments besides all business capacity and powers of drawing and design. The constant aim in his writings was to elevate the standard of the profession, both by pointing out the weak points in the constitution of architects as a body and by indicating the many ways by which they might protect themselves against the wrongs which they have been so long content to suffer at the hands of the British public.

Not only, however, was he a true friend to the practising portion of the profession by his advocacy of what he esteemed good, and his denunciation of what he regarded as bad, but his knowledge of the wants of students, and his sympathy with them, was strikingly shown by much that he said and did. He had, it is true, little sympathy for superficial brilliancy of attainments, but the earnest, painstaking student ever found in him a ready and sympathetic adviser. What could be more helpful, for instance, than his criticisms upon the work submitted to his examination from time to time by the members of the *British Architect* Art Club? That they were thoroughly appreciated, even when most condemnatory, we know for a fact. Take, also, the short series of letters to art students, [...], and note how much to the purpose are all his remarks. Certainly Godwin was as gifted in his power of imparting knowledge to others as he was in his accumulation of it. He arrested attention, first, by showing his readers he had something to tell them which they would like to know, and then he retained their interest by imparting it to them in that pleasant, crisp style, so peculiarly his own. [...]

The late
E·W·Godwin

Sketch of Godwin published with the British Architect *obituary.*

Of Godwin as a man, apart from his professional career; we can only say that his temperament was hardly calculated to attract close friendship, but he was extremely genial and pleasant company, and in all matters of art — of design, drawing and decoration his enthusiasm could always be drawn forth. He had a very dignified appearance, having a tall upright figure, dark moustachios and beard (the latter he recently discarded), and grey hair. He had a powerful voice and emphatic pronunciation and could read with considerable effect. Perhaps he never appeared to greater personal advantage than when he came upon the stage of his extemporised Greek theatre at Hengler's Cirque in response to calls for "Godwin" at the close of the performance. [...]

We have spoken of Godwin as we knew him. As an architect we consider he had no compeer in England. Other architects may be as clever in some respects, and may have produced designs as pleasing and correct, and have been infinitely more practical and skilled in the conduct of their professional engagements, but as an artist-architect of varied accomplishments and catholic sympathy Godwin was in our opinion without a rival. It must, however, be a matter for the keenest regret that through untoward circumstances (not altogether, perhaps, of his own creation) he failed to leave an impression on English art equivalent to his great capabilities.

The sketch likeness we give this week is not taken from a very recent photograph, but it exactly expresses his attitude of intent and careful observation when making a study of some object or other, notebook and pencil in hand.

Biographical Notes

Aitchison, George (1825–1910) Leading architect of the late Victorian period although very little of his work survives. Aitchison was best known for his interiors on which he employed many of the finest mural and decorative painters, including Frederic **Leighton**, Albert **Moore** and Thomas **Armstrong**. In 1864 Leighton returned to his old employer, commissioning a house from Aitchison at Melbury Road, the finest example of the architect's work. Aitchison became President of the **RIBA** in 1896.

Alma-Tadema, Sir Lawrence (1836–1912) Dutch-born painter who achieved great success after moving to Britain in 1870 for his pictures of daily life in the ancient world. A trip to Pompeii in 1863 converted him from medieval to Classical subjects, which he depicted as period genre scenes in elaborate architectural settings. His closely studied treatment of marble and textiles, linked to a smooth refined technique, lent his historical views great veracity, although his later work was criticised for moral vacuousness and overt sensuality. Such was his success by the 1880s that he was able to build a huge Pompeiian-style villa as a studio-house in St John's Wood.

Bibl: V. Swanson, *The Biography and Catalogue Raisonné of the Paintings of Sir Lawrence Alma Tadema*, London, 1990

The Architectural Association (AA) Founded in 1847 by a group of disaffected students from the Association of Architectural Draughtsmen. Led by Robert **Kerr** and Charles Grey the new organisation was 'an endeavour towards an improved system of architectural study – an endeavour on the part of the students themselves'. At a time when there was no formal training available, the AA became the first independent school of architecture in Britain although it was not until 1890 that it was able to offer formal qualifications. The early history of the AA was shaped by prominent visitors, notably **Ruskin** and G. G. **Scott**, but by the later 19th century it had developed a strong bias towards the Arts and Crafts Movement. Architects who studied there include Phillip **Webb**, Edwin Lutyens and C. F. A. Voysey.

Armstrong, Thomas (1832–1911) English painter and designer whose depictions of idealised women in classical and rural settings exemplified 'Aesthetic' taste of the 1870s and 80s. Armstrong trained in Paris in 1853–6 where he shared lodgings with J. M. **Whistler**, E. J. **Poynter** and George **Du Maurier**. This period of bohemian life furnished much of the material for Du Maurier's novel *Trilby* (1894). Armstrong took an active interest in domestic and ecclesiastical decoration, stained glass design and dress reform. He was also involved in art education, serving as Director of Art at the **South Kensington** Schools from 1881 to 1898.

Bibl: L. Lamont, *Thomas Armstrong, CB: A Memoir*, London, 1912

Arnold, Matthew (1822–88) Poet, critic and Oxford Professor of Poetry, also a school inspector for much of his life. Most of Arnold's poetry was written by 1855, after which he devoted himself to improving cultural standards in an age he felt was marked by materialism, narrowness and 'Philistinism'. His essays upheld ideals of aesthetic and moral quality, looking to literature and the arts to lead modern society to a higher spiritual level.

Bancroft, Squire (1841–1926) and **Marie** (1839–1921) Theatre managers who in 1875 brought Ellen **Terry** back to the London stage as Portia in *The Merchant of Venice*. As historical adviser Godwin attempted to implement his views on archaeological accuracy, basing the costumes on paintings by Veronese (although it seems likely that they were not made up entirely to his designs). Despite mixed reviews the production appealed to the Aesthetes. Terry later recalled that a 'poetic and artistic atmosphere pervaded the front of the house as well as the stage itself'.

Bibl: S. Bancroft, *The Bancrofts: Recollections of Sixty Years*, London, 1911

Barker, Lady Mary Anne (1831–1911) Author whose accounts of colonial life were very popular. She also worked as a journalist and wrote advice on household taste including *The Bedroom and the Boudoir* of 1878.

Barnard, Bishop & Barnard's Iron foundry established in Norwich in 1826 which became the leading producer of domestic metalwork in the second half of the 19th century. The 'Norwich Gates', designed by Thomas **Jeckyll**, were acclaimed at the 1862 International Exhibition in London, prompting a revival in wrought ironwork. Jeckyll also designed their pagoda-like pavilion in cast iron for the Philadelphia Centennial Exposition (1876) which was much admired and subsequently re-erected at Paris in 1878. Andirons adapted from the sunflower balustrade of this structure became icons of Aestheticism.

Barry, Sir Charles (1795–1860) Eclectic English architect whose travels in Italy fostered a taste for the Renaissance manner known as 'Anglo-Italian'. This is apparent in the Travellers' Club (1831) and the Reform Club (1837) in London, both of which emulate Renaissance palace designs. Following the destruction by fire of the Houses of Parliament in 1834, Barry won the competition for the new buildings. Working with **Pugin**, he was able to create a Gothic Revival masterpiece which met the terms of the brief although the basic form and plan of the buildings is essentially Italianate. Pugin's mastery of detail was largely responsible for the success of the building although Barry was the principal architect.

Beresford-Hope MP, Alexander (1820–87) Son of the Neo-classical designer Thomas Hope and ardent member of the **Cambridge Camden Society**, he was a founder and President of the **Ecclesiological Society** which advocated the Gothic as the only style appropriate for church buildings. High Tory and High Church Anglican, he campaigned for richer decoration in churches and gave funds for church building and improvements, notably at All Saints' Margaret Street and Kilndown in Surrey. He was elected President of the **RIBA** in 1865.

Blomfield, Arthur William (1829–99) English architect, son of the Bishop of London, who established his reputation with parish churches in the Gothic Revival style but moved on to a more eclectic manner in the 1880s. He was appointed President of the **AA** in 1861 and knighted in 1889.

Bloxam, Matthew (1805–88) Solicitor and antiquary who first reported the story of William Webb Ellis and the invention of Rugby football. His book *The Principles of Gothic Ecclesiastical Architecture* (1829) was a key source, going into many editions throughout the 19th century.

Bodley, George Frederick (1827–1907) Architect and designer whose training under G. G. **Scott** fostered a devotion to 14th-century English Gothic. He became one of the leading ecclesiastical architects of the high Victorian period, designing a series of impressive parish churches as well as cathedrals in San Francisco, Tasmania and Washington DC. Bodley's early friendship with

the Pre-Raphaelites and the leading figures of the Arts and Crafts Movement encouraged his interest in the domestic interior and he produced a number of striking designs for furniture, wallpaper and textiles.

Bibl: D. Verey, 'George Frederick Bodley: the climax of the Gothic Revival', in J. Fawcett, ed., *Seven Victorian Architects*, London, 1976

Boehm, Joseph Edgar (1834–90) Austro-Hungarian sculptor who trained in Vienna, London and Paris before settling in London and, in 1865, taking British nationality. Boehm was committed to progressive ideas and modern subject matter in sculpture believing that character should be revealed 'instinctively' instead of by sculptural conventions. He was a successful portraitist and undertook many statues including those of General Gordon in St Paul's Cathedral, and Wellington at Hyde Park Corner. Although a full RA, and eventually knighted, he was a popular figure in Aesthetic circles, a teacher of **Princess Louise** and a close friend of Godwin and **Whistler**.

Bowman, Henry (1814–83) **& Crowther, Joseph S.** (1832–93) Manchester-based architectural practice responsible for many Gothic Revival churches in the north of England between the 1840s and 1870s. They also wrote *The Ecclesiastical Architecture of Great Britain* (1845) and a series of illustrated books entitled *The Churches of the Middle Ages* (1845–53).

Brandon, David (1813–97) English architect, partner of T. H. **Wyatt** from 1838 to 1851, and designer of country houses such as Falconhurst Lodge, Kent (1851) in the Jacobean style.

Brandon, Raphael (1817–77) English architect and co-author, with his brother Joshua, of *An Analysis of Gothick Architecture* (1844).

Broughton, Rhoda (1840–1920) English novelist, whose characters, often female, were driven by strong psychological forces. Her novel *The Temple Bar* (1872) was of interest to Godwin, who wrote a pamphlet on the architecture of this monument.

Brown, Ford Madox (1821–93) English painter whose meticulous technique and use of 'primitive' sources was an inspiration to the younger artists who in 1848 formed the Pre-Raphaelite Brotherhood. Although never a member of the Brotherhood, Brown shared their principles and remained a close friend of their circle. In 1861, alongside William **Morris** and Dante Gabriel **Rossetti**, he became a founding partner of Morris, Marshall, Faulkner & Co. for whom he designed furniture and stained glass. In 1878 he was commissioned to undertake a series of murals for the interior of Manchester Town Hall.

Bibl: K. Bendiner, *The Art of Ford Madox Brown*, Philadelphia, 1997

Brunel, Isambard Kingdom (1806–59) Civil and marine engineer responsible for some of the most ambitious projects of the Victorian age including the Clifton Suspension Bridge (1839), the Great Eastern steamship (1852–8) and the Great Western Railway. Bold and experimental in approach, his control of projects was often wayward, leading to delays and increased expense.

Bibl: R. A. Buchanan, *The Life and Times of Isambard Kingdom Brunel*, London, 2002

Burges, William Burges (1827–81) English architect and designer notable for the eclecticism and flamboyance of his work, whether massive building projects or individual domestic items such as an inkstand. Son of a wealthy engineer, Burges pursued his interest in Gothic architecture on extensive travels across Europe which served him well in his future career. He trained in the office of Matthew Digby **Wyatt**, whom he assisted in various aspects of the Great Exhibition, including the two-volume record entitled *The Industrial Arts of the Nineteenth Century* (1851–3). Burges's early career as an architect was marked by a series of successes in major competitions, none of which was built until 1863, when he won the competition for St Finn Bar's Cathedral, Cork. Soon after this he met the Marquess of Bute, an aristocrat of colossal wealth who commissioned him to build a castle at Cardiff on the ruins of a medieval pile. Burges worked on the building for the rest of his life, adding new towers and wings to create a medieval fantasy in which the interiors were elaborately furnished and decorated in thematic schemes. In 1871 Bute commissioned Castell Coch from Burges, another castle outside Cardiff to be used as an occasional residence which was still unfinished at his death. Burges also designed houses and churches as well as individual items of furniture and decorative arts, each of which reveals something of his idiosyncratic yet masterly design skills. His own house, The Tower House (1875–81) at Melbury Road, London, has a plain brick exterior of bold interlocking forms, but the interior was an extravagant display of integrated design combining painted furniture, murals and decorative arts derived from a wide range of exotic and historical sources. This revealed

the wit and diversity of Burges, admired by Godwin, in contrast to the didacticism and moralising which dominated much design debate in the high Victorian period.

Bibl: J. M. Crook, *William Burges and the High Victorian Dream*, London, 1981

Burnand, Sir Francis (1836–1917) Editor of ***Punch*** and author of comic plays, including *The Colonel* (1881), with music by Arthur Sullivan, which anticipated **Gilbert and Sullivan**'s *Patience* in parodying the style and manners of the Aesthetes.

Burne-Jones, Edward Coley (1833–98) The greatest and most enigmatic of the later Pre-Raphaelites, Burne-Jones aspired to pure idealism in his art by depicting mythic themes using wistful androgynous figures. He began studying theology at Oxford alongside William **Morris** but the two students were recruited by **Rossetti** to assist in the decoration of the Oxford Union. This inspired Burne-Jones to become a painter and, with **Ruskin**'s support, he gradually achieved success. By the 1870s he had developed his mature style and attracted a circle of wealthy Aesthetic patrons, notably the Ionides family. He remained a close friend of William Morris, collaborating on many designs for stained glass, tapestries and books. In 1878 Burne-Jones gave evidence for Ruskin in the famous trial with **Whistler**, despite having exhibited alongside Whistler at the **Grosvenor Gallery**.

Bibl: S. Wildman & J. Christian, eds, *Edward Burne-Jones: Victorian Artist-Dreamer*, Birmingham, 1998

Burnet, John (1814–1901) Leading Glasgow architect responsible for several imposing Gothic churches and commercial building in the city. His Glasgow Stock Exchange (1875–7) was a close adaptation of Burges's design for the Law Courts (1866).

Butterfield, William (1814–1900) Leading architect of the Gothic Revival in the High Victorian period, noted for the strength of his convictions and for his attempts to forge a manner of building appropriate to modern life from the repertoire of the Gothic. Although he did serve part of an apprenticeship, Butterfield was largely self-taught. He set up his own practice in London in 1840 and four years later joined the **Ecclesiological Society**, which opened up several commissions for church building and restoration. His most famous church, All Saints' Margaret Street in London (1849–59), established the distinctive features of his architecture: local and modern building materials (brick), bold angular forms, and polychromatic decoration on the exterior and interior. A devout High Church Anglican, Butterfield designed several cathedrals (Perth in Scotland, Adelaide and Melbourne in Australia), but was equally famous for his university buildings, notably Keble College Oxford (1875). His Highbury Chapel, built opposite Godwin's school, inspired the youth to take up architecture. Godwin felt honoured, therefore, when in 1862 he won the competition to enlarge the building.

Bibl: P. Thompson, *William Butterfield*, Cambridge, Mass., 1971

Caldecott, Randolph (1846–86) English illustrator who took up an art career despite family opposition. After training at the **Slade** School under **Poynter**, he began illustrating books in 1874 and was soon contributing drawings to ***Punch*** and *The Graphic*. In 1878 he produced his first 'Shilling Toy Books' with coloured illustrations engraved by Edmund Evans, which appeared every year in pairs until his death. More naturalistic than Walter **Crane** and more amusing than Kate **Greenaway**, Caldecott's children's books have an earthy side while preserving the artistry of his drawings. He collaborated with his friend Thomas **Armstrong** on the murals for Bank Hall.

Cambridge Camden Society Founded in 1839 by a group of Cambridge University dons and students to revive interest in medieval church architecture and liturgy, the society was soon associated with the so-called 'Catholic Revival' in the Anglican church. Theological disputes aside, the CCS was notable for rallying the archaeological interests of Gothic Revival architects and antiquarians. The society's journal *The Ecclesiologist*, launched in 1841, became an important forum for research in medieval architecture and decorative arts. In 1845 the CCS was renamed the Ecclesiological Society and from its London base continued to exercise great influence over the design of churches and their furnishings.

Campbell, Lady Archibald (1845–1923) 'Lady Archie', née Janey Sevilla Callander, married Lord Archibald Campbell, 2nd son of the Duke of Argyll in 1869. From this position of wealth and social status she was able to pursue her interest in art, dress reform and the theatre, creating her own company of actors, the Pastoral Players, for which she wrote, directed and occasionally acted. She enlisted Godwin's support, giving him the opportunity to realise some of his most ambitious ideas about stage design and production in a series of plays performed in the open air, first at Coombe Wood, Surrey in 1884–5,

and then at Wimbledon in 1886. With **Whistler** she attended Godwin on his deathbed.

Carlyle, Thomas (1795–1881) Scottish historian and essayist whose impassioned writings had a powerful effect on Victorian values. His studies of Schiller, Goethe and Frederick the Great helped introduce German culture to British readers but he also wrote famous books on the French Revolution (1837) and Oliver Cromwell (1845), which expressed his views on the importance of 'Great Men'. *Sartor Resartus* (1834) demonstrated many of his distinctive qualities, not least the intuitive use of language ('Carlylese') which often led him to invent new words. He and his formidable wife, Jane Welsh, were neighbours of **Whistler** in Chelsea and the artist painted a portrait of Carlyle in 1873.

Carr, Jonathan (1845–1915) Merchant and property speculator responsible for the middle-class housing development called **Bedford Park** in west London. He employed both Godwin and R. Norman **Shaw** as architects.

Carr, Joseph W. Comyns (1849–1916) Journalist, critic and playwright who in 1877 became assistant manager of the **Grosvenor Gallery**, responsible for establishing its reputation as a centre of Aestheticism in the arts. In 1887 he set up the New Gallery with Charles Hallé which carried on the ideals of the Grosvenor. Comyns Carr's wife, **Alice** (1850–1927), was a novelist and friend of Ellen **Terry**, for whom she designed several costumes.

Bibl: J. Comyns Carr, *Some Eminent Victorians*, London, 1908; E. Adam, ed., *Mrs Comyns Carr's Reminiscences*, London, 1926

Champneys, Basil (1842–1935) English architect in the 'Queen Anne' style best known for schools and university buildings, including Newnham College Cambridge (1878–9). Despite his sympathy for the style, Godwin was critical of Champneys' work as attractive but occasionally crude and superficial.

Bibl: D. Watkin. *The Architecture of Basil Champneys*, Cambridge, 1989

Chaucer, Geoffrey (c.1343–1400) Courtier and poet best known for *The Canterbury Tales* (c.1387), a sequence of stories recounted by pilgrims on route to the shrine at Canterbury cathedral. Chaucer was much admired by Victorians, particularly those like the Pre-Raphaelites interested in the Middle Ages, and he came to be regarded as the father of the native tradition of English literature.

Chute, James Henry (d.1878) Manager of the Theatre Royal in King Street, Bristol, where the young Kate and Ellen **Terry** performed. Godwin regularly reviewed productions and occasionally advised on costume and stage design.

Clayton & Bell English stained glass manufacturers founded in 1857 by draughtsmen from G. G. **Scott**'s office. Working in a medievalising style, with clear primary colours, they soon became the leading firm supplying windows for the many Gothic Revival churches which were being built throughout Britain. They also produced mosaics and mural designs from their London studios.

Cockerell, Charles Robert (1788–1863) English architect and archaeologist whose early travels and excavations in Greece and Asia Minor laid the groundwork for his career as a Neoclassical architect. In 1837 he succeeded Soane as architect of the Bank of England, after which he was responsible for some important public, commercial and university buildings including the Ashmolean Museum in Oxford (1841–5). He was not indifferent to the Gothic although his buildings in that style, such as the chapel at Harrow, are less successful than his classical works. He was elected RA in 1836 and three years later became Professor of Architecture. His son F. P. Cockerell (1833–79) was an architect in the Queen Anne style.

Collcutt, Thomas E. (1840–1924) Architect-designer who worked with **Street** but developed a Free-Renaissance manner in his own practice. He designed the 1871 furniture catalogue for **Collinson & Lock** and their Fleet Street premises in the following year.

Collinson & Lock Firm of English Art Manufacturers noted for furniture and interiors in the Aesthetic style of the 1870s and 80s. Their 1871 catalogue, with designs by Thomas **Collcutt**, popularised the taste for furniture designed by artists and architects such as Godwin, **Burne-Jones** and Fairfax Murray. They undertook the fitting out of the Savoy Theatre in 1881. Having taken over **Jackson & Graham** in 1885, they were themselves subsumed within the firm of **Gillow & Co.** in 1897.

Bibl: J. Kinchin, 'Collinson and Lock', *Connoisseur*, 201, May 1979, pp. 47-53.

Cowlishaw, Nichol & Co. Manchester weaving firm noted for their heavy wool hangings. They produced textiles from Godwin's designs in the mid 1870s.

Cowper, Francis, Lord (1834–1905) 7th Earl, peer and landowner who in 1871 commissioned Godwin to design Beauvale, a substantial country house in Nottinghamshire in the Old English style. Despite problems during the construction, Cowper went on to commission several smaller houses on the estate from Godwin.

Crace Family firm of decorators and furnishing suppliers, founded in 1768 but achieving their greatest success during the Victorian period. They produced interior designs for many aristocratic and public buildings, working with **Pugin** on the Houses of Parliament and the Medieval Court at the Great Exhibition.

Bibl: M. Aldridge, *The Craces: Royal Decorators 1768–1899*, London, 1990

Craig, Edward Gordon (1872–1966) Son of Godwin and Ellen **Terry**, who followed his mother onto the stage, acting in the company of Henry Irving. Although he hardly knew his father, he took up many of Godwin's interests, becoming a notable printmaker and an innovative theatre designer. He edited *The Mask*, a magazine of art and drama which included unpublished writings by his father. After 1900 he turned increasingly to stage design and production, working in a bold minimalist style that had a great influence throughout Europe. He met and had an intense affair with the dancer Isadora Duncan in 1905–6, and in 1912 staged a famous production of Hamlet for Stanislavsky's company in Moscow.

Crane, Walter (1845–1915) English designer and author who trained as an engraver before achieving success in the 1870s as an illustrator of children's books. Thereafter he applied his skill in figural and pattern design to a range of media including ceramics, textiles, wallpapers and murals, becoming one of the most versatile and successful designers of the period. Crane grew close to Morris, and played an active role in several Arts and Crafts organisations. He also exerted considerable influence as a teacher and writer on design.

Bibl: G. Smith & S. Hyde, eds, *Walter Crane: Artist, Designer and Socialist*, London 1989

de Caumont, Comte Arcisse (1801–73) Archaeologist and architectural historian active in his native Normandy, whose *Histoire de l'architecture religieuse, civile et militaire* (6 vols, 1830–43) provided much of the terminology and classifications for medieval architecture. The Société française d'archéologie, which he founded in 1833, marks the beginning of architectural conservation in France.

de Honecourt, Wilars (Villard) (*fl.* c.1220s–30s) Author of a 13th-century manuscript in the Bibliotèque Nationale containing texts and drawings on medieval building, among other subjects. Published in Britain in 1859, at the height of the Gothic Revival, this seemed to be a manual on the working methods of medieval French masons, and therefore a link with the world of the cathedral builders. There was speculation as to whether Wilars was himself an architect and several Gothic buildings were ascribed to him: it is now thought that he was probably a clerk with a flair for drawing. Godwin and **Burges** consulted the original manuscript in Paris.

de Staël, Madame (1766–1816) French woman of letters whose salon in Paris at the time of the Revolution and Consulate was a focus for progressive ideas on art and literature. Her most famous book, *De l'Allemagne* (1810) was a study of Romanticism in German culture.

Deane, Thomas (1792–1871) **& Woodward, Benjamin** (1815–61) Irish architectural partnership formed in 1851 whose work closely reflected the principles of John **Ruskin**. Trinity College Museum in Dublin (1852–7) established their reputation, being one of the first public buildings in the Gothic style after the Houses of Parliament. This was followed by the influential University Museum in Oxford (1855–60) where they repeated their Ruskinian practice of allowing the stone carvers to design their own details and ornament. Woodward was the main designer although Deane carried on after 1861 in partnership with the former's son.

Dicksee, Frank (1853–1928) English artist who achieved early success at the **RA** for his painting *Harmony* (1877) which exploited the association of art and music as well as sentimental genre. In later years he was better known for historical and chivalric subjects, and society portraits which brought him considerable wealth. He lived in the artists' area of St John's Wood and eventually became President of the RA in 1924.

Disraeli, Benjamin (1805–81) English novelist and politician, famous for his flamboyant manner and brilliant debating skills. As leader of the Conservatives and Prime Minister 1874–9, he was a striking opponent and contrast to the austere Liberal, William **Gladstone**.

Dowdeswell, C. William (1832–1915) English art dealer whose gallery at 133 New Bond Street, opened 1878, specialised in prints by contemporary artists. **Walter**, the founder's son, was a friend of **Whistler**, arranging the

exhibitions known as 'Notes – Harmonies – Nocturnes' in 1884 and 1886.

Dresser, Christopher (1834–1904) An early independent designer, Dresser, like Godwin, worked for a variety of manufacturers producing designs for furniture, glass, ceramics, metalwork, wallpaper and carpets. Trained as a botanist, he applied his scientific knowledge to the principles of design, believing in simple organic forms and a sense of underlying structure to all patterns and artefacts. These ideas were published in several books including *The Art of Decorative Design* (1862) and *Principles of Decorative Design* (1873), as well as several books of ornament. In 1876–7 Dresser visited America and the Far East. His book *Japan: Its Architecture, Art and Art Manufactures* (1882) was one of the first authoritative accounts of Japanese art and culture in the west.

Bibl: W. Halen, *Christopher Dresser: a Pioneer of Modern Design*, London, 1993; M. Whiteway, *Christopher Dresser: a Design Revolution*, London, 2004

Du Maurier, George (1834–96) Illustrator and novelist, he trained in Paris 1856–8 in the company of **Whistler**, **Poynter** and **Armstrong**, an experience he called upon later when writing *Trilby*. On his return to London he produced illustrations for magazines and novels but was soon offered a position on the staff of ***Punch***. Almost immediately, Du Maurier's cartoons became famous for a cast of characters, including 'Mrs Cimabue Brown' and the poet 'Jellaby Postwaite', who frequented the artistic salons of London expressing opinions associated with the emerging Aesthetic Movement. Du Maurier was himself a prominent figure in artistic and literary circles and in 1889 he published his first novel *Peter Ibbetson*, followed by *Trilby* (1894) which became a huge best-seller.

Bibl: L. Ormond, *George Du Maurier*, London, 1969

Dudley Gallery (1865–1918) One of the earliest private galleries in London, the Dudley occupied the Egyptian Hall in Piccadilly from where it became a rival to the **RA**. Unlike the **Grosvenor Gallery**, which introduced a new approach to displaying pictures, the Dudley tended to show works in a conventional dense hang, but its themed exhibitions brought some distinction.

Eastlake, Charles Locke (1833–1906) Museum keeper and writer on architecture and taste. Nephew of the painter Sir Charles Eastlake (PRA), the younger Eastlake trained as an architect but turned to journalism. His articles in *The Queen* were published in 1868 as *Hints on*

Household Taste in Furniture, Upholstery and other Details, which promoted the Gothic style for domestic furniture in accordance with the views of the Design Reformers. In 1866 he became secretary of the **RIBA** and published *A History of the Gothic Revival in England* (1872). In 1878 he was appointed Keeper of the National Gallery but resigned in 1898 having been passed over for the directorship. Eastlake exerted a great influence on domestic taste in Britain and America, his illustrations of furniture becoming the basis for many modern interiors in the Gothic or reformed style.

The Ecclesiological Society (See Cambridge Camden Society)

Farmer & Rogers 'Shawl and Cloak Emporium' on Regent Street which opened up the popular market for Japanese goods following the International Exhibition of 1862. Much of this was due to Arthur **Liberty**, manager of their 'Oriental Warehouse', who left in 1875 to open his own store opposite. The Oriental Warehouse was frequented by many artists and designers including Godwin, **Burges**, **Whistler**, **Rossetti**, and **Moore**.

Fergusson, James (1808–86) Historian and theorist on architecture who championed new technology and modern styles in building, in opposition to the dominant Gothic Revivalists. His main publications include *An Historical Enquiry into the true Principles of Beauty in Art* (1849), an *Illustrated Handbook of Architecture* (1859) and *History of Architecture in all Countries from Earliest Times to the Present Day* (1865–7). He led the campaign opposing **Street**'s designs for the Law Courts in the 1870s.

Fildes, Samuel Luke (1844–1927) Successful painter and illustrator, best known for scenes of poverty and suffering. Fildes's early illustrations of the plight of the poor for *The Graphic* helped prepare him for a career as a genre painter, and he achieved success in 1874 with *Applicants for Admission to a Casual Ward*. Thereafter he became a successful society portraitist and history painter, and a member of the Costume Society. His status as a prominent figure on the art scene was confirmed in 1877 when he moved to a house commissioned from R. Norman **Shaw** in Melbury Road, Holland Park.

Bibl: L. V. Fildes, *Luke Fildes R.A.: a Victorian Painter*, London, 1968

The Fine Art Society Gallery, founded in 1876 by Marcus Huish, was notable for Aesthetic art and design as well as for the publication of prints. The FAS pioneered the one-man exhibition, holding important shows by **Whistler**, **Millais** and Stacy **Marks**. The façade of the New Bond Street gallery was remodelled by Godwin in 1881.

Frith, William Powell (1819–1909) English painter whose crowded genre scenes, such as *Derby Day* (1858) and *The Railway Station* (1862), presented a cross section of contemporary society. Frith's work was hugely popular with the public but its moral and anecdotal aspects attracted criticism and ridicule from the Aesthetes, including Godwin. Frith gave evidence on Ruskin's behalf at the libel trial of 1878.

Bibl: W. P. Frith, *My Autobiography and Reminiscences*, London, 1887

Garbett, Edward Lacy (1826–1901) Architect with an eclectic approach similar to Robert **Kerr**'s. His book, *A Rudimentary Treatise on the Principles of Design in Architecture as Deducible from Nature and Exemplified in the Works of the Greek and Gothic Architects* (1850) was an important touchstone in the debate over style and construction.

Garrett, Rhoda (1841–82) and **Agnes** (1845–1935) English decorators from an eminent progressive family whose *Suggestions for House Decoration* (1876) was the most ambitious manual in **Loftie**'s *Art at Home* series. After training with the designer Daniel Cottier and the architect J. M. Brydon, they established a successful business in Gower Street, furnishing many of the new women's university colleges. They exemplified Godwin's support for 'Lady Architects', although he was irked when they reproduced illustrations of his furniture designs.

Garrick, David (1717–79) English actor and theatre manager, responsible for the revival of interest in Shakespeare on the Georgian stage, largely through his affecting and emotional performances of the great roles.

Gilbert, William Schwenck (1836–1911) and **Sullivan, Arthur Seymour** (1842–1900) Lyricist and composer respectively of a series of 14 popular comic operas between 1871 and 1896, many of which were performed at the Savoy Theatre. *Patience, or Bunthorne's Bride*, produced in 1881, was a satire on the manners and mores of the Aesthetes, who had become prominent in London society during the previous decade. Many key features of Aesthetic taste were held up to ridicule, including the craze for things Japanese, 'blue and white' porcelain, lilies, sunflowers and a vocabulary ('utterly', 'consummate' and 'quite too') expressing the over-refined and affected manner of the group. Oscar **Wilde**, a relatively recent recruit to the Aesthetic Movement, was recognisable in the central character from his velvet knee-breeches.

Gillow & Co. Cabinetmakers founded in Lancaster in 1728, best known as suppliers of the leading styles for wealthy middle-class clients in the Georgian period. Their business thrived equally during the Victorian period maintaining their traditional designs but opening up new areas in collaboration with architect-designers including **Pugin**, Godwin and Bruce Talbert. They provided much of the furniture for the new Houses of Parliament (1837–67) and benefited from large contracts to furnish Government buildings throughout the empire. In 1877 they commissioned Godwin to design three houses on Chelsea Embankment as a speculative venture.

Gladstone, William Ewart (1809–98) Liberal politician and Prime Minister whose debates with the Conservative leader Benjamin **Disraeli** were famous. Gladstone supported reforms in various spheres of Victorian life, notably suffrage, education, health and agriculture, but his life-long attempts to achieve home rule in Ireland were unsuccessful.

Godwin, Beatrice *see* Philip, Beatrice

Greenaway, Kate (1846–1901) English illustrator and artist whose children's books were very popular in the 1880s. A rival to **Crane** and **Caldecott**, Greenaway's coloured illustrations of little girls in mob caps and Empire dresses encouraged the rising interest in design for children and helped popularise the taste for Aesthetic dress. Her watercolour drawings were much admired and she became a friend of John **Ruskin**. Success in children's books was very lucrative and she was able to commission a house from R. Norman **Shaw** in Hampstead.

Grosvenor Gallery Founded in 1877 by Sir Coutts and Lady Blanche **Lindsay**, the Grosvenor Gallery introduced a new type of exhibition in which a select few artists showed their pictures in a sympathetic environment, unlike the crowded displays typical of the **RA** and **Dudley** Gallery. The Grosvenor offered spacious galleries decorated with specially chosen wall coverings and furniture, creating a domestic environment attractive to their wealthy patrons. Aesthetic artists dominated the Grosvenor's early exhibitions, the most popular being **Whis-**

tler, **Burne-Jones**, **Watts** and **Moore**. It was comments by **Ruskin** on Whistler's work in the first Grosvenor Gallery exhibition of 1877 which prompted the famous libel trial. In the 1880s the gallery widened its range to include naturalist paintings but, after the initial sensation, it declined in importance and closed in 1890.

Bibl: C. Denney & S. Casteras, eds, *The Grosvenor Gallery: A Palace of Art in Victorian England*, New Haven, 1996

Guffens, Godfried (1833–1901) Belgian artist who, with Jan Sweerts, produced many historical murals for public buildings in Antwerp and Ypres. They were approached by **Waterhouse** to decorate Manchester Town Hall but a public outcry restored the commission to Ford Madox **Brown**.

Gwilt, Joseph (1784–1863) Scholar and editor whose works include *Rudiments of Architecture, Practical and Theoretical* (1826), the *Encyclopaedia of Architecture, Historical, Theoretical and Practical* (1842) and a translation of Vitruvius.

Haden, Sir Francis Seymour (1818–1910) Successful surgeon and amateur etcher, Haden was a leading figure in the revival of 'original' or artist-printmaking in Britain. He was already an accomplished printmaker and collector when his brother-in-law, J. M. **Whistler**, came to live with him in London in 1859, reawakening his interest in etching. The two worked closely together for several years producing innovative landscape etchings until differences in temperament drove them apart. In 1867 Whistler attacked Haden in Paris, pushing him through a plate glass window, which effectively ended their relationship. Haden continued to produce fairly repetitive etchings and became the founding president of the Royal Society of Painter-Etchers and Engravers.

Bibl: R. S. Schneiderman, *A Catalogue Raisonné of the Prints of Sir Francis Seymour Haden*, London, 1997

Hardman, John (1812–67) English metal and stained glass manufacturer who produced many of **Pugin**'s metalwork designs for both domestic and ecclesiastical settings. His products were shown in the Medieval Court at the Great Exhibition of 1851.

Hart, Solomon (1806–81) English painter of biblical subjects who occasionally depicted scenes of Jewish religious ritual. He was Professor of Painting at the **RA** schools.

Haweis, Mary Eliza (1848–98) Author and illustrator whose writings on household taste and dress for magazines such as *The Queen* and *The Lady* were widely read and followed. Her most important manuals on domestic design are *The Art of Beauty* (1878), *The Art of Decoration* (1881) and *Beautiful Houses* (1882). She and her husband, the Rev. Haweis, occupied Rossetti's house in Cheyne Walk, Chelsea following the artist's death.

Bibl: B. Howe, *Arbiter of Elegance*, London, 1967

Heaton, Butler & Bayne English stained glass manufacturers founded in 1862, although Heaton and Butler had already traded alongside **Clayton & Bell** from 1857. Bayne brought a disciplined, linear approach to design which was very effective alongside Heaton's technical expertise. With greater flexibility than many of the Gothic Revival glass manufacturers, by the late 1860s they were seen as leaders in design and technique with a wider range than ecclesiastical glass alone.

Hill, Amelia (1802–1904) Scottish sculptor, wife of D. O. Hill, the painter and pioneer photographer. She undertook portrait and architectural sculpture including several figures on the Walter Scott Monument in Edinburgh.

The Hogarth Club Exhibition society and club founded by the Pre-Raphaelite painters in 1858. It closed in 1861.

Holme, Myra (d.1919) English actress who performed in **Burnand**'s *The Colonel* at the Adelphi in 1881. She married the playwright Arthur Wing Pinero.

Howell, Charles Augustus (1840–90) Anglo-Portuguese art dealer whose period as secretary to John **Ruskin** introduced him to the Pre-Raphaelites and many leading figures in the art world. Unscrupulous and unpredictable, he seems to have led a precarious life as an art dealer but, despite dubious practices, remained on good terms with many artists. He fell out eventually with both **Rossetti** and **Whistler** over debts, yet he was one of Whistler's main creditors at the time of the bankruptcy in 1879 and helped save some of the artist's works from the bailiffs.

Bibl: H. R. Angeli, *Pre-Raphaelite Twilight*, London, 1954

Howell & James London furnishing firm associated with contemporary styles in the 1870s, particularly Jacobean and Queen Anne. Lewis Day and Thomas Harris produced designs for them and their shop was well known for its annual exhibition of china painting, which showed the work of many women designers.

Image, Selwyn (1849–1930) English designer and illustrator who abandoned a career in the church to devote himself to the Arts and Crafts. In 1883 Image and A. H. Mackmurdo opened the Century Guild Workshops for which Image produced furniture and stained glass, although he was best known for the design of the magazine *The Century Guild Hobby Horse* (1884). After the guild closed in 1888, Image continued to work in graphics and a variety of craft media. He became **Slade** Professor of Fine Art in 1910 and a founder of the Design and Industries Association in 1915.

Jackson & Graham London cabinet-making firm founded in 1836, which catered for the luxury market with richly ornamented furniture in the French and Renaissance manners. Designers who worked for them included Owen Jones and Bruce Talbert, and they won many prizes at International Exhibitions. By the 1870s they offered a full interior decorating service often incorporating elements of the new Aesthetic taste. They were taken over by rivals **Collinson & Lock** in 1885.

Jeckyll, Thomas (1827–81) English architect and designer who began his career in East Anglia working in the Gothic Revival manner. Moving to London in 1859 he entered leading artistic circles and adopted a new range of sources including Old English, Queen Anne and Anglo-Japanese. His dining room for Frederick **Leyland** at 49 Princes Gate was much altered by **Whistler** in 1876–7 and renamed *The Peacock Room*. Jeckyll was an innovative designer of metalwork for the Norwich firm of **Barnard, Bishop & Barnard**, examples of which were acclaimed at international exhibitions. He became ill in 1876 and spent his last years in insane asylums.

Bibl: S. Soros, ed., *Thomas Jeckyll: Architect and Designer*, New Haven, 2003

Jeffrey & Co. Wallpaper printers founded in 1836 who became the leading producers of high quality hand and machine printed art papers. William **Morris** used them for his first foray into wallpaper printing in 1862 and they were known for producing patterns by many of the leading architect-designers of the period, including Godwin, **Eastlake**, Owen Jones, Sedding, **Burges**, Voysey and **Crane**. From 1872 Jeffrey & Co. developed complementary papers for the tripartite wall divisions (dado, filling and frieze) which Godwin advocated in his interior designs. They won many awards at international exhibitions.

Johnson, Robert J. (1832–92) Architect and author of *Specimens of Early French Architecture* (1864), an important source for the High Victorian Gothic Revivalists.

Jopling, Louise (1843–1933) Artist friend of Godwin and **Whistler** who in 1886 appeared in the production of *Helena in Troas*. Her husband, Joseph (1831–84), also a painter, was employed by the **Fine Art Society**.
Bibl: L. Jopling. *Twenty Years of My Life: 1867 to 1887*, London, 1925

Kean, Edmund (1787?–1833) English actor famous for romantic renditions of classic roles in which he heightened the unique drama of each performance by strong emotional engagement. Coleridge reported that Kean had the power to reveal Shakespeare by 'flashes of lightning'.

Keeling, Enoch Bassett (1837–86) English Gothic Revival architect, pupil of Christopher **Dresser**, notable for the use of bold polychrome colours on the exterior and interior of his churches. He designed the Strand Musick Hall at the Aldwych (1864) in a Gothic style which attracted some criticism, not least from Godwin.

Keene, Charles Samuel (1823–91) English illustrator and printmaker whose work was highly admired in Aesthetic circles. He counted Godwin, **Whistler**, Degas and Legros among his friends.

Kemble, John Philip (1757–1823) English actor and manager of the Drury Lane and Covent Garden Theatres whose performances of Shakespeare set a standard for his period. In contrast to **Kean**, Kemble's acting style was in the heavy declamatory manner but he was noted for innovations in costume and stage design.

Kerr, Robert (1823–1904) Scots-born architect who worked in Aberdeen and New York before establishing a practice in London in the 1840s. Kerr went on to become one of the most successful architects in Britain, best known for his country houses and public buildings of the 1860s. These apart, Kerr's reputation rests primarily on his role in professional organisations, notably the **AA**, of which he was the first President, and the **RIBA**. He was also an important writer on style in architecture and his books, above all *The English Gentleman's House* (1864), were widely read and commented upon. Kerr had a combative side to his character and tended to adopt the role of official spokesman for the profession, a position which could not fail to attract criticism from figures like Godwin.

Langtry, Lillie (1853–1929) English actress and society figure who in the 1870s became the mistress of the Prince of Wales (future King Edward VII). After the failure of her first marriage in 1881 she went on the stage, achieving success as a celebrated beauty rather than for her dramatic skills. A friend of Godwin's, in 1882 she commissioned him to design a house but it was never built.

Leighton, Frederic, Lord (1830–96) English artist best known for his classical and mythological paintings. After a period studying in Italy and France, Leighton returned to Britain in 1859 where he undertook some decorative painting while exhibiting at the **RA**. His career was soon launched as the most successful history painter of the Victorian period. He became RA in 1855, PRA in 1878, and was made Baron in 1896, the first British artist to be ennobled. His house at Melbury Road, designed by George **Aitchison** in 1864, was the paradigm for British artists' studio-houses, famous especially for the Arab Hall which Leighton added in 1877.
Bibl: S. Jones et al., *Frederic, Lord Leighton: Eminent Victorian Artist*, London, 1996

Lescot, Pierre (c.1510–78) French Renaissance architect and theorist of the classical orders. He was responsible for the main design of the Louvre.

Leslie, George Dunlop (1835–1921) English painter of sentimental genre scenes whose depictions of Regency life, like the illustrations of Kate **Greenaway**, contributed to the taste for Queen Anne architecture. A friend of Fred **Walker** and Stacy **Marks**, he was a member of the group known as the St John's Wood Clique. He was made RA in 1876.

Leyland, Frederick Richards (1831–92) Liverpool ship owner and art collector whose support for **Whistler** in the 1870s was lavish, although it ended when the artist overstepped the mark. Leyland had already begun collecting pictures by **Rossetti** and Whistler, from whom he commissioned portraits of his family, when he began the decoration of his London house at 49 Princes Gate. Whistler, commissioned to decorate the hall in 1876, took over the decoration of the dining room in Leyland's absence, repainting it in blue and gold on a theme of peacocks. This far exceeded Leyland's wishes and when the artist demanded 2000 guineas, Leyland refused, paying him only £1000. This ended their relationship and the loss of support aggravated Whistler's financial problems.

Liberty, Arthur Lasenby (1843–1917) Shop owner and entrepreneur, who began work as a draper for **Farmer & Rogers** in Regent Street in 1862. Liberty saw the potential for oriental goods and, when refused a partnership by his employer, opened his own store in Regent Street in 1875. Liberty & Co. concentrated on the rising taste for Japanese and oriental goods and his premises soon expanded until in 1885 he had seven departments in two buildings. Textiles were the core of the business with Liberty pioneering the importation of various grades of cloth for upholstery, clothing and hangings, some of which he had dyed and printed in Britain using contemporary designs. 'Liberty Art Fabrics' were very popular in Aesthetic circles and in 1884 he introduced a costume department under the direction of Godwin as a rival to the Paris fashion houses. After Godwin's death this department continued to attract attention and in 1890 Liberty's opened a branch in Paris. Liberty's became synonymous with modern design to the extent that, in Italy, the popular term for Art Nouveau was 'Stile Liberty'.

Bibl: S. Calloway, *House of Liberty: Masters of Style and Decoration*, London, 1992

Limerick, Lord (3rd Earl) Anglo-Irish peer and (absentee) landowner who in 1866 commissioned Godwin to design Dromore Castle on his estate in Ireland. As chairman of the Bristol Society of Architects he had come to know Godwin early in his career.

Lindsay, Sir Coutts (1824–1913) and **Lady Blanche** (1844–1912) Wealthy socialites involved in the arts in London who, in 1877, founded the **Grosvenor Gallery** in New Bond Street. This quickly became a meeting place for wealthy aesthetes and artists, enhancing the Lindsays' position in society. After initial success, the gallery lost its prestige in the 1880s. Financial problems began in 1882 when Blanche withdrew her support following the Lindsays' separation and in 1888 a rival, the New Gallery, took many of the Grosvenor's artists. The Grosvenor Gallery closed in 1890.

Long, Edwin L. (1829–91) English painter of grand historical and biblical scenes whose reputation was established with *The Babylonian Marriage Market* (1875). His work was praised by Godwin for its archaeological accuracy.

Bibl: M. Bills, ed., *Edwin Longsden Long RA*, London, 1998

Loftie, Rev. W. J. Editor and commentator on household taste. Loftie edited *Art at Home*, a series of manuals published by Macmillan between 1876 and 1883 giving advice on domestic furnishing and decoration for the growing middle-class readership. Authors who contributed to the series include Loftie himself (*A Plea for Art in the Home*, 1876), Rhoda and Agnes **Garrett** (*Suggestions for House Decoration* 1876), Mrs **Orrinsmith** (*The Drawing Room*, 1877), Mrs Loftie (*The Dining Room*, 1878) and Lady **Barker** (*The Bedroom and Boudoir*, 1878).

Louise, Princess (1848–1939) Sculptor, daughter of Queen Victoria. She married John Campbell, Marquis of Lorne, in 1871 becoming Duchess of Argyll in 1900 when he became the 9th Duke. Taught sculpture by J. E. **Boehm**, Princess Louise had a talent for the arts and grew to know many of the artists associated with the **Grosvenor Gallery**. In 1878 she commissioned a modest studio from Godwin in the grounds of Kensington Palace. Her royal status denied her a public career but she executed several monuments including a statue of her mother the Queen in Kensington Palace.

MacBeth, Robert Walker (1848–1910) Scottish painter and etcher of landscape and genre scenes who began his career producing illustrations for *The Graphic*. After the 1870s he gave more time to his own art and achieved some success at the **RA** and as a printmaker through such journals as *The Portfolio*.

MacLaren, James M. (1843–1890) Scottish architect, a talented admirer of Godwin, who designed houses and public buildings in the evolving 'Free Style'.

Bibl: A. Service, 'James MacLaren and the Godwin Legacy', in *Edwardian Architecture and its Origins*, London, 1975

Maclise, Daniel (1806–70) Irish history and genre painter whose murals in the Palace of Westminster, including *The Death of Nelson* (1857) and *Wellington at Waterloo* (1864), were dismissed by Godwin as 'easel paintings magnified'.

Mandelgren, Nils Mansson (1813–99) Swedish historian and illustrator, author of *Monuments Scandinave du Moyen Age*, Paris, 1862.

Marks, Henry Stacy (1829–98) Painter and muralist who studied in Paris and at the **RA** before turning his hand to portraiture, wood engraving, furniture and glass painting. His early submissions to the RA, such as *Toothache in the Middle Ages*, were often light-hearted but he achieved success in 1860 with *The Franciscan Sculptor*. He was a highly regarded muralist, executing work at the South Kensington Museum and Eaton Hall (1877–80) as well as in Godwin's Dromore Castle in Ireland and the Midland Grand Hotel in London. He undertook a range of decorative work at **Burges**'s Tower House. He also exhibited paintings of birds, often with anecdotal titles, which he based on studies done at London Zoo. This combination of interests did not undermine his status and he was elected RA in 1878.

Miles, George Francis (1852–91) English portrait and genre painter who in 1879 shared rooms with Oscar **Wilde** in London. Miles had commissioned a house from Godwin at 1 Tite Street in Chelsea which the architect regarded as 'the best thing I ever did'. A bold and simple rectilinear design, it was rejected by the Metropolitan Board of Works, like its near neighbour the White House for **Whistler**. It was eventually approved with substantial revisions, including a Dutch gable and some decorative sculpture, and Miles and Wilde were able to move in.

Millais, John Everett (1829–96) A child prodigy in painting who became one of the Pre-Raphaelite Brotherhood in 1848 before establishing a successful career at the **RA**. Millais was a naturally gifted painter but his work was often criticised for its vacuous subject matter. This may have been a drawback among his PRB friends but not in the English art establishment, which he courted from the mid 1850s. In 1854 he painted a celebrated portrait of **Ruskin** and married the latter's wife Effie after the annulment of her marriage. Despite this awkwardness, Millais went on to become the President of the RA in 1896. He was a notable illustrator during the 1860s.

Millet, Jean-François (1814–75) French Realist painter best known for his depictions of peasant life in the vicinity of Barbizon. Although initially controversial, by the 1870s his art was universally admired.

Minton & Co. Staffordshire ceramics factory which became associated with the Design Reformers of the Victorian period. Tablewares had been the main part of their production but Minton increasingly dominated the market for encaustic and printed tiles which, in the wake of the Gothic Revival, became popular for ecclesiastical and domestic as well as commercial interiors. By the 1860s decorated tiles also began appearing in furniture. Minton's engaged many leading designers and artists to work for them and in 1871 opened its own Art Pottery Studio in London, employing J. Moyr Smith and Christopher

Dresser among others. Japanese designs figured prominently in their tablewares but, under the French designer Marc-Louis Solon, the range expanded in the 1870s to include other Aesthetic tastes such as Classical Greek.

Moore, Albert Joseph (1841–93) English painter and designer whose early interest in Pre-Raphaelitism gave way to a lifelong adherence to monumental figures derived from Greek classical sculpture. This was first seen in the domestic murals he painted for **Nesfield**, but soon appeared in Moore's easel paintings. Unlike other Victorian Classicists such as **Alma-Tadema**, Moore was uninterested in narrative or archaeology. Instead he sought an art of pure Aesthetic values in which the rhythmic composition of women in delicate colour harmonies is used to evoke abstract and musical qualities. Moore's art was close in spirit to that of **Whistler** and, after an uneasy period in the late 1860s when they were wary of each other, the two men became firm friends. Moore exhibited at the **Grosvenor Gallery** and testified for Whistler in the 'Ruskin Trial' of 1878.

Bibl: R. Asleson, *Albert Moore*, London, 2000

Morris, William (1834–96) Son of a wealthy stockbroker, Morris began studying for the ministry at Oxford, alongside Edward **Burne-Jones**, before devoting himself to art and design under the influence of **Rossetti** and **Ruskin**. He worked in G. E. **Street**'s office, where he met Phillip **Webb** and commissioned him to design the Red House at Bexley Heath (1859). Appalled by the standard of machine-made goods, he and his friends, including Webb, Burne-Jones, Rossetti and Ford Madox **Brown**, decided to decorate the house themselves in a medieval manner employing traditional craft techniques. From these efforts, Morris set up the firm Morris, Marshall, Faulkner & Co. in 1861 producing a range of furniture and decorative work. Stained glass was a major part of the firm's output but Morris, who was largely self-taught, developed great skill at pattern design, which he applied to printed textiles and wallpaper as well as furniture. In 1866 the firm designed the Green Dining Room at the **South Kensington** Museum which offered a showcase for their integrated decorative schemes. By the 1870s Morris had also turned his attention to carpets, embroidery, tapestry, illumination and calligraphy, mastering the techniques for each craft skill himself before introducing it to the studios and showroom of the firm. At the same time he was a prolific poet, author and translator of medieval and Norse texts. From the beginning Morris had been motivated as much by a desire to improve the moral and spiritual character of the domestic environment as by any simple ideal of taste. As a result he increasingly became an advocate of design as a force for social change and by the 1880s he had become a committed socialist as well as a campaigner for various causes, including architectural conservation under the aegis of the **SPAB**. His final venture was the Kelmscott Press (founded 1890), an attempt to reform the arts of the book which had a strong influence on the Private Press movement throughout Europe and the USA.

Bibl: F. MacCarthy, *William Morris: A Life for Our Time*, London, 1994; L. Parry, ed., *William Morris*, London, 1996

Nash, John (1752–1835) Architect and developer whose white stucco terraces and crescents in north-west London came to define the Regency style in English architecture. After a haphazard training, Nash worked with Humphrey Repton before attracting the attention of the Prince Regent who, in 1811, sponsored the development of the area round Regent's Park, including the Mall, Carlton House and Cumberland Terrace. Nash also designed the exotic Pavilion in Brighton for the Prince, and remodelled Buckingham Palace.

Nesfield, William Eden (1835–88) Educated at Eton, he trained in the office of William Burn where he met R. Norman **Shaw** and the two embarked on a detailed study of Gothic architecture. Nesfield's *Specimens of Mediaeval Architecture* (1862) was the result of a lengthy continental tour but he was already showing more eclectic interests than the High Victorian Gothic Revivalists. Setting up practice in London in 1859 he enjoyed a loose partnership with Shaw for many years but was also able to pursue his own commissions for large houses and the attendant minor buildings on English country estates. Cloverly Hall, Salop (1865–70), and Kinmel Park (1871–4) and Bodrhyddan Hall (1872–4), both in Wales, reveal Nesfield's gradual shift from a vernacular Old English style, rich in ornament, to a more confident and free eclectic manner employing French, English and Japanese elements. His design of the lodge at Kew Gardens (1866) in a manner sympathetic to the 17th-century Kew Palace was an important landmark in the 'Queen Anne Revival' of which Nesfield was a leading exponent. His later years were overshadowed by depression and he increasingly gave up architecture for painting.

Orrinsmith, Lucy Designer, craftswoman and author of *The Drawing Room* in the 'Art at Home' series edited by Rev. **Loftie**. She was an early collaborator with William **Morris**, her brother Charles Faulkner becoming a partner in 'the Firm'.

Ouida (1839–1908) Pseudonym of Louise de la Ramie, writer of flamboyant romantic fiction including *Under Two Flags* (1867) and *A Dog of Flanders* (1872).

Palmerston, Henry John Temple, Lord (1784–1865) Veteran Liberal politician, member of the House of Commons for 58 years and, apart from a brief gap, Prime Minister from 1855 to 1865. His opposition to Gothic as a style led to the dispute over G. G. **Scott**'s designs for the Foreign Office.

Parker, John Henry (1806–84) Antiquarian and author of important books on architecture including *A Glossary of Terms used in Grecian, Roman, Italian and Gothic Architecture* (1836) and *An Introduction to the Study of Gothic Architecture* (1849). He was an advocate of restoration of medieval buildings.

Parry, Thomas Gambier (1816–88) Artist, collector and authority on decorative painting who in 1859 invented the 'spirit fresco' process whereby murals could be executed using a medium of oil, wax and other solutions. This medium allowed artists to work in a manner similar to oils while offering the durability associated with 'true fresco'.

Bibl: D. Farr, ed., *Thomas Gambier Parry 1816–1888 as Artist and Collector*, London, 1993

Pater, Walter Horatio (1839–94) English critic and author who, despite his cloistered life as an Oxford don, became a great influence on taste and the arts in late Victorian Britain. A scholar of classical philosophy, Pater's collection of essays *Studies in the History of the Renaissance* (1873) celebrated 'Art for art's sake' in the heightened aesthetic responses of the refined spectator, an approach contrary to **Ruskin**'s emphasis on naturalism and morality. *The School of Giorgione*, first published in 1877, contained the famous dictum, 'All art constantly aspires towards the condition of music', an ideal of the Aesthetes including Godwin, **Whistler** and Oscar **Wilde**. Pater's notion of the 'aesthetic hero' was further explored in his novel *Marius the Epicurean* (1885), an important source for the 'Decadents' of the 1890s.

Pearson, John Loughborough (1817–97) Architect in the Gothic Revival style. Pearson's early devotion to **Pugin** and **Ruskin** matured into a more individual manner in which Gothic forms were adapted for modern requirements in church design. St Peter's at Vauxhall, London (1860–4), set a standard for practical and inexpensive brick churches, elaborated in many subsequent commissions. His success in this field led in 1878 to the commission for a new cathedral at Truro which was generally well received, although, like some of his restorations, it did attract criticism. His domestic work was more diverse and he designed several houses in the Old English and Jacobean styles. He became a Fellow of the **RIBA** in 1860, and RA in 1880.

Bibl: A. P. Quiney, *John Loughborough Pearson*, New Haven, 1980

Pecksniff, Seth Sanctimonious surveyor-architect, with a 'soft and oily' manner, from Dickens's novel *Martin Chuzzlewit* (1843–4), frequently used by Godwin as a shorthand for hypocrites in the profession. Described as 'fuller of virtuous precept than a copy book. Some people likened him to a direction-post, which is always telling the way to a place, and never goes there'.

Pellegrini, Carlo (1838–89) Italian-born draughtsman whose lithographed caricatures of politicians and celebrities appeared in *Vanity Fair* under the name of 'Ape'. Godwin designed a studio-house for him and Archibald Stuart **Wortley** at 60 Tite Street in 1878. Pellegrini was a friend of many modern artists including Degas who painted a portrait of him.

Philip, Beatrice (1857–96) Daughter of the Scottish sculptor John Birnie Philip. She took up art under Godwin's tutelage in 1875 and the two were married the following year. Beatrice worked alongside Godwin producing decorative designs for furniture, wallpaper and tiles as well as paintings and drawings. In 1884 **Whistler** began a full-length portrait of her (*Gaslight*, 1886) and she spent increasingly more time among his followers. Two years after Godwin's death in 1886 Beatrice and Whistler were married and enjoyed a very happy relationship until her death from cancer.

Bibl: M. MacDonald, *Beatrice Whistler: Artist & Designer*, Glasgow, 1997

Phipps, Charles John (1835–97) English theatre architect who worked for many leading theatrical personalities in Godwin's circle including the **Bancrofts**, Henry Irving and Beerbohm **Tree**. His Savoy Theatre for D'Oyly Carte opened in 1881 with the **Gilbert and Sullivan** operetta *Patience*. The interior, designed by **Collinson & Lock**, was the first public building to employ electric light.

Pinwell, George (1842–75) English illustrator and artist. A leading figure in the great boom in wood-engraved illustrations of the 1860s, Pinwell began to make a reputation for his watercolours at the **Dudley** Gallery but died before his potential as an artist was realised.

Planché, James Robinson (1796–1880) English author, theatre critic and antiquarian who wrote a *History of British Costume from the Earliest Period to the Close of the 18th Century* (1834). He was also a scene designer and prolific dramatist, writing over 170 plays, many of which were burlesques or pantomime.

Bibl: Planché, *Recollections and Reflections*, London, 1872

Poynter, Edward (1836–1919) Leading English painter and designer who trained in Paris (1856–9) in the company of **Whistler**, Thomas **Armstrong** and George **Du Maurier**. On his return to England he undertook some decorative work for William **Burges** and began to exhibit at the **RA**. His reputation was made from a series of classical and biblical subjects, notably *Faithful unto Death* (1865) and *Israel in Egypt* (1867), although he continued to undertake mural work such as that for the Grill Room at the **South Kensington** Museum (1866–74). Poynter was actively involved in art education becoming first **Slade** Professor at University College (1871–5), then Director of the National Art Training Schools at South Kensington (1875–83). He continued to exhibit large classical subject pictures at the RA and found time to be Director of the National Gallery (1894–1904) and President of the RA (1896–1918).

Princess Louise *see* Louise, Princess

Prinsep, Valentine Cameron (1838–1904) Brought up in the celebrated artistic and literary salon led by his mother, Sara (one of the Pattle sisters), at Little Holland House, Val Prinsep kept the company of **Tennyson**, **Carlyle**, Dickens and **Rossetti**. G. F. Watts, a lodger for some 25 years in the Prinsep household, inspired the boy to take up painting. He studied in Paris alongside **Whistler**, **Armstrong**, **Poynter** and **Du Maurier**. In 1857 he collaborated with Rossetti, **Burne-Jones** and **Morris** on the Oxford Union murals, and from then on achieved success painting historical subjects in a Pre-Raphaelite and later an 'Aesthetic' or classical manner. He married the daughter of the wealthy collector Frederick **Leyland**, which freed him from a necessity to pursue commissions. He did, however, achieve professional recognition, being elected a full academician in 1894 and Professor of Painting at the **RA** in 1900. He also wrote novels and plays.

Prout, Samuel (1783–1852) Topographical draughtsman and water-colourist whose illustrations of European landscape and architectural antiquities were collected by architects and travellers embarking on tours of the continent. Prout's subject matter and style were a great influence on John Ruskin's watercolour drawings.

Bibl: R. Lockett, *Samuel Prout, 1783–1852*, London, 1985

Pugin, Augustus Welby Northmore (1812–52) Architect, designer, theorist and the central figure in the Gothic Revival in England. Son of an architect and draughtsman, who was himself a pioneer in the Gothic taste, A. W. N. Pugin followed his father in the 1820s, undertaking designs for furniture and metalwork which were produced by leading manufacturers. From 1832 he devoted himself increasingly to architecture and, after his conversion to Catholicism in 1835, became a fervent polemicist for the Gothic as the only true style on moral, structural and theological grounds. His ideas were expressed in a series of famous books including *Contrasts* (1836), *The True Principles of Pointed or Christian Architecture* (1841) and *An Apology for the Revival of Christian Architecture* (1843). St Giles at Cheadle in Staffs (1841–6) was his most successful church, the large budget allowing for the elaborate detailing and interior decoration that Pugin regarded as essential for the full realisation of his ideas. Pugin continued to develop Gothic design in the applied arts, producing designs for furniture, textiles, metalwork, ceramics, glass and wallpaper. He was engaged by Charles **Barry** in 1835 as a collaborator on the new Houses of Parliament. Pugin's dedication and authority with regard to Gothic architecture and design also drew him into the '**South Kensington** Group' of Henry Cole and Thomas Digby **Wyatt**. He was one of the organisers of the Great Exhibition of 1851, responsible for the Mediaeval Court which was regarded as the finest display of British goods. Depressed and exhausted from overwork, he died at the threshold of the High Victorian period when younger architects like Godwin began looking to a wider range of Gothic sources than the 14th-century 'English Middle pointed' favoured by Pugin. His son E. W. Pugin (1834–

75) continued the practice, working mostly on R.C. church commissions.

Bibl: P. Atterbury and C. Wainwright, eds, *Pugin: a Gothic Passion*, London, 1994

Punch Humorous magazine launched in 1841 which commented on topical matters from politics to fashion in cartoons and satirical articles. Initially radical in its outlook, *Punch* became increasingly conservative after 1850 reflecting the views of its middle-class readership. From the 1860s, it employed a stable of cartoonists, including George **Du Maurier** and Linley Sambourne, who satirised fashionable and artistic society with insight gained from personal experience. Aesthetes and bohemians were regular targets, helping to popularise the manners and catch-phrases of these marginal groups among the middle classes.

Quilter, Harry (1851–1907) Journalist and art critic of the *Times*. Despite his hostility to Aestheticism, he bought the White House in Chelsea following **Whistler**'s bankruptcy in 1879. He was described by Oscar **Wilde** in *Pall Mall Gazette* (18 Nov. 1886) as 'The apostle of the middle classes ... [who] raises literature to the position of upholstery, and puts it on the level with the anti-macassar'.

Richardson, Charles James (1806–71) English architect, designer, writer and collector, regarded as an expert on Elizabethan architecture.

Roberts, David (1796–1864) Scottish landscape artist who began his career as a scene painter in the theatre alongside Clarkson **Stanfield**. He later achieved great success as a painter of dramatic views in Spain, Egypt and the Holy Land.

Rossetti, Dante Gabriel (1828–82) Artist and poet, founder of the Pre-Raphaelite Brotherhood and later a leading figure in the development of Aesthetic values in art. Son of an Italian émigré and Dante scholar, the young poet changed the order of his names to emphasise his identification with the medieval poet. Taking up painting at the **RA** schools, he formed the PRB with fellow students J. E. **Millais** and W. Holman Hunt to reform art in the spirit of **Ruskin**'s writings. Although the Brotherhood was dedicated to uncompromising naturalism, Rossetti was more interested in religious and literary themes. In the later 1850s he worked mostly in watercolour but in 1859 he recruited William **Morris** and Edward **Burne-Jones** to assist in painting murals of Arthurian subjects in the Oxford University Union. In the 1860s Rossetti returned to oil painting, producing a series of half-length pictures of sensual female figures inspired by personal and literary associations. Like many artists in his circle, especially **Whistler**, Rossetti was interested in interior decoration and an early collector of Japanese prints and 'Blue and White' porcelain. Although Ruskin had been a supporter of his early work, Rossetti was in Whistler's camp during the libel trial of 1878. His last years were overshadowed by declining health, partly due to excessive use of chloral and laudanum.

Bibl: V. Surtees, *Dante Gabriel Rossetti: the Paintings and Drawings*, Oxford, 1971; J. Treuherz et al., *Dante Gabriel Rossetti*, London, 2003

Rossetti, William Michael (1829–1919) Younger brother of D. G. **Rossetti** and a founder of the Pre-Raphaelite Brotherhood, who became an eminent art and literary critic alongside his main job as a civil servant.

The Royal Academy (RA) Founded in 1768 as a state-sponsored association of artists on the model of the European academies of art. It quickly became financially independent due to the success of its annual exhibitions and gained considerable prestige within the British art establishment. Unlike the French 'Académie Royale', the RA admitted architects from the outset, although they were always in a tiny minority compared to painters and sculptors. A major aspect of the Academy's role was the teaching of art and architecture, but by the early Victorian period this was widely felt to be seriously deficient. The RA continued to elect a Professor of Architecture, who delivered lectures to students, and to award a Gold Medal for architectural composition.

Royal Institute of British Architects (RIBA) Growing out of the Institute of British Architects (founded 1834) and the Architectural Society (founded 1831), the RIBA received its royal charter in 1866 after which it became the principal professional body for architects in Britain. The RIBA aimed to promote architecture in general but, more importantly, to establish standards in training which eventually became recognised in formal examinations. Although this served to improve the professional status of architects there were many, such as R. Norman **Shaw**, who opposed the RIBA in its attempts to enforce national standards on the basis of 'stale legislation'.

Royal School of Art Needlework Established in 1872 by Princess Christian, one of Queen Victoria's daughters, and Lady Welby Gregory to raise the standard of needle crafts in the face of machine-made textiles, the Royal School offered employment and training for gentlewomen in financial need. Advised by William **Morris** and Walter **Crane**, the school undertook embroidery commissions using quality materials and traditional skills in the spirit of the Arts and Crafts Movement.

Ruskin, John (1819–1900) English critic and artist who, aged 17, was moved to write in defence of Turner, thus embarking on a career as the most influential commentator on art and culture of the 19th century. The defence of Turner grew into the five-volume *Modern Painters* (1843–60) in which he put forward belief in undecorated nature as the basis for true art since this was the perfect expression of God's work. These writings had a great influence on the Pre-Raphaelites and in 1851 Ruskin befriended and supported many of the group. Polymathic and ambitious, Ruskin's interests extended to economics, politics, religion, geology and botany, on all of which he felt confident to write. *Seven Lamps of Architecture* (1849) and *The Stones of Venice* (1853) gave his support to the Gothic Revival but added elements of his own on the virtues of craftsmanship which influenced the Arts and Crafts Movement. By the 1870s, Ruskin was a grand and forbidding presence in the cultural landscape of Britain although alternative approaches to art and taste were emerging. The Aesthetes looked more to **Pater** for their inspiration, and in 1878 both **Whistler** and Godwin crossed swords with the great man. Godwin's exasperated question, 'Is Mr. Ruskin living too long?' (p.133) suggests the oppressive weight of moral reckoning which still clung to matters of art, but this was only a pinprick. By contrast, Whistler's libel action against Ruskin for a hostile and insulting comment did much damage to both men. Whistler won the case but, awarded only a farthing's damages, was soon declared bankrupt. Ruskin suffered the first of many debilitating mental attacks and largely withdrew from public life until his death in 1900.

Bibl: E. T. Cook & A. Wedderburn, eds, *Library Edition of the Works of John Ruskin* (42 vols), London, 1903–12; T. Hilton, *John Ruskin* (2 vols), New Haven, 1985, 2000

Salviati Glass factory founded in 1862 in Murano, the historic centre of glassmaking in Venice, which launched a revival of Italian mosaic and art glass based on traditional techniques and designs. In 1866 Antonio Salviati was joined by English investors who helped promote the firm's wares among wealthy travellers on the Grand Tour.

Ruskin was an admirer, seeing the revival of blown glass as an alternative to the cut glass he abhorred. As the business expanded the company split into several rival firms.

Scott, Sir George Gilbert (1811–78) The most successful British architect of the High Victorian period, Scott was flexible instead of doctrinaire and his large practice was run very efficiently with the result that he secured many of the principal public and ecclesiastical commissions. The son of an evangelical minister, he trained with several minor architects before launching his own career in 1834 with workhouses and churches. Under the influence of **Pugin** and the **Cambridge Camden Society**, he adopted an increasingly scholarly approach and gained several commissions for churches which were well received. His own views were put forward in *A Plea for the Faithful Restoration of our Ancient Churches* (1850), the first of several books proposing conservative principles in church design. In 1856 his Gothic design was well placed in the competition for the new government offices in Whitehall and despite changes in the brief he secured the commission, eventually completing the huge complex in an Italianate manner. From then on Scott's office undertook some of the largest and most famous commissions in the country including the Albert Memorial (1862), Glasgow University (1864–84), Brill's Baths in Brighton (1866), the Midland Grand Hotel at St Pancras Station in London (1866–76) and St Mary's Episcopal Cathedral in Edinburgh (1872–1916). Scott was active in many official organisations, such as the **RA**, and was knighted in 1872 which, alongside his great professional success, made him a figure of the establishment. He was not without controversy, however. In 1877 J. J. **Stevenson** and the **SPAB** took him to task over his approach to restoration, a dispute which undermined his lofty position.

Bibl: D. Cole, *The Work of Sir Gilbert Scott*, London, 1980

Scott, Sir Walter (1771–1832) Scottish novelist and poet whose books established the historical novel as one of the principal forms of Romantic fiction. Trained as a lawyer, his early interests were in the poetry and vernacular traditions of his native Borders. *Waverley* (1814) launched the series of historical novels, including *The Antiquary* (1816), *Ivanhoe* (1819) and *Quentin Durward* (1823), which were international best-sellers, making Scott's reputation and assisting his heroic struggle to repay the debts incurred by his publisher's bankruptcy. Abbotsford, his house near Selkirk, became a place of pilgrimage and a model of Romantic design and decoration.

Severn, Arthur (1842–1931) English painter whose wife, Joan Agnew, was **Ruskin**'s cousin. The Severns looked after Ruskin at Brantwood following his breakdown before the libel action brought by Whistler.

Shaw, Richard Norman (1831–1912) Leading architect of the 'Old English' and 'Queen Anne' Revivals, Shaw employed a wide range of sources and styles across his long career. Brought up in genteel poverty, he trained in the office of William Burn where he met W. E. **Nesfield**. The two studied Gothic buildings together, and in 1854 Shaw embarked on a European tour, the results of which were published as *Architectural Sketches from the Continent* (1858). In 1859 he succeeded Phillip **Webb** as assistant to G.E. **Street**, an experience from which he learned a great deal, although he increasingly turned away from Street's singular Gothic taste. In 1863 he set up in practice alongside Nesfield, the two architects pursuing parallel careers working mostly on houses in the picturesque 16th- to 17th-century vernacular style known as 'Old English'. Shaw's Cragside (1869–85) in Northumberland is the climax of this style, a huge house in a spectacular setting with furnishings designed partly by Shaw himself. His drawings for this and other country houses were published and much imitated, creating a considerable fashion at various levels of society. In an urban context, Shaw deployed the 'brick and sash' elements associated with 'Queen Anne' in New Zealand Chambers (1871–3) and at Bedford Park where, in the wake of Godwin, he was responsible for several houses and some of the public buildings. In the 1880s Shaw relied increasingly on his assistant Richard Lethaby but his practice continued to expand and develop into the 20th century. Although proud of his status as RA, Shaw was a bitter opponent of the **RIBA**, which he felt debased the creative side of architecture by recourse to professional qualifications.

Bibl: A. Saint, *Richard Norman Shaw*, London, 1976

Slade School of Art In 1868 Felix Slade bequeathed funds for three professorial chairs of fine art, at the universities of Oxford, Cambridge and London. Only London took up the challenge of teaching art and in 1871 the Slade School opened in University College under the directorship of Edward **Poynter**. In keeping with Poynter's own training in Paris, drawing from the model was a central feature of the classes. This was maintained by his successor, Alphonse Legros, a French Realist and friend of **Whistler**, who took over in 1876. For the next 40 years the Slade was the leading art school in England.

Small, William (b.1843) Prolific and accomplished illustrator whose best work was engraved in the 1860s for periodicals such as *Good Words* and *The Cornhill*. He also produced many book illustrations and a few paintings of religious subjects.

Smirke, Sir Robert (1780–1867) Leading architect of the Greek Revival, of which his British Museum (1823–47) is the most famous example, although he also designed many churches in the Gothic Revival style. His younger brother, **Sidney** Smirke (1798–1877), was also an architect, responsible for the circular reading room of the British Library (1854–7), Burlington House, home of the **RA** (1868), and the Carlton Club (1845).

Smith, Thomas Roger (1830–1903) Architect, author and editor of the *Architect*. As President of the **Architectural Association** (1860–1 and 1863–4), and Professor of Architecture at University College London, he exerted considerable influence on the profession.

Society for the Protection of Ancient Buildings (SPAB) Founded by **Morris** and **Webb** in 1877 to protect old buildings from destruction and, equally dangerous, the aggressive restoration promoted by many Gothic Revivalists. The SPAB encouraged preservation of all phases in a building's history, not merely the 'best period', thus allowing the variety and texture of different generations to remain part of its appearance. The society campaigned to save many old buildings, advocating sensitive restoration in favour of rebuilding whenever possible. Many of the leading architects and designers of the 1870s and 80s were members.

South Kensington schools and museums refers to the complex of buildings and agencies which were reorganised after the Great Exhibition of 1851 into the Science and Art Department of the government's Council on Education. Comprising the South Kensington Museum (renamed the Victoria & Albert Museum in 1899), the Schools of Science and Art and the National Art Training Schools, as well as a series of libraries and outstations, the department's remit was to set and maintain standards in art and design education throughout the country. The curriculum that was developed, involving a series of drawing exercises and copying from pattern books and historic artefacts, became known as the 'South Kensington System'. It had a great influence on British design practice in the late Victorian period although many artists and designers were critical of its effects. Edward

Poynter, G. D. **Leslie**. H. Stacy **Marks**. J. E. **Boehm**, J. J. **Stevenson** and Thomas **Armstrong** all played an active role in the schools.

Spenser, Edmund (c.1552–99) Poet of the English Renaissance noted for combining Italian and English sonnet forms. His epic allegory *The Faerie Queen* (1590–96) was written for Queen Elizabeth and her court.

Spiers, Richard Phené (1838–1916) British architect and author, draughtsman for William **Burges** in the 1860s and later an influential teacher of drawing at the **RA** Schools. He was responsible for organising the British contributions to several international exhibitions. An exponent of the Queen Anne style, he designed 'Board schools' and several houses in the 1870s and 80s.

Stanfield, Clarkson (1793–1867) English marine and landscape painter who had early success as a painter of theatre sets and dioramas.

Stevens, Alfred (1817–75) English sculptor best known for his decorative work at Dorchester House and for the Wellington Memorial in St Paul's Cathedral. The latter project, a huge complex of Italian and English Renaissance elements, is his greatest work although it was constantly delayed due to Stevens's slow working practices and government prevarication. The completion and relocation of the monument was a major source of friction in the British art establishment of the late 19th century. It was eventually completed in 1912.

Stevenson, John James (1831–1908) Scottish architect who showed early promise in a series of impressive Gothic Revival churches in Glasgow before withdrawing from his practice and embarking on a lengthy European tour. On his return in 1870 he set up in London, where the design of his own house in red brick (the Red House 1871), using the 'simple and homely' forms of the English Renaissance, set the tone for much of his later work. Over the next two decades he designed many houses, notably at Palace Gate, Kensington, and Pont Street, Chelsea, and a series of 'Board schools' in collaboration with E. R. Robson in the emerging 'Queen Anne' or 'Free Classic' style. Stevenson's book *House Architecture* (1880) did much to promote the new style and he himself was a considerable spokesman for advanced ideas in domestic architecture among his wide circle of friends in the artistic and intellectual worlds. Stevenson's later career was notable for his work in Oxford and Cambridge colleges, and his office was well known as a staging post for young Scots making their way in the capital.

Stone, Marcus (1840–1921) After a modest career as an illustrator, Stone turned to painting historical and anecdotal subjects for which he achieved considerable success at the **RA**. Specialising in romantic themes from the Regency period, his works were very popular through engravings. As a result, he became very wealthy and was one of the first artists to commission a studio-house from Norman **Shaw** in the famous enclave at Melbury Road, London.

Bibl: A. L. Baldry, *The Life and Work of Marcus Stone*, London, 1896

Stott of Oldham, William (1857–1900) English naturalist painter who trained in Paris, becoming a friend of **Whistler** and member of the New English Art Club. He was known for his paintings of figures in low-toned, atmospheric landscapes. Stott died on board ship, prompting Whistler, whom he had alienated, to remark, 'he died at sea – where he always was'.

Street, George Edmund (1824–81) Architect, designer and writer noted for his scholarly dedication to the Gothic Revival. In 1850 he made the first of many tours on the Continent from which he wrote articles in *The Ecclesiologist*. His book *Brick and Marble in the Middle Ages: Notes of a Tour in the North of Italy* (1855) was very influential, followed ten years later by *Some Account of Gothic Architecture in Spain*. He served as assistant to G.G. **Scott** but attracted attention on his own account for Cuddesdon College (1853), a work much admired by Godwin. Thereafter he relied mostly on church buildings and restoration through contacts in the **Ecclesiological Society**. 'St James the Less' (1860–1), his first important church in London, demonstrated his grasp of bold yet harmonious design and from then on he led a very successful practice combining clear architectural principles with great sensitivity to the interior fittings and decoration. The triumph of his career came in 1869 when he won the competition for the new Law Courts in the Strand (completed 1882), an enormous and controversial project which occupied him for the rest of his life. Street was meticulous in his handling of all aspects of the design but came in for considerable criticism in the architectural press. Despite his reputation as a severe Gothic Revivalist who refused to delegate responsibility, his office attracted many promising assistants. Phillip **Webb** and William **Morris** met in

Street's office and Norman **Shaw** and the Seddings also worked there, making it something of a breeding ground for the Arts and Crafts Movement.

Bibl: D. B. Brownlee, *The Law Courts: The Architecture of George Edmund Street*, Cambridge, Mass., 1984

Stuart & Revett Travellers to Greece in the 1750s whose publication *The Antiquities of Athens* (5 vols, 1762–1830), providing accurate drawings and dimensions of ancient Greek buildings, became the standard source for Neoclassical architects and antiquarians.

Swinburne, Algernon Charles (1837–1909) English poet whose precocious talent attracted **Tennyson** and the Aesthetes although his dissolute behaviour eventually exasperated even **Rossetti**, whose house he shared. His 'Algernonic exaggeration', drunkenness, sado-masochism and homosexuality have often obscured his genuine literary talents. Some of his best poetry was inspired by paintings and music, reflecting the widespread idea of synaesthesia and the 'unity of the arts'.

Taylor, George Warington (1835–70) Business manager of Morris & Co. (the reformed version of Morris, Marshall, Faulkner & Co.) from 1865–70, responsible for improving the organisation and profitability of the firm by concentrating on inexpensive, traditional furniture. Warington Taylor is sometimes credited with developing the 'Sussex' chair, one of the firm's most successful items. He was also a critic of architecture and design.

Taylor, Tom (1817–80) English journalist and playwright who was art critic of the *Times* and the *Graphic* in 1870s and editor of **Punch** from 1874 to 1880. His most notable plays are *Masks and Faces* (1852) and *The Ticket of Leave Man* (1863), although he will perhaps be best known for *Our American Cousin* (1858), the play that Abraham Lincoln was watching when he was assassinated. A friend of Ellen **Terry**, he was a witness for **Ruskin** at the libel trial of 1878.

Tennyson, Alfred, Lord (1809–92) The greatest English poet of the Victorian period and, although shy, something of a public figure and symbol of the abiding importance of literature. His early poems had a mixed reception but from the time he published *In Memoriam* (1850) he enjoyed both popular and critical success. The young Pre-Raphaelites were great admirers of Tennyson and his work was widely illustrated in books and paintings by them and other artists.

Terry, Ellen Alicia (1847–1928) English actress who became the leading lady of the British stage, famous for her performances of Shakespeare. She and her sister Kate went onto the stage as children but in 1864, aged 16, she married the 46-year-old painter G. F. **Watts**. Separating after a year she returned briefly to the stage before setting up house in 1868 with Godwin. Although never married, they lived together for six years at Harpenden in a modest house decorated in a modern Japanese style, where they had two children (Edith and Edward Gordon **Craig**). Financial problems led Ellen to return to the stage in 1875, for which Godwin undertook set and costume designs. They separated later that year and in 1876 Godwin married Beatrice **Philip**. Terry's stage career flourished, especially after 1878 when she joined Henry Irving's company, creating a celebrated stage partnership which lasted for 24 years. In later life, she was made a Dame and continued to perform in Shakespeare and modern plays, including those of Bernard Shaw. At her death she is reported as saying that her period with Godwin was the happiest of her life.

Bibl: E. Terry, *The Story of my Life*, London, 1908; E. Terry, *Memoirs*, London, 1932

Thackeray, William Makepeace (1811–63) English novelist and magazine editor whose success arrived with *Vanity Fair* (1847) after an uncertain period as an investor, gambler, artist and journalist. His novels were published as monthly serials illustrated by himself and leading draughtsmen of the period. Thackeray's writings were credited with popularising the Queen Anne style.

Thomas, William Cave (1820–c.1884) Painter and writer on art including *The Techniques of Mural Decoration*.

Tredgold, Thomas (1788–1829) English architect and engineer who wrote several books on technology and craft, including *Elementary Principles of Carpentry* (1820).

Tree, Herbert Beerbohm (1853–1917) English actor-manager, half-brother of Max Beerbohm, famous for his Shakespearean roles from the 1870s. In 1887 he took over the Haymarket Theatre in London where he successfully produced *Trilby* by George **Du Maurier** and *A Woman of No Importance* by Oscar **Wilde**.

Verdier & Cattois French government architect and physician respectively whose book *Architecture civile et domestique au moyen age et à la renaissance* (2 vols Paris 1855 & 1857) pioneered the study of medieval domestic, as opposed to ecclesiastic, buildings.

Viollet-le-Duc, Eugène Emmanuel (1814–79) Architect, writer and restorer, the central figure of the Gothic Revival in France and a powerful influence on the understanding of the middle ages and of architecture in general. Brought up in a cultured, well-connected family, he chose to train as an architect through practical engagement with building and extensive travels rather than in the Ecole des Beaux-Arts. Joining the Conseil des Batiments Civils in 1838 he began restoring medieval towns as well as the principal Gothic abbeys and cathedrals, including Nôtre Dame de Paris, Saint-Denis, Amiens and Reims. Viollet-le-Duc's approach was based on archaeological research but combined with a belief that Gothic structural principles had an inner coherence which linked the medieval and modern worlds – ideas which he put forward in his *Dictionnaire raisonné de l'architecture française du XIe au XVIe siècle* (1854–68) and *Entretiens sur l'architecture* (9 vols, 1863–72). These theories gave him great confidence in undertaking extensive restoration projects, although many are now regarded as doctrinaire and insensitive. He was responsible for the design of many churches and secular buildings, including several houses in Paris, and wrote a second *Dictionnaire* on furniture and the decorative arts (6 vols, 1858–75).

Bibl: Exhibition Catalogue, *Viollet-le-Duc*, Grand Palais, Paris, 1980

Vulliamy, George J. V. (1817–86) Architect in partnership with his uncle, **Lewis Vulliamy**, who sponsored Godwin's admission to the Archaeological Institute in 1851. He later sat on the Metropolitan Board of Works which in 1879 rejected Godwin's designs for both The White House and the Miles House.

Vulliamy, Lewis (1791–1871) Eclectic architect and garden designer commissioned by Sir Robert Holford to design Dorchester House in London (1848–63) in an Italianate manner (with sculptural decoration by Alfred **Stevens**) and Westonbirt (1863–70), a country house in Gloucestershire, in an Elizabethan style. The designer Owen Jones was a pupil in his office.

Walker, Frederick (1840–75) English painter and illustrator whose early death after great promise was much lamented. Walker was one of the leading draughtsmen of the 1860s, a period when wood-engraved illustrations for books and periodicals were of very high quality. Turning increasingly to oil painting in a poetic but naturalistic manner, he died before his work had fully matured.

Waterhouse, Alfred (1830–1905) English architect, designer and painter whose pioneering use of terra-cotta encouraged the tendency towards richer surface decoration in Victorian public buildings. His early career was spent in Manchester during the 1850s and, although he moved to London in 1865, it was success in the competitions for Manchester Assize Courts (1859) and Town Hall (1869) which confirmed his position as a leading architect-designer. For both these and the Natural History Museum (1868–81) he also designed much of the furniture and fittings as well as the external sculptural decoration. Unlike his contemporaries, Waterhouse was never committed to one style alone. At Eaton Hall, Cheshire (1870–82), and in his college buildings for Oxford and Cambridge, he combined Gothic, Renaissance and vernacular elements. From 1877 he designed a series of offices for the Prudential Insurance Company using red brick and terracotta which attracted much interest. Over the next two decades he employed this combination of materials for a range of public and commercial buildings. Waterhouse was a popular and respected figure in the art world becoming RA in 1885 and President of the **RIBA** in 1888–91.

Bibl: C. J. K. Cunningham & P. Waterhouse, *Alfred Waterhouse: Biography of a Practice*, Oxford, 1992

Watt, William Art furniture manufacturer of Grafton Street in London who worked with Godwin from c.1867, publishing his designs in his catalogues and putting numerous pieces into production. 'The Butterfly Suite', designed by Godwin and painted by **Whistler**, was made for Watt's stand at the Paris Exposition Universelle of 1878.

Watts, George Frederick (1817–1904) English painter whose long career spanned several phases in British art although his work remained topical to the end. Watts emerged in the 1840s after a prolonged period of study in Italy but his retiring manner made him nervous and depressed. In 1851 he withdrew to the home of Thoby and Sara Prinsep at Little Holland House, which offered security as well as informal contact with the leading artists and writers of the day who attended their salon. Watts began to make a reputation for his portraits but his allegorical paintings only became well known after the **Grosvenor Gallery** opened in 1877. In 1864 Watts

married the young actress Ellen **Terry**: given their differing personalities, this was an unlikely match. After a year they had parted although they were not divorced until 1877. Watts became a celebrity during the last quarter of the 19th century, a grand old man of high Victorian art whose house at Compton was already a museum before his death, complete with mortuary chapel designed by his second wife.

Bibl: B. Bryant. *G. F. Watts Portraits: Fame and Beauty in Victorian Society*, London, 2004

Webb, Philip (1831–1915) Architect and designer closely associated with the Arts and Crafts Movement although he remained independent in many of the stylistic disputes of the period. Webb trained with John Billing in Reading 1849–51 and, after a short sojourn in Wolverhampton where the effects of industrialisation appalled him, he became an assistant in G. E. **Street**'s office in Oxford. It was here that he met William **Morris** who became a lifelong friend and commissioned his first work, the Red House at Bexley Heath (1859). From the collaborative effort of Webb, Morris and their friends, the Pre-Raphaelite painters, in designing and decorating this house, the firm of 'Morris, Marshall, Faulkner & Co.' was set up with Webb as one of the partners. The Red House established Webb's abiding interests: a preference for vernacular forms and materials, control over all aspects of the building and an approach to design and room arrangement appropriate for informal domestic living. His later and grander houses, such as Clouds in Wiltshire (1879–91), all reflect aspects of these principles. The studio-house at Palace Green at Kensington (1868) is often cited as an early example of the 'Queen Anne Revival', although Webb dismissed any such label. Alongside Morris, Webb became a committed socialist and a champion of sensitive, archaeological restoration under the auspices of the **SPAB**.

Bibl: W. R. Lethaby, *Philip Webb and his Work*, London, 1935 (repr. 1979)

Whistler, James McNeill (1834–1903) American-born painter and printmaker who lived in both Paris and London, becoming a leading figure in the Aesthetic Movement, a famous polemicist and the most progressive artist in late Victorian Britain. His early etchings in the circle of Courbet were remarkable but in the 1860s he rejected Realism, turning to Japanese and Classical sources to pursue the doctrine of 'Art for art's sake'. This was first seen in his three 'Symphonies in White' (1862–7) and the abandoned 'Six Projects', depictions of women which suggested abstract musical qualities similar to the work of Albert **Moore**. In the 1870s Whistler developed a sophisticated tonal manner of painting best seen in a series of portraits and evening landscapes which he described as 'Arrangements' and 'Nocturnes' respectively. The 1870s were the period when Whistler was most engaged with the decorative arts. In 1876 he took over the redecoration of Frederick **Leyland**'s dining room at Princes Gate from Thomas **Jeckyll**, a project which became his most ambitious interior (The Peacock Room), although a dispute over the extent of the work and the fee led to a break with his principal patron. The following year he commissioned a studio house (The White House) in Tite Street, Chelsea from Godwin and the two men collaborated on the *Harmony in Yellow and Gold*, or 'Butterfly Suite', for William **Watt**'s stand at the Paris Exposition Universelle 1878. Whistler was well represented at the first **Grosvenor Gallery** exhibition (1877) but an insulting review from **Ruskin** prompted him to sue the critic for libel. The trial was a *cause célèbre* in the British art world. Whistler won but was awarded only a farthing's damages. The legal costs and his own extravagant lifestyle led to bankruptcy in May 1879 and the sale of his property including the White House. Commissioned by the **Fine Art Society** to make a suite of etchings, he went to Venice for over a year. On his return the exhibitions of his Venice prints and pastels were a triumph, as were the watercolours shown at **Dowdeswell**'s in 1884 as 'Notes – Harmonies – Nocturnes'. The following year he delivered his *Ten O'Clock Lecture*, a polished and wide-ranging exposition of his ideas on art including many now famous statements and aphorisms. Whistler's return to prominence was accompanied by a number of portrait commissions from figures in society and the arts such as Lady Archibald **Campbell**. In 1884 he began a portrait of Beatrice **Godwin** and, following Godwin's death in 1886, he married Beatrice in 1898. Living mostly in Paris, Beatrice gave Whistler's life greater stability and their marriage was very happy until in 1895 her diagnosis with cancer forced them to return to London, where she died the following year. By the time of his own death Whistler was a celebrated figure and one of the most influential artists in Europe and America.

Bibl: R. Dorment & M. McDonald, *James McNeill Whistler 1834–1903*, London, 1994; www.whistler.arts.gla.ac.uk

White, William (1825–1900) Architect and writer who promoted certain features of the Gothic style, notably asymmetry, polychromy and the bold expression of structure, which became hallmarks of the full-blown Gothic Revival in the High Victorian period. He trained in the office of George Gilbert **Scott**, where he befriended G. E. **Street**, after which he set up his own practice concentrating on the design and restoration of churches. His writings in *The Ecclesiologist*, such as 'Modern Design' (1853) and 'On Windows' (1856), emphasised abstract architectural qualities rather than slavish attention to archaeological accuracy.

Bibl: P. Thompson, 'The Writings of William White', in J. Summerson, ed., *Concerning Architecture*, London, 1968

Wilde, Oscar Fingal O'Flahertie (1854–1900) Anglo-Irish author, dramatist and critic, born in Dublin but celebrated and eventually banished from London society in 1895 following a sensational trial in which he was convicted of gross indecency and sentenced to two years hard labour. Wilde was a prodigy, publishing poetry and reviews while still a student in Dublin and Oxford. Coming to London in 1879, he shared rooms with Frank **Miles** and adopted an extreme 'Aesthetic' position in his taste, dress and social manner, much of which was derived from the circle of Godwin and **Whistler**. In 1880 Miles and Wilde moved to Keats House at 1 Tite Street which Miles had commissioned from Godwin. George **Du Maurier**'s cartoons in ***Punch*** and **Gilbert and Sullivan**'s operetta *Patience* (1881) satirised this Aesthetic circle, with Wilde the most identifiable figure. In 1884, following his marriage to Constance Lloyd, Wilde moved to a house at 16 (now 34) Tite Street which Godwin remodelled and decorated. Wilde's greatest success came from his plays in the early 1890s but his fall in 1895 was rapid and, on release from prison, he travelled on the continent until his death in 1900 in a Paris hotel.

Bibl: C. Gere & L. Hoskins, *The House Beautiful: Oscar Wilde and the Aesthetic Interior*, London, 2000; R. Ellman, *Oscar Wilde*, London, 1987

Willis, Rev. Robert (1800–75) Jacksonian Professor of Natural and Experimental Philosophy at Cambridge whose writings and lectures on the history of architecture, including *Architecture of the Middle Ages, especially of Italy* (1835) and *Gothic Mouldings* (1842), were an inspiration to Godwin and others of his generation. Willis translated and edited the first English edition of Wilars (Villard) **de Honecourt** (1859).

Woodward See Deane & Woodward.

Woolner, Thomas (1825–92) The only sculptor among the founding members of the Pre-Raphaelite Brotherhood, Woolner found little support for his work and in 1854 emigrated to Australia. Achieving some success in the colony, he returned to London three years later and established a successful career as a portrait sculptor. Although noted for the harsh naturalism of his portraits, some of the most eminent figures in Victorian society, politics and the arts sat to him. He was elected RA in 1875 and became Professor of Sculpture in 1877.

Worth, Charles Frederick (1825–95) English-born dress designer who founded the first *haute couture* house in 1859, thus establishing Paris as the centre of high fashion. The House of Worth made dresses for the empresses and queens of Europe as well as the wealthiest middle-class women. Worth is credited with inventing the fashion show, presenting four collections each year which stimulated interest in the latest designs and styles.

Worthington, Thomas (1826–1909) Manchester-based architect noted for his innovative use of new materials in Gothic Revival buildings. He trained with **Bowman & Crowther**, after which he was responsible for a wide variety of building types, including churches, workhouses, tenements, country houses, baths and hospitals, (on the design of which he corresponded with Florence Nightingale). Although unsuccessful in the Manchester Town Hall competition, his public projects include the Albert Memorial (1862), the Memorial Hall (1865) and the Police Courts (1868), all in a variety of Gothic styles, which did much to establish the character of Manchester city centre.

Wortley, Archibald Stuart (1849–1905) Aristocratic artist who trained under **Millais**, after which he specialised in portraiture and hunting scenes. Wortley moved in Aesthetic circles and in 1878 commissioned Godwin to design Chelsea Lodge, a double studio house at 60 Tite Street for himself and Carlo **Pellegrini**. This arrangement broke down after six months' residence together and in August 1879 Wortley commissioned another house from Godwin, at 9 (now 29) Tite Street, for himself alone.

Wren, Sir Christopher (1632–1723) The greatest English architect of the baroque period, he was responsible for a plan to rebuild London after the great fire of 1666 which was only partly realised. Proposals to 'complete' St Paul's Cathedral, Wren's greatest building, prompted much debate in the 1860s, especially since **Burges**, a 'Goth', was put in charge. **Leighton** and **Poynter** prepared plans to decorate the interior with murals, which Godwin opposed on the basis that this would compromise the architecture. Godwin campaigned to save Wren's Temple Bar but it was dismantled in the 1870s to make way for the Law Courts.

Wyatt, Sir Matthew Digby (1820–77) Member of the Wyatt dynasty of architects, Matthew Digby was more diverse than many of his relatives, and exerted an important influence on Victorian design although personally responsible for few buildings. His early training at the **RA** was dominated by research and travel and he quickly made a reputation as a scholar of the applied arts. His lectures and writings, including *Specimens of Geometrical Mosaic of the Middle Ages* (1848), drew him into the circle of Henry Cole, Owen Jones and the Prince Consort, the so-called 'South Kensington Group', who were then engaged in planning the Great Exhibition of 1851. Wyatt, who became Secretary to the exhibition, oversaw the construction of Paxton's Crystal Palace in Hyde Park and the design of the Courts of Architecture inside. He continued to work on committees to reform design in Britain and produced designs for firms like **Minton**'s. He also undertook architectural projects in Britain and India employing an eclectic range of styles, his most important building being the India Office in Whitehall. By the 1870s his health had deteriorated from overwork.

Bibl: N. Pevsner, *Matthew Digby Wyatt*, Cambridge, 1950

Wyatt, Thomas Henry (1807–80) Prolific architect whose large and efficient office offered clients an appealing, if unimaginative, version of the late Tudor style well-suited to the expanding country house market in mid-Victorian Britain. His career was launched with a series of public and domestic buildings for the Beaufort estates in South Wales, after which he designed many churches in the dominant Gothic Revival style alongside his lucrative country house practice. Like his brother, Matthew Digby **Wyatt**, Thomas Henry was active in committees to reform and institutionalise the architectural profession.

E.W. Godwin's Writings

Those entries from which an extract has been made are followed by a square-bracketed reference to the page on which the extract begins.

The following abbreviations have been used:

Arch. – *The Architect*
BA – *The British Architect and Northern Engineer*
BN – *Building News and Engineering Journal*

1851

With Edward William, James Hine, & William Corbett Burder, *The Architectural Antiquities of Bristol and its Neighbourhood*, Bristol: Burder, Hine & Godwin, 1851

1853

'Notes, historical and architectural, of the Priory of Dominicans, Bristol', in *Memoirs Illustrative of the History and Antiquities of Bristol, and the Western Counties of Great Britain ...*, by the Royal Archaeological Institute of Great Britain and London, London, 1853
'Ancient coffin-slab in St. Philip's Church, Bristol', *Archaeological Journal* 10, Dec. 1853, pp.182-3
'Notes on some examples of church architecture in Cornwall', *Archaeological Journal* 10, Dec. 1853, pp.317-24

1856

'Account of a Roman villa discovered at Colerne, in the County of Wilts', *Archaeological Journal* 13, Dec. 1856, pp.328-32

1857

'An account of the Church of St. John the Baptist, Colerne', *Wiltshire Archaeological and Natural History Magazine* 3, no.9, 1857, pp.358-66
'Answers to queries: Earl's Meadows', Letter to *Ulster Journal of Archaeology* 5, 1857, pp.163-4
'Antiquarian notes and queries: "Augustinians" and "Augustine Canons"', *Ulster Journal of Archaeology* 5, 1857, pp.157-8
'Gothic and Classic', *Builder* 15, 28 March 1857, p.176

1858

'An account of the Church of Biddeston St. Nicholas,

Wilts', *Wiltshire Archaeological and Natural History Magazine* 4, 1858, pp.143-6
'An account of Ditchridge Church, Wilts', *Wiltshire Archaeological and Natural History Magazine* 4, 1858, pp.146-8
'Notice of the castle at Dudley', *Archaeological Journal* 15, 1858, pp.47-54
'The Taunton Tower, or a word for restoration', *Builder* 16, 21 August 1858, p.572

1860

The Court-house, Clapton-in-Gordano, Somersetshire', *Archaeological Journal* 17, 1860, pp.128-31

1861

'Notes on some of the churches in the deaneries of Kerrier and Penwith, Cornwall', Pts 1 & 2, *Archaeological Journal* 18, Sept. 1861, pp.231-52; Oct. 1861, pp.325-41
'Notice of an example of domestic architecture at Colerne, Wiltshire', *Archaeological Journal* 18, June 1861, pp.125-7 **[p.145]**

1862

'Excursion of the Bristol Society of Architects', *Western Daily Press* 20 Aug. 1862, p.3
'Theatrical Jottings' in the *Western Daily Press*: 'The new burlesque', 16 Oct. 1862, p.4; 21 Oct. 1862, p.2; 30 Oct. 1862, p.2; 6 Nov. 1862, p.3; 15 Nov. 1862, p.3; '*Romeo and Juliet*', 24 Nov. 1862, p.3; 28 Nov. 1862, p.3; 1 Dec. 1862, p.3; '*Macbeth*', 4 Dec. 1862, p.2; 8 Dec. 1862, p.3; 17 Dec. 1862, p.4; 'Christmas at the Theatre Royal: *Cinderella and the Cruel Sisters*', 26 Dec. 1862, p.4

1863

'Bristol Cathedral', *Archaeological Journal* 20, 1863, pp.38-63
'The destroyed monasteries of Bristol', *Western Daily Press* 16 Feb. 1863, p.3; 23 Feb. 1863, p.3
'Theatrical Jottings' in the *Western Daily Press*: 'The Pantomime', 3 Jan. 1863, p.4; '*The Little Treasure*', 7 Jan. 1863, p.2; 13 Jan. 1863, p.3; 'The London Pantomime', 21 Jan. 1863, p.4; 27 Jan. 1863, p.3; 11 Feb. 1863, p.3; 17 Feb. 1863, p.2; 23 Feb. 1863,

p.2; 26 Feb. 1863, p.2; 5 March 1863, p.3; 11 March 1863, p.4

'The sister arts and their relation to architecture', 1863 news-cutting in Archive of Art and Design AAD 4/561 **[p.36]**

1864

'The theatre', *Western Daily Press*, 4 April 1864, p.3

'The churches of Somersetshire', *BN* 11, 24 June 1864, pp.479-80

'The Savoy chapel, Strand', *BN* 11, 15 July 1864, p.539

'An antiquarian tramp through Old Bristol', *Western Daily Press* 10 Sept. 1864, p.4

'Theatrical Jottings' in the *Western Daily Press*: 21 March 1864, p.3; 5 April 1864, p.3; 18 July 1864; 31 Aug. 1864, p.2; 6 Sept. 1864, p.3; 10 Sept. 1864; 19 Sept. 1864, p.2; 22 Sept. 1864, p.3; '*Romeo and Juliet*', 5 Oct. 1864, p.2 **[p.330]**; 11 Oct. 1864, p.2 **[pp.328, 329]**; 'Theatre Royal, Bath: *The Merchant of Venice*', 18 Oct. 1864, p.4 **[p.329]**; 'Drury Lane and the Lyceum Theatres', 2 Nov. 1864, p.2; 'The Olympic', 9 Nov. 1864, p.3

'Mr. E. W. Godwin on architecture and Somerset churches', c.1864, lecture to the Bristol Society of Architects, V&A AAD 4/560-1988: cuttings book [probably from the *Western Daily Press*] **[pp.84, 146]**

1865

A Handbook of Floral Decoration for Churches, London: J. Masters & Son, 1865 **[p.232]**

'A few notes on some churches near Warwick', *Archaeological Journal* 22, March 1865, pp.33-40

'Plymouth', *BN* 12, 18 Aug. 1865, pp.574-5

'Art Cliques', Pts 1-8 of 12, *BN* 12, 15 Sept. 1865, pp.642-3 **[p.5]**; 22 Sept. 1865, p.657 **[p.55]**; 29 Sept. 1865, p.673 **[p.57]**; 13 Oct.1865, p.707 **[p.58]**; 20 Oct. 1865, pp.725-6 **[p.60]**; 3 Nov. 1865, p.766-7 **[pp.61, 63]**; 1 Dec. 1865, p.843; 'No. VII', 8 Dec. 1865, p.843 **[p.62]**; 15 Dec. 1865, p.876 **[p.65]**

1866

'Art Cliques', Pts 9-12 of 12, *BN* 13, 19 Jan. 1866, p.33 **[p.66]**; 2 Feb. 1866, pp.62-3 **[p.68]**; 9 March 1866, pp.146-7 **[p.69]**; 23 March 1866, pp.177-8 **[p.70]**

'(Notes on) Painted Decoration(s)', Pts 1-8 of 12, *BN* 13, 20 April 1866, pp.247-8; 4 May 1866, pp.282-3; 25 May 1866, pp.334-5; 22 June 1866, p.405 **[p.233]**; 3 Aug. 1866, p.507; 10 Aug. 1866, pp.526-7; 7 Sept. 1866, p.590; 16 Nov. 1866, pp.756-8

'Three modern architects', *BN* 13, 30 Nov. 1866, pp.799-800 **[p.251]**

1867

'(Notes on) Painted Decoration(s)', Pts 9-11 of 12, *BN* 14, 4 Jan. 1867, pp.4-5; July 1867, pp.490-1; 18 Oct. 1867, pp.715-17 **[p.234]**

'The photographs of the Architectural Photographic association for 1867', Pts 1 & 2, *BN* 14, 22 Feb. 1867, pp.147-8; 1 March 1867, pp.164-6

'Dromore Castle', *BN* 14, 29 March 1867, pp.222, 224-5; 1 Nov. 1867, pp.755, 758-9

'St. Alban's Abbey Church reviewed', *Civil Engineer and Architect's Journal*, 1 April 1867, pp.117-19

'The Architectural Exhibition, 1867', *BN* 14, 17 May 1867, pp.335-8

'A paper read by E. W. Godwin F.S.A. at the Country Meeting of the Waynflete Society in the Abbey of S. Albans on June 15, 1867', *The Annual Report of the Waynflete Society*, London, 1867

'Mr Street on the Bristol cathedral', *BN* 14, 9 Aug. 1867, pp.549-51

'Leicester and its Clock Tower Competition', *BN* 14, 20 Dec. 1867, pp.877-8

1868

'(Notes on) Painted Decoration(s)', Pt 12, *BN* 15, 3 Jan. 1868, pp.6-8

1869

'Foundation of S. Mary and S. Mark, now the Mayor's Chapel, Bristol', in *Somersetshire Archaeological and Natural History Society. Proceedings During the Year 1867*, Vol. 14, pt 1, Taunton, 1869

'On ancient Bristol', in *Somersetshire Archaeological and Natural History Society. Proceedings During the Year 1867*, Vol. 14, pt 2, Taunton, 1869

'Mr. Marks's work at the Gaiety Theatre', *Arch.* 1, 2 Jan. 1869, pp.3-4 **[p.340]**

'The Royal Academy', *Arch.* 1, 1 May 1869, pp.229-30 **[p.102]**

'Architecture at the Royal Academy', *Arch.* 1, 8 May 1869, pp.242-3

'The Architectural Association's Screen at the Exhibition, Conduit Street', *Arch.* 1, 15 May 1869, p.253

'The Royal Academy Exhibition', *Arch.* 1, 5 June 1869, pp.289-90 **[p.351]**

Letter, 'Bradford Town Hall', *Arch.* 2, 27 Nov. 1869, p.266

'Bradford Town Hall Competition', Letter, *Arch.* 2, 18 Dec. 1869, p.302

Caesar', 19 June 1875, pp.358-9; 'The Roman Plays – III. Antony and Cleopatra', 26 June 1875, pp.372-3

'Competitions and professional referees', *Arch.* 13, 9 Jan. 1875, pp.15-17

Illustration, 'Someries Castle', *BN* 28, 22 Jan. 1875, pp.90, 92

'First impressions on a private view of the Dudley Gallery', *BN* 28, 5 Feb. 1875, pp.146-7 **[p.352]**

'Japanese wood construction', Pts 5 & 6 of 'Woodwork', *BN* 28, 12 Feb. 1875, pp.173-4; 19 Feb. 1875, pp.200-1, 214 **[p.269]**

Obituary. 'Professor Willis', *Arch.* 13, 6 March 1875, pp.134-5

'Theatrical Jottings', Pts 1& 2, *BN* 28, 19 March 1875, pp.311-12 **[p.341]**; 18 June 1875, pp.683-5 **[p.343]**

'Specimens of Glazing', *BN* 28, 19 March 1875, p.316 and illustration

'The ex-Classic style called "Queen Anne"', *BN* 28, 16 April 1875, pp.441-2 **[p.91]**

Letter, *The Times*, 23 April 1875, p.10

'Notes on the costumes in the pictures at the Royal Academy', *Arch.* 13, 29 May 1875, pp.314-15 **[p.315]**

'Wall paintings in 1875: Mr. Armstrong and Mr. V. Prinsep', *Arch.* 14, 3 July 1875, pp.2-3 **[p.243]**

'Architectura vulgata', *Arch.* 14, 10 July 1875, pp.16-17

'Curiosities of architecture', *Arch.* 14, 17 July 1875, pp.30-1 **[p.94]**

'Harold's Church at Waltham', *Arch.* 14, 24 July 1875, pp.42-5

'Old English or Saxon Building', Pts 1-4, *Arch.* 14, 7 Aug. 1875, pp.70-1 **[p.96]**; 14 Aug. 1875, pp.84-5; 21 Aug. 1875, pp.98-9; 28 Aug. 1875, pp.112-14

'Bristol', *Arch.* 14, 4 Sept. 1875, p.126

'The present aspect of decorative painting', *Arch.* 14, 11 Sept. 1875, pp.140-1 **[p.238]**

'More words on Saxon architecture', *Arch.* 14, 18 Sept. 1875, p.154

Letter, 'The improvement of London Bridge', *Arch.* 14, 25 Sept. 1875, pp.179-80

'The cyclopaedia of Costume', *Arch.* 14, 16 Oct. 1875, pp.208-9

'The "mise-en-scène" at the Lyceum', *Arch.* 14, 23 Oct. 1875, p.222 **[p.337]**

'The Bayeux Tapestry', *Arch.* 14, 6 Nov. 1875, pp.250-1

'The "Daily News" versus Art', *Arch.* 14, 20 Nov. 1875, pp.281-2 **[p.40]**

'The hope of the family', *Arch.* 14, 18 Dec. 1875, pp.342-3

1876

'Some stray notes on the modern field of art', *Arch.* 15, 1 Jan. 1876, pp.2-3 **[p.39]**

'A painter and a sculptor', *Arch.* 15, 15 Jan. 1876, p.30 **[pp.133, 319, 355]**

'Correspondence: The Walker Exhibition', *Arch.* 15, 22 Jan. 1876, p.58

'Frozen music', *Arch.* 15, 5 Feb. 1876, pp.76-7 **[p.43]**

'Notes on English mediaeval architecture', *Arch.* 15, 19 Feb. 1876, pp.107-8

'In the studios of some "Outsiders"', Pts 1 & 2, *Arch.* 15, 11 March 1876, pp.156-7 **[p.353]**; 18 March 1876, pp.172-3

'A church in the way', *Arch.* 13, 25 March 1876, pp.190-1 **[p.150]**

'The popular novelist on art', *Arch.* 15, 8 April 1876, pp.221-2 **[p.270]**

[Attributed] '"Artistic" furnishing', *The Furniture Gazette*, 8 April 1876, p.222 **[p.275]**

'Scraps for students', Pts 1-6, *Arch.* 15, 15 April 1876, p.237-8 **[p.178]**; 'II. Out-door sketching', 22 April 1876, pp.252-3 **[p.182]**; 'III. Selection of studies', 6 May 1876, p.284-5 **[p.175]**; 'The office', 13 May 1876, pp.303-5 **[p.110]**; 'Competitions and clients', 20 May 1876, p.320 **[p.117]**; 'At home', 27 May 1876, pp.338-9 **[p.115]**

'Bristol blunders', *Arch.* 15, 29 April 1876, pp.267-8

'Mantelpieces', *Arch.* 15, 3 June 1876, p.353 **[p.296]**

'Modern dress', *Arch.* 15, 10 June 1876, p.368 **[p.319]**

'Greek art at the conference', *Arch.* 15, 24 June 1876, pp.396-7

'My chambers and what I did to them', Pts 1&2, *Arch.* 16, 'Chapter I: A.D. 1867', 1 July 1876, pp.4-5 **[p.192]**; 'Chapter II. A.D. 1872', 8 July 1876, pp.18-19 **[p.197]**

'My house "in" London', Pts 1-6, *Arch.* 16, 'Chapter I', 15 July 1876, pp.33-4 **[p.201]**; 'Chapter II.—the hall', 22 July 1876, pp.45-6 **[p.205]**; 'Chapter III.—the dining-room', 29 July 1876, pp.58-9 **[p.209]**; 'Chapter IV.—the drawing-room', 5 Aug. 1876, pp.72-3 **[p.214]**; 'Chapter V.—the bedrooms', 12 Aug. 1876, p.86 **[p.217]**; 'Chapter VI.—tops and bottoms', 19 Aug. 1876, pp.100-1 **[p.220]**

'From the house-top', *Arch.* 16, 26 Aug. 1876, pp.112-13

'Floorcloths', *Arch.* 16, 2 Sept. 1876, p.128 **[p.299]**

'*Henry V*: an archaeological experience', *Arch.* 16, 9 Sept. 1876, pp.142-3

'Lintel architecture', *Arch.* 16, 16 Sept. 1876, p.157

'The bell turrets of North Wilts', *Arch.* 16, 23 Sept. 1876, pp.174-5

'Theatrical notes', *BA* 17, 3 Feb. 1882, p.53

'*British Architect* Art Club: second session', *BA* 17, 10 March 1882, p.117

'Irish sketches by E. W. Godwin, F.S.A.' *BA* 17, 31 March 1882, p.149

'*British Architect* Art Club: fifth series', *BA* 17, 28 April 1882, p.199

Copy of letter dated 2 Oct. 1882, to Louis Fagan **[p.322]**

1883

'*Claudian*', *A Few Notes on the Architecture and Costume: A Letter to Wilson Barrett Esq., by E. W. Godwin.* Pamphlet, London, privately printed, 1883. Copy in V&A TA, Godwin collection, box 1

Review, '*The Tale of Troy*', *Royal Society of Painters in Water Colours*, 1883

'*British Architect* Art Club', *BA* 19, 19 Jan. 1883, pp.32-3

'Colours and cloths of the middle ages', *BN* 7 Sept. 1883, p.357 **[p.280]**

Letter, *The World*, 7 Nov. 1883, written from the New Athenaeum Club **[p.262]**

'A few notes on the architecture and costume of the period of the play of *Claudian*, A.D.360–460', *BA* 20, 7 Dec. 1883, pp.267-70 and illustration

'The first act of Claudian ...', *BA* 20, 21 Dec. 1883, p.290

'The third act of Claudian ...', *BA* 20, 28 Dec. 1883, p.300

'*British Architect* Art Club: second session, analysis of merit and award', *BA* 20, 28 Dec. 1883, pp.302-4

1884

Dress and its Relation to Health and Climate, London, 1884 **[p.323]**

'Notes on current events', *BA* 21, 4 Jan. 1884, p.4

'Notes on current events', *BA* 21, 22 Feb. 1884, p.86

'Notes on current events', *BA* 21, 21 March. 1884, p.134

'Notes on current events', *BA* 21, 28 March 1884, p.146

'The new Admiralty and War Offices competition', *BA* 21, 4 April 1884, p.165

'To Art Students', Pts 1-10 (2 pts are numbered 'Letter No.4). 'Letter No. 1', *BA* 21, 2 May 1884, p.215 **[pp.47, 364]**; 'Letter No. 2', 9 May 1884, p.225 **[p.365]**; 'Letter No. 3', 16 May 1884, p.238; 'Letter No. 4', 30 May 1884, p.262 **[p.187]**; 'Letter No. 4', 6 June 1884, p.273 **[p.149]**; 'Letter No. 5', 13 June 1884, p.285 **[p.161]**; ' Letter No. 6', 20 June 1884,

p.297 **[p.157]**; ' Letter No. 7', 27 June 1884, pp.309-10 **[p.334]**; *BA* 22, 'Letter No. 8', 4 July 1884, pp.1-2 **[p.128]**; 'Letter No. 9', 11 July 1884, p.13 **[p.248]**

Letter, 'My dear Atlas', *The World*, 30 July 1884

'Tenders: The Tower House, Chelsea', *Builder* 47, 2 Aug. 1884, p.179

Letter, 'Westminster Hall', *Times* 4 Dec. 1884, p.10. Reprinted *BN* 47, 5 Dec. 1884, pp.902-3

Letter, 'The restoration of Westminster Hall', *Times*, 10 Dec. 1884, p.6

'The restoration of Westminster Hall', *BA* 22, 19 Dec. 1884, pp.302-3

1885

Godwin, E. W., ed., *The Faithfull Shepherdesse, by John Fletcher. Adapted and Arranged in Three Acts for the Open Air*, London, 1885

'Archaeology on the stage', Pts 1-7, *Dramatic Review*, 8 Feb. 1885, pp.19-20 **[p.335]**; 22 Feb. 1885, p53; 7 March 1885, pp.84-5; 5 Sept. 1885, p.42; 19 Sept. 1885, pp.60-1; 10 Oct. 1885, pp.92-3; 24 Oct. 1885, p.112-13 **[p.148]**

'The Tower House', *BA* 23, 22 May 1885, p.252

'*British Architect* Special correspondence', *BA* 24, 18 Dec. 1885, p.262

1886

'Ancient Greek, Assyrian and Phoenician furniture' c.1886. British Architectural Library Manuscripts Collection, RIBA, MS GoE/5/1

'The Greek house according to Homer: its furniture and the costume of its inhabitants', c.1886. British Architectural Library Manuscripts Collection, RIBA, MS GoE/5/1

'Fine Art', Review of F. W. Fairholt, *Costume in England. Academy* 29, 27 March 1886, pp.225-6

'Dramatic and musical gossip', *Referee*, 23 May 1886

'The Greek home according to Homer', *Nineteenth Century* 19, June 1886, pp.301-5

'The home of an English architect', Pts 1&2, *Art Journal* June 1886, pp.170-3 **[p.140]**; Oct.1886, pp.301-5

'Whistler and the Philistines. What is a "Master"?', unpublished letter to the editor of the *Court and Society Review*, 22 July 1886, Library of Congress PWC 14/1336-7 **[p.366]**

1914

'A lecture on dress by E. W. Godwin, F.S.A. 1868', *Mask* 6 no.4, April 1914, pp.335-52 **[pp.145, 309]**

Index

Page numbers in *italics* refer to illustrations. The Biographical Notes (pp. 378-400) are not indexed.

CONTENTS

Front cover photograph: Le Creux Harbour
Back cover photograph: Carriage at La Moinerie
Title page: Grande Grève

Published by
GATEWAY PUBLISHING LTD
La Heche, Sark
Channel Islands
Typeset by Colophon
Colour by Riverline, Oxford
Printed in England

The Island Described

ARK is near the centre of the Channel Islands archipelago, which lies off the coast of France in the Bay of Avranches, north of Saint Malo. From Sark all the other principal Islands and the coast of France are visible in clear weather, but between the Islands and England lies the English Channel at its widest.

The Channel Islands are British only through several accidents of history; they are within the British Isles but they are not part of the United Kingdom and they remain something of an anomaly in today's world. Sark is perhaps the strangest of all the Islands, for its way of life and its constitution are as arcane as its granite coast is unassailable. Access to the Islands has always been difficult because of their rocky coasts and the treacherous currents surrounding them; for the larger Islands these obstacles have now disappeared with the introduction of air services, but not for Sark, which remains almost as inaccessible as ever with its huge cliffs, the scarcity of safe landing places for any vessel bigger than a rowing boat, and the refusal of the islanders to permit a helicopter service to operate from Guernsey.

Sark is a small plateau of irregular shape mostly at a height of between 60 and 100 metres. Above the massive cliffs, though hardly visible from the sea, is a luxuriant green country of small fields, with here and there thickly wooded valleys leading down to small bays or coves – some with sandy beaches – between craggy headlands and almost vertical fissured cliff-faces. From the earliest times explorers and travellers have been awed by Sark's forbidding aspect from the sea, and enchanted by its unexpectedly verdant interior and the abundance of its wild flowers. Writers and painters of the nineteenth century, keenly alive to the beauty of untamed Nature, were much taken with Sark. Victor Hugo, for example, visited the Island several times when he was living in exile in Guernsey; Swinburne was moved by its wildness; and J. M. W. Turner made La Coupée the subject of a drawing.

La Coupée is perhaps the most dramatic of Sark's many impressive features; it is a very narrow isthmus of 85 metres' length between Sark and Little Sark, carrying a three-metre wide road at a height of some 60 metres above the sea. Its sides are almost vertical and are under continual threat of landslides. It is mentioned again later.

Arriving in Sark. The normal way into Sark is by boat to Maseline Harbour, a deep-water mooring for all tides; construction of the jetty was begun in 1938, interrupted by the German occupation, and completed in 1949. The old harbour of Le Creux is more picturesque but suffers from being very shallow or even dry at low tide. The two harbours almost adjoin each other, and both are connected with the interior of the Island by L' Amont du Creux, a steep road up, also known as Harbour Hill.

There are no motor cars in Sark. Visitors who arrive by a regular boat service, whether to stay or for a day's excursion, may ride up Harbour Hill in a sort of *char-à-bancs* trailer – known as a 'toast-rack' – attached to a tractor, or they may walk; the distance to the top is about 800 metres and the rise is 90 metres.

Maseline Harbour

At the top of the hill is the electricity station operating in a building dated 1895; also the Information Bureau of the Sark Tourism Committee; the Aval du Creux Hotel, the Bel Air Tavern; and from this point onwards, as far as the crossroads known as La Collinette, horse-drawn carriages wait to pick up visitors.

Seeing Sark. The carriages are used for conducted tours of the accessible parts of the Island, including the gardens of La Seigneurie (the Manor House) on certain days. Carriages are also available for specific journeys; for instance, visitors wishing to go to lunch or dinner at one of the hotels may arrange a carriage for the purpose.

The top of Harbour Hill and La Collinette

Sark is only some 5 km from north to south, including Little Sark, and 2.5 km from east to west, excluding Brecqhou. There is a simple grid road pattern serving the central, populated, part of the Island. La Collinette, the commercial centre of the village, is at the south-east corner of a roughly rectangular section of the road system; this section includes The Avenue, which has the Post Office and most of the shops; it also includes the Anglican Church of St. Peter, the Island Hall, the world's smallest prison, the Greffe Office, the two schools, two banks, the Telephone Exchange, and such other representations of the modern world as have reached Sark.

The curious little barrel-vaulted prison at the western end of The Avenue was built in 1856 to replace a much older one that formerly stood beside the church; it has two cells; there are no windows, but electric light has been installed.

The Prison

Across the road from the school beside the prison there is a row of ancient cottages; this is the surviving part of the original Manor House or Seigneurie built by the first Lord of the Fief, Helier de Carteret of Jersey, soon after 1565 (see *History*). The building is in the style of Jersey farmsteads of the period; it not only housed the de Carteret family but also included a chapel and a school-room. What is now the principal part of this house is on the other side of the cottages, past the bend in the road; it is a handsome Jersey-style farm-house built in the 17th century by a later de Carteret, who placed the family arms* on the west gable. This property is called Le Manoir, but it is no longer the Manor house or Seigneurie, which in the 18th century was established at another house, La Perronerie, where it is today.

Some two hundred metres farther along this same road – Rue du Moulin – stands the windmill, now without sails, built by Helier de Carteret in 1571; the date and the family arms* are just discernible on the stone lintel of the doorway. Helier decreed a monopoly for his mill, but this was challenged by one of the tenants in Little Sark, who built another mill for himself and his neighbours; only the stump of this other mill remains.

The western side of the central rectangle of roads – a lane called Chasse-Marais – leads to the parish church of St. Peter (1820), then to the Island Hall, obviously 20th-century, and finally to the Senior School, formerly the boys' school, solidly 19th-century and complete with bell; this is where the Island's parliament, the Court of Chief Pleas, meets.

Next to the boys' school is the new ambulance and fire station, which also houses the Greffe Office. The Greffier or Registrar is Clerk to the Court and records all legislative and administrative documents and proceedings. There is a notice-board stating when the office is open. On the eastern side of the rectangle is the Telephone Exchange – now automated and impersonal, to the regret of some residents.

---

* Four fusils conjoined in fesse – or four vertically elongated diamond shapes touching each other in a horizontal row.

Remains of the mill on Little Sark

The seventeenth-century Manoir

La Seigneurie and garden

La Seigneurie

Houses and Farms. The present Seigneurie, with its splendid gardens, lies about 400 metres to the north-west of the central rectangle of roads. La Perronerie was one of the forty land-holdings into which the Island was divided in 1565; it became the Seigneurie or Manor in 1730 when the holder, Susanne Le Pelley, acquired the Fief of Sark and became Dame. The main body of the house dates from 1675; it was enlarged in the 1730s by Susanne's son Nicholas, who also asserted his ancient manorial right and built a dovecote. The house was further embellished by the Revd. W. T. Collings, Seigneur from 1853 to 1882; he added the massive watch-tower, with the intention of being able to signal to Guernsey.

The original Sark farm-houses built in the 16th and 17th centuries were modelled on the traditional Jersey long-house of one storey; many of them have later been enlarged by the addition of a second storey, and some have been entirely rebuilt. At first the houses were thatched, and continued to be so until the beginning of the 20th century, by which time grain farming had ceased to be economic in Sark, and straw for thatching was no longer readily available. A rather unaesthetic consequence of this is that the appearance of many attractive old granite houses is somewhat marred by their being roofed in corrugated iron or with too neat slates or tiles.

The older houses have a stone ledge projecting from the chimney-stack over the roof ridge; its purpose was to cover the ridge of the thatch where it abutted the chimney. Now that roofs are no longer thatched the ledges serve no practical purpose, but they have not lost their significance in folk-lore, for, as every guide-book reports, they are known as 'witches' seats' and are used as resting places by passing witches who, in gratitude, will refrain from doing the house any harm; the ledges remain as a kind of insurance policy.

North of La Seigneurie

In some of the old farm-yards there are traces of the traditional island method of hanging gates; that is, projecting from the corner of a barn or other thick wall, some two metres from the ground, a large flat stone with a round hole in it, and, at ground level immediately below it, a similar stone with a cup-shaped hollow serving as a bearing for the gate's main upright post – which of course projected upwards through the pierced stone.

Duval Farm, Little Sark

Butter-making at Le Grand Fort

Some of the original land-holdings – known as *tenements* – are still worked as farms, chiefly with dairy cattle and horses. The cattle are Guernseys and, as in Guernsey, they are tethered in these diminutive fields to regulate their grazing. Even so, with such luxuriant pasture they yield a very rich milk from which the characteristically bright yellow butter is made by hand. Some of the farming women still have, and occasionally wear, traditional black bonnets as used by their grandmothers.

Horses have been to some extent displaced by tractors for the heavier farm work and transport jobs, but they are still much in use for the tourist business, especially for the carriage trips. The care and maintenance of the carriages and harness, as well as the grooming of the horses, are now important ancillary occupations at the farms.

Other livestock, such as sheep and pigs, now have a less important place in the economy than they did in earlier centuries when the Island had to be virtually self-supporting in food and clothing; they are still useful, however, in mixed farming.

Mixed farming

At Le Grand Fort

9

Blacksmiths in Rue du Moulin

The Avenue

Flora. The lush pastures, the densely wooded valleys, and above all the abundant wild flowers, indicate the mild climate and fertile soil; another factor, now that farming is virtually confined to grazing, is that herbicides, fungicides, artificial fertilizers and other noxious substances are used very little or not at all.

In the interior of the Island the abundance of ash trees and Turkey oaks lends a bright feathery touch to the landscape. On the cliff tops the most prominent growth is gorse, which strongly colours the whole coast, intermixed according to season with bluebells, ox-eye daisies, foxgloves of an exceptionally dark colour, sea-pinks, and a wealth of other flowers many of which are seldom seen elsewhere.

R. M. Lockley, in *The Charm of the Channel Islands* has a chapter on the wild flowering plants of the Islands where he says that 700 species have been recorded; of these, 80 species are

Path to Pignon Landing, Little Sark

peculiar to Jersey, 35 to Guernsey, 11 to Alderney, and 2 to Sark. This was written about 1949 and, as Lockley himself remarks, such figures need frequent revision as species appear or die out in each Island.

A useful guide to Channel Island flora is the two-volume, pocket-sized, *Wild Flowers of the Channel Islands* by E. A. Ellis containing good colour photographs of 94 species, most of which are found in Sark.

Birds. Sark and the other Islands are visited by many migrating birds, occasionally including Siberian and American migrants off their normal routes; also the Islands and outlying rocks are the breeding grounds of more than a dozen species of sea-bird, including cormorant and shag, fulmar, gannet, guillemot, oyster-catcher, petrel, puffin, razor-bill, and tern. Besides these, Lockley in *The Charm of the Channel Islands* records over sixty passerine species, some resident, others visiting or migrating; he also mentions kestrel, sparrow-hawk, and peregrine falcon. As with the changing patterns of the flora, any record of the bird population – especially the breeding species – should be frequently revised.

The Lighthouse at Point Robert

Footpaths and cliff walks. The original land-holdings, or *tenements*, were arranged by Helier de Carteret so that each should have enough land to support a family and should also include a stretch of the coast to be defended against invasion, as required in Queen Elizabeth's founding charter. Except for Le Manoir in the centre of the Island, each land-holding therefore included an area of cliff grazing known as *côtil*; today these cliff-tops are where the roads and cart-tracks end and the footpaths begin. The coast of the Island, with many paths leading to its headlands and bays, affords attractive walks and superb views of cliffs and sea, with the other principal Islands and even the coast of France often visible in the distance, and opportunities for swimming, marine exploration, bird-watching, and botanical study.

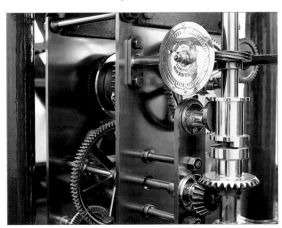

Inside the Lighthouse

Where a path traverses what is clearly private land, walkers should exercise tact and discretion, and in farm land they should remember that grass is the cattle-farmer's livelihood and they should not stray from the path. On cliff walks it may be dangerous to leave the path, since rocks are not always as stable as they may seem.

Cliff Walks. *Eperquerie Common.* At the northern tip of the Island is Eperquerie Common, a rocky but not very precipitous promontory with several footpaths leading to the Boutiques caves which are accessible at low tide; to L' Eperquerie landing; and to Les Fontaines Bay.

La Banquette. South of the Common the land rises to its mean height of about 90 metres. At Le Fort there are two paths leading eastwards towards the coast; one to a promontory with a wide view to the east and north, where a Napoleonic period cannon has been mounted; the other down to La Banquette landing. Near the landing is a *souffleur* or blow-hole – a rock formation that in certain states of wind and tide causes a jet of spray to be blown into the air. There are other *souffleurs* round the coast.

Grève de la Ville. From La Ville Roussel a pathway zig-zags down, partly through trees and with increasingly fine views, to the sheltered but stony beach of La Grève de la Ville, where a slightly Gothic-looking rock formation is known as *La Chapelle des Mauves,* the Gulls' Chapel.

Point Robert. On this high exposed promontory, reached from La Vallette, stands the Lighthouse, built in 1912. From this point to Maseline Harbour the coast is high and precipitous, and there is no way down to the sea. There is another *souffleur* across the bay from Maseline Jetty.

Le Creux Harbour. This is said to be the world's smallest harbour, and it is surely the most attractive; from the bottom of Harbour Hill it is reached through either of two tunnels, one made by Philippe de Carteret in 1588 – it bears the date over the arch at the seaward end – and the other by the Revd. W. T. Collings in 1866. The harbour encloses a small beach and is clean enough and safe enough to be used as a swimming pool.

Derrible and Dixcart. There are several paths; one begins a short way up Harbour Hill, on the left, with a branch to Les Lâches; another at La Forge, and others at the Dixcart group of houses; these paths traverse the beautiful area of Derrible Bay, Dixcart Bay, and the Hog's Back between these two bays. Derrible Bay and Point, and Point du Château, are precipitous, but the path down the wooded valley to Dixcart Bay is an easy and idyllic walk.

Little Sark from the Pilcher Monument

13

The Island from the East

The Island from the West

The buildings of La Seigneurie and the Rue La Rade

La Coupée

La Coupée. From Dixcart Bay southwards to La Coupée the coast is precipitous; there are several caves and another *souffleur,* but no pathway down. La Coupée is a high and narrow neck of land between Sark and Little Sark, in places barely three metres wide, with precipices on both sides. It seems alarming despite the solid concrete roadway that now spans it; this road was built – as a plaque explains – by German prisoners of war in 1945 under the direction of the Royal Engineers. The road is some 60 metres above the sea, but it is lower than the land at either end because in 1811, and again in 1862, there were landslides that left the path too narrow for safety; the level consequently had to be lowered to reach a wider base. Before 1900 there were no railings, and children going to school in windy weather used to cross La Coupée on their hands and knees.

The eastern face of La Coupée is so nearly vertical that it is not safely accessible; the western face has a steep, but safe, zig-zag path down to La Grande Grève, the largest of Sark's beaches. Near La Coupée, on the east side, is the Caverne de la Lamente, Lamentation Cave, not accessible from the land but, according to The Revd. J.L.V. Cachemaille,* terrifyingly audible when a particular conjunction of wind and tide causes a wailing and moaning as of lost souls in Hell.

Le Pot. From La Coupée southwards in Little Sark the first footpath is reached after 500 metres opposite a house called Clos de la Pointe, a pathway leads to Cider Press Cottage and Le Pot; this is a large cauldron-like pit or cavity in the land with the sea at the bottom.

Plat Rue Bay and Port Gorey. There are several paths over the southern part of Little Sark; they branch off the track that goes from La Sablonnerie to La Clôture, the Barracks; one leads to the 'Venus' pool, a large natural rock pool that is left full of water when the tide recedes and is much enjoyed by swimmers. Other paths go near the remains of the silver-mining venture that came to an end in 1845, and to Port Gorey from where silver ores were shipped. The promontory is not very precipitous, but the coast is rocky and there are no beaches. There are paths as far as Rouge Câne, or Caneau, and another natural pool known as 'Adonis'.

Le Havre Gosselin. With the exception of the pathway down the west face of La Coupée, there are no public footpaths between La Fontaine and Le Havre Gosselin; this may be reached either by a

---

* The Revd. J. L. V. Cachemaille, Vicar of Sark 1835-77. *The Island of Sark,* trans Louisa Harvey (1928).

path from the Pilcher Monument* down to the landing, or by one from Petit Beauregard to the bay. Le Havre Gosselin is the only landing alternative to those on the east coast, but it is of limited usefulness as there is no road and the declivity is very steep at this point.

Gouliot. The headland projecting towards the island of Brecqhou is accessible from Petit Beauregard. Below the headland there are caves where certain rare sea-anemones may be found; the approach is steep and calls for agility as well as for a watchful eye on the tide. *(For note on Brecqhou see page 26).*

Port à la Jument. To the north of Gouliot headland is a low-tide peninsula, Moie de Mouton, with long tunnel-like caves in it; adjoining it is Port à la Jument, a sheltered bay with a sandy beach.

Port du Moulin. Pegâne Bay and Port du Moulin are separated by the promontory that ends at the rock known as Tintageu and is noted for the 'window' in a rock wall, cut in the 19th century to provide a view of Port du Moulin. There are several delightful footpaths in this area, partly through woods, beginning at the end of the road that runs along the north side of the grounds of La Seigneurie and leads to L'Ecluse. There are no more cliff paths between here and Eperquerie Common.

The 'Non Pareil'

Boat-Trips and Fishing. Fishing is no longer the important activity for the islanders that it once was, but there are several fishing boats still working, and there is no better way of seeing the formidable grandeur of Sark's precipitous coast and hearing the strange names of its headlands, rocks, bays, caves and chasms, than to take a boat trip round the Island with a local boatman. Besides the amazing rock formations and the towering cliffs, there are many uncommon sea-birds, as already mentioned, and glimpses into mysterious caves. The boatmen normally take a course close in-shore, following the deeply indented coastline and going round the outside of Brecqhou, with the consequence that the trip covers some 24 km and takes four to five hours.

La Seigneurie. Visitors to La Seigneurie will find it useful to acquire a copy of the pamphlet *Brief History and Guide to Grounds,* which succinctly conveys much interesting information.

* This obelisk commemorates Jeremiah Pilcher, a London merchant, who was drowned in Gouliot Passage in 1868.

History Briefly Related

Early History. Stone-age man was in Sark 3000-2000 BC and left a few minor megalithic structures; over centuries these have been eroded by the islanders in their search for suitable building stone, and little now remains. The Romans may briefly have maintained a garrison in Sark; they, or possibly some Gauls trying to escape from them, left a few artifacts and some coins, but no durable buildings. The existence of a Visigothic settlement, probably of the 5th century, has been deduced from the remains of a bronze foundry discovered in the 19th century.

The recorded history of Sark begins about AD 557, when the Channel Islands were incorporated into the Celtic Diocese of Dol in Brittany and were visited by the Bishop, St Sampson, by St Helier, and by St Magloire (Macglorius, son of glory, a Breton monk of Welsh origin who later succeeded St Sampson as Bishop of Dol). St Magloire came again in AD 565 and established in Sark a community of some sixty Breton monks; they built a chapel and living quarters; they dammed a small stream to make fishponds and to drive a water-mill; and they enclosed some pasture land. This community continued in existence for some eight centuries.

The next certain date is 933, when the Channel Islands were granted by the French King in fief to William Long-sword (d. 943) who had succeeded his father Rollo, the first Duke of Normandy. About this time the Islands were transferred from the Diocese of Dol, in the Celtic Church, to that of Coutances in the Roman Church. St Magloire's monastery in Sark then came under the Abbey of Mont St Michel, and it was rebuilt as a priory.

In 1066 William the Conqueror added the Kingdom of England to his Duchy of Normandy; this made little difference to the islanders who continued to pay homage to him as Duke even after he became King of England. In 1199 Richard Coeur de Lion was succeeded by John as King of England and Duke of Normandy, but the French invaded Normandy and John lost his mainland Duchy. The Islands, however, have never belonged to France but remain an unconquered part of the old Duchy; as such, they are possessions of the English Crown, but the islanders to this day maintain a formal allegiance to the Duke of Normandy.

Following this French invasion of Normandy the larger islands were heavily fortified, but Sark, being naturally almost impregnable, was given no more than a simple tower or keep; a length of very thick ancient wall at La Seigneurie is thought to be a fragment of such a fort.

The lawlessness of the Hundred Years' War continued into the 14th century and made life untenable for the monks in Sark, so that by the middle of the century they had all returned to France. Of the priory or monastery, dating from the 10th and later centuries, little now remains.

The departure of the monks seems to have left the islanders without guidance or leadership, and in 1369 the French raided Sark so devastatingly that it remained virtually uninhabited. There is a well-entrenched legend that the Island then fell into the hands of pirates and wreckers, who with false lights would lure ships onto the rocks and plunder them. Rabelais, who had an ear for folk-lore, refers to it as an island of thieves and murderers.

The same, or a related, legend – for which reputable historians* assert there is no basis in fact – has it that the crew of a boat from Jersey, or possibly from Rye or Winchelsea in Sussex, cunningly sought permission to land, ostensibly to bury their captain who, they said, had died at sea;

---

* Ewen & de Carteret: *The Fief of Sark* Guernsey 1969.

the islanders agreed on condition that the landing party were not armed. The crew came ashore bearing a coffin containing not a body but weapons, with which they repaired to the chapel; having privily armed themselves, they emerged in strength and wrought havoc on the unsuspecting islanders. This picturesque story appears again in the 16th century and is cited by Sir Walter Raleigh in his account of the Channel Islands.

French Occupation. From the latter part of the 14th century, after the French raid, until the middle of the 16th century, over a span of nearly two hundred years, Sark appears to have been uninhabited, or at least uncivilized and without government. In 1549 a large French force landed and set up a garrison of some two hundred conscripts, convicts, or

The West coast and Brecqhou

mercenaries, under Captain François Bruel. He built three forts: Le Grand Fort in the north of the Island to cover the landings at L'Eperquerie and La Banquette, Le Château de Quénevêts on the headland above Dixcart Bay, and a third at Vermondaye in Little Sark.

The garrison was soon reduced, by desertions or escapes, to a mere handful, and in 1553 it was easily overcome by the Flemish adventurer Adrian Crole, to whom the coffin story is sometimes attributed. He took some French prisoners and landed them in Guernsey; he then went on to London to report his deeds to the Ambassador of the Emperor Charles V, hoping for a handsome reward. The Emperor, it seems, was not interested and Crole was referred to Queen Mary Tudor; she ignored his request and he went back to Sark disappointed. He collected 'ordnance' and other valuables from the French forts and then returned to Holland, stopping on the way to sell some of his booty to the Captain of Alderney. The Governor of Jersey sent a party to demolish the French forts, and Sark was then again left untenanted.

In 1560, when the Island had been unoccupied for six or seven years, the Seigneur of Glatigny in Normandy obtained a lease from the King of France – who was hardly entitled to grant it – and set up a colony of tenants from his Normandy estates. In 1562, however, war again broke out between England and France; it may be supposed that Glatigny thought his tenure none too secure, for he took his people back to Normandy. Sark was once again left uninhabited.

The following year, 1563, may be said to mark the beginning of Sark's modern history with the colonizing venture of Helier de Carteret under the patronage of Queen Elizabeth I.

The de Carteret family. Helier de Carteret was the hereditary Seigneur of the Manor of St Ouen, the principal fief of Jersey, which his family had handed down from father to son for over five hundred years. St Ouen is in the north-west corner of Jersey facing towards Sark; Helier, with Glatigny in mind, saw a threat of French encroachment in an unoccupied island, and he decided that Sark must be colonized. The Island was in the Bailiwick of Guernsey, and Helier therefore had to obtain the authority of the Governor of Guernsey, who acted for the Crown, to occupy Sark. With the help of a Guernsey friend, Nicholas Gosselin, Helier obtained the concession in 1563 and the following year took a party of his tenants from St Ouen to Sark. They made some trial grain sowings and, finding the land fertile, were encouraged to press on with the colonizing scheme.

Road from La Seigneurie

A couple of years later, in 1565, Helier was in London on Jersey affairs; he took this opportunity to seek royal confirmation of his tenure of Sark. From Queen Elizabeth he obtained Letters Patent granting him the Island of Sark as an addition to his fief of St Ouen. For this he undertook to pay a small annual rent and to provide at any time forty men armed with muskets for the defence of the Island.

The settlers, led by Helier and his redoubtable wife Margaret, faced a forbidding task; the ruined chapel of St Magloire was patched up for the de Carteret household to live in; there were otherwise no houses, though the stones from the demolished French forts were quickly put to good use. There had been no orderly cultivation for nearly two hundred years, and the land was a wilderness of gorse and brambles, riddled with rabbits. All the settlers' livestock, seed grain, tools, timber for building, and supplies for subsistence had to be shipped from Jersey and unloaded at one or another of Sark's precarious landing places. Helier had proved at the beginning how fertile the land was; he believed that efforts to cultivate it would be rewarded and that the huge expense of the venture would be justified, as indeed it was.

On Little Sark

To ensure that he could at all times muster the forty men required in the Queen's charter, Helier divided the Island into forty land-holdings, collectively known as *La Quarantaine*, comprising his own manorial land and thirty-nine sub-fiefs or *tenements* leased to tenants under obligation of tithe and labour and the service, when required, of an armed man for the defence of the Island – who in practice would be the Sieur (tenant) himself or a member of his family. The system of land-tenure that evolved out of this arrangement became the basis of the Island's constitution and government.

Helier set up his own holding, Le Manoir,* in the centre of the Island near a spring at the head of the valley that goes down to Dixcart Bay. The thirty-nine *tenements* were arranged so that each included a stretch of the coast with possible landing places to be defended, as well as enough workable land to support a family, and some *côtils* or cliff-top grazing. Helier entrusted four tenements in the west of the Island to his friend Nicholas Gosselin of Guernsey, who had helped him to obtain the preliminary concession in 1563. These four *tenements* were held by Guernsey people brought by Nicholas, after whom Le Havre Gosselin is named.

---

* The house known as Le Manoir is not now the Manor or Seigneurie, as explained in *The Island Described*, page 4. See also page 23, *The Le Pelley family*.

Helier was again in London in 1572, when he gave the Queen an account of his achievements over the seven years of his tenure. She rewarded him by making Sark a Fief Haubert* and giving him six bronze cannons from the Tower of London, one of which, suitably inscribed, is preserved at La Seigneurie. Two of the others were melted down in the 19th century and re-cast as the church bell.

Another of Helier's undertakings, begun in 1570, was the building of Le Creux Harbour at Baie de la Motte, which he regarded as more accessible for boats from Jersey than the unprotected landings at L'Eperquerie and La Banquette in the north of the Island. Le Creux, however, was almost inaccessible from the land until Philippe de Carteret (Helier's son and successor) cut the tunnel, dated 1588, and made the road up to La Collinette. Helier also built the windmill which stands in Rue du Moulin a short distance to the west of Le Manoir.

Royal visit, in Chasse-Marais

After some fifteen years as active Seigneur, Helier in 1579 conferred the governing of Sark on his son Philippe and retired to his St Ouen estate. Philippe achieved nothing very remarkable beyond improving the access to Le Creux Harbour. His attempt to make Sark an independent bailiwick, separate from Guernsey, was unsuccessful.

The Fief of Sark continued to be held, but was seldom visited, by successive generations of the de Carteret family. A difficult situation arose during the English Civil War; Jersey was Royalist, as also the de Carteret family and, by implication, most of the Sieurs of the Quarantaine in Sark. Guernsey, however, was Parliamentarian, and Sark was in its Bailiwick. Under the Commonwealth the royal fiefs were confiscated by Parliament, and the de Carterets could not go to Sark, which was governed from Guernsey; in particular the Guernsey family of Le Gros became *de facto* rulers of Sark.

After the Restoration of the Monarchy in 1660 the Seigneur, Sir Philippe de Carteret III, regained possession of his fiefs, and Sark's former system of government was more or less restored. In 1693 the fief passed to Sir Charles de Carteret, then aged about 15; he managed Sark's affairs no better than he did his own life, and he died childless and heavily in debt in 1715. He was the last of the de Carterets who had held the Fief of St Ouen in Jersey for seven centuries.

---

*A Fief Haubert, or Knight Service, is held direct from the Crown; the fee is the service for a twentieth part of the year of a mounted and armed knight clad in a coat of chain mail, or *haubert* (English: hauberk). A Fief Haubert cannot be sold or mortgaged without the assent of the Crown.

The Fief of Sark, encumbered with debts, then passed to Lord John Carteret, a member of the anglicized branch of the family, who never went to the Channel Islands and was not interested in the affairs of Sark beyond eliminating the debts. In 1720 he sold the Fief, with Royal Assent, to Colonel John Johnson of Guernsey, who was the principal creditor; the Colonel died in 1723 and the Fief passed through several hands until it was bought in 1730 by Susanne Le Pelley, née Le Gros, widow of Nicholas Le Pelley and tenant of La Perronerie, one of the forty holdings.

The Le Pelley tenure. Susanne Le Pelley, of the Le Gros family, thus became in 1730 the first Dame of Sark; she founded a dynasty that continued until 1852 – for almost as long as the century-and-a-half of the de Carteret tenure. The Le Gros and the Le Pelley families were Guernsey people, and Sark thus became more closely attached to Guernsey, while the Jersey influence waned.

Susanne, on becoming Dame, decided to remain in her family house at La Perronerie, rather than move to Le Manoir, which was the traditional residence of the Seigneur. She accordingly set up the Seigneurie at La Perronerie, and the house of Le Manoir became the residence of the Minister or Vicar, which it continued to be until 1934, when a new Vicarage was built. The house of La Perronerie, built about 1675 and much added-to over the years, succeeds an earlier building on or near the site of the Priory established by the Abbey of Mont St Michel in the late 10th or early 11th century. As mentioned earlier, the monks abandoned the Priory in the 14th century, and the buildings were dismantled by the islanders wanting stone for their houses.

Susanne's successors in the 18th century lived in Guernsey for most of the year and used their Sark estate as a summer resort. The Island became fashionable for week-end parties and wedding celebrations – said to have been riotous at times – engendering among the islanders no little resentment. This coincided, at the turn of the century, with anti-feudal and anti-aristocratic sentiments inspired by the French Revolution, and with the rise in England of Methodism and its stricter moral standards. The islanders readily welcomed a Methodist missionary from Guernsey, who in 1789 preached in the evenings in the kitchen at Clos à Jaôn (at the corner of Chasse Marais and Rue du Sermon). The Methodist Ebenezer Chapel was built in 1796 – twenty-four years before the Anglican church of St Peter. The chapel was popularly known as *Le Sermon*, whence Rue du Sermon is named.

It is recorded that in the late 18th century, and into the early 19th, scant attention was paid to Sunday observance. In the 1820s the Minister, Jean de Jaux, succeeded in having the taverns closed on Sundays – as they still are – and one of the *Quarantaine*, Sieur Elie Guille, obtained an order forbidding field work on Sundays. Sark remains to this day very quiet on Sundays, since there are no day-trip boats and only the hotels are open.

Pierre Le Pelley II (great-grandson of Susanne) gave the land and arranged for the building of St Peter's Church, to replace the 'rotten old barn' at Le Manoir that was still being used. St Peter's was completed in 1820 and consecrated in 1829; the cost was in part met by selling the pew tenures and entailing them with the *tenements* and *clos* (other farms) properties; the ownership of the entailed pews is today indicated by the names and emblems of the properties worked on the cushions. The Church Building Society too contributed to the costs of building St Peter's, provided that half the pews in the church should be kept 'free', as they remain today.

The Silver Mine. In the early 1830s traces of copper were found at Le Pot, but the fact was overshadowed by the discovery in 1835 of silver ore near-by at Port Gorey. A company was formed to exploit the lode; some two hundred Cornish miners were brought in, and four shafts were sunk to amazing depths as great as 180 metres, which is 120 metres below water level, with immense

Remains of the silver mines

lateral galleries following the silver veins, some stretching out under the sea. A massive 120 horse-power steam pumping-engine was installed, with other machinery for treating the ores. The young Seigneur, Pierre Le Pelley III, was persuaded to invest in the mining venture; the company claimed to be finding ever-richer ores requiring ever-greater capital outlay, and prospects were made to look very promising.

Pierre was drowned in a storm off the Bec du Nez* in 1839 and was succeeded as Seigneur by his younger brother Ernest, who inherited Pierre's shareholding in the silver mine and even made a further investment in it. In 1845, when the company's prospects had never seemed better, first a valuable cargo of silver ore was lost at sea, and soon afterwards the lower, richer, galleries were flooded and lost beyond hope of recovery. The value of the ore produced up to then was £4,000, from a capital expenditure of £34,000. The company was wound up a few years later.

Ernest Le Pelley was bankrupt; with Royal Assent he mortgaged the Fief to a rich Guernsey financier named Jean Allaire, whose fortune was reputedly derived from privateering during the Napoleonic Wars. When Ernest died in 1849 his son Peter Carey Le Pelley, aged 19, inherited the Fief and the debts; he was unable to meet the interest charges on the mortgage, and in 1852 he surrendered the Fief to Allaire's daughter Marie, the widow of Thomas Guerin Collings. Marie thus became the second Dame of Sark, but she died in the following year and was succeeded by her son The Revd. William Thomas Collings. It was he who established the dynasty that continues today and has already exceeded the duration of the Le Pelley family.

The Collings-Beaumont family. The Revd. William T. Collings was perhaps the most dedicated Seigneur since Helier de Carteret; he loved Sark, lived here much of the time, and was interested in the Island's affairs. He organized the rebuilding of Le Creux Harbour and he cut the second tunnel in 1866; he added the chancel to St Peter's Church in 1878, and he gave a parcel of Seigneurie land for an extension of the cemetery. He also had the ancient prison removed from alongside the church in 1856 and rebuilt where it now stands at the western end of The Avenue; he bought the *tenement* of L'Ecluse, which adjoins La Perronerie; and he added the watch-tower to the Seigneurie house – considered by subsequent generations to be a rather regrettable lapse of taste.

* The Minister of Sark at the time, the Revd. J. L. V. Cachemaille, actually witnessed this event from the land and vividly described it in his book *The Island of Sark,* trans Louisa Harvey *1928.* It is said that he so feared the sea that he never left the Island during the forty-odd years that he was Minister.

On Little Sark

The Revd. William was succeeded in 1882 by his son William Frederick, whose tenure of the Fief lasted for 45 years; during this time the tourist business became important; excursion steamers used to come from Jersey and Guernsey two or three times a week; the hotel trade flourished, and Sark began to be known in the world.

William Frederick died in 1927 and was succeeded by his daughter Sibyl Mary, the widow of Mr Dudley Beaumont; she was thus the third Dame in Sark's history, and she was by far the most notable. Two years after becoming Dame she married Mr Robert W. Hathaway, an American citizen naturalized British; he was thus legally Seigneur, but in practice he preferred to leave the government of the Island to his wife. Sibyl Hathaway was the Dame of Sark who became a legend and is still justly renowned; she was a person of strong character who governed her Fief wisely and devotedly for 47 years, and lived to the age of 90.

She was never more formidable than during the German occupation of Sark, 1940-45; she refused to leave the Island, and when the occupying German officers arrived she told them, in fluent German, what they were allowed and not allowed to do on her Island. They recognized authoriy when they met it, and they treated her with respect. The German occupation of the Channel Islands is a horrifying chapter in their history; Sark, it seems, suffered somewhat less than did the larger Islands, partly because of its very small population and its geographical unimportance, and partly – perhaps chiefly – because of the Dame's authoritarian presence.

When in 1957 Queen Elizabeth II, with Prince Philip, visited Sark she was the first Sovereign to do so (Queen Victoria had tried in 1859 but the sea was too heavy for her to land). On this occasion the Dame was able to render her homage to her Sovereign in the very terms in which Helier de Carteret had paid homage to Queen Elizabeth I. A few years later, when celebrating the 400th anniversary of the first charter, Sibyl Hathaway became, as she put it, a 'double Dame' when she was created Dame of the British Empire.

Dame Sibyl died in 1974 and was succeeded by her grandson John Michael Beaumont. He has continued her policy of preserving traditions that serve a good purpose, or are at least harmless, while conceding change where advantages lie. The islanders' views appear to run on the same lines.

Thus their long-established refusal to admit motor-cars to the Island was later endorsed and extended by their rejection of proposals for a helicopter service from Guernsey. On the other hand, the practical advantages of allowing tractors were presumably found to outweigh the disadvantages of the consequent pollution.

Sark has so far managed to avoid becoming entirely part of the modern world, and it consequently has enormous but vulnerable charm. Nobody appreciates this more than the Seigneur and the islanders themselves.

The Church

Brecqhou. The Fief conferred by Queen Elizabeth's Charter of 1565 consists of the Island of Sark and all adjacent islets and rocks. Brecqhou, though part of the Fief, was not included in the original distribution of land among the thirty-nine Sieurs or tenant farmers (see page 21). It became a *tenement* in 1927 when Dame Sibyl sold its lease and transferred to it the vote pertaining to La Moinerie de Haut, a *tenement* that had become part of La Seigneurie.

Government

Constitution. The Channel Islands are constitutionally the last remaining part of the lost Duchy of Normandy, to which William the Conqueror added the Kingdom of England. The Islands are included in the British Isles and are dependencies of the English Crown, but they have never been incorporated into the Kingdom of England, nor into the United Kingdom; their largely autonomous governments are responsible only to the Sovereign in Council, not to the Parliament of Westminster, and the Islands' legislation is subject only to the Royal Assent.

The Islands are grouped in two Bailiwicks: Jersey and Guernsey, the latter including Alderney and Sark; the principal officer in each Bailiwick is the Bailiff, who is both Judge and President of the legislative assembly.

Sark has its own legislative assembly, called *Le Cour des Chefs Plaids* or Court of Chief Pleas, presided over by the Seneschal who appoints the Court's five officers. The Royal Court of Guernsey, with jurisdiction over the Bailiwick, may lay down rules of procedure for Sark, and the Court of Chief Pleas, may also decide its own rules; the Crown Officers of Guernsey may, and do, give advice to the officers of the Chief Pleas, who are not usually professional lawyers.

The Court is composed of the Seigneur and the five officers approved by him, the thirty-nine tenants of the *Quarantaine* as established by Helier de Carteret, and twelve People's Deputies elected by the Island's residents. As a representative system Sark's constitution is probably unique; apart from the Seigneur and the Officers of the Court, the voting members of the Chief Pleas are the thirty-nine Sieurs and the twelve People's Deputies. These amount in practice to some fifty representatives for a population of fewer than six hundred; even if only the People's Deputies are regarded as genuinely elected representatives, the electoral constituencies average about fifty voters.

An important feature of the Island's administration is the *Douzaine*; twelve members of the Chief Pleas are elected for six-year terms, and the body so formed is responsible for the maintenance of footpaths, roads, and publicly owned equipment. The *Douzaine* employs labour for public work and sees to general administration; most important of all, the *Douzaine* collects the Direct Tax and handles Parish Relief, Sark's equivalent of income support.

Land Tenure and Taxation. By the 17th century it had become evident that the feudal system of dividing property on inheritance threatened to fragment Sark's forty land-holdings into impractically small parcels. In 1611 Letters Patent were obtained from King James entailing the *tenements* and so ensuring that they would be handed down entire, thus re-enforcing the terms of the 1565 charter.

If a tenant dies leaving no known heirs, the *tenement* reverts to the Seigneur; if a *tenement* is sold out of the hereditary family, a relative may exercise *retraite*, or the right to repossess the property on payment to the buyer of the price paid. The system may seem cumbersome, but it can provide safeguards to back up the vigilance of the Seigneur against the predations of property developers.

The tax system, as it has developed over the years, has progressively separated the Island's public fiscal business from the private finances of the Seigneur. The manorial income from tithes, milling dues, contributions of live hens (the *poulade*), and similar ancient levies, has virtually disappeared.

There remains the *treizième* – the thirteenth part of any property sale – which the Seigneur may claim when he approves such a sale; and there are *rentes* from certain freeholds leased to tenants other than the *Quarantaine*. None of these levies produces a large income, and the Seigneur personally depends on other resources outside the Island.

Sark's public finances are self-sufficient at a modest level. There is a Direct Tax, not very onerous, levied on land and capital resources; it is managed by the *Douzaine* and revenue is wholly applied to Parish Relief.

General Revenue, derived principally from excise duty (the *Impôt*) and the landing fee levied from some 50,000 visitors a year, is used to fund all other public expenditure; this embraces education, including schooling in Guernsey for selected pupils, a Medical Officer of Health or resident doctor, and the maintenance of harbours and roads.

The islanders have been criticized for keeping the *Impôt* too low to improve public services, but since both revenue and expenditure are managed by the same people in the Chief Pleas, it is understandable – as the Seigneur has observed – that they should refrain from taxing themselves more than is strictly necessary.

Language. Up to the end of the eighteenth century the islanders of Sark spoke only their own *patois* and standard French; none spoke English. From 1835 the presence of the Cornish miners at the silver workings meant that English had to be used in the schools, and in church. This led to a decline in the use of the *patois* and of French. During the twentieth century the modernization of island life under British influence has furthered the prevalence of English, except in ceremonial and legal utterances. However, at the turn of the century the development of European unity and the growth of tourism are encouraging the islanders in the use of French, chiefly to attract visitors from near-by mainland France.

For much of the information we are indebted to the Seigneur, Mr. Michael Beaumont, whose book *The Constitution and Administration of Sark* lucidly covers this complex subject.